Revenue Law

Principles and Practice

Third Edition

Revenue Law

Principles and Practice

Third Edition

Professor Abimbola A. Olowofoyeku, Professor James Kirkbride
and Dr Deborah Butler

Liverpool Academic Press

Preface to the third edition

Nearly ten years since the publication of the first edition, it is a pleasure to welcome Dr Deborah Butler to the team. Since the previous edition there have been significant developments in many aspects of revenue law. A substantial part of these developments have occurred since the New Labour landslide election victory in 1997. With the election of the Labour government for a second term in May 2001, the pace of development and change is unlikely to abate, and New Labour's tax policies are set to become entrenched. We have already witnessed significant changes in Corporation Tax (removal of advance corporation tax), in Capital Gains Tax (indexation allowance and taper relief), and Income Tax (the IR35 legislation).

Additionally, the Human Rights Act 1998 is beginning to impact on revenue law as cases challenging actions of the Inland Revenue and Customs and Excise departments start to trickle into the courts. The first fruits of the efforts of the Tax Law Rewrite project are beginning to emerge, as witnessed in the new Capital Allowances Act 2001. The House of Lords continue to develop their judicial anti-avoidance doctrines and take it to new heights in *Westmoreland Investments Ltd v MacNiven*, and the Labour government seems to be undecided about their earlier plans to introduce a general statutory anti-avoidance rule. Things have never been more confusing and fraught for taxpayers and their advisers respectively, as new offences of defrauding the Revenue are introduced and tax advisers who devise tax-saving schemes start to get dragged into the courts by a newly empowered Inland Revenue, to be charged with defrauding the Revenue.

Revenue law has never gone through a more exciting period of development and change. This edition takes on these developments, and, while retaining the "principles" approach, expands on the critical and scholarly analyses of the issues. Many parts of the book have been substantially rewritten and extended, and a new VAT section has been added. Those who are familiar with the previous editions would have noticed that the size of the book has increased greatly. This increase has been necessary to accommodate the new sections and widening of the analysis of the taxes that were already covered.

As with the previous editions, we are convinced of the benefits of a principles approach to the study of revenue law and this edition seeks to further this through its expansion of discussion of theoretical issues, taxation policy and economics, and through its inclusion of comparative material. We hope that the reader finds our reflections in this area of interest.

The chapters in this book are up to date at the end of March 2002.

Prof. Abimbola Olowofoyeku
Prof. James Kirkbride
Dr Deborah Butler
March 2002

© Professor Abimbola A. Olowofoyeku, Professor James Kirkbride
and Dr Deborah Butler, 2003

First published in Great Britain by Liverpool Academic Press in 1993
Second Edition in 1997

A CIP catalogue for this book is available from the British Library

ISBN 1 903499-09-7 (Paperback)
ISBN 1 903499-05-4 (Hardback)

Typeset by Bitter & Twisted N. Wales. bitter@cybase.co.uk

Printed and Bound in Great Britain by Lightning Source, Milton Keynes.

Table of Cases

Table of Statutes

Taxation of Chargeable Gains Act 1992

contents

chapter one
History, Functions and Systems

Although the majority of this book is devoted to an examination of the principles and policy surrounding VAT and the direct taxes of income, capital gains, inheritance and corporation tax, it is important to develop an awareness of the history of taxation and the declared or presumed functions of tax. It is also of interest to be aware of the ad hoc nature of the UK tax system and opportunities and choices for reform. It is suggested that the sections on "functions" and on "systems" ought to be revisited once the reader has acquired and developed a working knowledge of the principles and operation of some of the direct taxes. The reader's ability to constructively analyse suggested reforms will be enhanced by his/her understanding of some of the substantive taxes.

The final part of this chapter considers some of the implications for revenue law of our membership of the European Communities. These are considered further in the sections on corporation tax and VAT.

History and functions

Income tax was introduced in this country by Pitt in 1799.[1] Its purpose was to finance the cost of the war against France. It was charged on the world-wide income of British residents and the British income of non-residents. This "temporary measure" was repealed in 1802 (a temporary peace in the war with France) but reintroduced by Addington in 1803. Addington made a number of adjustments and reforms to Pitt's system, in particular, Addington introduced a Schedular system of taxation and assessment – a system that remains today.[2] Peace in 1815 resulted in the expiration of the 1803 Act. A tax-free period was then enjoyed until 1842 when Peel re-imposed taxes broadly on the previous lines. Once again, it was believed to be a "temporary" measure but was periodically re-imposed and remains today. The development of tax law and taxation has extended

---

[1] Although it should be noted that taxes and their influences might have been felt at an earlier time. For example, King John's demand for "scrutage" contributed to the crisis of 1215 and the subsequent submission and the issue of Magna Carta. It should be appreciated that "tax" has proved difficult to define. The OECD's definition is, "the term taxes is confined to compulsory, unrequited payments to general government". This is perhaps the most useful working definition of tax.

[2] The details of today's Schedules are presented in later discussion.

from pure income tax on individuals to encompass taxes on the income of companies (corporation tax) and taxes on the capital receipts and gains of individuals and companies through the introduction of capital gains tax, inheritance tax and corporation tax. As we shall see later, the various taxes and their methods of introduction and application have created many opportunities for tax planning and avoidance.

Apart from the above direct taxes introduced on the capital and income of individuals and companies, a number of indirect taxes have been introduced into the United Kingdom. Generally, indirect taxes do not apply directly to our income but are paid indirectly through our expenditure. For example, they are often found to be included in the final price we might pay for goods. Value added tax (VAT) is the more well-known and apparent indirect tax. It is also the tax that is causing concern at European level and is subject to reform.

Finally, it is interesting to note that although income tax in the United Kingdom reflected the development of many overseas systems of taxation – they also commenced life in response to the need to raise finances for periods of war and developed into a complex system imposing tax on most low income individuals – it has been suggested that the British tax system differs from its overseas equivalents in two ways.[3] First it raises taxes under a system of schedules.[4] Second, its system of collection at source is widespread and sophisticated. The PAYE system is a familiar example of the latter. A further example of collection at source and an indication of the system's expansion is apparent in the "net" interest payments received on ordinary Building Society and Bank Saving accounts. Collection at source necessarily results in a hidden cost. For example, one only needs to reflect on the administration costs to the employer of "agreeing" to act as tax collector through the imposition of the PAYE system. Recently this has been subject to calls for reform from the British Chamber of Commerce under the umbrella of reducing the regulatory burdens on business, particularly small business.

Functions and principles of taxation

It has been suggested that tax system has become the "maid of all work".[5] This description emphasises the range of functions that taxes and the tax system might perform or be asked to perform. These functions often include a combination of a management function, a redistributive function and a general need to raise revenue. We saw the need to raise revenue in the introduction of income tax to finance warfare. Today, that need might

---

3   See S James and C Nobes, "The Economics of Taxation", at Chapter 8.
4   See later discussion of the Schedular system.
5   In the Budget of March 1993, the Chancellor of the Exchequer, announced that in looking for extra revenue he had to be guided by three principles :
    "... that where possible money should be raised in a way that will not damage the working of the economy"
    "... this means reducing the value of allowances and broadening the tax base ... and ..."
    "... that taxation should support social, health and environmental objectives".

still be one of maintaining the armed forces along with a wider range of services such as law and order and education. But today the raising of revenue is not the sole function of tax – this was strikingly illustrated in the suggestion that a slight increase in income tax rates would compensate for any lost revenue that might ensue if we agreed the removal of capital gains tax and inheritance tax. Of course, the removal of capital taxation per se is unlikely. It exists for its own reasons and supports other general objectives and functions of our tax system. It is the choice of treatment of capital that invites discussion of the concept of optimal taxation and the choice between a consumption tax and an income tax (see Broadway and Wildasin).

The redistributive function will find differing degrees of support reflecting political persuasions and pressures. The progressive tax rates are often perceived as a reflection of the equitable imposition of higher rates of tax upon those who enjoy the greatest ability to pay those rates. Similarly, one could refer to the introduction of capital gains tax as an example of imposing tax on these who were fortunate enough to enjoy their "wealth" in a form other than as income. An interesting redistributive proposal was the suggestion that a number of tax deductions ought to be replaced by a system of tax credits. It was believed that "tax credits" would be much more useful to low income families[6] – particularly because the absence of taxable income removed the usefulness of a tax deduction. In recent years in the UK we have seen an expansion of the use of tax credits, including the Working Family tax credit.

Contribution to the management of the economy is a widely accepted function of taxation. Examples of this can be found in the way in which tax rules and allowances are used to control expenditure and inflation; and in the way in which we are encouraged to invest in the UK economy through tax exempt or advantageous savings schemes. For example, Personal Equity Plans (PEPs) have proliferated in the UK since their introduction in the late 1980s. They provide an opportunity to invest stocks and shares with the advantages of tax free profits.

In introducing a "Saver's Budget" in 1986 the Chancellor of the Exchequer increased the annual limit on a PEP investment to £6,000 and limited the requirement that the monies must be invested in UK equities to 50% of the portfolio. The Chancellor declared his intention of encouraging long-term investment in share-ownership. In the same Budget, the Chancellor introduced the "Tax Exempt Special Savings Budget" and the TESSAs. These also have become very popular. The stated

---

[6]   This was a recommendation of the Carter Report in respect of taxation in Canada, the Report of the Royal Commission on Taxation, RC Canada (1966). The UK also considered a tax credit system in the 1972 Green Paper, "Proposals for a Tax Credit System".

intention of the TESSA is to

> introduce a wholly new tax incentive which will reward saving and encourage people to build up a stock of capital.

The management of the economy and the use of tax often involves aspects of credit control, customs duties and to a lesser extent the control of, or influence on, behaviour. The latter is apparent in the investment and savings behaviour of PEPs, TESSAs and ISAs but might also include social behaviour such as taxation of alcohol, tobacco and car fuel.

Finally, we need to mention the link between taxation and the environment. A number of studies have shown that environmental hold out the prospect of more cost-effective pollution control than regulatory policies which are limited by the informational capacity of regulatory authorities (Smith, 1992). Once that is accepted, the political process then needs to explore the scope for the practical application of environmental taxes. The choice is between pollution taxes based on measured emission quantities and environmental taxes with an indirect linkage between the tax base and pollution. The choice and effectiveness of introducing new "pollution taxes" or restructuring existing taxes is political but is supported through a number of empirical studies (Smith, 1992).

The Principles of Taxation

In developing a tax system to facilitate the above functions (or any other functions) it is normal to consider the "principles" upon which a tax system ought to be based. These principles are often the measure against which one would judge whether a tax system is good or bad. In considering and developing such principles, the accepted starting point is Adam Smith's proposed canons of taxation[7].

1. Equity – people should contribute taxes proportionate to their incomes and wealth.
2. Certainty – taxes should be certain and not arbitrary.
3. Convenience – the timing and manner of payment of taxes must be convenient.
4. Efficiency – the costs of collecting and imposing taxes must be kept to a minimum. The costs of collection should represent a small proportion of the revenue collected. The taxes should be efficient in that they do not distort behaviour – the principle of "neutrality".

---

[7]   Adam Smith, "An Inquiry into the Nature and Causes of the Wealth of Nations" (1776).

Over the years, these canons of taxation have been reviewed and discussed and have occasionally been presented under similar or revised headings. For example, in 1978 the Meade Committee considered the "Characteristics of a Good Tax Structure" as representing six heads:[8]

1. Incentives and economic efficiency.
2. Distributional effects.
3. International aspects.
4. Simplicity and costs of administration and compliance.
5. Flexibility and stability.
6. Transitional problems.

The principles proposed by Adam Smith still dictate and influence thinking in this area.[9] We shall consider aspects of those principles together with aspects of the "characteristics" proposed by the Meade Committee, under four heads :

1. efficiency
2. incentives
3. equity
4. stability considerations.

Our choice of these "heads" reflects the economic influences on tax system and reform.

1. *Efficiency* – the efficiency of the tax system often involves consideration of its economic efficiency and contributions, and its efficiency measured in terms of administration and costs of compliance. The costs of compliance are the easier to appreciate and recognise. Adam Smith expressed concern over the proportional costs of collection. Similar concerns were expressed by the Meade Committee. The Committee emphasised the need to consider the potential costs of administrative complexity and the pure costs of administration. The latter should incorporate official administrative costs and also the (often neglected) tax compliance costs incurred by the private taxpayer. The Meade Committee believed that private compliance costs were often in excess of the official administrative costs – but often ignored when judging and analysing the

---

[8] "The Structure and Reform of Direct Taxation: Report of a Committee chaired by Professor J E Meade", The Institute of Fiscal Studies (1978) at Chapter 2.
[9] For a useful introduction, see James and Nobes, "The Economics of Taxation". See also, Kay and King, The British Tax System.

operation of the tax system. Examples of the private costs of compliance would include the costs of the employer in operating as a tax collector under the PAYE system; the costs imposed on a trader in complying with any VAT system; and the social costs to the community of the investment of manpower in developing a tax advisory and avoidance industry and the costs to the public sector in trying to hinder or prevent any process of tax avoidance. The process of tax change also brings with it the costs to the taxpayers and the authorities of adaptation and response.

The actual costs of compliance ("the hidden costs of taxation") are more difficult to calculate than administrative costs, although attempted calculations and estimates do support the Meade Committee's conclusions that compliance costs are "substantial".[10]   The Meade Committee's conclusions included the advice that we "tip the balance away from compliance costs on to official administrative costs" and develop a coherent tax system that is simple and easy to understand with the consequent advantages of acceptability.

Economic efficiency (or contributions) often invites recognition of what is known as the excess burden of taxation. Economists regard "efficiency" in terms of contributions to the "optimal allocation of scarce resources".   Such an allocation demands the existence of perfect competition; and that market forces (supply and demand) dictate the price of goods and services and the allocation of scarce resources of factors of production. In the "real" world perfect competition does not exist and influences on supply or demand can distort allocations and price – with the accompanying inefficient effects on the economy. The imposition and use of tax can distort choices and subsequent allocations.   It is that "distortion" that amounts to the "excess burden" of tax. The traditional example is the avoidance of window tax in 1747 when many taxpayers bricked-up their windows rather than pay tax. This "cost" resulted in a lack of amenity with no consequent benefit to the Government or the economy – it represented the excess burden of the window tax.

Similarly, the Meade Report refers to the "substitution effect" whereby, taxes contribute to economic inefficiency by interfering with consumer choice. The Meade Report cites the examples of the

wage earner reducing his hours of work in order to substitute untaxed leisure or do-it-yourself activity at home for taxed work;

---

[10]   Sandford, "Hidden Costs of Taxation", Institute of Fiscal Studies (1973) estimated compliance costs to represent 2.5 4.4 per cent of the revenue collected during 1970.

the housewife who may substitute untaxed domestic work for taxed earnings outside the home; and

the business executive who refuses promotion and thus substitutes his present occupation for the alternative more productive job, because the low post-tax increases in his earnings do not compensate for the social costs of moving.

These examples, and others, represent the loss or "costs" (the excess burden) of tax.

Similarly, it was reported in the *Financial Times* (28 November 1986) that compliance costs represented 3.3 per cent of the tax yield for 1983-84.

Two particular examples of "excess burden" that we will consider in detail in later chapters, are (i) the use of fringe benefits; and (ii) tax evasion and avoidance.

Fringe benefits represent those benefits in kind that employees receive instead of salary or income. The hope is that the benefits in kind will escape tax. If the "benefit" had been received as income or as part of the salary it would probably be taxable. We will examine in later chapters, the detailed rules for the taxation and assessment of benefits in kind, but at this point it is important to appreciate the potential inefficiency of fringe benefits. If, for example, instead of receiving a company car (a fringe benefit) an employee was provided with the cash equivalent, he would then have the choice on how he might spend that money. That freedom of choice would accord with the economist's concept of "perfect competition" and his choice would better influence the factors of supply and demand and the allocation of scarce resources. For instance, he could choose to buy a cheaper form of transport (a used car) and invest the remainder or spend it on consumer goods of a different kind.

Tax evasion and avoidance is difficult to measure. The "loss" or "costs" represents the effort and the monies expanded in avoiding or even evading liability. It is estimated that evasion, and thus the "cost" and "loss", is widespread. For example, in 1979 the Chairman of the Board of Inland Revenue suggested that it was "not implausible" that tax evasion monies could amount to 7.5 per cent of the gross domestic product.

2. *Incentives* - many regard the concept and consideration of incentives as an aspect and measure of tax efficiency, and to that extent "incentives" belong to principle 1. above. "Incentives" examine the way in which the tax system should or does encourage people to work, save and invest, and

accept risks of enterprise and innovation.

We previously mentioned the "substitution effect" of taxation and the taxpayer's surrender of work and effort in favour of other benefits such as leisure, hobby and do-it-yourself crafts. Similarly, the tax system might contribute to a substitution effect in relation to forms of business organisation. One might choose to operate as an unincorporated association rather than an incorporated business - depending upon the tax regimes and advantages. Alternatively, one might opt for a less profitable but relatively risk free business instead of the development of a risky venture, albeit that such a development would provide wider benefits to the economy and the community (if successful).

In relation to savings and investment, the "substitution effect" is often discussed in terms of the "double taxation of savings": "savings" often come from earned income that has already been subject to taxation, and those savings and any interest returned will be subject to further tax. One can point to our discussion on PEPs and TESSAs as examples of Government attempts to encourage savings and investment in a particular direction through the removal of a "double taxation" principle.

It is widely believed that an expenditure tax would provide a wider incentive to save essentially because it would, like PEPs and TESSAs, remove any "double taxation" fear.

In terms of incentive effects much discussion and emphasis is placed upon comparing the incentive effects of different forms of taxation. For example, it is widely believed that a progressive tax rate has potentially a higher disincentive effect on work effort than a proportional income tax system or a poll tax system. Similarly, it is believed that indirect taxes are more attractive to savers than progressive income tax rates which contribute to "double taxation".

The major difficulty in relation to incentives and tax is measurement. It is difficult to measure incentive responses to tax systems and change. For example, although there have been many studies whose conclusions and reports appear to support the widely believed views on incentives, tax rates and work effort; the methodology, precision and accuracy of the studies have caused concern.[11]

3. *Equity* - equity initially demands a consideration of whether a tax is "fair" and equitable. "Fairness" involves subjective judgments although some objective acceptance and perception of the "fairness" of a tax and a tax system is necessary in order to avoid adverse consequences. For example, evasion and taxpayer resistance to taxation can dramatically increase if the system or the tax is perceived to be unfair.

[11] See Atkinson and Stiglitz, "Lectures on Public Economies", (1980); Brown, "Taxation and the Incentive to Work", (1983).

In considering "fairness" it is normal to recognise the importance of "horizontal" and "vertical" equity. "Horizontal" equity demands that tax systems treat equal people in equal circumstances in an equal way. "Vertical" equity permits discrimination between taxpayers in order to facilitate a redistribution between rich and poor. The Meade Committee reported that

1. A good tax system should be horizontally equitable, i.e. it should treat like with like.

2. A modern tax system must be so constructed as to be capable of use for vertical redistribution between rich and poor.[12]

An example of an equity argument supporting the introduction of a tax is apparent in the case of capital gains tax. During its introduction in 1964, the Chancellor of the Exchequer, stated that :

Capital gains confer much the same kind of benefit on the recipient as taxed earnings more hardly won. Yet earnings pay full tax while capital gains go free. This is unfair to the wage and salary earner.[13]

The development and promotion of "equity" of tax, incorporates problems of the definition of "income", "wealth" and "ability to pay". It also invites discussion of the need to consider tax capitalisation; distribution and the incidence of tax; inflation; and tax avoidance and evasion. Tax capitalisation involves tax benefits being incorporated in and reflected in the capital value of an asset.

The distribution and incidence of tax is difficult to measure. It is assumed that a progressive tax rate coupled with the extension of tax beyond pure income tax has reflected a movement towards equality of liability. However, in determining equality of distribution it is important to appreciate the "incidence" of tax (who really pays for tax changes and increases?). The "incidence" of tax might include the "economic" incidence in that the economy and the consumer might suffer if a progressive income tax induces more leisure and less work effort. The consumer might also suffer if the "incidence" is "shifted" from the producer to the consumer; for example, through the incorporation of tax rises into the market price of the product or service.

[12] Supra n8, at Chapter 2.
[13] Hansard, vol. 710, col. 245.

Inflation and its effects on "equity" is apparent in relation to both earned and unearned income. In relation to earned income it is important under a progressive tax rate system to make proportional adjustments to counter the effects of inflation. Thus, the Chancellor might seek to raise personal allowances and rate bands by the amount of inflation in order to seek to avoid any fall in "real incomes". In relation to unearned income, we find complex rules to allow an indexation system to apply to capital gains in order that taxpayers pay for "real" rather than inflationary gains.

Tax avoidance and tax evasion[14] often contribute to the "hidden costs" of taxation, but more importantly they have an adverse effect on redistribution because of the retention of wealth by those who successfully operate or contribute to avoidance schemes – an unintended distribution! In addition to the redistribution "inequity", widespread tax avoidance and tax evasion might contribute to the development of a perception of the "acceptability" of avoidance (or worse still, evasion!) which might find further wasteful avoidance and evasion. It is necessary for the legislature and the Courts to respond appropriately to artificial avoidance schemes in an attempt to curtail and prevent any perceptions of "acceptability" – unless, of course, we wish to follow some of our European partners in accepting evasion as a moral duty!

4.   *Stability* – We mentioned earlier, that one of the functions of tax and tax systems is a contribution to the management of the economy. To economists and others, the use of the tax system in managing the economy ought to promote "stability". The Meade Report emphasised the need

for a certain stability in taxation in order that persons may be in a position to make reasonably far-sighted plans. Fundamental uncertainty breeds lack of confidence and is a serious impediment to production and prosperity.[15]

In promoting stability in the economy, taxation is a useful part of any Government's armoury – yet, at a apparently contradictory level, taxation must allow flexibility and change. The flexibility and change is required in order to respond to different political views and changes and different trends and thinking in economic policy. The tax system must be able to respond and adjust to monetary policy or fiscal policy while providing and supporting economic stability. Economic stability and stabilisation demands recognition of the relative merits of the various taxes; the size of the tax base; the speed of adjustment and influence of tax changes (the "implementation" and "response" "lag"); and the development of built-in

---

[14] See later discussion on the concepts of evasion and avoidance.
[15] Supra.

flexibility methods, such as progressive tax rates. Within these considerations it is clear that a good tax system must permit a change of emphasis in economic policy in order to reflect changes in government and thinking but appreciate that,

Such changes of emphasis will show themselves in the trade-off which is preferred among the various objectives of a good tax system.[16]

Tax Reform

Tax reform requires "a tax system which looks like someone designed it on purpose" (W E Simon, former Secretary to US Treasury).

Such a system would, presumably, address the principles and functions of taxation and demonstrate and achieve appropriate distributions and contributions. In the United Kingdom we have, at times, seen aspects of reform and consolidation, but little in terms of a co-ordinated review and reform of our overall tax system and burdens[17] - perhaps, because the process of review and reform contains a number of fundamental difficulties. An interesting, unofficial review of the UK Tax System was conducted by the Meade Committee, on behalf of the Institute of Fiscal Studies.[18] Although both the Committee and its Report have been subject to much criticism and comment, the Report is useful in identifying anomalies and areas of concern in the UK tax system, and in providing a comparison with an Expenditure Tax System. It is also believed that the Report will influence and make a contribution to future tax reform.

The Meade Committee was set up in mid-1975 and reported in 1978. Its brief was to "take a fundamental look at the UK tax structure". It must be noted that to make its task "manageable" the Committee quickly decided to exclude consideration of some taxes, in particular excise taxes, local rates, stamp duties, petroleum revenue taxes and aspects of value added tax. In reaching its conclusions, the Meade Committee considered that the present anomalies in the UK system ought not to remain and that it would be necessary to move to a pure income tax or to a pure expenditure tax.[19] The Committee, for reasons that we shall explore, preferred the option of an expenditure tax. An expenditure tax involves a calculation of an individual's consumption expenditure not an individual's expenditure per se. For example, one might start by calculating an individual's income for any period and add to that income any capital

---

[16] The Meade Committee Report, supra.

[17] We have experienced periods of consolidation, and periods of occasional and limited reforms, such as the reform of the unit of assessment to permit independent taxation of husband and wife (introduced on 6 April 1990).

[18] Supra. See also Kay & King, "The British Tax System".

[19] The anomalies and concessions that concerned the Committee included, (i) the distortions in the capital markets through preferential treatment of some investments (e.g. Pensions), (ii) the disincentive of progressive rate tax and the use of wasteful fringe benefits, (iii) the tax capitalisation problems of some concessions, such as mortgage interest relief. Others have suggested that the UK tax system ought to be considered for reform because (i) the costs of administration are comparatively high, (ii) the system is not internationally compatible; and (iii) historically, the PAYE system is out-of-date and unnecessary.

receipts and borrowing. This would enable us to calculate an individual's "spending power". Sensible and desirable spending in the form of savings and investment would then be deducted from that "spending power". The remaining balance would represent the individual's consumption expenditure and it is that "expenditure" (consumption) which would be subject to tax – progressive or otherwise.[20]

The concept of an expenditure tax is not new. It can be traced back to the writings of Thomas Hobbes and of John Stuart Mill. Nor is the concept of an expenditure tax confined to this country. In 1977 the US Treasury produced a "Blueprint for Basic Tax Reforms" based on expenditure tax principles; similarly in 1978 the Swedish Royal Commission on Taxation proposed reforms along the lines of an expenditure tax. Despite these proposals the only known experience of expenditure tax systems were in India and Ceylon in the 1950s. In both instances, the systems were impractical and were abandoned – an event that was not considered by the Meade Committee.

The perceived advantages of an expenditure tax are that it would increase incentives to save and invest; it avoids the need to distinguish capital from income (although one would have to distinguish "saving" from "expenditure or consumption"); it would provide a base to tax an individual on what he takes out of (or "consumes") rather than on what he puts into the economy (although some economists believe "consumption" is economically beneficial and ought to be encouraged rather than penalised); and that it provides a basis for the development of a co-ordinated system of taxation based on proper principles rather than on ad hoc anomalies and concessions.

Even if one accepts the basis and principles of an expenditure tax, one wonders whether it is practically possible to consider its total introduction into the United Kingdom. For example, some tax concessions have been capitalised into assets. A sweeping removal of those concessions would remove the value of those assets and penalise those who had purchased or invested on the basis of existing concessions. Similarly, those individual enjoying retirement might constantly be "taking out" of the economy monies to support their day-to-day activities. Those monies might derive from lifelong capital investments and pensions. To penalise such "consumption" might be perceived as inequitable. When he was Chancellor of the Exchequer, Mr N Lawson was caused to remark that a system of expenditure tax was "quite impracticable, even if it was desirable"[21].

---

[20]   An "expenditure tax" ought to be regarded as (or even called) a "cash-flow income tax". See Kay, "Fiscal Studies", Vol. 7, No 4, page 9.
[21]   1984 Budget Speech.

Credit must be given to the Meade Committee in recognising possible transitional problems and responding by suggesting two alternative approaches to the introduction of an expenditure tax. The first approach involved the introduction of a universal expenditure tax based on the consumption principle and applicable to all taxpayers. The second approach involved the introduction of a two-tier expenditure tax. The lower tier would consist of a single rate of tax levied on expenditure or consumption through a form of value added tax (VAT or ITVAT as the Committee calls it). the upper tier would be a "universal expenditure tax" but limited in its "universal" application to higher rate taxpayers with higher levels of expenditure – a sort of surtax on the higher level consumers. It would be intended that over time the threshold for the application of the universal tax to those in the upper tier would eventually be lowered to a degree where the universal tax would be truly universal in its coverage and then the special VAT would be removed – proposal one, the favoured proposal, would then have been achieved.

As mentioned earlier, the Meade Committee and its Report were subject to criticism and comment.[22] Some critics referred to the unofficial nature and actual composition of the Committee; many critics commentated on the practical problems of the introduction of an expenditure tax – particularly transitional problems and the ultimately heavy reliance on a process of self-assessment; and some critics were concerned over the suggested benefits of an expenditure tax : some economists perceive that consumption is economically beneficial and ought not to be discouraged or penalised.

Similarly some particular (alleged) benefits of an expenditure based tax have come under scrutiny. For example, it has been suggested that although an expenditure tax might increase the return to saving there was little evidence to suggest that it would substantially increase the level of saving. There is also some belief that expenditure tax would result in higher tax rates (needed to offset the loss of capital tax receipts) which in turn might present a disincentive to work, especially in instances of immediate consumption. Nor is it firmly believed that an expenditure tax would necessarily promote equity; a person's wealth might indicate a person's ability to pay but careful placing of that wealth (through exempt savings and investments) removes the obligation and liability to pay.

It is interesting to note that one of the driving forces behind the Meade Committee's appointment and proposals, the need to consider the removal of anomalies and concessions and the development of a co-ordinated and principled tax system, might itself be in danger should the Committee's

---

[22] See Prest [1978] BTR 176.

proposals ever be formally adopted. It is clear that in any process of tax reform special interest groups are capable of obtaining ad hoc concessions and contribute to the development of anomalies through the process of "pressurising". There is little to suggest that such interest group concessions and anomalies would not be present in the process of change to an expenditure tax.

Finally, although their has not been a wholesale introduction of expenditure tax into the United Kingdom it is beginning to appear in the form of influencing recent tax developments. For example, the introduction of Personal Equity Plans (PEPs) in the 1986 Budget stirred the reaction that this represented

> ... the transfer of quoted shares from the category of "no fiscal privilege" to that of "Expenditure Tax" or better ... the principle that direct personal investment in equities is intended to be a privileged form of saving has now been clearly established ....[23]

A comprehensive income tax

The Meade Committee reported that the UK tax system fell somewhere between a pure (or comprehensive) income tax system and an expenditure tax system. Its principal reason for dismissing reform in favour of the former was that

> ... it would be extremely difficult, if not impossible, to introduce all the features of a comprehensive tax. In particular, we think that many of the measures which would theoretically be necessary to index the system for proper capital income adjustments against inflation would not be practicable.[24]

Despite any apparent practical difficulties, the development of a comprehensive income tax has been the subject of serious consideration – particular in Canada.[25] In essence a comprehensive income tax, often referred to as a tax on the "accretion of economic power", requires that tax is imposed on actual or imputed increases in wealth or economic power. The increase in wealth would include consideration of "wealth" at the beginning and at the end of the tax period together with a consideration of consumption during that period.

---

[23] J A Kay, "Fiscal Studies", 1986 Vol. 7, No 2, at page 35.

[24] at p500.

[25] It must be recognised that the debate and discussions of the Carter Commission will influence the reform debate in other countries. This was apparent in the tax base rate reforms in the United States in 1986.

In 1966, the Carter Report[26] was presented to the Federal Government of Canada with the recommendation that a comprehensive income tax be introduced. The Report attracted the accolade that,

It must rank as the most comprehensive and detailed blueprint for tax reform ever created.[27]

The recommendations of the Carter Commission included the introduction of a new comprehensive base for income tax. This new base would enable tax to be imposed on all gains in purchasing power. Such gains, whether they occurred from actual or deemed capital disposals, would be classed as taxable "income". At the same time, the Commission proposed a general reduction of the tax rate : a reduction that could be achieved through the widening of the tax base.

Other recommendations of the Carter Commission included the integration of personal and corporate income tax and the removal of capital investment and allowance incentives. The latter were perceived as important in removing major sources of tax avoidance.

It is interesting to note that the Carter Commission considered the functions and principles of tax and was concerned at the need to reconcile any conflicts in terms of economic growth, stability, individual freedoms and Government Policy. The Commission's overriding objective in supporting the introduction of a comprehensive income tax was the promotion of "horizontal equity". It was the Commission's view that the development of "fair taxes should override all other objectives" – the comprehensive income tax was perceived as providing a good indicator and measure of the ability to pay.

Although the Carter Commission's Report was initially welcomed, it appears that little of it has been implemented or enacted.[28] Much of that "failure" must be accounted for by the particular political changes in Canada; however, it is probable that the Carter proposals, like the Meade Committee proposals, would face common problems and barriers in the process of tax reform. These include :

1. Pressures from special interest groups – we mentioned in relation to expenditure tax that anomalies and concessions could develop as a consequence of special interest groups. Examples of the "pressurising" that might be experienced are found in some of the responses to the Carter proposals. It is reported that the "business lobby" and the "farm lobby" made strong representation in respect of the proposed treatment of death and gift taxes. Similarly, one would expect that financial institutions in the

---

[26] The Report of the Royal Commission on Taxation, Canada, 1966. Chaired by Kenneth Le M Carter.
[27] Sandford [1987] BTR 148.
[28] See Sandford, ibid.

UK would strongly respond to any attempts to remove mortgage interest relief – although the March Budget (1993) saw some weakening of the mortgage interest relief position.

2. Social and economic views – it has been suggested that one of the reasons why the Carter proposals may have failed to have been implemented is that the economic arguments and base of the proposals are no longer "vogue". Social attitudes change in terms of priorities and "horizontal equity" might not now be appropriate. Regional policies; selective investment policies and redistribution might now be priorities. An extreme example of difference in social attitudes can be found in some jurisdictions where tax evasion is socially acceptable and often encouraged. By contrast, in the United Kingdom, tax evasion and avoidance is believed to attract social stigma.

3. Short-term political goods – it is clear that if any sweeping tax reforms are to succeed, they must enjoy political support. This need raises two problems. First, the proposals themselves ought to be as a consequence of political initiative and emanate from an official Committee. The Meade Committee Report, initiated and appointed by the Institute of Fiscal Studies, failed to enjoy the necessary "official" status. Second, both the expenditure tax system and the comprehensive income tax system require a long term commitment and ability to withstand public criticisms and concerns. Despite the long term benefits of enjoying a tax system based on a coherent set of principles, it is highly probable that those who suffer during the transition would vehemently pursue their own short term goals of defeating the changes and restoring their benefits. That "short termism" might also apply to the politicians. Apart from the amount of Parliamentary time that sweeping changes would absorb, it is unlikely that the Parliamentary term of a Government would be sufficient to facilitate long term changes and withstand short-term unpopularity. Any attempt at introducing "wholesale changes might realistically be viewed as political suicide",

British politicians used to be told that if they changed the tax system, the gainers would not thank them and the losers would not forgive them. If a Chancellor really wanted to make a reputation as tax reformer, he was advised to lie down until the feeling had passed.[29]

4. It has been suggested that tax reform in Britain will never substantially take place unless we reform the Inland Revenue first.[30] Criticism is placed at the dominant policymaking role performed by the Inland Revenue. Not only is this comparatively unique, but also inappropriate. The Inland Revenue does not possess the necessary awareness or expertise to contribute to and consider the socio-economic and political realities of

[29]   J A Kay, "Fiscal Studies", 1990, Vol. 7, No 4, at p1.
[30]   Ibid. at p3.

reform – it is merely equipped to consider administrative criteria and perform administrative functions. It has been suggested that the Inland Revenue's role should be confined to the latter and that tax policy and reform should clearly be placed in the hands of the Treasury – perhaps assisted by a body of advisors. Recent developments, Mr Lamont's body of wise men, might constitute a tangible response to this area criticisms and concerns. This body of independent tax advisors (the "wise men") has been continued by Mr Lamont's successors.

Finally, despite these procedural and process difficulties it is widely accepted that the "British tax system is complex, inefficient and unfair" and that reform is necessary.[31] The manner and method of reform is subject to opinion and debate but it is agreed that it must be coherent and caused on principle; and probably incremental in approach and implementation.

The plain language and structure of tax legislation

One of the criticisms and perceived barriers to the reform of tax law is directed at the language and mass of detail of tax legislation: in fact it was reported that in November 1995 there were nearly 6,000 pages of Inland Revenue primary legislation, representing an increase of over 50 per cent since 1988. The language of the tax statutes is also notoriously convoluted at times and has often been described as "unintelligible". The following words of Rowlatt J are apt:

> This Section 31 is a Section which in five pages introduces piece-meal amendments into Section 21 with the result that the latter Section is made perfectly unintelligible to any layman or any lawyer who has not made a prolonged study with all his law books at his elbow, and it is a crying scandal that legislation by which the subject is taxed should appear in the Statute Book in that utterly unintelligible form. I am told, and rightly told, by the Attorney-General – he understands it as much as anybody – that it is only in this form that legislation can be carried through at all. Then all I have to say is that the price of getting his legislation through is that the people of this country are taxed by laws which they cannot possibly understand, and I must say I think that this is the worst possible example that has ever been put on the Statute Book.[32]

A number of initiatives have been taken to address concerns over language,

---

[31] For a useful discussion on reform and principle see M Wilson, Taxation, Chapter 12.
[32] *Lionel Sutcliffe Ltd v IRC* (1928) 14 TC 171 at 187.

structure and volume. The Institute of Fiscal Studies set up a committee back in 1994 to examine these concerns. It subsequently recommended that a pilot project be adopted to see if an expensive rewrite could be justified: it estimated that a rewrite would take about five years and involve a team of up to 40 people. The Institute's Final Report on Tax Legislation was published in June 1996. In the meantime the Inland Revenue delivered to Parliament its report "The Path to Tax Simplification" in December 1995. Subsequently the Inland Revenue has published another consultative document, August 1996, setting out proposals for carrying out the review and rewrite recommended in the Institute of Fiscal Studies Final Report on Tax Legislation. The Revenue aims to make the rewritten laws as easy as possible to understand, through logical ordering of the provisions, directness of expression and clear and simple layout. Difficult decisions exist in terms of layout: should we take an activity-based approach or one that reflects type of taxpayer, or type of tax or subject-base? Should we rewrite all the legislation at the same time and go for a "big-bang" introduction, or should we seek to reap the benefits of incremental reform through a staged introduction? Who should comprise the reform/rewrite team: public/private sector experts or a combination?

Whatever the answer to these and the many other questions raised by the Reports, it is interesting to note the recognition of the problems and of the time-scale to achieve a revision of the problems of language, detail and volume. Perhaps the system and experiences of "self-assessment" might increase public awareness and experiences of the problem. One suspects that until public opinion is strong enough that successive Governments will avoid the costs and disruption of a sweeping rewrite of tax legislation whatever the perceived long term benefits - albeit that the "Tax Law Rewrite" project has commenced.

Commentators on the early experiences of the rewrite suggest that the rewrite is likely to be an extremely long document in that it is an attempt to rewrite the law and practice of income tax, not just current legislation. The essence is an attempt to change the wording of laws without trying to change the meaning. It should embrace extra-statutory concessions and rules for practice in addition to principles from case law and legislation. It is indeed a big challenge although the Government has confirmed that it is "committed to proceeding with the rewrite project on the basis of full consultation in that the aim is to prepare a series of rewrite Bills, the first Bill likely to be ready for enactment is the capital allowances rewrite Bill." The following main Acts are to result, but from a steady progressive introduction rather than any "big bang" event:

1. Income Tax (either tax-based or individual-based)
2. Corporation Tax (either tax or company-based)
3. Capital Allowances
4. Capital Gains (computational provisions)
5. Stamp Duties
6. Inheritance Tax; and
7. Management.

The Capital Allowances Act 2001 is a product of the Tax Law Re-write project.

EC and international influence

The operation of our tax system and the development and reform of our tax system must consider EC and International influences. International influences have always been present. For example, there is a need to consider comparative treatment of the taxation of individuals and corporations. High tax rates might result in emigration of individuals and corporations. Similarly, the tax treatment of capital will influence investment decisions and locations. It is clear that the tax induced mobility of these factors of production will have a distorting effect on the locality and transfer of these factors – the tax system is not neutral but is influential in determining the allocation and location of scarce resources. One need only refer to the intentions of the government in the Republic of Ireland when it set a corporation tax of 10% in the hope of attracting manufacturing industry and corporations, to illustrate the distorting effect of taxation.

Other international effects of taxation include concerns over jurisdiction and enforcement. These involve the difficulty of negotiating double tax treaties and international co-operation. The fiscal and economic needs of some countries present difficult, and at times insurmountable, hurdles to co-operation on jurisdiction and enforcement matters. The OECD has a model code and agreement but this model is not binding and is often viewed as biased in favour of the economies of Western Europe. Other models have been suggested and developed, but they also suffer from perceived prejudice and favour. It is the US tax officials who seem to attract a lot of criticism for the methods by which they seek to pursue profits across frontiers in the interest of their own revenue chests. Davies suggests (1969) that they frequently flout the spirit of international tax treaties and adopt investigatory methods slightly less offensive than the activities of the Gestapo or the Russian secret policy.

Through its membership of the European Community, the United Kingdom has participated in the debate on aspects of tax reform in areas where barriers and distortions are apparent. It is important to appreciate that tax reform is necessary if the Community aim to facilitate the free movement of goods, services, people and capital and the freedom of establishment is to be fulfilled. This demands that the European Community considers and embarks on an ambitious harmonisation programme of both direct and indirect taxes. Thus far the Community has been progressing reform and harmonisation in areas of corporation tax and indirect tax in the form of VAT reforms. The Community's progress in the area of corporation tax reform will be considered at a later stage in the chapter on Corporation Tax - suffice to say at the moment that the Commission's progress has been slow and somewhat disappointing. The issue of indirect tax reforms have also been slow but are beginning to come to fruition. The operation and rates of VAT have had a distorting effect on the transfer of goods and services.[33] In a series of Directives the European Community has accepted a framework for a common system of VAT and the Community countries are working toward the ultimate aim of a harmonised system of rate bands : although political difficulties remain. As part of the push for the creation of the "internal market", transitional measures came into force on 1 January 1993 and remain in force until 31 December 1996. These transitional measures involve a limited harmonisation and a response to the abolition of fiscal frontiers. The "measures" were included in the Finance Bill 1992[34] and involve (broadly) amendments whereby exports from a member state to other European Community countries will no longer be subject to VAT, while imports from other European Community countries would be (an "acquisitions" principle). Tax charged in one member state will be deductible in another member state ("reverse charge" principle); whereas imports from non-EC countries will still be subject to taxation. More detail can be found on the sections of this book dealing with VAT.

Increasingly there has been a call for European tax powers giving to Europe its own "tax sovereignty". Thus far this has been resisted, although some countries, including Belgium, believe that some formula must be found for a Europe-wide tax to replace contributions to the EU budget. That latest budget committee report (March 1999) suggests that the EU should gain direct responsibility both for raising and spending revenue with the conclusion that EU taxes would have to come "sooner or later".

---

[33]   Since 1967, the Community has been working on the approximation of VAT and to this effect it adopted a long line of directives. For example, see the First and Second Directives (67/227/EEC and 67/228/EEC) which required member states to adopt a system of VAT. The comprehensive rules on VAT are to be found in the Sixth Directive (77/388/EEC) entitled "harmonisation of the laws of the Member States relating to turnover taxes - common system of value added tax and uniform basis of assessment". Numerous directives and decisions have been adopted to limit or amend Directive 77/388 (see Directive 83/181).

[34]   The transitional system is an amendment of Directive 77/388 (Directive 91/680/EEC).

The Human Rights Act and Revenue Practice

The Human Rights Act 1998 came into force throughout the UK on October 2000, giving effect to the European Convention for the Protection of Human Rights and Fundamental Freedoms in UK law. Essentially the Act requires that:

a. legislation will have to be interpreted subject to Convention rights, if it is possible to do so;

b. public authorities will have to respect Convention rights;

c. courts and tribunals will have to give remedies for human rights violations.

Already the Human Rights Act has impacted on revenue law and practice. For example the Court of Appeal recently declared that defendants facing allegations of tax evasion must be given the same rights as defendants in a criminal case. *Han and Yau v Customs and Excise Commissioners* [35] arose from a £67,000 penalty imposed by Customs and Excise on George Han and David Yau, restaurant owners of a Chinese takeaway, for non–payment of VAT. This was in line with the practice adopted in the mid–1980s under which Customs impose civil penalties and defendants are spared a criminal record. Customs can offer the inducement of a reduced penalty, depending on the amount of co–operation shown towards the VAT investigation. Lawyers acting for Mr Han and Mr Yau, agreed that such a system penalised the two men because it deprived them of the normal rights of a defendant, such as access to an interpreter or adequate explanation of the alleged offence. The Court of Appeal agreed and held that the civil VAT evasion penalties under VATA 1994 s.60 were criminal charges which entitle defendants to the protection offered by art. 6(1) of the European Convention on Human Rights. [36]

Further Reading

Beighton LJH, *The Simplification of Tax Legislation* [1996] BTR 50.

Sandford C, Carter *Twenty Years On* 1987 [BTR] 148.

Bensusan-Butt DM, *The Target for Tax Reform* [1979] BTR 168-77.

Nelson-Jones J, *Tax Re-Distribution and Reality* [1977] BTR 362-70.

Prest AR, *Proposals for a Tax-Credit System* 1973 [BTR] 6-16.

---

[35] [2001] BTC 5328

[36] See also *King v Walden* (HMIT) [2001] BTC 170.

chapter two
The Territorial Scope

United Kingdom taxation is subject to a territorial limit, the cardinal principle being that the tax legislation does not extend beyond the jurisdiction. As far as income tax is concerned, this territorial aspect of income tax can be formalised into two propositions, which were given voice by Lord Wrenbury in *Whitney v IRC*[1]:

> The policy of the Act is to tax the person resident in the United Kingdom upon all his income whencesoever derived, and to tax the person not resident in the United Kingdom upon all income derived from property in the United Kingdom.

The rules applicable in respect of other taxes are roughly similar, although they may differ in important respects (discussed below).

This territorial limit to income tax was approved as still being a correct statement of the law by Lord Hailsham LC in *National Bank of Greece SA v Westminster Bank Executor and Trustee Co (Channel Islands) Ltd*.[2] More recently, in *Clark v Oceanic Contractors Inc*[3], a case in which the principle of territoriality was applied to UK legislation generally, Lord Wilberforce said[4] that, as a statement in respect of liability to pay income tax, it is "still broadly correct". The territoriality principle, as far as it applies to U.K legislation generally, is a principle of construction only, and can give way to express words or necessary implication. As far as it relates to income tax, it is to be found in the income tax Acts themselves.[5] This principle is also the doctrine of the Supreme Court of the United States.[6]

Lord Wrenbury provides the justification for the tax gatherers' so dipping their hands into the pockets of those whose activities or properties fall within their reach. He said in *Whitney v IRC*[7]:

---

[1] (1925) 10 TC 88 at 112; see also Lord Herschell in *Colquhoun v Brooks* (1889) 14 App. Cas. 493 at 504; also, the Royal Commission on the Taxation of Profits and Income, First Report, Cmnd 8761 para. 8 (1953).

[2] [1971] All ER 233 at 236.

[3] [1983] 1 All ER 133.

[4] at pages 143-144

[5] See Lord Scarman in *Clark v Oceanic Contractors Inc* [1983] 1 All ER at page 139.

[6] See for example, *People of the State of New York ex. Re. Cohn v Graves*, 81 L.ed. 666; *Lawrence v State Tax Comm. of the State of Mississippi*, 76 L.ed. 1102; *International Harvester Co. v Wisconsin Dept. of Taxation*, 88 L.ed. 1373.

[7] (1925) 10 TC 88 at 112.

The person who is resident in the UK is taxed because (whether he be a British subject or not) he enjoys the benefit of our laws for the protection of his person and his property. The non-resident with UK property is taxed because in respect of his property in the United Kingdom he enjoys the benefit of our laws for the protection of that property.

There are a number of possible explanations for the existence of this territorial limit in the tax statutes. First, it may be, as Lord Scarman said in *Clark v Oceanic Contractors Inc* that Parliament is simply recognising the "almost universally accepted principle that fiscal legislation is not enforceable outside the limits of the territorial sovereignty of the kingdom", and that fiscal legislation is therefore drafted in the knowledge that "it is the practice of nations not to enforce the fiscal legislation of other nations".[8] On the other hand, it may be a case of Parliament not wanting to "go beyond its rights with regard to the comity of nations."[9] It may also be a question of practicality. It is unlikely that the UK tax gatherer will be able to collect any tax charged on a person who is not present in the UK, and who has no UK income or property.[10]

In the USA, the taxing power is a constitutional issue and the question of territoriality has been treated as an issue of due process (i.e., possible violation of the 14th Amendment to the US Constitution).[11] The state has no power to tax unless it has jurisdiction of the person to be taxed or the property that produced the income to be taxed[12] and so, for example, an attempt to tax the income of a non-resident derived from sources outside the state is unconstitutional and void.[13] The Supreme Court has however repeatedly asserted that the power of the state to tax where there is a territorial connection is not a deprivation of property without due process. Thus the court said in *People of the State of New York ex. Re. Cohn v Graves*[14]:

Enjoyment of the privileges of residence in the state and the attendant right to invoke the protection of its laws are inseparable from the responsibility for sharing the costs of government. "Taxes are what we pay for civilized society ..."

[8]   ibid.
[9]   See Lord Esher MR in *Colquhoun (Surveyor of Taxes) v Heddon*, (1890) 2 TC 621, at 625; compare Fry LJ at page 630.
[10]   See generally E C D Norfolk [1980] BTR 70.
[11]   See for example *State of Wisconsin v JC Penney & Co.*, 85 L.ed. 267 at 270: "The test is whether property was taken without due process of law, or ... whether the taxing power exerted by the state bears fiscal relation to protection, opportunities and benefits given by the state." (per Frankfurter J).
[12]   *Chrysler Corp. v Oklahoma Tax Commission*, 173 P.2d. 933; *Curle Clothing Co. v Oklahoma Tax Commission*, 68 P.2d.834.
[13]   *Standard Oil Co., Indiana v Thoresen*, 29 F.2d. 708; *Montgomery Ward & Co. v State Tax Commission*, 98 P.2d. 143; *McCutcheon v Oklahoma Tax Commission*, 132 P.2d. 337.
[14]   81 L.ed. 666 at 670 (per Stone J); see also *Lawrence v State Tax Comm. of the State of Mississippi*, 76 L.ed. 1102 at 1105.

Residence or domicile within the state is a valid basis for imposing tax,[15] as are the presence in the state of the source of income[16] and the performance in the state of the taxed transactions.[17] Ultimately, it is a question of equity among those who are privileged to enjoy the benefits provided by the state who ought all to support the state financially[18] and the true test is "whether the state has given anything for which it can ask return."[19] If the question is answered in the affirmative, it is part of the sovereign powers of the state to extract a contribution from those who enjoy its benefits.[20]

The connecting factors

The main factors which connect a person to the UK's territorial limits for tax purposes are residence, ordinary residence, nationality (or citizenship), and domicile. Of these, residence is by far the most important, while nationality is, by itself, not of great significance. Practicality, as referred to above, and yield may be the most important reasons why residence, as opposed to nationality, is preferred by the tax system as the main connector. Using nationality as the connector would result in substantial loss of tax because foreign citizens working in the UK would escape tax, while it might be impossible to collect tax from UK citizens who live and work abroad. This result may of course be commended by the fact that it would attract foreigners to the UK and thereby generate more revenue to circulate within the economy generally – but the loss of tax revenue to the exchequer may not be recouped by the spending power of the foreigners, and there may be reasons why the UK might not want to encourage such an influx of fiscal refugees. The residence connector avoids the problems inherent in the nationality connector, but both might, for different reasons, lead to adverse results for the exchequer in cases of increased emigration and/or reduced birth rate.[21]

As connecting factors, the terms "residence" and "ordinarily resident" are normally used in United Kingdom tax legislation, to describe a situation arising in a year of assessment, and not in relation to some longer or shorter period. The question that has to be decided is generally whether or not a person is resident or ordinarily resident in the United Kingdom in the year of assessment. This is generally the same question that has to be decided in respect of the domicile of a person. The "United Kingdom" in

---

[15] *People of the State of New York ex. Re. Cohn v Graves*, 81 L.ed. 666; Guaranty Trust Co. of New York v Commonwealth of Virginia, 83 L.ed. 16; *Lawrence v State Tax Comm. of the State of Mississippi*, 76 L.ed. 1102.

[16] *Chestnut Securities Co. v Oklahoma Tax Commission*, 125 F.2d. 571; *Scobie v Wisconsin Tax Commission*, 275 NW531; *Reynolds Metal Co. v Martin*, 107 SW.2d. 251; *First Wisconsin Trust Co. v Wisconsin Dept. of Taxation*, 294 NW 868.

[17] *International Harvester Co. v Wisconsin Dept. of Taxation*, 88 L.ed. 1373; *Youngstown Sheet & Tube Co. v City of Youngstown*, 108 NE.2d. 571.

[18] *People of the State of New York ex. Re. Cohn v Graves*, 81 L.ed. 666 at 670.

[19] *State of Wisconsin v JC Penney & Co.*, 85 L.ed. 267 at 270 - 271

[20] *Lawrence v State Tax Comm. of the State of Mississippi*, 76 L.ed. 1102 at 1105; *International Harvester Co. v Wisconsin Dept. of Taxation*, 88 L.ed. 1373 at 1381.

[21] For a discussion about the emigration of persons and capital see A Park [1976] BTR 20.

this context refers to England, Scotland, Wales and Northern Ireland and does not include the Isle of Man and the Channel Islands.[22]

There are a number of general points to note with respect to the territorial scope of United Kingdom tax. As has been seen earlier, generally, a United Kingdom resident is taxable in respect of all income (and capital gains) wherever arising. Such a person will also be liable to inheritance tax, unless he is not domiciled in the United Kingdom and he has no United Kingdom property. A non-resident will be taxable on income arising from sources within the United Kingdom, and will be liable to capital gains tax if he is ordinarily resident, or if he is trading through a branch or agency in the United Kingdom and he disposes of assets used for the purposes of that branch or agency. There may be liability to inheritance tax unless the non-resident is also not domiciled here, and has no property here.

Residence[23]

While residence is the most important of the territorial connectors for liability to United Kingdom tax, the term is not defined by statute. This lack of a definition serves to ensure that the application of legislation in which the term is used "is haphazard and beyond all forecast"[24], leading Viscount Sumner to voice this powerful criticism[25]:

> [T]he subject ought to be told, in statutory and plain terms, when he is chargeable and when he is not. The words "resident in the United Kingdom", "ordinarily" or otherwise, and the words "leaving the United Kingdom for the purpose only of occasional residence abroad", simple as they look, guide the subject remarkably little as to the limits within which he must pay and beyond which he is free. This is the more likely to be a subject of grievance and to provoke a sense of injustice when, as is now the case, the facility of communications, the fluid and restless character of social habits, and the pressure of taxation have made these intricate and doubtful questions of residence important and urgent in a manner undreamt of by [the introducers of income tax]. The Legislature has, however, left the language of the Acts substantially as it was in their days, nor can I confidently say that the decided cases have always illuminated matters. In substance persons are chargeable or exempt, as the case may be, according as they are deemed by this body of Commissioners or that to be resident or the reverse, whatever resident may mean in

---

[22] Inland Revenue Statement of Practice, IR 20, page 3
[23] For a general discussion see A Sumption [1973] BTR 155.
[24] Viscount Sumner in *Levene v IRC* (1928) 13 TC 486 at 502.
[25] ibid.

the particular circumstances of each case. The tribunal thus provided is neither bound by the findings of other similar tribunals in other cases nor is it open to review, so long as it commits no palpable error of law, and the Legislature practically transfers to it the function of imposing taxes on individuals, since it empowers them in terms so general that no one can be certainly advised in advance whether he must pay or can escape payment. The way of taxpayers is hard and the Legislature does not go out of its way to make it any easier.

In spite of the criticisms, Viscount Sumner was of the view that the statutory provisions in which the terms referred to are employed are "plain".[26] Thus for example, Lord Warrington of Clyffe said in the same case that the term "has no special or technical meaning" for tax purposes,[27] and it is often said that, since "residence" has no special meaning for tax purposes, it has to be given its plain and ordinary meaning. This view found its earliest expression in *Re Young* where the Lord President said[28] that the court must deal entirely with the statute in reference to the "natural and proper meaning" of the words. In *Lysaght v IRC*[29] Viscount Sumner said that the meaning of the word is its meaning in the speech of plain men, and that the question to be asked is whether plain men would find that the result of the facts found is "residence" in its plain sense. The best known formulation is however found the words of Viscount Cave LC who said in *Levene v IRC*[30]:

> [T]he word "reside" is a familiar English word and is defined in the Oxford English Dictionary as meaning "to dwell permanently or for a considerable time, to have ones settled or usual abode, to live in a particular place". No doubt this definition must for present purposes be taken, subject to any modification which may result from the terms of the Income Tax Act and schedules, but, subject to that observation, it may be accepted as an accurate indication of the meaning of the word "reside".

The concept of residence being related to the individual's "home" is evident from this definition – for it refers to the place where the individual has his or her usual place of abode, or where he or she lives. This concept also appears frequently in judicial dicta. For example, the Lord President in *Lloyd v Sulley*[31] referred to the place where a person's "ordinary place of abode" and "home" is situated. Similarly in *Levene v IRC* Viscount Sumner said[32] that the taxpayer "continued to go to and fro during the years in

[26] ibid.
[27] 13 TC 486 at 509. The terms "resident" and "ordinarily resident" have the same meanings for Capital Gains Tax purposes as they have under the Income Tax Acts (see TCGA 1992, s.9(1)).
[28] (1875) 1 TC 57 at page 59.
[29] (1928) 13 TC 511 at 529.
[30] 13 TC at page 505.
[31] (1884) 2 TC 37 at 42.
[32] 13 TC at page 501.

question, leaving at the beginning of winter and coming back in summer. His home thus remained as before. He changed his sky but not his home". On this basis, the taxpayer was resident in the UK even during long trips abroad. While this concept of where the taxpayer's home is located is seen in many cases[33], as we shall see, the dictionary definition of residence is often undermined, and the view that the word must be given its ordinary meaning, is often honoured as much in the breach as in the observance. There have been cases in which individuals have been held to be resident in the United Kingdom who could neither be regarded as dwelling here "permanently or for a considerable time", nor as having their "settled or usual abode", or their "home" here, nor indeed, as "living" here. This situation is of course largely due to the factors pointed out by Viscount Sumner in his powerful criticism of the lack of statutory definitions in *Levene v IRC* (above). It nevertheless does sometimes contradict the assertion that the plain and ordinary meaning of the term is to be used.

The principal question with regard to residence is whether a person is resident in the United Kingdom, and not whether a person is resident in this country or in another country. That is to say, the question is "is X resident in the United Kingdom?" and not for example, "is X resident in France or in the United Kingdom?", for X may well be resident in the United Kingdom for United Kingdom tax purposes while at the same time she may be resident in France under French law, and in Germany under German law. The Revenue and the courts in this country are not generally concerned with the last two situations, except perhaps in the context of double taxation agreements. As the Lord President said in *Cooper v Cadwalader*[34], it is not necessary in order for a person to be chargeable that he shall have his sole residence in the United Kingdom, and, it has been recognised as far back as the 19th century that "a man cannot have two domiciles at the same time, but he certainly can have two residences."[35] This principle has been incorporated into the Inland Revenue's code which states thus:

> It is possible to be resident (or ordinarily resident) in both the UK and some other country (or countries) at the same time. If you are resident (or ordinarily resident) in another country, this does *not* mean that you cannot *also* be resident (or ordinarily resident) in the UK.[36]

While it is clear that a person may be resident in more than one place, it may be that an individual cannot be resident nowhere. According to the Lord President in *Rogers v IRC*,[37] "a man must have a residence

---

[33] See for example, Viscount Cave LC (dissenting) in *Lysaght v IRC*, 13 TC 511 at page 532.

[34] (1904) 5 TC 101 at 106-107.

[35] Per the Lord President in *Lloyd v Sulley* (1884) 2 TC 37 at 41. For an even earlier expression of the principle, see *AG v Coote* (1817) 2 TC 385 at 386 (Wood B).

[36] IR 20, para. 1.4 (emphasis supplied). Note that the situations in which a person may be resident in the United Kingdom and in another country in the same year are normally covered by double taxation agreements.

somewhere." Why this is so is not clear, but as early as 1875, it was stated that this proposition does not require the aid of decisions or authority.[38] Thus a sailor who spends most of his time at sea nevertheless must have a residence on land, because a residence is a dwelling place on land,[39] and the court cannot recognise "that he lives so entirely on the sea as to have no residence on the land."[40] Since both *Rogers v IRC* and *Re Young* involved sailors, it may be that this principle applies to sailors only,[41] although it is difficult to see why that should be so. In the modern world of high technology, anything is possible. With the advent of the first American "space tourist" early in 2001, the prospect of people living in outer space starts to loom. However, one does not need to go that far to present an example that would question the correctness of these decisions, at least, in modern times. For example, in July 2001 the proprietors of the large luxury cruise liner *The World* were still taking orders for the purchase of apartments on the ship. These were luxury apartments large and facilitied enough to be the owners' permanent homes, and the ship itself featured a mini-village and high street complete with post office, newsagents, etc. When these purchasers, who each paid millions of pounds for the apartments, take up residence in their apartments on the ship and sell all their terrestrial property, would it be said that they have their residences on land and that they must have a residence on land? That would be a questionable result – unless they were treated as being in the same category as sailors (also a questionable result). A better approach would be to recognise that there would or might be exceptional situations in which an individual has no residence at all (at least, not on land). So, while it may have been correct over 125 years ago to say that "a ship cannot be called a residence"[42] it is arguable that such an absolute statement cannot be correct today.

Grammatically, the word "resident" indicates a quality of the person to be charged to tax – it is not descriptive of his property, real or personal.[43] The relation between a person and a place which is predicated by saying that a person "resides" there includes, *inter alia*, the element of time, duration, or permanence. However, that element, essential and importance as it is, is not the sole criterion[44], and thus whether a person is resident in the United Kingdom or not is essentially a question of fact and degree. The determination of whether or not the degree extends so far as to make a person resident or ordinarily resident here is for the Commissioners and it is not for the courts to say whether they would have reached the same conclusion.[45]

---

[37]   (1879) 1 TC 225 at 227.
[38]   See Lord Deas in *Re Young* (1875) 1 TC 57 at 61-62.
[39]   Per the Lord President in *Re Young*, 1 TC 57 at 59.
[40]   Per Lord Ardmillan in *Re Young*, 1 TC 57 at 63.
[41]   In *Rogers v IRC* (1 TC 225 at 226) the Lord President said that "every sailor has his residence on land".
[42]   Per the Lord President in *Young v IRC*, 1 TC 57 at 59.
[43]   Per Viscount Sumner in *Lysaght v IRC* 13 TC at page 528.
[44]   Lord President Clyde in *Reid v IRC* (1926) 10 TC 673 at 678.
[45]   Per Lord Buckmaster in *Lysaght v IRC* 13 TC at page 534.

The residence of individuals

The determination of an individual's residence must be made for each relevant year of assessment (Viscount Cave in *Levene v IRC*). However, the taxpayer's conduct in years previous and subsequent to the relevant year of assessment is often relevant in determining whether the taxpayer was resident in that year. The Inland Revenue have produced a fairly detailed Statement of Practice on the residence and ordinary residence of individuals (IR 20), which contains a code of principles that seems to be based largely on decisions in their favour. We shall refer to this code at various stages of our discussion.

The Revenue's position is that, strictly speaking, each tax year must be looked at as a whole, that an individual is to be treated as either resident or not resident for the whole year, and that he cannot be regarded as resident for part of the year and not resident for the remainder.[46] The Revenue will however split the year, by concession[47], if the individual is a new permanent resident, or if the individual comes to the United Kingdom for at least two years (provided that he has not been ordinarily resident in the United Kingdom); or if the individual has left the United Kingdom for permanent residence abroad (provided that in so doing he ceases to be ordinarily resident in the United Kingdom); or, subject to certain conditions,[48] if the individual goes abroad under a contract of employment. In the first two cases the individual is treated as resident only from the date of arrival in the United Kingdom, and in the last two, he is treated as not resident from the date of departure.

There are a number of factors (derived both from case law and the Inland Revenue code IR 20) which are applied in the determination of the residence status of an individual. Some of them are of conclusive effect in themselves, while some others, while not necessarily conclusive may, in combination with others, suffice to make an individual resident in the United Kingdom in a relevant year of assessment. Furthermore, some of the factors apply only to certain classes of individual while others apply generally. The discussion that follows examines these factors.

Period of physical presence in the United Kingdom

Section 336(1) of the ICTA 1988 provides that an individual who is in the United Kingdom for some temporary purpose only and not with a view to establishing his residence there will not be charged to income tax as a person resident in the United Kingdom in any year of assessment, if he has

---

[46] IR 20, para. 1.5.
[47] See ESC A11.
[48] The conditions are that, the absence from the United Kingdom and the employment itself both extend beyond a complete tax year, and, any interim visits to the United Kingdom during the period do not amount to 183 days or more, in any tax year, or, an average of 91 days or more in a tax year. In this respect, the average will be taken over the period of absence up to a maximum of 4 years.

not "actually" resided in the United Kingdom for a period equal in the whole to six months in that year.[49] The corollary to this is that if an individual has actually resided in the United Kingdom for a period amounting to six months in any tax year, he will be taxed as a resident.[50] This provision relates only to the taxation, under Schedule D, of profits or gains received in respect of foreign possessions or securities. However s.336(2) extends the rule to tax charged under Cases I, II and III of Schedule E (income from offices, employments, etc), and the Revenue code IR 20 applies the rule generally.

The rule as stated could be seen as an exempting clause. In this context, its import was succinctly expressed by the Lord President in *Lloyd v Sulley*[51]:

> The meaning of it is this, if a foreigner comes here for merely temporary purposes connected with business or pleasure, or something else, and does not remain for a period altogether within the year of six months, he shall not be liable for a certain portion of taxation imposed by Schedule D. He would have been liable but for this exemption; he would have been a person de facto residing in Great Britain. But it is thought that it would be rather hard to charge him when it is merely a visit here for a temporary purpose, and therefore this exemption is introduced. But that so far from derogating from the force of the words by which the tax is laid on in Schedule D., only confirms the view which I have taken of the true force of these words, because it shows that residence for a temporary purpose would have subjected to the tax if it had not been for this clause of exemption.

On the other hand, it could also be seen as a charging clause. Consider these words of Lord Shand in *Lloyd v Sulley*[52:]

> [I]t rather occurs to me that although the provision in section (336(1)) is in the language of exemption, as I have indicated in the course of the argument, it rather appears to me to be a section which is intended to impose liability, or to show that liability will be imposed upon persons who come to this country, but who are the subjects of other realms.

Lord Shand's is a lone voice, since most of the authorities assume that the rule is an exempting clause. However, the provisions of s.336(1)(b) that an individual who has actually resided in the UK for six months will be

---

[49]   See also s 9(3) of the Taxation of Chargeable Gains Act 1992 for a similar provision in respect of Capital Gains Tax.
[50]   s.336(1)(b).
[51]   (1884) 2 TC 37 at 42.
[52]   2 TC 37 at 44.

chargeable as a person residing here can be seen (because of the form of words employed) as one which does impose a charge.

What constitutes six months?

The period of six months referred to in s.336 is calculated in terms of calendar months, rather than lunar months. In *Wilkie v IRC*[53] the Revenue argued for the use of lunar months (i.e., 28-day months), whereby six months would be equal to 168 days. Donovan J rejected this, saying:

> I see no rational purpose behind a provision that the months shall be lunar months. When one is determining how long a foreigner or a Briton from abroad should be allowed to stay in the United Kingdom before contributing, through income tax, to the expenses of the State, there is something at least intelligible, if arbitrary, about selecting one-half of the fiscal year. But to tax him because he has been here for 168 days out of 365 is unintelligible and merely whimsical.[54]

In *Wilkie* the taxpayer was of Scottish origin and was domiciled in Scotland, but lived in India. He arrived in the United Kingdom for temporary purposes at about 2 p.m. on 2 June 1947. He left the United Kingdom on at about 10 a.m. 2 December 1947, his departure having been delayed for about two days as a result of a compulsory cancellation by the airline of his earlier departure reservation. The question was whether he had "actually" resided in the UK for six months in that tax year. Donovan J said[55] that it was right to add up the number of days in which an individual had been actually resident in order to see whether those days, continuous or discontinuous, equalled the number of days in six calendar months. There was however the problem of what to do about fractions of a day, since an individual's stay will almost always begin and end with a fraction of a day. The Revenue had argued for treating fractions of a day as a whole day, with the effect, as they argued, that both the days of arrival and departure were whole days within which the taxpayer was actually resident in the UK. By this interpretation, the taxpayer would have been resident in the UK for 184 days in the year 1947-48 and so would have been here for more than six months. This of course leads to difficulties. There is no reason why taxpayer could not also also claim under that principle to have been actually resident outside the UK on the days of arrival and departure, since he was actually outside the UK for

---

[53]   [1952] 1 All ER 92.
[54]   at page 94.
[55]   ibid.

fractions of those days. The problem was thus presented by Donovan J[56]:

> [B]y applying the rule about fractions of a day one gets the absurdity that the taxpayer is actually resident outside the UK for more than six months and actually resident inside the UK for more than six months. In other words, he is both exempt and chargeable under the rule.

Unsurprisingly, Donovan J rejected the rule about fractions in favour of a rule taking account of a lower unit of time than a complete day "to arrive at the truth and avoid a fiction".[57] This required an examination of the actual number of hours spent here – which in this case was some four hours below the limit. Arguments by the Revenue as to the administrative inconvenience that such a rule would cause were rejected on the basis that the burden of proving the facts justifying exemption under the six month rule lay on the taxpayer who has to establish his case for exemption.[58]

No doubt in consequence of this decision, the Revenue practice now is to consider only whole days, but leaving the days of arrival and departure out of the calculation, thus avoiding the type of problems encountered in *Wilkie*. Under the IR 20, six months is equated with 183 days, whether or not the year is a leap year, ignoring the days of arrival and departure, and a person is who in the United Kingdom for this 183 day period in one year of assessment will, without exception, be treated as resident.[59]

The exemption

It is noteworthy that the six-month period specified in the rule relates to the time spent in the UK in each year of assessment – so it is possible in theory for a visitor to actually spend more than six months in the United Kingdom without being resident, if the period is spread over two years of assessment (for example, from February to August). This point should be taken with care, because if the visits become regular, even though each one is for a duration which is less than six months in each tax year, it is still possible, taking into account other factors, for an individual to be resident. It is also quite easy to fall foul of the terms of the exemption itself. According to Lord McLaren in *Cooper v Cadwalader*[60] this six month exemption is "one that walks upon two legs". It requires, first, that the party is here for a temporary purpose only, and secondly, that he is here not with a view or intent of establishing a residence. If the argument is lame on one of the legs, then the party does not get the benefit of the

---

[56] at page 96.
[57] ibid.
[58] at page 97.
[59] IR 20, para. 1.2.
[60] (1904) 5 TC 101 at 108-109.

exemption, because he must be able to affirm both members of the double proposition.

The interpretation of the first part of the exemption – the meaning of "temporary purpose" – is pertinent to the issue of visits being spread over two years of assessment. In this respect Lord McLaren said[61]:

> [T]emporary purposes mean casual purposes as distinguished from the case of a person who is here in the pursuance of his regular habits of life. Temporary purpose means the opposite of continuous and permanent residence. Nobody ever supposed that you must reside twelve months in the year in order to be liable for Income Tax, and therefore "temporary" does not mean the negation of perpetuity, but means that it is casual or transitory residence, as distinguished from a residence, of which there may be more than one, but which may be habitual or permanent.

The vital words here are "regular habits", "casual" and "transitory". An individual who spends eight months in the United Kingdom spread over two years of assessment may well be stretching those words to their limits, since it is not entirely clear when the visit may be considered to have ceased to be casual or transitory. That the courts sometimes take a strict view of the matter is evident from *AG v Coote*.[62] In that case the taxpayer was domiciled in Ireland, and lived there for most of the year. He bought and furnished a house in London, where he stayed for a few weeks from time to time. The question was whether he was taxable as a UK resident in respect of his profits received here from his possessions in Ireland. The Barons of the Court of Exchequer held that he was. Graham B said[63] that it was "quite impossible to say that the residence of the defendant in England was occasional, or for a temporary purpose" since at any period of the year he might have come to London, where he would have found his house ready for him. Wood B said that if the taxpayer had come to reside in London for a temporary purpose, he might have qualified for exemption, but said that "it is clear that his residence here, while it continued, was for all manner of purposes."[64] With regard to the taxpayer's house, he said[65] that "if this were a temporary residence, he would probably change it sometimes, but in fact it is his own house." If not for recent legislation (see the discussions below on the "place of abode rule"), this type of statement would have raised serious issues as to whether any foreigner who owns a house in this country would ever be able to qualify for this exemption. However, more pertinent to this present discussion is

[61] at page 109.
[62] (1817) 2 TC 385.
[63] at page 385.
[64] ibid.
[65] at page 386.

Wood B's statement that the taxpayer was here for "all manner of purposes." Presumably then, "temporary purposes" is not the same thing as "all manner of purposes", or to put it differently, "all manner of purposes" extends beyond "temporary purposes", and is therefore not permissible. Temporary purposes may therefore signify some sort of cohesiveness or singularity of purposes, all of which are "temporary".

With respect to the words "view or intent of establishing his residence" in the second part of the exemption, the situation is just as interesting. In *AG v Coote*,[66] Richards CB said:

> The fact of the defendant's domicile has nothing to do with the question, nor has the time of his residence any effect on the construction of the words of the Act; for if the defendant came here for the purpose of establishing a residence, it were enough, although he should reside here only two weeks. The sole question is, whether he came here to reside with such a view as exempts him.

In the same case Graham B asked rhetorically, "if a man dies two days after forming his establishment, is he not within the Act?"[67] The answer presumably was "yes, he is within the Act". Thus in this context, Lord McLaren said in *Cooper v Cadwalader* that there seemed to be a recognition of what may be called "a constructive residence as distinguished from actual residence". According to him[68]:

> It is not that you take a house or country place with a view or an intention of establishing a residence, although you may not have had time to become a resident. Still, if you are looking forward to it, apparently that makes you liable to taxation, because in order to get the benefit of the exemption you must say that you have no view and no intention of acquiring a residence there.

What Lord McLaren is saying is that this part of the exemption contains a very subjective element – i.e., did the taxpayer in fact have the view or intention of establishing his residence here? – and if subjectively this is found to be so, then he cannot claim the benefit of s.336(1). It therefore seems that the exemption thus granted to people who visit the United Kingdom is fairly limited in scope. Those who visit the United Kingdom for temporary purposes will be well advised to actively seek not to "look forward to" establishing a residence here, and to avoid actively all activities which may be so construed.

[66]   2 TC 385.
[67]   ibid.
[68]   5 TC at page 109.

Absence for a whole tax year

It is possible for an individual to be resident in the UK even when he or she has not been physically present in the UK at any time during that year.[69] However, if an individual is absent from the United Kingdom for the whole of a year of assessment, it is more difficult for the Revenue to assert that he is resident in the UK in that tax year. This point is illustrated by *Turnbull v Foster*.[70] The taxpayer carried on business for about 40 years as a merchant in Madras where he had his residence. His children lived in the family home in the United Kingdom and he had over the years visited them for short periods nearly every year. The taxpayer and his wife were not in the United Kingdom at any time during the year in which the revenue sought to assess him as a person residing in the United Kingdom. Not surprisingly, the Revenue's attempt failed. The fact that he was never in the country during the year was vital. The Lord Justice Clerk said that to hold the taxpayer resident in those circumstances "would require a pretty strong case indeed".[71]

It is important to note however that the taxpayer in *Turnbull v Foster* had not previously been ordinarily resident in the United Kingdom, a fact noted by the court. For example, the Lord Justice Clerk said[72] "this gentleman has a usual residence in Madras – a usual residence – and he was in that usual residence for the whole of the year of assessment." Lord Trayner also referred to the taxpayer's "usual residence" being in Madras, and equated his usual residence with ordinary residence.[73] In the case of an individual who has previously been ordinarily resident, other factors may apply to make him resident, even though absent from the United Kingdom throughout the tax year. One of these is the "place of abode" rule (below), and another is the principle that an individual must have a residence somewhere. So for example, in *Rogers v IRC* (above), a master mariner whose wife and family lived in the United Kingdom throughout the year in which he was abroad was taxed as a resident notwithstanding his absence for the whole year. According to the Lord President[74]:

> The circumstance that Captain Rogers has been absent from the country during the whole year to which the assessment applies does not seem to me to be a speciality of the least consequence. That is a mere accident. He is not a bit the less a resident in Great Britain because the exigencies of his business have happened to carry him away for a somewhat longer time than usual during this particular voyage.

[69] See Nicholls J in *Reed v Clark* (1985) 58 TC 528 at 547.
[70] (1904) 6 TC 206.
[71] at page 209.
[72] at page 210.
[73] ibid.
[74] 1 TC 225 at 227.

Ordinary residence in previous years

An individual's ordinary residence in the United Kingdom in years prior to a year of assessment in which his residence status is at issue is statutorily relevant now only in respect of Commonwealth citizens or citizens of the Republic of Ireland. The relevant rule is in s.334, which provides that, if a Commonwealth citizen or a citizen of the Republic of Ireland who has been ordinarily resident in the United Kingdom leaves the United Kingdom for the purpose only of occasional residence abroad, he shall be assessed and charged to income tax as a person residing in the United Kingdom, notwithstanding such absence. The Revenue's version of this rule is in para. 2.1 of IR 20 which simply states that "you are resident and ordinarily resident in the UK if you usually live in this country and only go abroad for short periods only – for example, on holiday or on business trips." This paragraph says nothing about the individual being a Commonwealth citizen or a citizen of the Irish Republic and it is questionable whether the Revenue can extend the provisions of s.334 in this way. It is possible of course for the Revenue to take refuge in a statement of the Lord President in *Young v IRC*,[75] where he said:

> I have no doubt myself that if a man has his ordinary residence in this country, it does not matter much whether he is absent for a greater or shorter period of each year from that residence or from the country itself. That is a thing that depends a good deal on a man's occupation, or it may be on his tastes and habits, especially in the latter case, if he is a man not requiring to be engaged in business for his maintenance.

However, this statement was made in the context of a taxpayer who was in fact a British citizen, and so its application should be confined to that context, except as extended now by statute to other Commonwealth and Irish citizens.

This rule is, in spite of its wording (starting as it does with a reference to assessments, thereby appearing to be of a procedural nature), a substantive charging provision.[76] The rationale therefore has been thus expressed

> Now that is a very important provision as extending the meaning of the words in the taxing clause, "residing in the United Kingdom." It extends it to a person who is not for a time actually residing in the United Kingdom, but who has constructively his residence there

---

[75] (1875) 1 TC 57 at 59.
[76] Per Nicholls J in *Reed v Clark*, 58 TC 528 at 552.

because his ordinary place of abode and his home is there, although he is absent for a time from it, however long continued that absence may be.[77]

With respect to the terms used in this rule, the individuals who have the status of "Commonwealth citizen" are described in s.37 of the British Nationality Act 1981. We shall discuss the meaning of "ordinary residence" later in this chapter, and we shall consider now the meaning of "occasional residence" abroad.

Occasional residence

Section 334 applies to Commonwealth or Irish citizens who have left the UK for the "purposes of occasional residence" abroad. What does this phrase mean in this context? The term been considered in a number of cases. It seems that the words "purpose", "residence", and "occasional" are each vital here. Combined, they seem to refer to what the individual was seeking to achieve by going abroad. In ascertaining this, it is valid to examine the taxpayer's conduct in the relevant year of assessment as well as in other years of assessment, as this may throw light on the purpose with which the first departure from the UK took place. Such examination may go to show "method and system" and so remove doubt which might be entertained if the years were examined in isolation one from the other.[78] It has been held that all the reasons underlying a person's being in a particular place are relevant.[79] So for example, a master mariner who has a home in this country, but spends considerable amounts of time abroad with his ship, cannot be considered to have gone abroad for the purposes of occasional residence. According to Lord Deas in *Re Young*[80]:

> [H]e does not go into foreign parts beyond the seas for the purpose of occasional residence. He must live at the port he trades to for a considerable time. He may live on shore or on board the ship according to his mind, but he goes there, not for occasional residence, not for residence at all, but for the purposes of his trade.

By this token, it would seem that a business person who is merely going abroad on a business trip, no matter for how long, is only going abroad for his or her trade, and not for the purpose of residence – "occasional" or not.

---

[77] Per the Lord President in *Lloyd v Sulley* (1884) 2 TC 37 at 42.
[78] See Viscount Sumner in *Levene v IRC* 13 TC 486 at 501.
[79] Per Nicholls J in *Reed v Clark*, 58 TC 528 at 556.
[80] 1 TC 57 at 62.

Lord Deas seems to require that, in order for that phrase to be satisfied, there must at least be a purpose to reside abroad. This is the same thing as saying that the individual must be purposing or intending to live abroad, or to make his home abroad. So, a trading purpose is not necessarily a residence purpose, since trading abroad does not necessarily imply living abroad or making one's home abroad. It seems clear also that a prolonged stay abroad due only to enforced circumstances does not equate to a residence purpose.[81] In this respect, Nicholls J said in *Reed v Clark*[82]:

> There is nothing in the language or in my view the context of (s 334) to show that regardless of the circumstances a person can never be said to have left for the purpose only of occasional residence abroad if his residence abroad extends throughout an entire tax year. A man ordinarily resident here may go to live abroad in March intending to return some months later but through serious illness of himself or others or other unforeseen change of circumstances not return until the end of the following March. I can see no reason why, depending upon all the facts, such a man may not fall within (s. 334). If that is right, it would be absurd that such a man should fall outside (s. 334) if the emergency which kept him abroad should chance to last for a week or two longer and not permit his return until after 5 April.

But if an individual is actually purposing to reside or live abroad, can this correctly be considered to be a purpose of occasional residence only? Since residence refers to a person's "home", would an individual who purposes to live or make her home in France for a defined period – say, six months – be living in France for occasional residence only, or would the intention to make a home abroad necessarily connote something else? What then is a purpose of occasional residence? Let us examine some interesting cases. In *Levene v IRC*[83] a retired businessman who had previously been both resident and ordinarily resident in the United Kingdom went (in December 1919) to "live abroad". From the date of departure until some time more than five years later, he maintained no fixed place of abode anywhere, but stayed in various hotels, both in this country and abroad. In 1925, he finally was able to secure a flat in Monte Carlo for himself and his wife. During the years that he spend abroad, he spent an average of twenty weeks each year in the United Kingdom, his purpose being to obtain medical advice, to visit relatives, to take part in certain Jewish religious observances, and to deal with his income tax affairs. It was held by the House of Lords that the taxpayer originally left the United Kingdom and went to live abroad for occasional residence

---

[81]   See Hanna J in *Iveagh v Revenue Commissioners* [1930] IR 386 at 422.
[82]   58 TC at 553.
[83]   (1928) 13 TC 486.

only, and so was resident in the United Kingdom in the years in question. According to Viscount Sumner[84]:

> The evidence as a whole disclosed that Mr. Levene continued to go to and fro during the years in question, leaving at the beginning of winter and coming back in summer, his home thus remaining as before. He changed his sky but not his home. On this I see no error in law in saying of each year that his purpose in leaving the United Kingdom was occasional residence only. The occasion was the approach of an English winter and when with the promise of summer here that occasion passed away back came Mr. Levene to attend calls of interest, of friendship and of piety.

In this case, the court thought that it could identify an "occasion" which led to the occasional residence abroad – the English winter. In another case, no such occasion was identifiable, and thus the decision went the other way. In *IRC v Combe*[85] the taxpayer, who had been both resident and ordinarily resident in the United Kingdom left for the purpose of a three year apprenticeship under a New York employer. The object of his apprenticeship was to qualify him as European Representative of the New York firm, and his employment accordingly made it necessary for him to visit Europe, and especially the United Kingdom from time to time on his employer's business (at times spending almost six months). On these visits he lived in hotels and throughout the three years he had no house and no fixed place of abode in this country. Instead, his business and residential headquarters were permanently in New York throughout the three years. It was held that the taxpayer's departure was not a departure for the purpose of occasional residence abroad and he was not resident in the United Kingdom in the years in question. Lord President Clyde said[86] that "occasional residence" is residence taken up or happening as passing opportunity requires in one case, or admits, in another, and contrasts with the residence, or ordinary residence, of a person who is "resident" or "ordinarily resident" in some place or country. Lord Sands, concurring, noted that there was a "distinct break" in the nature of the taxpayer's residence when he departed for America.[87]

This concept of distinct (or definite) break was applied by Nicholls J in *Reed v Clark*.[88] The taxpayer left the United Kingdom for the USA with the firm intention of living in Los Angeles throughout the relevant year of assessment but to return to the United Kingdom shortly after the end of that year. He was away for a 13-month period which spanned the whole

---

[84] at page 501.
[85] (1932) 17 TC 405.
[86] at page 410.
[87] at page 411.
[88] 58 TC 528; [1985] 3 WLR 142.

of the tax year, living for the most part in a house rented for him by a company under his control. Nicholls J held that, considering all the circumstances underlying the taxpayer's departure, including the fact that there was a definite break in the pattern of his life, his departure for the USA. was not for occasional residence only. He ceased living in London, and for the whole tax year, he lived in or near Los Angeles, mostly in one fixed place of abode. He worked from there, and for that year, Los Angeles was his headquarters. The inescapable conclusion from the primary facts was that for the whole of the relevant year his home and place of business were in Los Angeles. He was thus not resident in the United Kingdom in the year in question. Nicholls J said that the meaning to be given to "occasional residence" in the context of the relevant section was a question of law[89] and that occasional residence was the converse of ordinary or usual residence.[90] According to Nicholls J[91] a British resident's departure abroad for a period of a few weeks or months with the firm intention of returning to live here as before at the end of that period would most likely be always a departure for the purpose only of occasional residence. However, a firm intention to return to live as before is not necessarily indicative of occasional residence.[92] The difference is a question of degree, and "there is an area where different minds may reach different conclusions."[93] So, a period of one year is "long enough for a person's purpose of living where he does to be capable of having a sufficient degree of continuity to be properly described as settled".[94] Nicholls J thus concluded that the foreign country could be the place where, for that period, the individual was ordinarily and not just occasionally resident.[95]

In this case the Commissioners had found that the taxpayer's journey to America was not made as a matter of "passing opportunity". His business activities had previously taken him, and still took him to America every year, and on that particular trip he had established himself in a way which would make him both resident and ordinarily resident there under the United Kingdom rules. Summing up the matter Nicholls J said[96]:

> In this case there was a distinct break in the pattern of Mr. Clark's life which lasted (as from the outset he intended) for just over a year. He ceased living in London and for that year he lived in or near Los Angeles, mostly in one fixed place of abode, and he worked from there. For that year Los Angeles was his headquarters. He did not visit this country at all. On the whole I do not think that he can be said to have left the United Kingdom for the purpose only of occasional residence abroad. In my judgment the conclusion of the Commissioners on this was correct.

---

[89]   58 TC at 554.
[90]   ibid.
[91]   at page 555.
[92]   ibid.
[93]   ibid.
[94]   ibid.
[95]   ibid.
[96]   at page 556.

Thus perhaps it is easiest to look at "occasional residence" first from the point of view of what it is not. It seems that a purpose to establish a settled residence (or to settle) abroad is not a purpose of occasional residence. Neither, it seems, is a purpose to establish a planned residence, not as passing opportunity requires or admits, but as part of a defined plan for a new lifestyle, either forever or for a specific limited period. A purpose of occasional residence on the other hand seems to be a purpose to reside abroad, but not for settled purposes – or perhaps a purpose to live, but not to settle abroad. The duration of the actual residence abroad does not seem to be the crucial factor,[97] since for example prolonged residence abroad due to ill health does not necessarily impact on the original purpose for leaving this country. However, the duration of the proposed residence abroad may be important, as this may be indicative of whether there was a plan to settle (for a defined or indefinite term). Furthermore, the fact that the plan to reside abroad is motivated by fiscal reasons is not material. As Nicholls J said in *Reed v Clark*[98]:

> The presence of a tax avoidance intention may help to show, for instance, why a person went abroad at all, or at the particular time he did, how long he intended to remain away, or where his home in fact was in the year of assessment. But residence abroad for a carefully chosen limited period of work there (if that is what the facts establish) is no less residence abroad for that period because the major reason for it was the avoidance of tax. Likewise with ordinary residence.

The concept of a plan or purpose to live abroad seems clear enough. But the case of *Levene v IRC* appears to muddy the waters. Mr Levene and his wife had formed an "intention to live abroad". Both he and his wife had indifferent health, and had been advised by their doctors to live in the South of France and to avoid the UK in winter. In pursuance of his intention to "live abroad", he sold his furniture, surrendered the lease of his house, and eventually went abroad. While abroad, he endeavoured to find a suitable flat in Monaco, but failed to find one until several years later. Viscount Sumner referred[99] to the rule charging the taxpayer as a UK resident if he had left the UK for the purpose only of occasional residence abroad, and asked "Was that the only purpose of his leaving so far as residence is concerned?" This presumably presupposes that, if Mr Levene had any residential purpose which was not "occasional", then the rule would not apply. The Special Commissioners had answered Viscount Sumner's question in the affirmative – and he felt that there was evidence

---

[97] See *Iveagh v Revenue Commissioners*, above.
[98] 58 TC at 556.
[99] 13 TC 486 at 500.

before them on which they could so decide. According to Viscount Sumner[100]:

> His only declaration was that he meant to live abroad, not saying whether it was to be an occasional or a constant, a part time or a whole time sojourn. He was advised by his doctor to seek a better climate, which is consistent with returning to England when English weather minds. He had gone out of business in England and had broken up his establishment, but he still had in England business interests connected with his Income Tax assessments, and ties of filial piety and religious observance, for his father was buried at Southampton and he was himself a member of the English community of Jews.

With all respect to Viscount Sumner, it is difficult to see why any of these factors should matter. It seems clear that the taxpayer had formed an intention to live abroad, and to stop living in England. The fact that he had closed his English establishment and was looking for suitable accommodation in Monaco would be indicative of that. This fact was pointed out by Lord Warrington of Clyffe who said[101] that "Since he gave up his house in 1918 he has had no intention of again taking a house or flat in the United Kingdom." It is clear that an individual may easily decide to settle in another country while maintaining ties with his country of origin. Most emigrants do just that, and it would be quite odd if they did not. It would be impossible for an emigrant to also transplant all of his or her family and friends, even if they were agreeable to the idea. Many emigrants will (financial and political considerations permitting) continue to visit their countries of origin frequently and for any number of reasons. Expatriate academics often do this during the summer vacations. Neither the retained ties nor the visits necessarily have any bearing on their original intention or purpose to emigrate from their home country and settle in another country.

In *Levene's* case, the Commissioners were "satisfied" that Mr Levene had formed the intention of living abroad for the greater part of the year, but of returning to the UK each year and remaining here "for considerable periods" in the year. Therefore, taking into account his past and present habits of life, the regularity and length of his visits here, his ties with this country, and his "freedom from attachments" abroad, they came to the conclusion that, until 1925 when he took a lease of a flat in Monte Carlo, he continued to be resident in the UK. It seems that it was generally agreed that he ceased to be resident in the UK from the time that he

---

[100] ibid.
[101] at page 509.

acquired the flat.[102] Viscount Cave LC made reference to this 1925 event[103].

> He then went abroad from time to time, but continued to live in hotels either here or in France and he did not actually find a home abroad until the month of January, 1925, when he took a lease of a flat at Monte Carlo. The result is that during the period from the end of 1919 until January, 1925, he went much abroad, partly for the sake of his own and his wife's health, partly no doubt to search for a house or flat, and partly (as may be inferred from the finding of the Commissioners) in the hope of escaping liability to the English Income Tax.

Viscount Cave then went on to say that none of these purposes of going abroad was "more than a temporary purpose". In so doing, he referred to the fact that Mr Levene "regularly returned to England for the greater part of the summer months though for less than one half of each year".

Again, with all respect to Viscount Cave, the fact that Mr Levene did not succeed in finding "a home abroad" (obviously not from want of trying) does not seem to be a valid criterion for deciding what his purpose was in going abroad. It is not entirely clear how Viscount Cave came to the conclusion that none of Mr Levene's purposes was more than a "temporary purpose". If it was accepted that his leasing of a flat in 1925 changed his purpose of going abroad from temporary residence to a settled residence, what actually precipitated that change? Suppose that Mr Levene had succeeded in finding a suitable flat in 1920 – would this have meant that he had not gone abroad for occasional residence only? That would seem to follow from the reasoning of the Commissioners and the courts. It is of course true that a temporary purpose can change to a settled one. This would be the case if for example an individual went abroad to learn a foreign language for say, four months, and while there, fell in love, got married, and decided to settle in that country. However, a lot of this would be directly related to the individual's own intentions. Clearly, Mr Levene had "formed an intention to live abroad". He had sought for accommodation, but only succeeded in finding one after a few years. It would seem to be obvious that his lack of success had nothing to do with his intentions, which seemed clear enough. The inescapable conclusion is that his inability to secure adequate accommodation operated against him by being somehow linked by the courts to his intentions or purposes in going abroad. This does not seem to be a correct way to looking at the matter.

---

[102] Contrast Lord Warrington of Clyffe (at page 510), who preferred to leave that particular question open.
[103] at page 506.

Perhaps *Levene v IRC* can be explained from the point of view that the question involved was a question of fact and the courts were not prepared to disturb the Commissioners findings of fact without compelling reasons – a factor of some prominence in the speeches in the House of Lords. However, in applying this principle, statements were made which raise as many questions as they answer.

Regularity of visits to the United Kingdom

The case of *Levene v IRC* (above) shows that where an individual makes regular visits to the United Kingdom for periods which are less than six months in any year of assessment, such an individual can still be treated as resident even if he has no home, business, or residential establishment in the UK. The crucial question is whether the visits are sufficiently regular to be part of his normal life. This point is illustrated even more vividly in *Lysaght v IRC*.[104] The taxpayer, born in England of Irish parents, was a Managing Director of an English company. After retiring from this post, he was appointed an advisory director to the company. He thereupon sold his house in England and went to live in Ireland, maintaining no definite place of abode in this country. His new position as a consultant to the company brought him to England every month for directors' meetings, on which visits he stayed for about one week, in hotels. The commissioners held that he was resident and ordinarily resident in the United Kingdom in the year in question and this was upheld by the House of Lords (Viscount Cave LC dissenting). Viscount Sumner noted[105] that it was the shortness of the aggregate time during which Mr Lysaght was in the United Kingdom that constituted the principal point in his favour, but also noted that the question of longer or shorter time, like other questions of degree, is one peculiarly for the commissioners. He did not doubt that the commissioners had understood the word "resident" in its proper legal signification and so applied it. Therefore their decision could not be interfered with. It is interesting however that Viscount Cave LC (dissenting) thought that the Commissioners could not rightly have arrived at their decision. His argument was powerful[106].

> In the present case the Respondent, Mr. Lysaght, has a permanent home in Southern Ireland where he lives with his family; but he comes to England once a month for business purposes, stays at an hotel and, when his business (which usually occupies about a week) is concluded, he returns home. It is unnecessary for me to repeat the observations which I have made in the previous case (*Levene v IRC*) as to the meaning of the expressions "reside" and "ordinarily reside";

[104] 13 TC 511.
[105] at page 581.
[106] 13 TC at page 532.

and it is enough to say that, on the view which in that case I have taken as to the meaning of those expressions, there appears to me to be no reason whatever for holding that the Respondent is resident or ordinarily resident in this country. It is true that he comes here at regular intervals and for recurrent business purposes; but these facts, while they explain the frequency of his visits, do not make them more than temporary visits or give them the character of residence in this country. That he has a small account at a bank in Bristol – doubtless for use during his visits to this country – and a club in London to which he hardly ever goes, appear to me to be trivial circumstances which cannot affect the decision. If the Respondent is held to reside here and to be taxable accordingly, there would appear to be no reason why those many foreigners who periodically visit this country for business purposes, and having concluded their business go away, should not be made subject to a like burden.

Viscount Cave was a lone voice, although his position seems to accord better with common sense than the position of the majority. Thus Mr Lysaght found himself to be a resident of two countries for tax purposes. The result then is that an individual may be held resident even if he has no place of abode (or home) at all (*Levene v IRC*) or no place of abode (or home) in the United Kingdom (*Lysaght v IRC*) if he makes habitual and substantial visits to the United Kingdom. For these purposes, "substantial" means (per the Revenue code IR 20) that the average annual period(s) of the visits amounts to three months (91 days) or more per tax year[107] (no doubt derived from Mr Lysaght's visits of one week every month amounting to twelve weeks in a year), and "habitual" means that this pattern has been followed for four consecutive years. In such a case, the Revenue will treat the individual as being resident from the fifth year.[108] If it is clear that the individual intends to follow this pattern from the beginning, he may be treated as resident from the beginning.[109] Presumably, the decision of whether an individual "intends" to follow the pattern from the beginning can take cognisance of subsequent events.

The purpose of the visits to the United Kingdom

Closely connected with the last point is the purpose of the taxpayer's visits to the United Kingdom. If the person is merely in the United Kingdom as a traveller, and not as part of his regular order of life, the visits *per se* will

---

[107] Days spent in the U.K for exceptional purposes beyond the taxpayer's control will be discounted for these purposes (see IR 20, para. 3.3). An example given in IR 20 of this scenario relates to illness of the taxpayer or a member of his family. The question here is what happens if the whole purpose of the visit is for medical treatment.
[108] See IR 20, para. 3.3.
[109] ibid.

probably not be sufficient to make him resident. For example in *IRC v Zorab*[110] the taxpayer was a retired member of the Indian civil service, who in the course of his habitual travels in Europe spent about five months in England each year, the sole purpose being to visit friends. He was held not to be resident by the commissioners, and this was upheld by Rowlatt J. Rowlatt J said[111] that one had to consider not only the time that the taxpayer was here but also the nature of his visit and his connection with this country. According to Rowlatt J, in this case the gentleman seemed to be a mere traveller. He was a native of India and had retired from his work there, after which be began to travel extensively in Europe. In these circumstances there was sufficient evidence for the commissioners to hold that he was not resident.

It should be noted that this test as to the purpose of the taxpayer's visit is not conclusive, since a person may still be resident in the United Kingdom even if he is here for reasons beyond his control. That this is so can be established from the cases. In *Lysaght v IRC* (above) for example, the taxpayer only came to the United Kingdom for the purpose of board meetings, and not for the purpose of living here. This fact seemed to influence the Court of Appeal, which decided (by a majority) in his favour. However, that decision was reversed by the House of Lords. The inconclusiveness of volition is further illustrated by *Inchiquin v IRC*.[112] The taxpayer was an Irish peer, who had succeeded to the ancestral titles and estates (including a castle in Ireland) on the death of his father, but who was living in England. On the outbreak of the Second World War in 1939 he was called up for military service and became an officer in the British Army. In 1940, during the course of the war his mother, who was living in the castle in Ireland, died. The prevailing circumstances made it desirable that he should return to Ireland to live in the castle and look after the estate, and in particular to avoid being called an absentee landlord. However his military duties occupied him and he was not relieved until 1942 upon which he took up permanent residence in the castle in Ireland. The commissioners held that he was resident in the years 1940–41 and 1941–42, in spite of the fact that he had always wanted to return to Ireland but was forced to stay here. This decision was upheld by the Court of Appeal. Tucker LJ said[113] that he derived most assistance from the speech of Lord Buckmaster in Lysaght's case in which Lord Buckmaster said:

A man might well be compelled to reside here completely against his will; the exigencies of business often forbid the choice of residence and though a man may make his home elsewhere and stay in this country only because business compels him, yet ... if the periods for

---

[110] (1926) 11 TC 289.
[111] at page 291.
[112] (1946–50) 31 TC 125.
[113] at 133-134.

which and the conditions under which he stays are such that they may be regarded as constituting residence, it is open to the commissioners to find that in fact he does so reside.

In this case there was sufficient evidence for the commissioners to decide as they did.

Place of abode in the United Kingdom

The availability of accommodation or a place of abode to an individual is a factor that often points strongly to residence, because it indicates some sort of psychological or emotional connection with the place where the place of abode is located. It may be indicative of an intention to establish a residence in that place. However, as we have seen in the context of regular visitors to the UK (*Levene and Lysaght* above), it is possible for an individual to be resident in the United Kingdom even though he has no home or place of abode here. The Lord President (Lord Clyde) noted this point in Reid v IRC[114].

> Take the case of a homeless tramp, who shelters to-night under a bridge, to-morrow in the greenwood and as the unwelcome occupant of a farm outhouse the night after. He wanders in this way all over the United Kingdom. But will anyone say he does not live in the United Kingdom? – and will anyone regard it as a misuse of language to say he resides in the United Kingdom? In his case there may be no relations with family or friends, no business ties, and none of the ordinary circumstances which create a link between the life of a British subject and the United Kingdom; but, even so, I do not think it could be disputed that he resides in the United Kingdom.

The point was reiterated by Viscount Cave LC in *Levene v IRC*[115].

> [W]here the person sought to be charged has no home or establishment in any country but lives his life in hotels or at the houses of his friends, and if such a man spends the whole of the year in hotels in the United Kingdom, then he is held to reside in this country; for it is not necessary for that purpose that he should

---

[114] (1926) 10 TC 673 at 679.
[115] 13 TC 486 at 505.

continue to live in one place in this country but only that he should reside in the United Kingdom.

So, the lack of living accommodation or of an "establishment" does not necessarily operate in favour of a taxpayer as pointing to non-residence. However, availability thereof may operate against the taxpayer as pointing to residence. We have noted earlier in this chapter that the concept of where an individual's "home" is located appears regularly in the cases. It may be difficult for an individual who has a home or a residential establishment in a country to claim that he does not have a view or intention to establish his residence in that country. Why then would he have an establishment there? Furthermore, the lack of a residential establishment anywhere abroad might operate against an individual who has left the UK to live abroad to indicate that he is still resident here.[116] But once such an establishment is acquired, the taxation situation may change miraculously.[117] Thus the presence of living accommodation may introduce a presumption as to the individual's intentions – but of course this presumption, if it exists at all, must be rebuttable. Is this really the case?

It is interesting to examine the Revenue's practice in this respect. The Revenue's position used to be that, if an individual has a permanent place of abode or accommodation available in the United Kingdom for his use, he is resident here for any tax year in which he visits the United Kingdom, however short the visit may be.[118] There may have been a number of explanations for this type of rule. The sailors' cases referred to earlier (*Rogers v IRC* and *Re Young*) both involved individuals who had residential establishments in the UK, and this fact played a role in the decisions to hold them resident even though they were out of the UK for long periods (indeed, in *Rogers*, the absence was for the whole tax year). It was of course material in these cases that the sailors had no home or establishment anywhere else on land. *AG v Coote* (above) was another case in which the existence of a residential establishment in the UK played a major role in the decision to hold the taxpayer resident, even though his visits to the UK were for relatively short periods. This time, the fact that the taxpayer possessed a house in London went to establish that he had not come to visit the UK for "temporary purposes" only, and so could be held resident even though he was here for less than six months. A more celebrated case in point is *Cooper v Cadwalader*.[119] The taxpayer in this case was an American barrister who had his ordinary residence in New York and who rented a house in Scotland, with exclusive shooting and sporting rights over the grouse shootings of the property, and fishing rights in the rivers and streams within the bounds of its territory. The house was furnished and

---

[116] *Levene v IRC* (above).
[117] ibid.
[118] This rule, as far as it relates to temporary visitors, has recently been changed by statute - see ICTA 1988, s.336(3).
[119] (1904) 5 TC 101.

was kept up for the taxpayer and placed at his disposal to go to at any time of the year that he chose. He and his valet, whom he brought with him from America, normally resided at this property continuously for a period of about two months each year during the grouse shooting season. He had no place of business in the United Kingdom, and, during his stay here, maintained and kept open his residence in New York so he could return to it at any time. It was held that he was resident in the United Kingdom. According to the Lord President[120] the taxpayer had, in effect, a lease of heritage in Scotland, occupied personally the properties let to him for a considerable portion of each year, and when he was absent in America, these properties were kept in readiness for his return. It was clear that his occupation of the property was not of a casual or temporary character. Rather, it was substantial, and as regards some of its incidents, it was continuous.

The Lord President said[121] that if a person continues to have a residence in the United Kingdom, he is resident there in the sense of the Acts, and that a person may have more than one residence, if he maintains an establishment at each. This is may be regarded as strong support for the proposition that the existence of accommodation introduces a presumption as to intention to establish a residence. Although the context in which the statement was made does not suggest that any visit, no matter how brief, will be sufficient, it is arguable that cases like *AG v Coote* could be interpreted as pointing to such a result (at least, perhaps in respect of property owned by the taxpayer). It also seems that dicta in *Thomson v Bensted*[122] provide support for the proposition. In that case the taxpayer had his home in Hawick, wherein lived his wife and family. He worked for a company which required him to live in Nigeria, where he spent eight months in the relevant year, the remaining four months being spent at his Hawick home in the UK. The question was whether he was resident in the UK during the relevant year. The taxpayer argued that he was not resident in this country inasmuch as he was required to reside in Southern Nigeria during the whole period of his employment by the company, and that his residence must therefore be deemed to be in that country. The Court of Session held that he was resident in the UK. Lord Dundas referred to his home in Hawick, and said "That is a place of residence, and if he occupies that place of residence for a portion of a year, he then is within the meaning of this clause, as I read it, residing there in the course of the year."[123] This was so far the most direct statement of the "place of abode" rule, and it may have been the direct source of the revenue's original position on the matter. The Court of Session in this case placed

---

[120] at page 105.
[121] at page 106.
[122] (1918) 7 TC 137.
[123] 7 TC at page 146.

reliance on *Cooper v Cadwalader*. However, there is nothing in *Cooper v Cadwalader* that justifies this statement by Lord Dundas. The statement seems to be an extension of *Cooper v Cadwalader*, and that in a way that was not necessary for the decision in *Thomson v Bensted* itself. That the statement is not supported by *Cooper v Cadwalader* itself is clear. For example, there was nothing in the statement of the Lord President in *Cooper v Cadwalader* to suggest that the six month rule in s.336(1) cannot apply in appropriate cases to negate the rule that he had stated. This would seem to indicate that any presumption that may exist as to intention to establish a residence is rebuttable. Indeed the possibility of the six month rule being applicable to negate the place of abode rule was explored, albeit unsuccessfully, by counsel in *Cooper v Cadwalader* itself. In response to the argument of counsel that Mr Cadwalader fell within the six month exemption, the Lord President said[124]:

> This provision appears to be directed to prevent temporary residents for less than six months in one year from being charged in respect of profits received from abroad, but it does not appear to me to apply to a case like the present. I do not think that the Appellant can reasonably maintain that he is in the United Kingdom "for some temporary purpose only, and not with any view or intent of establishing his residence therein", in the sense of the section, as he took (the property in which he had shooting rights) with the view of establishing his residence there during a material part of each year and maintaining his connection with it as tenant during the rest of the years, and he has a residence always ready for him if he should choose to come to it.

What may be deduced from this answer is that, if Mr Cadwalader's visit had been for some temporary purpose only, and if he had never had any intention of establishing his residence in the rented property, s.336(1) may have availed him, notwithstanding that he had an establishment or place of abode available for his use. This is very far from Lord Dundas' statement in *Thomas v Bensted* (and the Revenue's old stance) that any visit will automatically be sufficient to attract a resident status if an individual has a place of abode. Indeed, none of the early cases which may be regarded as favourable to the Revenue (e.g., *AG v Coote, Re Young, Rogers v IRC*) expressed any universal and immutable principle in this respect. While some of them did indicate that the existence of a residential establishment may be strongly indicative of the taxpayer's state of mind (or purpose) when coming to this country, it was never stated that any presumption in

---

[124] ibid.

that respect could not be displaced by clear evidence.

The Revenue rule could clearly work hardship to foreign visitors who just happened to have some available accommodation in the UK, and it might even have eventually served as a strong disincentive to property deals in the UK. It is not surprising therefore that the rules governing the application of the place of abode were changed.[125] The change relates only to those who are in the United Kingdom for temporary purposes only. In this respect, s.336(3) provides that the question whether an individual is in the United Kingdom for some temporary purpose only and not with the intention of establishing his residence there shall be decided without regard to any living accommodation available in the United Kingdom for his use.[126] Thus, an individual whose normal place of residence is outside the UK and who comes to visit the UK will not be resident here simply because he has accommodation available here for his use. However, other factors may still apply to make him resident. The only real change introduced by s.336(3) is simply to remove, in respect of visitors to the UK, any presumption that seemed to arise out of the availability of accommodation that (a) they are not here for temporary purposes only, and (b) they have an intention to establish a residence here – and the effect is simply that the availability of accommodation is in itself no longer a sufficient criterion to make a visitor resident. The situation is thus now much the same as that which was envisaged in *Cooper v Cadwalader* – i.e., the place of abode rule affects those who have some stronger connection with the United Kingdom than the mere availability of accommodation here. This stronger connection is most likely to be found in the lifestyles of the individuals concerned, vis-a-vis the UK (for example, that they come here every year, have business or family connections here, etc). The connection, if it exists, may then be fortified (but not established) by the availability of accommodation, which may operate in addition to the other factors to indicate a particular lifestyle or intention (of residence here).[127]

The issue of the taxpayer's intentions in respect of the UK then becomes a distinct matter to be established by evidence, as does the issue of whether he is in the UK for some temporary purpose only. This may have taken the real sting out of the place of abode rule, for it's original sting (at least, as far as the Revenue's rule was concerned) was in relation to temporary visitors who happened to have accommodation available for their use. It is of course arguable that the sting never ought to have been there at all. The Revenue's old rule seems to bear no relationship to the ratio of the authority (*Cooper*) that it was supposed to have been based on, since it seems clear that *Cooper* never intended to apply any presumption

---

[125] The changes took effect on 6th April 1993; see ICTA 1988, s.336(3).

[126] Compare s 9(4) of the TCGA 1992 for similar provisions with respect to Capital Gains Tax.

[127] Compare the Revenue code IR 20 (paras. 3.7 and 3.11) which now applies a variation of the place of abode rule to "longer term visitors" (i.e., those who visit for a purpose that will entail a stay of at least 2 years). In such cases the fact that accommodation is owned or leased by the visitor will render him from the date of arrival. For those who "come to and remain" in the U.K availability of accommodation is also said to be relevant in determining their ordinary residence status (para. 3.11).

to people who were clearly temporary visitors. In *Cooper* it was clear to the court that the taxpayer was not here for "temporary purposes." The evidence for this lay not in any presumption that the availability of the accommodation raised, but rather, in the lifestyle of Mr Cadwalader. That lifestyle may itself have been sufficient to make him resident, even if he had lived in hotels when he came here (*Lysaght v IRC*). That he also had a "home" in the UK made his case even weaker. Viewed in this light, it is questionable whether the place of abode rule now serves any purpose in its own right. It is not really appropriate for people whose homes are in the UK, since the fact that this is where they "live" means that they are resident here. It is not relevant to those who have no "home" at all (e.g., wanderers and vagrants). It no longer raises any presumption in respect of those whose homes are outside the UK but who come to visit the UK temporarily. It appears that the availability of accommodation in the UK now merely serves as a corroborative factor, where other factors are present. The Revenue's new rule of treating it as establishing residence in certain situations seems suspect.

Question of fact

Whether or not an individual has a place of abode available for his use is a question of fact, and as *Lowenstein v De Salis*[128] shows, an individual does not even have to own or rent the property if it is de facto available for his use. In that case a Belgian national, who had his residence in Brussels, visited the United Kingdom each year, and occupied for varying periods property in England, which comprised of a hunting box, together with the hunting stables, garage and gardens, and which belonged to a company of which he was a director and majority shareholder. It was admitted that the taxpayer could, when in the United Kingdom, use the said residence, stables and garage, without obtaining formal permission. In no year was he in this country for up to six months.

The main factor that distinguished this from *Cooper v Cadwalader* was that in this case the taxpayer was neither the owner nor the lessee of the property. According to Rowlatt J, it really came to this – whether it is of the essence of the case that a man should be treated as coming here with a view to establishing his residence, and not for a temporary purpose only, that he should have at any rate a proprietary interest, such as a lease or something of that sort, in the house which he occupies when he is here. Rowlatt J held that it was not. He could not see what difference it made. The house was *de facto* available for the taxpayer's occupation whenever he came to this country and that was sufficient. Rowlatt J, concluding the

[128] (1926) 10 TC 424.

matter, said[129]:

> [W]hen you are considering a question like residence, you are considering just a bundle of actual facts, and it seems to me that in a case like this you can quite well say that here this man had this house at his disposal, with everything in it or for his convenience, kept going all the year round, although he only wanted it for a short time. Luckily, he was in relation with a Company who were the owners of it, and he could do that without owning it. It is an accident. It might have been that he could do that with a relation, or a friend, or a philanthropist, or anybody; but in fact there was this house for him; and a lease would not put him in any better position so far as having the house and the availability of it, and the power of coming to it were concerned, so far as I understand the facts. Now I think that it is a case in which you do say you look at the substance of the matter. You do not look at the substance of the matter and say the man is the Company, – that is inaccurate, but you look at the substance of the matter and say: This is the house in which he could reside and did reside. It might have been held that he must not do it any longer, but up to the present time in history there has been no change for the last two or three years. There it is. He has got this house to come to when he likes; he does not own it; he has got no proprietary interest in it, but it is just as good as if he had for the purpose of having it for a residence, and there it is. I am bound to say that I do not think there can be any question upon the facts as clearly found in this case, giving the Appellant the benefit of anything that may be doubtful upon the case … stated.

The latest incarnation of the Revenue code IR20[130] seems to dispense with this de facto availability rule in favour of a rule that considers whether the taxpayer owns or leases the place of abode. Para. 3.7 claims that a "longer term visitor" will be resident from the date of arrival in the UK if he owns or leases accommodation here. The paragraph then refers to para. 3.11 which provides:

If you come to, and remain in, the UK, you will be treated as ordinarily resident

a. from the day you arrive, if

- you already own accommodation here

---

[129] at pages 437-438.
[130] The preface claims that it "reflects the law and practice at October 1999".

- you buy accommodation during the tax year of arrival, or
- you have or acquire accommodation on a lease of three years or more during the tax year of arrival; or

b. from 6 April of the tax year in which such accommodation becomes available, when this occurs after the year of arrival.

Presumably the reference by para. 3.7 to para. 3.11 is intended to indicate that similar principles apply to residence. While the reference that these rules apply to "longer term visitors" is consistent with the view expressed earlier that the accommodation rule has now been consigned to a corroborative role,[131] it is not clear what the change of emphasis from de facto availability to ownership (or leasehold interests) is intended to achieve. It is clear that the Revenue do not have the authority to override decided cases – and we must therefore assume that this change of emphasis only indicates a policy not to press the issue where the taxpayer does not own or lease accommodation which is in fact available for his use. There would of course be nothing to stop them from applying the principle in *Lowenstein v De Salis*.

Overseas duties

Apart from s.336(3) ICTA 1988 (availability of a place of abode disregarded for certain purposes in respect of temporary visitors), there is another statutory qualification to the place of abode rule. S.335(1) ICTA 1988 provides that, where a person works full-time in a trade, profession, vocation, office or employment, and no part of the person's duties are carried on in the United Kingdom, then the question whether he is resident in the United Kingdom shall be determined without regard to any place of abode maintained in the United Kingdom for his use.

With respect to the question whether, for the purposes of this statutory qualification, any part of the duties of an office or employment was performed in the United Kingdom, an allowance is made for "incidental" duties. S.335(2) provides that where the duties of an office or employment fall substantially to be performed outside the United Kingdom in any year of assessment, duties performed within the United Kingdom which are merely incidental to the performance of the duties performed abroad will be treated as if performed outside the United Kingdom.[132] The question when a duty performed in the United Kingdom can be taken to be "merely incidental" to one which is performed abroad was confronted in

---

[131] Para. 3.2 indicates that a person is a longer term visitor where he comes to the UK intending to remain indefinitely or for an extended period, perhaps stretching over several tax years. That intention alone is sufficient to take the visitor outside s.336(1).
[132] See also IR 20, para. 5.5.

Robson v Dixon.[133] The taxpayer was employed as a pilot by KLM Airlines, his base being at Schiphol Airport, Amsterdam. He and his wife had their family home in Hertfordshire, meaning that he had a place of abode in the United Kingdom. His duties always commenced in Amsterdam but he would sometimes land at Heathrow en-route to Amsterdam. In the years in question the total number of take-offs and landings made by the taxpayer in all the countries that his flights took him to was 811. Of this number, only 38 took place in the United Kingdom and such stop overs were normally for a duration of some 40 to 60 minutes. It was held that, while the duties performed by the taxpayer in the United Kingdom were small quantitatively in comparison with the duties performed by him outside the United Kingdom, they were qualitatively of a nature similar to those duties, and were not duties the performance of which was merely incidental to the performance of the duties performed abroad. According to Pennycuick V-C[134] the expression "merely incidental to" must be given effect according to the ordinary meaning of those words. The words are on their ordinary use apt to denote an activity (here the performance of duties) which does not serve any independent purpose but is carried out in order to further some other purpose. He concluded[135]:

> [T]he duties performed by the taxpayer, apart from his duties at Schiphol, mainly consisted of taking a plane up at Schiphol, flying it to whatever its destination was and then bringing it down. In the case of the flights from Schiphol to some destination (normally in America) on which there was a stop at England, his duties consisted of taking the plane up at Schiphol, flying it to England, bringing it down at Heathrow or elsewhere, and then taking it up again and flying it again to the next destination, in America. With the best will in the world, I find it impossible to say that the activities carried on in or over England are merely incidental to the performance of the comparable activities carried on in or over Holland or in or over the ultimate destination in America. The activities are precisely co-ordinate, and I cannot see how it can properly be said that the activities in England are in some way incidental to the other activities.

It was said however[136] that a single landing might be disregarded under the *de minimis* rule. Furthermore, landings due to an emergency, such as weather conditions or mechanical trouble, or due to a diversion, might be regarded as incidental to the performance of the duties performed abroad. A

---

[133] [1972] 3 All ER 671.
[134] at page 677.
[135] ibid.
[136] at page 677.

situation that presents borderline questions would be one in which "a pilot's normal route did not touch on the United Kingdom but on one or two occasions he landed in the United Kingdom while acting as substitute for some other pilot who was ill".[137]

There exists an argument that this provision in s.335(1) speaks only in respect of a place of abode which is maintained in the United Kingdom (as opposed to one which is actually used), such that if the place of abode is not used at all, then the provision may assist the taxpayer, but that if a person visits that place of abode then the provision will not help him. This type of issue was not raised in *Robson v Dixon* and, considering that, if correct, it would by itself alone have been fatal to the taxpayer's case, it seems that the argument is of doubtful force.

Partnerships

Section 111(2) of the ICTA 1988 provides that, where a trade or profession is carried on by persons in partnership, and any of those persons is chargeable to income tax, the profits, gains, or losses arising from the trade or profession will be computed for income tax purposes as if the partnership were an individual who is resident in the United Kingdom. If any of the partners is not resident in the United Kingdom, then s.111 would apply in respect of that person as if the partnership were an individual who is not resident in the United Kingdom.[138]

Corporations

According to Lord Loreburn LC in *De Beers Consolidated Gold Mines v Howe*[139] it is easy to ascertain where an individual resides, but when the inquiry relates to a company, which, "in a natural sense, does not reside anywhere, some artificial test must be applied."[140] In applying such an artificial test, one may adopt a number of approaches. First, one may take a company to be resident where it was incorporated. Such an approach would have the "merits of simplicity and certitude."[141] It would however open up tremendous planning opportunities. For as long as UK taxes remain residence-based, a company would be able to avoid UK (and other) taxes by the simple expedient of being incorporated in a tax haven. Secondly, one may take a company to be resident where its directors (or the majority of them) are resident. This might raise a number of problems, and would

[137] Pennycuick V-C at page 677.
[138] S.112(1). The section also deals generally with partnerships which are controlled abroad.
[139] (1906) 5 TC 198 at 212.
[140] J Prebble in "Should Tax Legislation be written from a Principles and Purpose Point of View or a Precise and Detailed Point of View" ([1988] BTR 112 at 116) talks about the "unreality" of the process of ascribing a notional residence to companies. The author states that it "becomes even more divorced from facts and fictions that exist in the world or in the legal system when one bears in mind that companies are themselves already artificial, fictitious, creations".
[141] per Lord Loreburn LC, ibid.

also have planning implications. Thirdly, a company might be taken to be resident wherever its centre of operations is. This would accord with the reality of the company's situation.

The UK, pragmatic as always, adopts a mixture of the first and third approaches. The third approach was given voice by Lord Loreburn LC in the De Beers case, when he said[142]:

> In applying the conception of residence to a Company, we ought, I think, to proceed as nearly as we can upon the analogy of an individual. A company cannot eat or sleep, but it can keep house and do business. We ought, therefore, to see whether it really keeps house and does business. An individual may be of foreign nationality, and yet reside in the United Kingdom. So may a Company. Otherwise, it might have its chief seat of management and its centre of trading in England, under the protection of English law, and yet escape the appropriate taxation by the simple expenditure of being registered abroad and distributing its dividends abroad ... (A) Company resides, for purposes of Income Tax, where its real business is carried on ... and the real business is carried on where the central management and control actually abides.

This is acknowledged to be the basic common law test for the residence of corporations. What the test means, is, according to Madden J in *John Hood & Co Ltd v W E Magee*,[143] that the residence of a company is to be determined, "not by the place of abode for the time being of its managing director, but by the place where the company permanently keeps house, where it can make and re-make its officers, including its managing director, prescribe their duties, including the place of their residence, and call them to account."

The first approach referred to earlier in this discussion was adopted by the UK as a further test for the residence of corporations by s.66(1) of the FA 1988.[144] By this provision, any company which is incorporated in the United Kingdom is resident here with effect from 15 March 1988 and the place of central management and control will no longer be taken into account. Transitional provisions existed in Sch. 7 of the FA 1988, for example, providing a five year period of grace for existing companies. There is however no corollary to this statutory test for residence. The *De Beers* test has been described as still being "alive and well".[145] Thus it would seem that companies which were incorporated outside the United

---

[142] 5 TC at pages 212-213.
[143] (1918) 7 TC 327 at 355.
[144] See generally, D Sheridan [1990] BTR 78.
[145] See J D B Oliver [1996] BTR 505; compare D Sheridan [1990] BTR 78.

Kingdom would still be subject to the common law rule of control and management. Thus the Exchequer can "have it both ways" in that those companies which were incorporated here are resident here automatically, and those which were not incorporated here are still resident here if their central management and control is exercised here.

Ordinary Residence

Ordinary residence is of far less importance for the purposes of United Kingdom tax than residence. It is however important in several respects. First, as we have seen above, s.334 ICTA 1988 applies to treat Commonwealth citizens and citizens of the Republic of Ireland, who are ordinarily resident in the United Kingdom, and who go abroad for the purposes of occasional residence, as being resident in the United Kingdom during their absence. Secondly, s.65(4) and s.65(5) ICTA 1988 provide that a Commonwealth citizen or a citizen of the Republic of Ireland who satisfies the Board that he is not ordinarily resident in the United Kingdom is to be taxed on foreign income under Cases IV and V of Schedule D only on income which is remitted here (and not on all income arising). Thirdly there is a general anti-avoidance provision in s.739(1) of the ICTA 1988 which deals with the transfer of assets by a person who is ordinarily resident to a person who is not resident or not domiciled in the United Kingdom. And fourthly, the persons chargeable to United Kingdom capital gains tax are defined by s.2(1) of the Taxation of Chargeable Gains Act 1992 as persons who are resident or ordinarily resident in the United Kingdom.

In spite of its importance in the contexts mentioned above, the term "ordinary residence" is not defined in statute. Like "residence", it does not have a special or technical meaning for tax purposes.[146] The words must bear their natural and ordinary meaning as words of common usage in the English language.[147] It is clear from the discussions above that ordinary residence is not synonymous with residence, that the word "ordinary" qualifies the word "residence",[148] and that there is thus a need to examine the judicial definitions. The early cases equated ordinary residence with an individual's "usual" residence.[149] In *Levene v IRC*, Viscount Cave said that ordinary residence "connotes residence in a place with a degree of continuity and apart from accidental or temporary absences".[150] Worryingly, he then added that, so understood, the expression "differs little" from the meaning of the word "residence" as used in the tax

---

[146] See Lord Warrington of Clyffe in *Levene v IRC* 13 TC at page 509.
[147] See Lord Scarman in *R v Barnett LBC, ex parte Shah* [1983] 2 AC 309 at 341.
[148] Lord President Clyde in *Reid v IRC* (1926) 10 TC 673 at 678.
[149] See for example *Turnbull v Foster* (6 TC 206) - the Lord Justice Clerk at page 210; Lord Trayner, ibid.
[150] 13 TC at page 507.

legislation, and that he found it difficult to imagine a case "in which a man while not resident here is yet ordinarily resident here".[151] In the same case Lord Warrington of Clyffe[152] defined it as meaning residence "according to the way in which a man's life is usually ordered". In Lysaght v IRC[153] Viscount Sumner said that the converse of "ordinarily" is "extraordinarily", and that part of the regular order of a man's life, adopted voluntarily and for settled purposes, is not "extraordinary". In the non-tax case of *R v Barnet LBC ex parte Shah*[154] Lord Scarman, after a review of the case law (including Lysaght and Levene) said:

> Unless, therefore, it can be shown that the statutory framework or the legal context in which the words are used requires a different meaning ... 'ordinarily resident' refers to a man's abode in a particular place or country which he has adopted voluntarily and for settled purposes as part of the regular order of his life for the time being, whether of short or of long duration.

Lord Scarman added[155] that a settled purpose does not require an intention to stay indefinitely, but that the purpose, while settled, might be for a limited period only. All that is necessary is that the purpose of living where one does live has a sufficient degree of continuity to be properly described as "settled". In this context, a specific limited purpose, such as education, can be a settled purpose. However, in spite of the reference to a voluntary adoption of a way of life, volition is no more a necessary ingredient of ordinary residence than it is of residence. Thus, in *Re Mackenzie*[156] for example, a woman who was domiciled in Australia and who came to visit this country and who was detained as a person of unsound mind, was held to be ordinarily resident in the United Kingdom when she died here, still detained, some 50 years later. According to Norton J,[157] "If ... she was not ordinarily resident in England during the last 52 years of her life, she was not ordinarily resident anywhere else".

This question, like that of residence, is a question of fact, and there are many examples in the cases. The taxpayers in Levene and Lysaght for example, were held to be ordinarily resident as well as resident. These cases have already been discussed earlier. We will examine a couple of other cases. First, *Reid v IRC*.[158] The taxpayer, a British subject, was in the habit of travelling abroad on the Continent of Europe for the greater part of the year, spending only the summer months in the United Kingdom. While abroad, she had no fixed place of abode in this country, staying in hotels

---

[151] ibid.
[152] at page 509.
[153] 13 TC at page 528.
[154] [1983] 2 AC 309 at 343. For comment, see J L Wosner [1983] BTR 347.
[155] at page 344.
[156] [1941] Ch 69.
[157] at page 77.
[158] (1926) 10 TC 673.

both when she was here and when she was abroad. She however had family and business ties here, and her personal belongings, which were not required when she was travelling, were kept in store in London. It was held by the commissioners that she was ordinarily resident in the United Kingdom and this decision was upheld by the Court of Session. The Lord President (Lord Clyde) rejected the suggestion that the meaning of the word "ordinary" is governed wholly or mainly by the test of time or duration.[159] According to Lord Clyde,[160] from the point of view of time, "ordinary" would stand in contrast to "casually". In this case the taxpayer was not a "casual" visitor to her home country. Lord Clyde said he would hesitate to give the word "ordinary" any more precise interpretation than "in the customary course of events".[161]

In response to the argument of counsel that the taxpayer "ordinarily resided" on the Continent rather than in this country because she spent nearly three times as much of her life abroad as here, Lord Clyde said that there was nothing impossible in a person ordinarily residing in two places. Lord Blackburn, concurring, said[162] "[i]t is quite true a man may have more than one ordinary residence; he may have half-a-dozen; and each might be described quite fairly as an ordinary residence." He also noted[163] that a person may be ordinarily resident in the United Kingdom without having any particular house or spot in the United Kingdom which could be described as his "ordinary residence". According to Lord Blackburn, such a person may stay in a different hotel every day of the 365 days in the year. Nobody could say in such situation that the person had an ordinary residence, but everyone would agree in saying that he had been "ordinarily resident" for the whole of the year within the confines of the United Kingdom. That conclusion would be reached entirely from the fact that he had physically resided in the United Kingdom and no other fact, as far as Lord Blackburn could see, is material in construing the expression "ordinarily resident".

The second case that we shall examine is *Miesegaes v IRC*.[164] The taxpayer was a Dutch national. He and his father had originally come to this country as refugees at the beginning of the Second World War. When his father left this country for Switzerland at the end of the war, he remained at boarding school in England. He was at all material times domiciled outside the United Kingdom, and spent his school holidays with his father in Switzerland. It was held that he was ordinarily resident in the United Kingdom. Wynn Parry J at first instance said[165] that the correct test was whether the taxpayer had been here in the ordinary course of his life during his adolescence. The commissioners had applied the test correctly and he could see no justification for interfering with their decision. He

[159] See also Lord Warrington of Clyffe in *Levene v IRC* 13 TC at page 509.
[160] at page 680.
[161] ibid.
[162] at page 682.
[163] at page 681.
[164] (1957) 37 TC, 493.
[165] at page 499.

was upheld by the Court of Appeal. Pearce LJ, referring to the statement of Lord Buckmaster in *Lysaght v IRC* that volition was immaterial, said[166]:

> Lord Buckmaster's remarks as to the exigencies of business seem equally applicable to the exigencies of education. Education is a large, necessary and normal ingredient in the lives of adolescent members of the community, just as work or business is in the lives of its adult members. During the years of youth education plays a definite and dominating part in a boy's ordinary life. In this case the school terms at Harrow dictated the main residential pattern of the boy's life. Education is too extensive and universal a phase to justify such descriptions as 'unusual' or 'extraordinary'. It would be as erroneous to endow educational residence with some esoteric quality that must, as a matter of law, remove it from the category of residence, or ordinary residence, as it would be to do so in the case of business residence. The argument based on the institutional or compulsory nature of a boy's life at school is misleading. The compulsion is merely the will of his parents, who voluntarily send him to that school. It would be hazardous, and in my opinion relevant, to investigate whether adolescents are residing voluntarily where their lot is cast and how far they approve of their parents' choice of a home or school. The Appellant's argument might lead to the unreal conclusion that a boy whose parents were in the Far East and who was therefore boarded with a tutor, or at an educational establishment where boys remain all the year round, would not reside anywhere at all. The educational and institutional nature of the residence are, of course, factors to be taken into account; but it would be wrong to hold that such residence cannot be ordinary residence.

The Revenue practice is to treat ordinary residence as being equal to habitual residence[167] (usually for three successive years). A person who is non resident for a year because he is physically absent from this country for that whole year may still be treated by the revenue as ordinarily resident, if he "usually" lives here.[168] It may be that the only case in which an individual would be held to be resident but not ordinarily resident is when he comes from abroad to this country for some temporary purpose but remains for more than six months in the tax year.[169]

With respect to students, a person who comes to the United Kingdom for a period of study or education which is expected to last for more than four years will be treated by the Revenue as resident and ordinarily

---

[166] at page 501.
[167] IR 20, para. 1.3 ("if you are resident in the UK year after year"); para. 2.1 ("if you usually live in this country"). See also paras. 3.4 to 3.13.
[168] para. 1.3.
[169] ibid.

resident from the date of his arrival.[170] If the period of study is not expected to exceed four years, the person may be treated as not ordinarily resident, but the result will depend on whether or not he has accommodation available here, whether he intends to remain here at the end of his period of education, or whether he proposes to visit the United Kingdom in future years for periods of three months or more per year of assessment.[171] And with respect to other long term visitors, a person who comes here (whether to work or not) will be treated as ordinarily resident from the date of his arrival if it is clear that he intends to remain here for three years or more.[172]

Domicile

The domicile of a person is often of much less importance than his residence or ordinary residence. However, it is still important for certain purposes. First, s.65(4) and (5) of the ICTA 1988 charge the foreign income of a non-domiciled person on a remittance basis.[173] Secondly s.192(1) of the ICTA 1988 defines "foreign emoluments" as the emoluments of a non-domiciled person from an office or employment with an employer who is non-resident (excluding employers in the Republic of Ireland), and thirdly, s.6(1) of the Inheritance Tax Act 1984 defines "excluded property" as property situated outside the United Kingdom, of which the person beneficial entitled thereto is domiciled outside the United Kingdom.

Domicile bears its general Conflicts of Laws meaning. The common law of domicile in the U.K has been described as being "of a highly capricious nature".[174] Detailed discussion is beyond the scope of this book and can be found in books on Private International Law.[175] Here, we will just identify a number of general features. Domicile generally refers to a person's permanent home. Every one must have a domicile and only one.[176] A domicile of origin is acquired at birth and a domicile of choice can be acquired by adults, the requirements being a change of residence to another place and an intention to stay there permanently. The domicile of choice can be abandoned by acquiring another one or by revival of the domicile of origin.

---

[170] paras. 3.8 and 3.13.
[171] para. 3.8..
[172] ibid.
[173] Compare s 12(1) of the TCGA 1992.
[174] S Green [1991] BTR 21. See also D Sheridan's analysis of the Joint Report of the Law Commission and the Scottish Law Commission of 31 July 1987 [1989] BTR 230.
[175] See also IR 20, paras. 4.1 to 4.8, for the Revenue's summary of the position.
[176] See for example the Lord President in *Lloyd v Sulley* (2TC 37 at 41) - "A man cannot have two domiciles at the same time"

Citizenship

Citizenship is largely relevant only in respect of Commonwealth citizens or citizens of the Republic of Ireland, and then only in certain clearly defined situations (see for example, s.65 and s.334 of the ICTA 1988 – both discussed above). Citizenship is determined according to general law. Relevant provisions can be found in the British Nationality Acts.

Further Reading

Lyons T, *The Reform of the Law of Domicile* [1993] BTR 42.

Green S, *Domicile and Revenue Law: The Continuing Need for Reform* [1991] BTR 21.

Sheridan D, *The Residence of Companies for Taxation Purposes* [1990] BTR 78.

Oliver JDB, *Some Aspects of the Territorial Scope of Double Tax Treaties* [1990] BTR 303.

Sheridan D, *Private International Law: The Law of Domicile: Observations on the Joint Report* [1989] BTR 230.

Prebble J, *Should Tax Legislation be written from a Principles and Purpose Point of View or a Precise and Detailed Point of View* [1988] BTR 112.

Chopin LF & Granwell AW, *The New Concept of Residence for Federal Income Tax Purposes* [1985] BTR 62 (discussion on American law).

Wosner JL, Ordinary Residence, *The Law and Practice* [1983] BTR 347.

Oliver JDB, *Double Tax Treaties in United Kingdom Tax Law* [1970] BTR 388.

chapter three
Income Tax - Introduction and General Concepts

Income Tax - the Concept

By comparison to other taxes, income tax is by far the largest source of revenue in the United Kingdom. For example, in 1989 income tax accounted for approximately 26% of the total tax revenue; Corporation tax accounted for 11%; and the combined revenue of capital gains tax and inheritance tax accounted for 2% of the total tax revenue.

It is in the first part of this book that we develop a consideration of the rules and principles that apply to income tax. The problem we initially face is that of seeking to ascertain and present a definition of income. It has often been stated that income tax is a tax on income; but an economist would reply and explain that the flow of revenue from capital is also income. Clearly income tax for our purposes (and for the purposes of the Inland Revenue) does not include income from capital. This calls for a consideration of the distinction between income and capital. Exhaustive and conclusive definitions of income and capital are not provided by the Legislature. There exists a further need to consider the Schedular system and the definitions within that and the roles that the various Schedules perform. It is unfortunate that distinctions in tax law between kinds of income create avoidance problems, because it pays to pretend that one sort of income is really another sort bearing lower tax. Efforts to counter tax-avoidance then inevitably lead to further complexity in the tax system.

Capital v Income : The Distinction and its Importance

The distinction between an income and a capital item of expenditure or receipt, has assumed a lesser importance than it previously enjoyed. Its past importance reflected the absence of a capital gains tax (until its introduction in 1965) and the consequent ability, prior to 1965, to enjoy tax free capital gains. It was eventually conceded that the absence of a capital gains tax presented not only an avenue for tax planning or avoidance, but also supported the possible "injustice" of not taxing those with the ability to pay on the grounds that their income was of a particular type and derived from a particular source (a capital gain).

The introduction of a capital gains tax has not removed the need to recognise the distinction between income and capital – at the very least the distinction is of importance in recognising and advising upon the correct tax principles. The distinction may have practical importance in that the rates applicable to income gains and those applicable to capital gains have not always been the same.[1] For example, capital gains tax enjoyed a maximum rate of 30% for a number of years, whereas income tax rates reached 60% during the same period. Today's assimilation of the rates provides stronger recognition of the often indistinguishable, distinction between income and capital and of the need to tax the latter.[2]

In doing so it raises the issue of whether the capital/income distinction matters? In response to this one must acknowledge that the assimilation of rates does not amount to as assimilation of taxes: the income and capital tax regimes remain distinct and separate. For example, differences remain in the following areas:

1. The bases of computation

2. The annual CGT exemption is higher than the income tax personal allowance

3. The ability to use "losses"

4. The dates for payment

5. Different reliefs.

---

[1] Today the rates are the same, except that any capital gain is always to be taxed as the top slice of one's income and thus at any marginal rate of income tax.

[2] It is widely believed that the previous practice of taxing income and capital gains at different rates distorted investment decisions and contributed to the development of a tax avoidance industry.

One of the major problems in determining the distinction between income and capital is the absence of precise definitions or determining theories.   Judicial comments have confirmed that the question must depend in large measure upon the particular facts of the particular case[3] and it has been said that "in many cases it is almost true to say that a spin of a coin would decide the matter almost as satisfactorily as an attempt to find reasons."[4]

Although one should recognise the difficulties in this area, one must also possess an awareness of the application of the distinction in relevant case-law. We will present a discussion of the more important cases when we consider income receipts and revenue expenditure in Schedule D Cases I and II. For the moment, we will simply highlight the competing theories that have been presented as assisting or explaining the distinctions between capital and income.

Fixed and circulating capital

This theory has enjoyed a great deal of support and involves a recognition that fixed capital is "capital" whereas circulating capital is merely "income". The fixed capital is the   structure (permanent or semi-permanent) that generates the income. The income is often represented through the disposal of the circulating capital items. Those circulating capital items are the creation of the fixed capital.

For example, in *Golden Horse Shoe (New) Ltd v Thurgood*[5], the court was required to decide whether the sale of dumps generated at a Gold Mine was a sale of capital.   Romer LJ summarised the issue by stating that the question to be decided in the case was whether the dumps should be regarded as fixed capital or circulating capital. In conclusion, the dumps were regarded as circulating capital: their existence and creation was caused by and was an aside to the fixed capital - the mines.

Fruit of the tree

In a similar fashion to fixed and circulating capital theory, the "fruit of the tree" theory suggests that the tree represents the capital and the fruit represents income items that are generated by and grow out of and from the capital.

[3]   Per Abbott J in *Oxford Motors Ltd v Minister of National Revenue* (1959) 18 DLR 712.
[4]   Per Sir Wilfred Greene MR in *IRC v British Salmson Aero Engines Ltd* [1938] 2 KB 482 at 498; (1938) 22 TC 29 at 43.
[5]   [1933] All ER 402.

Accretion to economic power

This theory involves a recognition that income is the gain generated out of the application of capital. It has been suggested that the accretion to economic power theory is perhaps a more accurate description of the distinction between income and capital, albeit that the other theories are more frequently cited by the judiciary.

Ultimately the issue is one of fact and, as we shall see in our later discussions, the suggestion that the matter could, as easily and as predictably, be determined by a "spin of a coin" is very close to the truth! For the moment is useful to look at a few cases (some of which are also discussed in later chapters) as an illustration of the difficulties in this area.

In *Gray (Inspector of Taxes) v Seymours Garden Centre*[6] the taxpayers, who carried on the trade of nurserymen, erected a "planteria" to protect growing plants and to maintain the quality of the plants until they were sold. The planteria enjoyed an internal layout that permitted customers to view and select plants. The taxpayer sought to claim allowances on the cost of the construction of the planteria on the grounds that it constituted "plant".

The case ultimately revolved around the meaning of "plant". This is were we begin to see the limits of our capital allowance system. To enjoy the allowances, investments must be channelled in certain directions. Included in the permitted directions is "plant". Unfortunately no statutory definition of this term is provided and it is left to the judiciary to determine its meaning and scope and hence the scope of this element of our capital allowance system. As one might expect, the meaning of "plant" has caused much debate and concern over the years. In the current case, Vinelott J was prepared to conclude that the planteria was not just plant and thus not deserving of allowance status, saying that "on the evidence before the Commissioners a planteria falls well on the premises side of the line wherever it may be drawn."[7] The dividing line referred to was the consequence of the application of the business test and the premises test as explained and applied by Hoffman J in *Wimpey International Ltd v Warland*.[8] In fact, Vinelott was at pains to point out that in *Gray* "the Commissioners overlooked the crucial distinctions recently emphasised by Hoffmann J. Those tests and the distinctions are found in a long line of decisions, summarised and referred to by Hoffmann J, and emanate from the often-quoted *dictum* of Lindley LJ, that plant:

---

[6]   [1993] 2 All ER 809
[7]   at page 814.
[8]   [1988] STC 149 at 172

... in its ordinary sense, includes whatever apparatus is used by a businessman for carrying on his business, not his stock-in-trade which be buys or makes for sale; but all goods and chattels, fixed or moveable, live or dead, which he keeps for permanent employment in his business.[9]

Subsequent acceptance and application of this dictum evolved into a recognition of a number of tests and distinctions (and a lot of confusion and ambiguity). These tests and their application invite a two-tier approach to the determination of the meaning of "plant". The first tier (the "business test") demands that the item in question is used in the carrying on of the business. The second tier (the "premises test") disallows items that are used in the business as premises or as the place upon which the business is conducted. This second tier could also be called the "stock-in-trade test", for following the distinctions adopted by Lindley LJ, stock-in-trade would also be disallowed at tier two.

Vinelott J's overriding acceptance of the two-tier approach with the emphasis on the prevailing nature of the premises test, is disappointing in that it creates the impression that premises can never constitute plant, and it ignores the value of the "functional" approach. It has been through the proper use of the functional approach that some structures that could be described as "premises" have in the past succeeded as being "plant". The case of *IRC v Barclay, Curle and Co*[10] is a well-known example where the costs of excavating and constructing a dry dock were allowed as expenditure on "plant". The Revenue had argued, unsuccessfully, that the excavation and construction related to an industrial building and not plant. The taxpayers were able to succeed with their claim in *IRC v Barclay, Curle* because the court properly considered the role of "function". Lord Reid correctly suggested that if a structure fulfilled the function of "plant" then it should be presumed to be "plant"[11]. The scope of the functional approach is enhanced if we recognise that the function can be performed passively and that the same item could constitute both "plant" and "premises".

The difficulty raised by this decision is how to incorporate the "functional" approach into the business premises dichotomy and approaches in *Wimpey* and *Gray*. Interestingly, in *Gray* Vinelott J was prepared to recognise that the property in question, a planteria, could constitute "plant", but did not explain the relationship between this possibility and the business/premises dichotomy adopted in the case. One suspects that the possibility was based on "function". It is likely that the functional approach will operate as an exception to the prevailing nature of the tier-two premises test. As such it will provided proper recognition

---

[9]   *Yarmouth v France* (1887) 19 QBD 647 at p 658.
[10]   [1969] 1 All ER 732.
[11]   At page 740.

that premises can constitute and function as plant. In a sense it also completes the circle, in that the business/premises approach begins by considering whether the asset functions as part of the carrying on of the business (the business test), and then moves to consider (negatively) whether that contribution is as an excluded item, such as stock-in-trade or premises. The functional approach completes the circle and returns us to our functional beginnings (the business test) by allowing function to prevail in the determination of excluded assets: i.e., a *prima facie* excluded asset, premises, will not be excluded if it functions as part of the business (the "business test" and performs the particular functions of "plant" (the functional approach).

Another case that we shall examine is *Lawson v Johnson Matthey Plc.*[12] A parent company's (Johnson Matthew plc) injected £50 million into one of its wholly-owned subsidiaries, Johnson Matthey Bankers Limited (JMB). The cash injection was part of a scheme to facilitate the disposal of JMB to the Bank of England. The background of the scheme revealed that JMB had fallen into difficulties on its commercial loan business; large advanced h ad been made on what turned out to be inadequate security. The parent company, Johnson Matthey plc, discussed these difficulties at a board meeting on the night of September 30/October 1, 1984, and concluded that:

- JMB was insolvent and could not open its doors for business later that day unless further financing, which Johnson Matthew plc could not afford to supply, was made available;
- the cessation of business by JMB, and the resulting damage to confidence in Johnson Matthey plc, was likely to lead to demands by lending institutions for the repayment of metals and moneys owed to them by Johnson Matthew plc and that Johnson Matthey plc would be unable to meet its obligations as they fell due in the absence of further financial support, which did not seem to be available. Johnson Matthey plc would therefore have to cease trading;
- there was no alternative to the winding up of JMB and that a liquidator should be appointed;
- they should do everything in their power to protect the interests of Johnson Matthey plc's shareholders and employees and to facilitate the orderly disposal of Johnson Matthey's plc's assets, in which unsecured creditors would be dealt with on an equitable basis, and that therefore they would ask for the appointment of a receiver for Johnson Matthey plc;

---

[12] This case is discussed in more detail in the chapter on trading expenditure.

- these decisions to ask for a liquidator for JMB and a receiver for Johnson Matthey plc should be implemented an hour later at 1.30am.

The Bank of England was immediately informed of this decision and, concerned at the possible effects on the stability of the United Kingdom banking sector, the Bank of England proposed a "rescue package". This consisted of two elements:

1. the Bank would acquire the issued share capital of JMB for the sum of 1; and

2. prior to this sale, Johnson Matthew plc must inject £50 million into JMB.

Johnson Matthew plc responded to this scheme by noting that the only practical alternative to the Bank's proposals was to implement the previous decision to ask for the appointment of a receiver and that, in the circumstances, the injection of 50 million might appropriately be regarded as expenditure necessary to retain goodwill and confidence in all the remaining group companies and enable them to stay in business. Consequently, Johnson Matthey plc agreed to inject £50 million into its wholly-owned subsidiary and then transferred the whole of the issued share capital of that subsidiary, JMB, to the Bank of England for £1. Johnson Matthey plc then sought to deduct the £50 million injection monies as a trading expense in its accounts for the year ending March 31, 1985. It was that deduction and the nature of the expenditure that formed the basis of this dispute. It is clear that in order to be deductible the expenditure must be of a revenue nature and that it must be "wholly and exclusively" incurred for the purposes of the trade.

The General Commissioners held that the £50 million payment was of a revenue and not capital nature because its purpose was to preserve the trade of Johnson Matthey plc from collapse.[13] The High Court disagreed, preferring to treat the expenditure as part of the disposal of a capital asset – the shares in JMB. The Court of Appeal followed the High Court's opinion in treating the expenditure as capital expenditure. The Court of Appeal was reversed by the House of Lords.[14] The speeches in the House of Lords appear to present two very different approaches to the determination of the capital v revenue expenditure issue – albeit both approaches, in this particular instance, admit of the same conclusion: the expenditure was of a revenue nature. The first approach we can attribute to Lord Templeman. Lord Templeman began by confirming that the

---

[13]   [1990] STC 149.
[14]   [1992] BTC 324.

purpose of the expenditure has a limited use in contributing to the requirement of "wholly and exclusively," but that the finding that the purpose of the expenditure was to "preserve the trade" of Johnson Matthew plc did "... not automatically enable the taxpayer company to deduct 50 million ... the deduction can only be made if the 50 million was a revenue expenditure and not a capital expenditure."[15] Thus the nature of the expenditure is not determined, nor perhaps even influenced, by the purpose of the expenditure. The nature of the expenditure was determined by Lord Templeman by consideration of and application of existing authorities – despite an earlier acknowledgement and approval of Lord MacMillan's observation o n the fallibility of the criteria adopted in those authorities. The first authority referred to by Lord Templeman was that of *British Insulated and Helsby Cables Ltd v Atherton*[16] and the proposition of Viscount Cave L.C. that a "once and for all payment bringing into existence an asset or advantage for the enduring benefit of the trade" was capital expenditure. On the basis of that proposition, Lord Templeman was able to conclude that the protection of the taxpayer company from insolvency was not expenditure on an "advantage for the enduring benefit of the trade."[17] Some might quite reasonably disagree with Lord Templeman's perception of the benefit received by the taxpayer company, unless Lord Templeman's emphasis on the need to directly relate the expenditure to the transfer of an existing identifiable and tangible asset is a narrowing of Viscount Cave's enduring test to include only the bringing, or the procurement, of an asset into existence – not the protection of an existing asset of the existence, the goodwill and the business of Johnson Matthey plc.

In a similar vein, Lord Templeman distinguished *Associated Portland Cement Manufacturers Ltd v IRC*[18] in that the payment in that case was capital. The expenditure in that case was designed to improve the goodwill of the business and would thus follow earlier categories of capital expenditure being expenditure on the acquisition or the improvement of capital assets. In *Johnson Matthey* the expenditure was not to acquire or improve its goodwill, but to preserve it – a vital distinction according to Lord Templeman[19]; although one might question the degree of difference between the preservation and the improvement of goodwill.

Finally, reference was made to Lord Wilberforce's *dicta* in *Tucker (Inspector of Taxes) v Granada Motorway Services Ltd*[20] that, in determining the distinction between capital and revenue expenditure, the courts can do little better than form an opinion as to where the balance of indicators lie. In *Johnson Matthey plc*, Lord Templeman formed the opinion that the balance of

---

[15] At page 327.
[16] [1926] AC 205 at 212 et. seq.
[17] At page 328.
[18] [1946] 1 All ER 68.
[19] At page 329.
[20] [1979] 1 WLR 683.

indicators supported the conclusion that the 50 million was paid, and paid solely, to enable the taxpayer company to continue in business. As such it was a revenue expense and not a capital expense attributable to the disposal of the worthless shares in JMB.

The other approach apparent in the House of Lords can be found in the speech of Lord Goff. Lord Goff acknowledged that the agreement between the taxpayer and the Bank of England was reduced to a written document that made no mention of the rescue plan but referred solely to the agreement for the sale and purchase of the shares of the wholly-owned subsidiary, JMB. If that agreement was the sole matter that the court elected to examine, then the logical conclusion would be to treat the expenditure as capital expenditure attached to the disposal of a capital asset. Lord Goff concluded that that type of analysis is too narrowly construed, and ignores the reality of the situation.[21] The "reality" and the true analysis according to Lord Goff was that the payment was a "contribution to the rescue of JMB planned by the Bank, which was a prerequisite of the transfer of the shares in JMB to the Bank for a nominal consideration. As such it was a revenue payment." The conclusion reached was the same as that of Lord Templeman but with a less mechanistic and perhaps more practical reality approach.

Sources of Income and the Schedular System

Having ascertained that the funds received are of an income nature, the next stage in determining any tax liability is the need to ascertain whether that type of income is taxable. Some guidance is provided by the legislature through the declaration that certain types of income are non-taxable. These include an array of items representing political and policy considerations; for example among the items are : certain social security benefits; War widows pension; Redundancy payments; Education Scholarship and foreign services allowances for civil servants.

Apart from the statutory declared non-taxable incomes, income will be taxable or non-taxable depending upon the application of the doctrine of source and recognition of the schedular system. The Schedular system reflects an historical contribution to the UK tax system having been originally developed by Addington during the early 1800s. The Schedular system remains today – subject to a number of refinements and the pending "tax law rewrite" (which may threaten its future existence). The significance of this system is that income in any tax year will not be taxable unless it can be traced to a source identified in a Schedule. Thus, for

---

[21]   At page 332.

income to be taxable it must be caused, for example, by employment (Schedular E) or trade (Schedule D). Section 1, (TA 1988), supports this conclusion by declaring that "Income is taxable if it falls within one or other of the Schedules".

Today's Schedules are as follows[22]

Schedule A	Income from rents and other receipts from land in the UK
Schedule D	
Case I	Profits of a trade in UK
Case II	Profits of a profession or vocation in UK
Case III	Interest, annuities and other annual payments
Case IV	Securities out of the UK
Case V	Profits from foreign possessions
Case VI	Annual profits or gains not falling under Cases I-V and not charged by virtue of any other Schedule
Schedule E	Income from offices, employments
Cases I, II and III	and pensions
Schedule F	Dividends and distributions by companies.

Exclusivity

Although income tax is one tax[23] its computation must reflect the individual contributions from the Schedules A-F, and the computations within those Schedules. This leads us onto the need to recognise the mutual exclusivity of the Schedules and the rules therein. For example, assessment of income under Schedule E will prevent the assessment of the same income under Schedule D (or vice versa). This was confirmed at an early stage by the House of Lords in *Fry v Salisbury House Estate Ltd.*[24] Here the taxpayer owned a building and let parts of it. The taxpayer was initially assessed under Schedule A on the basis of the building and services and then reassessed for the services under Schedule D. The House of Lords dismissed the reassessment on the grounds that, having assessed the rental incomes under Schedule A, there was no possibility of subsequently dealing with them under Schedule D. According to Viscount Dunedin "once assigned to its appropriate Schedule, the same income cannot be

---

[22]   Schedule B was repealed by the FA 1988. Schedule C was repealed by s.79 FA 1996 and the income previously charged under it was assigned to Schedule D.

[23]   Lord MacNaghten said in *London County Council v A.G.* ([1901] AC 26 at 35): "Income Tax ... is one tax, not a collection of taxes essentially distinct. There is no difference in kind between the duties of income tax assessed under Schedule D and those under Schedule A or any of the other Schedules of charge".

[24]   [1930] AC 432.

attributed to another Schedule".[25] This principle was explained by Lord Radcliffe in *Mitchell & Edon v Ross*[26] by the statement that "the sources of profit in the different schedules are mutually exclusive".

As between the Cases within the Schedules, it appears that, subject to statutory direction to the contrary, the Inland Revenue may elect under which case to charge income. For example, in *Liverpool and London and Globe Insurance Co v Bennett*[27] a fire and life insurance company was entitled to "invest money, not immediately required, in such manner as might from time to time be determined." Using this power the Company invested money in the USA and those investments subsequently yielded interest. The interest was received by the Company abroad but never remitted to the UK (although it did appear on the Company's balance sheet). The Company was assessed under Case 1 of Schedule D (ITA 1842) in respect of the 'interest received'. The assessment was upheld by the court. The Company had unsuccessfully argued that they ought to be assessed under Case IV only. The advantage of Case IV was that it would only attach to interest from securities abroad if that interest had been received in the UK in the current year.

In hearing the case, Lord Shaw of Dunfermline stressed[28] that:

> ... it is well settled that if a sufficient warrant be found in the statute for taxation under alternative heads the alternative lies with the taxing authority. They have selected Case 1. It appears to me that this selection is ... founded upon the soundest and most elementary principle of business ...

Doctrine of Source

The Schedular system led to the development of the source doctrine. The doctrine demands that in the current tax year, the source of the income must be an identifiable activity and that activity must be recognised as falling within one of the Schedules.[29] This doctrine has proved problematic when income is identifiable but the source of that income (the activity) is no longer identifiable in the current tax year. For example, in *Bray v Best*[30], a payment in respect of employment that no longer was in existence, nor had it been in existence during the year of assessment, was not taxable. The payment referred to previous employment. Lord Oliver stressed that for an emolument to be chargeable to income tax under Schedule E not only must it be an emolument from employment but it must be an emolument for the year of assessment in which the charge is sought to be

---

[25] At page 442.
[26] [1962] AC 814 at 838.
[27] [1913] AC 610.
[28] at page 616.
[29] See for example *Carson v Cheyney's Executor* [1959] AC 412.
[30] [1989] 1 All ER 969.

raised. This particular payment is now dealt with by statute[31] – but it is still a useful illustration of the requirements of the doctrine of source.

One of the logical developments from the doctrine of source requirements is the development of a residual Schedule or Case to catch and sweep-up all sources of income other than those specified in the other Schedules or Cases. The provision of a "catch-all" or "sweeping" case would prevent the possible non-taxable income or source (other than those to be declared as exempt by statute). On first impressions Schedule D, Case VI (see later discussion) might be regarded as that residual, catch-all case, but on closer examination its comprehensiveness appears to be incomplete and defective.

The Tax Unit

Before we examine some of the detailed rules and principles of the various Schedules, we must briefly consider the unit of assessment. In essence, the unit of assessment requires that we make a choice as to how we tax husbands and wives. We may, for example, wish to adopt separate taxation, whereby we treat husbands and wives as if they were single people. Under a system of separate taxation marriage would attract no fiscal incentives or disincentives, nor would there be any disincentives to a married woman seeking and obtaining employment.

An alternative to a system of separate taxation, might be a system of splitting income. This would involve computing the total joint income and splitting (or dividing) that income by two. Tax liability would then be assessed on an individual basis with each partner's taxable income representing their share of the split income. For example, a disproportionate individual income of £20,000 for one partner (husband) and £15,000 for the other partner (wife) would be split to represent taxable income of £17,500 per partner (individual). Under a split system fiscal advantages are apparent where income is unequally earned or if one partner only is working.

Finally, a system of aggregation could apply to the income of husbands and wives. Under the principles of aggregation the income of the husband and wife are summed to represent joint income. Tax liability would then be assessed and determined according to the joint income. For instance, if we use the example above, the assessable income would not be £17,500 per individual but £35,000 per married couple.

Until 1990, the system of aggregation applied in the United Kingdom.

---

[31] See TA 1988 s.19(1)(4A). See also s.103(1) with respect to Schedule D.

Legislation declared that "a woman's income chargeable to tax shall be deemed for income tax purposes to be his [the husband's] income and not to be her income".[32]

The selection of the family unit as the tax unit was not all bad news: the husband became entitled to a married man's personal allowance to help him support his "dependent" wife.

The system of aggregation was subject to much criticism and concern. In the Meade Report, reference was made to the perceptions of dependency as "becoming less and less compatible with modern attitudes to the relationships between men and women".[33]

The Government announced the possibility of change through its Green Paper in 1980[34], and changes were introduced in the treatment of husbands and wives in the reforms of 1990. These reforms abolished the system of aggregation, and husbands and wives are not subject to individual assessment on their income (both earned and investment income). However, an element of discrimination does remain in that a "married couple's allowance" is available to either the husband or the wife. In practice it is normally attributed to the husband and as such may represent an implicit acceptance of "dependence".

Critics of the 1990 reforms emphasise that the married couple's allowance does little to recognise or assist the needs of the family unit. It is suggested that if the "married couple's allowance" was abolished, then child benefit provision could be doubled. The belief is that a change in that direction would move adequately and effectively represent and assist the needs of the family unit.

Further criticisms of the 1990 reforms are directed at the treatment of investment income. It is now possible for the transfer between husband and wife of investment income profit to reduce tax liability. A higher rate tax partner might transfer his investment income to his wife in order that the income is subject to basic rate liability in her hands (assuming she is a basic rate taxpayer). Some critics believe that investment income ought still (on equitable grounds) remain subject to a system of aggregation.

In a budget declared to give to families support when they needed it, the Chancellor announced on 9 March 1999 that a child tax credit would replace the married couple's allowance from April 2001. Nothing is offered to assist childless married couples.

---

[32]   TA 1988, s.279. Repealed by FA 1988, s.32 for the year 1990-91 and subsequent years of assessment.

[33]   The Structure and Reform of Direct Taxation : Report of a Committee chaired by Professor J E Meade. The Institute of Fiscal Studies (1978) page 377.

[34]   "The Taxation of Husband and Wife", 1980 Cmnd 8093.

The System of Self-Assessment

In March 1993, the Chancellor of the Exchequer announced that the direct tax system would move to a system of self-assessment. The intention was that the procedures for assessment and collection would be more "straightforward and fairer." It was also expected that the new system would free up time for the Revenue to investigate matters rather than be involved in detailed tax calculations. Self-assessment applies to tax returns for the 1996/97 tax year onwards. In essence the system allows the taxpayer a choice as to whether they want the Inland Revenue to calculate their tax liability or whether they wish to calculate their own liability. Different deadlines exist for the completion of complex forms (or free of charge floppy disk) for Schedule E taxpayers with automatic penalties for late returns.[35]

In February 1998 the Revenue issued an invitation (contained in a press release) for people to send in views and suggestions on the operation of the Self-assessment scheme. Over 400 responses were received and a report was issued in December 1998 (Assessing Self-Assessment. Response to Public Consultation on Self-Assessment). It was concluded that there was a considerable degree of consensus on the main aspect in need of improvement which was summarised thus

The new system is an improvement on the old system. With a little more attention to the organisation with tax offices and a little more clarity of the notices which are issued to taxpayers, the new system could be a very considerable improvement on the old.[36]

Labour Supply and Taxation

There have been many studies on the effects of taxation on the labour supply. The overall picture of labour supply responses, especially for married women, is now fairly well understood[37]. These studies tend to focus on the positive consequences of tax reforms to encourage participation (changes to the benefit structure, for example) or the mixed response to measures designed to encourage more work from those already in employment (reductions in basic and higher rates of tax, for example). In recent years the political debate in this area has been caught-up in the debate on marriage and the family. The choice is one between independent taxation and individual freedom versus tax breaks and transferable allowances for families. At the moment there is scant evidence of an incentive effect of independent taxation but clear evidence on the

---

[35] The Revenue will provide "Help Sheets" providing guidance on particular topics.
[36] page 33.
[37] See Blundell, R, "Labour Supply and Taxation", (1992) *Fiscal Studies*, 15-40.

cost-effectiveness of a family based transferable allowance system. It is estimated that some 13 million UK families would gain from a tax relief for marriage, so even a £100 incentive would cost the treasury £1.3 billion.

Further Reading

Blundell R, *Labour Supply and Taxation* (1992) Fiscal Studies, 15.

chapter four

Income Tax - Schedule E - Offices, Employments and Emoluments

Tax under Schedule E is charged by TA 1988 s.19(1) in respect of "any office or employment", on "emoluments therefrom".[1] Schedule E contains three *Cases* of which only Case I is discussed in this chapter. Case I applies to any emoluments for any year of assessment in which the person holding the office or employment is resident and ordinarily resident in the United Kingdom. Case II and Case III cover cases involving a foreign element.

Office

One of the initial problems to be determined in discussion of the scope of Schedule E is the meaning of "office" or employment". In the absence of any statutory definition or guidelines, we need to turn to judicial comment and guidance. The accepted meaning, or perhaps the characteristics, of an office appear to be those enumerated by Rowlatt J in *Great Western Railway Co v Bater*[2] and repeated in *Davies v Braithwaite*[3]. In *Great Western Railway Co v Bater* Rowlatt J defined an office as

> a subsisting, permanent, substantive position which [has] an existence independent of the person who [fills] it, and which [is] filled in succession by successive holders.[4]

In *Davies v Braithwaite* Rowlatt J emphasised the non-personal nature of an office, reiterating that need for an existence independent of the person who fills it.[5] Despite this apparent clarity, "office" is a difficult concept. In *McMillan v Guest*[6] Lord Wright said[7] that the word "office" is of "indefinite content"[8] the various meanings of which covered four columns of the

---

[1] As we shall discuss later, not all income from employment is caught under Schedule E. Schedule E is concerned with the taxation of income caused by the employment: a principle that is of vital importance.

[2] [1920] 3 KB 266; 8 TC 231.

[3] (1931)18 TC 198; [1931] 2 KB 628.

[4] [1920] KB at page 274.

[5] Ibid. at 635.

[6] [1942] AC 561; 24 TC 190.

[7] At page 566.

[8] In the American case of *State v Wilson* (29 Ohio St. 347 at 349) the court admitted that "it is impossible to give a definition of an office that will be applicable to all offices."

New English Dictionary. He said that he imagined that the words of Rowlatt J in *Great Western Railway Co v Bater* were deliberately left vague and that the words should be applied "according to the ordinary use of language and the dictates of common sense with due regard to the requirements that there must be some degree of permanence and publicity in the office". American courts are no less vague in their definitions. For example, in *Kendall v Raybould*,[9] it was said that an office embraces the idea of tenure, duration, emoluments, and duties, and these ideas or elements cannot be separated, and each considered abstractly, and that, all taken together constitute the office. However the element of continuance also features in American definitions,[10] and, interestingly, the American hold that an office is a creation of law (instead of contract)[11] and involves an exercise of portions of the state's sovereign power.[12]

In the UK, the characteristics of an office identified in *Great Western Railway Co v Bater* were approved in *Edwards v Clinch*[13]. Mr Clinch had been appointed as inspector at a number of separate public local inquiries. The issue was one of whether Mr Clinch held an "office" at each inquiry or was he merely exercising his profession. It was held that Mr Clinch's appointment at each inquiry was not the appointment to an "office". Having repeated the accepted characteristics of an office, Lord Salmon accepted[14] the words of Ackner LJ[15] that Mr Clinch's appointment was a temporary, ad hoc, appointment confined to the taxpayer, and to a position that did not have an existence of its own, nor any quality of permanency.

This strict adherence to the suggested characteristics of an "office" might result in few offices being accepted as such.[16] One wonders as to extent to which the decision in *Edwards v Clinch* gives effect to the suggestion that the deliberately vague term (office)[17] should be applied according to the ordinary use of language and the dictates of common sense.

---

[9] 44 P. 1034 at 1036. See also *US v Fisher*, 8 F. 414 at 415; *Hawthorne v Fisher*, 33 F.Supp. 891 at 895.

[10] See *Mosby v Board of Commissioners of Vanderburgh County*, 186 NE.2d. 18 at 20.

[11] See for example *Mosby v Board of Commissioners of Vanderburgh County*, supra; *Ray v Stevenson*, 111 P.2d. 824 at 830 ("an employment arising out of contract is not an office"); *Stapleton v Frohmiller*, 85 P.2d. 49 at 53 (an office as distinct from an employment may be created only by the legislative branch of the government, either directly or by necessary implication); *Hudson v Annear*, 75 P.2d. 587 at 588.

[12] *Oklahoma City v Century Indemnity Co.*, 62 P.2d. 94 at 97; *Mosby v Board of Commissioners of Vanderburgh County*, supra.

[13] [1981] 3 All ER 543; 56 TC 367. Lord Salmon (56 TC at page 414) confirmed the meaning of the word 'office' as, "a subsisting, permanent, substantive position which has an existence independent of the person who fills it."

[14] 56 TC at page 415.

[15] [1981] Ch 1 at 17-18.

[16] Examples of office holders include, a director of a company (*MacMillan v Guest*, supra); executors and trustees of a will (*Dale v IRC* (1951) 34 TC 468); and a company auditor (*Ellis v Lucas* [1966] 2 All ER 935; 43 TC 276).

[17] Lord Salmon in *Edwards v Clinch* did not think that the dictionary meaning was helpful, although Lord Bridge (dissenting) thought that it was.

Employment

"Employment" is an "unhappy word"[18] the meaning of which cannot always be the same as that of "office" in Schedule E.[19] But it has to be construed with, and takes its colour from the word "office".[20] It has been suggested that its inclusion was to extend the scope of Schedule E and that it might possibly be viewed as a residual category.[21] The proposition that "employment" is wider than "office" is clearly correct, since the meaning of office is so narrow. Thus although an office is an employment, it does not follow that every employment is an office.[22]

For present purposes, the real bone of contention is not the distinction between an office and an employment (since both fall under Schedule E[23]), but between employments and professions. In this context, the determination of employment now focuses on the distinction between a contract of service and a contract for services. The former is equated with employment[24] and the latter signifies a profession. Previous analysis of employment centred on the suggestion that employment "means something analogous" to an office, and in the nature of a "post".[25] It is now clear that a person employed by a company is an employee - except where the company and the individual might in fact be treated as the same. Employment lawyers will remind us that a difficulty exists when an employee is seconded to work for another an "office" and neither earnings from a profession or vocation. firm. This situation involves a determination of fact and a recognition of tax concessions.[26]

It has been recognised that the exercise of a profession or trade can co-exist with the exercise and engagement of employment. For example, *Mitchell and Edon v Ross*[27] raised the possibility that a consultant radiologist could be in private practice exercising his profession and, in the same year of assessment, receive income from employment with a Regional Hospital Board. The income attributed to the profession (the private practice) would be assessed under Schedule D Case II whereas the employment income would be assessed under Schedule E.[28]

Concerning the distinction between employments and professions, in *Davies v Braithwaite* the issue was whether an actress who performed in plays,

---

[18] Per Rowlatt J in *Davies v Braithwaite* 18 TC 198 at 203.
[19] Per Lord Salmon in *Edwards v Clinch* (56 TC at page 414).
[20] Per Lord Wright in *McMillan v Guest* (at page 566).
[21] Rowlatt J in *Davies v Braithwaite* (18 TC at page 202) suggested that it was found "convenient" to put "employment" expressly in Schedule E and that it can be viewed as something that was not an "office" nor earnings from a profession or vocation.
[22] *Hudson v Annear*, supra; *Pardue v Miller*, 206 SW.2d. 75 at 76.
[23] This distinction can sometimes be of some importance – for example, s.291(2) TA 1988 disqualifies an employee but not an officer from holding shares, under the BES scheme, in a connected company.
[24] *Fall v Hitchen* [1973] 1 All ER 368; *Andrews v King* [1991] STC 481. American case law also applies this principle. See *Malloy v Board of Education of City of San Jose*, 36 P. 948 at 949, and *Birmingham Trust & Savings Co. v Atlanta B. & A. Ry. Co.*, 271 F. 743 at 744.
[25] Rowlatt J in *Davies v Braithwaite* (18 TC at page 204).
[26] Extra-statutory concession A37 (1988) declares that fees paid to the individual but accounted for to his firm should not be treated as his taxable income and subject to PAYE.
[27] [1961] 3 All ER 49.
[28] See also *IRC v Brander & Cruickshank* [1971] 1 All ER 36; 46 TC 574.

films and radio productions was exercising a profession in doing so (Schedule D Case II) or merely engaging in contracts of employment (Schedule E). In determining the matter, the court preferred to look at the context of the activities (rather than each isolated activity) and the general arrangements and activities of the taxpayer. By taking such a wide perspective the court was able to conclude that:

> ... where one finds a method of earning a livelihood which does not consist of the obtaining of a post and staying in it, but consists of a series of engagements and moving from one to another ... then each of those engagements cannot be considered an employment, but is a mere engagement in the course of exercising a profession ...[29]

More recently, in *Fall v Hitchen* (above) the court was prepared to take a more restrictive approach in concluding that the engagement of a ballet dancer involved a contract of employment. This decision is difficult to reconcile with that in *Davies v Braithwaite*. In both instances one would suggest that the nature of the livelihood envisaged and contemplated the entering into of a series of engagement and that each engagement ought not to be viewed in isolation from the nature of the livelihood and from the arrangements and activities of the taxpayer. Perhaps any reconciliation or explanation lies in the apparent change of focus. The focus today appears to involve the analysis of the isolated contract under dispute in an attempt to determine whether that contract – irrespective of other commitments or expectations – was one for services or of service.[30] The emphasis, therefore, appears to be one of determining whether that is a contract of employment rather than consider whether it is in one sense employment but in reality part of the arrangement and exercise of a profession.[31]

Further guidance on the relevance of this distinction can be seen in *Hall v Lorimer*[32] where Nolan J provided a list of indicators on the issue of employee v self-employed. These included such matters as whether the person performing the services had set up a business-like organisation of his own; the degree of continuity in the relationship between the person performing the services and the person for whom he performs them; how many engagements he performed and whether they were performed mainly for one person or for a number of different people.

---

[29] Per Rowlatt J (18 TC at page 204). Although Rowlatt J did, rather unhelpfully add : "... every profession and every trade does involve the making of successive engagements and successive contracts and, in one sense of the work, employments ...".

[30] On the basis of such an analysis the conclusion of employment was unavoidable in *Fall v Hitchen*. The contractual details indicated that it was a full-time contract and prohibited the employee from taking on outside activities without the employer's consent.

[31] A further element of explanation can be found in the judgement of Rowlatt J in *Davies v Braithwaite*, where emphasis is placed on the historical background to the introduction of the word 'employment' to Schedule E. Rowlatt J appears to suggest that 'employment' is a residual category. If the activity is neither an office nor the exercise of a trade or profession, then we must turn to 'employment' to plug the gap and catch the activity. If that suggestion is accepted, then Rowlatt J's analysis of the activities in *Davies v Braithwaite* would begin and end with 'trade or profession'.

[32] [1993] BTC 473.

On the issue of compiling a list we are warned that:

> No exhaustive list has been compiled and perhaps no exhaustive list can be compiled of considerations which are relevant in determining that question [distinguishing between a contract of service and a contract for services], nor can strict rules be laid down as to the relative weight which the various considerations should carry in particular cases.[33]

This appears to have been confirmed by the Court of Appeal in *Hall v Lorimer* where the emphasis was placed on the overall effect and circumstances of the particular case rather than on any definitive checklist.

The recent "IR35" litigation provides a modern example of the tensions between employments and professions. The dispute rumbled on for two years before being settled before Burton J in *R (on the application of Professional Contractors Group Ltd) & Ors v IRC.*[34] The story started when the Revenue issued a press release in March 1999 to announce a planned clampdown on tax-avoidance by personal service companies (one-person businesses through which consultants such as information technology specialists provide service to clients). The government argued that some people used these businesses as vehicles to escape tax and cited the examples of employees of large companies who left their posts on Friday and returned on Monday to do the same job but operating through one-person companies. By doing this, they could avoid national insurance contributions by paying their salary as dividends and using other devices such as paying spouses a nominal salary to take advantages of their tax allowances. The government claimed that IR35 was aimed at stopping consultants who treated the tax rules with contempt – such people would find themselves redefined as employees of their clients and pay tax accordingly. The Revenue estimated that the change could push the tax and national insurance bill of a consultant earning £50,000 a year from £10,500 to about £17,500.

The Professional Contractors Group, set up to represent consultants, applied for judicial review, seeking a declaration that the IR35 legislation was incompatible with the European Convention on Human Rights and was contrary to Community law, in that it was unlawful State aid within Art. 87 of the EC Treaty, and was a hindrance to the free movement of workers, freedom of establishment and freedom to provide services. Burton J, in a long judgment, rejected these claims. He held that IR35 was not discriminatory, and that it fulfilled the requirements of proportionality.

---

[33] Per Cooke J in *Market Investigations Ltd v Minister of Social Security* [1969] 2QB 173.
[34] [2001] BTC 240.

Also, the legislation was justified since its objective was to combat tax avoidance. He viewed the issue as ultimately a political rather than legal question, stating: "It is not for me to enter into the political arena".[35]

The decision has been applauded as endorsing the government's right to set tax policy, but the dispute illustrates a number of tensions. First, the case showed that the Inland Revenue was out of touch with events in a changing economy in which flexible employment and contracting practices had seriously blurred the boundary between employment and self-employment. Second, the once advanced PAYE system was inappropriate to this new economy. Every year, fewer people have the simple employment patterns expected by the PAYE system. People move jobs more frequently. They often work for more than one employer. Free-lancing and contracting is more common. Self-employment is growing. And in each case the PAYE system struggles to cope.

In response to these suggestions, it has been suggested that the government should consider an American-style simple withholding tax on labour income with end-of-the year tax reconciliation. With modern record-keeping, there would be no need for everyone to fill in an annual tax return. That would help constrain the Inland Revenue from classifying everyone as an employee.

The detail of the IR35 legislation, as far as it relates to income tax, can be found in FA 2000, s.60 and Sch.12. The provisions apply if three conditions are satisfied.[36] The first condition is that an individual (referred to in the legislation as "the worker") personally performs, or is under an obligation personally to perform services for the purposes of a business[37] carried on by another person (referred to as "the client"). Secondly, the services are provided not under a contract directly between "the client" and "the worker" but under arrangements involving a third party[38] (referred to as "the intermediary"), and, thirdly, the circumstances are such that, if the services were provided under a contract directly between the client and the worker, the worker would be regarded for income tax purposes as an employee of the client. In such cases, and subject to certain conditions[39], the worker is treated as receiving a payment chargeable to tax under Schedule E if he or an associate of his receives from the intermediary, directly or indirectly, a payment or other benefit that does not fall to be taxed under Schedule E, or has rights entitling him, or which in any circumstances would entitle him, to receive from the intermediary, directly or indirectly, any such payment or other benefit.[40]

---

[35] At page 281.

[36] See FA 2000, Sch.12 para 1(1).

[37] "Business" for these purposes includes any activity carried on by a government or public or local authority, or by a body corporate, unincorporated body, or partnership – FA 2000, Sch.12 para 1(2).

[38] A "third party" includes a partnership or unincorporated body of which the worker is a member – FA 2000, Sch.12 para 1(3).

[39] Where the intermediary is a company, the conditions relate to material interest (generally a 5% beneficial interest) owned by the worker in the company or to the worker's receipt of money from the intermediary that can reasonably be taken to represent remuneration for services provided by the worker to the client (Sch.12 para 3). There are other conditions where the intermediary is a partnership (Sch.12 para 4) or an individual (Sch.12 para 5).

[40] FA 2000, Sch.12 para 2.

The practical effect of these provisions when they apply is to treat a person who would otherwise be treated as a professional person taxable under Schedule D Case II as an employee taxable under Schedule E.

Emoluments

As indicated earlier, tax under Schedule E is charged on "emoluments" from the office or employment. Emoluments are defined as including "all salaries, fees, wages, perquisites and profits whatsoever."[41] American case law defines emoluments as pecuniary profit, gain or advantage[42] and confirms that the meaning is more extensive than just salary or fees, but rather, it "imports any perquisite, advantage, profit or gain arising from the possession of an office".[43]

TA 1988 s.19(1) requires that the emolument must, for the purposes of Schedule E[44], be "from" the office or employment. The insistence on "from" or "therefrom" (by reference to the office or employment) is acknowledged to represent a test of causation[45] and demands consideration of the question: when is a fee, salary, reward etc received in respect of the employment, or in respect of a personal characteristic or circumstance?

The importance of the test of causation is that is correctly places the focus on the cause and reason for the receipt rather than on the timing of the receipt or the status of the giver. Thus, receipts from non–employers and/or receipts received before or after employment are capable of being treated as caused by the employment and therefore "emoluments" taxable under Schedule E.[46]

One of the tests of causation can be found in the celebrated statement of Upjohn J in *Hochstrasser v Mayes:*

---

[41] TA 1988 s.131.

[42] *Irwin v State*, 177 SW.2d. 970 at 973.

[43] *Taxpayers' League of Carbon County Wyoming v McPherson*, 54 P.2d. 897 at 901; *Dugger v Board of Supervisors of Panola County*, 104 So. 459 at 461. *Scharrenbroich v Lewis & Clarke County*, 83 P. 482 at 483.

[44] In accordance with the Schedular system, emoluments not caused by and, therefore, not caught under Schedule E might be assessed to tax elsewhere. It has even been suggested that they might be regarded as capital as opposed to income, and conceivably taxable as capital. See *Jarrold v Boustead* [1964] 3 All ER 76.

[45] See Viscount Simonds in *Hochstrasser v Mayes* [1960] AC 376 at 389: "... the issue turns ... upon whether the fact of employment is the causa causans, or only the sine qua non ...". There is a suggestion that the test is simply one of 'emolument' and that in applying such a test we are necessarily establishing that the source is one of employment. See Kerridge [1991] BTR 313. Perhaps this suggestion does not recognise the distinction between an emolument flowing from employment and an emolument caused by the employment. See more recently in *Mairs v Haughey* ([1993] BTC 339) where it was decided that a payment made to employees to relinquish their contingent rights under a non-statutory redundancy scheme was not taxable because the character of the payment took that of the payment it replaced, namely a redundancy payment. Such a payment was caused through being unemployed rather than being employed!

[46] Practical problems can result from a future sum being received following the termination of employment, or vice versa. The Finance Act 1989 provided some relief by adopting a receipts basis and charging tax by reference to the year of receipt irrespective of the fact that that receipt might not have any source in that year, i.e. the taxpayer is not an employee in that year of receipt and assessment. Objections to the absence of source can be answered by understanding that the tax liability will be by reference to the relevant year of employment.

. ...not every payment made to an employee is necessarily made to him as a profit arising from the employment, the payment must be made in reference to the services the employee renders by virtue of his office and it must be something in the nature of a reward for services past, present or future.[47]

The facts of *Hochstrasser v Mayes* provide a useful illustration of the causation requirement. Here the employer, ICI Ltd, operated a relocation scheme for its employees whereby ICI Ltd would reimburse any loss suffered on the selling price of the employees house. An employee, Mayes, was required to relocate by ICI Ltd. He did so and sold his house for £350 less than the purchasing price of three years earlier. The Inland Revenue's attempt to assess the £350 receipt as an emolument under Schedule E failed. The House of Lords emphasised that the sum of £350 was paid to the taxpayer in respect of his personal situation as a house–owner and not because of or caused by any services given by him. Emphasis was also placed on the "favourable" salary of the employee (the £350 was not a disguised salary payment) and on the fact that the onus is on the Revenue to establish that the reward was for the employees' services.[48] Lord Radcliffe provided another statement of the test for causation.

... while it is not sufficient to render a payment assessable that an employee would not have received it unless he had been an employee, it is assessable if it had been paid to him in return for him acting as or being an employee. [49]

The Court of Appeal had the opportunity to apply these tests in *Hamblett v Godfrey*.[50] Employees at GCHQ who wished to continue in employment following the removal of their rights to belong to a Trade Union were given £1,000 each in recognition of the withdrawal of those rights. The Court of Appeal agreed with the Revenue that the sum of £1,000 was an emolument caused by their employment and thus assessable to tax under Schedule E. Purchas LJ noted that in *Hochstrasser*, the status of the payment and the employee was important (i.e., payment in return for acting as or being an employee").Thus the approach that the court should adopt is one

---

[47] [1959] Ch 22 at 33. Although it should be noted that the causation test has not enjoyed overwhelming support. Lord Simon criticised it as "outmoded and ambiguous" and subsequently suggested a "far less begging test" by asking was it paid to taxpayer as an employee? (see *Brumby v Milner* [1976] 2 All ER 636). Lord Simon's criticisms were not followed in the subsequent case of *Tyrer v Smart* ([1979] STC 34) nor in *Mairs v Haughey* ([1993] STC 569) where the House of Lords relied on Lord Radcliffe's speech in *Hochstrasser* where he considered that the test was whether the payment had been made for acting as or being an employee.

[48] Concern has been expressed at the anomaly consequent on this decision. Depending on the nature and manner of provision, housing benefit or contribution may be taxable. For example, the provision of rent free (full or partial) would attract a tax assessment. Similarly mortgage contributions and concessions will attract the attention of an assessment - but contributions in the form of a guarantee against loss or relocation will not (according to the decision in *Hochstrasser v Mayes*).

[49] [1960] AC 376 at 391-392 (emphasis added).

[50] [1987] 1 All ER 916; (1986) 59 TC 694. See also *Bird v Maitland* [1982] STC 603 where a compensatory sum paid to employees following the withdrawal of a hire care provision was an emolument.

of considering the "status of the payment and the context" in which it was made. The status of the payment was one of compensation for loss or rights as an employee. The context was one of employment.[51] Purchas LJ explained that, if the employment did not exist, there would be no need for the rights in the particular contract in which the taxpayer found herself.[52]

One might respond that the context of the payment in *Hochstrasser v Mayes* was also one of employment. If Mayes had not been in employment with ICI Ltd he would not have been in the situation of the need to relocate albeit on favourable terms. Perhaps the solution, or at least reconciliation, lies in the emphasis and degree placed on the dominant cause of the payment.[53] In *Hamblett v Godfrey* the rights subject to compensation were stated as being "directly connected with the fact of the taxpayer's employment". That "direct connection" places emphasis on and indicates the dominant cause of the payment – the employment situation and the employee status. The decision can thus be rationalised on the basis that the payment concerned was a payment for continuing as an employee, or, in the words of Lord Radcliffe in *Hochstrasser v Mayes*, a payment "for being an employee". In contrast, the emphasis in *Hochstrasser v Mayes* was placed on the status of house-owner as the dominant reason and cause for the receipt. This type of analysis indicates the fine line and distinctions that are necessary and not all too obvious in this area of law.

The categories of cases selected below are used as a matter of convenience to place and introduce some decisions that illustrate the fine distinctions and degrees of emphasis adopted by the Courts. The cases also illustrate the breadth of coverage of s.19, including payments from non-employees and payments by reference to past, present and future services.[54] It must be appreciated that the distinctions are issues of fact and, in determining fact, the courts will look to the reality of the situation. Thus in *O'Leary v McKinlay*[55] the court looked beyond a trust to the reality of the provision of funds to an employee. Similarly, in *Shilton v Wilmshurst*[56] Southampton paid a £325,000 transfer fee to Nottingham Forest in order to secure the services of Peter Shilton, a well-known professional footballer. Southampton also paid an £80,000 signing-on fee to Shilton. In addition, Nottingham Forest paid £75,000 to Shilton in order to secure the transfer to Southampton. The reality of the situation was that Nottingham Forest was to receive a net sum of £250,000 (£405,000 – £80,000 – £75,000) and Shilton was to receive £155,000 (75,000 + £80,000). This case is discussed in more detail below. It suffices at this

---

[51]   59 TC at page 723.

[52]   Ibid.

[53]   Apportionment suggests itself as an equitable, if not practically onerous, solution.

[54]   It is possible that the scope for the inclusion of payments for past services as emoluments has been limited. Lord Templeman in *Shilton v Wilmshurst* ([1991] 1 AC 684 at 689) indicated that s.19 includes (inter alia) as emoluments sums paid "as a reward for past services and as an inducement to continue to perform services". Although Lord Templeman stated that the 'authorities are consistent' with his analysis, it is not entirely settled that payments for past services must also be an inducement as to future services in order to be treated as an emolument under s.19.

[55]   [1991] STC 42.

[56]   [1991] 1 AC 684; STC 88. Noted by R Kerridge, [1991] BTR at 311.

point to note that the final outcome of a series of appeals gave effect to the arithmetic reality and the taxpayer was assessed on the basis that the sum paid too him by his old club, Nottingham Forest, was an emolument from his new employment with Southampton. And Lord Templeman explained that an emolument "from employment" means an emolument "from being or becoming an employee".[57]

Thus, an "emolument from employment" means a payment as reward for services[58], a payment in return for acting as or being an employee[59], a payment for remaining an employee[60], and a payment from being or becoming an employee.[61] We shall now examine this in closer detail under a number of headings.

Inducement payments/signing-on fees

The courts have been required to determine the status of inducement payments paid in return for persuading one to adopt employment or leave employment. In most cases, the payments are made by the new employer. Although the inducement payments appear to have made in return for an agreement to enter into employment, it has been possible for the courts to conclude that such payments, albeit "flowing" from employment, were not caused by the employment – as different causes might be identifiable, such as the foregoing of some personal advantage or right such as amateur status and rights appertaining to such status.

In *Jarrold v Boustead*[62] the taxpayer received a signing-on fee from Hull Rugby League Club of £3,000. In determining the status of this signing-on fee the Court of Appeal were prepared to look outside the terms of the agreement under which it was paid[63] to conclude that the signing-on fee was not an emolument but an award of compensation to Mr Boustead for relinquishing for ever his amateur status and the advantages that flowed from that status.[64] Lord Denning MR said[65]:

> Suppose there was a man who was an expert organist but was very fond of playing golf on Sundays. He is asked to become the organist of the parish church for the ensuing seven months at a salary of £10 a month for the seven months, but it is expressly stipulated by this

---

[57]   [1991] 1 AC at page 689.
[58]   Upjohn J in *Hochstrasser v Mayes*, supra.
[59]   Lord Radcliffe in *Hochstrasser v Mayes*, supra.
[60]   *Hamblett v Godfrey*, supra.
[61]   Lord Templeman in *Shilton v Wilmshurst*, supra.
[62]   [1964] 3 All ER 76; 41 TC 701.
[63]   At first instance Pennycuick J held that it was not permissible to look outside the terms of the agreement under which the £3,000 was paid. It is submitted that the Court of Appeal's approach was correct in ignoring expressions of consideration and agreement but focusing on the reality of the payment.
[64]   By relinquishing his amateur status, Mr Boustead, was barred from playing for or visiting and using the facilities of a rugby union club. Byelaw 24 of the Rugby League provided that "A player who relinquishes his amateur status is permitted to receive a signing-on fee from the club with which he first registers as a professional player. No club shall pay, or offer to pay a signing-on fee to a player who has previously been registered as a professional player with the League."
[65]   41 TC at page729.

strange parish council that, if he takes up the post, he is to give up Sunday golf for the rest of his life. Thereupon he says that, if he is to give up golf, he wants an extra £500 and they agree to pay it. In such a case the £500 is not a payment for his services as organist for seven months. It is a payment for relinquishing what he considered to be an advantage to him.

By contrast, in *Riley v Coglan*[66] a sum of £500 paid as a signing-on fee by York Rugby League Club was treated as an emolument from and caused by the employment. The distinction appears to be that in *Riley* the sum was clearly related to the services to be performed: it was repayable if the player failed to serve for the stipulated period (proportionate repayment) and was classified as "a running payment for making himself available to serve the club when required to do so".[67]

In *Pritchard v Arundale*[68], a senior chartered accountant (Mr Arundale) surrendered his accountant and senior partner status, and took up an appointment as a joint managing director of a company. In return Mr Arundale received a full salary and a stake in the business consisting of 4,000 shares. On the issue of whether the transfer of the shares amounted to an "emolument from employment" the court concluded that it did not. Factors influencing this conclusion included (1) the shares were transferred not by Mr Arundale's new employer but by a third party[69]; (2) under the agreement Mr Arundale was entitled to the transfer of shares "forthwith" (a full six months in advance of entering into employment as a joint managing director)[70]; and (3) Mr Arundale was to receive a full salary at a commercial rate as an employee.

This analysis was confirmed and followed in *Glantre Engineering v Goodhand*[71] where a £10,000 sum paid to Mr Wells in return for his agreeing to leave a firm of accountants and join another company was held to be an emolument from employment. In this case, Mr Wells received the payment direct from his new employers and it was not regarded as severable from the other benefits to which Mr Wells became entitled under the employment agreement – it was an emolument from that employment agreement and that employment situation. Following an analysis of the arguments that the sum of £10,000 was to compensate Mr Wells for the surrendering of his chartered accountant status (a *Jarrold v Boustead* attempted analogy), the court remained unconvinced: the loss of status was

---

[66] [1968] 1 All ER 314.
[67] Ibid, per Ungoed-Thomas J.
[68] [1972] Ch. 229; [1971] 3 All ER 1011.
[69] The third party consisted of the major shareholder of the company. One might suggest that the major shareholder was for all intents and purposes the Company - although the decision in *Salomon v Salomon & Co Ltd*. [1897] AC 22, illustrates the difficulty in supporting that suggestion.
[70] It was suggested that the distinction was apparent in that the taxpayer might have died between receiving the shares and entering into the contract of employment. The suggestion was that the shares would still be part of the deceased's estate.
[71] [1983] 1 All ER 542.

a less important factor than the loss of security that Mr Wells would suffer as a result of leaving the employment of the firm of accountants.

Shilton v Wilmshurst is relevant here. As indicated above, the case involved the transfer of Peter Shilton from Nottingham Forest to Southampton Football Club. Under the transfer arrangement, Southampton were to pay a transfer fee of £325,000 to Nottingham Forest, and a signing-on fee of £80,000 to Peter Shilton. Peter Shilton also demanded and received a fee of £75,000 from Nottingham Forest. The courts were required to determine the status of the £75,000 fee and concluded that it was a fee paid for "being or becoming an employee" and therefore an emolument from employment and taxable irrespective of the fact that it came from Nottingham Forest rather than from Southampton. The decision clearly permits a signing-on fee as taxable even if paid by one's ex-employer[72]. The difficulty is in determining when a payment made as a signing-on fee will not be classed as an emolument from employment. The distinctions adopted in *Pritchard v Arundale* and in *Jarrold v Boustead* remain valid and are a guide in this area. The decision in the *Shilton* case appears to be chipping away at those distinctions (without removing them) and widening the scope of the "emolument" to include payments and signing-on (leaving-fees) fees paid by ex-employers. The decision in the Shilton case made fiscal sense when one views the financial and arithmetic reality of the situation. It also makes sense by closing the door on an area of potential in tax planning and evasion – but, what the decision fails to do is provide sufficient guidance on its own limitations; in particular, when we can apply a *Pritchard v Arundale* or *Jarrold v Boustead* analysis in the determination of whether a payment, from a third party in particular, is made in return for one "being or agreeing to become an employee"?

If we search the judicial reasoning in *Shilton v Wilmshurst* we begin to find some, albeit inconclusive, guidance. The Court of Appeal agreed with Morritt J that the emolument from a third party (here an ex-employer) would only be an emolument "from the employment" if that third party could be shown to have an "interest" in the performance of the employment contract.[73] The problem with that analysis was that it gave the wrong result; Nottingham Forest had no interest in the performance of the contract: Nottingham Forest's interest was in the formation of the contract only. Adopting the requirement of "interest" and the distinction between "interest in performance" and an "interest in formation" led the Court of Appeal to the conclusion that the payment of £75,000 was not an "emolument from employment" (arithmetically incorrect!). The House of Lords[74] rejected the Court of Appeal's analysis and held the £75,000 to be

---

[72]   Cf. *Pritchard v Arundale*, supra.

[73]   [1990] STC 55 at 62.

[74]   [1991] 1 AC 684.

taxable as an "emolument from employment" (arithmetically correct!). Lord Templeman in rejecting the "interest" requirement, emphasised that it should not and did not matter whether the payment be received from Southampton or from Nottingham Forest; the crucial analysis was whether it was paid for "acting, being or becoming an employee".

> In determining this we are to include emoluments which are paid as inducements to enter into contracts of employment and to perform services in the future.[75]

The use of the word "and" is significant. It perhaps sets the boundaries and acts as guidance for later courts (it might also raise doubts as to the correctness of the *Shilton* case). One might suggest that the requirement of having to show that payment was not only a signing-on fee (or leaving-fee) but also paid on the basis of the "performance of services in the future" (albeit those services might be performed for a new employer) is analogous to the need to establish an "interest" in the employment contract, the interest being one of the "performance of services". If that is so, then we have not, in substance, removed the Court of Appeal's requirement of the need to establish an "interest of performance".

Rewards and Gifts

It is possible that rewards and gifts received by employees might be treated as not being caused by the office or employment and that therefore they would not be taxable under s.19.[76] Such "gifts", rewards and other payments have been found to have been caused by the desire to recognise and acknowledge achievements[77] or to indicate one's appreciation or goodwill at times of celebration or occasion.[78]

The issue is one of fact and degree and is illustrated by a number of decisions which we shall now examine. First, *Moore v Griffiths*[79]. Here, Bobby Moore captained the England Football team that won the World Cup championship in 1966. He then received a bonus of £1,000 from the Football Association. The Court decided that this bonus was not taxable

---

[75] At page 689.

[76] Although some judges and commentators have referred to the 'testimonial principle', it has been emphasised that the 'testimonial principle and the personal gift principle' are not categories to be defined or explained, but merely examples of transactions that do not fall within the taxable category of remuneration for services (per Megarry J in *Pritchard v Arundale* (1972) 47 TC 680 at 686). Megarry J clearly emphasised that there does not exist a range of categories: "... the question is not one of which of two [or more] straitjackets the transaction best fits, but whether it comes within the statutory language, or else, failing to do so, falls into the undefined residuary class of cases not caught by Statute."

[77] See discussion on *Moore v Griffiths* and *Seymour v Reed* above. Note also the non-taxable award to a bank employee in recognition of his achievements in his professional examination: *Ball v Johnson* (1971) 47 TC 155.

[78] In *Calvert v Wainwright* [1947] 1 All ER 282, a tip to a taxi driver was held to be taxable. Atkinson J stated that it was a tip "... given in the ordinary way as remuneration for services ...". Atkinson J, further stated that: "... supposing at Christmas, or, when the man is going for a holiday, the hirer says : "You have been very attentive to me, here is a £10 note", he would be making a present, and I should say it would not be assessable because it has been given to the man because of his qualities, his faithfulness, and the way he has stuck to the passenger ...". It is that distinction that is of importance!

[79] [1972] 3 All ER 399.

as a reward for services; it was of the nature of a testimonial. Brightman J identified six factors that contributed to this conclusion: (1) the payment had no foreseeable element of recurrence (2) there was no expectation of award – it came as a surprise to Mr Moore. It was not a contractual right or expectation (3) the payment was not made or announced until after the World Cup had been won and the Association had dispensed with the services of the players (4) a gift was consistent with the Association's nature and functions of promoting the sport and recognising appropriate achievements (5) the intention of the giver (the Association) was clearly one of benevolence and not one of employer; (6) all players, irrespective of the service rendered, received the same award of £1,000 – it was not proportionate to services rendered.

By contrast, a proportionate "gift" in *Laidler v Perry*[80] was held to be an emolument from employment. Here an employing company gave each of its 2,300 employees a Christmas "gift" of a £10 voucher. Any employee who had not been with the company for one full year would not receive the full £10 but a proportionately reduced amount. The Court concluded that, despite the expression of "gift" and the time of year of its presentation, Christmas, the voucher was taxable. It did not distinguish between the personal achievements and contributions of the employees (upon qualifying, they would all received a flat rate of £10) but did relate the payment to length of employment.

In *Seymour v Reed*[81] a professional cricketer with Kent County Cricket Club was, under the club regulations, granted a benefit match. The grant of the benefit match was not of right but discretionary. It was the Committee of the County Cricket Club that exercised the discretion in favour of the taxpayer. Following the benefit match, the taxpayer received the gate monies and subscriptions. The Revenue claimed the money was taxable as an emolument from the taxpayer's employment. The Court disagreed. The benefit match and monies collected were an appreciation and acknowledgement of the cricketer's contributions and personal qualities. The income was more in the nature of a testimonial to mark appreciation at the end of a professional cricketer's career.

In *Moorhouse v Dooland*[82] the Revenue successfully persuaded the Court that monies and gifts received by a professional cricketer employed by Lancashire Cricket Club were taxable as emoluments from employment. The monies and gifts here consisted of a contractual entitlement to receive one guinea for every 50 runs scored or six wickets taken, and a right to "collections" for meritorious performance.[83] In concluding that these sums were emoluments from employment, Jenkins LJ identified four issues for consideration: (1) the perceptions of the receiver. Did he believe it to be

---

[80]   [1965] 2 All ER 121.
[81]   [1927] AC 554; 11 TC 625.
[82]   [1955] 1 All ER 93; 36 TC 12.
[83]   The latter was a right found in the League rules rather than expressly in the contract with Lancashire Council Cricket Club.

a gift or testimonial, or did he believe it be derived from or caused by his employment?; (2) Was the income part of a contractual entitlement and expectation or was it a purely voluntary payment?; (3) Was the payment of a recurring nature?; (4) Did the circumstances indicate a gift, a payment according to personal needs or qualities?[84]

Payments for Entering into Restrictive Covenants

Under TA 1988 s.313, a payment made in respect of an undertaking given by the employee to restrict his activities is treated as an emolument of the employment chargeable to tax under Schedule E in the year of assessment in which it is made. The restriction(s) must be caused by the undertaking as opposed to interest or professional restrictions on the employee or their position.[85] The sums paid are deductible income expenses of the employer.[86]

Payments Made in Respect of the Variation and/or Termination of Employment

It is necessary to have an awareness of the general principles and of the statutory rules. The general principles attempt to give effect to the issue of causation. They respect the need to consider, as a matter of reality and fact, whether the payment was an emolument caused by the employment in accordance with the requirements of TA 1988, s.19. Thus we find that on the matter of payments in respect of the variation and removal of contractual rights we need to carefully consider the "right" and its context. For example, a payment made in respect of the removal of pension rights was not a payment caused by employment, as required by s.19.[87] Strictly speaking the pension is not paid in return for services rendered – albeit it tends to be viewed today as part of the remuneration package.

The need to focus on the exact variation and the focus of the payment or compensation received is illustrated in *Holland v Geoghegan*.[88] In that case the "totting" rights (rights to sell salvaged property) of refuse collectors were terminated. The refuse collectors went on strike and subsequently received a lump sum in respect of terminated rights. The court, however, viewed the lump sum payment as a inducement to return to work and not,

---

[84] These issues can be contrasted with the six factors identified by Brightman J in *Moore v Griffiths* (see discussion, above).

[85] In *Vaughan-Neil v IRC* [1979] 3 All ER 481, a payment made to a barrister for his agreeing not to practice escaped\ tax. The payment was made upon the barrister taking-up an appointment with a building contractor - inherent in taking-up such employment was a prohibition on a barrister practicing at the bar (professional restriction and prohibition).

[86] FA 1988 s.73(2) and (3).

[87] See *Tilley v Wales* [1943] 1 All ER 280.

[88] [1972] 3 All ER 333.

primarily, as a payment of compensation. On that basis the lump sum paid was taxable as an emolument from employment.

In *Hunter v Dewhurst*[89] a taxpayer waived his retirement rights under the contract and thereby, continued in his office as director. In return he received £10,000 and agreed to renounce all rights of compensation. The House of Lords held that this sum was not an emolument caused by the office or employment. The House of Lords treated this sum as a payment of compensation for the surrender of retirement rights.

When payments are received in respect of the termination of the employment, *Dale v De Soissons*[90] indicates the danger of including termination rights and payments in the initial contractual terms. The contractual terms stipulated that the company would have the right to terminate the contract after only one year. The contract also stated that if the company did exercise their right to terminate after only one year's service, the company would pay a sum in respect of the services and a further sum on the termination. In *Dale v De Soissons*, the company exercised this contractual right and terminated the employment after only one year. The company also paid a sum of £10,000 to the employee, at termination, caused by the employment (albeit paid at termination) because is was part of the employee's rights under the terms and contract of employment.

Finally, as part of the general principles, we must again mention *Shilton v Wilmshurst*. The decision of the House of Lords seems to suggest that a payment made (by one's employer) at the termination of the employment will be a taxable emolument if paid by reference to the beginning of an employment with another employer (Southampton Football Club).

The relevant statutory principles are to be found in TA 1988, s.148 which was subject to some redrafting in the FA 1998. S.148 is an important residual section in that it applies to payments that are not taxable as emoluments under the general principles (experience as "not otherwise chargeable to tax"). It applies to payments and other benefits not otherwise chargeable to tax which are received in connection with (a) the termination of a person's employment, or (b) any change in the duties of or emoluments from a person's employment. Such payments are chargeable to tax under the section if and to the extent that their amount exceeds £30,000.[91] "Benefits" are defined to include items which, if received for the performance of the duties of the employment, would be an emolument of the employment or would be chargeable to tax as an emolument of the employment.[92] Any amount chargeable under s.148 is

---

[89] (1932) 16 TC 605. There is some concern over the status of the decision in *Hunter v Dewhurst*. In the case, four judges found for the taxpayer (three being in the House of Lords) and five found for the Revenue. In later cases, it has been suggested that *Hunter v Dewhurst* be confined to its special facts. This illustrates the difficulties and uncertainties faced in this area.

[90] [1950] 2 All ER 460. See also *EMI Group Electronics Ltd. v Coldicott* [1999] BTC 294 (CA); *Richardson v Delaney* [2001] STI 936.

[91] S.148(1). Hence in *Shilton v Wilmshurst*, the debate took place in recognition that, if the sum paid by Nottingham Forest was not an emolument under the general principles, then it would be caught by s.148 subject to the £30,000 exemption.

[92] S.148(2).

income chargeable under Schedule E for the year of assessment in which the payment or benefit is received.[93]

Fringe Benefits ("Benefits in Kind")

According to TA 1988 s.131, in addition to salaries, fees and wages, the term "emoluments" includes benefits in kind.[94] These are described in s.131 as "perquisites" and "profits". For these purposes, "perquisite" means "something that benefits a man by going into his own pocket."[95] The rationale for including the value of perquisites ("perks") in calculating Schedule E tax liability was expressed by the Royal Commission on the Taxation of Profits and Income as being the promotion of equality and equity between taxpayers. According to the Commission

> If advantage can be taken of any weakness in the tax treatment of such benefits, there is an obvious temptation to resort to them as a means of part remuneration. And the harm that results is not merely the absolute loss of revenue: it is unfairness in the distribution of tax as between one taxpayer and another.[96]

The above statement also indicates the importance of not leaving any "gaps" in the taxation of benefits. One assumes that any "gaps" will promote tax planning and tax advantages to the detriment of the equality and equity among taxpayers. Whether the rules on the taxation of fringe benefits achieves or substantially contributes to any desired equal treatment of taxpayers is debatable.[97] Economists point out that an income tax system which exempts or fails to "catch" income in kind will encourage individuals toward self-sufficiency and trade by barter and influence the allocation of resources. An often given example of that influence on the allocation of resources is of a man painting his own house rather than employing someone else to paint his home. The latter transaction would attract tax. The result is an incentive towards do-it-yourself work where it may be more efficient for individuals to specialise in the occupations at which they have a comparative advantage. The complexity of the rules and principles applying to the taxation of fringe benefits illustrate, or perhaps contribute to, the difficulties in this area. The principles demand that we ask two questions: (1) Is the benefit taxable in the hands of that particular taxpayer? (a "status" and "benefit" issue); (2) If the benefit is taxable, what is the appropriate value of the benefit? In answering these questions we must consider both common law and statutory rules. Our starting point is consideration of the principle of convertibility.

---

[93]   S.148(3).

[94]   An appropriate definition of a benefit in kind can be found in the Final Report of the Royal Commission on the Taxation of Profits and Income, Cmnd 9474 (1055) at para 208: "... the law includes in its conception of income a benefit having money's worth even though it is only received in kind."

[95]   Per Lord Pearce in *Owen v Pook*, 45 TC 571 at 592.

[96]   Ibid.

[97]   Cf. the Royal Commission's Report, ibid. at para. 211: "... all benefits in kind received in the course of employment and attributable to it are a form of remuneration and should rank as taxable income, since otherwise one taxpayer's income is not equitably balanced against another's."

Convertibility

The principle of convertibility was established by the House of Lords in *Tennant v Smith*.[98] At its purest level, this principle states that a benefit is taxable only if the taxpayer is able to convert the benefit into money. Thus in *Tennant v Smith* the provision of free accommodation (valued at £50) to a bank employee was not taxable because it was non-convertible. The bank employee was to act as custodian of the premises and conduct special bank business after bank hours. He was not allowed to sublet the premises nor to use them for any purpose other than the bank's business. The House of Lords that the benefit was not taxable. According to Lord Halsbury, a benefit cannot be taxed unless it can be turned to money.[99] Lord Watson thus explained the principle;[100]

It is clear that the benefit, if any, which a bank agent may derive from his residence in the business premises of the bank is neither salary, fee, nor wages. Is it then a perquisite or a profit of his office? I do not think it comes within the category of profits, because that word in its ordinary acceptation appears to me to denote something acquired which the acquirer becomes possessed of; and can dispose of to his advantage, in other words money, or that which can be turned to pecuniary account.

The principle of convertibility has subsequently developed to include the convertible value of benefits that could not be assigned or sold but could be converted into monetary value. For example, in Heaton v Bell the taxpayer partook of his employer's car loan scheme. In return for the use of a car, the taxpayer received an amended lower wages (a deduction of just over £2 per week). It is important to appreciate that the employer would enjoy the use of the car but it was an unassignable (to a third party) right. The House of Lords held that the benefit was convertible. It could, at any time, be converted into money by the employee giving notice to his employers that he wished to relinquish his right to use the car and his employers would then be obliged to increase his wages by an amount equal to the amount by which his wages had been reduced by the car loan scheme (£2 per week).[101] Similarly, in *Abbott v Philbin*[102] a non-assignable share option was convertible in that it could be used to raise monies. Alternatively, the right to exercise the option enabled the taxpayer to obtain shares from the company. Those shares would be property rights of value and freely convertible into money.

It is interesting that in both *Abbott v Philbin* and in *Heaton v Bell*, the benefit was expressed to, or appeared to be, unassignable (directly) to a third party. It is perhaps asking too much of one to accept that both decisions are authorities for allowing the Revenue to ignore expressed or actual restrictions on assignment. In *Tennant v Smith* the Court did not

---

[98] [1892] AC 150; 3 TC 158.
[99] 3 TC at page 164.
[100] 3 TC at page 167.
[101] Lord Upjohn dissented explaining that the benefit (the use of the car) could not be turned into money: "In my opinion, this personal unassignable right for use of the car was not equivalent to money while it continued and that, surely must be the test ...".
[102] [1961] AC 352.

appear to look beyond the expressed non-assignability of the benefit as found in the terms of employment and occupation. In *Abbott v Philbin* Lord Radcliffe criticised the "not very precise language" used in *Tennant v Smith*, and suggested that there exist many uncertainties that have yet to be cleared up, including the issue:

> must the inconvertibility arise from the nature of the thing itself, or can it be imposed merely by contractual stipulation? Does it matter that the circumstances are such that conversion into money is a practical, though not a theoretical, impossibility; or, on the other hand, that conversion, though forbidden, is the most probable assumption.[103]

The test of convertibility not only determines the taxability or otherwise of the benefit, but it also provides the answer to the question of the "value" of the benefit provided. The value of the benefit provided equals the convertible value at the date of provision. Thus in *Wilkins v Rogerson*[104] an employee who was provided with a suit was assessed on the second hand value of the suit at the date of provision (the convertible value). The second hand value was lower than the cost to the employer of providing the benefit but it reflected the value that the employee would expect if he elected to convert the benefit into money.[105] In *Heaton v Bell* the converted value was of £2 per week - the amount by which the taxpayer's wages would increase if he had elected to withdraw from the car loan scheme and the amended lower wage benefit.

Statutory rules

Despite judicial efforts, the convertibility rule remains limited in its scope and, particularly in times of high tax rates, ineffective in controlling and dealing with the growth in fringe benefits.[106] The Legislature has responded to this situation by declaring that certain types of benefit, and, benefits provided to certain types of employee, will be taxable irrespective of the fact that those benefits would not be convertible under the principle established in *Tennant v Smith*.

---

[103] [1961] AC at pages 378-379.
[104] [1961] 1 All ER 358.
[105] The suit cost the employer £14 15s to provide, but the taxpayer was attributed as receiving a benefit to the value of £5 only (the second hand value of the suit).
[106] It has been reported that the use of recognised fringe benefits is far higher in the UK than in any other European country. The limitations of the principle in *Tennant v Smith* may not have been of concern in 1892 when the standard rate of income tax was only 2.5%: the incentive to substitute income with a fringe benefit was clearly not prominent or strong.

Living accommodation[107]

Where living accommodation is provided for a person "by reason of his employment", its value to him, less anything that he pays himself, is taxed under Schedule E.[108] Accommodation provided for members of the taxpayer's family or household by reason of his employment is treated as being provided for the taxpayer.[109] The charge only applies to the provision of living accommodation: not to ancillary services such as heating, lighting and furniture (although the provision of such services to "higher paid employees" may be assessable under other statutory provisions). It is important to establish that the accommodation was provided by reason of the employment. For these purposes, accommodation provided by the taxpayer's employer is deemed to be provided by reason of the employment.[110] There are exceptions for cases (a) where the employer is an individual and it can be shown that he makes the provision in the normal course of his family or personal relationships, and (b) where the employer is a local authority providing accommodation for its employees on terms which are not more favourable than the terms under which other council tenants hold their accommodation.[111]

As indicated earlier, the assessment is based on the value to the employee of the accommodation provided. S.145(2) provides that the value to the employee is the "annual value" of the accommodation under s.837[112] – but where the rent paid by the providers of the accommodation exceeds the annual value, then the amount of the rent is the value of the accommodation.

An additional charge is imposed on employees who are provided with living accommodation that cost more than £75,000 to provide.[113] The additional charge involves the application of a formula taking into account the actual cost of provision, the official rate of interest prescribed by the Treasury, and any rent paid by the employee.[114]

Section 145(4) provides some relief for those who occupy living accommodation provided by their employer in "non-beneficial circumstances". The following classes of non-beneficial (or representative) occupation and provision will not be chargeable:

    a.   where living in the accommodation provided is necessary for the proper performance of the employee's duties;

---

[107] TA 1988, ss.145, 146.

[108] S.145(1). Note that this rule does not apply if the accommodation is made subject to a charge to him as income tax elsewhere. For example, if the benefit of the accommodation is convertible then it will be taxed in accordance with the *Tennant v Smith* principles and not by an application of these statutory rules and valuations.

[109] S.145(6).

[110] S.145(7).

[111] Ibid.

[112] Section 837 initially provides that the annual value is a "fictitious rent" equating to that "which might reasonably be expected to be obtained on a yearly letting if the tenant undertook to pay rates and taxes and the landlord undertook to pay for repairs and insurance." In practice, it is the rateable value rather than the value of the 'fictitious rent' that is used for assessment purposes.

[113] TA 1988, s.146 (introduced by FA 1983, s.21).

[114] The formula provides: [(cost of providing accommodation) minus £75,000 x official rate of interest] minus any excess rent paid by the employee.

b. where the employment is one where it is customary to provide living accommodation and the accommodation is provided for the better performance of the employment duties;

c. where the occupation of the premises are part of special security arrangements.

Each exception is "quite separate"[115], and the nature of the employment and the contractual responsibilities will help determine whether the employee is able to enjoy the "non–beneficial" occupation exceptions. For example, it is probable that hotel staff will enjoy exception (a). Similarly, in *Tennant v Smith* the obligation to occupy the premises was related to the performance of contractual duties. The requirements in situation (b) of "customary" and "better performance" might present an additional burden. "Customary" will demand an examination of "industry wide" practices and an examination of the history and length of those practices.[116] This burden can be compared with the requirement in exception (a) to show that the occupation was "necessary" for "proper performance" rather than merely promoting "better performance".

In *Vertigan v Brady*, Mr Vertigan was a very experienced nurseryman and a "Icey worker." His employer bought him a bungalow in which he lived rent free (he could not afford to buy his own bungalow). He was assessed under s.145, and appealed on the grounds that the provision was either necessary for the proper performance of his duties, or that it was for the better performance of duties of his employment, which was the kind employment in which it was customary to make such provision. The Special Commissioner, not being convinced that the provision of accommodation had become an established custom (even though it was practised by about 2/3 of the industry) rejected his appeal. Knox J, upholding the Special Commissioner, explained[117] that the "necessity" required for ground (a) was a necessity based on the relationship between proper performance and the dwelling house, not a "necessity based on the personal exigencies of the taxpayer in the shape of his inability to finance the acquisition of suitable accommodation." According to him[118]:

Where, as here, there are rather more than 78 square miles of inhabited countryside in which geographically and physically suitable accommodation existed, it seems to me impossible to contend that it was necessary for the proper performance of Mr. Vertigan's duties for him to reside where he did. No doubt it was necessary for [the employer] to buy the particular bungalow in order to secure Mr. Vertigan's services, but that is a different matter altogether.

[115] Per Knox J in *Vertigan v Brady* [1988] BTC 99 at 106; STC 91.
[116] See *Vertigan v Brady*, supra.
[117] [1988] BTC at page 107.
[118] Ibid.

The claim on the second ground also failed. It was accepted that the provision of the bungalow was for the better performance of Mr Vertigan's duties but the prudent practice had not become "customary". In this sense, "customary" was not used in a technical legal sense but "as a normal English word."[119] According to Knox J a useful approach would be to seek to identify what is involved "in the concept of a practice being customary for employers to follow".[120] In his opinion, there were three "constituent factors". First, the statistical evidence — i.e., how common is the practice statistically? In this case the answer was that two-thirds of workers in that industry were provided with accommodation. Secondly, there was the issue of longevity — how long has the practice gone on? "A custom can hardly into existence overnight."[121] Thirdly, trade acceptance — has it achieved acceptance generally by the relevant employers? Knox J said that if regard is had to these three factors, then it was up to the commissioners to make up their minds as to whether the practice is properly called customary. In this case, the Special Commissioner had not been convinced that "a custom had been established". According to Knox J, this "points to a conclusion on his part as a matter of fact that although the statistical requirement may well be met the practice, prevalent though it is, has not become customary".[122] He did not think that it followed that a 66.6% recurring frequency must necessarily be high enough to constitute a custom, seeing that considerations other than statistical ones could be determinant.[123]

Vouchers and credit-tokens

If an employee receives a voucher or credit token that can be exchanged for goods and/or services, he will be taxed on the cost of provision, i.e., the amount that it cost the employer to provide the voucher or token[124] (except in the case of a cash voucher where the exchange value will apply).[125] Prior to the introduction of legislation covering this area, the convertibility principle would have caught many vouchers and, possibly, credit tokens.[126] Problems did occur with the growing use of non-convertible credit-tokens, such as credit-cards and non–transferable season tickets. Here the voucher or token remained in the physical possession of the employee and, although it may have been used to acquire goods or services, it remained non-converted: under today's legislation,

---

[119] At page 109.
[120] Ibid.
[121] Ibid.
[122] Ibid.
[123] At page 107.
[124] TA 1988 s.141.
[125] TA 1988, s.143. A cash voucher is one which can be exchanged for a sum of money greater than, equal to, or not substantially less than the expense incurred in providing it (s.143(3)).
[126] The "convertibility" principle did develop to recognise an element of the cost of provision or, more accurately, the debts incurred by the employer in providing the benefit. For example, in *Nicholl v Austin* (1935) 19 TC 531, a company paid an employee's debts and the court held that the benefits provided were convertible into a sum equating with the costs to the employer of providing those benefits (the cost of settling those debts).

convertibility is irrelevant and the credit token or voucher will be taxable on the value of "the cost of provision."

Special statutory provisions applying only to directors and "higher paid employees"

In 1948 special rules were introduced to tax certain benefits that were not "otherwise chargeable to tax" provided to directors and higher paid employees. In other words, these benefits will be taxable even though they are not convertible within the principle of *Tennant v Smith*. The relevant rules can now be found in TA 1988, Part V, Chapter II[127] and Schedules 6 and 7. The statutory rules began life in 1948 as an attempt to control the tax avoidance opportunities provided through the use of expense account provisions. Today the rules apply to a wider range of benefits and attempt to provide some recognition of the practice of providing remuneration and benefit packages. The main specific benefits which are chargeable to income tax by the TA 1988, Part V, Chapter II are (a) expense allowances, (b) benefits in general, (c) beneficial loan arrangements, (d) expenses connected with living accommodation, (e) cars and petrol, and (f) scholarships.

By virtue of TA 1988 s.167(1), this special code only applies to (a) Directors and employees with emoluments of £8,500 or more, per annum[128] and (b) Directors with emoluments of less than £8,500, except where those directors work full-time in the company and control less than 5% of the company,[129] or the company is non-profit making, or is established for charitable purposes only.[130] In computing the employees emoluments for the purposes of the £8,500 threshold level, it is assumed that the rules of the special code are applicable and sums computed on that basis are included within the computation of the employees' emolument level. Such sums will later be ignored if the final emolument level does not reach the £8,500 threshold level.[131]

Payments for expenses and expense allowances[132]

Any sum paid to an employee, by reason of his employment, in respect of expenses is treated as income of that employee or director. This includes expense allowances and the reimbursement of expenses. The expenses are caught under this provision unless "otherwise chargeable to tax".

---

[127] See especially ss.153-167.
[128] The FA 1989, s.53, explains that employees earning over £8,500 are no longer to be described as "higher paid". We shall continue to use the term as one of convenience.
[129] 'Directors' need not be formally appointed as 'directors' in order to be caught by the legislation (TA 1988, s.168). The 5% requirement relates to 5% of ordinary share capital or distribution rights and satisfies the statutory requirement of 'material interest' (TA 1988, s.167).
[130] See s.167(5).
[131] S.167(2).
[132] TA 1988, s.153.

Furthermore genuine expenses[133] are deductible and are not treated as emoluments.

Benefits in general[134]

TA 1988, s.154 requires that the "cash equivalent"[135] of certain benefits provided to directors or higher paid employees or to members of their families or households are to be treated as emoluments from their office or employment, if those benefits are provided "by reason of the employment". The benefits caught by s.154 include sums spent in or in connection with the provision of (a) accommodation, other than living accommodation, (b) entertainment, (c) domestic or other services; and (d) other benefits and facilities "of whatsoever nature".[136] There are some exceptions to this charge in s.155.[137] The charge also does not apply to sums chargeable under the general principle of convertibility under *Tennant v Smith*, since those sums would represent sums "otherwise chargeable to tax" (although non-convertible excess amounts will be assessed for liability under the section).

Section 154 applies to the "provision" of benefits irrespective of whether those benefits were requested, used, even in cases wherein the "provision" was greater in cost than an alternative or self-provision. So, for example, in *Rendell v Went*[138] a taxpayer was assessed on the cost of a benefit of legal expenses provided by his employers. The cost of that benefit was £641. The employee's objection that his own provision of such services would only have cost £60 and the fact that he might even have obtained legal aid were ignored as irrelevant under the wording of s.154.

According to TA 1988 s.156(2) the "cost of a benefit" is generally the amount of any expense incurred in or in connection with its provision. Thus in *Rendell v Went* the value of the benefit provided was the full cost to the employer of £641. Assessing the cost of the provision of an in-house service, such as reduced rate or free travel to airline employees, has proved difficult and might possibly lead to absurd results. The obvious (and perhaps logical) solution would be to follow the approach of most other OECD countries and insert market-value as the cost of provision. Another sensible choice would be to use the "marginal cost" of the provision as the relevant employer's cost. Unfortunately, the legislation appears to indicate that the appropriate cost is the "actual cost" of provision. The cost of the benefit, according to s.156(2), must include "a proper proportion of any expenses relating partly to the benefit and partly to other matters." The

---

[133] To be deductible, expenses must satisfy the tests laid down in TA 1988 ss.198, 201 and 203.

[134] TA 1988, s.154.

[135] S.156(1) provides that the cash equivalent of any benefit chargeable under s.154 is the "cost of the benefit" less any amount paid for it by the employee.

[136] S.154(2).

[137] Examples include the provision of meals in a canteen in which meals are provided for the staff generally (s.155(5)), and the provision of medical treatment outside the UK where the need for treatment arises when the employee is abroad on official duties, or medical insurance against the cost of such treatment outside the UK (s.155(6)).

[138] [1964] 2 All ER 464.

effect of this provision can be seen in *Pepper v Hart*.[139] Here, employees of
Malvern College had taken the benefit of a scheme whereby their sons
were educated at the school at one-fifth of the fees normally charged. The
employees submitted that the cost of the benefit should be the marginal
cost, and that in this instance, the marginal cost of the boys' education
represented some additional expenditure on items such as food, laundry
and stationery. It was clear that the presence of the boys did not increase
the other expenses of running the school: staff salaries, insurance, heating
and maintenance of buildings, maintenance of grounds, remuneration of
administrative and other staff, and so on. Nor would the absence of the
boys have reduced these "other expenses". The Court of Appeal
unanimously rejected the submissions of the taxpayers. Nicholls LJ
explained[140] that the

> statutory formula is concerned with one specific calculation: the
> amount of the expense incurred by the employer in providing the
> benefit.

Applying that calculation it was clear that each place in the school cost the
school as much as every other place. Thus the expense incurred by the
school in providing the benefits to the assistant school masters and bursar
must include a proper portion of the general running expenses of the
school; that portion represents the statutory requirement of including

> a proper proportion of any expenses relating partly to the benefit and
> partly to other matters.

The taxpayers were properly assessed on the full cost rather than the
marginal cost of the benefit; Nicholls LJ admitted[141] that the necessary
rateable apportionment of the relevant expenses would produce a figure
close to the amount of the ordinary school fees - thus removing the
benefit.

Initial academic and press response suggested that this decision may have
adverse and absurd effects on existing fringe-benefit concessions.[142] The
suggestion was that employees may be assessed on a cost basis that may
exceed the cost of the benefit to non-employees. For example, airline staff
occupying otherwise empty seats on an aircraft amounts to very little in
marginal costs but amounts to an excessive amount if the cost is to include
an apportionment of full costs.

---

[139] [1990] STC 786.
[140] at page 791.
[141] at page 788.
[142] For initial responses see J Dyson, [1990] BTR 122 and D Wright, *The Sunday Times*, 18 November 1990, at 11.

An appeal by the taxpayers to the House of Lords[143] was successful. The taxpayers were charged on the marginal cost of provision. The House of Lord's decision is important in a wider context in the pronouncements made on the issue of statutory interpretation and the use of supplementary material, including the use of *Hansard*. On the less important issue of the value to be attributed to the benefit provided there appear to be two approaches. In the minority, Lord Mackay LC insisted that, once the benefit to be taxed has been identified, one must then consider whether that benefit was received as of right or as result of the exercise of the provider's discretion.[144] If it was as a result of the exercise of discretion, then the surplus (marginal) costs of exercising that discretion and providing, in this case the surplus school places, must be the cost of provision.

Lord Browne-Wilkinson (representing the majority) disagreed with the approach of Lord Mackay on the ground that the distinction proposed was "not reflected in the parliamentary proceedings". He preferred the approach of accepting that the relevant statutory provisions were ambiguous and thus, he referred to the debate in Hansard and in particular to the responses given by the, then, Financial Secretary to the Treasury, which made it clear that the absurd consequence of apportioning total costs to those enjoying an in-house provision or benefit was never intended. Nor was it intended that market-price should apply (an original provision that was withdrawn during debate). Lord Browne-Wilkinson concluded that parliamentary debate reveals that the value of the benefit provided (in-house) was intended to be and should represent and reflect the marginal costs of provision. Commenting on the difficulties that a reference to *Hansard* and parliamentary debate might cause, Lord Browne-Wilkinson suggested that he did not believe that the practical difficulties arising from this approach to statutory interpretation were "sufficient to outweigh the basic need for the courts to give effect to the words enacted by Parliament in the sense that they were intended by Parliament to hear".[145]

The Legislature has been able to predict and make provision in other potentially difficult areas. For example, where the provided benefit remains the property of the employer, the employee is taxed on the "annual value" of the asset, plus any other expenses of provision excluding acquisition and production costs.[146] The "annual value" for the provision of land is its rateable value. For other assets, the annual value is 20% of their market value at the time that it is first provided by the employer.[147] If the ownership of the asset is subsequently transferred to the employee the employee may be charged on the value of the item when he first received it less any annual value charges that may have been applied.[148] This is an

---

[143] [1992] STC 898.
[144] [1992] STC 898 at 901.
[145] [1992] STC 898 at 921.
[146] TA 1988, s.156(5).
[147] TA 1988, s.156(6).
[148] TA 1988, s.156(4).

anti-avoidance provision preventing the abuse of the normal rule[149] of market value at the date of transfer in circumstances of depreciating assets.

If the expense incurred by the employer is partly to provide a benefit to the employee and partly for some other identifiable purpose, s.156 allows "apportionment" to take place. The employee is only taxed on the proper proportion of the expense and the benefit. For example, in *Westcott v Bryan*[150] a managing director was required by his employers to live in a large house, close to the Potteries in Staffordshire. The Managing Director would have preferred to have lived in London and would have preferred a much smaller property. His employers were concerned over the need to entertain clients and the convenience of the location. The employers paid most of the running costs of the house. The Court held that the taxpayer was to be assessed on only a proportion of the running costs provided by his employers. The money spent by his employers was partly for the taxpayer's benefit and partly for the benefit of others.[151]

Living accommodation (ancillary services)[152]

The general rules in TA 1988 s.145 covering the provision of living accommodation are supplemented in the case of directors and higher paid employees to facilitate the taxation of services provided with the accommodation (such as furniture, heating, telephone etc). The "general benefits" provisions in s.154 will normally attach to the provision of "ancillary services". However, where those ancillary services are provided in relation to non-beneficial occupation some relief is provided in s.163 which provides that[153] in instances of non-beneficial occupation the provision of sums in respect of heating, lighting, cleaning, repairs, furniture etc, the amount that falls to be included in the emoluments will not exceed 10% of the emoluments of the employment - a maximum charge for the provision of those services and benefits.

Low interest or beneficial loans[154]

If the employer provides the employee or a relative of the employee with a low interest or interest free loan, the employee is taxed on the cash equivalent of that loan. The cash equivalent represents a computation of the benefit received by calculating the difference between the amount of interest that would have been paid at the official rate and any interest actually paid.[155] Some relief is provided in that a *de minimis* exception

---

[149]   TA 1988, s.156(3).
[150]   [1969] 3 All ER 564.
[151]   It is significant that in *Rendell v Went*, apportionment of the legal fees was not allowed on the grounds that "no part of the money was spent on something that did not benefit the taxpayer". The taxpayer enjoyed all the money in that it was all spent to cover his legal fees.
[152]   TA 1988, s.163.
[153]   S.163(2).
[154]   TA 1988, s.160 and Sch. 7.
[155]   See Sch. 7 para. 3.

applies[156] and there is also relief in respect of loans to relatives of the employee if the employee can show that he derived no benefit from the loan.[157]

Should the employer release or write-off (whole or in part) a loan to the employee which was obtained by reason of the employment, a charge will be imposed on the amount so released or written off (the benefit provided).[158]

Cars and car fuel[159]

If an employee has a car available to him or members of his family or household for his or their private use by reason of the employment, the cash equivalent of that benefit will be taxable.[160] This cash equivalent is fixed by statute and depends on the price[161] and age[162] of the car. From the year 2002-2003 it will simply be fixed at the appropriate percentage of the price of the car as regards the year.[163]

There is an exception where the car is a "pooled car". [164] A pooled car is one that is genuinely available to more than one employee, is not regularly kept overnight at or in the vicinity an employee's residence, and any private use thereof is purely incidental to its business use. Such cars are treated by s.159(3) as not being available for the private use of any of the employees, and therefore not taxable.

There were concerns as to the whether the statutory regime adequately taxes the private value of the "company car" and some changes have been introduced to try to reflect concerns. The old rules were in effect from 6 April 1994, and tax cars on a cash equivalent of 35% of the list price of the car based on the full cost (i.e., car price including VAT and cost of any accessories and delivery) subject to a list price ceiling of £80,000 with a one-third reduction for 2,500 plus business miles and a reduction of two-thirds for over 18,000 business miles per annum. A further reduction of one-third may be made if the car is four years old or more at the end of the year.

[156] TA 1988, s.161. The *de minimis* limit means that the employee is not treated as receiving an emolument where the aggregate amount of all beneficial loans outstanding in a tax year does not exceed £5000.
[157] S.161(4).
[158] S.160(2).
[159] TA 1988, ss.157 and 158. On 30 July 1992, the Inland Revenue issued a Consultative Document, "Company Cars Reform of Income Tax Treatment". The Document contained the broad aims of (1) ensuring that the tax charged is a fair reflection of the benefit received; (2) avoiding distortions in the car market; (3) minimising incentives to drive less fuel efficient cars; (4) keeping administrative costs to a minimum. The central proposal was that the car cash equivalents should be based on a percentage of the price of the car supplied. No charges were proposed to the apportionment rules or to the "business deductions" rules. Although the general aim of "neutrality" is accepted, some critics suggested that the proposals fell short of satisfying the declared aims, and that the proposals failed to recognise that the majority of company cars are work cars - figures reveal that less than 8% of "company cars" travel less than 2,500 business miles per annum whereas over 26% travel 18,000 plus, business miles per annum (see K Paterson [1992] BTR 368).
[160] TA 1988 S.157(1).
[161] See Sch. 6 para. 1.
[162] See Sch. 6 para. 5.
[163] Sch. 6 para. 1, as substituted by FA 2000 s.59 and Sch. 11 para. 1(2) with effect from 2002-2003.
[164] TA 1988, s.159.

Subsequently, in cases of business travel of at least 18,000 miles in the year, the cash equivalent was 15% of the price of the car as regards the year[165], and for business travel of between 2,500 and 18,000 miles, the cash equivalent was reduced by 25%.[166] There were also reductions in respect of any part of the year in which the car was "unavailable" to the employee.[167] Different scales apply from 2002 -2003.

The car-related benefit of fuel for private use raises a tax charge under s.158. The cash equivalent of the benefit of the fuel is statutorily fixed according to a table in s.158(2).

Scholarships[168]

Ordinarily, income arising from a scholarship held by a person receiving full time education at a university, college, or other educational institution is exempted from tax.[169] However this exemption does not apply to scholarships provided for the family or household of a directory or higher-paid employee. In such cases, only the holder of the scholarship is entitled to a tax exemption[170] – meaning that a charge under s.154 normally arises. Scholarships provided for a member of the employee's family or household are deemed to be provided by reason of the employment if provided under arrangements made by the employer or any person connected with the employer.[171] Some relief is available in that the charge can be avoided if it is shown that the scholarship was from a trust or similar scheme and that such payments do not represent more than 25% of payments made from that fund in that year.[172]

Employee shareholdings

TA 1988 s.162 introduced controls to recognise the growing use of employee share schemes. This "use" often reflected elements of the following:

1. the use of partly paid shares or shares acquired at less than market value; and

2. the use of "stop loss" arrangements consisting of arrangements to protect against a fall in the value of the shares after the employee acquired them (for example, through an option for the company to buy back the shares at the employee's acquisition cost).

---

[165] Sch. 6 para. 2(1).
[166] Sch. 6 para. 2(2).
[167] Sch. 6 para. 3. See para. 9 for definitions of "unavailable".
[168] TA 1988, s.165.
[169] TA 1988 s.331(1).
[170] S.165(1).
[171] S.165(2).
[172] S.165(3).

S.162 imposes a charge on the benefits connected with employee shareholdings where an employee (or a person about to be employed) acquires shares at an "undervalue" in a company (whether from the employer or not) in pursuance of a right or opportunity available by reason of the employee's employment. The charge applies by deeming there to be a "notional loan" to which the "beneficial loan" provisions under s.160 apply.[173] The amount of the notional loan is the amount of the undervalue represented by the difference between the market value of fully paid shares at the date of acquisition and the price actually paid by the employee for those shares. For these purposes, "undervalue" means the postponement of payment or payment at less than the market value of the shares.[174] The notional loan continues until the amount outstanding is made good or the shares are disposed of.[175] Section 162(3) and (11) indicate that this is a remedial charging provision, applicable only where the benefit of the shareholding is not otherwise taxable.

Further Reading

Ward J, *What Can it Matter? Why Should it Matter?* The Taxation of Offices [1989] BTR 281.

Bandal S, *The Legacy of Tennant v Smith* [1984] BTR 333.

Kerridge R, *Emoluments and Causation—Hochstrasser Investigated* [1982] BTR 272.

---

[173]   S.162(1).
[174]   S.162(2).
[175]   S.162(4).

chapter five

Income Tax -
Schedule E - Allowable Expenditure

The provisions for deductible expenses under Schedule E are contained in TA 1988, s.198. These rules have been subject to amendments in recent times, the most exciting of which was the removal of the ancient provision for deducting the expenses of keeping and maintaining a horse. The amendments operate to clarify the rules relating to deductible expenditure, and do not change the substance of the rules. The TA 1988, s.198(1) provides that if the holder of an office or employment is obliged to incur and defray out of the enrolments of the office or employment

a. qualifying travelling expenses, or
b. any amount (other than qualifying travelling expenses) expended wholly, exclusively and necessarily in the performance of the duties of the office or employment,

there may be deducted from the emoluments to be assessed the amount so incurred and defrayed.

These rules have been described as "notoriously narrow in their application" and "notoriously rigid, narrow and restricted in their operation".[1] Certainly when one compares the deductibility rules in Schedule E with the Schedule D taxpayer, the Schedule E taxpayer does appear to be at a significant disadvantage that is hard to justify.

The application of s.198(1) involves the application of two tests:
1. was the taxpayer necessarily obliged to incur those expenses? and,
2. were the expenses necessarily incurred in the performance of the taxpayer's duties?

---

[1] See the Final Report of the Royal Commission on Taxation of Profits and Income: Cmnd 9474 (1955). The Report also reveals opinion that the 'existing rule drew the line as fairly as could be expected of any general rule and that no other form of wording would be an improvement upon it'.

As seen above, the wording of s.198 draws a distinction between expenses connected with travelling (qualifying travelling expenses), and other expenses. We shall first examine the law relating to deductibility of travelling expenses.

Travelling Expenses

For present purposes, the term "qualifying travelling expenses" means:

a.   amounts necessarily expended on travelling in the performance of the duties of the office or employment, or

b.   other expenses of travelling which

    i.   are attributable to the necessary attendance at any place of the holder of the office or employment in the performance of the duties of the office or employment, and

    ii.   are not expenses of ordinary commuting or private travel.[2]

Thus it appears from these provisions that travelling expenses need only be incurred "necessarily" and "in the performance of the duties", or be expenses which are not expenses of "ordinary commuting" but which are "attributable" to the necessary attendance at a place of work. This is different to the "wholly, exclusively and necessarily" incurred requirement for the deduction of other expenses.

With respect to both travelling and other expenses, the test of necessity appears to be an objective test demanding consideration of whether the class of employee (or potential employee) would necessarily incur those expenses as part of their duties.[3] In some instances, the class of employee might be so small as to demand an assessment of whether it was necessary for an individual to incur those expenses as part of his or her duties. In *Ricketts v Colquhoun*[4] the taxpayer was a barrister who resided in London. His earnings from the bar were assessable under Schedule D Case II. He also took up an appointment as Recorder of Portsmouth (a Schedule E appointment). His claim to deduct the costs of travelling from his home in London to Portsmouth failed. The costs of travel were not necessarily incurred, since he could have lived in Portsmouth. Neither were the costs incurred in the performance of his duties: his duties as Recorder did not

---

[2]   See s.198(1A).

[3]   See Lord Blanesburgh in *Ricketts v Colquhoun* [1926] AC 1 at 7 - the expense has to be one "which each and every occupant of the particular office is necessarily obliged to incur".

[4]   [1926] AC 1.

commence until he reached the office in Portsmouth – when travelling to that office he was travelling to his employment, and not in the course of that employment. Here the class of employee (or potential employee) was wide and could have included those who lived in the Portsmouth area where the taxpayer's work was to be undertaken rather than in London. The taxpayer's decision to reside in London was a personal decision and his travel expenses from London to Portsmouth were not necessarily incurred as a consequence of his employment or office in Portsmouth.[5]

By contrast in *Taylor v Provan*[6] (discussed in more detail below) the class of potential employee was very narrow; it consisted of the need to acquire the services of one particular individual. The question of whether that individual would necessarily have to incur travel expenses from Canada to London in the performance of his duties, became a personal question and was answered in the affirmative: the employers could employ only him and must accept his decision on residence.

The second part of the s.198 test demands consideration of whether the travel expenses were incurred in the performance of the duties of the employment. The application of this part of the test invites the following general principles:

1.   The costs of travelling to work from home are not deductible on the grounds that the travel does not involve the "performance of duties"[7]: an employee's duties commence when he arrives at work, not when on the way to work. The travel from home to work is simply an expense of ordinary commuting.[8]

2.   The costs of travelling from one place of employment to a place of different employment are not deductible. Once again this does not amount to travelling in the course of the employment: it is simply travelling from one employment to another employment. Once again, this falls within the statutory definition of "ordinary commuting".[9] However, if the travel is between different places of employment with two companies in the same group, the travel expenses can be deducted.[10]

3.   In contrast to (2) above, if the employee is travelling from one place of employment to another place of work with regard to the same employment, it is likely that this is travelling in the performance of the employee's duties. In such a case, it is likely that any expenses incurred will

---

[5]   This decision has been described by Lord Pearce in *Owen v Pook* (45 TC 571 at 592) as "very unsatisfactory both in its result and in its reasoning". According to Lord Pearce, "In order to carry out his duties as Recorder, the taxpayer had to travel to Portsmouth, since he was a London practitioner (and it was, no doubt, by virtue of his London practice that he was appointed Recorder). It was, therefore, unreasonable to tax him on the emoluments of his office without allowing the travelling expenses. For that would be to tax him on a sum larger than the true profit of the office. Rowlatt J. described the position as unreasonable, but felt compelled by the rules to come to an unreasonable conclusion."

[6]   [1974] 1 All ER 1201.

[7]   See *Ricketts v Colquhoun*, supra.

[8]   See TA 1988 Sch. 12A (2) (1).

[9]   TA 1988 Sch. 12A (2) (1).

[10]   TA 1988 s.198(1B).

be deductible as necessarily incurred in the performance of the duties (provided, of course, that the employee is obliged to travel within the same employment).[11]

4. It is possible that the employee's "home" can be classed as a point where work commences (a place of work) and travel between that point to another point of the same work will be deductible, as a continuation of those duties.[12]

The complexity of the above rules and of the distinctions adopted therein emerge clearly from a number of leading decisions of the House of Lords. First, *Owen v Pook*. The taxpayer, a medical practitioner, worked as a general practitioner at his home in Fishguard. He also held a part-time appointment as an obstetrician and anaesthetist at Haverfordwest, 15 miles from Fishguard. The part-time appointments included "stand-by" duties. These duties required the taxpayer to be accessible by telephone :he often gave advice by phone. The costs of travelling between the taxpayer's home in Fishguard and the hospital in Haverfordwest were held to be deductible. Lord Guest explained that the taxpayer here had, in contrast to the taxpayer in *Ricketts v Colquhoun*, two places where the duties were performed. Dr Owen's duties commenced at the moment he was first contacted by the hospital authorities. He took responsibility for a patient as soon as he received a telephone call. He often advised treatment by telephone:

> There were thus two places where his duty is performed, the hospital and his telephone in his consulting room. If he was performing his duties at both places then it is difficult to see why, on the journey between the two places, he was not equally performing his duties.[13]

In *Taylor v Provan* the taxpayer was appointed as a director of an English Brewery Company. The taxpayer was resident in Canada but was appointed by the English Company because of his very special knowledge and skills on matters of amalgamation and merger within the brewing industry. The taxpayer completed most of his work in Canada but frequently made visits to England. He did not receive any remuneration for the work completed, but he did receive income to cover the travel expenses to England. The House of Lords held by a majority of 3:2 that the expenses were an allowable deduction. The reasoning of the majority is not altogether clear. Lord Morris and Lord Salmon appear to accept that

---

[11]   See *Taylor v Provan*, supra.
[12]   See *Owen v Pook* [1970] AC 244; (1969) 45 TC 571.
[13]   45 TC at page 590.

the taxpayer was travelling between two places of the same employment and was thus travelling in the course of, and in the performance of, his duties of employment. More controversially, Lord Reid in his search for the ratio of *Owen v Pook* appeared to accept that the expenses were deductible on the grounds of "necessity".[14] If the latter is the sole reasoning of Lord Reid and of *Owen v Pook*, then it fails to recognise the dual requirements of "necessity" and "performance" of s.198 – unless the latter requirement was implicitly accepted as present on the facts presented in both cases.

One of the more interesting concerns expressed by Lord Reid was the danger of adopting a test on the ground of one's home being regarded as a place of work. Lord Reid expressed concern that the majority in *Owen v Pook* did not intend to

> decide that in all cases where the employee's contract requires him to work at home he is entitled to deduct travelling expenses between his home and his other place of work. Plainly that would open the door widely for evasion of the rule. There must be something more.[15]

It has been suggested that the emphasis should not be upon where the work started (is one's home a place of work?) but on when the work started.[16] If the emphasis is then placed on the issue of when duties will be deemed to have commenced any necessary travelling will be in the performance of those duties.

Finally, it is generally accepted that if travel expenses are allowable then any incidental expenses of the travel will also be allowed.[17]

TA 1988 s.198(1A)(b) permits expenses of "triangular travel" and enables those employees who do not have a normal place of work but who perform their duties at a number of different sites to get relief for their travelling expenses. The detail covers travelling expenditure which does not comprise "ordinary commuting" or "private travel" but which is attributable to the necessary attendance by the employee at "any place" where his or her attendance at that place is in performance of the duties of the office or employment.

Other Expenses

Expenses, other than travel expenses, are deductible if they are "wholly, exclusively and necessarily incurred in the performance of the duties".[18]

---

[14]   [1974] 1 All ER 1201 at 1207.
[15]   Ibid.
[16]   Simon's Tiley and Collision: UK Tax Guide (2000-2001) para. 6:123.
[17]   The normal example is the allowance for airline pilots and staff. See *Nolder v Walters* (1930) 15 TC 380.
[18]   TA 1988, s.198(1).

Judicial interpretations render this a hard test to comply with. As Warner J said in *Smith v Abbott*[19]

> It is notorious that the provision is rigid, narrow, and to some extent unfair in its operation. In order to satisfy its requirements, an office-holder or employee has to show four things. First, he has to show that he has incurred the expenses in question "in the performance of the duties of the office or employment" .... Second, an office-holder or employee has to show that the expenses he seeks to deduct are expenses that he has been "necessarily obliged" to incur and defray in the performance of the duties of the office or employment. Third, he has to show that the expenses have been "wholly" so incurred. The better view seems to be that that goes only to quantum. Last, he has to show that they have been "exclusively" so incurred".

This notoriety and strictness was long ago alluded to by Vaisey J in his celebrated statement in *Lomax v Newton*[20].

> In order to satisfy the terms of the rule it must be shown that the expenditure incurred was not only necessarily but wholly and exclusively incurred in the performance of the relevant official duties. And it is certainly not enough to merely assert that a particular payment satisfies the requirements of the rule without specifying the detailed facts upon which the finding is based. An expenditure may be necessary for the holder of an office without being necessary to him in the performance of the duties of that office. It may be necessary in the performance of those duties without being exclusively referable to those duties. It may perhaps be both necessarily and exclusively but still not wholly so referable. The words are indeed stringent and exacting, compliance with each and everyone of them is obligatory if the benefit of the rule is to be claimed successfully. They are, to my mind, deceptive words in the sense that that when examined they are found to come to nearly nothing at all.

These statements show that the test can be broken down into three parts:

1. *In the performance of duties*

As with travel expenses, other expenses are only deductible if those expenses are incurred in the performance of the employee's duties. This

---

[19] [1991] STC 661 at 674(approved by Nolan LJ ([1993] 2 All ER 417 at 420).
[20] [1953] 2 All ER 801 at 802; 34 TC 558.

requirement excludes expenses incurred in enabling an employee to acquire qualifications or training to facilitate later performance or performance at a different level of employment – preparation costs. For example, in *Lupton v Potts*[21] a solicitor's clerk was not allowed to deduct the expenses of Law Society Examination fees, partly on the ground that the fees and the examinations were not part of the performance of his duties – they were part of preparation costs for new duties.

Similarly, a school teacher in *Humbles v Brooks*[22] was not allowed to deduct the costs of a weekend course in history on the grounds that he was not performing his duties by attending the course merely getting background information.

In *Simpson v Tate*[23] the medical officer for a county sought to deduct the cost of subscriptions to medical and scientific societies. The subscriptions had been taken up in order to keep him up-to-date with scientific advances. It was held that the expenses were not incurred in the performance of his official duties, but were rather incurred for the purposes of enabling him to continue to be qualified for his job.

In *Ansell v Brown*[24] a professional rugby player's claim to deduct expenditure incurred on dietary supplements failed. His argument that his profession required him to maintain certain levels of fitness and weight was of no consequence. Lightman J held that the expenditure had merely enabled him to perform his duties, and had not been incurred in the performance of his duties.

Finally, in *Smith v Abbott*[25] journalists had to read other newspapers as part of their job. The purpose of the reading was to give them some ideas for stories and to ensure that they did not repeat news which had been reported by competitors. The question was whether the cost of these newspapers was deductible. The House of Lords held that the reading was not done in the performance of the duties of the journalists, but was rather done in order to enable them to carry out the duties more efficiently. Thus it was merely preparatory for doing the work. The House of Lords held that the question whether expenses were necessarily incurred in the performance of duties was a mixed question of fact and law.

2. Necessarily incurred

As explained earlier, the test of whether an expense is necessarily incurred is an objective test based upon the question of "whether the duties could be performed without incurring that expense".[26] Thus, we ignore the personal attributes of the individual employee, and look to the attributes

---

[21] [1969] 3 All ER 1083.
[22] (1962) 40 TC 500.
[23] [1925] 2 KB 214.
[24] [2001] STC 1166.
[25] [1994] 1 All ER 673. For a critical analysis of this decision see Olowofoyeku [1996] BTR 28.
[26] *Brown v Bullock* [1961] 3 All ER 129; 40 TC 1; "The test is not whether the employer imposes the expense but whether the duties do, in the sense that, irrespective of what the employer may prescribe, the duties cannot be performed without incurring the particular outlay." (per Donovan LJ [1961] 3 All ER at page 133).

of a reasonable class of employees and the requirements of the employment. For example, one employee with defective eyesight could not recover the costs of glasses on the ground that the expense would not necessarily have been incurred by the employment: the objective test would raise the issue of the reasonable class of employee, including many good sighted persons.[27] In *Lupton v Potts* (above) Plowman J explained that the duties of the taxpayer under the contrast of employment were perfectly capable of being performed without incurring the expense of Law Society Examination fees. In *Humbles v Brooks*, the course fee was not deductible, the court explained that he was not "necessarily obliged" to attend the weekend course.

The existence of personal choice and benefit is a strong indicator that it is not objectively necessary for an employee to incur an expense.[28] However, the fact that the employer requires the expense or even that incurring the expense is a stipulated condition of the employment is not sufficient to make it "necessary". This principle amounts to an application of an objective principle in the abstract and in isolation from the context of the particular employment. This can work hardship on employees, who thereby have to suffer loss. The principle is illustrated by a number of cases. First, *Griffiths v Mockler*.[29] Here the taxpayer was a major in the Royal Army Pay Corps. He was obliged under the army rules to be a member of his regimental mess, and to pay an annual mess subscription fee. Refusal to pay these fees would have led to disciplinary action. The subscriptions were held not to be deductible.

Also, in *Brown v Bullock*, a bank manager was required by his employer to join a club in order to foster local contacts. This was virtually a condition of managerial appointment. His claim to deduct the cost of subscribing to one such club failed because the expense was not necessarily incurred in the performance of his duties as bank manager. According to Lord Evershed MR[30], what his employers may think it desirable for him to do, socially, is one thing, but performance of the duties of branch manager was something else.

We have already referred to the statement of Diplock LJ in this case that the correct test is whether, regardless of what the employer may prescribe, the duties cannot be performed without incurring the expense. This construction of the test makes it almost impossible to succeed in proving that an expense was "necessary". For example, the job of a bank manager is to manage a bank branch. It is hard to imagine what expense can be considered "necessary" in the abstract in the performance of that specific job. In fact, apart from necessary travel expenses, it is hard to imagine other

---

[27] *Roskams v Bennett* (1950) 32 TC 129.
[28] Per Laddie J in *Baird v Williams* (HMIT) [1999] BTC 228 at 233.
[29] [1953] 2 All ER 805.
[30] [1961] 3 All ER at page 132.

expenses that can be considered necessary in the sense that the job cannot be done by anybody without incurring that particular expense. This renders the statutory deduction provision virtually meaningless, and it is difficult to argue with the conclusion of Vaisey J in *Lomax v Newton* (above) that the words of the statutory provision are "deceptive words in the sense that that when examined they are found to come to nearly nothing at all." Nolan LJ endeavoured to bring some sense and meaning into it in *Smith v Abbott*[31] when he said

> [T]he test is whether the expenses are dictated by the nature of the employment, as distinct from the personal choice of the taxpayer. The question whether the taxpayer is necessarily obliged to incur them is to be answered not simply by reference to the legal obligations imposed by the contract of employment (though these may be highly relevant) but by considering once again what the employee has to do as a practical matter in performing the work of his employment.

If this test of practicality is adopted, the court would be able to take all the circumstances of the particular employment into account in determining whether specific expenses are necessary for that employment. This would remove the artificiality of an abstract analysis of a job, divorced from the real life issues relating to it. In such a scenario, the journalists in *Smith v Abbott* might well succeed (as they did in the Court of Appeal), the bank manager in *Brown v Bullock* may or may not succeed, the army officer in *Griffiths v Mockler* would succeed, and the rugby player in *Ansell v Brown* might succeed.. The House of Lords in *Smith v Abbott* reversed the Court of Appeal – hence the status of Nolan LJ's "practicality" test is in doubt. It is submitted however that such a test would bring some meaning into the currently meaningless statutory provision.

3. *Wholly and exclusively*

The test of "wholly and exclusively" imports the same test of "remoteness and duality" that is found in the expenses rule for Schedule D Cases I and II. The test of remoteness is that the expense must be incurred for the purposes of the employment. The test of duality (or singularity) is that it must be incurred only for the purposes of the employment. The term "wholly" refers to *quantum*, and the *dictum* of Romer LJ in *Bentleys, Stokes & Lowless v Beeson*[32] in respect of the similar Schedule D test was approved for Schedule E by Nolan LJ in *Smith v Abbott*.[33] The exclusivity test means that

---

[31] [1993] 2 All ER 417 at 431.
[32] [1952] 2 All ER 82 at 84.
[33] [1993] 2 All ER at page 431.

expenditure of a personal nature or expenditure for mixed purposes[34] will not be deductible. So for example in *Ricketts v Colquhoun* (above) Lord Blanesburgh said that charges for food and refreshments incurred in the course of a recorder's duties were not deductible, being at best, personal expenses. One question that needs to be considered is whether the individual derives any personal, private, benefit or advantage from the expenditure. Thus, for example, in *Brown v Bullock* the bank manager would obtain the private benefits of club membership and in *Ansell v Brown* the rugby player would derive nourishment and strength from the dietary supplements. The test of wholly and exclusively does, however, permit some private benefit provided that the sole object of the expenditure was the performance of the employee's duties and that any private benefit was an unintended but inescapable incidental result or effect of that expenditure[35] – a test that is very difficult to satisfy. For example, in *Ward v Dunn*[36] a taxpayer claimed an allowance in respect of clothing worn for work purposes. The claim failed. Walton J explained that the expenditure on the clothing was not only for the purposes of his employment.

> ... when Mr Dunn purchases a suit he purchases it, maybe partly with a view to going round the sites [his employment] but, at any rate, partly with a view to wearing it in the ordinary course as one wears clothing for comfort and for covering one's nakedness [intended private benefit] ...[37]

It could of course be argued that the nourishment derived from food supplements by the rugby player in *Ansell v Brown* was only an unavoidable effect of the expenditure on the supplements and not a purpose of the expenditure. Whether this type of argument will ever commend itself to a court is debatable.

The requirement of "wholly and exclusively" is not without relief in that apportionment appears to be available in appropriate instances. For example, where a telephone is used partly for business calls the taxpayer can deduct the expenses of those business calls as they are "wholly and exclusively" intended for business purposes: costs of private calls are obviously not deductible. Any telephone rental charges are not deductible because the intention of the rental agreement and expenses is a dual intention of business and private use.[38]

---

[34] See for example *Baird v Williams* (HMIT) [1999] BTC 228: interest paid on mortgage of building purchased by Clerk to general commissioners for office space was not exclusively for the purposes of his employment because part of the purposes were to provide a *pied-a-terre* and too assist the Clerk in acquiring a capital asset.

[35] See for example Nolan LJ in *Smith v Abbott* [1993] 2 All ER at page 431.

[36] [1979] STC 178.

[37] Walton J did appear to suggest that the matter would be very different if the clothes that Mr Dunn wore were special clothing worn only at, and for, places of work, rather than clothing that could be used for ordinary wear.

[38] *Lucas v Cattell* (1972) 48 TC 353.

Entertainment Expenses

Legislation has been introduced to supplement the s.198 requirements in relation to entertainment expenses. TA 1988, s.577 prohibits the deduction of entertainment expenses subject to a number of exceptions including a de minimis exception. However, should an employee receive an entertainment allowance s.577 allows the employee to escape liability on that part of the expenditure that satisfies the requirements of s.198 that the expenditure was incurred wholly, exclusively and necessarily in the performance of duties.

Concessions

A number of extra-statutory concessions exist to assist the employee. This includes allowances for the cost of upkeep of tools or special clothing (ESC A1), travel by directors and other "higher paid" employees between two or more group companies (ESC A4), and the cost of meals purchased away from home by lorry drivers (SP 16/80).

Further Reading

Olowofoyeku AA, *In the Performance of Duties: Fact, Law or Both?* [1996] BTR 28.

Smith PF, *Travelling Expenses* [1977] BTR 290-301.

chapter six

Income Tax -
Schedule D Cases I and II
Introduction and General Concepts

The income tax charge on the profits of trades, professions and vocations is to be found in s.18 of the ICTA 1988. By s.18(3), tax is charged under Case I of Schedule D on the "annual profits or gains" of a trade carried on in the United Kingdom or elsewhere[1], and tax is charged under Case II on the annual profits or gains of a profession or vocation[2] not contained in any other Schedule. Taxpayers who are resident in the UK are charged in respect of annual profits or gains arising or accruing

i.   from any property whatever, whether situate in the UK or elsewhere, and

ii. from any trade, profession or vocation whether carried on in the UK or elsewhere.[3]

Non-residents are charged on profits from any property whatever in the UK, or from any trade, profession or vocation exercised within the UK.[4] Generally, the tax is chargeable on and paid by the persons entitled to or receiving the relevant income.[5]

Scope of the Charge

As we have just seen, the charge under Schedule D Cases I and II is limited to persons carrying on or exercising either a "trade", or a "profession", or a "vocation". We will now examine the meaning of each of these terms.

---

[1]   S.18 TA 1988. The term "elsewhere" is redundant in that the House of Lords have declared that Sch. Case I does not apply to a trade carried on wholly outside the United Kingdom (See *Colquhoun v Brooks*, (1889) 2 TC 490).

[2]   Note that although section 18 refers to "profits or gains", "gains" do not include capital gains.

[3]   ICTA 1988, s.18(1).

[4]   ibid.

[5]   s.59(1). Compare the American case of *Brandon v State Revenue Commission*, 186 SE 872 (Georgia).

Profession

The word "profession" is not a term of art, and does not appear to have any special or technical meaning for income tax purposes. It used to be confined to the three "learned" professions – clergy, medicine, and law.[6] However, it now has a much wider meaning[7] and can include all sorts of occupations. Judges quite rightly are wary of attempting to produce a comprehensive definition.[8] The rationale for such wariness, according to Scrutton LJ in *Currie v IRC*,[9] is that "it is impossible to lay down any strict legal definition of what is a profession, because people carry on such infinite varieties of trades and businesses that it is a question of degree in nearly every case whether the form of business that particular man carries on is, or is not, a profession". While the vastness of the range of activities in which humans may engage would preclude an all embracing definition, general principles are ascertainable. Some of these emerge from this statement of Scrutton LJ in *IRC v Maxse*[10]:

> [A] "profession" in the present use of language involves the idea of an occupation requiring either purely intellectual skill, or of any manual skill, as in painting and sculpture, or surgery, skill controlled by the intellectual skill of the operator, as distinguished from an occupation which is substantially the production, or sale, or arrangements for the production or sale of commodities. The line of demarcation may vary from time to time.

Similar ideas are found elsewhere. For example in *Teague v Graves*[11] it was said that a profession implies professed attainments in special knowledge, as distinguished from mere skill. It has also been said that the term: is applied to an occupation or calling which requires learned and special preparation in the acquirement of scientific knowledge and skill[12]; refers to status which requires knowledge of an advanced type in a given field of science or learning gained by a prolonged course of specialised instruction and study[13]; and is a calling in which one professes to have acquired some special knowledge used by way of either instruction, guiding or advising others, or of serving them in some art.[14]

A journalist is exercising a profession.[15] So is an author,[16] a "man of letters",[17] an actress,[18] an editor,[19] a painter, sculptor, and, of course, anyone

---

6   See Scrutton LJ in *IRC v Maxse* (1919) 12 TC 41 at 61; see also *People v Maggi*, 33 NE.2d. 925 at 927 (Illinois).
7   Scrutton LJ, ibid.
8   Scrutton LJ, ibid.
9   (1921) 12 TC 245 at 264.
10 12 TC at page 61.
11 27 NYS.2d. 762 at 765.
12 *Commonwealth v Fitler*, 10 Pa. Co. Ct. Rep. 144 at 147.
13 *Traub v Goodrich*, 143 NYS.2d. 334 at 335.
14 *Stoor v City of Seattle*, 267 P.2d. 902 at 904.
15 *IRC v Maxse*, supra.
16 Swinfen Eady MR in *IRC v Maxse* 12 TC at page 58.
17 Swinfen Eady MR, ibid.
18 *Davies v Braithwaite* [1931] 2 KB 628; 18 TC 198.
19 Scrutton LJ in *IRC v Maxse*, 12 TC at page 61.

in the three "learned professions".[20] An accountant may or may not be exercising a profession – no hard and fast rule can be laid down about it.[21] On the other hand, a proprietor of a periodical or newspaper who is not responsible for the selection of the artistic or literary contents is not exercising a profession.[22] A company cannot carry on a profession even if its members are professionals.[23]

Although it appears that it is a question of fact whether or not an individual is carrying on a profession, the issue is not so straightforward, as was thus explained by Lord Sterndale MR in *Currie v IRC*[24]:

> Is the question whether a man is carrying on a profession or not, a matter of law or a matter of fact? I do not know that it is possible to give a positive answer to that question, because it must depend upon the circumstances with which the Court is dealing. There may be circumstances in which nobody could arrive at any other finding than that what the man was doing was carrying on a profession; and therefore, taking it from the point of view of a judge directing a Jury, or any other tribunal which has to find the facts, the judge would be bound to direct them that on the facts they could only find that he was carrying on a profession. That reduces it to a question of law. On the other hand, there might be facts on which the direction would have to be given the other way. But between those two extremes there is a very large tract of country in which the matter becomes a question of degree; and where it becomes a question of degree, it is then undoubtedly, in my opinion, a question of fact; and if the Commissioners come to a conclusion of fact without having applied any wrong principle, then their decision is final upon the matter.

In the same case Scrutton LJ said[25] that the question "in the last resort" is a question of fact. So it seems that the correct answer is that "it is *prima facie* and in the last resort a question of fact – but it depends on the circumstances." It is clear from *Currie v IRC* (above) that a finding of the Commissioners on the question will not be overturned unless there is either no evidence to support their finding, or they have misdirected

---

[20] Scrutton LJ in *IRC v Maxse*.

[21] *Currie v IRC* 12 TC 245. See especially Scrutton LJ at page 264. In this case, the Commissioners found that an accountant who was practising as a tax consultant was not carrying on a profession. Rowlatt J held that the issue was one of law, and that the Commissioners were wrong. On appeal, both Lord Sterndale MR and Scrutton LJ had "great difficulties" with the Commissioners' finding that a man who was a member of an organised profession with recognised standard of ability was himself not exercising a profession, but still upheld the findings on the ground that it was a question of fact. With respect, this is a questionable outcome.

[22] Scrutton LJ in *IRC v Maxse*, 12 TC at page 62; compare Warrington LJ at page 60.

[23] See *William Esplen v IRC* [1919] 2 KB 731. According to Rowlatt J (at page 734), "it is of the essence of a profession that the profits should be dependent mainly upon the personal qualifications of the person by whom it is carried on, and that can only be an individual. There can be no professional qualifications except in an individual".

[24] (1921) 12 TC 245 at 259.

[25] 12 TC at page 263.

themselves in law.

Vocation

Again, the word "vocation" does not appear to be a term of art. For income tax purposes, it is normally given its plain and ordinary meaning "according to common sense and according to the ordinary use of language".[26] In *Partridge v Mallandaine*[27] Hawkins J said that "vocation" and "calling" are synonymous terms.[28] Denman J said in the same case[29] that "vocation" is a strong word, that it is analogous to the word "calling", which is "a very large word indeed", and that "it means the way in which a person passes his life".[30] In this case, the taxpayers attended races, and systematically and annually carried on the business of bookmakers. It was held that they were carrying on a vocation. According to Hawkins J,[31] "if anybody were asked what was the calling or vocation of these gentlemen, the answer would be 'professional bookmakers.' Everybody knows what professional bookmakers are".[32] A jockey is carrying on a vocation.[33] But a film producer is not carrying on a vocation[34] – neither is a man who is "continually betting with great shrewdness and good results, from his house or from any place where he could get access to the telegraph office".[35] According to Rowlatt J in *Graham v Green*[36], to say that such a person was carrying on a vocation would produce very startling results – because

> a loss in a vocation or a trade or an adventure can be set off against other profits and we are face to face with this result, that a gentleman earning a profit in some recognised form of industry but having the bad habit of frequently, persistently, continuously and systematically betting with bookmakers, might set off the losses by which he squandered the fruits of his industry, for Income Tax purposes, against his profits – a very remarkable result indeed.[37]

---

[26] Denman J in *Partridge v Mallandaine* (1886) 2 TC 179 at 181.
[27] 2 TC 179 at 181.
[28] Compare *Mutual Life Ins. Co. of New York v Enecks*, 154 SE 198 at 199 (Georgia): vocation "means one's regular calling or business".
[29] 2 TC at page 180.
[30] Compare *Frierson v Ewing*, 222 SW.2d. 678 at 680 (Tenn.); *Steinbeck v Gerosa*, 151 NE.2d. 170 at 173 (NY) – "the activity on which [a person] spends the major portion of his time, and out of which he makes a living."
[31] 2 TC at page 181.
[32] Compare *Graham v Arnott* (1941) 24 TC 157.
[33] *Wing v O'Connell* [1927] IR 84.
[34] *Asher v London Film Productions Ltd.* [1944] KB 133.
[35] *Graham v Green* (1915) 9 TC 309.
[36] 9 TC at pages 312 - 313.
[37] Contrast the American case of *C.I.R v Groetzinger* (94 L. ed. 2d. 25), where the US Supreme Court held that a full time gambler was engaged in a "trade" or "business".

Trade

Atypically, the Taxes Act attempts to define "trade". S.832(1) provides that trade "includes every trade, manufacture, adventure or concern in the nature of trade". From this startling definition[38] we can extract a number of principles. First, trade includes every trade. This is of course circular and rather unhelpful.[39] It still leaves us with the question "what then is a trade?". However, the expression "trade includes every trade" may be construed partly to refer to those activities which have specifically been declared to be trades by the statute, in addition to those which may be construed to be trades in particular instances by the courts. There are several such statutory trades, examples of which are; all farming and market gardening in the UK[40]; the occupation of land for any purpose other than farming or market gardening, if the land is managed on a commercial basis with a view to the realization of profits[41]; mines, quarries, railways, and other specified concerns (e.g., fishings, railways and other ways, ironworks, gasworks, alum mines, canals, etc.).[42]

Secondly, by virtue of Scott LJ's statement in *Smith Barry v Cordy* (above) that the word must be used in its ordinary dictionary sense (as enlarged by the other words in the statutory definition), it may also be construed partly to refer to those things which fit within the ordinary dictionary definition of trade. *The Concise Oxford Dictionary* defines trade as a "business", and as the "exchange of commodities for money or other commodities".

So we learn that, first of all, for the purposes of the charge to tax under Schedule D Cases I and II, "trade" includes all those statutory trades referred to above, and to businesses and exchanges of commodities for reward. Inclusion of the last two might need to be qualified in some circumstances. The second thing that we learn from the statutory definition is that trade includes every "manufacture",[43] thereby bringing a whole range of manufacturing industries within the charge under Sch. D Case I.[44] According to Lord Donovan in *Ingram v Callaghan*,[45] the definition shows that manufacture is to be regarded as more than a means to an end. Thirdly, we learn that trade includes every "adventure" in the nature of trade, and fourthly, we learn that it includes every "concern" in the nature of trade. The last two points presuppose that we already know what a trade is, before we can begin to consider whether a particular "adventure" or "concern" has the nature of a trade. – which may well provide support for Scott LJ's view that the word is used *prima facie* in its ordinary sense.

[38] In *Van Den Berghs Ltd v Clark* (1935) 19 TC 390 at 428, Lord Macmillan said that this definition involves "a fine disregard of logic".
[39] Note however the statement of Scott LJ in *Smith Barry v Cordy* ((1946) 28 TC 250 at 257) that, since the definition includes the very word "trade" without qualification, that word must be used in its ordinary dictionary sense, and the other words must necessarily be intended to enlarge the statutory scope to be given to the word "trade" in Schedule D.
[40] s.53(1), ICTA 1988.
[41] s.53(3).
[42] s.55.
[43] In *Ingram v Callaghan*, (45 TC at page 166) Lord Donovan said that this definition is not worth very much, unless it is to be implied that the definition assumes in this respect that the goods manufactured will be sold.
[44] 45 TC at page 166.
[45] ibid.

It may be that the words "adventure" and "concern" relate to different things. *The Concise Oxford Dictionary*[46] defines concern as "a business" or "a firm", and defines adventure as "a daring enterprise", "a hazardous activity", and "a commercial speculation". Thus, an "adventure" seems refer to an isolated activity, whereas a "concern" may relate to an on-going or continuous activity. This means that any single speculative activity or continuous activity which has the nature of a trade is caught within the Sch. D Case I charge. This is a major factor distinguishing trades from professions and vocations, since the last two presuppose continuity. Thus, there is no such thing as an adventure in the nature of profession, or an adventure in the nature of vocation.

After analysing the statutory definition of trade, which seems to enlarge the ordinary meaning of the words, we are still left with the task of ascertaining what exactly constitutes a trade within the statutory language.[47] The authorities indicate that there is no single, infallible test for determining this question. A few examples will suffice. Lord Denning famously said in *Griffith v J.P Harrison (Watford) Ltd*[48]:

> Try as you will, the word "trade" is one of those common English words which do not lend themselves readily to definition, but which all of us think we can understand well enough. We can recognize a "trade" when we see it, and also an "adventure in the nature of a trade." But we are hard pressed to define it ... short of a definition, the only thing to do is to look at the usual characteristics of a "trade" and see how this transaction measures up to them.

Similarly, Lord Wilberforce said in *Ransom v Higgs*[49]:

> Trade cannot be precisely defined, but certain characteristics can be identified which trade normally has. Equally some indicia can be found which prevent a profit from being regarded as a profit of a trade.

While the courts have often stated that precise definition of trade is not possible, they have not shied away from venturing opinions on the characteristics of a trading activity. This is not surprising seeing that Lord Denning suggested in *Griffith v J.P Harrison (Watford) Ltd*[50] that we should try to identify the characteristics of trade and measure any transaction against those characteristics. With respect to what those characteristics are, Lord Wilberforce said in *Ransom v Higgs*[51]:

---

[46] 9th edn, 1995.
[47] See generally D de M Carey [1972] BTR 6.
[48] [1963] AC 11 at 20.
[49] [1974] 1 WLR 1594 at 1610.
[50] [1963] AC at page 20.
[51] [1974] 1 WLR 1594 at 1611.

Trade involves normally, the exchange of goods, or of services, for reward, not of all services, since some qualify as a profession, or employment, or vocation, but there must be something which the trade offers to provide by way of business. Trade moreover presupposes a customer.[52]

Lord Reid said in the same case that trade is "commonly used to denote operations of a commercial character by which the trader provides to customers for reward some kind of goods or services"[53]. Finally, in the American case of *State v Worth*[54], it was held that trade, as used in the provisions of the Constitution authorising the legislature to tax "trades, professions, franchises and income" includes all who are engaged in buying and selling merchandise, all whose occupation or business it is to manufacture and sell the products of their plants, and businesses embarked in for gain or profit.

From all these *dicta* we observe that one who is involved in a trade has "something" (goods or services) to trade in, and that a trader must have "someone" (a customer, or, exceptionally, himself or herself[55]) to trade with. While these points are helpful, they do not tell the whole story. The question whether a person is trading or not is a question of fact and each case depends on its own circumstances. In analysing such circumstances, there are several factors which may legitimately be taken into account. These factors are the so-called "badges of trade". The Royal Commission on the Taxation of Profits and Income (the Radcliffe Commission) identified six such badges[56] which we will use as the basis of the discussion that follows.

The Commission, after an analysis of competing principles and methods of ascertaining which profits to charge to income tax, concluded that there should be no single fixed rule.[57] It pointed out that the general line of enquiry that has been favoured by Commissioners and encouraged by the courts is to see whether a transaction bears any of the badges of trade. According to the Commission,[58] this is the right line, which has the advantage "that it bases itself on objective test of what is a trading adventure instead of concentrating itself directly with the unravelling of motive".[59] The Commission therefore set out to produce a summary of what it regarded as "the major relevant considerations that bear upon the identification" of the badges of trade.

While the avowed intention of the Commission was to address the

---

[52] Compare Palles CB in *Dublin Corporation v M'Adam* (2 TC 387 at 397) - "No man, in my opinion, can trade with himself; he cannot, in my opinion, make, in what is its true sense or meaning, taxable profit by dealing with himself..."
[53] [1974] 1 WLR at page 1600.
[54] 21 SE 204 at 205. See also *Nesbitt v Gill*, 41 SE 646 at 649.
[55] See *Sharkey v Wernher* [1955] 3 All ER 493.
[56] Cmnd 9474, para 116.
[57] ibid.
[58] ibid.
[59] ibid.

issue of "lack of uniformity in the treatment of different cases according to the tribunals before which they have been brought"[60], it is important to note that these badges of trade harbour no magic. None of the badges is conclusive in itself [61], and some of them are of negligible value. The question which the Commissioners and the courts must answer in every case is, whether, on a true analysis of the activities and circumstances of the taxpayer, the taxpayer is trading. This seemingly simple question may rightly lead to different results on apparently similar facts. It may even rightly lead to results which may be considered by others to be suspect. According to Browne-Wilkinson VC in *Marson v Morton*[62] the most that is detectable from the reading of the authorities is that there are certain features or badges which may point to one conclusion rather than another. The discussion that follows needs to be viewed in this context.

The Badges of Trade

1. The subject matter of the realisation

This particular badge addresses itself to the situations where the "thing" which the taxpayer is alleged to have traded in consists of goods (as opposed to services). It is a "very important" badge, and "may in some cases be decisive, or almost decisive".[63] The badge normally comes into play when a person has disposed of goods at a profit, without having been running an established business of dealing in those goods. In such cases, the transaction is either a trading transaction (i.e., an adventure that has the nature of a trading transaction) or a capital transaction.[64] The latter would not be subject to income tax, but may (given the right factors) be subject to capital gains tax. It is not difficult to see the position which the revenue would take in such matters. If the transaction results in a profit, the revenue would almost certainly claim that it is a trading transaction. On the other hand, if it results in a loss, the revenue would almost certainly claim that it is a capital transaction not eligible for loss relief. For a taxpayer who has made a profit, the resolution of the question would no longer in most cases result in a significant difference in tax liability. Before the introduction of capital gains tax in 1965, a decision against the revenue would have resulted in the taxpayer completely escaping tax on the transaction. This result would only follow today if the capital transaction also somehow manages to escape capital gains tax. However, even if capital gains tax is chargeable, there may still be a benefit to the taxpayer in having the

---

[60] ibid. The Commission suggested that, in future, all tax appeals that raise this issue should go before the Special Commissioners, instead of various bodies of General Commissioners (see para. 117).

[61] See Browne-Wilkinson VC in *Marson v Morton*, (1986) 59 TC 381 at 392.

[62] (1986) 59 TC 381 at 391.

[63] Per Robert Walker LJ in *Clark (HMIT) v BT Pension Scheme Trustees* [2000] BTC 64 at 72.

[64] See generally Rowlatt J in *Ryall v Hoare* (1923) 8 TC 521 at 525; Lord Keith in *IRC v Reinhold*, (1953) 34 TC 389 at 396.

transaction classified as a capital transaction – the taxpayer might be able to benefit from the capital gains tax "annual exemption". Thus, the question is not entirely moot.

The badge of trade under discussion involves an examination of the nature of the goods which the taxpayer is alleged to have traded in. The purpose is to ascertain whether there could be any valid explanation other than commercial speculation ("adventure") for the taxpayer's initial acquisition of the goods. The essence of the question is: is this a speculative deal or adventure, or, is it an investment? The application of this badge is based on certain premises. First, that certain types of property are more likely to be acquired as investments than with the view to trading in them. This is typically true of income yielding assets. Some other types of goods, while yielding no income, might provide aesthetic enjoyment and pride of possession for the owner. With these types of goods, the inference of trading is difficult to draw from an isolated transaction of selling them at a profit. On the other hand, there are commodities which give no pride of possession, provide no aesthetic enjoyment, and which are unsuitable for long term investment. When such goods are bought and sold (especially if bought in large quantities exceeding the taxpayer's personal requirements), the inference of trading is easier to draw. The nature and/or quantity of the goods may be such that they could only have been acquired as the subject of a "deal" (i.e., a commercial speculation).

The explanation of this badge by the Radcliffe Commission is thus[65]:

> While almost any form of property can be acquired to be dealt in, those forms of property, such as commodities or manufactured articles, which are normally the subject of trading are only very exceptionally the subject of investment. Again, property which does not yield to its owner an income or personal enjoyment merely by virtue of its ownership is more likely to have been acquired with the object of a deal than property that does.

While the Commission's explanation does not deal with the issue of quantity, as we shall see, the quantity of the items purchased can be a decisive factor against the taxpayer.

The case law relevant to this badge is both interesting and sometimes conflicting. Some cases are quite clear in pointing to a speculative deal. Some for example involve the purchase and sale of goods of such quantity that they could never have been intended for personal consumption. In *Martin v Lowry*[66] the taxpayer was a wholesale agricultural machinery

---

[65]   1955, Cmnd 9474 para 116.
[66]   (1927) 11 TC 297 (HL).

merchant who had never had any connection with the linen trade. He purchased from the Government some 44 million yards of its surplus stock of aeroplane linen, "with the sole intention of selling it again at a profit". He proceeded to sell the linen piecemeal by an extensive series of transactions spread over a period of seven months, using an organisation set up for that purpose. The Revenue argued that the profits derived from the sale were profits from a trade. The taxpayer on the other hand argued that he did not carry on a trade or business, but only engaged in a single adventure not involving trading operations. The Commissioners held that he did carry on a trade. Upholding this finding, Viscount Cave LC said[67] that, having regard to the methods adopted for the resale of the linen, to the number of operations into which the taxpayer entered, and to the time occupied by the resale, the Commissioners could not possibly have come to any other conclusion.

Rutledge v IRC[68] was similar. The taxpayer was a money lender and cinema proprietor. On a business trip to Berlin, he made a deal with a bankrupt firm of paper manufacturers to purchase one million rolls of toilet paper for £1,000. Within a short time after his return to the United Kingdom, he sold the whole consignment to one person at a substantial profit. The Court of Session held that he had been involved in an adventure in the nature of trade. The Lord President (Clyde) said[69] that the taxpayer had certainly been in an adventure - for he had made himself liable for the purchase of this vast quantity of toilet paper obviously for no other conceivable purpose than that of re-selling it at a profit. Thus, the element of adventure entered into the purchase from the first. On the question whether this adventure was "in the nature of trade", Lord Clyde said[70] that the question was not whether the taxpayer's isolated speculation in toilet paper was a trade, but whether it was an "adventure ... in the nature of trade". He said that the question whether a particular adventure is "in the nature of trade" or not must depend on its character and circumstances. However, if, as in this case, the purchase is made for no purpose except that of re-sale at a profit, there was little difficulty in arriving at the conclusion that the deal was in the nature of trade, even though it may be wholly insufficient to constitute by itself a trade.[71] In the circumstances, it was

> quite plain (1) that the [taxpayer], in buying the large stock of toilet paper, entered upon a commercial adventure or speculation; (2) that this adventure or speculation was carried through in exactly the same way as any regular trader or dealer would carry through any of the adventures or speculations in which it is his regular business to

[67]   11 TC at page 320.
[68]   (1929) 14 TC 490.
[69]   at page 496.
[70]   at pages 496-497.
[71]   at page 497.

engage; and therefore (3) that the purchase and re-sale of the toilet paper was an "adventure … in the nature of trade" within the meaning of the Income Tax Act …

Whilst expounding on the issue of adventures and their nature, Lord Clyde did not say much about the subject matter. It was Lord Sands who dealt with that point. He said [72] that the nature and quantity of the subject dealt with exclude the suggestion that it could have been disposed of otherwise than as a trade transaction. According to him, "neither the purchaser nor any purchaser from him was likely to require such a quantity for his private use", thus it was quite a reasonable view for the Commissioners to have taken that the transaction was in the nature of trade.

The third case in point is *IRC v Fraser*.[73] The taxpayer, a woodcutter, bought three lots of whisky, which he sold at a profit. He had no special knowledge of the whisky trade, did not take delivery of the whisky, nor did he have it blended or advertised. The purchases and sales were operated through an agent, and this type of purchase was a common type of transaction in the neighbourhood. This was an isolated transaction on the taxpayer's part, but it was still held to be an adventure in the nature of trade. The Lord President (Normand) in a most enlightening passage said[74]:

But what is a good deal more important is the nature of the transaction with reference to the commodity dealt in. The individual who enters into a purchase of an article or commodity may have in view the resale of it at a profit, and yet it may be that that is not the only purpose for which he purchased the article or the commodity, nor the only purpose to which he might turn it if favourable opportunity of sale does not occur. In some of the cases the purchase of a picture has been given as an illustration. An amateur may purchase a picture with a view to its resale at a profit, and yet he may recognise at the time or afterwards that the possession of the picture will give him aesthetic enjoyment if he is unable ultimately, or at his chosen time, to realise it at a profit A man may purchase stocks and shares with a view to selling them at an early date at a profit, but, if he does so, he is purchasing something which is itself an investment, a potential source of revenue to him while he holds it. A man may purchase land with a view to realising it at a profit, but it also may yield him an income while he continues to hold it. If he continues to hold it, there may be also a certain pride of possession. But the purchaser of a large quantity of a commodity like whisky, greatly in

---

[72] 14 TC at page 497.
[73] (1924) 24 TC 498.
[74] at pages 502-503.

excess of what could be used by himself, his family and friends, a commodity which yields no pride of possession, which cannot be turned to account except by a process of realisation, I can scarcely consider to be other than an adventurer in a transaction in the nature of a trade ... In my opinion the fact that the transaction was not in the way of the business (whatever it was) of the Respondent in no way alters the character which almost necessarily belongs to a transaction like this. Most important of all, the actual dealings of the Respondent with the whisky were exactly of the kind that take place in ordinary trade.

These three cases are straightforward. Regardless of the intentions of the taxpayers at the time of purchase, the nature of the items was that they could not be held as investments, and they yielded no aesthetic enjoyment or pride of possession. Furthermore, the sheer quantity of the items purchased was a giveaway. These two factors could not have led to any conclusion other than that the taxpayers had been engaged in commercial speculations. *Fraser's* case was even stronger, because the taxpayer in that case did not even take delivery of the goods, acting all the time through an agent. It could not be clearer that the taxpayer never intended to drink the whisky himself.

What is not so straightforward however is the case of land. Lord Normand in the passage just referred to indicated that land by its nature is capable of yielding income and pride of possession. But it is also something of which no more is being created (except by expensive reclamation programmes) and therefore it tends to appreciate in value. Land is thus often a sound investment. Does this then mean that sales and purchases of land inevitably will be capital and not trading transactions? Such a proposition cannot possibly be right, for after all, there is an abundance of real estate speculators. So the result here also depends on the circumstances, and cases dealing with land can often produce conflicting outcomes. We will examine a few of them.

In *IRC v Reinhold*[75] the taxpayer, a company director, bought four houses in 1945 and sold them almost three years later at a profit. He admitted that he had bought the property with the view to resale and that he had instructed his agents to sell whenever a suitable opportunity arose. The Revenue assessed him to tax on the profits on the basis that that they were profits from an adventure in the nature of trade. The General Commissioners, being equally divided on the issue, allowed his appeal. The Revenue's appeal against this decision failed. The Revenue had contended

---

[75] (1953) 34 TC 389.

that, if a person buys anything with a view to sale that is a transaction in the nature of trade. They argued that the purpose of the acquisition in the mind of the purchaser is all-important and conclusive, and that the nature of the thing purchased and the other surrounding circumstances do not and cannot operate so as to render the transaction other than an adventure in the nature of trade. This argument was rejected. According to Lord Russell,[76] the argument, as formulated, was "too absolute". Lord Russell said that it took no account of a variety of circumstances which are or may be relevant to the determination of such a question.[77] Such factors included whether the article purchased, in kind and in quantity, is capable only of commercial disposal and not of retention as an investment or of use by the purchaser personally, and whether the transaction is in the line of business or trade carried on by the purchaser.[78] These factors were not present in the case, and the mere fact of the intention to resell was not conclusive. The transaction was prima facie an investment capable of yielding an income[79], and the Revenue had not discharged the burden of showing that it was an adventure in the nature of trade. Lord Keith agreed that it was not enough for the Revenue to show that the subjects were purchased with the intention of realising them some day at a profit.[80] He said that this is the expectation of most, if not all, people who make investments. According to him, "heritable property is a not uncommon subject of investment and generally has the feature, expected of investments, of yielding an income while it is being highway."[81] In the present case the property yielded an income from rents, and so was clearly capable of being held as an investment. Lord Carmont dealt in greater depth with the question of the subject matter of the transaction. Referring to property which can be held as an "investment", he said[82] that this referred to the purchase of "something normally used to produce an annual return such as lands, houses, or stocks and shares." He said that the term would cover the purchase of houses as in the present case, but would not cover "a situation in which a purchaser bought a commodity which from its nature can give no annual return."[83] According to him, this is just another way of saying that certain transactions show inherently that they are not investments but incursions into the realm of trade or adventures of that nature, and that it is because of the character of such transactions that it can be said with additional definiteness that certain profits are income from trade and not capital accretion of an investment.[84] The conclusion therefore was that "although in certain cases it is important to know whether a venture is isolated or not, that information is really superfluous

---

[76] at pages 394-395.
[77] at page 395.
[78] ibid.
[79] at pages 395-396.
[80] at page 397.
[81] ibid.
[82] at page 392.
[83] ibid.
[84] ibid. Lord Carmont gave as an example the purchase and sale of whisky in *IRC v Fraser*, supra.

in many cases where the commodity itself stamps the transaction as a trading venture, and the profits and gains are plainly income liable to tax."

A similar case is *Marson v Morton*.[85] A potato merchant bought land with the benefit of planning permission in July 1977 and sold it in September 1977 at a profit. The General Commissioners, relying on *IRC v Reinhold*, held that the transaction was not an adventure in the nature of trade, because it was in the same category as normal investments in stocks and shares, and it was far removed from the taxpayer's normal trading activities. Browne-Wilkinson VC upheld their decision. He said that the case fell in the "no-man's-land", where different minds might reach different conclusions on the facts found.[86] The subject matter – land with planning permission – is an item of property which is "neutral" (in the sense that it could have been bought for investment purposes). Although it is a commodity which is dealt with by way of property deals, it is not the same as whisky or toilet paper, which is incapable of realisation or in relation to which profit is incapable of being realised other than by a quick sale.[87] With respect to the Revenue's argument that the land did not yield any income, Browne-Wilkinson VC said[88] that "in 1986 it is not any longer self-evident that unless land is producing income it cannot be an investment", and added that the mere fact that land is not income-producing should not be decisive or even virtually decisive on the question whether it was bought as an investment.

Reinhold seems to decide that, in the case of real estate that has investment value, a transaction of buying and selling will *prima facie* be presumed to be an investment, the onus falling on the Revenue to rebut that presumption.[89] This may of course be easy for the Revenue to do where for example a taxpayer buys 1,000 plots of land, or 10 million acres. By the same token, it appears that there is an opposite presumption in respect of other commodities. This *Reinhold* analysis is one that focuses sharply on real estate, not in a general sense, but in respect of the specific property in issue, and its specific character or potential. This presumably means that there may be specific items of real estate that do not have the necessary character or potential, in which case, would the presumption then be the same as that in respect of non-investment commodities? *Cooke v Haddock*[90] may give an indication of the answer. The taxpayer, a solicitor, purchased 72 acres of farm and land. He obtained planning permission in respect of the property. The rental value of the property was £167 per annum, while the interest charged on the mortgage secured to purchase it was £320 per annum. He did not take any steps to advertise the property. He later sold the property at a profit. The taxpayer claimed that the

---

[85] (1986) 59 TC 381.
[86] at page 392.
[87] at page 393.
[88] ibid.
[89] See Lord Russell at pages 395-396; Lord Carmont at page 392. Lord Carmont seemed to extend this proposition to stocks and shares.
[90] (1960) 39 TC 64.

property had been bought as a long-term investment. The Special Commissioners held that the transaction was an adventure in the nature of trade. They held that it must, have been obvious to the taxpayer at the time of the purchase that he must either himself develop the land or sell it in whole or in part to developers, because the transaction would otherwise have been quite un-economic due to high level of the interest payment compared to the rental value. This decision was upheld by Pennycuick J, largely on the basis that there was sufficient evidence before the Commissioners on which they could have reached their decision. Pennycuick J mentioned[91] in particular a number of facts found by the Commissioners − first, the land was ripe for building subject to the necessary licences being obtained, and it was unsuitable for occupation by the taxpayer or for retention as an income-producing investment by the taxpayer. Also important was the fact that the taxpayer obtained planning permission for the development of the land (although this was to safeguard himself against the threat of compulsory purchase and not with a view to developing the site himself), as was the fact that the taxpayer sold parts of the land piecemeal.

So the taxpayer here had real estate with no obvious income-yielding potential. Indeed, in terms of running costs, the land was a liability rather than an asset. But does that necessarily render it unsuitable for long term investment? One would imagine not. It is common in modern times to invest in property with low yields in terms of rental income, but with the anticipation of a rise in the capital value of the property in the future. This type of investment has been richly rewarding for those who saw significant rises in the capital values of their properties in the late 1990s. This is just another way of saying that the reasoning of the Commissioners in *Cooke v Haddock* might not be very convincing today. Nevertheless, it would be impossible for a judge to say, even today, that the Commissioners in *Cooke v Haddock* had no evidence on which they could base such a decision. There is clearly sufficient evidence for that purpose. *Cooke v Haddock* may well be considered good authority for the proposition that a transaction in real estate with no income-yielding potential, but with development potential would prima facie be presumed to be a commercial speculation and not an investment.

These cases can be contrasted with *Page v Pogson*.[92] The taxpayer, who was at the time an unemployed former clerk of works and local authority building inspector, bought some land and built a house on it for himself and his wife. After completing it, he lived in it with his wife, and then sold it six months later. He then bought another piece of land and built another house on it. He and his wife lived in this house until he was able to secure

---

[91]   At page 71.
[92]   (1954) 35 TC 545.

employment in another part of the country, upon which he sold the house in order to take up residence where his new job was located. The Commissioners held that he had not built his first house with the idea of resale or of carrying on the business of a builder, but that the success of the first transaction encouraged the him to build the second house as a business venture and that the profits on the second house were taxable. Upjohn J felt himself unable to reverse the Commissioners decision that with respect to the second house, although he felt that the taxpayer showed a number of "cogent reasons" why the Commissioners were wrong, and although doubting whether he himself would have reached that decision.

It is not clear what lessons can be learnt from *Page v Pogson*. It is probably best consigned to the murky realms of decisions on their own facts, since one cannot help feeling that the right result might not have been reached in the case. Perhaps this case just goes to illustrate further the principle that this issue is essentially a question of fact.

The sum of the preceding discussion is that when property is dealt in in an isolated transaction, much depends on the nature of that property in the determination of the question whether the transaction is an adventure in the nature of trade. Where the nature and/or quantity of the property is such that it is only capable of commercial realisation, this might be decisive of the question – the adventure or speculation in respect of that property would be in the nature of trade. With respect to other types of property, one would have to examine the whole range of circumstances, although it may be possible to start with some presumptions. In this respect, Browne-Wilkinson VC suggested in *Marson v Morton* that, "in some cases perhaps more homely language might be appropriate by asking the question, was the taxpayer investing the money or was he doing a deal?"[93]

2. Length of the period of ownership

The Radcliffe Commission said in respect of this badge that "generally speaking, property meant to be dealt in is realised within a short time after acquisition. But there are many exceptions from this as a universal rule."[94]

Normally, investment items presuppose an intention to hold onto an item for a long period. On the contrary, if property is resold "very swiftly after the purchase", this would, in the ordinary case point to an intention to trade rather than invest.[95] However, the last statement in the explanation by the Radcliffe Commission (above) is pertinent. This badge is not of very much value because of the "many exceptions". For example, a long period between acquisition and sale will only negative a finding of trading where

---

[93] (1986) 59 TC 381 at 392.
[94] 1955, Cmnd 9474 para 116.
[95] See Browne-Wilkinson VC in *Marson v Morton*, 59 TC at page 393.

other factors do not lead to an opposite conclusion – and the fact of a quick resale is of itself inconclusive. The best that can be said is that a quick resale attracts attention. Cross J presented a helpful assessment of this badge in *Turner v Last*[96]:

> The fact that [the taxpayer] did resell [the property] very soon is obviously not conclusive. A man may buy something, whether it be land or a chattel, for his own use and enjoyment with no idea of a quick resale, and then, quite unexpectedly, he may receive an offer to buy which is too tempting to refuse. That is a perfectly possible state of facts: but the fact that there was a quick resale naturally leads one to scrutinise the evidence that it was not envisaged from the first very carefully.

3. The frequency or number of similar transactions by the same person
According to the Radcliffe Commission[97]:

> If realisations of the same sort of property occur in succession over a period of years or there are several such realisations at about the same date a presumption arises that there has been dealing in respect of each.

This badge deals with a question which is different from that which was raised in the "adventure in the nature of trade" discussions. A person who has been held to be chargeable to income tax in respect of an isolated speculative activity does not thereby become a trader in the subject matter of the transaction. He or she would have been on an adventure and no more. Income tax is chargeable in those cases simply because Parliament has decreed that it be so if the adventure had the nature of trade. As we have seen earlier, not all speculative adventures have the nature or character of trade. In fact, many may not even properly fit the description of an "adventure", but would fall better within the description of an "investment". What the present badge deals with is those situations where a single transaction in a thing is not an adventure in the nature of trade, but then the transaction is repeated. This repetition takes us from the realm of adventure into the realm of pattern. Traders trade according to patterns, and the existence of a pattern of profitable deals, speculations, or "investments" may mean that the person engaged therein has now become a trader in the subject matter. This principle can be seen in the judgment of the Lord President (Clyde) in *IRC v Livingston*[98].

---

[96]   (1946) 42 TC 517 at 522-523.
[97]   1955, Cmnd 9474 para 116.
[98]   (1926) 11 TC 538 at 542.

I think the profits of an isolated venture ... may be taxable under
Schedule D provided the venture is "in the nature of trade." ... If the
venture was one consisting simply in an isolated purchase of some
article against an expected rise in price and a subsequent sale it might
be impossible to say that the venture was "in the nature of trade";
because the only trade in the nature of which it could participate
would be the trade of a dealer in such articles, and a single transaction
falls as far short of constituting a dealer's trade, as the appearance of a
single swallow does of making a summer. The trade of a dealer
necessarily consists of a course of dealing, either actually engaged in
or at any rate contemplated and intended to continue.

Thus the presence of a pattern of dealing is strongly indicative of trading.
The courts may even categorise retrospectively an activity as trading by
examining subsequent, similar, acts. Consider the following words of
Rowlatt J in *Pickford v Quirke*[99]:

Now, of course, it is very well known that one transaction of buying
and selling a thing does not make a man a trader, but if it is repeated
and becomes systematic, then he becomes a trader and the profits of
the transaction, not taxable as long as they remain isolated, become
taxable as items in a trade as a whole, setting losses against profits, of
course, and combining them all into one trade.

In *Pickford v Quirke*, the taxpayer had, during a boom in the Lancashire
cotton spinning industry, engaged in transactions which were known in
the area as "turning over a mill". The transactions usually involved the
purchase by a syndicate of the shares of an existing mill, liquidation of the
company, and formation of a new company to purchase the old company's
assets at a profit to the syndicate. The taxpayer engaged in this on four
different occasions. In each of the transactions he formed a syndicate with
different people for the purpose of the transactions, making a profit in each
one. The Commissioners found that the four transactions, considered
separately, were capital transactions, and the first transaction, considered by
itself, would not have constituted a trade. However, since there was more
than one transaction, they asked the question whether, when all the four
transactions were regarded together, the taxpayer could be said to have
entered "habitually" into profitable contracts in such a sense as to
constitute the four transactions into a trade – i.e., "did he make a business
of turning mills over?". This question they answered in the affirmative,

---

[99] (1927) 13 TC 251 at 263.

meaning that the profits were taxable. They were upheld by Rowlatt J and the Court of Appeal. Lord Hanworth MR said that the Commissioners had addressed their minds to the right questions, and the point could not be taken that they were adverting their minds to facts known to them beforehand in previous related cases involving the taxpayer.[100] According to him[101]:

> [Y]ou may have an isolated transaction so independent and separate that it does not give you any indication of carrying on a trade ... When, however, you come to look at four successive transactions you may hold that what was, considered separately and apart, a transaction to which the words "trade or concern in the nature of trade" could not be applied, yet when you have that transaction repeated, not once nor twice but three times, at least, you may draw a completely different inference from those incidents taken together.

A similar approach was taken in *Leach v Pogson*.[102] The taxpayer established a driving school, and sold it to a company at a profit, in return for cash and shares. This type of transaction was repeated this 29 more times. The Special Commissioners found that he carried on one trade of turning motoring schools, by way of selling driving lessons and selling schools. Thus the receipts from the sale of the driving schools were taxable as receipts from a trade. On appeal to the High Court, the taxpayer admitted that the Commissioners' decision was correct in respect of all the transactions except the first, but argued that the first was of a different character. Ungoed-Thomas J held that the Commissioners were entitled to take into consideration the subsequent 29 transactions to throw light upon the nature of the original transaction, and to come to the conclusion that, at the time the of the first transaction, the taxpayer had intended to embark, and was in fact embarking, upon a course of trade consisting of selling driving schools of motoring.

Finally, in *Smith Barry v Cordy*[103] a man spent a substantial part of his fortune in purchasing about 63 endowment policies taken out on the lives of other people. The purpose of the purchases was to enable him to derive an annual income sufficient for him to live on. Consequent upon war injuries he was advised to seek warmer climes, upon which he decided to settle in India. He thereupon sold most of the policies which had not matured. He was assessed to income tax on the profits of "dealing in insurance policies". On appeal to the Special Commissioners, the Commissioners held that he had been engaged in a "concern in the nature of trade", and was therefore taxable on the profits. The Court of Appeal

---

[100]   13 TC at pages 269-270.
[101]   at page 269; compare Sargant LJ at page 275.
[102]   (1962) 40 TC 585.
[103]   (1946) 28 TC 250; 2 All ER 396.

held that the Commissioners' finding was conclusive unless there was no evidence to support it. According to Scott LJ[104]:

> There appears to us to be abundant evidence to support this finding. The Case is conclusive that he made up his mind to utilise the commercial market in endowment life policies for the express purpose of getting a means of livelihood at the average rate of £7,000 a year over a long period of years. He showed great mathematical skill – an element in the business of an average adjuster, an underwriter, a banker or a financier. He continued to make his purchases in the commercial market over a period of eighteen months, i.e., until he had planted enough trees to yield him the fruit he wanted over the series of seasons for which he was making his purchases.

All these decisions clearly establish that repetition points strongly to trading. The difficult question here concerns how many times a transaction in a thing has to be repeated before the repetition leads to a finding that the taxpayer is "dealing in" that thing. On one view, *Page v Pogson* (above) may indicate that one instance of repetition may be sufficient. This raises questions about those activities which people may not consider to be dealing in a thing – e.g., the pensioner who makes home-made tarts and who occasionally sells some of them to her friends, or a man who occasionally sells things at car boot sales. Such individuals may well find themselves being regarded as by the Revenue as traders.

However, while repetition may be indicative of trading, it is important to appreciate that "frequency cannot by itself be decisive".[105] One cannot simply look at repetition in isolation from the whole context of the taxpayer's transactions. As Jenkins said LJ in *Davies v Shell Company of China Ltd*[106]:

> [T]he mere fact that a certain type of operation is done in the ordinary course of a company's business and is frequently repeated, does not show that the transaction in question was a trading transaction; you have to look at the transaction and see what its nature was.

Jenkins LJ gave[107] the example of a retail trader who, as and when he opens new branches, buys shops in which to carry on his business, and from time

---

[104] at page 260.
[105] Per Robert Walker LJ in *Clark (HMIT) v BT Pension Scheme Trustees* [2000] BTC at page 72.
[106] (1951) 32 TC at pages 155-156.
[107] (1951) 32 TC at page 156.

to, time may make a profit by selling one of the shops so bought, and said:

> Now it may, be said of such a trader that he buys shops and from time
> to time disposes of shops that he no longer wants to operate, in the
> ordinary course of business but it would by no means follow that the
> price he spends on a shop when he buys it is an outgoing of his trade
> or that the price he gets for a shop when he sells it is a trading receipt.
> In fact in the case of an ordinary retail trader the contrary would be
> the case and expenditure and receipts such a these would, I
> apprehend, clearly be in respect of fixed capital.

Thus an investor may change his investments frequently, without the
investments losing their character.[108] This is a strong warning against
treating the simple fact of repetition as being anything more than an
indicator.

4. Supplementary work on or in connection with the property realised

This badge often comes into play in connection with isolated activities –
i.e., adventures or speculations. As with the "subject matter" badge, the
question when applying this badge is often whether the relevant adventure
or speculative activity has the nature of trade. The essence of the badge was
thus explained by the Radcliffe Commission[109]:

> If the property is worked up in any way during the ownership so as
> to bring it into a more marketable condition; or if any special
> exertions are made to find or attract purchasers, such as the opening
> of an office or large-scale advertising, there is some evidence of
> dealing. For when there is an organised effort to obtain profit there
> is a source of taxable income. But if nothing at all is done, the
> suggestion tends the other way.

The implication of this statement is that supplementary work on an item
of sale may convert what would have been a capital transaction into one
having the nature of a trade. This is not self-evident, and it is clearly not a
conclusive factor. However, there is ample authority for its applicability.
One aspect of this badge – special exertions to find or attract purchasers –
is exemplified by *Martin v Lowry* (above), which involved the purchase of 44
million yards of aircraft linen. In order to facilitate the disposal of the linen
the taxpayer created a business structure, including the appointment of

---

[108] Per Robert Walker LJ in *Clark (HMIT) v BT Pension Scheme Trustees* [2000] BTC at page 72.
[109] 1955, Cmnd 9474 para 116.

sales staff and the rental of premises. This, in addition to the nature and quantity of the materials dealt in, provided a strong indication of trading.

The other aspect of the badge – i.e., that property is worked up in any way during the ownership so as to bring it into a more marketable condition - is illustrated by several cases. In *Cape Brandy Syndicate v IRC*[110] the taxpayers, a group of wine merchants, formed a syndicate to buy what amounted in total to 3100 casks of brandy from the Cape Government. They then proceeded to blend the brandy with French brandy and recask it, before resale in lots over a period of some 18 months. None of the taxpayers had previously or since been engaged in a similar transaction, and they contended that they carried out an isolated transaction of a speculative nature, which was not a trade or business. The Special Commissioners held that they were trading and were upheld by Rowlatt J and the Court of Appeal. According to Rowlatt J[111], the case presented some curious features.

> It is quite clear that these gentlemen did far more than simply buy an article which they thought was going cheap, and re-sell it. They bought it with a view to transport it, with a view to modify its character by skilful manipulation, by blending, with a view to alter, not only the amounts by which it could be sold as a man might split up an estate, but by altering the character in the way it was done up so that it could be sold in smaller quantities. They employed experts – and were experts themselves – to dispose of it over a long period of time. When I say over a long period of time I mean by sales which began at once but which extended over some period of time. They did not buy it and put it away, they never intended to buy it and put it away and keep it. They bought it to turn over at once obviously and to turn over advantageously by means of the operations which I have indicated.

IRC v Livingston[112] provides another illustration of the principle. In this case, three individuals purchased as a joint venture a cargo vessel, with a view to converting it into a steamer-drifter before resale. They completed the conversion after extensive repairs and alterations, and sold it at a profit. It was held that this was an adventure in the nature of trade. The Lord President (Clyde)[113] compared the case with *Martin v Lowry* (above). According to him, the disposal of the aircraft linen in that case involved the organisation of a number of selling agencies similar to those required for the purpose of marketing a large stock in the course of any ordinary

[110] [1921] 2 KB 403; 12 TC 358.
[111] 12 TC 358 at page 364.
[112] (1926) 11 TC 538.
[113] at page 542.

trade, and lasted seven months. Similarly, in the present case, the conversion of the cargo-vessel into a steam-drifter required a more or less extensive reconstruction and alteration of the vessel similar to what is required in order to market second-hand vessels in the ship-building and ship-repairing trades, and the operation of the venture lasted for nearly four months. Lord Clyde said[114] that the test which must be used to determine whether a venture such as was undertaken in the case was in the nature of trade is "whether the operations involved in it are of the same kind, and carried on in the same way, as those which are characteristic of ordinary trading in the line of business in which the venture was made". In this case, the activities of the taxpayers fell within the test, and they were trading.[115]

However, as indicated earlier, it not necessarily the case that that supplementary work will always convert an isolated transaction from a mere capital speculation into an adventure in the nature of trade. There is nothing magical about supplementary work in itself, if it does not show a pattern of operation that is consistent with ordinary trading in the line of business wherein the property is dealt. Even if the supplementary work is consistent with the activities of those who ordinarily trade in that property, that still is not conclusive.[116] For example, a man who wishes to sell the family car, and who proceeds to get it serviced, cleaned, repainted, and fitted with new tyres, does not thereby engage in an adventure in the nature of trade, even if he takes steps to advertise the car for sale. However, these are the normal steps that any sensible dealer in used cars might take before selling a car. So what would be the decisive factor? The answer would lie in the whole set of circumstances surrounding the transactions. So for example, if the same man who had taken the above steps in respect of the family car had instead taken the same steps in respect of a used car recently purchased by him, that might very well constitute an adventure in the nature of trade. The distinction between the two scenarios is simply that the circumstances are quite different. On the one hand (the case of the purchase and sale of a used car), the whole transaction from the beginning (purchase) to the end (sale) is no different from what a used car dealer would do. On the other hand (the sale of the family car), only the end (sale) showed any resemblance with the normal activities of a used car dealer. The beginning (purchase) was of a totally different character.

This means that the circumstances of the purchase of an asset may negative any inference of trading that may be drawn from supplementary work done on it before sale. This is illustrated by *Jenkinson v Freedland*.[117] The taxpayer bought two metal stills which were covered with a thick coating of sticky, tenacious, and highly inflammable resinous substance. He

---

[114] ibid.
[115] See also *Iswera v CTC*, [1965] 1 WLR 663.
[116] See for example Wynn-Parry J in *West v Phillips* (1958) 38 TC 203 at 213-214.
[117] (1961) 39 TC 636.

removed the resinous substance by a process of his own invention, and restored them to good working order. He thereafter sold them to companies under his control. The Commissioners held that this was not trading, and they were upheld by the Court of Appeal. With regard to the question whether the adventure was an adventure in the nature of trade, Harman LJ said that the first question which arose was, "whose trade?".[118] He said that it must be profits of the taxpayer's trade which are to be taxed. So far as the evidence went, the taxpayer never engaged in the trade of buying or selling equipment for the chemical trade except in connection with the two companies to which he sold the stills. According to Harman LJ, further inferences that could be drawn from the facts were that the taxpayer would never have embarked on the deal except with a view to the advantage of the companies, that he never intended to market the stills in the ordinary course of trade but rather to supply them as equipment for the companies (which although an advantage to him having regard to his interest in the companies, was not a trading advantage to himself), and, that the so-called profit on the sale was the result of fiscal and not trading considerations (viz, that the high price would allow the companies to claim greater tax allowances).

A stronger case is *Taylor v Good*[119]. The taxpayer and his wife carried on two retail businesses, one as a grocer, and the other as a newsagent and post office. He bought a house at an auction for possible residence with his wife. On inspection, the condition of the house was such that it was not practicable for them to live in it. He subsequently obtained planning permission and sold it at a profit. The Special Commissioners held that the transaction was an adventure in the nature of trade. On appeal, the Revenue conceded that the circumstances of the purchase could not be regarded as having been part of an adventure in the nature of trade. However, they argued that the subsequent activities of the taxpayer pointed to such an adventure. The Court of Appeal rejected the Revenue's claim. Russell LJ, after reviewing some of the relevant cases said[120]:

> All these cases, it seems to me, point strongly against the theory of law that a man who owns or buys without present intention to sell land is engaged in trade if he subsequently, not being himself a developer, merely takes steps to enhance the value of the property in the eyes of a developer who might wish to buy for development.

He therefore concluded[121] that there was no ground at all for holding that activities such as those in the present case, designed only to enhance the

---

[118] at page 646.
[119] (1974) 49 TC 277.
[120] at page 296.
[121] at page 297.

value of the land in the market, are to be taken as pointing to, still less as establishing, an adventure in the nature of trade.

In short, merely taking steps to enhance the value of something that one has decided to sell does not point to (much less establish) an adventure in the nature of trade. According to Wynn-Parry J in *West v Phillips*,[122] such steps are by themselves "colourless".

5. The circumstances that were responsible for the realisation

The Radcliffe Commission said in respect of this badge[123]:

> There may be some explanation, such as a sudden emergency or opportunity calling for ready money, that negatives the idea that any plan of dealing prompted the original purchase.

This badge is essentially a negative badge. The circumstances for realisation might point to reasons of disposal other than for trading profit. In such a case, the proceeds of the disposal might well constitute capital in the hands of the taxpayer.[124] In *West v Phillips*[125] the taxpayer, a builder, built a large number of houses to hold as an investment (the "A" houses). He also built others for sale (the "B" houses). When faced with rent controls, high taxation, and high cost of repairs which meant that the "A" houses were no longer a profitable investment, he changed his mind and sold them. Wynn-Parry J, reversing the Special Commissioners, held that the profits on the "A" houses were not taxable as income of a trade. He said that the circumstances of the sales precluded any finding that the "A" houses had been incorporated into trading stock with the "B" houses. He referred to some of the findings of the Commissioners[126].

> Mr. West changed his intention in regard to class "A" houses and decided to sell such of them as became vacant or whenever a sitting tenant made a suitable offer. There was a number of reasons for this change of policy. The combination of a rise in the cost of repairs and of higher taxation with the existence of rent control during and after the war made the class "A" houses no longer a profitable investment. Furthermore, all hope of paying off his mortgages to building societies out of the net yield from rents had ... entirely disappeared ...

---

[122] 38 TC 203 at 214.

[123] 1955, Cmnd 9474 para 116.

[124] For example in the American case of *Pfister v US* (102 F.Supp. 640) it was held that, where heifers, raised by the taxpayer and held as part of his breeding stock for breeding purposes from birth until they were more than one year old, were sold because of prevailing shortage of necessary ranch help, the proceeds of their sale constituted capital gains.

[125] (1958) 38 TC 203.

[126] at page 212.

With respect to these findings of the Commissioners, Wynn-Parry J said[127]:

> It is those reasons which in my view must be borne in mind all through the consideration of this case. It comes to this. The house property had become more of a liability than a profit; he had to find moneys to clear his liabilities to his bankers, to the building societies, and in respect of arrears of taxation ...

All these points could be taken as part of the particular facts of the case to which regard is had by the court in determining as a question of fact whether this taxpayer was trading.

This principle can also work against the taxpayer, as is illustrated by *Stott v Hoddinott*.[128] The taxpayer, an architect, surveyor and engineer, was contractually obliged to take up shares in milling companies granting him contracts. The shares were subsequently sold at a loss. The sales were necessary to finance the purchase of shares from other companies under similar contracts. The General Commissioners held that the taxpayer was not a dealer in shares, that it was not a part of his business to deal in shares, and that the losses on sales by him of shares so taken up by him were a loss on capital and could not be allowed to he set against or deducted from the profits or gains of his business as an architect, surveyor and engineer. Their decision was upheld by Atkin J.

Like other badges, the fact that there exists an explanation for the sale does not necessarily always lead to a conclusion that the taxpayer was not trading. We saw this earlier in *Page v Pogson* (above), where a decision of the Commissioners that the taxpayer was trading when he sold a house occupied by him and his wife was upheld by the court even though he clearly had a good and reasonable explanation – the fact that he had secured a job in another part of the country – for selling his house.[129]

6. Motive[130]

The final badge of trade referred to by the Radcliffe Commission is motive.[131] According to the Commission[132]:

> There are cases in which the purpose of the transaction of purchase and sale is clearly discernible. Motive is never irrelevant in any of these cases. What is desirable is that it should be realised clearly that it [i.e., motive] can be inferred from surrounding circumstances in the

---

[127] At pages 212-213.
[128] (1916) 7 TC 85.
[129] See also *Mitchell Bros v Tomlinson* (1957) 37 TC 224; *Wisdom v Chamberlain* (1968) 45 TC 92.
[130] A substantial part of this discussion on motive was first published in Olowofoyeku A: "A Century of Doubt: Profit Motive in the UK Income Tax Law" (2000) *New Zealand Journal of Taxation Law and Policy*, Vol. 6, 40-60.
[131] See generally, J F Avery-Jones [1983] BTR 9; I Saunders [1990] BTR 168.
[132] 1955, Cmnd 9474 para 116.

absence of direct evidence of the seller's intentions and even, if necessary, in the face of his own evidence.

There are many problems with this statement which we shall presently give attention to, and it is important to note at this point that the modern case law is often confusing and the state of the authorities leaves much to be desired. Part of the problem may lie in changes in statutory terminology. Other Commonwealth countries have, like the U.K., had to contend with the question of the proper role (if any) of profit motive in its income tax system. Unlike countries such as Australia and New Zealand which apply the general term "business" to represent the various activities that may attract income tax, the U.K. brings now income from enterprise to charge if the income represents profit derived from "a trade, profession, or vocation". However, early U.K. cases on the issue of motive did refer to "business". In this context, the change of terminology from "business" to "trade", etc., has not been a happy one. The earliest cases were quite clear on the issue of the relevance of profit motive. More than a century ago, Jessel MR said in *Bramwell v Lacy*[133]:

> The first question is, is this a "business", or "in the nature of a business"? ... The question whether it is a business carried on for the purposes of profit or not, is not, in my opinion, material.

This case involved a non-profit hospital that was established for poor persons suffering from throat and chest diseases. It was entirely free to the poor but those who could afford to pay contributed voluntarily according to their means. The question was whether the running of the hospital amounted to the carrying on of a "trade or business" in violation of covenants in the lease of the property which was used for the hospital. The question was answered in the affirmative, in spite of the fact that there was no intention to make any profit from the running of the hospital. Jessel MR decided similarly in *Portman v Home Hospital Association*[134] – a case involving similar facts. In this case, Jessel MR, speaking about a physician at the hospital, said:

> For what purpose does he use the consulting room of the hospital? Surely in the exercise of his occupation or calling, his calling being that of a physician. It cannot make any difference that he gets no fees; that he does not get paid, and does not attempt to get paid.[135]

[133] (1879) 10 Ch. D 691 at 694-695.
[134] (1879) 27 Ch. D 81.
[135] (1879) 27 Ch. D at page 83. Compare *Rolls v Miller* (1884) 27 Ch. D 71 – a residential home established for working girls by a charity was a business even if no fees were charged, because (per Cotton LJ at page 85) it is not essential that there should be payment for there to be a business.

These were not tax cases but they did establish that the making of profits and the intention to make a profit are not essential to the carrying on of a trade or business. The courts soon had the opportunity to consider these issues in the tax context. The setting was again that of provision for the poor. In *The Burial Board for Paddington, Middlesex v IRC*,[136] the burial board established under statute a burial ground with money secured on the poor-rates of the Parish of Paddington. The surplus of income (derived from burial fees) over expenditure was applied in aid and in reduction of the poor-rate, which would otherwise be levied on individual ratepayers. It was held that the surplus was the profit of a business and was liable to income tax. Day J said that the board was in fact carrying on a business (burying of the dead) for the benefit of the ratepayers of the parish[137], and that this was a "fortunate speculation" which the parish was justified in entering upon.[138] Significantly, Day J said that "we need not trouble ourselves about the destination of the profits".[139] This was significant because the courts had held in income tax cases, even before the *Bramwell v Lacy* line of cases, that the proposed or actual use of the profits was not relevant to the question whether tax was chargeable thereon. This principle was established in 1871 in *A-G v Black*.[140] There, Improvement Commissioners for Brighton had statutory powers to levy a charge on coal landed on the beach or brought into the town. The charge was for certain statutory purposes – viz., to form a common fund for the general purposes of the statute, including erecting and maintaining groyns against the sea, paving, lighting, etc. It was held that the Commissioners were liable to pay income tax in respect of the surplus of income over expenditure. According to Montague Smith J[141] the purpose to which the levy is applied cannot be taken into consideration if it in its nature it is a property or profit. This decision was subsequently approved and applied by the House of Lords in *Mersey Docks and Harbour Board v Lucas*,[142] where Lord Selborne LC noted that a gain is a gain, "for whatever purposes it is used, whether it is gained for the benefit of a community, or for the benefit of an individual".[143] There was a similar outcome in *St Andrew's Hospital, Northhampton v Shearsmith*[144], a case which was somewhat to *Bramwell v Lacy*. A hospital was founded by voluntary contributions, as a charity for the treatment of mental diseases. Fees paid by wealthy patients were applied to fund the treatment of poor patients, and to bring the hospital up to standards advised by the Lunacy Commissioners. It was held that the profits from the undertaking were taxable.

While it could be contended that the tax cases were not about profit motive, it is also arguable that the question of profit motive was an

---

[136] (1884) 13 QBD 9.
[137] at page 13.
[138] at page 14.
[139] at page 13.
[140] (1871) 6 LR Exch. 78, 308.
[141] (1871) 6 LR Exch. 308 at 311.
[142] (1883) 8 App. Cas. 891 (cited by Smith J in *The Burial Board for Paddington, Middlesex v IRC* (1884) 13 QBD 9 at 14).
[143] at page 905.
[144] (1887) 2 TC 219.

underlying (if unspoken) theme, centering around the fact that the taxpayers in these cases were not acting out of a profit motive, but rather for statutory or charitable purposes or objects. Therefore on one analysis, these cases, by a somewhat different route from the landlord and tenant cases earlier referred to, can be explained on the basis that, it is not essential to the carrying on of a trade or business (with the attendant income tax consequences) that there should be a view or desire or an intention to make profit. This principle was clear enough in the latter part of the last century, wherein the courts seemed more concerned with the activities of the taxpayer than with the taxpayer's intentions or motives.

As already indicated, the situation now has shifted and the 20th century has witnessed an increasing sophistication in the judicial analyses of this issue. Unfortunately this increased sophistication of analysis has not resulted in increased clarity, but has rather often tended to obfuscate the issue. This may itself be a result of the fact that the issues have themselves become more complicated as the activities of taxpayers take on greater sophistication and complexity. Today the courts are faced with a myriad of activities by taxable persons. Some clearly (from beginning to end) form an integral part of the taxpayer's trade, profession or vocation. Some clearly do not. Some are entered into and concluded with a profit motive. Some are entered into and concluded without such a motive, while others are entered into without a profit motive but are concluded after a profit motive has arisen. Some are undertaken in the course of a continuous activity, while others are isolated "one-off" transactions. Some are "straightforward" transactions, while others have been engineered to secure a tax advantage. Faced with such an array of activities and an ever more sophisticated tax avoidance industry, it may be said that the UK courts are right in developing more sophisticated rules of engagement. It is however questionable whether these rules have developed in the right direction.

We have seen earlier the Radcliffe Commission's explanation of the role of profit motive. This statement, if correct, would seem to mark a departure from the trend of the 19th century cases that we have referred to above, and it is not at all certain that the difference in terminology ("trade" as opposed to "business") warrants such departure. It is also not entirely clear what the Commission's statement actually means. The Commission claimed that motive is "never irrelevant", but it is not clear whether they were stating that as an absolute principle, or whether the stated principle only relates to those cases "in which the purpose of the transaction and sale is clearly discernible." Presumably, the meaning of the statement also depends much on what the Commission meant by "motive". First, they may have been referring to the taxpayer's conscious subjective motives. In that case, if the statement was intended as an absolute principle, then it may be considered incorrect, for the UK courts have consistently maintained that such motive by itself is not relevant; and if the statement refers only to cases in which the purpose of the transaction is clear, then it is still difficult to see how motive can under the current law be relevant in cases of such clarity. On the other hand, the Commissioners may have been referring to an objective motive (which seems nonsensical), or, to a constructive motive (i.e., attributed to the parties by others) – hence the statement that motive can be inferred from surrounding circumstances. If this is the correct interpretation of the Commission's use of the word "motive" (and it is not the sense in which the courts have normally used the word) then the statement that it is "never irrelevant" may, on some analyses, be correct. However, even in that case, and whatever the statement means, it does not reveal very much, because it says nothing about the weight to be accorded to motive.

As we have seen earlier in this chapter, the Radcliffe Commission took the view that objective tests of what is a trading adventure are preferable to a test that concerns itself directly with "the unravelling of motive".[145] That approach however seems to be compromised by the Commission's explanation of the relevance of motive, and, as regards that explanation, the task of inferring motive in the "absence of direct evidence of the seller's own intentions" must be unsavoury.[146] The task of inferring motive "in the face of" the seller's own evidence must be even more unedifying, for such a task must involve an assumption that the seller is lying.[147] Nevertheless, it is clear that the Commission, while itself preferring an objective approach, was attempting to formalise the principles enunciated in the cases. But how clear is the case law itself?

On one hand, we can see from the cases an attempt to apply an objective standard that represents that the presence or absence of a profit motive is inconclusive. This we can see from *IRC v Reinhold* (which we have discussed earlier) where the House of Lords rejected the Revenue's contention that, if a person buys anything with a view to sale, that is a transaction in the nature of trade and that the purpose of the acquisition in the mind of the purchaser is all-important and conclusive, and that the nature of the thing purchased and the other surrounding circumstances cannot operate so as to render the transaction other than an adventure in the nature of trade. Their Lordships rather preferred some more objective criteria, such as whether the article purchased, in kind and in quantity, is

---

[145] 1955, Cmnd 9474, para. 116.

[146] This point may however be superfluous, for the seller is likely to be available in most cases to give direct evidence as to his/her/its intentions.

[147] It seems that Canadian case law agrees with the Radcliffe Commission's suggestion. One commentator has noted in this respect that one of the themes in the Canadian case law is that "statements made by the taxpayer himself with regard to his own intention must be treated with caution". (I Saunders, The Role of Intention in Identifying Trade or Business Income: the United Kingdom and Canadian Approaches [1990] BTR 168, at 175).

capable only of commercial disposal and not of retention as an investment or of use by the purchaser personally, and whether the transaction is in the line of business or trade carried on by the purchaser;[148] and the nature of the property and whether it is income-yielding and is capable of being held as an investment.[149]

A similar objective standard was applied with respect to large quantities of whisky in *IRC v Fraser*, which we have also examined in detail earlier in this chapter. We have a clear indication from these cases of the inconclusiveness of the profit motive. In *IRC v Reinhold*, Lord Keith said[150] that the facts were, at the worst for the taxpayer, "equivocal". This meant that the Revenue had to tilt the scales in their favour by showing other factors (apart from the intention to make a profit) that pointed to trading. Such a factor (the nature and quantity of the whisky bought and sold) was present in *IRC v Fraser*, and so, objectively, it could be held that the taxpayer was trading in the whisky.

On the other hand, some cases have accorded much weight to the presence of an intention to make profit. In *Wisdom v Chamberlain*[151] the actor Norman Wisdom had a substantial amount of savings. With this he bought a quantity of silver bullion, as a "hedge" against the devaluation of sterling that seemed imminent. In the event, the expected devaluation did not materialise, but other events led to a marked appreciation in the value of the silver bullion. He subsequently sold the bullion at a profit. The taxpayer had contended that silver was not a commodity which he would have bought if he had intended to make a quick profit, and that the object of the transactions was to minimise possible loss through devaluation. However, the Commissioners held that the profit was taxable as the profit of an adventure in the nature of trade. Goff J reversed them on the grounds that the silver was purchased as a hedge against devaluation, but the Court of Appeal restored the Commissioners' decision. Harman LJ said[152]:

[I]t seems to me that, supposing it was a hedge against devaluation, it was nevertheless a transaction entered into on a short-term basis for the purpose of making a profit out of the purchase and sale of a commodity, and if that is not an adventure in the nature of trade I do not really know what is. The whole object of the transaction was to make a profit. It was expected that there would be devaluation, and the reason for wanting to make a profit was that there would be a loss on devaluation; but that does not make any difference, it seems to me, to the fact that the motive and object of the whole transaction was to buy on a short-term basis a commodity with a view to its resale at a profit. That, as it seems to me, is an adventure in the nature of trade.[153]

---

[148] Lord Russell (34 TC 389 at page 395).
[149] Lord Carmont at page 392; Lord Keith at page 397.
[150] 34 TC at page 397.
[151] (1968) 45 TC 92.
[152] at page 106.
[153] Compare *Californian Copper Syndicate v Harris* (1924) 5 TC 159. See also *Ducker v Rees Roturbo Development Syndicate* [1928] AC 132 (especially Lord Buckmaster at page 140).

It is difficult to know what exactly to make of this statement, for it seems unduly wide and sweeping. But two things seem to emerge therefrom. First, although the taxpayer disclaimed any profit motive, Harman LJ ascribed such a motive to him. This supports the Radcliffe Commission's statement that a particular motive may be attributed to the seller in the face of the seller's own evidence. Secondly, Harman LJ appeared to be suggesting that the presence of a profit motive is decisive – a statement that cannot possibly be correct, especially when viewed in the light of *IRC v Reinhold*. This cannot have escaped Harman LJ and so the question arises what he was seeking to do. Was he trying to apply some kind of objective standard involving a constructive profit motive? Was he presenting an objective formula whereby we should look to the "whole object of the transaction" rather than the object of the taxpayer? (the significance of the difference will be discussed later). And how does the absence (or alleged absence) of a profit motive in the taxpayer fit into an objective standard?

It seems clear from the authorities that the absence of a profit motive in the taxpayer does not necessarily mean that the taxpayer is not trading. That much is discernible from the 19th century cases that we have referred to earlier. If those cases do not seem to present the principle clearly enough, a direct statement of the principle can be seen from the following passage in the judgment of Lord Coleridge CJ in *IRC v Incorporated Council of Law Reporting*[154].

[I]t is not essential to the carrying on of a trade that the persons engaged in it should make, or desire to make, a profit by it. Though it may be true that in the great majority of cases, the carrying on of a trade does in fact, include the idea of profit, yet the definition of the mere word "trade" does not necessarily mean something by which a profit is made.[155]

The principle so expressed has been applied in a long line of cases. In *Mersey Docks and Harbour Board v Lucas*[156] (another "destination of profits" case) the board had to use its profits for certain statutory purposes. It was still held that its profits were taxable. In *Grove v YMCA*[157] the YMCA was a society established for the improvement of the spiritual, mental, social and physical condition of young men. It established a restaurant, operated on the usual commercial principles, which was open to the public. It was held

---

[154] (1888) 22 QBD 279 at 293.
[155] Contrast Lord Wilberforce in *Fletcher v Income Tax Commissioner* [1971] 3 All ER 1185 at 1189 – "one of the criteria of a trade is the intention to make profits." However, this statement was made in the context of the mutuality principle, to show that contributors to a mutual fund are not trading with each other. It was not intended as a general statement of principle – but if it was, then it must be considered suspect. Contrast also the statement of Barwick CJ in the Australian case of *White v FCT* (1968) 120 CLR 191, at 216, that merely to realise a capital asset may involve money making as distinct from profit making but that a business "of necessity involves the earning or the intention to earn profits." The differences between the UK and the Australian and New Zealand case law will be considered later.
[156] (1883) 2 TC 25 (HL).
[157] (1903) 4 TC 613.

that the restaurant was a trade although it was clear that it would still have been kept running even if it did not make a profit. Presumably the idea was that running a restaurant is an ordinary trading activity, which could not be viewed otherwise.

This objective principle, which seems clear enough, was applied to dubious effect in *Iswera v CTC*[158], a decision the correctness of which must now be in doubt. Here the taxpayer wished to be near her daughters' school. She negotiated to buy a plot on a building site close to the school, but the owner would only sell the whole site. She accordingly bought the whole site, and sold off nine of the other ten lots to sub-purchasers. She retained two lots, while the remaining one was reconveyed to the vendor. The sale of the lots yielded a profit. The Ceylon Board of Review held that the dominant motivation of the transaction which she ultimately undertook appeared to be (a) a blocking-up of the premises, (b) the selling of these blocks so as to make a profit on the transaction, and (c) obtaining a block for herself below the market value. Therefore, it was an adventure in the nature of trade. This decision was upheld by the Supreme Court of Ceylon, and by the Privy Council. Lord Reid in a famous statement said[159]:

> Before their Lordships, counsel for the appellant came near to submitting that, if it is a purpose of the taxpayer to acquire something for his own use and enjoyment, that is sufficient to show that the steps which he takes in order to acquire it cannot be an adventure in the nature of trade. In their Lordships' judgment that is going much too far. If, in order to get what he wants, the taxpayer has to embark on an adventure which has all the characteristics of trading, his purpose or object alone cannot prevail over what he in fact does. But if his acts are equivocal his purpose or object may be a very material factor when weighing the total effect of all the circumstances. In the present case not only has it been held that the appellant's dominant motive was to make a profit, but her actions are suggestive of trading as regards the greater part of the site which she bought. She had to and did make arrangements for its subdivision and immediate sale to the nine sub-purchasers before she could carry out her contract with the vendor of the site.

In this case, as in *Wisdom v Chamberlain*, it seems that that the taxpayer was attributed a profit motive, in the face of her own evidence as to her motives or purposes. It is clear that she only bought any land in the area because of a desire to live near the school attended by her daughters. It is also clear that, had she had the option, she would only have bought one or

---

[158] [1965] 1 WLR 663 (PC).
[159] at page 668.

two plots, and that she only bought the whole site because that was what the vendor demanded. Furthermore, she did nothing more than the minimum necessary to sell the blocks that she had been lumbered with. Her actions subsequent to the agreement to purchase the land might have been anything, but certainly it seems harsh to attach a profit motive to the purchase itself. An alternative analysis of the facts (and one which seems more supportable and more consistent with the actual facts) is that, having been forced to purchase a quantity of land which she neither wanted nor needed, the taxpayer only proceeded to take steps, which were sensible in the circumstances, to obtain the best price for the "excess baggage" that had been forced upon her. On that analysis, it is difficult to see how a profit motive (actual or constructive) could have been attributed to her purchase and/or sale of the land.

This type of analysis can be seen in *Taylor v Good* (above) where the mere fact of the taking of steps to enhance the value of land before resale did not convert the transaction into a trading transaction. There is stronger Commonwealth support for this type of approach. In *White v FCT*, a decision of the High Court of Australia, Barwick CJ said[160]:

> It is not enough, in my opinion, to make the proceeds of the realization taxable income, that the taxpayer in realizing his capital asset has taken steps to increase the amount it will realize, even if those steps are clearly commercial steps, and even if they are of an organized or repetitive nature.

If this approach had been applied in *Iswera v CTC*, the decision might have gone in the taxpayer's favour. However, in *Iswera*, Lord Reid also stated that the taxpayer's purpose or object alone could not prevail over what she had in fact done, and that her actions were suggestive of trading. Thus, it may be said that, independently of her motives, her activities, viewed objectively in the light of other badges of trade, pointed to trading. On this analysis, her motives were not relevant at all. On the other hand, it is not self-evident that activities such as those of the taxpayer in *Iswera* objectively point to trading. We have already referred in this respect to a pertinent statement by Barwick CJ in *White v FCT*. In the same case, Taylor and Owen JJ said[161]:

> [T]here is no doubt that a person who purchases land not for the purpose of profit making by resale does not engage in business merely by reselling it. And the same must be true whether he resells it in one

[160] (1968) 120 CLR 191, at 216.
[161] at page 222.

parcel or in several parcels.

From this point of view, it is difficult to see why it should be supposed that Iswera's actions in acquiring and splitting up the land spoke clearly for themselves. This is an indication that an objective test may not be any easier to apply in practice than a subjective test. It may also be that the test was wrongly applied in *Iswera v CTC*.

Terminology

This present discussion concerns profit motive and the role that it plays in determining whether an activity amounts to a trading transaction. In this respect, complications arise from the loose usage of terminology.[162] We see that in *Iswera v CTC* Lord Reid said that the taxpayer's "purpose or object" alone could not prevail over what she had in fact done. In that case, the taxpayer's "purpose or object" was to be near her daughters' school. However, it was held that she also had a profit motive. Does this presuppose that a person's motive is a different thing from his or her purpose or object.[163] If so, a question that arises is "what is the difference?". And if there is indeed a real difference, which, in cases of conflicting motives and purposes, prevails for tax purposes?

There is authority for the view that, as far as the question whether a person is trading is concerned, there is a difference. This can be found in the judgment of Millet J (as he then was) in *Ensign Tankers (Leasing) Ltd v Stokes*.[164] Millet J said that, in order to constitute a transaction in the nature of trade, the transaction in question must possess not only the outward badges of trade but also a genuine commercial purpose.[165] This point had earlier been made by Browne-Wilkinson VC (as he then was) in *Overseas Containers (Finance) Ltd v Stoker*,[166] where Browne-Wilkinson VC also said that the commercial character of a transaction is normally determined objectively by the nature of the transaction itself (i.e., whether it is a transaction of a similar kind to transactions of the same nature in the commercial world, and whether it is carried on in the same way).[167] Millet J then went on to say in Ensign Tankers that the purpose or object of a transaction must not be confused with the motive of the taxpayer in

---

[162] A classic example of the confusion of terminology can be seen in another context in the speech of Lord Brightman in *Mallalieu v Drummond* [1983] 2 AC 861 at 870 et seq., where Lord Brightman seemed in a muddle over the terms "object" "purpose", "intention", and "motive".

[163] This is not an easy question to answer, and the answer may well depend in many cases on the context. Avery-Jones has produced an interesting analysis of this issue in the context of anti-avoidance legislation (see JF Avery-Jones, Nothing either good or bad- but thinking makes it so – The Mental Element in Anti-Avoidance Legislation [1983] BTR 9, and 113).

[164] [1989] BTC 410; 1 WLR 1222 (reversed on other grounds [1991] BTC 74). For a critical view of Millet J's approach, see V Shrubsall, Note of Case: Trading – Commercial Purpose and Fiscal Motive [1990] BTR 52, especially at 58-59, where the author describes Millet J's distinction as "artificial".

[165] [1989] BTC at page 469.

[166] [1989] BTC 153 at 159.

[167] ibid.

entering into it.[168] According to him, the question is not why the taxpayer was trading, but whether he was trading.[169] Thus, if the sole purpose of a transaction is to obtain a fiscal advantage, it is logically impossible to postulate the existence of any commercial purpose.[170] However, it is possible to "predicate a situation in which a taxpayer whose sole motive is the desire to obtain a fiscal advantage invests or becomes a sleeping partner with others in an ordinary trading activity carried on by them for a commercial purpose and with a view of profit".[171] Millet J also said that where both commercial and fiscal purposes are present the question is not which purpose was predominant, but whether the transaction can fairly be described as being in the nature of trade.[172] Therefore, motive is different from purpose – but as we shall see, this statement in itself might be misleading if both terms are applied in relation to the taxpayer as opposed to some other thing.

The view of Millet J in *Ensign Tankers* that the taxpayer's motive is not relevant to the issue was disapproved by the Court of Appeal, which held that motive is relevant in certain circumstances.[173] Browne-Wilkinson VC confirmed that "a transaction which has all the features of trade must also have a commercial purpose".[174] He also confirmed Millet J's view that motive, as such, is irrelevant.[175] According to him, the only relevant question is "what was the purpose or object of the transaction"? Browne-Wilkinson VC said that it does not follow however that, in deciding the purpose of the transaction, the motives or intentions of the parties are immaterial.[176] In his view (and in line with the statement of Lord Reid in *Iswera v CTC*) where the acts of the taxpayer are equivocal, and the purpose may or may not have been commercial, the Commissioners are entitled to look at evidence of the subjective intention or motives of the relevant party. This is not because the legally relevant question is "with what motive did the parties enter into the transaction", but because such motive is evidence, sometimes compelling, on which to decide the legally relevant question (i.e., was the purpose of the transaction a trading purpose?),[177] and because "the character of the transaction may be ambiguous until resolved by reference to purpose or motivation".[178]

We have already raised the question that, if there are mixed motives, or if there is a conflict between purpose and motive, which is to prevail for tax purposes? Browne-Wilkinson VC attempted a resolution of such questions in *Ensign Tankers*, saying[179]:

---

[168] [1989] BTC at page 469.
[169] ibid (emphasis supplied).
[170] ibid.
[171] at pages 469-470.
[172] at page 469.
[173] [1991] BTC 74 (reversed on other grounds by the House of Lords, [1992] BTC 110).
[174] [1991] BTC at page 83.
[175] ibid.
[176] ibid.
[177] at page 84 (emphasis supplied).
[178] See Robert Walker LJ in *Clark (HMIT) v BT Pension Scheme Trustees* [2000] BTC at page 72.
[179] at page 85 (emphasis supplied); compare Browne-Wilkinson VC in *Overseas Containers (Finance) Ltd. v Stoker* [1989] BTC, at page 160.

If the Commissioners find as a fact that the sole object of the transaction was fiscal advantage, that finding can in law only lead to one conclusion, viz. that it was not a trading transaction. Since a fiscal advantage was the sole purpose there is no place for there being any commercial purpose; but ... if the Commissioners find as a fact only that the *paramount* intention was fiscal advantage, as a matter of law that is not decisive since it postulates the existence of some other purpose (albeit not paramount) which may be commercial. In such a case, the Commissioners have to weigh the paramount fiscal intention against the non-fiscal elements and decide as a question of fact whether in essence the transaction constitutes trading for commercial purposes.

In other words, the question cannot be answered definitively by any statement of principle – other than to say that the Commissioners have to weigh all the factors. This statement was rejected by Lord Templeman in the House of Lords. Lord Templeman did not consider that the commissioners or the courts were competent or obliged to decide whether there was a sole object or paramount intention, or to weigh fiscal intentions against non-fiscal intentions.[180] Rather, "the task of the commissioners is to find the facts and apply the law".[181] In the present case, he felt that the facts were undisputed and the law was clear. With due respect to Lord Templeman, this does not advance the situation at all. The facts are quite often undisputed. This is often why the Revenue would argue that the absence of an intention to make a profit does not prevent a finding of trading. Lord Templeman's response does not answer the question of the correct approach in cases of conflicting motives and purposes. It may be that the Commissioners ought not to be facing the task of unravelling a person's paramount intention (and any subsidiary thereto) but it may be better still to relieve them of the burden of looking into the matter of intention at all, therefore rendering redundant the question which intention is to prevail.

Furthermore, contrary to Lord Templeman's claim, the law is, with respect, not so clear – particularly with regard to the question of the relevance of, and the weight to be accorded to, a seller's motives. The proof of this can be seen in the apparent inability of Lord Templeman to provide a clearer and better solution than that proposed by Browne-Wilkinson VC, which Lord Templeman was rejecting. That the law is not so clear is especially evident when considering the confusion engendered by the loose usage of terminology in the courts. To further compound matters, Lord Reid in *Iswera v CTC* used the words "purpose or object" to refer to

---

[180] [1992] BTC at 125.
[181] ibid.

the same things that Browne-Wilkinson VC described in *Ensign Tankers* as "motive or subjective intention". We recall the statement of Lord Reid in *Iswera v CTC* that, if the taxpayer's acts clearly point to trading, her purpose or object alone cannot prevail over what she in fact does, but if her acts are equivocal, her purpose or object may be a very material factor when weighing the total effect of all the circumstances.[182] But as we have seen above, motive might well be a different thing from purpose. The issue has then variously been described as involving, (a) the motive of the taxpayer, (b) the object of the taxpayer, (c) the intention of the taxpayer (d) the purpose of the taxpayer, (e) the object of the transaction, and, (f) the purpose of the transaction. Which of these formulations actually represents correctly the relevant issue?

None of the *dicta* referred to above gives any indication as to what precisely is meant by the purpose of the transaction. However, one may deduce from the *dicta* that the motive of the taxpayer and the subjective intention of the taxpayer both refer to the same thing – possibly the taxpayer's state of mind. Thus, the issue of a person's motive would logically seem to be an entirely subjective matter. If this be so, then it is difficult to see how any board of Commissioners or court could sensibly attribute any motive to a person "in the face of" that person's own evidence. Even more interesting is the question how one would attribute a motive to an artificial person, as many taxpayers are.

So where does this lead? Perhaps the answer to this apparent confusion of terminology in formulating the question lies not in an analysis of the differences (if any) between motive, purpose, and object, but in an examination of what these terms are attached to. Thus, the motive of the taxpayer may be interpreted as referring to the same things as the purpose of the taxpayer, the object of the taxpayer, and, the intentions of the taxpayer, in entering into the relevant transaction.[183] All of these may then be contrasted with the purpose of the transaction or the object of the transaction itself. The former concepts would appear to be subjective (although they may be imputable) – but the latter would primarily be objective[184], involving subjective factors only if the transactions themselves are equivocal, and their purpose or object cannot be ascertained definitively from the facts alone. While this analysis advances the situation somewhat, it is not entirely convincing to pretend that one can ascertain the purpose or object of the transaction just by examining a state of facts, and without reference to the purpose, object, intention, or motive of the taxpayer, for it may be argued that one necessarily colours the other.[185]

---

[182] [1965] 1 WLR 663 at 668.

[183] In the Australian case of *White v FCT* ((1968) 120 CLR at page 218) Taylor and Owen JJ seemed to equate the purposes of the taxpayer with the taxpayer's subjective intentions or motives. Contrast this with the approach of McCarthy J in the New Zealand case of *Graham v IRC* (NZ) ((1961) AITR 309). McCarthy J took the view that the taxpayer's motive is different from his or her intention, saying (at page 314) that motive, as distinct from intention is not the concern of the law. He then went on to say: "the essential test as to whether a business exists is the intention of the taxpayer as evidenced by his conduct, and ... the various tests discussed in the decided cases are merely tests to ascertain the existence of that intention".

[184] See Browne-Wilkinson VC in *Ensign Tankers*, at page 87.

[185] Compare Lord Brightman in *Mallalieu v Drummond* [1983] 2 AC 861 at 870.

Having submitted that the way forward may lie in an examination of the subject of the terms motive and purpose rather than in focusing on those terms themselves, the next question relates to the dynamics of the relationship or interconnection between motive (i.e., the subjective intentions of the taxpayer) and purpose (i.e., the purpose of the transaction into which the taxpayer has entered). That there is such an interconnection is clear from the statement of Lord Reid in *Iswera v CTC* and the statement of Browne-Wilkinson VC in *Ensign Tankers*. The statements relate to the part played by motive in the context of the equivocal acts (Lord Reid), or the equivocal transactions (Browne-Wilkinson VC) of the taxpayer. In that context, Lord Reid said in *Iswera v CTC* that the taxpayer's "purpose or object [i.e., motive] may be a very material factor when weighing the total effect of all the circumstances".[186] It was however Browne-Wilkinson VC who in *Ensign Tankers* brought this general point into sharper focus, saying that, in this context, the taxpayer's motive is evidence, sometimes compelling, to decide the question "what was the purpose of the transaction?"[187] To take this even further, there is some authority for the proposition that the taxpayer's motive, subjective intention, object or purpose may, in some cases, be decisive as to the purpose of the transaction into which he or she has entered.

This principle was applied to questionable effect in *Religious Tract & Book Society of Scotland v Forbes*[188] – a case which also illustrates the other aspect of the principle – viz., that when a transaction has all the hallmarks of trade, the motive of the taxpayer is not relevant. In this case the object of the society was "by the circulation of religious tracts and books, to diffuse a pure and religious literature among all classes of the community". This object was to be carried out "by the establishment of central and branch depositories and of auxiliary societies and by means of colportage and other agencies." These "depositories" were basically bookshops, which were found to be run according to commercial principles. On the other hand, the society's colporteurs were to a certain extent cottage missionaries, who were often found reading the Scriptures, praying with the sick and others, or conversing with them on spiritual matters, and the directors attached importance to that aspect of their work. Instructions to colporteurs were to the effect that "as the Society exists to spread the knowledge of the Gospel and promote the Kingdom of Christ by means of the press, and to circulate pure and healthy general literature, a colporteur's chief duty is to sell Bibles and the books and periodicals which are supplied to him." The bookshops or "depositories" were operated at a profit, but the colportage resulted in losses, and the question was whether these were trading losses that could be set against the profits

---

[186] [1965] 1 WLR 663 at 668.
[187] [1991] BTC 74 at 84.
[188] (1896) 3 TC 415.

from the bookshops. It was held that the colportage was not a trade, but that the bookshops were. The Lord President pointed out[189] that the object of the Society was not that of making profit, but the diffusion of religious literature. However, "the business of bookselling cannot be taxable or not taxable according to the motive of the bookseller". As far as the colportage was concerned, he said that the issue must depend entirely on whether it, as well as the shops, is a business, trade, or adventure, carried on for commercial purposes and on commercial principles. The facts negatived that view. The methods of the colportage were not commercial methods – "that is to say, that the business carried on is not purely that of pushing the sale of their goods, but that on the contrary the duty of the salesman is to dwell over the purchase and make it the occasion of administering religious advice and counsel."[190] Lord Adam concurred, saying:

> I think the true question is whether this colportage system to which the profits of the shops are applied is or is not part of the trade of bookselling carried on by the Society. Now, we are told in this case that this colportage system is not a commercial system at all. It is not carried on for the purpose of making profit. It is not carried on as a trade speculation, because *we are told in this case that it could not be carried on at a profit*. It appears to me to be a very remarkable trade as to which those who carry it on admit that they could not possibly make any profit out of it. It shows clearly that it is not carried on as part of the business of bookselling, but they carry on the business of bookselling for the purpose of making profit, and having made profit, they expend it on the charitable purpose for which this Society exists, namely, the sale of books by colporteurs. [191]

It is not clear whether the ratio of this decision is that evangelism is not a trade, or whether it is that the colportage was not operated along commercial lines. Browne-Wilkinson VC thus explained the decision in *Ensign Tankers* – "A seller of religious tracts who travels from door to door selling his wares, appears to be conducting an ordinary business of sale and purchase. Yet if his object is to engage the customer in religious discussion so as to spread the gospel that *intention is decisive* and the selling of the tracts does not constitute trading."[192] Lord Templeman in the same case explained the case as deciding that a colporteur "was a missionary and not a trader".[193] If this be the true *ratio*, with due respect, it does not follow that a missionary or evangelist cannot at the same time be a trader. An illustration of this can be seen in the New Zealand case of *Graham v IRC*

---

[189] at page 418.
[190] ibid.
[191] at page 419 (emphasis added).
[192] [1991] BTC at page 83 (emphasis added).
[193] [1992] BTC at page 125.

(NZ)[194], where an itinerant evangelist whose principal source of livelihood consisted of voluntary payments from various assemblies where he preached, was held to be carrying on a business the profits of which were liable to income tax. Secondly, if the *ratio* of *Forbes* is that the colportage was not operated on commercial lines, that is not very convincing either. It begs the question what "commercial lines" means in this context. It also raises questions as to the basis of application of that definition to the action of selling books from door to door, as opposed to selling books from a fixed location. Finally, if the analysis of *Browne-Wilkinson VC* (that the intention to evangelise is conclusive against trading) is the true *ratio* of *Forbes*, that would seem quite odd, considering the fact that the courts have always maintained that the absence of a profit motive does not prevent trading. It is also worth noting that in *Graham v IRC (NZ)* the court accepted that the taxpayer was a true evangelist – however, the fact of his intention to evangelise did not lead to an inference that he was not carrying on a business for profit.

Equivocal transactions

Whatever the ratio of *Forbes*, it seems a questionable decision. If, as indicated by *Iswera v CTC* and *Ensign Tankers*, a taxpayer's subjective intention is only relevant where the facts are equivocal, then it is not clear how that subjective intention could have been relevant in this case. Viewed objectively, the act of going from door to door to sell things seems to be very clearly an ordinary trading activity, particularly where this is not an isolated transaction but a continuous operation. Many businesses are run today on those lines – including milk delivery, pizza delivery, newspapers, etc. If a person ran a pizza-selling-and-delivery operation with the main or sole aim of engaging customers in religious discussion, and the operation was run at a profit, it is difficult to see how such an operation would not amount to trading. Similarly, if an individual operated a taxi-cab with the same objective, and this was operated at a profit, it is difficult to see why it would not be a trade. There is nothing equivocal about these activities in themselves. It is only when viewed in the light of the seller's motives that questions of whether they are equivocal arise – but then that motive is only relevant where the activity itself is equivocal. It seems that a major factor in *Forbes* was the fact that the colportage was operated at a loss. If it had operated at a profit, it is not certain that the decision would not have been that it was a trade.[195] The role played by the fact that the operation was loss-

---

[194] (1961) 8 AITR 309.
[195] Contrast *Grove v YMCA*, supra.

making can be observed from the statement of Lord Adam (above) that the colportage could not be carried on at a profit, leading him to state that it would be a remarkable trade if those who carry it on admit that they could not possibly make a profit out of it. But arguably, the fact that a profit cannot be made does not inevitably lead to non-trading. To contend otherwise would be to contend that profitability or the prospect of profit is a necessary ingredient of trade. While there is strong Commonwealth authority for that proposition, that is arguably not what the U.K. authorities decide. The New Zealand courts hold that a reasonable possibility of profit it essential to business. In *Prosser v IRC (NZ)*[196] an undertaking was held to have ceased to be a business from the date that it became clear to its proprietors that there was no longer any reasonable prospect of profit. Quilliam J said[197]:

> I do not consider that our statute entitles a taxpayer to create or persist in any entirely unrealistic venture and then, because it has the outward semblance of a business, to be able to assert that it is one.

Quilliam J then went on to say that he accepted the proposition that the expression "business" involves "both the intention of making profit and at least the reasonable prospect of doing so",[198] and in *Harley v IRC (NZ)*[199] North P said that "if the enterprise had no prospect of earning a profit, it may be wrong to describe the enterprise as a business".[200]

The position in Australia is not so clear. While the Australian courts hold that the intention to make profit is essential,[201] persistent loss–makers have also been held to be carrying on a business. In one of such cases (*Tweddle v FCT*[202]) Williams J said:

> The Act must operate on the taxpayer's activities as it finds them. If a taxpayer is in fact engaged in two businesses, one profitable and the other showing a loss, the Commissioner is not entitled to say he must close down the unprofitable business and cut his losses even if it might be better in his own interests.[203]

It might however be said that the Australian cases are not conclusive on the issue of prospect of profit because in these cases of persistent loss-making, the taxpayers claimed to expect their activities to return a profit in the long term. Whether this is significant or not is not clear, especially as such claims

---

[196] (1972) 3 ATR 371.
[197] at page 375.
[198] ibid.
[199] [1971] NZLR 482 at 486 (CA).
[200] Note that it is not necessary for a profit to be made - but there must at least be an intention to earn profit (per Henry J in *IRC (NZ) v Watson* [1960] NZLR 259 at 262).
[201] *White v FCT* (1968) 120 CLR 191 (High Court); *FCT v The Myer Emporium Ltd* (1987) 87 ATC 4363 (High Court); *Westfield Ltd v FCT* (1991) 91 ATC 4234 (Full Court, Federal Court).
[202] (1942) 2 AITR 360 at 364.
[203] See also *Scott v FCT* (1939) 1 AITR 495.

can easily be made by any persistent loss–maker.

In the event, Australian case law is, at best, equivocal, but New Zealand case law clearly supports Lord Adam's approach in *Forbes*. It is important to note however that the Australian and New Zealand cases are closely tied to the wordings of their legislation, which require an intention to profit in order to bring transactions within the income tax charge. The significance of the form of statutory words was pointed out by McCarthy J in *Graham v IRC (NZ)*[204] where he doubted whether it could be maintained that "where the word is unaffected by statutory definition, the purpose of producing profits must necessarily be present".[205] As far as UK law is concerned, we should recall that Jessel MR said of a physician in 1879, "it cannot make any difference that he gets no fees; that he does not get paid, and does not attempt to get paid".[206] If a business man or woman does not get paid and does not attempt to get paid, that can hardly be taken to represent a reasonable prospect of profit. Yet this was said to make no difference to whether a business is being carried on or not. Perhaps the closest that we can get to Lord Adam's approach in the UK is the statement of Rowlatt J in *Royal Agricultural Society of England v Wilson*[207] that "if you do the operation of trading *and make a profit* you are carrying on a trade which in that case becomes taxable, and you are carrying on a trade whether you make a profit or not, and whether you want to make a profit or not, because it is not a mere question of motive". The phrase "and make a profit" in this statement may possibly be taken as qualifying both the preceding and succeeding words, such that, if you do the operation of trading and do not make a profit, then whether you make or profit or not, and whether you want to make a profit or not, become pertinent. Such an interpretation would however be quite nonsensical. If the words "and make a profit" are significant, then the words "and you are carrying on a trade whether you make a profit or not" become meaningless. Neither can the proposition "if you do the operation of trading and do not make a profit you are not carrying on a trade, which in that case denies you loss relief" be inferred from the statement just quoted. Rather, Rowlatt J would seem to be restating the general principle that the activities of the taxpayer, rather than the taxpayer's motives should be the focus of attention.

The real difficulty as far as activities and motives are concerned lies in the point which has been made earlier, that it may not be possible (especially where an operation is carried on at a loss) to determine what the purpose of the transaction is, or whether the taxpayer's activities are equivocal (for the purpose of admitting his or her motives) without prior reference to those motives. Yet it is clear that motive or subjective intention

---

[204] (1961) 8 AITR 309 at 313.
[205] See also the decision of the High Court of Australia in *White v FCT*, supra.
[206] *Portman v Home Hospital Association* (1879) 27 Ch. D 81 at 83.
[207] (1924) 9 TC 62 at 67 (emphasis added).

is only relevant where the transactions are equivocal. Is the analysis of that issue then to fall prey to a consideration of motive (thereby engendering great circularity), or is it a self-standing analysis?

This issue was addressed directly by the Court of Appeal in *Kirkham v Williams*.[208] The taxpayer in this case was a general dealer and demolition contractor. His storage of some demolition equipment at his mother's house led to some problems with the local planning authorities. Subsequently, he contracted to purchase some land, "principally to provide office and storage space" for his demolition and plant hire business. He used the site for the storage of materials for his business, and he used part of a mill situated on it as his office. He grew a few crops on the land and bought a few calves for fattening up for resale. The level of the taxpayer's farming activities in this regard were very limited, to the extent that they were never recorded in his account books. After obtaining planning permission for the erection of an industrial/agricultural dwelling house he built over a period of nine months a substantial four-bedroomed house on the site, although he never actually intended to live in it, and only occupied it temporarily. The taxpayer sold this property at a profit and soon completed the purchase of another piece of property from where he continued his business. The Revenue contended that the profit on the sale was derived from a trading activity. The Commissioners found that the site was acquired *principally*[209] to provide office and storage facilities for the taxpayer's business but nevertheless decided that the sale was a trading venture and was thus assessable under Schedule D Case I. No reason was given for this conclusion.

The Court of Appeal reversed the decision and held that the taxpayer was not trading. The issue of the taxpayer's intentions or purposes was crucial. Nourse LJ said[210] that the Commissioners' most significant finding was that the site was acquired principally to provide office and storage space for the taxpayer's business. But, according to him, the finding of a principal purpose also presupposes the co-existence with it of some subsidiary purpose, which the Commissioners had failed to specify. Possible subsidiary purposes were agricultural use of the whole or some part of the land available for such use, development and sale of some part or parts of the site, and, development and sale of the whole site. Nourse LJ said that it was open to the Commissioners to infer from their findings of primary fact that the taxpayer's subsidiary purpose in acquiring the site was the development and sale of part or the whole of the property. This however did not answer the question and an analysis of the primary facts was essential. The facts showed clearly that the taxpayer had contracted to purchase the site before making any application for planning permission.

---

[208] [1991] BTC 196; 64 TC 253.
[209] The import of this will soon appear.
[210] [1991] BTC 196 at 200.

It was not possible for him to develop the site without planning permission, and at the date of the contract, he was not certain as to whether or not he would be able to obtain such permission. Furthermore, if the principal purpose of the acquisition was the provision of office and storage space for his business, he must have intended to retain the site for the immediate future, perhaps for longer, and certainly not to dispose of it unless and until he had made alternative provision. Thus, if one were to look at the primary facts found by the Commissioners, and "the inferences that could be properly drawn from them in the light that is least favourable to the taxpayer",[211] the position was thus: the taxpayer acquired the site in order to provide the office and storage space which he needed for his business as a result of the difficulties which he had experienced with the local authority over storage at his mother's address. He could also have intended to develop and sell the site as a whole if he could obtain planning permission to do so and if and when he had been able to provide himself with suitable office and storage space elsewhere. This was an event which could not occur in the immediate future, and might not occur for some time. Was this state of affairs a sufficient basis in law for the conclusion that the site was acquired as trading stock and not as a capital asset of the taxpayer's business? Nourse LJ said that the authorities were to the effect that the first question to be asked was whether a transaction was equivocal or unequivocal. If it is unequivocal, that is, if it has all the characteristics of trading, then the taxpayer's "purpose or object alone cannot prevail over what he in fact does."[212] If an equivocal transaction is entered into for two different purposes, both must be taken into account when weighing the total effects of all the circumstances in order to decide as a question of fact whether the transaction constitutes trading for commercial purposes. With regard to a trading or profit making intention, the material intention was that which the taxpayer had at the time when he acquired the property.[213]

According to Nourse LJ, the taxpayer's acquisition of the site was an equivocal transaction. This was because:

> If viewed on its own, it does not tell you whether the property was acquired as trading stock or as a capital asset of the taxpayer's business. It might have been either. So account must be taken of the two purposes which the commissioners had attributed to the taxpayer, in the one case by express finding and in the other by presumed inference.[214]

In His Lordship's view, any "subsidiary purpose" which the taxpayer may have had here of developing and selling the site could not have been

---

[211] Nourse LJ at page 201.
[212] at page 203.
[213] ibid.
[214] ibid.

implemented concurrently with his "principal purpose" of providing office and storage space for his business[215] - first, there was no certainty that he would succeed in obtaining planning permission, and even if he did, he would not have been able to sell the site unless and until he had been able to provide himself with suitable office and storage space elsewhere. This was an event which might not have occurred for some time. This, according to him, meant that the taxpayer's 'object' or "purpose" or "intention" with respect to the development and sale was severely circumscribed, and its implementation indefinite in point of time. It was therefore not capable of amounting in law to an intention sufficient to give the property the character of trading stock. Nourse LJ therefore concluded that it was not open to the Commissioners, having made a finding which was apt to characterise the transaction as an acquisition of a capital asset, to deny it that character by reason of an intention thus circumscribed and indefinite.

Lloyd LJ concurred with the outcome, but on a different analysis of the facts. On the issue of a subsidiary purpose, he said that the most conspicuous feature of the case was the absence of any finding as to the subsidiary purpose.[216] He felt that if the Commissioners had intended to find that the subsidiary purpose was a trading purpose they would have made an express finding to that effect, bearing in mind their express findings as to the principal purpose, and their conclusion. Thus, it was not open to anyone to draw an inference that the Commissioners had found that the subsidiary purpose was a trading purpose. He was convinced that the only subsidiary purpose which the Commissioners could have had in mind was the farming purpose. Although they had found that the level of farming was very limited, this limited nature of the purpose was irrelevant. A principal purpose implies a subsidiary purpose, but does not exclude a very subsidiary purpose.[217] On a fair reading of the case, Lloyd LJ was of the view that the case was not a dual-purpose case at all, since neither of the two purposes found or implied by the Commissioners was a trading purpose. The Commissioners, according to him, must have held that the taxpayer was assessable because of a subsequent change of intention, but there was no evidence to support such a finding and it was not part of the Revenue's case.

So in this case, the transactions were equivocal, and the taxpayer's intentions or purposes became relevant. Why were the transactions equivocal? Because it was not clear whether the taxpayer had acquired the site as stock-in-trade, or as a fixed capital asset. Why was this not clear? Because it was not clear whether he had embarked on an adventure which had all the characteristics of trading. Why was this not clear? Because his

---

[215] at page 204.
[216] at page 209.
[217] ibid.

activities, viewed on their own, could have been interpreted in many ways. Thus, it seems that a transaction is only unequivocal if, viewed by itself and without reference to any other factor, it clearly points in one direction.

Motive: conclusions

The sum of the preceding discussions is that the law on the role of profit motive in ascertaining whether a person is trading is based on a number of principles the application of which in practice can be quite problematic. We can take the following propositions as established. First, profit motive is not essential to the carrying on of a trade.[218] Second, profit motive (or lack of it) by itself is, at worst, irrelevant, and, at best, inconclusive. Thus, a person may be trading even if he or she had no profit motive[219] and a person may not be trading even if he or she had a profit motive.[220] Third, where a person's activities bear all the hallmarks of trading, then the person's motive cannot prevail over an objective analysis of those activities[221] – or, alternatively, if that motive is important at all, then there is a constructive profit motive based on the fact that the activities clearly amount to trading.[222] Fourth, where the activities bear the hallmarks of trading, there must still be a commercial purpose.[223] Fifth, "commercial purpose" in this context relates not to the purposes or motives of the taxpayer, but to the purposes of the transaction.[224] Sixth, where the activities of the parties are unequivocal, commercial purpose is objectively deduced from those activities themselves.[225] Seventh, where the activities of the parties are equivocal, commercial purpose may be deduced subjectively by reference to the taxpayer's motives.[226] The principle in this respect is that the taxpayer must have had a profit motive, and that, at the time when the transaction is entered into. In a simple case of purchase and sale by a taxpayer, the relevant time is the time when the article was purchased by him or her.[227] In other cases (e.g., continuing operations as in *Forbes*) it is not entirely clear how the timing would be decided.

---

[218] The *Burial Board for Paddington, Middlesex v IRC* (1884) 13 QBD 9; *Mersey Docks and Harbour Board v Lucas* (1883) 2 TC 25; *IRC v Incorporated Council of Law Reporting* (1888) 22 QBD 297; *Grove v YMCA* (1903) 4 TC 613; *Royal Agricultural Society of England v Wilson* (1924) 9 TC 62.

[219] *Grove v YMCA*; *Mersey Docks and Harbour Board v Lucas*; *IRC v Incorporated Council of Law Reporting*; ; *Royal Agricultural Society of England v Wilson*.

[220] *IRC v Reinhold*. In New Zealand (see for example *Graham v IRC (NZ)* (1961) 8 AITR 309) and Australia, the presence of such a motive will amount to the carrying on of a business (see for example *FCT v The Myer Emporium Ltd* (1987) 87 ATC 4363; note that in *Westfield Ltd v FCT* ((1991) 91 ATC 4234) the full Federal Court emphasised that the profit making purpose must exist in relation to the particular operation which in fact led to the profit - see Hill J at page 4242).

[221] *Iswera v CTC*; *Royal Agricultural Society of England v Wilson*; *Grove v YMCA*.

[222] *Iswera v CTC*; *Wisdom v Chamberlain*.

[222] *Iswera v CTC*; *Wisdom v Chamberlain*.

[223] Browne-Wilkinson VC in *Overseas Containers v Stoker* [1989] BTC 153 at 159; Browne-Wilkinson VC in *Ensign Tankers (Leasing) Ltd v Stokes* [1991] BTC 74 at 83. The Australian cases also emphasise that the taxpayer's transactions need to be "commercial" in order to constitute a business. See *FCT v The Myer Emporium Ltd* (supra); *Westfield Ltd v FCT* (supra).

[224] *Ensign Tankers (Leasing) Ltd v Stokes*.

[225] *Ensign Tankers (Leasing) Ltd v Stokes*; Lord Reid in *Iswera v CTC* ; *Kirkham v Williams*.

[226] See the cases in the preceding footnote.

[227] The Australian case law (see for example, *FCT v The Myer Emporium Ltd*, and *Westfield Ltd v FCT*, supra) also establishes this timing principle.

These principles are, in the main, straightforward enough, but the number of questionable decisions and dicta (for example in *Forbes* and *Iswera*) and the apparent confusion over motives and purposes (for example in *Ensign Tankers*) indicate that the simplicity may be more apparent than real. By keeping an objective principle as a starting point, the courts have kept some of the spirit of the old cases. But by admitting motive in certain situations, it would seem that they have departed somewhat from that spirit – or, at least, that they have modified it. Of course this may be seen as simply an expedient and sensible extension of the principle of the 19th century cases. However, linking the admission of motive to the question whether or not the taxpayer's activities are equivocal is likely to continue to be problematic. The differing analyses of the facts in *Kirkham v Williams* in indicative of this. This would seem an area ripe for reform the object of which is clarification. The current hybrid principle does not provide that clarity. Clarity would come in the form of a total abandonment of motive, or, acceptance of motive as vital in all cases. The latter would, it is submitted, be preferable and more practical. Perhaps the way forward is a principle similar to that applied in Australia and New Zealand, where the intention to make profit is considered to be necessary to bring an operation within the scope of income tax.[228] It might also be helpful to indicate clearly (as in New Zealand) that a reasonable prospect of profit is also essential. In application, when a transaction takes place as part of the ordinary business of the taxpayer, the requisite intention could be presumed. This is the principle applied in Australia.[229] With respect to other transactions, a principle such as the one thus formulated by Hill J in *Westfield Ltd v FCT*[230] could be applied:

> [W]here a transaction falls outside the ordinary scope of the business, so as not to be a part of that business, there must exist ... a purpose of profit-making by the very means by which the profit was in fact made.[231]

Such formulations will not eliminate controversy in borderline cases, as they clearly have not done in Australia, New Zealand, or Canada. They might also encourage planning. However, they would have one advantage – clarity, and they would avoid some of the anomalies that we have observed, for example, in *Forbes*. Obviously the adoption of these principles would (as in Australia and New Zealand) require a statutory basis.

---

[228] Canadian case law seems to be similar in this respect – i.e., "intention is all important" (see I Saunders, above (1990) BTR, 168 at 186).

[229] *FCT v The Myer Emporium Ltd* (1987) 87 ATC 4363 at 4366 (per curiam); *Westfield Ltd v FCT* (1991) 91 ATC 4234 at 4242 (per Hill J). Hill J said in *Warner Music Australia Pty Ltd v FCT* ((1996) 70 FCR 197 at 210) that, in seeking to determine whether a gain is one made in the ordinary course of carrying on a business, it will be necessary to examine in detail both the scope and nature of a taxpayer's business. In *London Australia Investment Co Ltd v FCT* ((1977) 138 CLR 106 at 116 (High Court)) Gibbs J said that, in such cases, it would be necessary to make "both a wide survey and an exact scrutiny of the taxpayer's activities" (see also Dixon and Evatt JJ in *Western Gold Mines N.L v Commissioner of Taxation (Western Australia)* (1938) 59 CLR 729 at 740 (High Court)).

[230] (1991) 91 ATC at page 4243.

[231] Compare the High Court of Australia in *FCT v The Myer Emporium Ltd* (1987) 87 ATC at page 4367.

Mutual trading

We have noted at the beginning of this chapter the suggestion that trade is bilateral, in the sense that the trader must trade with someone. The principle that (subject to specific exceptions) no one can trade with himself or herself has led to the recognition of tax free surpluses of mutual associations.[232] The question in cases of alleged "mutuality" is, according to Lord Wilberforce in *Fletcher v Income Tax Commissioner*,[233] "is the activity, on the one hand, a trade, or an adventure in the nature of trade, producing a profit, or is it, on the other, a mutual arrangement which, at most, gives rise to a surplus?"

The mutuality principle applies where a number of people contribute to a common fund for their mutual benefit, and there is any refund of the surplus contributions.[234] According to Lord MacMillan in *Municipal Mutual Insurance Ltd v Hills*,[235] since the common fund is composed of sums provided by the contributors out of their own moneys, any surplus arising after satisfying claims obviously remains their own money, and "such a surplus resulting merely from mis-calculation or unexpected immunity cannot in any sense be regarded as taxable profit." Thus for example, if ten tenants contribute regularly to a fund for the maintenance and improvement of the facilities of their block of flats, and at the end of a certain period, they discover that the expenses of such maintenance were lower than their contributions to-date, if they then distribute the surplus between themselves, the Revenue cannot be heard to say that the sums so distributed are the profits of a trade. This principle is illustrated by *New York Life Insurance Co. v Styles*.[236] In this case, the only members of the taxpayer life insurance company were the holders of participating policies, who also owned all the assets of the company. Every year, surpluses of the premiums over the expenditure referable to the policies was returned to the policy holders as bonuses. The House of Lords held that these were not taxable as profits arising from a trade. Lord Watson said[237]:

> When a number of individuals agree to contribute funds for a common purpose, such as the payment of annuities, or of capital sums, to some or all of them, on the occurrence of events certain or uncertain, and stipulate that their contributions, so far as not required for that purpose, shall be repaid to them, I cannot conceive why they should be regarded as traders, or why contributions returned to them should be regarded as profits.

In order to obtain recognition as a mutual association, or to obtain

---

[232] This has naturally attracted increasing attention from the Revenue - see D Harris [1998] BTR 24. One effect of this attention can be seen in s.21C(3) TA 1988, in respect of "mutual businesses" under Schedule A.
[233] [1971] 3 All ER 1185 at 1189.
[234] See generally R Burgess [1976] BTR 361.
[235] (1932) 16 TC 430 at 448.
[236] (1889) 2 TC 460.
[237] at page 471.

recognition of mutual trading, the situation must be such that an identifiable class of persons (members) contribute to funds and enjoy and participate in the surplus, and there must be complete identity between the contributors and participators. Lord Macmillan said in *Municipal Mutual Insurance Ltd v Hills*[238] that the cardinal requirement is that all the contributors to the common fund must be entitled to participate in the surplus and that all the participators in the surplus must be contributors to the common fund; this is just another way of saying that there must be complete identity between the contributors and the participators. If this requirement is satisfied, the particular form which the association takes is immaterial.[239] Thus, such an identity, if it exists, is not destroyed or even impaired by the fact that the members form themselves into a corporation,[240] or by the fact that the contributions of members are not equal.[241]

Two points must be noted in relation to mutual trading. First, if a mutual association trades with outsiders (non-contributors) then any surplus from those dealings will be trading profits and thus taxable. For example in *Carlisle and Silloth Golf Club v Smith*[242] although the annual subscriptions received from members were not taxable because those members were also participators, the green fees from non-members were taxable as trading income. As the non-members were not entitled to participate in profits or surpluses, there was no mutuality. Secondly, it has been suggested that the mutuality, and, in particular, the participation, must be genuine. For example, in *Fletcher v Income Tax Commissioner*,[243] hotel owners paid subscription fees to a members' club as part of an arrangement to allow the hotel guest access to some private bathing areas. The Privy Council declared that no mutuality was present. Lord Wilberforce said[244] that it is not an essential condition of mutuality that contribution to the funds and rights in it should be equal. However, "if mutuality is to have any meaning there must be a reasonable relationship, contemplated or in result, between what a member contributes and what ... he may expect or be entitled to draw from the fund: between his liabilities and his rights".[245] In the present case it was clear that such a relationship was not reasonable. The hotel owners were required to contribute much more and were entitled to much less than the other members of the club. The disparity, as regards surpluses, between their interest and that of ordinary members was of a substantial scale, and the result was a distortion of the mutuality principle.

[238] 16 TC at page 448
[239] ibid.
[240] See Lord Watson in New York Life Insurance Co. v Styles, 2 TC at page 471.
[241] See Lord Wilberforce in Fletcher v Income Tax Commissioner, [1971] 3 All ER at page 1190.
[242] [1913] 3 KB 75; 6 TC 198.
[243] [1971] 3 All ER 1185.
[244] at page 1191.
[245] ibid.

Illegal trading

The issue of whether the profits of illegal or criminal activities are or should be taxable has long been debated.[246] It is however clearly established now that a taxpayer cannot raise the illegality of his or her activities as a defence to an assessment to income tax. In effect, trade, profession, or vocation does not necessarily presuppose legality. This principle was recognised even in the 19th century. It was Denman J who said in *Partridge v Mallandaine*[247]:

> But I go the whole length of saying that, in my opinion, if a man were to make a systematic business of receiving stolen goods, and to do nothing else, and he thereby systematically carried on a business and made a profit of £2,000 a year, the Income Tax Commissioners would be quite right in assessing him if it were in fact his vocation. There is no limit as to its being a lawful vocation, nor do I think that the fact that it is unlawful can be set up in favour of these persons as against the rights of the revenue to have payment in respect of the profits that are made. I think this does come within the definition of the word "vocation" according to common sense and according to the ordinary use of language.

In this case, a book maker's profits were taxable as the profits of a vocation, even though wagering contracts were unlawful. In *Minister of Finance v Smith*[248] the profits of illegal brewing were held to be taxable, and in *Mann v Nash*[249] the profits of automatic "fruit" and "diddler" machines used for illegal gambling activities were held to be taxable. It is interesting to note that the court does not necessarily view the taxing of proceeds of illegal activities as the State participating in unlawful gains. Rowlatt J explained that the State would merely be taxing a man in respect of his resources.[250] More recently, in *IRC v Aken*[251] the profits of prostitution were held to be taxable.[252] In the USA it is also long established that income is taxable notwithstanding that it may have accrued or been received in connection with an illegal transaction.[253] Thus, money obtained by extortion has been held to be taxable in the hands of the extortioners.[254] Notwithstanding that a person who has been defrauded might be able to recover the funds from an embezzler, also taxable are embezzled funds and profits earned by the embezzler through the use of those funds,[255] as are kickbacks to obtain

---

[246] See generally, G Graham [1966] BTR 309; K Day [1971] BTR 104; M Mulholland and R Cockfield [1995] BTR 572.
[247] (1886) 2 TC 179 at 181.
[248] [1927] AC 193.
[249] (1923) 16 TC 523.
[250] *Mann v Nash* (1923) 16 TC 523 at 530-531.
[251] [1990] BTC 352; STC 497.
[252] Note that Parker LJ said ([1990] BTC at page 359) that, in England, prostitution is not illegal - the deal between a prostitute and her client is immoral and unenforceable, but it is not illegal.
[253] *Barker v US*, 26 F.Supp. 1004 at 1005-1006.
[254] *Rutkin v US*, 343 US 130; 96 L.ed. 833 (US Supreme Court).
[255] *Rutkin v US*, supra; *Kurrle v Helvering*, 126 F.2d. 723 at 724-725; *McNight v CIR*, 127 F.2d. 572.

contracts[256] and the receipt of ransom.[257]

It is well enough to state that the profits of illegal activities are taxable in principle. This however raises questions. How, for example, would one ascertain those profits? The Taxes Act does not levy tax on proceeds, but on profits. Profits presuppose expenses. The question is, what expenses of illegal activities (if any) are deductible? For example, if a man rents some premises and buys personal computers and peripherals for the purpose of making illegal copies of computer software, which illegal copies he then sells systematically at a huge profit, can he claim any deductible expenses? Presumably the expenses of the running premises would be deductible – and presumably, he would be able to claim capital allowances in respect of the plant and machinery used for the copying. If not, why not? Presumably also, he will be able to deduct any costs incurred in avoiding detection by the police – and if not, why not? And what happens if there is a police raid, all his equipment and "trading stock" are all confiscated, and he is forced to pay substantial damages to those whose copyright he is breaching by his illegal copying? Would any of these be deductible? If the principle of taxing illegal trades is to be carried to its logical conclusion, there is no reason why such expenses cannot be deducted. If they are deductible, that raises all sorts of other questions, both moral and legal.

Let us examine another example that arises from recent convictions in England. Suppose, as has recently happened, that a group of foreign smugglers import illegally large quantities of "bush meat" from abroad to sell in this country. One would presume that the profits of such activities would be taxable. Now, suppose that the smugglers' storage premises are raided, the unsold "bush meat" is seized by Customs and Excise officers, and the individuals concerned in the smuggling are all convicted and fined. All these activities result in the smugglers incurring a "loss" in their "trade". Would they be entitled to loss relief? Would they be entitled to claim as deductible expenses the cost of purchasing and transporting the meat to this country? Would the fines be losses that arise out of or are connected with their "trade"?[258]

Finally, supposing that, in the example given by Denman J in *Partridge v Mallandaine* above, some of the stolen goods are later recovered by the police or by their rightful owners before the "trader" can sell them, can the "trader" then deduct the cost of having knowingly bought these stolen goods? There would appear to be no reason in principle why this should not be the case.

Some of the questions that may be asked in respect of illegal trading have been answered by the legislature. Parliament has stepped in to

---

[256] *Caldwell v CIR*, 135 F.2d. 488 at 491.

[257] *Humphreys v CIR*, 125 F.2d. 340 at 341.

[258] The answer to this last question is "no" – *McKnight (HMIT) v Sheppard* [1999] BTC 236; also *IRC v E C Warnes & Co. Ltd* [1919] 2 KB 444; 12 TC 227; *IRC v Alexander von Glehn & Co Ltd.* [1920] 2 KB 553; 12 TC 232. Lord Sterndale MR said (12 TC at page 238) "It is perhaps a little difficult to put the distinction into very exact language, but there seems to me to be a difference between a commercial loss in trading and a penalty imposed upon a person or a company for a breach of the law which they have committed in that trading."

determine that, in certain situations, expenses will not be deductible. S.577A(1) of the Taxes Act provides that no deduction shall be made for any expenditure incurred in making a payment the making of which constitutes the commission of a criminal offence. S.577A(2) provides that payments induced by demands constituting the offences of blackmail and extortion cannot be deducted. This would cover a situation such as a person paying for knowingly receiving stolen goods – but it would not cover the case of the dealer in illegal copies of computer software referred to above, since there is nothing criminal in paying for computer software or hardware. Would it cover the cost of buying bush meat in Africa, seeing that that activity is normal and lawful in many African countries? (See below). Would it cover the cost of shipping the bush meat to the UK? The answer to both questions may well be "yes", since it is arguable that the illegality begins only with the attempt to take the goods surreptitiously past the Customs and Excise officers (i.e., only after the bush meat has arrived in this country). But there are too many questions, and, it would seem that this whole question of illegal activities needs to be investigated properly and resolved (by Parliament) once and for all.

When Parliament comes to address the question, it will be faced with many instinctive and "obvious" responses. One such instinctive response can be found in the statement of Lord Denning in *J P Harrison (Watford) Ltd v Griffiths*[259].

> [T]ake a gang of burglars. Are they engaged in trade or an adventure in the nature of trade? They have an organisation. They spend money on equipment. They acquire goods by their efforts. They sell the goods. They make a profits What detail is lacking in their adventure? You may say it lacks legality, but it has been held that legality is not an essential characteristic of a trade. You cannot point to any detail that it lacks. But still it is not a trade, nor an adventure in the nature of trade. And how does it help to ask the question: If it is not a trade, what is it? It is burglary, and that is all there is to say about it.

This seems to go against the trend of the authorities, although it seems to be a "sensible" approach to the question. But if it indeed be true that burglary is not a trade, why does the same principle not apply to receiving stolen property, smuggling bush meat, or supplying illegal gambling machines? And, if receiving stolen property can amount to a trade, why not burglary?

The problem with instinctive responses to such legal questions was

---

[259] (1962) 40 TC 281 at 299.

highlighted (in the context of deductibility of fines imposed for illegal conduct during the course of a trade) by Scrutton LJ in *IRC v Alexander Von Glehn & Co Ltd* in these words[260]:

> The question which this case raises is whether a trader in presenting the balance of profits and gains for Income Tax can deduct, either in getting at the balance or after he has got at the balance, fines in the way of penalties which have been imposed on him for carrying on his trade in an unlawful way, and I confess that the way that the question so stated strikes me is that the obvious answer is "Of course he cannot." But, as Lord Macnaghten said in the House of Lords once, the clearer a proposition is the more difficult it often is to find authority in support of it, and when one comes to state the reasons-why that obvious answer should be given, perhaps it is not so easy as saying, "Of course he cannot."

The government is already taking steps to tighten the noose in this area, with a new provision in the Finance Act 2002 adding to the prohibition in s.577A(1) discussed above the making of any payment outside the United Kingdom where the making of a corresponding payment in any part of the United Kingdom would constitute a criminal offence there. Whether this new prohibition would cover the cost of buying bush meat in Africa is debatable.

The Basis of Assessment

The basis of assessment under Schedule D Cases I and II used to be known as the "preceding year" basis. In practice, application of the preceding year basis of assessment would mean that the owner of a business will be assessed for every year of assessment ending 5 April on the profits of his or her accounting year ending in the previous year of assessment. For example, if a trader makes up his or her accounts to 31 December in each year, he or she would be assessed for the year 2001-2002 (i.e., the year ending 5 April 2002) on the profits of the account ending 31 December 2000. The rationale for this type of assessment was simple – the profits of a year which has already ended are easily ascertainable since the trading activities of that year are concluded and set in stone. This basis of assessment also gives businesses some "breathing space" in which to finalise their accounts. However, the preceding year basis of assessment can lead to

---

[260] 12 TC at page 242.

anomalies and difficulties. Some of the anomalies were addressed by differential rules for opening and closing years of trading. One major problem however was the propensity of the preceding year basis to engender cash flow problems for the trader in years of falling profits or high investment costs. Another problem was the delay in recovering tax revenues in years of increasing profits. While this particular problem might have been seen as problematic for the Revenue, traders could benefit immensely by paying tax on the profits of a year of low profits, in a year of high profits.

The choice and application of basis of assessment has been a source of debate and concern. Prior to the introduction of the preceding year basis, a rather complicated system of assessing the average profits of the three accounts years preceding the year of assessment existed. The preceding year basis was introduced in 1927-28 (by the Finance Act 1926) following the recommendations of the Royal Commission on Income Tax, 1920. One alternative to the preceding year basis is the "current year" basis – one which charges tax in each year of assessment on the profits of the trader's accounting period ending in that year. Theoretically, this would avoid the anomalies and difficulties inherent in the preceding year basis. However, it would also lose one of the benefits of the preceding year basis – the "breathing space" would be gone, and businesses would have to rush to finalise their accounts. Some may find it difficult to meet the deadlines for submission of returns. Also, in this type of rush, mistakes may be made. The Revenue can then capitalise on either of these scenarios and impose penalties. It is interesting in this respect to note that both the Radcliffe Committee[261] and the Committee on the Taxation of Trading Profits[262] concluded that a true current year basis of assessment of profits under Schedule D could not be achieved.

To add to the debate on the issue, in the 1991 Budget speech, a consultative document on the basis of assessment was proposed. The document, "A simpler system for taxing the self-employed: Proposals for the reform of the administrative arrangements for taxing the self-employed and the basis of assessment", was published on 14 August 1991. As the title of the document suggests, the broad aim was to make the system of assessment "easier and cheaper to administer and to reduce dealings between the Inland Revenue and the taxpayer". Two options for changing the basis of assessment were proposed: (1) Current Year basis, and (2) Accounting Period basis. The proposals relating to the current year basis still took the preceding year into account. The proposal was for interim payments to be made on 1 January and on 1 July (before actual profits are known) with an adjustment following the computation of actual profits,

---

[261] Cmnd 9474, (1955).
[262] Cmnd 8189 (1951).

on 1 January of the following year. The profits and performance of the preceding year were to be the basis for the calculations needed to ascertain these "interim payments". On the other hand, the proposals relating to the Accounting Period basis were an attempt to follow the corporation tax rules of demanding a return of income in respect of a stated accounting period. However, unlike corporation tax, payments would be made either (1) by two instalments, nine and 15 months after the start of the accounting periods, each equal to 50% of the final liability for the last period; or (2) one payment, twelve months after the start of the accounting period. This attempt to bring the basis of assessment in line with that operated in relation to companies contributed to the declared aim of "neutrality". The proposals represented an attempt to bring the basis of assessment for all businesses "into line", so that "the form of business vehicle chosen would be irrelevant from a tax perspective". Initial response to these proposals suggested that the detail would not achieve the stated aims, and that further consultation and clarifications was needed.[263]

In the March 1993 Budget, the Chancellor announced further developments, including the introduction of a self-assessment system. The Chancellor also explained that the preceding year basis of taxation was "one of the least attractive features of our present tax system", and declared that he proposed a "major simplification" through the introduction of a current year basis of assessment and taxation of the self-employed. These two proposals are now in effect. The Finance Act 1994[264] introduced a new s.60 into the Taxes Act 1988. This took effect in the 1994-95 year of assessment, with respect to trades, professions and vocations commenced on or after 6 April 1994. With respect to other trades, professions and vocations, it took effect in the 1996-97 year of assessment.[265] S.60(1) of the ICTA 1988 provides that income "tax shall be charged under Cases I and II of Schedule D on the full amounts of the profits of the year of assessment." Thus, the normal basis of assessment is now the current year basis.

Special rules still exist for the opening and closing years of trading. In respect of the first year of trading (referred to in the statute as "the commencement year"), the computation of the profits chargeable to income tax is made on "the profits arising in that year".[266] In respect of the second year of trading (described as "the year next following the commencement year"), tax is charged generally on the profits of the first 12 months of trading.[267] In situations of cessation of trading (where a trade, profession or vocation is "permanently discontinued"), tax is charged on the profits of the period from the end of the basis period for the preceding

---

[263] See A J Shipwright [1992] BTR 12.

[264] s.200.

[265] There are some transitional provisions in Sch. 20, para 3, FA 1994.

[266] S.61(1) TA 1988.

[267] S.61(2) TA 1988.

year of assessment to the date of cessation[268] except where the cessation takes place in the second year of trading, in which case tax is charged on the profits of the period starting immediately after the end of the commencement year to the date of cessation.[269]

Application of opening and closing year rules

We have seen that, in spite of the change of the basis of assessment from the preceding to the current year basis, special rules still apply to the opening and closing years of the business. This means that the question whether and when a trade, profession or vocation was actually commenced or discontinued is pertinent. The commencement of a business is usually easy to ascertain. One of the major problems about commencement dates (eligibility for deductible expenses) has been rendered moot by s.401(1) if the Taxes Act. This subsection allows a trader to deduct expenditure incurred in the seven years before commencement of the trade by treating the expenditure has having been incurred on the date of commencement. However, the date of commencement is still important in respect of the application of the opening year rules.

Discontinuance

The question whether there has been a discontinuance of the business is more involved. It has been said that there is a discontinuance where a trader ceases to carry on the trade and where the trader ceases to trade in the way that he or she had previously traded.[270] The first point is trite but the second raises questions. Obviously, not every change in trading practices will amount to a discontinuance, so the question necessarily arises as to how to determine whether a change has led to a discontinuance. The question whether a trade has been permanently discontinued within the meaning of the statute may, on one view of the matter, be a question of law. In *Kirk and Randall v Dunn*[271] Rowlatt J asserted that the question was one of law – "the finding is that upon the construction of the Rule this case is not within it". However, the question whether a change of activities results in a trade being permanently discontinued or whether it was merely suspended for a time, is a question of fact[272] and degree.[273] This seems a different question from that posed by Rowlatt J in *Kirk and Randall v Dunn*,

---

[268] S.63(b) TA 1988.

[269] S.63(a) TA 1988.

[270] Simon's Tiley and Collison: UK Tax Guide (2000-2001) para. 7:50 (2000, Butterworths, London).

[271] (1924) 8 TC 663 at 670.

[272] See The Lord President (Clyde) in Gordon and Blair Ltd. v IRC, (1962) 40 TC 358 at 362; compare Lord Donovan in *Ingram v Callaghan* (1968) 45 TC 151 at 165.

[273] Lord Guthrie in *Gordon and Blair Ltd. v IRC*, 40 TC at page 364; compare Lord Carmont (at page 363). Note that "a question of degree is typically a question of fact, and a decision on it is not in effect open to review" - per The Lord President (Normand) in *IRC v Fraser*, 24 TC at page 502.

and to that extent, that statement is perhaps of doubtful authority.[274] The better view seems that the whole issue is one of fact and degree.

Some principles are discernible from the cases. First, the expression "permanently discontinued" does not connote a discontinuance which is everlasting[275] even though a trade which is discontinued indefinitely would come within that expression.[276] Secondly, it seems that a trade is not discontinued if it is merely in abeyance[277], or if it lapses into a period of quiescence (i.e., if there has been a temporary cessation in activities). In *Kirk and Randall Ltd v Dunn*[278] the taxpayer company was the new owner of the business of a firm of contractors. It was engaged in the completion of the old contracts of the business but was unable to obtain new contracts. From December 1914 until February 1920, the it had neither works nor plant, but during that period persistent but unsuccessful efforts were made by its directors to obtain contracts. The company at all times retained a registered office and held its statutory meetings yearly. The secretary's salary and directors' fees were paid, and substantial payments made for expenses, including those incurred by the directors in connection with their abortive efforts to obtain contracts. In 1920, with the introduction of fresh capital into the company, and the adoption of a different business policy, a number of profitable contracts were obtained, and fresh plant was acquired.

The special commissioners held that the trade ceased between 1914 and 1920, and that a new trade was commenced in 1920. This decision was reversed by Rowlatt J. Rowlatt J said[279] that the question here was "Is what this Company is doing carrying on a trade or business, or nothing at all?" because there is "no question about it being anything else but a trade or business if it is carrying on anything".[280] He noted that the company had "persisted in seeking for business – business which, if they got, they would have had to finance somehow and to carry out which they would have had to acquire plant and workmen whether the business was in this country or elsewhere."[281] He also noted that, at all times, they still had directors and a secretary who drew fees, typing, legal, and travelling expenses. Rowlatt J said that the contention was unarguable that they only began their business in 1920 merely because for the first time somebody yielded to their solicitations for a contract – just as it would be unarguable to say that a person who in the middle of a great career failed for some time to obtain business despite all efforts had therefore ceased to be in business.[282] He thus concluded:

---

[274] Contrast Rowlatt J in *Seldon v Croom-Johnson* (16 TC 740 at 746), where he said that the question whether a barrister who had been appointed as King's Counsel was carrying on a new and different profession was "to a certain extent" a question of fact.
[275] See Lord Donovan, in *Ingram v Callaghan* (1968) 45 TC 151 at 165.
[276] Lord Donovan, ibid.
[277] ibid.
[278] (1924) 8 TC 663.
[279] at page 669.
[280] ibid.
[281] ibid.
[282] at pages 669-670.

As far as I understand it it is not a question that the field of business was not precisely the same. The Company solicited precisely the same class of business they did in the old days. They solicited just the same sort of business, and they got some. That is all there is.[283]

This case can be contrasted with *Ingram v Callaghan*.[284] The taxpayer company manufactured surgical and pharmaceutical rubber goods. It incurred losses due to competition from the plastics industry. In 1960 it was acquired by another company (R Ltd) which later decided to switch the company's business to plastics. In 1961 it ceased to produce rubber goods, sold off its stock and dismissed most of its staff. For a time, it sold plastic components manufactured by another company in the group (M Ltd), for products which were indistinguishable from those the company had previously been marketing. They were sold under the same brand name and the company's profits during this period were profits on goods invoiced to it by M Ltd. In 1962, the company was sold to another company (P Ltd), after which its trade, was exactly the same as it was originally, except that the components which it manufactured (in factory space rented from P Ltd) were plastic instead of rubber. It claimed that it was carrying on the same trade as before and was entitled to carry forward losses incurred before 1961. The Special Commissioners held that, in 1961, the company had permanently discontinued the trade of manufacturing and selling rubber goods, that the trade of selling goods made by another company was a different trade, and yet a new trade was commenced in 1962. The company argued that the original trade had merely been in abeyance. Goff J accepted the company's argument and reversed the Commissioners. The Court of Appeal upheld the Commissioners' decision. Harman LJ said[285]:

[T]he learned Judge [held] that the conclusion reached by the Commissioners was an "impossible" one, and that what had happened was in truth that there had been a mere suspension of the Company's business between 1961 and 1962 and no "permanent discontinuance", so that the new business could be regarded as the same as the old one. I am unable to take this view of the facts. I cannot see any evidence that, when the Company's factory was closed and its machinery disposed of and its staff dismissed in 1961, there was any intention of merely keeping it in abeyance to resume at a favourable opportunity. I think that at that time anyone would have said that the business was at an end. If the receipt by the Company from [M Ltd] during the next year of some part of the

---

[283] at page 670.
[284] (1968) 45 TC 151.
[285] 45 TC 151 at 169-170.

proceeds of [M Ltd's] activities is to be regarded as a trading activity, I think it was a different and new trade, and the manufacturing business started up in the [P Ltd] factory in 1962 seems to me to have been a fresh venture. Even if this be to go too far and supposing it to be wrong, I cannot see how there was no basis for such a conclusion so that it was one at which the Commissioners were not entitled to arrive. It was, in my judgment, a justifiable conclusion.

Gordon and Blair Ltd v IRC[286] was another case involving a change from one type of activity to another. The taxpayer company carried on business as brewers. It also sold beer on the open market. In October 1953, after making losses, it ceased to brew its own beer. At this time, some of its staff became redundant and were dismissed. The company continued to bottle and sell beer, but this was in respect of beer supplied to its specification by another brewery Company. The company claimed that it carried on the same trade before and after October 1953, so that losses sustained prior to that date could be set against subsequent profits under s.342(1) ICTA 1952. The Special Commissioners held that, as from 1953, the Company ceased trading as brewers, and commenced a fresh trade of selling beer. The Court of Session held that the Commissioners were entitled to decide as they did. The Lord President (Clyde) said[287] that the question was primarily, if not wholly, a question of fact, depending on the circumstances of each case.

The last two cases show the types of problems that can arise in respect of new activities taken on by trader. In the context of a change in the nature of the taxpayer's activities, as seen in the cases just examined, the real question in such cases is whether the taxpayer is thereby discontinuing one trade and commencing a new one, or whether the original one is in abeyance, waiting to be revived at some future date. There are situations however wherein the taxpayer does not stop any particular activity, but still takes on a new role. In such cases, is the taxpayer merely extending his or her business or commencing a new one? This issue came up for decision in *Seldon v Croom - Johnson*.[288] The taxpayer was a barrister and he was appointed as a King's Counsel during the year of assessment. Before his appointment as King's Counsel, the taxpayer carried on his practice partly in Bristol and partly in London. Before making his application to be appointed as King's Counsel, he was given to understand that his application would not be considered unless he was prepared, in case he should be appointed, to have professional chambers and a professional address in London only. Immediately upon his appointment, he accordingly gave up the occupation of his chambers at Bristol and

---

[286] (1962) 40 TC 358.
[287] 40 TC 358 at 362.
[288] [1932] 1 KB 759; 16 TC 740.

commenced to practice from London only. By the practice of the Bar, a King's Counsel was not allowed to draw pleadings, to settle interrogatories or a notice of appeal, to advise on evidence, or to appear before any court without junior counsel, except in cases in which he may have already been engaged before his appointment. From the date of his appointment as King's Counsel, the taxpayer began to appear in a class of cases in which he had not appeared for some years before his appointment and to be instructed by clients, many of whom were different from those by whom he had been previously instructed. He was also engaged in few, if any, of the class of cases in which he had normally been engaged as a junior counsel in the years immediately preceding his appointment. His earnings in the relevant year were lower than those of the preceding year and he contended that the profession he carried on as a King's counsel was different from the one that he carried on as barrister-at-law. The General Commissioners held that the taxpayer had permanently discontinued his profession as barriser-in-law and had commenced a new profession as King's Counsel. Their decision was reversed by Rowlatt J. He said[289] that a change of residence or a change of chambers from one town to another did not throw any light on the question of identity of profession. He further said[290] that the position involved in becoming a King's Counsel in all ordinary cases of practising barristers is quite simple – they always fall under the same rule. They carry on the same profession – "only they occupy a higher rank or degree within it and therefore are in fact more selective in the business which they do. That is all it comes to." Thus, there was no evidence upon which the Commissioners could properly come to the conclusion to which they did.

These cases all go to illustrate that, in the final analysis, the question must depend on the available evidence (and perhaps also on what the judges know, since Rowlatt J's knowledge of the barristers' profession may be seen as having had a significant effect on the decision in *Seldon v Croom-Johnson*). Therefore decisions will normally be taken on a case by case basis, and decided cases will be useful mainly as illustrations.[291]

Succession and changes in ownership

A change in the ownership of a business results, for income tax purposes, in the business being permanently discontinued, and a new business being commenced on date of the change. This principle is mainly relevant to cases where the business is being carried on in partnership, but it is also

---

[289] 16 TC 740 at 746.
[290] at page 747.
[291] See Lord President Clyde in *Gordon and Blair Ltd. v IRC*, 40 TC 358 at 362.

relevant in cases of succession (i.e., where a business carried on by one person is transferred as a going concern to another[292]). The relevant provision is s.113(1) of the Taxes Act which provides:

> Where there is a change in the persons engaged in carrying on any trade, profession or vocation chargeable under Case I or Case II of Sch. D ... the amount of the profits of the trade, profession or vocation on which income tax is chargeable for any year of assessment and the persons on whom it is chargeable, shall be determined as if the trade, profession or vocation had been permanently discontinued, and a new one set up and commenced, at the date of the change.

However, where there is a continuing partner after the change, the trade, profession or vocation is not treated as discontinued.[293]

Partnerships

Before we go further, it is useful at this stage to note some general issues in respect of the income tax treatment of partnerships. Unless the contrary intention appears, a partnership is not treated as entity separate and distinct from the partners.[294] If any of the partners is liable to income tax, then the profits of the partnership's business will be computed for income tax purposes as if the partnership were an individual who is resident in the UK.[295] Each partner's share in the profits and losses of the business will be determined according to his or her interest in the partnership.[296]

Where a partnership is a "limited liability partnership" that carries on a trade, profession or other business with a view to profit, all the activities of the partnership are treated as carried on in partnership by its members and not by the partnership as such,[297] and, except otherwise provided, references to a partnership in the Tax Acts include a limited liability partnership, but references to a company do not include a limited liability partnership.[298]

Where a partnership includes a company, the profits of the partnership's trade are computed, for Corporation Tax purposes, as if the partnership were a company.[299] The share of the profits attributable to the member

---

[292] See *Watson Bros v Lothian* (1902) 4 TC 441.
[293] s.113(2) TA 1988.
[294] TA 1988, s.111(1).
[295] s.111(2).
[296] s.111(3).
[297] s.118ZA (1). This also applies to a limited partnership that has temporarily ceased trading, or (subject to exceptions relating to tax avoidance and unreasonable prolongation of winding up) to a limited partnership that is in a period of winding up following a permanent cessation (s.118ZA (3)).
[298] s. 118ZA (2).
[299] s.114(1).

company will be subjected to Corporation tax[300], and income tax will be charged on the profits of the partners who are not companies.[301]

As already seen above, a change in the partners leads to a discontinuance of the existing trade, and a commencement of a new trade by different people, except where there is continuing partner. However, by virtue of s.114(1)(c), where a company joins a partnership which did not originally include a company, there is a discontinuance, even if there are continuing partners.

Ascertainment of Profits

As indicated earlier in this discussion, income tax is charged under Cases I and II of Sch. D on the "annual profits or gains arising or accruing" from the trade, profession or vocation.[302] The measure of the income that is charged is described as "the full amount of the profits of the year of assessment."[303] Typically, the statute does not define "annual profits or gains". It is established however that, in this context, the word "annual" means "in any year," and the words "annual profits or gains" mean "profits or gains in "any year as the succession of the years comes round."[304] This definition was approved by the House of Lords in *Martin v Lowry*[305] in which case Viscount Cave LC also made the point that "annual" does not denote any need for recurrence.[306]

For the purposes of the Sch. D charge, the words "profits" and "gains" bear the same meaning,[307] i.e., the net increase (if any) enjoyed by the business in the relevant period. The word "profits" is to be understood in its natural and proper sense – in a sense which no commercial man would misunderstand.[308] Judicial comment explains that it is the "difference between the price received on a sale and the cost of what is sold."[309] According to Fletcher-Moulton LJ in *Re Spanish Prospecting Co Ltd*[310]:

> Profits implies a comparison between the state of a business at two specific dates usually separated by an interval of a year. The fundamental meaning is the amount of gain made by a business during the year. This can only be ascertained by a comparison of the assets of the business at the two dates ... if the total of the assets of the business at the two dates are compared, the increase which they show

---

[300] s.114(2).
[301] s.114(3).
[302] S.18(1) TA 1988.
[303] S.60(1) TA 1988.
[304] Rowlatt J in *Ryall v Hoare* (1923) 8 TC 521 at 526.
[305] (1927) 11 TC 297. See Viscount Cave LC at page 320; Viscount Sumner at page 321.
[306] at pages 320-321.
[307] See Lord Selborne LC in *Mersey Docks and Harbour Board v Lucas* (1883) 2 TC 25 at 29; compare Lord Halsbury LC in *Gresham Life Assurance Society v Styles*, (1892) 3 TC 185 at 188 and 189.
[308] Lord Halsbury LC in *Gresham Life Assurance Society v Styles* (1892) 3 TC 185 at page 188.
[309] Sir George Jessel MR in *Erichsen v Last* (1881) 8 QBD 414.
[310] [1911] 1 Ch 92 at 98-99.

at the later date as compared with the earlier date (due allowance of course being made for any capital introduced or taken out of the business in the meanwhile) represents in strictness, the profits of the business during the period in question.

The issue of the amount of the profits or gains made by a business is basically a question of fact. Profits and gains must be ascertained on ordinary principles of commercial trading.[311] This was confirmed by the Committee on the Taxation of Trading Profits when it reported the need to compute a balance of a profit and loss account[312]. The Committee also reported that it was settled that profits should be computed in accordance with established commercial accountancy principles[313] As such, there is a clear principle that business accounts should be made up in accordance with ordinary accountancy practice, unless these contravene some legal rule.[314] Viscount Haldane explained this principle in *Sun Insurance Office Ltd. v Clark*[315]

It is plain that the question of what is or is not profit or gain must primarily be one of fact to be ascertained by the tests applied in ordinary business. Questions of law can only arise when ... some express statutory direction applies and excludes ordinary commercial practice, or where, by reason of its being impracticable to ascertain the facts sufficiently, some presumption has to be invoked to fill the gap.[316]

Cash or Earnings Basis?

Ordinary principles of commercial trading pointed to two methods of ascertaining the profits of a business. First, the cash basis (or the conventional basis). This requires profits to be ascertained by simply deducting all sums actually expended from the sums actually received during the relevant period.[317] This was the normal method of computing the profits of authors and barristers[318] – the latter because of an archaic principle that they cannot sue for their fees, and the former because they are remunerated by royalties which cannot be computed accurately in advance. The cash basis, being a simple arithmetical calculation of incoming and outgoing sums has simplicity as its main virtue. However, it runs into problems in cases where the taxpayer both gives and receives credit, or carries trading stock at the beginning and the end of the relevant period. The earnings basis is more appropriate for these types of situations.

---

[311] Lord Halsbury LC in *Gresham Life Assurance Society v Styles* 3 TC at page 189; see also J Freedman [1995] BTR 434; G MacDonald [1995] BTR 484.
[312] Cmd 8189 (1951).
[313] Ibid. According to the Committee, this was settled following the House of Lords' decision in *Usher's Wiltshire Brewery Ltd v Bruce* [1915] AC 433.
[314] For a general discussion see J Freedman [1994] BTR 468; R Burgess [1972] BTR 308.
[315] [1912] AC 443 at 455.
[316] See also *Odeon Associated Theatres v Jones* [1972] 2 WLR 331.
[317] See generally, Lord Denning MR in *Mason v Innes* (1967) 44 TC 326 at 339.
[318] See the Revenue Statements of Practice A3 (barristers), and A27 (others).

This basis requires the business to bring into account its debts, credits, and trading stock, at the beginning and at the end of the relevant period. The resulting figure represents a more accurate profit figure. Originally the idea was that neither of these bases is necessarily more correct than the other, although the Revenue seemed to prefer the earnings basis. However, the principle was established that, an assessment on a particular basis for any year necessarily precludes the application of the other. In *Rankine v IRC*[319] Lord Keith thus explained this point:

> [A]nd if the taxpayer and the revenue agree, in circumstances of full disclosure, to the computation of the profits and gains upon a certain basis it is not, I think, open to the revenue to seek to reopen an assessment made on this agreed basis merely because the revenue finds that it would have been more profitable to the tax gatherer to have made the assessment on another basis.

The Labour Government announced in December 1997 that it was going to withdraw the cash basis. The promised reforms were implemented in the Finance Act 1998, the effect of which seems to be the imposition of the earnings basis in virtually all cases. S.42(1) FA 1998 provides that, for the purposes of Case I or II of Sch. D, the profits of a trade, profession or vocation must be computed on an accounting basis which gives a "true and fair view". Exemption from this rule is given for barristers and advocates who are in the first seven years of practice.[320] The Revenue in a March 1998 Budget Press Release[321] explained the significance of the "true and fair view" by saying that the approach's only concern is the computation of taxable profits and losses – in other words, it does not require accounts to be drawn up in any particular way – as long as the tax computations are made according to the true and fair view. Thus, a trader can still make up his trading accounts on a cash basis if he so chooses – but when the tax calculations start, he will then have to "convert the profit to an earnings basis profit in the tax computations". The Release went on to state that the true and fair view does not require a true and fair view balance sheet to be prepared.[322] The question of course is why a trader would want to keep accounts on the cash basis knowing fully well that, for tax purposes, he or she would have to do the calculations on the earnings basis. More recently, the Revenue, in a joint statement with the Tax Faculty of the Institute of Chartered Accountants[323], claimed that this true and fair view imposed by the FA 1998 is nothing new at all, but is rather a mere adoption by Parliament of an approach which has been adopted by the courts over several years.[324] They pointed out that the concept is one which

---

[319] (1952) 32 TC 520 at 531.
[320] S.43 FA 1998.
[321] IR 29, para. 26.
[322] ibid.
[323] IR Tax Bulletin, December 1998, page 606 et seq.
[324] The statement refers for example to the Court of Appeal's decision in *Gallagher v Jones* (1993), 66 TC 77, and the decision of Knox J in *Johnston v Britannia Airways Ltd* (1994) 67 TC 99.

is well known to accountants, and that the Accounting Standards published by the professional bodies have recognised that certain accounts should be prepared in this way. In terms of practicality, the tax requirement for "documents to show a true and fair view requires them to comply only with those parts of Accounting Standards that are germane to the calculation of profits."[325]

It is not clear whether "the true and fair view" necessarily equates to "the earnings basis", as the Revenue and the ICA seem to think. It is arguable that if this is what Parliament intended, they could have said so in so many words. Is it the case that the cash basis can never present the true and fair view, or that the earnings basis always will? What for example would represent a true and fair view in respect of an author who is only paid by yearly royalties, but who regularly incurs business expenses on credit? Presumably such royalties are normally known to the author only when they are paid/received. Therefore it is sensible to bring them into account upon receipt (cash basis), as opposed to when they are arguably "earned" (when the books are being sold in the bookshops). On the other hand, would such an author be able to brings his or her debts into account at the time when they are incurred (and not wait until he has paid the debts)? This might have to be so in order to present a true and fair view. But here we might have an application of a mixture of the cash basis and the earnings basis in the same trade – an idea which sounds odd – and this in order to present a true and fair view! Perhaps a better approach is to say that s.42(1) FA 1998 is just advocating a common sense approach wherein Accounting Standards are influential.

To conclude this part of the discussion, trading profits are, broadly speaking, equal to trading receipts minus trading expenditure. In *Mersey Docks and Harbour Board v Lucas*[326], Lord Selborne LC said that the word "profits" as used in the statute means the incomings of the concern, after deducting the expenses of earning and obtaining them. As Lord Herschell put it in *Gresham Life Assurance Society v Styles*, "whether there be such a thing as profit or gain can only be ascertained by setting against the receipts the expenditure or obligations to which they have given rise."[327] This seemingly simple arithmetical formula for ascertaining the profits of a trade, profession or vocation actually involves a number of detailed legal principles, for once a person has been found to be trading, it is not the law that everything which he or she receives or earns is a trading receipt, or that everything that he or she spends or owes is a trading expense. There is a glut of case law relating to these points just mentioned – whether something received or earned is a trading receipt, and whether something spent or owed is a trading expense. The next two chapters will address these questions.

---

[325] ibid, para. 11.
[326] 2 TC 25 at 28.
[327] 3 TC at 194. See also Lightman J in *McManus v Griffiths* [1997] BTC 412 at 419: "Profit for [the purposes of Sch D] is the balance of income over deductable expenditure."

Further Reading

Olowofoyeku A, *A Century of Doubt: Profit Motive in the UK Income Tax Law* (2000) New Zealand Journal of Taxation Law and Policy, Vol. 6, 40.

Harris D, *Mutuality and Temporary Membership* [1998] BTR 24.

Olowofoyeku A, *In the Performance of the Duties: Fact, Law or Both?* [1996] BTR 28.

Freedman J, *Defining Taxable Profit in a Changing Accounting Environment* [1995] BTR 434.

MacDonald G, *Matching Accounting and Taxable Profits: Reflections on Gallagher v Jones* [1995] BTR 484.

Mulholland M and Cockfield R, *The Implications of Illegal Trading* [1995] BTR 572.

Shipwright AJ, *Consultative Document on a Simpler System for Taxing the Self Employed* [1992] BTR 12.

I Saunders, *The Role of Intention in Identifying Trade or Business Income: the United Kingdom and Canadian Approaches* [1990] BTR 168.

Shrubsall V, *Note of Case: Trading – Commercial Purpose and Fiscal Motive* [1990] BTR 52

Avery-Jones JF, *Nothing either good or bad- but thinking makes it so – The Mental Element in Anti-Avoidance Legislation* [1983] BTR 9 and 113

Burgess R, *The Mutuality Principle* [1976] BTR 361.

D de M Carey D, *Trade – The Elusive Concept* [1972] BTR 6.

Day K, *The Tax Consequences of Illegal Transactions* [1971] BTR 104;

Graham G, *Taxes on Betting and Games* [1966] BTR 309.

chapter seven

Income Tax -
Schedule D Cases I and II
Trading Receipts

Trading receipts represent the consideration for the goods and services provided by a person carrying on a trade, profession or vocation. While the discussions in this chapter will focus almost entirely on the nature of sums of money received by a trader, payments in money's worth such as shares[1] or a "rent charge"[2] (to be brought into account at market value) also fall within the income tax charge and may well fall within a trader's trading receipts.

The phrase "trading receipts" is not defined in statute. Simply put, it implies that "there is a trader carrying on a trade or profession and that the payment is received in the course of his trade or profession."[3] However, it is not the rule that every sum of money received by a trader is to be brought into account as a receipt of the trade. This is one area where the distinction between capital and income comes into play, for the cardinal principle is that only receipts of an income or revenue nature fall to be taken into account as trading receipts. When a trader receives a sum of money, two main questions arise – whether the money is income or capital in nature, and whether it is a receipt of the trader's business. Sums which represent capital in the hands of the taxpayer necessarily escape a tax which is only charged on income. Consider the famous words of Lord MacNaghten in *A-G v London County Council*[4]: "income tax, if I may be pardoned for saying so, is a tax on income. It is not meant to be a tax on anything else."[5] This is not to say that capital receipts will always escape the tax gatherer. There was a time when capital receipts escaped tax altogether, but today, capital receipts may well fall within the charge to capital gains tax. In spite of the fact that capital gains tax may be chargeable today, the distinction between capital and income is still important – and this, despite

---

[1]   *Gold Coast Selection Trust Ltd. v Humphrey* [1948] 2 All ER 379; AC 459.
[2]   *Emery & Sons v IRC* [1937] AC 91.
[3]   Per Lord Cameron in *IRC v Falkirk Ice Rink Ltd* (1975) 51 TC 42 at page 51.
[4]   (1901) 4 TC 265 at 293.
[5]   Compare Sir Wilfred Greene MR said in *IRC v British Salmson Aero Engines Ltd* (1938) 22 TC 29 at 42.

the harmonisation of income and capital gains tax rates. For example, the differential rules for allowances and deductions for income tax and capital gains tax may be significant.

As indicated earlier, two questions arise when a trader receives a sum of money – is the sum income or capital, and, is it "a receipt of the recipient's business"?[6] And there are two possible approaches to these two questions. First, it may be that the question whether a sum received by a trader is income or capital in nature comes first – the idea being that if it is capital in nature, then that is decisive, and the question whether it is a receipt of the taxpayer's trade or business does not arise. This is the approach that has been taken in many leading cases[7], and, more recently, by Lord Hoffmann in *Deeny v Gooda Walker Ltd*.[8] However, doubt was cast on this manner of ordering the questions by the other Law Lords in the case. Lord Browne-Wilkinson seemed to reverse the order, putting the question whether the sum is a receipt of the business first, and the question whether it is income or capital, second.[9] It is not clear whether he was thereby seeking to particularise this as the correct order, or whether he was simply listing the questions as it suited him. However, Lord Mustill was quite definite in preferring the second approach to the questions. He said that the question whether a particular receipt was a receipt of the taxpayer's trade "must always come first."[10] He admitted that, in practice, the question will often be so closely linked to the question whether, if it is a receipt of the trade, it is in the nature of income or capital, that an affirmative answer to one will demand an affirmative answer to the other. He said however that this need not always be so.

Is there actually any significant difference between these two approaches, and, if so, which is to be preferred? It may be that much depends on what is meant by the phrase "a receipt of the taxpayer's business". On one view of the matter, it might seem odd (except perhaps in respect of cases which clearly have no connection at all with the taxpayer's trade) that the question whether a sum is a receipt of the trade can come before the question whether it is capital or income – because it is arguable that, by definition, a capital sum cannot ever be a receipt of the trade (or "business") for income tax purposes. On this basis, it might be that Lord Hoffmann's approach, which seeks first to determine whether the sum is income or capital, is to be preferred. In this case, it is only after this hurdle has been crossed that the question whether the payment is a receipt of the trade (which is an issue of causation) will arise. However, as already indicated, much depends on what their Lordships meant by "receipt of the business". If the term was employed loosely (to refer to anything that arises out of or is connected with the taxpayer's trading

---

[6] See Lord Browne-Wilkinson in *Deeny v Gooda Walker Ltd* [1996] BTC 144 at 146.
[7] See for example, *Glenboig Union Fireclay Co. Ltd v IRC* (1922) 12 TC 427; *Van Den Berghs v Clark* (1935) 19 TC 390.
[8] [1996] BTC 144 at 152-153.
[9] at page 146.
[10] ibid.

activities), then perhaps Lord Mustill's ordering is to be preferred because, presumably, the idea is that a trader can have capital receipts of the trade, and income receipts of the trade, and receipts which have nothing at all to do with the trade. In this case, it is right first to consider whether the receipt had any connection with the trade (i.e., whether it was a receipt of the trade) before considering whether it was a capital or income receipt of the trade. If, however, the term was employed technically (referring to what amounts in law to a trading receipt chargeable to income tax) then Lord Hoffmann's approach is preferable. Nevertheless, perhaps an even better approach to the issue is to treat both questions as part and parcel of one single question (whether the sum is taxable as a trading receipt), in which case the question which of them "comes first" must depend on the circumstances of each case. Thus, if a trader wins a "jackpot" in the National Lottery, the question whether the prize money is a receipt of his business would come first, in the sense of whether it actually has any relationship with his business. The situation might be the same if a trader receives an unsolicited gift from a former customer (see below), or if he sells an item of machinery used in his trade. However, all these situations also arguably raise the question whether the sums are income or capital. Indeed, one might rightly say that if a sum is not a receipt of the trade, then it is capital[11] (or "a windfall"[12]) and so, the jackpot or unsolicited gift referred to above might rightly be described as capital sums, by which token the question whether they arose out of the trade is irrelevant. This of course begs the question why they are capital sums. As a corollary, one might also say that if the sum is capital, then it is not a receipt of the trade – a point that hardly needs authority. In short, it does not seem to be an edifying task to take this issue too far as the argument can quickly become circular. Perhaps the courts should just take first the question that seems most appropriate to be so taken and not bother too much about the "right" order (if there is one). As Lord Mustill said, for practical purposes, in most cases, the answer to both questions is likely to be the same., regardless of which issue is considered first. For present purposes, we prefer to look first at the income/capital question – not because it is necessarily the "right" one to consider first, but simply as a matter of convenience.

Income or Capital?

We have already identified and discussed at an earlier stage various theories relating to the proper distinction between income and capital. This distinction has been described as "artificial"[13], and, according to Kay[14],

---

[11] See for example Lord Blackburn in *Burmah Steamship Company Ltd v IRC*, 16 TC at page 75.

[12] per Lord Sands, ibid.

[13] See Lord Sands in *Burmah Steamship Company Ltd v IRC* (1931) 16 TC 67 at 73; contrast Lord Macmillan in *Van Den Berghs Ltd v Clark*, (1935) 19 TC 390 at 428 - "in general the distinction is well recognised and easily applied".

[14] J A Kay, "The Economics of Taxation" [1979] BTR 354 at 357.

neither legislation nor case law has succeeded in creating an economically defensible justification for the distinction. Nevertheless, it is still necessary to ascertain whether a sum of money is income or capital. The word "income" is not defined anywhere in the statute. American courts have taken the bull by the horns and have bravely tried to provide definitions – for example, it has been held, that its meaning is the same as in "the common speech of men" and every day usage;[15] that it is to be given a broad meaning, and must be "rationally construed" and not stretched to include purely theoretical as distinguished from practical conceptions[16]; that it is equipollent with "harvest" or "product"[17]; that it is the return or gain from business, labour, capital[18], skill, ingenuity, sound judgment, or from two or more of them in combination[19], and that it denotes an increase in wealth.[20] However, it seems that the best that the UK courts can provide is the definition by Lord Wrenbury in *Whitney v IRC*[21] where he said that the word "income" means "such income as is within the Act taxable under the Act". Unfortunately, this statement does not really advance the situation. The American definitions referred to above provide interesting insights into the matter, but it seems that, in the UK, the term is acquiring an increasingly technical meaning. In the UK we have applied concepts such as the "tree" and the "fruit", and fixed and circulating capital and such other formulations, which may be helpful in specific cases to resolve the matter. However there are many transactions which do not fit readily into these categories, and care must be taken not to accord undue weight to these tests. Lord Radcliffe's warning in this respect is poignant[22].

These phrases are, of course, used with intended reference to earlier judicial decisions that distinguish between capital and income for the purpose of assessing profit. Since a question of capital or income is always capable of giving rise to a question of law, such a form of argument is unavoidable in any legal system that governs itself by appeal to precedent. Nevertheless, it has to be remembered that all these phrases ... are essentially descriptive rather than definitive, and, as each new case arises for adjudication and it is sought to reason by analogy from its facts to those of one previously decided, a court's primary duty is to inquire how far a description that was both relevant and significant in one set of circumstances is either

---

[15] *US v Safety Car Heating and Lighting Co*, 297 US 88 at 99; *Roberts v CIR*, 176 F.2d. 221 at 225; *Mahama v US*, 88 F.Supp. 285 at 288. In *Union Trust Co. of Pittsburgh v CIR* (115 F.2d. 86 at 87) the court referred to the economists' definition of income as "the money value of the net accretion in one's economic power between two points of time".

[16] *State v Flenner*, 181 So. 786 at 790.

[17] *In Re Baum's Will*, 91 NYS.2d. 649 at 654.

[18] *Wells v Wells*, 148 P.2d. 126 at 128; *Woodhouse v Woodhouse*, 100 A.2d. 211 at 212; *Cheley v CIR*, 131 F.2d. 1018 at 1020; *US v Safety Car Heating and Lighting Co*, 297 US 88 at 99.

[19] *Diefendorf v Gallet*, 10 P.2d. 307 at 310; *Towne v Towne*, 159 P.2d. 352 at 357.

[20] *Commr. of Corporations and Taxation v Williston*, 54 NE.2d 43 at 44-46; *State v Flenner*, 181 So. 786 at 790.

[21] (1925) 10 TC 88 at 113.

[22] *Commrs. of Taxes v Nchanga Consolidated Copper Mines* [1964] AC 948 at 959.

significant or relevant in those which are presently before it.

There are many cases wherein the distinction between income and capital has been at issue and the decisions have not always been consistent – which can hardly be unexpected given the absence of clear definitions or guidance. Indeed, Lord Sands has said in *Burmah Steamship Company Ltd v IRC*[23] that "some of the decisions may appear to be arbitrary", and, Sir Wilfred Greene MR said in *IRC v British Salmson Aero Engines Ltd*[24] that there have been many cases which fall on the borderline, and "in many cases it is almost true to say that the spin of a coin would decide the matter almost as satisfactorily as an attempt to find reasons." Presumably, judges are not in the habit of spinning coins to decide matters such as these, and so attempts have been made to rationalise the case law under a number of categories of consideration. The discussion that follows employs some of these categories as a foundation for its analysis.

1. Payments in lieu of trading receipts

Sometimes sums that a trader might normally expect to earn from his trade may fail to reach his hands due to the acts or omissions of others. In such cases the trader may have a cause of action against or some other right or entitlement to compensation from those others, as redress for the loss occasioned by the trader's failure to earn the sums that he would normally have earned. Where a trader receives such compensation payments in lieu of what would have fallen to be classified as receipts of his or her trade, the authorities have consistently held such payments to be of the same nature as the payments that they are replacing – in other words, income or revenue receipts, which will also be classified as trading receipts. The relevant principle was explained by Diplock LJ in *London and Thames Haven Oil Wharves Ltd v Attwooll*[25]

> Where, pursuant to a legal right, a trader receives from another person compensation for the trader's failure to receive a sum of money which, if it had been received, would have been credited to the amount of profits (if any) arising in any year from the trade carried on by him at the time when the compensation is so received, the compensation is to be treated for income tax purposes in the same way as that sum of money would have been treated if it had been received instead of the compensation.[26]

---

[23] 16 TC at page 73.
[24] (1938) 22 TC 29 at 43.
[25] (1966) 43 TC 491 at 515.
[26] For a similar principle in the USA see *Swastika Oil and Gas Co v CIR*, 123 F.2d. 382 at 384.

The principle of this statement was approved and applied by Lord Hoffmann in its entirety in *Deeny v Gooda Walker Ltd*.[27] It was also approved by Lord Browne-Wilkinson (the rest of their Lordships other than Lord Hoffmann concurring) in respect of the question "whether such compensation falls to be treated as income or capital of the taxpayer's trade".[28] However, Lord Browne-Wilkinson had some reservations about the applicability of the statement to the question whether the compensation was a receipt of the taxpayer's business.[29] According to Lord Browne-Wilkinson, in the ordinary run of cases the receipt of a sum by a trader as compensation for the failure to receive what would have been a receipt of his trade will normally demonstrate that the compensation is itself a receipt of that business. However he felt that "there may be unusual cases where the test propounded by Diplock LJ might not be appropriate to the correct determination of the question whether the compensation is a receipt of the taxpayer's business."[30]

In other words , the principle, as explained by Diplock LJ, is correct as a general principle, but it admits of exceptions, perhaps in relation to the question whether the compensation is a receipt of the business (i.e., with respect to the issue of causation). The Diplock principle applies, not only in respect of compensation for failure to receive a sum of money, but also to compensation for liability to pay a revenue expense.[31] It can be seen in operation in a long line of cases. For example, in *Gray v Lord Penrhyn*[32], two employees of the taxpayer trader had misappropriated money by falsifying the wages accounts over a number of years. The taxpayer's auditors admitted negligence on their part in not making certain inquiries and paid compensation of a sum equal to the misappropriated amounts to the taxpayer. Finlay J held that the compensation payment had to be treated as simply a business payment and a business receipt. In *London & Thames Haven Oil Wharves Ltd v Attwooll* itself, the taxpayer owned jetties for discharging oil from tankers. One of its jetties was damaged by the negligent handling of a tanker and was out of service for over one year. The tanker owners admitted liability and the taxpayer recovered from the owners and its insurers the cost of repairing jetty and compensation for the loss of use of the jetty during its repair. The combined compensation received exceeded the cost of repairing the jetty by some £21,000, which the Revenue sought to tax as a trading receipt. The compensation for the loss of profit was held to be taxable as a trading receipt. Willmer LJ said[33] that if there had been no collision, the profits which the taxpayer would have earned by the use of the jetty would plainly have been taxable as a trading receipt. He then wondered why the same should not apply to "the sum of money recovered from the wrongdoer in partial replacement of those profits". If

[27]   [1996] BTC 144 at 153.
[28]   See Lord Browne-Wilkinson at page 146.
[29]   ibid.
[30]   ibid; compare Lord Mustill, ibid.
[31]   See *Donald Fisher (Ealing) Ltd v Spencer* (1989) 63 TC 168; BTC 112 (CA); *Deeny v Gooda Walker Ltd* [1996] BTC 144.
[32]   (1937) 21 TC 252.
[33]   43 TC at page 507.

the taxpayer could escape tax in this type of case, Willmer LJ said that there would be "something very much wrong with the law, for the consequence would be that a jetty-owner, such as the taxpayer company, would be better off by being subjected to a casualty of this sort (that is, by losing the use of his jetty and recovering damages therefor) than he would be if he were able to use it continuously for the purpose of making profits"[34], which would be "a very strange result indeed."

These cases both involved payments agreed between the parties (no doubt to avoid costly litigation). However, the way in which the payment came to be made is not material. The principle can apply in respect of payments made after litigation, compromised or otherwise.[35] It also applies to statutory payments. This can be seen in a number of cases. First, *IRC v Newcastle Breweries Ltd.*[36] Here, the government requisitioned one-thirds of the total stock of raw rum belonging to the taxpayers who were wine and spirit merchants. Compensation was paid for the rum. The taxpayers argued that the compensation was not a profit from the their business at all, but was a sum payable by way of compensation for the compulsory taking by the Crown of a part of the their capital. The House of Lords disagreed and held that this must be treated as a sale of the rum and the fact that it was compulsory made no difference. Viscount Cave LC said[37]:

> It is true that the rum taken by the Crown had not been refined or blended and was not, therefore, in the state in which rum was usually sold by the Appellants; but it was rum which they had bought for the purposes of their business, and the cost of the rum was no doubt treated as an outgoing of the business. If the raw rum had been voluntarily sold to other traders, the price must clearly have come into the computation of the Appellants' profits, and the circumstance that the sale was compulsory and was to the Crown makes no difference in principle ... The transaction was a sale in the business, and although no doubt it affected the circulating capital of the Appellants it was none the less proper to be brought into their profit and loss account.

Similarly, in *Sutherland v IRC*[38] a steam-drifter used for herring fishing by the taxpayer was requisitioned by the Admiralty for hire. The taxpayer argued that his fishing industry was brought to an end by the intervention of the Admiralty and that the hiring by the Admiralty subsequently must be viewed as compensation to him for the stoppage of his business. The compensation (hire) payments were held to be trading receipts. The Lord

---

[34] ibid.
[35] See for example, *Roberts v WS Electronics Ltd* (1967) 44 TC 525; *Donald Fisher (Ealing) Ltd v Spencer* (1989) 63 TC 168;
[36] (1927) 12 TC 927.
[37] at page 953.
[38] (1918) 12 TC 63.

President (Strathclyde) said[39]:

> The Appellant acquired this ship, he acquired her as an instrument, or
> as ... a commercial asset, susceptible of being put to a variety of
> different uses in which gain might be acquired, and whichever of
> these uses it was put to by the Appellant and profits earned, he was
> carrying on the same business, even although alterations were
> necessary on the vessel for the changed purpose, provided that each
> of these uses was one for which she as a ship was adapted. It is true
> in a sense that fishing is a different industry from mine sweeping, or
> trading or patrolling, or watching a gap in a boom, or the like, but
> viewed form the standpoint of the ship-owner, they are the same
> business because in each his vessel, if she earns profits, is employed for
> gain. It is the same piece of machinery, or implement, or commercial
> asset which is used to acquire profit. In short the business is that of
> the employment of a ship for gain in ordinary ship owning business.

Finally, in *Lang v Rice*[40] the taxpayer ran cabaret clubs in Belfast which were
completely destroyed by bombs. The Northern Ireland Office paid
compensation for, *inter alia*, "consequential loss". This part of the
compensation was "confined to loss of net profit" in respect of a period of
about 18 months. The Court of Appeal in Northern Ireland held that this
was revenue payment because it was made in lieu of trading profits.

In fact, the principle that a payment in lieu of trading profits is income
and taxable as a trading receipt is applicable regardless of the source of the
legal right of the trader to recover the compensation. This was clearly
stated by Diplock LJ in *London & Thames Haven Oil Wharves Ltd v Attwooll*[41].

> It may arise from a primary obligation under a contract, such as a
> contract of insurance, from a secondary obligation arising out of
> non-performance of a contract, such as a right to damages, either
> liquidated, as under the demurrage clause in a charter-party, or
> unliquidated, from an obligation to pay damages for tort, as in the
> present case, from a statutory obligation, or in any other way in which
> legal obligations arise.[42]

In order to apply this principle to a particular case, it is necessary first to
identify what the compensation was paid for.[43] The answer to this question
also provides the answer to the question whether the compensation arose

---

[39] at pages 69-70.

[40] [1984] STC 172; 57 TC 80.

[41] 43 TC at page 515.

[42] Note however that payments under an insurance contract may sometimes be treated a capital receipts - see for example *Crabb v Blue Star Line* Ltd [1961] 2 ALL ER 424; 39 TC 482.

[43] Diplock LJ in *London & Thames Haven Oil Wharves Ltd v Attwooll* (ibid); compare Kerr LJ in *Donald Fisher (Ealing) Ltd v Spencer*, 63 TC at page 186.

out of the trade.[44] If the compensation was paid for the failure of the trader to receive a sum of money, then the question has to be asked whether, if that sum of money had been received by the trader, it would have been credited to the amount of profits (if any) arising in any year from the trade carried on by him at the date of receipt.[45] For these purposes, the method by which the compensation has been assessed in the particular case does not identify what it was paid for; it is no more than a factor which may assist in the solution of the problem of identification.[46] Lord Hoffmann put it slightly differently in *Deeny v Gooda Walker Ltd*[47].

> The fact that damages are computed by reference to income which could have been earned does not mean that they are compensation for the loss of that income. The income which might have been expected to be received may be merely an element in the valuation of a different asset or interest.[48]

2. Compensation for the sterilisation of assets

Sometimes a trader is prevented from using a business asset for the purpose of earning profits, because the asset has been damaged, destroyed or otherwise sterilised by the actions of others. Compensation may be received by the trader in respect of the damage to or the loss or destruction of his asset. In such cases (where a trader has received compensation for the sterilisation of business assets), the courts have normally held the compensation to be capital in nature.[49] In *Glenboig Union Fireclay Co Ltd v IRC*[50] the taxpayer manufactured fireclay goods and sold raw fireclay. They were lessees of some fireclay fields in the neighbourhood of the Caledonian Railway, some of which ran under the lines of the Railway. The Caledonian Railway, after some litigation, in exercise of a statutory power, and upon payment of compensation, required the taxpayer to leave part of the fireclay unworked. The compensation payment was calculated on the basis of projected lost profits. In this case, it was the taxpayer (rather than the Revenue) that was claiming that the compensation was a trading receipt. The House of Lords held that the compensation was not a profit earned in the course of the taxpayer's trade, but was a capital receipt, being a payment made for the sterilisation of a capital asset. The taxpayer had referred to the fact that the compensation was in fact assessed by considering that the fireclay to which it related could only be worked for some two and a-half years before it would be exhausted, and had argued

---

[44] Lord Hoffmann in *Deeny v Gooda Walker Ltd* [1996] BTC at page 153.
[45] Diplock LJ in *London & Thames Haven Oil Wharves Ltd v Attwooll*, ibid.
[46] ibid.
[47] [1996] BTC at page 153.
[48] Lord Hoffmann referred to *British Transport Commission v Gourley* ([1956] AC 185) and *Lewis v Daily Telegraph* ([1964] AC 234) as examples of the proof of this proposition. For a general discussion of the Gourley principle see G Dworkin [1967] BTR 315 and G Dworkin [1967] BTR 373.
[49] In the USA the principle has been stated in very strong terms. In *H. Liebes and Co v CIR* it was said that compensation for injury to capital "is never income" (90 F.2d. 932).
[50] (1922) 12 TC 427.

that the compensation therefore represented nothing more than the actual profit for two and a half years received in one lump sum. Lord Buckmaster[51] rejected that argument as fallacious. He said that the compensation was a sum paid to prevent the taxpayer from obtaining the full benefit of the capital value of that part of the mines which it was prevented from working by the railway company. He said that it made no difference whether it is regarded as a sale of the asset out and out, or whether it is treated merely as a means of preventing the acquisition of profit that would otherwise be gained – because in either case, the capital asset of the taxpayer has, to that extent, been sterilised and destroyed, and it was in respect of that action that the compensation was paid. Lord Buckmaster concluded[52]:

> It is unsound to consider the fact that the measure, adopted for the purpose of seeing what the total amount should be, was based on considering what are the profits that would have been earned. That, no doubt, is a perfectly exact and accurate way of determining the compensation, for it is now well settled that the compensation payable in such circumstances is the full value of the minerals that are to be left unworked, less the cost of working, and that is, of course, the profit that would be obtained were they in fact worked. But there is no relation between the measure that is used for the purpose of calculating a particular result and the quality of the figure that is arrived at by means of the application of that test. I am unable to regard this sum of money as anything but capital money.

Lord Wrenbury, concurring, said[53] that the answer to the question "was that compensation profit?" may be supplied by the answer to the question "Is a sum profit which is paid to an owner of property on the terms that he shall not use his property so as to make a profit?" He said that the answer must be in the negative. According to him, the whole point is that such an owner is not to make a profit and is paid for abstaining from seeking to make a profit. Lord Wrenbury presented[54] two ways of looking at the question, each of which pointed to a capital payment.

> The matter may be regarded from another point of view : the right to work the area in which the working was to be abandoned was part of the capital asset consisting of the right to work the whole area demised. Had the abandonment extended to the whole area all subsequent profit by working would, of course, have been impossible,

---

[51]   at page 463.
[52]   at pages 463-464.
[53]   at pages 465-466.
[54]   ibid.

but it would be impossible to contend that the compensation would be other than capital. It was the price paid for sterilising the asset from which otherwise profit might have been obtained. What is true of the whole must be equally true of part. Again, a further point of view is this: had the working not been interfered with, the profit by the working would have extended over, say, three years; it would have been an annual sum. The payment may be regarded as a redemption of that annuity. Is the redemption of an annuity itself an annuity? If the currency of the annuity had been, say, ten years, and the beneficiaries were A for three years and B for seven years, could A have claimed all the compensation money on the ground that it was income of the first year? Clearly not.

This case can be contrasted with *Burmah Steamship Company Ltd v IRC.*[55] The taxpayers bought a second-hand ship which they committed to repairers for overhaul. The repairers exceeded the contractual time for completion of the overhaul and the taxpayers recovered damages (calculated on the basis of estimated loss of profits) for the late delivery of the ship. Here, it was the taxpayers that were claiming that the compensation was not a receipt of their trade, because it did not arise out of any actual trading with the vessel. They claimed that, on the contrary, it arose out of the breach of a contract, the object of which was not trading, but rather the acquisition of a capital instrument of trade. The Court of Session held that the compensation was a trading receipt. The Lord President (Clyde) gave[56] the example of someone who chartered one of the taxpayers' vessels then breaching the charter, thereby exposing himself to a claim of damages. He said that in such a situation, there would be no doubt that the damages recovered would be regarded as a trading receipt, the reason being that the breach of the charter was an injury inflicted on the taxpayers' trading, making a "hole" in the profit. Thus the damages recovered could not therefore he reasonably or appropriately put by the taxpayer to any other purpose than to fill that "hole". He said that, if, on the other hand, one of the taxpayers' vessels was negligently run down and sunk by a vessel belonging to some other shipowner, and the taxpayers recovered as damages the value of the sunken vessel, there would be no doubt that the damages so recovered could not be regarded as a trading receipt, the reason being that the destruction of the vessel would be an injury inflicted, not on the taxpayers' trading, but on the capital assets of their trade, making a hole in those capital assets. The damages could therefore only be used to fill that hole.[57] What then was the position in this case? Lord Clyde said[58]:

---

[55] (1931) 16 TC 67.
[56] at page 71.
[57] at pages 71-72.
[58] at page 72.

Now in the present case, the injury inflicted on the Appellant by the repairers failure to make timeous delivery of the vessel is obviously not an injury to the Appellant's capital assets. Time sounds in money no doubt but the loss to the Appellant by the late delivery was in the form of loss of trading opportunities, not in the form of the loss of fixed capital ... it is very relevant to enquire whether the thing in respect of which the taxpayer has recovered damages or compensation is deprivation of one of the capital assets of his trading enterprise, or – short of that – a mere restriction of his trading opportunities.

It was stressed in both cases was that the measure by which the compensation is calculated is not the deciding factor – rather the crucial factor relates to the subject matter of the "injury" or damage. If the injury or damage occurs in respect of a capital asset so as to make a "hole" in that asset, compensation will be capital, since it will only go to fill the "hole" in the capital asset (i.e., to restore the capital asset, or to provide funds to replace it). If the injury or damage occurs in respect of trading opportunities, then compensation will be a receipt of the trade, filling, as it were, the hole in the trading opportunities. This all sounds straightforward enough. However, it would be a mistake to assume that the issue is so clear–cut that it can be expressed so definitively for all situations. It is not at all self-evident that a hole in a capital asset cannot by the same token constitute a hole in trading opportunities. In which case it has to be ascertained what exactly the compensation is paid for – the hole in the asset, or the hole in the trading opportunities, or both.

Finally, it is important to note that the asset in respect of which compensation is paid need not be tangible – for example in the American case of *Raytheon Production Corp. v CIR*[59] it was held that compensation awarded in an anti–trust action for loss of goodwill represents a return of capital.

3. Compensation for cancellation of business contracts

Where compensation is received in return for the premature termination of a business contract one might reasonably assume that the receipt is of an income nature – after all, businesses sell their goods and services by entering into contracts. However the matter is not as simple as that. It is possible for a contract to be so important to a business that it might be regarded as a capital asset of the business – in which case compensation for the termination of such a contract might well be of a capital nature. For a

---

[59]   144 F.2d. 110.

contract to be so regarded, it appears that it must be more than just a profit-earning contract. The contract must constitute, or contribute substantially to the provision of, the profit earning apparatus of the trade.

The leading case is *Van Den Berghs Ltd v Clark.*[60] In this case, the taxpayers entered into agreements with a Dutch company to regulate competition between them. The agreements detailed prices and areas of supply of margarine. They also provided for a sharing of profits, and for a management arrangement. A dispute arose and the agreements were eventually terminated on the understanding that the Dutch company would pay compensation of £450,000 to the taxpayers for the termination. The House of Lords held that the deal between the two companies was a capital asset, and the payment for its cancellation was capital. Lord Macmillan[61] noted that the taxpayers were giving up "their whole rights under the agreements for thirteen years ahead", and that the agreements which the taxpayers consented to cancel were not ordinary commercial contracts made in the course of carrying on their trade. Neither were they contracts for the disposal of their products, for the engagement of agents or other employees necessary for the conduct of their business, nor were they merely agreements as to how their trading profits when earned should be distributed as between the parties. Rather, the cancelled agreements related to the whole structure of the taxpayers' profit-making apparatus, regulated their activities, defined what they might and what they might not do, and affected the whole conduct of their business.[62] Lord Macmillan thus concluded[63]:

> The agreements formed the fixed framework within which their circulating capital operated; they were not incidental to the working of their profit-making machine but were essential parts of the mechanism itself. They provided the means of making profits, but they themselves did not yield profits. The profits of the Appellants arose from manufacturing and dealing in margarine.

A similar result was reached in *Barr Crombie & Co Ltd v IRC.*[64] The taxpayer company managed ships under certain agreements with a particular shipping company. About 98% of its business came from a 15 year agreement with this company. The shipping company went into liquidation about seven years into the agreement was, and the taxpayer company was paid compensation in respect of the eight years still to run before the expiry of the agreement. It was held that the compensation payment was capital and was not a trading receipt of the taxpayer company.

---

[60] (1935) 19 TC 390.
[61] at page 431.
[62] at pages 431-432.
[63] at page 432.
[64] (1945) 26 TC 406.

The Lord President (Normand) noted[65] that virtually the whole assets of the taxpayer company consisted in the cancelled agreement, and that, when the agreement was surrendered or abandoned, practically nothing remained of the taxpayer company's business. Thus this fell within the principle of *Van Den Berghs v Clark*.

As indicated earlier, this principle relates strictly to contracts affecting the whole structure of the taxpayer's trade. If a contract is an ordinary trading contract, payments for cancellation will be income, and will form part of the trading receipts. This principle can be seen in *Kelsall Parsons & Co v IRC*.[66] The taxpayers were manufacturers' agents who held a number of contracts for several manufacturers. They would arrange, under these contracts, to sell the manufacturers' products in return for a commission. One of the agency contracts, a three-year agreement, was terminated at the end of the second year, and the taxpayers received compensation amounting to £1,500 for the termination. The Court of Session held that the compensation was an income receipt from trading. The loss of one agency contract did not affect the profit making apparatus of the business. Such contracts were not part of the "fixed framework" of the taxpayers' business. Rather, it was a contract which was incidental to the normal course of their business – a business which was to obtain as many contracts of this kind as they could. Also important was the fact that the cancelled contract had only one year left to run.[67]

4. Compensation for restriction of activities

A sum of money might be received in return for foregoing or giving up business and trade opportunity or activity. If the restriction is substantial or results in removal of the profit-making apparatus (the "tree") then sums received in compensation will be capital. In *Higgs v Olivier*[68], Sir Laurence Olivier starred in the film *Henry V* and received a sum of £15,000 in return for agreeing that he would not, for a period of 18 months, appear as an actor in or act as producer or director of any film to be made anywhere by any other company. The Court of Appeal held that the sum of £15,000 was a capital receipt for a substantial restriction on the professional activities of the taxpayer. Sir Raymond Evershed MR said[69] that there is a true analogy between such an arrangement as that or between a sale of one of a trader's capital assets and a restrictive covenant of a substantial character entered into by a trader relating to trading. This was to be contrasted with a restriction of "a very limited or partial character". In this case, even though the taxpayer was still free to act upon the stage and to take broadcasting work, the restriction on him still took a "substantial piece" out of the ordinary scope of the professional activities which

---

[65]   at page 411.

[66]   (1938) 21 TC 608; see also *Rolfe v Nagel* (1981) 55 TC 585 (CA).

[67]   See generally, the Lord President (Normand) at page 621; Lord Fleming at page 622.

[68]   [1952] 1 Ch 311; 33 TC 136. Note that this case has been described as one which "depended on its own particular facts" (per Lord Cameron in *IRC v Biggar* (1982) 56 TC 254 at 274. Some doubt has also been cast on it ("the Court of Appeal held, rightly or wrongly") by Lord Browne-Wilkinson in *Deeny v Gooda Walker Ltd* [1996] BTC 144 at 146.

[69]   33 TC at page 146.

otherwise were open to him.[70] Since the agreement was "a restriction extending to a substantial portion of the professional activities which were open to" the taxpayer, the sum he that received for it could not properly be regarded as money which came to him from the ordinary course of the exercise of his profession. Singleton LJ said[71] that the money was not a profit or gain from the vocation of the taxpayer, but rather it was a payment for abstaining from his vocation.[72]

The crucial point in respect of this line of authority lies in the concept of "substantial restriction". Where an agreement is more regulatory than restrictive (for example, where it only determines the way in which a trader conducts his activities especially in a form in which it could be interpreted as an ordinary trading agreement), payments for the agreement may be income. For example, in *White v G & M Davies*[73] a farmer received an EEC subsidy for agreeing not to sell milk products and to restrict his dairy farming activities. Browne-Wilkinson J held that the subsidy represented trading income. It was a sum received for agreeing to work (trade) in a particular way. The facts also indicated that there was no substantial restriction on the farmer's activities. He could still farm the land, albeit not wholly for dairy farming purposes. Similarly, in *IRC v Biggar*[74] a farmer was paid some money under the EEC Dairy Herd Conversion Scheme for agreeing to switch from dairy farming to raising cattle for beef. The Court of Session, approving the decision of Browne-Wilkinson J in *White v G & M Davies*, held that the sum was a trading receipt. The Lord President (Emslie)[75] distinguished the case from *Higgs v Olivier*. He said that in *Higgs v Olivier*, Sir Laurence Olivier would, but for the restrictive covenant, have carried on acting in and producing and directing films as well as carrying on his vocation on the legitimate stage on radio and elsewhere. Thus the restriction which he accepted severely limited his ability to exploit his art and exposed him to inevitable loss. However, in the present case there was no question of there being a restriction of this kind which is capable of being equiparated with sterilisation of part of a taxpayer's capital assets.[76] According to Lord Emslie[77]:

> The Scheme was a conversion scheme in terms of which on the one hand the taxpayers agreed to stop producing milk and milk products and, on the other hand, to begin producing meat instead. They agreed, in short, to continue to farm to their full capacity. Only the product changed. There was no question, but for their entry into the

---

[70] Sir Raymond Evershed MR at page 147.

[71] at page 149.

[72] See also *Murray v ICI* [1967] 2 All ER 980 (CA) - payments in return for "keep out" agreements (agreements not to trade in specific countries) were capital.

[73] [1979] STC 415; 52 TC 597.

[74] (1982) 56 TC 254.

[75] at page 264.

[76] ibid.

[77] at pages 264-265.

Scheme, of the taxpayers producing both milk and meat and in any event there was no question of their being able to farm to better advantage. The Scheme itself recognised that those who entered it should not suffer, as a result of changing their product, any appreciable reduction in their income, and so far as the Case discloses, the taxpayers' entry to the Scheme exposed them to no loss of any kind. Their capital assets were not, in any sense, sterilised. They sold one herd (at a profit) and replaced it with another.

Finally, in *Thompson v Magnesium Elektron Ltd*[78] the taxpayers used chlorine in the production of magnesium. They were also able to produce caustic soda, a by-product of the use of chlorine. ICI then agreed to supply chlorine to the taxpayer at below market price in return for the taxpayer agreeing not to produce its own chlorine and caustic soda. ICI also paid a sum to the taxpayer to reflect the loss of caustic soda sales that the taxpayer was likely to suffer. ICI wished to protect its own market position in the production and sales of caustic soda. The Court of Appeal held that the payment was trading income representing the loss of trading profit on the sale of caustic soda. The agreement with ICI was simply a trading arrangement for the supply of chlorine.[79]

5. Sale of information or know-how

Statute has been introduced to deal with this type of receipt. Previously case law had suggested that if a trader disposed of a patent or know-how the sum received would be trade income unless the disposal was part of the disposal of a business interest and assets in a distinct area, normally a foreign country. The latter disposal would be one of capital (in part).[80] TA 1988 ss.530-531 now provide that the receipts from the sale of know how will be treated as trading income[81] unless the sale is consequent on the sale of the business entity, in which case it will then be treated as a capital receipt[82] - although even here the taxpayer can elect to treat the sum received as an income receipt.[83]

Other Factors Affecting Trading Receipts

We have so far been concerned primarily with the question whether a sum received by a taxpayer has the character of income or capital. As we have seen, this question can be (and is often) determinative of another question - whether the payment is a receipt of the taxpayer's business. This

---

[78]   [1944] 1 All ER 126; 26 TC 1.
[79]   See Lord Greene MR, 26 TC at page 11.
[80]   See *Evans Medical Supplies Ltd v Moriarty* [1957] 3 All ER 718.
[81]   S.531(1).
[82]   S.531(2).
[83]   S.531(3).

particular issue sometimes concerns the question whether the sum is really one that arises from the taxpayer's trade, or whether it derives from something else. In other words, it often raises the question of causation – for if a sum coming into a trader's hands is caused to come into his hands by something other than the business in which the trader is engaged, the sum, whatever its character, may not be a receipt of that business. As indicated earlier, this question is quite often linked inextricably with the question whether the sum is income or capital. However, for present purposes (and for convenience) we have herein treated these questions in different sections. In the remaining part of this chapter, we will examine the issue of causation, followed by an analysis of other factors that may fall to be taken into account in deciding whether a sum is a receipt of the taxpayer's trade.

1. Voluntary receipts

This point concerns a question of causation. Not only must sums alleged to be trading receipts be of an income or revenue nature, they must also be derived from the trade.[84] Thus, voluntary payments (even from present or past trading customers) are usually not trading receipts because there is often no causal link between the trade and the payment. For example, if a farmer meets a stranger on the road who then proceeds to give the farmer £20, this sum, regardless of whether it is considered to be income or capital, is not a receipt of the farmer's trade because of the absence of a causal link between the gift and the farming business. Now, supposing that the benefactor is not a stranger at all, but rather a former customer of the farmer. This would not change the character of the gift unless the money amounts to a late payment for goods or services already delivered. Now, supposing that the benefactor is not a former customer, but is rather a current customer. Again, unless the sum is remuneration for goods or services supplied by the farmer in the course of his farming business, there would still be no causal link which would turn the money into a receipt of the farming business. In other words, it is necessary to distinguish between a gift and a profit of the trade. [85]

The issue of voluntary payments has been addressed in a number of cases and we can glean a number of principles from these cases. First, *Walker v Carnaby Harrower et al*.[86] A firm of accountants had been auditors to a group of companies for some years. As a result of a group reorganization, the taxpayers were asked not to seek reappointment as auditors. The firm later received an unsolicited ex-gratia payment of an amount equal to their last fees "as solatium for the loss of the office of auditors". That sum was not a

---

[84] See generally D R Davies [1979] BTR 212.

[85] In the American case of *Connor v State*, 2 NW.2d. 852, it was held that in the absence of any provision to the contrary in a statute imposing tax on incomes, ordinarily, a gift of money or property is not income of the donee so as to be subject to taxation. See also *Miller v Wisconsin Dept. of Taxation*, 299 NW 28.

[86] [1970] 1 All ER 502; 46 TC 561.

gift to any individual partner. It was held that the sum was not a trading receipt. Pennycuick J explained the decision[87].

> At the end of their final term of office they had no legal claim of any description to receive any further payment from the companies. The companies then proceeded to make a wholly voluntary payment to the Respondent firm. It is, I think, irrelevant that the companies elected to make that payment in an amount identical to a penny with the fees paid to the firm during their last year of office. It seems to me that a gift of that kind made by a former client cannot reasonably be treated as a receipt of a business which consists in rendering professional services. The subject-matter of the assessment under Cases I and II is the full amount of the profits or gains of the trade or profession. Those profits have to be computed, it is well established, upon ordinary commercial principles. It does not seem to me that ordinary commercial principles require the bringing into account of this sort of voluntary payment, not made as the consideration for any services rendered by the firm, but by way of recognition of past services or by way of consolation for the termination of a contract. It is difficult to amplify the point any further.

A similar result was reached in *Simpson v John Reynolds & Co Insurance Ltd*.[88] The taxpayers were a firm of insurance brokers. When one of their longstanding clients was acquired by a public company, the client was required by the new owners to place all its insurance with one particular insurance group. The client then made a voluntary payment to the taxpayers, in recognition of the long period during which the taxpayers had acted as its broker and adviser on insurance matters. The Court of Appeal held that the payment was not a trading receipt. It was accepted by all the three judges in the Court that that the mere fact that the payment was made voluntarily is not of itself decisive of the question. However, the fact that the payment was voluntary, coupled with the facts that it was made after the business relationship had terminated[89], that it was wholly unexpected[90], "came out of the blue",[91] was not made by way of additional reward for any particular service rendered by the brokers or for their services generally,[92] was made in recognition of past services rendered to the client company over a long period, though not because those past services were considered to have been inadequately remunerated,[93] was made as a consolation for the fact that those remunerative services were no longer to be performed by the taxpayer for the donor[94], and the fact that

[87] 46 TC at pages 572-573.
[88] (1975) 49 TC 693.
[89] See Russell LJ at page 712; Stamp LJ at page 713.
[90] per Russell LJ at page 712.
[91] per Stamp LJ at page 713.
[92] ibid.
[93] Russell LJ at page 712.
[94] ibid.

there was no suggestion that at a future date the business connection might be renewed[95], all made it plain that this was not a trading receipt. Walton J captured the spirit of the decision, saying[96]:

> But when a payment is made purely voluntarily, on the termination of a trading relationship, that termination being so far as the parties can possibly foresee a permanent termination, and is made for no other reason than that the party making the payment is sorry that the relationship has had to terminate, and is grateful for the excellent service which the payee has given to it over a very long period of years, then it appears to me quite clear that the payment does not arise or accrue to the payee by reason of any trade carried on by it.[97]

In *Simpson*, the point was made that voluntariness does not stop a payment being a trading receipt. In *IRC v Falkirk Ice Rink Ltd*[98] the Lord President (Emslie) said that the fact that a payment was voluntary is "neutral". In this case the taxpayer company operated an ice rink on a commercial basis and provided curling facilities to the public. The income from curling did not cover the cost of providing ice of the quality that was required. A members' club which made use of facilities provided by the taxpayers made a donation to it in order to cover the additional cost of the curling and to enable it to continue to provide curling facilities in future. The payment was held to be a trading receipt. Lord Emslie said[99] that the payment was made in order that the taxpayer company might use it in its business, and that in substance and in form, it was a payment made to a trading company, artificially to supplement its trading revenue from curling, in the interests of the club and its members, to preserve the taxpayer company's ability to continue to provide curling facilities in the future. "In its quality and nature this payment was of a business nature."[100]

In *McGowan v Brown & Cousins*[101], another case in which a voluntary payment was held to be a trading receipt, Templeman J reviewed the authorities and put together some principles which we may be able to apply in reconciling the two lines of authority. The taxpayers in this case were estate agents who had acted for a company in connection with the acquisition of a site for development. The fee which they were paid for this work was acknowledged to be quite low for the work involved, but the taxpayers were prepared to accept the low fee because of a custom that the same agents would be engaged to sell the houses when they were eventually developed (this was a much more lucrative work). The site was eventually bought by another company which made an *ex gratia* payment

---

[95] ibid.
[96] at page 714.
[97] See also *Murray v Goodhews* [1978] 2 All ER 40; (1977) 52 TC 86.
[98] (1975) 51 TC 42 at 49; noted by P Skitmore [1978] BTR 250.
[99] at pages 49-50.
[100] at page 50.
[101] (1977) 52 TC 8.

to the taxpayers to compensate them for not using their services again. It was held that the sum was a trading receipt. It was a reward for services even though it was paid in pursuance of a moral rather than a legal obligation. In an enlightening passage Templeman J said[102]:

> [I]t seems to me that the broad line of distinction so far as taxability on this kind of voluntary gift is concerned, is a distinction which takes its origin in the question of whether the payment is attributable to specific work carried out by the recipient. If work is carried out then the payment, although voluntary, is made because payment has been earned. If the payment does not relate to specific past work then the payment is made, not because payment has been earned by work, but because the payment is intended for a deserving recipient. If the payment relates to work then, although the recipient may not be legally entitled, yet if he has a moral claim the payment is a receipt by him and a profit of his trade. When the payment is earned by work which has not been paid for or has not been adequately paid for then the payment has the quality of an income receipt liable to tax. On the other hand, if payment is not earned but is deserved, it is not income. If the recipient has been paid in full for past work, but the person making the gift wishes to acknowledge the past conduct of the recipient or to give some token of regret at the termination of a business association and to acknowledge the fact that this termination of business association will not be entirely welcome to the recipient either for financial or other reasons, the payment is not earned but is deserved. It is not taxable ... In determining whether a gift is earned and therefore taxable, or deserved and therefore not taxable, the test seems to me to be to enquire whether the gift can be referred to the work of the recipient or whether it can be referred to the conduct of the recipient.

2. Unclaimed balances and deposits

Most people are probably familiar with the marketing strategy whereby traders endeavour to extract a commitment from potential customers who appear to be interested to purchase certain goods or services, by requesting a "deposit". This type of sales strategy is common in the furniture and household goods, holiday, and travel industries. Typically, the potential customer is encouraged to "reserve" the relevant goods or services by making a "down payment", the full price to be paid later. The assumption is that, after making such a financial commitment, the customer is unlikely

---

[102] at pages 15-16.

to want to lose the deposit by not completing the transaction. Also, we might be familiar with the concept of appointing agents to sell goods and services. The agent takes a commission and pays the balance to the vendor. This practice is commonplace, indeed, normal, in the property and auctioneering industries. The question then arises as to what happens if the potential customer fails to take delivery of the goods and does not bother to claim the deposit back, or, if a vendor fails to claim the proceeds of sale from the agent appointed to sell the goods or service. If the trader later appropriates the funds, are they trading receipts?

The authorities indicate that the matter is decided by the nature of the money at the time of receipt. This was the principle applied in *Morley v Tattersall*.[103] The taxpayers were a firm of horse auctioneers. Some of the sums which they received from sales of horses on behalf of vendors were never collected by the vendors and were subsequently distributed among the partners of the firm. The Court of Appeal held that these sums were not trading receipts of the firm. According to Sir Wilfred Greene MR[104]:

> The money which was received was money which had not got any profit-making quality about it; it was money which, in a business sense, was the client's money and nobody else's. It was money for which they were liable to account to the client, and the fact that they paid it into their own account, as they clearly did, and the fact that it remained among their assets until paid out do not alter that circumstance ... It seems to me that the quality and nature of a receipt for income tax purposes is fixed once and for all when it is received.

So the question is "whose money is the money at the time of receipt"? Obviously in the case of someone selling goods on behalf of another, the money belongs to the owner of the goods. However, this principle is not so easily applied to other situations. This is particularly so in the case of advances or deposits. This issue was confronted in *Smart v Lincolnshire Sugar Company Ltd*.[105] In this case, statutory advances were made by the government to some sugar manufacturing companies, subject to repayment in certain prescribed conditions. The taxpayer company was one of such companies, and the question was whether these advances were trading receipts. The House of Lords held that they were – and that they were trading receipts of the year of receipt and not of the year in which the contingency of repayment ceased. Lord Macmillan said[106] that the decisive factor was the fact that the payments were made to the taxpayer company, "in order that the money might be used in their business." They

---

[103] (1938) 22 TC 51.
[104] at page 65.
[105] (1937) 20 TC 643.
[106] at page 670.

were intended artificially to supplement the company's trading receipts so as to enable them to maintain their trading solvency. According to him[107]:

> In the year with which your Lordships are concerned ... "advances" were received by the Company which were intended to be used and could properly have been used to meet their current trading obligations, and in that year the contingency of possible repayment did not in fact arise.

It therefore seems that the relevant question in these cases concerns the purpose for which the payment was made. If the money was paid so that it would be used in the taxpayer's trade, then this would point to a trading receipt – even if it was repayable.

The principles of both cases were applied applied in *Elson v Prices Tailors Ltd.*[108] The taxpayers carried on business as tailors. They normally took deposits from customers who ordered made-to-measure garments. These deposits would normally be returned to customers who were dissatisfied with the garments. However, the garments and deposits were sometimes not collected. In such cases, the deposits were transferred to a separate account. About 5% of the deposits to transferred were subsequently refunded to the customers, and the question was whether the ones that were never claimed at all were trading receipts. Ungoed-Thomas J held that the deposits on the facts were irrecoverable by the customers even if the taxpayers would normally refund them. He said[109] that the Lord Macmillan's statement in *Smart v Lincolnshire Sugar Company Ltd* applied, "with the possible qualification that they were not in this case strictly paid in order to be used in the Company's business but subject to the consequence that they would be so used – but nothing turns on that distinction." In this case, the deposits became the property of the taxpayer at the time of payment, and were therefore trading receipts.

It is well enough to say that sums paid so that they would be used in the taxpayer's trade thereby become trading receipts. Nothing is made of the point of what would be the position if the taxpayer subsequently pays the money back. Would this then be a trading expense or loss?[110]

In *Morley v Tattersall Ltd*, Sir Wilfred Greene MR indicated that the nature and quality of a payment is "fixed once and for all" when it is made. While this may be so under normal circumstances, it is important to note that the nature and quality may change subsequently by some event, or by operation of law. Sir Wilfred Greene MR himself contemplated this possibility, when, referring to some of the arguments of the Revenue in

---

[107] at page 671.
[108] (1963) 40 TC 671.
[109] at page 679.
[110] Perhaps the best solution is to pay the money into a "suspense account", and not bring them into the annual trading account, until such a time (if any) as the contingency of repayment ceases to exist (see Atkinson J in *Jay's - The Jewellers v IRC*, (1947) 29 TC 274 at 286).

the case, he said[111]:

> It was essential, of course, for the argument, to discover some act of
> receipt within the Income Tax year for which the assessment was
> made, and, in order to get an act of receipt, the metaphorical
> expressions were used such as I have described, the holding in a new
> capacity of something which the partners had previously held in a
> different capacity, the turning into a trading asset of something which
> had previously not been a trading asset, and things of that kind,
> which, if they accurately represented the facts, might form some basis
> for an argument that, at the moment when they took place, a receipt
> had taken place.

An example of changes in the quality of a payment by operation of law
can be seen in *Jay's The Jewellers v IRC.*[112] The taxpayers were jewellers and
pawn brokers. In the course of their pawnbroking business, they sold
unredeemed pledges. Under the Pawn Brokers Act 1872, pledgers were
entitled, within three years, to demand any surpluses of sale proceeds over
the amounts due to the pawnbroker. For various reasons, in practice, the
greater part of surpluses in respect of the sales of the unredeemed pledges
were never demanded, and ultimately they became in fact the property of
the pawnbroker. The question in the case was whether these unclaimed
surpluses were trading receipts. Atkinson J held that the surpluses were not
trading receipts in the year in which they were received, because that
point was governed completely by *Morley v Tattersall.* According to him,[113] "as
a matter of law, these monies when received were not their monies at all;
they belonged to their clients, and if a client came in the next day and
demanded his money they would have to pay it away." However,
something important happened at the end of the three-year period
specified in the 1872 Act.

> [A]t the end of three years, the money in question, the
> three-years-old surplus, did attain a totally different quality; a different
> quality was imprinted on surpluses three years old. I think there was
> then a definite trade receipt. At the end of the three years a new asset
> came into existence, an asset which had arisen out of a trade
> transaction ...[114]

Thus, from that point, the sums, which were then irrecoverable by the

---

[111] 22 TC at page 67.
[112] (1947) 29 TC 274.
[113] at page 285.
[114] at page 287.

pledgers, became the pawnbrokers' property, and thereby became trading receipts of the year.

3. Released debts

This point relates to those situations in which a trader has claimed and received some tax relief in respect of a debt owed by the trade, and the debt is subsequently released in whole or part by the creditor. In the USA a release or cancellation of indebtedness may result in taxable income.[115] A similar principle applies to a discharge of a debt or other obligation.[116] It has however been held that, in order for cancellation of indebtedness to result in taxable income on the theory that assets are thereby freed for the debtor's general use, the obligation to be returned must be one which unconditionally subjects the obligor's assets to liability for payment of a fixed amount.[117] It seems that, where the debtor taxpayer is in financial trouble so that the release of part of a debt is to allow the taxpayer to pay the balance[118], or where the debtor is insolvent[119], then the released debt is not taxable.

In the UK the amount of a released debt is always taxable as a trading receipt, as the situation is governed by a specific statutory provision. The relevant provision is in TA 1988, s.94(1), which provides:

> Where, in computing for tax purposes the profits or gains of a trade, profession or vocation, a deduction has been allowed for any debt incurred for the purpose of the trade, profession or vocation, then, if the whole or any part of the debt is thereafter released otherwise than as part of a relevant arrangement or compromise, the amount released shall be treated as a receipt of the trade, profession or vocation arising in the period in which the release is affected.

For this purpose, "relevant arrangement or compromise" has the same meaning as in TA 1988, s.74.[120]

4. Watson Bros. v Hornby[121]

This case is one of the exceptions to the principle that a person cannot trade with himself or herself. It established the principle that, where one trader has two distinct trades and transfers goods from one trade to the other, that transfer must be treated as a sale and purchase at a "reasonable price". The taxpayers in the case had a farm from which they carried on

---

[115] *Clarke v State*, 51 So.2d. 882; *Helvering v A. L. Killian Co.*, 128 F.2d. 433 at 434.
[116] *Commr. of Corporations and Taxation v Williston*, 54 NE.2d. 43.
[117] *Corporacion de Ventas de Salitre Y Yoda de Chile v CIR*, 130 F.2d., 141 at 143.
[118] *Burnett v John F. Campbell*, 50 F.2d. 487 at 488.
[119] *CIR v Simmons Gin Co.*, 43 F.2d. 327 at 329.
[120] S.94(2). By s.74(2), the term refers to certain voluntary arrangements under the insolvency legislations, and to arrangements and compromises under the companies legislations.
[121] [1942] 2 All ER 506; 24 TC 506; approved by the House of Lords in *Sharkey v Wernher* [1955] 3 All ER 493; 36 TC 275.

the business of poultry dealers and breeders. They also ran a chicken hatchery for selling day-old chicks. They transferred some of the stock from the hatchery to the farm. The cost of producing saleable day-old chicks was more than the market value of the chicks at the time of the transfer. They succeeded in establishing a trading loss. MacNaghten J thus explained the decision[122]:

> The question now before the Court is: What is the price at which the chicks should be deemed to have been bought by the farm from the hatchery? The Appellants are the proprietors of both the hatchery and the farm and it is said that a person cannot trade with himself. That, no doubt, is quite true; but for the present purpose it is, I think, necessary to regard the hatchery and the farm as separate entities. Where one person buys goods from another but the contract of sale does not specify the price to be paid, the contract is, nevertheless, valid and enforceable. The law provided that the purchaser must pay a reasonable price ... The cost of the production of an article, whether it is a day-old chick or anything else, might no doubt happen to be its reasonable price, but there is no ground for saying that in the absence of any agreement it should be taken as the reasonable price. On the contrary, the market price would as a general rule be the reasonable price.

5. *Sharkey v Wernher*[123]

This case presents another exception to the principle that one cannot trade with oneself. The case establishes the principle that where a trader appropriates part of his or her trading stock for personal use, this must be brought into account at market value as a trading receipt. In the case, Lady Wernher transferred five horses from her business of a stud farm to her racing stables, which she kept for purely recreational purposes. The cost of breeding the horses had been debited in the stud farm accounts. In accordance with accounting practice, the transfer was entered into her accounts at cost price, thereby cancelling the initial entry of cost price of the stock in trade. The insertion of cost price would mean that the business would be in a no-gain, no-loss situation. The initial expense of cost would be offset by the credit of a transfer at cost. The Revenue successfully claimed that "cost price" was not the correct figure for such a transfer, and that "market value" was better economics and would present a fairer measure of assessable profits. Viscount Simonds confirmed the general proposition that one cannot trade with oneself, but said that this did not

---

[122] 24 TC at pages 509-510.
[123] [1955] 3 All ER 493; 36 TC 275.

mean that "a man cannot make a profit out of himself".[124] According to Viscount Simonds,[125] once it is admitted or determined that an article forms part of the stock-in-trade of the trader, and that upon his parting with it so that it no longer forms part of his stock-in-trade, some sum must appear in his trading account as having been received in respect of it, the only logical way to treat it is to regard it as having been disposed of by way of trade, at its market value. Lord Radcliffe explained[126] that there were three possible methods of resolving the question. First, there might be no entry of a receipt at all. This method would be commended by the logic that nothing in fact is received in consideration of the transfer, and there is no general principle of taxation that assesses a person on the basis of business profits that he might have made but has not chosen to make. However, it would give an unfair advantage to the self-supplier. Secondly, a figure might be brought in at cost, and thirdly, a figure might be brought it at market value. His preference was thus expressed[127]:

> In a situation where everything is to some extent fictitious, I think that we should prefer the third alternative of entering as a receipt a figure equivalent to the current realisable value of the stock item transferred ... The realisable value figure is neither more nor less "real" than the cost figure, and in my opinion it is to be preferred for two reasons. First, it gives a fairer measure of assessable trading profit as between one taxpayer and another, for it eliminates variations which are due to no other cause than any one taxpayer's decision as to what proportion of his total product he will supply to himself. A formula which achieves this makes for a more equitable distribution of the burden of tax, and is to be preferred on that account. Secondly, it seems to me better economics to credit the trading owner with the current realisable value of any stock which he has chosen to dispose of without commercial disposal than to credit him with an amount equivalent to the accumulated expenses in respect of that stock. In that sense, the trader's choice is itself the receipt, in that he appropriates value to himself or his donee direct, instead of adopting the alternative method of a commercial sale and subsequent appropriation of the proceeds.

Sharkey v Wernher has not been accepted without criticism. It has been suggested that the reasoning in the case conflicts with established principles of mutuality, with the existence of statutory transfer pricing rules, and with the principle that one should be taxed on what one receives not on what one could or might have received.[128] However, the

---

[124] 36 TC at page 296, 298.
[125] at page 299.
[126] at page 306.
[127] at page 307.
[128] See Simon's Tiley and Collison: "UK Tax Guide 2000-2001", para. 7:153. For further comment on the decision see Potter [1964] BTR 438.

rule is now well established. It also applies to all disposals of trading stock otherwise than in the course of trade, e.g., by gift to members of the trader's family, or friends. This was clearly established in *Petrotim Securities Ltd v Ayres*.[129] In this case, the taxpayer company, a dealer in securities, sold (in transactions described by Lord Denning MR as "somewhat surprising") some securities to an associated company at a gross undervalue (this transaction was labelled the "X" transactions in the case). The Court of Appeal held that these X transactions were not in the normal course of trade, that the figures should be disregarded for tax purposes, and that a market value should be substituted. Lord Denning MR referred[130] to *Sharkey v Wernher*, and said that it is not confined to cases where a person is a "self-supplier". According to him, "it applies to any case where a trader may, for no reason, choose to give things away or throw them into the sea". So, when a trader "puts securities through his books at a derisory price, the figures are to be regarded as struck out for tax purposes; and in their place you must put in the market realisable value at the time."[131] Lord Denning MR subsequently explained fully the scope of this rule in *Mason v Innes*[132].

> I start with the elementary principle of income tax law that a man cannot be taxed on profits that he might have, but has not, made ... in the case of a trader there is an exception to that principle. I take for simplicity the trade of a grocer. He makes out his accounts on an "earnings basis". He brings in the value of his stock-in-trade at the beginning and end of the year; he brings in his purchases and sales; the debts owed by him and to him; and so arrives at his profit or loss. If such a trader appropriates to himself part of his stock-in-trade, such as tins of beans, and uses them for his own purposes, he must bring them into his accounts at their market value. A trader who supplies himself is accountable for the market value. That is established by *Sharkey v Wernher* itself. Now, suppose that such a trader does not supply himself with tins of beans, but gives them away to a friend or relative. Again he has to bring them in at their market value.[133]

The rule in *Sharkey v Wernher*, itself being an exception to the principle that one cannot trade with oneself, is subject to exceptions. The exceptions or limits of the rule themselves raise questions. The first limit or exception to note is that the rule is limited to Schedule D, and, perhaps even to Case I of Schedule D. Thus it would be possible to confer benefits on oneself in relation to activities within other Schedules (perhaps rent free accommodation under Schedule A) without fear of *Sharkey v Wernher*

---

[129] [1964] 1 WLR 190; (1963) 41 TC 389.
[130] 41 TC at page 407.
[131] ibid. See also *Ridge Securities v IRC* [1964] 1 All ER 275; 44 TC 373; *Skinner v Berry Head Lands Ltd* (1960) 46 TC 377.
[132] [1967] 2 All ER 926; 44 TC 326.
[133] 44 TC at page 339.

attributing a market value to that transaction. The suggestion that the rule in *Sharkey v Wernher* might be confined to Case I of Schedule D arises out of *Mason v Innes* (above). In this case Hammond Innes, a famous author, had written a book called "The Doomed Oasis", and had incurred and deducted travelling expenses to and from the Persian Gulf in obtaining background material used in the book. He then assigned the copyright to his father by way of a gift. The market value of the copyright was around £15,400. The Revenue claimed that, under the rule in *Sharkey v Wernher*, the market value of the copyright was a receipt of the taxpayer's profession. Their contention was that liability to tax does not, and should not, depend on the way in which a man keeps his accounts. Thus there is no difference in principle between a trader and a professional person. They argued that the appropriation of an asset, which has been produced in the ordinary course of a trade or profession, to the trader's or professional man's own purposes amounts to a realisation of that asset or the receipt of its value, and the taxpayer must bring it into account. It was held that the rule in *Sharkey v Wernher* did not apply. Lord Denning MR emphasised that the nature of a profession and the nature of a trade were very different, in that traders do have stock in trade but professional people normally do not.[134] He also emphasised that, in *Sharkey v Wernher* the accounts were presented on an earnings basis, whereas in *Mason v Innes* the accounts were presented on a cash basis.[135] Lord Denning MR, rejecting the Revenue's arguments highlighted above, said[136]:

> Suppose an artist paints a picture of his mother and gives it to her. He does not receive a penny for it. Is he to pay tax on the value of it? It is unthinkable. Suppose be paints a picture which he does not like when he has finished it and destroys it. Is he liable to pay tax on the value of it? Clearly not. These instances – and they could be extended endlessly show that the proposition in *Sharkey v Wernher* does not apply to professional men. It is confined to the case of traders who keep stock-in-trade and whose accounts are, or should be, kept on an earnings basis, whereas a professional man comes within the general principle that when nothing is received there is nothing to be brought into account.

The result was that, at the end of the day, Hammond Innes was able to enjoy the benefits of the deductible expenses in relation to the production of "The Doomed Oasis", and to confer the benefits of future sales to his father.

---

[134] 44 TC at page 339.
[135] ibid.
[136] ibid.

There are number of possible approaches to the interpretation of this decision. On one hand, one may focus on the distinctions, highlighted in the case, between trades and professions, and take view that the discussion on that point is sufficient to indicate that *Mason v Innes* clearly establishes that *Sharkey v Wernher* has no role to play in respect of professions. This approach is clear from the statement of Lord Denning MR, above. Another possible and closely linked interpretation is that the case simply highlights that *Sharkey v Wernher* is concerned only with goods - particularly, the value of the goods which it is a person's business to sell. Thus when a person is selling skills rather than goods, a principle developed in respect of the value of goods has no application. In this context it is useful to note the statement of Russell LJ that the copyright and other rights in the book in question in no sense formed stock-in-trade of Mr Innes, and that before the assignment to his father they had no part in any computation of profits and gains.[137] These two interpretations converge in the concept that traders sell their goods and professionals sell their skills.

A third possible interpretation of *Mason v Innes* is one that focuses on the manner and method of presentation of accounts. One could view *Sharkey v Wernher* as simply establishing that the correct manner of accounting for transfers "other than for trading purposes", is, when accounts are presented on an earnings basis, to enter market values of the transferred items. Thus, the accounting practice employed by Lady Wernher was tested and declared to be wrong. On that interpretation, *Sharkey v Wernher* was not saying anything about the correct practice in relation to accounts presented on a cash basis (such as was the case in *Mason v Innes*). The court in *Mason v Innes* was correct therefore in refusing to regard itself bound by the decision in *Sharkey v Wernher*.[138] This approach can also be supported from the judgment of Lord Denning MR.[139]

The third approach should probably be avoided even though the point being made therein is clear and sensible. The problem with it is that a sum of money is, by its nature, and in principle, either a trading receipt or not. The same sum cannot sensibly be a trading receipt given one accounting method, and not a trading receipt given a different accounting method. The issue is not one of quantum or calculation but of principle. The sense of the first approach is also clear – but just to say that trades are different from professions is to state the obvious and does not necessarily help to clarify why *Sharkey* should not apply to professions. Thus the second interpretation (i.e., focusing on the notion of what it is the taxpayer's business to sell – goods or skills) is preferable.

A further limitation to the rule in *Sharkey v Wernher* is that it does not apply to a *bona fide* commercial transaction, even if that transaction

---

[137] at page 341.
[138] See generally, Potter [1964] BTR 483.
[139] Compare Davies LJ at page 341; Russell LJ, ibid.

represents a "bad bargain" in terms of a sale at below market value. This principle emerges from *Jacgilden (Weston Hall) Ltd v Castle*.[140] Here, one Mr Rowe, a property developer, agreed to buy an hotel for £72,000. He later transferred the right to buy the hotel at this price to a company formed for that purpose, the shareholders of which were he and his wife. Accordingly, the hotel was conveyed by the vendors to the company, at Mr Rowe's direction, for the price of £72,000. At the time of the conveyance to the company, the hotel was worth £150,000. The company subsequently sold the hotel for £155,000, and was wound up. The Special Commissioners found that the deal between Mr Rowe and the vendors of the hotel was a genuine commercial deal. The question was the amount that should be entered into the company's books as the purchase price of the hotel. The company contended that, under *Sharkey v Wernher*, the market value at the time of the transfer of the right to buy the hotel (i.e., £150,000) should be used rather than the actual price paid (£72,000). This would have the effect of reducing the company's profits for tax purposes. Plowman J rejected the company's argument and held that the true purchase price should be entered. Plowman J[141] distinguished *Sharkey v Wernher*. First, that case, the court was concerned there with a disposal of property and not an acquisition, and therefore the question was what figure was to be credited, not debited, in the trading account. Also, in *Sharkey v Wernher*, there was a finding that the property in question was not sold or otherwise disposed of by way of trade, whereas in the present case there was a finding that the acquisition of the hotel was a commercial acquisition. Plowman J said[142] that the Commissioners were entitled to conclude, as a matter of business common sense and notwithstanding any element of gift there may have been, that the transaction with which they were concerned was not a gift or a sale by Mr Rowe to the company at an undervalue, but a purchase by the company of trading stock at a price which had been fairly negotiated between Mr Rowe and the vendors. He also said that the *Sharkey v Wernher* line of authority has never, been applied to a case where the price at which the property passed had been negotiated as a fair and proper price, and "because it is an exceptional line of authority I think that the Court should be slow to extend it."[143]

It is not clear from this case what point Plowman J was trying to make of the fact that *Sharkey v Wernher* involved a disposal, while this case involved an acquisition. Plowman J clearly indicated that this was a factor that distinguished the present case from *Sharkey v Wernher*. However, it is not entirely clear whether he was also trying to establish another exception to the *Sharkey v Wernher* principle. Such a rule, if introduced, would raise serious questions, and would also go against the decision of Pennycuick J

[140] [1969] 3 All ER 1110; 45 TC 685.
[141] 45 TC at pages 694-695.
[142] at page 700.
[143] ibid. See also *Julius Bendit Ltd v IRC* (1945) 27 TC 44; *Craddock v Zevo Finance* (1946) 27 TC 267.

in *Ridge Securities Ltd v IRC*.[144] As Pennycuick J said in that case,[145] "if a trader starts a business with stock provided gratuitously, it would not be right to charge him with tax on the basis that the value of his opening stock was nil". Thus it is doubtful whether it is correct that *Sharkey v Wernher* does not apply to acquisitions.

Also questionable is the conclusion that there was no gift by Mr Rowe to the taxpayer company. While the deal between Mr Rowe and the hotel vendors might have been a genuine commercial deal and the price fairly negotiated, the same cannot be said for the scenario whereby the company came to acquire the hotel. It is not clear how this could be said not to amount to a gift from Mr Rowe to the company. The company did not negotiate anything with the vendors and so was not a party to that original "genuine commercial deal". The facts do not show that the company paid a commercial price to Mr Rowe for the transfer to it of the right to buy the hotel at the price which Mr Rowe negotiated for his own purposes before the company was even formed. That Mr Rowe and his wife were the only shareholders of the company is of no consequence. It would seem that this was a case where the Commissioners' findings could not be justified by the facts and in which the court would have been right to intervene. Be that as it may, the principle that *Sharkey v Wernher* does not apply to a genuine commercial transaction can now be regarded as established and the criticisms of the reasoning of Plowman J does not affect the validity of this principle.

There are other exceptions to the *Sharkey v Wernher* principle. The first relates to the valuation of trading stock on the discontinuance of a trade. By virtue of s.100 TA 1988, if the stock is sold to another UK trader who is not connected with the seller, and the purchase price of the stock is deductible as an expense for the purchaser, the value of the stock will be the actual price for the sale. A similar rule applies to the valuation of work in progress at the discontinuance of a profession or vocation.[146] A final exception can be seen in s.84 TA 1988. This section applies to gifts of stock in trade to educational establishments, if that stock in trade would be plant or machinery in the hands of the educational institution. In this case, the donor is not required to enter any amount into his books as consideration for the sale.

6. Transfer pricing (TA 1988, s.770A and Sch. 28AA[147])

The transfer pricing rules deal with dealings between associated persons, at an undervalue or overvalue. Sch. 28AA(1) provides that, where provision has been made or imposed in a transaction or series of transactions

[144] [1964] 1 All ER 275.
[145] at page 289.
[146] S.101, TA 1988.
[147] See generally J Elliot [1995] BTR 348.

between any two persons, and the provision is not such as would be made between independent enterprises, and the provision confers a potential UK tax advantage on one or both of the parties, the profits and losses of the persons so advantaged would be computed as if an arm's length provision had been made. This transfer pricing only applies where, at the time of the provision, one of the parties was directly or indirectly participating in the management, control or capital of the other, or the same person were so involved, in respect of each of the parties. For these purposes, "transaction" includes arrangements, understandings and mutual practices, whether or not they are, or are intended to be, legally enforceable.[148] This rule is different from that in *Sharkey v Wernher* in that, in this case, the rule relates only to bodies corporate and partnerships[149] who are associated with each other. Such bodies are "associated" for these purposes if one controls the other or both are controlled by the same third party. On the other hand, *Sharkey v Wernher* applies to as much to individuals as it applies to bodies of persons, applies even where the parties are not "associated", and even applies where the "parties" to the transaction are one and the same person.

8. Trading stock

In addition to sums already received or earned, traders who operate their accounts on an earnings basis must also bring the value of their trading stock that remains unsold at the end of the accounting period into account as a trading receipt. If this not done, the result would be a distortion of the true state of the business. Similarly, the same trading stock would be entered as expense in the accounts in the following year, in order to avoid the danger of the same assets suffering double taxation. Subject to the provisions of s.100 TA 1988 (above) the trader may bring in each individual item at cost or market value, whichever is the lower, and may indeed pick and choose, bringing in some at cost, and others at market value[150] (again, whichever is lower).

In this context, the market value refers to the best price available in the market in which the trader sells.[151] Thus a wholesaler would be applying the value of the stock in the wholesale market, while a retailer would be applying the value in the retail market. Where stock is purchased at different times and at different prices during the year leaving a residue that cannot be connected to any specific purchase, the normal method of valuing such stock is known as "first in, first out" (FIFO), whereby the remaining stock is attributed to the latest purchases.

---

[148] Sch. 28AA(3).
[149] Sch. 28AA(4).
[150] See *IRC v Cock Russell & Co. Ltd* [1949] 2 All ER 889; 29 TC 387.
[151] See *B.S.C. Footwear Ltd. v Ridgeway* (1972) 47 TC 495.

8. Work-in-progress

At any point in time it is usual for traders and professional people to have unfinished work. For example a furniture manufacturer may have any number of partly-completed chairs. These items of unfinished work are often referred to as work-in-progress, and the value thereof also has to be brought into account in ascertaining the trading receipts. So, how does one value work-in-progress? In a Joint Statement issued by the Inland Revenue and the Tax Faculty of the Institute of Chartered Accountants[152] it is claimed that work-in-progress, like stock, is an accounting concept – "it is not for the Revenue to determine how to value it; it is solely a matter of the appropriate application of accountancy principles."[153] The purpose of valuation, according to the Statement, is to relate expenditure on such work to the period in which the income that it produces is earned,[154] such that if there is no expenditure, then there is no work-in-progress to be matched with income of later periods. The Statement also said that a sole trader or partnership with no fee-earning employees will have no work-in-progress,[155] and that there "can be no work-in-progress in relation to a proprietors' labour".[156]

When work-in-progress is actually found, the "basic principle" of valuation is said to be that it should be stated at the lower of cost and net realisable value.[157] In ascertaining these, one may apply the direct cost method, which values the work in progress by reference only to the costs of the materials and labour, or one may apply the on cost method, which adds overheads to the direct costs. It has been held that neither of these methods is necessarily more correct than the other.[158] However, the Joint Statement by the Revenue and the ICA questions whether that view would be correct today.[159] It points out that in *Duple Motor Bodies Ltd v Ostime* the Commissioners had found that the taxpayer's policy of applying the direct cost method accorded with generally accepted accounting practice, but that such a policy would no longer accord with generally accepted accounting practice. It is clear that the Revenue and the ICA do not have the authority to question *Duple Motor Bodies Ltd v Ostime* in this way. However, their Statement in relation to that case may lead to an unwelcome re-opening of the debate on whether overheads must be included or whether the direct cost method is valid. That the issue is far from settled even among accountants is evident from later passages in the joint statement. It is stated (*inter alia*) that there are "no rigid rules", and some of the passages then presented complicated rules to assist in deciding whether to add overheads of not. Since it seems that it is the policy of the taxpayer in *Duple Motor Bodies Ltd v Ostime* rather than the direct cost method

---

[152] "The new system for Taxing Professional Businesses: What is meant by 'true and fair view'?", IR Tax Bulletin, December 1998, page 606 at 607.
[153] ibid.
[154] para. 22.
[155] para. 23.
[156] para. 29.
[157] para. 20.
[158] See *Duple Motor Bodies Ltd v Ostime* [1961] 2 All ER 167; 39 TC 537.
[159] para. 25.

itself that the joint statement takes issue with, it would seem that the direct cost method itself might still be valid. If so, the remaining passages of the joint statement as to the issue of overheads can only lead one to the conclusion that the taxpayer in *Duple Motor Bodies Ltd v Ostime* was right to have steered clear of that issue.

Profits from Land: "Schedule A Businesses"

This section deals briefly with the principles governing the taxation of rents and other income derived from land under Sch. A. It may seem odd that this topic is being covered in a discussion on the taxation of trading income, but as we shall soon see, similar principles apply to income from Sch. A businesses and other types of business under Sch. D Cases I and II.

This area of law has undergone significant change in recent times. First, s.39 and Sch. 6 FA 1995 introduced a new Sch. A with respect to income tax only, effective from the year 1995-96. This meant that there were two versions of Sch. A - the "old" version, which applied to corporation tax, and the "new" version, which applied to income tax only. S.38 and Sch. 5 FA 1998 introduced yet another Sch. A, with effect for income tax purposes for the 1998-99 and future years of assessment, and with effect for corporation tax from 1 April 1998 (subject to some transitional provisions). By this amendment, the profits of companies under Sch. A fall to be calculated on the same basis as that for income tax.

The Schedule A Charge

Section 15(1)(1) TA 1998 charges tax under Sch. A on "the annual profits arising from a business carried on for the exploitation, as a source of rents or other receipts,[160] of any estate, interest or rights in or over land in the United Kingdom".[161] The words "arising from a business" in this provision are misleading and are not as limiting as they might first appear to be. This is because the statute clearly indicates that any transaction entered into for the exploitation, as a source of rents or other receipts of interests, estates or rights in land is deemed to be entered into in the course of such a business.[162] This means that an isolated transaction of letting, without any business structure, is caught by Sch. A. For these purposes, all businesses and activities of a particular person that are chargeable under Sch. A are (with some qualifications or exceptions in the cases of foreign companies and insurance companies) treated as one single business.[163]

---

[160] This term includes payments in respect of licenses to occupy, use, or exercise any rights over land, and rent charges, ground annual and feu duties and other annual payments in respect of land (s.15(1)(4)).

[161] For the meaning of "other receipts ..." see *Lowe v Ashmore* (1970) 46 TC 597.

[162] s.15(1)(2).

[163] s.15(1)(3).

The Schedule A charge includes profits arising from the right to use a caravan[164] or houseboat[165] at a single location in the UK.[166] It also covers sums payable for the use of furniture in cases of furnished lettings (in which case the sums paid for the use of the furniture are treated in the same way as rents).[167] In respect of leases for terms not exceeding 50 years, in respect of which the payment of a premium is required, a certain proportion of the premium is treated as rent received when the lease was granted.[168]

Exceptions to the charge include profits arising from the occupation of land,[169] profits charged under Case I of Sch. D under s.53(1) or s.55,[170] receipts treated as trading receipts in respect of tied premises,[171] or rent charged under Sch. D under s.119 or s.120(1).[172]

As under Sch. D Cases I and II, income tax is charged under Sch. A on the persons receiving or entitled to the income[173], and is charged on current year basis – i.e., "the full amount of the profits arising in the year of assessment".[174] Generally, the profits of a "Sch. A business" are computed in the same way as trading profits under Sch. D Case I,[175] thus a large number of provisions applying to trades under Sch. D Case I also apply to Sch. A (e.g., rules relating to deductible expenses, the rules relating to business entertainment, repairs of premises, post-cessation receipts and expenses, changes in partnerships, commencement and cessation of trades, etc).[176] In spite of this similarity of treatment, s.21C makes exception in the case of mutual trading. Transactions and relationships involved in "mutual business" are treated by s.21C(2) as if they took place between persons with no relationship of mutuality. By that token, surpluses or deficits are regarded as profits and losses if they would be so regarded if the business were not mutual.[177]

Further Reading

Elliot J, *Developments in Transfer Pricing* [1995] BTR 348.

Kay JA, *The Economics of Taxation* [1979] BTR 354.

Dworkin G, *Damages and Tax – A Comparative Survey* [1967] BTR 315 and 373.

---

[164] As defined under s.29(1) of the Caravan Sites and Control of Development Act 1960.
[165] Defined as "a boat or similar structure designed or adapted for use as a place of human habitation" (s.15(3)(2)).
[166] s.15(3)(1).
[167] s.15(4)(1).
[168] s.34(1).
[169] s.15(2)(1).
[170] s.15(2)(2)(a).
[169] s.15(2)(1).
[170] s.15(2)(2)(a).
[171] s.15(2)(2)(b).
[172] s.15(2)(2)(c).
[173] s.21(1).
[174] s.21(2).
[175] s.21A(1).
[176] s.21A and s.21B. See generally also the Inland Revenue Statement of Practice, "Taxation of Rents", IR50, para. 119 et seq.
[177] s.21C(3).

chapter eight

Income Tax -
Schedule D Cases I and II
Trading Expenditure

We have seen in the preceding chapters that the computation of trading profit involves the deduction of allowable expenditure from trading receipts. This chapter is concerned with the question of the types of expenses and losses which can be set against trading receipts in order to arrive at a profit figure. There are three qualifications for an item of expense to be allowable against trading receipts:

i.   the expense must be of an income and not capital nature;[1] and
ii. the expense must be incurred wholly and exclusively for the purposes of the taxpayer's trade, profession or vocation;[2] and
iii. the particular expense must not be prohibited by statute[3].

The discussion that follows addresses these issues in turn.

Income or Capital?

It stands to reason that a tax on income which only takes into account receipts of an income nature will not allow expenses of a capital nature to be set against those income receipts. This principle was recognised by the Barons of the Exchequer as far back as the late 19th century.[4] Therefore, the requirement that an item of expenditure be income in nature invites the same distinction and discussion that took place when considering the need to take into account only income receipts and not capital receipts. We have seen in the previous chapter the difficulties inherent in the classification of payments received by a trader. Similar difficulties exist in

---

[1] See generally Lord Templeman in *Lawson v Johnson Matthey Plc* [1992] BTC 324 at 327.
[2] See TA 1988, s.74(1).
[3] TA 1988, s.74(1).
[4] See for example, Huddleston B in *Forder v Andrew Handyside and Co Ltd.* (1876) 1 TC 65 at 70; compare Pollock B at page 69.

the classification of the trader's outgoings. As with trading receipts, there have been a range of approaches or tests. The distinction between the "tree" (e.g., the machinery) and the "fruit" (e.g., the things produced by the machinery) also comes into play here – expenses incurred on the tree will be capital, but those incurred on the fruit will be income. Then there is the dichotomy between fixed capital and circulating capital. The dichotomy has been variously described. One such description is by Lord Hanworth MR in *Mallet v Staveley Coal & Iron Company Ltd*[5]: "in dealing with any business, there are two kinds of capital, one fixed capital which is laid out in fixed plant, and the other circulating capital, which is turned over and over in the course of the business which is carried on." Lord Haldane in *John Smith v Moore*[6] preferred to refer to the economist Adam Smith: "Adam Smith described fixed capital as what the owner turns to profit by keeping it in his possession and circulating capital as what he makes profit of by parting with it and letting it change masters. The latter capital circulates in this sense." The application of the dichotomy in this context is to the effect that the cost of purchasing circulating capital assets will be income and may then qualify for relief.[7] On the other hand, the cost of purchasing fixed capital assets (e.g., permanent or semi–permanent investment items, such as plant and machinery) would normally be treated as capital expenditure which will not generally (excluding any Capital Allowances) be deductible. However, the term "fixed capital", which conjures an image of fixed plant and machinery, is deceptive, for it does not follow that fixed plant and machinery are always items of fixed capital. Consider these words of Romer LJ in *Golden Horse Shoe (New) Ltd v Thurgood*[8]

> Land may in certain circumstances be circulating capital. A chattel or a chose in action may in certain circumstances be fixed capital. The determining factor must be the nature of the trade in which the asset is employed. The land upon which a manufacturer carries on his business is part of his fixed capital. The land with which a dealer in real estate carries on his business is part of his circulating capital. The machinery with which a manufacturer makes the articles which he sells is part of his fixed capital. The machinery that a dealer in machinery buys and sells is part of his circulating capital, as is the coal that a coal merchant buys and sells in the course of his trade.

Another test for capital expenditure is the so-called "enduring benefit" test. This was propounded by Viscount Cave LC in *British Insulated and Helsby Cables Ltd v Atherton*[9].

---

5   [1928] 2 KB 405 at 413.
6   [1912] 2 AC 13 at 19.
7   See for example, *Ammonia Soda Co v Chamberlain* [1918] 1 Ch 266; *Golden Horseshoe (New) Ltd v Thurgood* [1934] 1 KB 548; 18 TC 280.
8   [1934] 1 KB 548 at 563.
9   [1926] AC 205 at 213-214.

When an expenditure is made not only once and for all, but with the view to bringing into existence an asset or advantage for the enduring benefit of a trade. I think there is very good reason ... for treating such an expenditure as being properly attributable not to revenue but to capital.

To the natural question "what is an enduring benefit?" Rowlatt J provides an answer in *Anglo-Persian Oil Co Ltd v Dale*[10].

What Lord Cave is quite clearly speaking of is a benefit which endures, in the way that fixed capital endures; not a benefit that endures in the sense that for a good number of years it relieves you of a revenue payment. It means a thing which endures in the way that fixed capital endures. It is not always an actual asset, but it endures in the way that getting rid of a lease or getting rid of onerous capital assets or something of that sort as we have had in the cases, endures. I think that the Commissioners, with great respect, have been misled by the way in which they have taken "enduring" to mean merely something that extends over a number of years.[11]

Viscount Cave LC was talking in *Atherton's* case about expenditure incurred "with a view" to bringing into existence an asset or advantage. However, the courts have often considered, not the "view" of the person who incurred the expenditure, but rather, the questions (a) whether any asset was actually brought into existence by the expenditure, and (b) whether the expenditure actually conferred an enduring benefit on the trade.[12] Thus the enduring benefit test enables the court to consider the nature and effects of the expenditure and of the asset, outside the traditional accountancy practice of categorisation and balance sheet representation of fixed and current assets. It also enables the court to deal with the actual effects of the expenditure. The enduring benefit test is not without criticism. For one, it is clear that "money spent on income account, for example on durable repairs, may often yield an enduring advantage."[13] It is also not clear what the correct approach is to the difference between a "view" to create an asset or advantage on one hand, and, on the other hand, whether such an asset or advantage was created successfully.

Yet another test is the "identifiable asset" test. The test requires an examination of the nature and subject matter of the expenditure. The purpose of this examination is to ascertain whether an asset is identifiable as the subject of the expenditure. If such an asset can be identified, sums

---

[10]   (1932) 16 TC 253 at 262.
[11]   Approved by Romer LJ in the same case, at page 274.
[12]   See for example Lawrence LJ in *Anglo-Persian Oil Co, Ltd v Dale*, at page 271; Lord Macmillan in *Rhodesia Railways Ltd v Bechuanaland Protectorate IT Collector* [1933] AC 368 at 374; Lord Reid in *IRC v Carron Company* (1968) 45 TC 18 at 68; Lord Templeman in *Lawson v Johnson Matthey plc* [1992] BTC at page 328.
[13]   See Lord Reid in *IRC v Carron Company* 45 TC at page 68. According to Lord Reid (ibid), what matters in a case of this kind is the nature of the advantage for which the money was spent.

spent on the acquisition or improvement of that asset will be capital. This test was confirmed in *Tucker v Granada Motorway Services Ltd*.[14] In this case the taxpayer company paid a sum of £122,000 in order to secure a reduction in the rent paid by them under a 50-year lease of a motorway service area, for the unexpired term of 40 years. The House of Lords held that the payment was capital expenditure. Lord Wilberforce referred[15] to the observations of Rowlatt J about the enduring benefit test (above), and said that the fact that the benefit obtained was enduring, in the sense that it might last for over 40 years, was not sufficient to make the payment a capital payment. However, a payment to get rid of a lease or a disadvantage in a lease might be so sufficient. He proceeded to explain the principle[16].

> I think that the key to the present case is to be found in those cases which have sought to identify an asset. In them it seems reasonably logical to start with the assumption that the money spent on the acquisition of the asset should be regarded as capital expenditure. Extensions from this are, first, to regard the money spent on getting rid of a disadvantageous asset as capital expenditure and, secondly, to regard money spent on improving the asset, or making it more advantageous, as capital expenditure. In the latter type of case it will have to be considered whether the expenditure has the result stated or whether it should be regarded as expenditure on maintenance or upkeep, and some cases may pose difficult problems.

In this case, the payment was a once-for-all expenditure on a capital asset designed to make it more advantageous. Although the lease was non-assignable so that it had no balance sheet value before or after the modification, it was none the less an asset and a valuable one for the taxpayer's trade. If an asset, it was a capital asset.[17] Thus the expenditure had been incurred on a capital asset (the lease), making it a more valuable asset for the taxpayer's trade.[18] Similarly, in *Pitt v Castle Hill Warehousing Co Ltd*[19] expenditure on an asset, a road, was held to be capital expenditure.[20]

With respect to the identifiable asset test, it seems that the word "asset" is given a wide meaning, and is not restricted to tangible property. So for example, goodwill is an asset, and a payment to protect or preserve goodwill is capital.[21] A credit agreement is also an asset, and a payment to secure release from onerous terms in such an agreement is capital.[22]

---

[14]   [1979] 2 All ER 801; 53 TC 92.
[15]   53 TC at page 107.
[16]   ibid.
[17]   at page 108.
[18]   Lord Salmon dissented, saying that while the lease was an asset of the company, he did not consider it to be a capital asset (at page 109).
[19]   [1974] 3 All ER 146.
[20]   The particular expenditure on the road related to its construction. If the expenditure on the same asset had been for its maintenance and upkeep, such expenditure might conceivably have been classed as revenue expenditure and deductible.
[21]   *Walker v Joint Credit Card Co. Ltd* [1982] STC 427; 55 TC 617; *Associated Portland Cement Manufacturers Ltd v IRC* [1946] 1 All ER 68.

The whole basis of this test is that, unlike the fixed and circulating capital test, the item of expenditure is not categorised and fixed exclusively by the nature of the asset. For example, we have seen that in *Pitt v Castle Hill Warehousing Co Ltd*, expenditure on the same asset might be revenue or capital nature depending on the nature of the expenditure in relation to the asset. The same fixed asset might invite both capital and revenue expenditure. One might suggest that this test also has elements of a merging of some of the other tests. We need to identify the asset and its nature (fixed or circulating) and then we need to consider the nature of the expenditure on that asset, presumably also examining whether it brings into the business an enduring benefit or advantage. For example, the expenditure in Pitt on the construction of the road (to facilitate access to an industrial site without disturbing residents) brought in an enduring asset and a benefit and advantage in terms of public relations and goodwill.

Despite all these tests, it has been held that a payment to get rid of an employee, who it is not in the company's interest to retain, is income in nature.[23] Similarly, a payment to secure the termination of an agency contract which later proved burdensome (because unexpectedly high fees became payable to the agents) has been held to be income,[24] as has a payment to remove "insurmountable obstacles to the profitable development" of the taxpayer's business "in contemporary economic and commercial conditions."[25] One might well regard an employee as an asset of the trade and therefore regard a payment to get rid of such an asset as a capital payment. One might also regard an agent as an asset of the business. Furthermore, one might arguably regard the departure of such an employee, or the freedom from such an agent, as conferring an enduring benefit (as defined).[26] So when the decisions are examined, we may be tempted to concur with Lord Greene's suggestion that the matter might as well be determined by a "spin of a coin". Equally, one might just consider that the matter is simply one of common sense and/or reality, although as we shall presently see, such an analysis might just be another way of spinning the coin.

The Court of Appeal seemed to favour the common sense approach in *Lawson v Johnson Matthey plc*[27] while Lord Goff of Chieveley in the House of Lords[28] in the same case talked about "the reality of the situation".[29] However, in applying that common sense and reality the Court of Appeal and the House of Lords reached different conclusions as to the status of the expenditure in the case. The expenditure in this case consisted of a £50 million injection by a parent company (Johnson Matthey plc) into one of

[22] *Whitehead v Tubbs* [1984] STC 1; 57 TC 472.

[23] *Mitchell v B W Noble Ltd* [1927] 1 KB 719; compare Lord Keith of Kinkel in *Lawson v Johnson Matthey Plc* [1992] BTC at page 326 - "... a payment to get rid of an obstacle to successful trading is a revenue and not a capital payment ... This must be no less true of a payment made to save the whole of an existing business from collapse."

[24] *Anglo-Persian Oil Co. Ltd v Dale*, supra.

[25] *IRC v Carron Company* (1968) 45 TC 18 (HL), following *Anglo-Persian Oil Co. Ltd v Dale*.

[26] The courts did not subscribe to this analysis - see for example Lawrence LJ in *Anglo-Persian Oil Co. Ltd v Dale*, 16 TC at page 271.

[27] [1991] BTC 150.

[28] [1992] BTC 324.

[29] at page 332.

its wholly-owned subsidiaries, Johnson Matthey Bankers Limited (JMB). This cash injection was part of a scheme to facilitate the disposal of the wholly-owned subsidiary to the Bank of England. The Bank of England was not willing to buy the (worthless) shares of JMB unless, immediately prior to the purchase and transfer of the shares and the company, Johnson Matthey plc would inject the £50 million. Johnson Matthey plc was willing to do this in order to facilitate the disposal and avoid the insolvent liquidation of JMB. If Johnson Matthey plc had held onto JMB, JMB would have faced insolvency with severe ramifications for the goodwill and trade of the rest of the companies in the Johnson Matthey group. There was even a suggestion that it might lead to a closure of Johnson Matthey plc itself.

The General Commissioners took the view that the £50 million payment by Johnson Matthey plc was of a revenue and not capital nature because its purpose was "to preserve the trade of Johnson Matthey plc from collapse" and further noted that the link between the £50 million expenditure and the subsequent transfer of shares to the Bank of England did not operate to convert the £50 million into expenditure of a capital nature. On appeal, the High Court disagreed with the Commissioners, and declared that the nature of the expenditure must be determined objectively and that its determination must recognise the nature of what it could achieve.[30] Such an analysis would facilitate the recognition of the achieved disposal of the shares and business of the subsidiary, JMB. That recognition would objectively indicate the expenditure to be of a capital nature; being part of the disposal of a capital asset. On further appeal to the Court of Appeal, the Court reviewed the long history of judicial comment in this area, noting that the "enduring benefit" test of Viscount Cave has been undermined by subsequent judicial comment.

The Court noted the absence of any definitive test for the determination of the income versus capital issue. Consequently the court decided to follow the "common sense" approach.[31] The position, according to Fox LJ[32], was as follows (i) JMB was a capital asset to the taxpayer company; (ii) the taxpayer company disposed of JMB to the Bank; (iii) the only terms on which the Bank was willing to acquire JMB was on payment of the £50m by the taxpayer company to JMB. Taking account of these factors, the situation, according to him was "in reality, the same as if the Bank had said "We will take over JMB if you pay us £50m". Whichever way it was done, the payment seemed to be a payment by the taxpayer company to enable it to get rid of a capital asset the continued retention of which was harmful to the plc. Thus the "common sense of the matter" was that the £50m was capital expenditure.[33]

---

[30]   [1990] STC 160.
[31]   See Fox LJ, [1991] BTC 150 at 156. The common sense approach was advocated by Lord Reid in *Strick (Inspector of Taxes) v Regent Oil Co Ltd* [1966] AC 295 at 313.
[32]   [1991] BTC at 156.

On further appeal to the House of Lords their Lordships differed from the conclusion reached by the Court of Appeal and held that the payment was revenue expenditure and deductible. The reality of the situation, according to Lord Goff of Chieveley was that the payment was a contribution towards the rescue of JMB which the taxpayer knew that the Bank of England was going to mount immediately in the public interest.[34] Similarly, Lord Keith of Kinkel said that the payment was, "on a proper analysis", not the payment of the price for getting rid of a burdensome asset, but a contribution required by the Bank of England towards its planned rescue operation.[35] Lord Templeman, who delivered the main speech, proceeded by drawing analogies from the authorities. According to him, the payment of £50m did not bring an asset into existence and did not procure an advantage for the enduring benefit of the trade.[36] The items of fixed capital which were disposed of (the shares in JMB) were not themselves of an onerous character, and the payment of £50m had no enduring effect on the capital of the taxpayer.[37] The goodwill of the taxpayer was not improved, but was saved from extinction.[38] In this case, the payment was made solely to enable the taxpayer to continue in business.[39]

One is hard pressed to find a neat categorisation for the approach of the House of Lords in this case. While the "reality of the situation" is one theme, the speech of Lord Templeman seemed to contain an amalgam of a number of the available tests – particularly the enduring benefit and identifiable asset tests. Thus perhaps the real answer to the question "how does one distinguish income expenditure from capital expenditure" is now that one has to look at all the circumstances of the case and apply any mixture of the enduring benefit and identifiable asset tests that appears appropriate in the light of the reality the situation. This, it is submitted, does not advance the situation very much at all and is more or less tantamount to saying that the issue should be decided on a case-by-case basis. Perhaps that is as much as one is entitled to expect in matters such as the income/capital divide in respect of which there will inevitably be hard and borderline cases – as long as any case-by-case analysis takes account of established tests, particularly, the two just referred to.

Statutory Provisions

Having examined the dichotomy between capital and income with respect to the characterisation of expenses, it remains to be examined the other factors that are relevant to the determination of whether an item of

---

[33] ibid.
[34] [1992] BTC at pages 332-3. Lord Goff referred to the Court of Appeal's analysis as "attractive", but on reflection came to the conclusion that it was too narrowly based, and ignored the reality of the situation. Compare Lord Emslie (at page 326) who also found the analysis of the Court of Appeal attractive, but too narrowly based.
[35] at page 326.
[36] at page 328; compare Lord Reid in *IRC v Carron Company*, 45 TC at page 68.
[37] ibid.
[38] at page 329.
[39] ibid.

expenditure is allowable as a deduction. The starting point for this discussion is s.817(1) of the Taxes Act, which provides that, in arriving at the amount of profits or gains for tax purposes, no other deductions shall be made than such as are expressly enumerated in the Tax Acts. This is a misleading provision insofar as it purports that the allowable deductions are expressly enumerated in the statute. In actual fact, in most cases, the Taxes Act does not specifically provide for a deduction to be made. Rather, deductions are allowed by implication, first, because this is inherent in the concept that it is the "profits", not the receipts of the trade that are charged to income tax, and, secondly, because the Taxes Act does contain an enumeration of the items which are disallowed. In this respect, the principle is that an item of expenditure that is not disallowed is allowed by implication. This principle can be found in the following passage in the judgment of Jenkins LJ in *Morgan v Tate & Lyle*[40].

> [The rule] does not provide that money wholly and exclusively laid out or expended for the purposes of the trade may be deducted, but that no sum shall be deducted in respect of any disbursements or expenses not being money wholly and exclusively laid out or expended for the purposes of the trade. It is, however, obvious that if no deduction at all of expenses from gross receipts was allowed, it would be impossible to arrive at the balance of the profits and gains of a trade upon which tax under Case I of Schedule D is to be assessed. Accordingly, it has long been well settled that the effect of these provisions as to deductions is that the balance of the profits and gains of a trade must be ascertained in accordance with the ordinary principles of commercial trading, by deducting from the gross receipts all expenditure properly deductible from them on those principles, save in so far as any amount so deducted falls within any of the statutory prohibitions contained in the relevant Rules, in which case it must be added back for the purpose of arriving at the balance of profits and gains assessable to tax.

This passage, while explaining the reason why deductions can be made also points to a very important principle with regard to the deductibility of expenditure – that which relates to the so-called principles of "remoteness and duality" (wholly and exclusively). This was referred to at the beginning of this chapter. This issue is examined in the next section.

---

[40] (1954) 35 TC 367 at 393-394.

"Wholly and exclusively"

The relevant statutory provision is in s.74(1)(a) which provides that no sum shall be deducted in respect of any disbursements of expenses, not being money wholly and exclusively laid out or expended for the purposes of the trade, profession, or vocation. This provision forms the backbone of the statutory deduction rules. Judicial responses to the provision result in the view that it incorporates the concepts of remoteness and duality.[41] Each item of expenditure must have been incurred for the purposes of the trade, etc. This is the principle of remoteness. The relevant item of expenditure must also have been incurred only for the purposes of the trade. This is the principle of duality (or perhaps more correctly, singularity – for the principle is that expenditure incurred for dual purposes is not allowable).

Let us examine the terminology employed within the provision. First, "wholly". In *Bentleys, Stokes & Lowless v Beeson*[42] Romer LJ, delivering the judgment of the Court of Appeal, said[43] that the adverb "wholly" refers to the quantum of the sums expended. This presumably means that the "whole" of the amount claimed as an expense must have been expended for business purposes. Secondly, "exclusively". Romer LJ[44] said in the same case that this word concerns the "motive or object in the mind" of the person making the expenditure. He said that this was a question of fact. Finally, what does the phrase "for the purposes of the trade" mean? In *Bentleys, Stokes & Lowless v Beeson,* Romer LJ seemed to link it with "the object of promoting the business or its profit earning capacity".[45] However, in *Strong & Co of Romsey Ltd v Woodifield*[46] Lord Davey said[47] that these words mean "for the purpose of enabling a person to carry on and earn profits in the trade". According to him, it is not enough that the disbursement is made in the course of, or arises out of, or is connected with, the trade or is made out of the profits of the trade – it must be made for the purpose of earning the profits.[48] It is not clear whether these two formulations will lead to different outcomes in practice, and if so, which should be preferred. Both Lord Davey and Romer LJ seem to be introducing their own glosses on the statutory words.[49] It is doubtful whether the statutory words justify or necessitate their formulations. When the statute speaks of the purposes of the trade, etc., it would seem that the intention was to distinguish a business purpose from a personal purpose. The scheme of the s.74(1) itself proves this – for a large part of it seems to be preoccupied with the distinction between business and domestic or private purposes.[50] Thus

---

[41]   For a general discussion see V Grout [1979] BTR 44, and 96.

[42]   [1952] 2 All ER 82; 33 TC 491.

[43]   33 TC 491 at 503.

[44]   at pages 503-504; approved by Lord Elwyn-Jones (dissenting) in *Mallalieu v Drummond* [1983] 2 All ER 1095 at 1097 1098.

[45]   at page 504.

[46]   (1906) 5 TC 215.

[47]   at page 220. Referred to with approval by Lord Brightman in *Mallalieu v Drummond* [1983] 2 All ER 1095 at 1099; see also Romer LJ in *Newsom v Robertson* [1952] 2 All ER 728 at 732-733.

[48]   ibid.

[49]   Lord Davey's gloss has been criticised by the Committee on the Taxation of Trading Profits (1951 Cmnd 8189), as being "much too narrow" (para. 152), and "unsatisfactory in its operation" (para. 153). The Radcliffe Commission was also highly critical of it (1955, Cmnd para. 127).

[50]   See for example, s.74(1)(b), (d), and (e).

there is no reason to link the statutory provision with the purposes of earning profits or promoting the business. So, the provision could well be referring to expenses which are incurred in connection with the trade, profession or vocation. This would of course just amount to one introducing one's own gloss, as would any other attempt to define the phrase. Perhaps the best approach is that the phrase needs no interpretation at all, since it is plain enough for all to see. If anything requires interpretation at all, it would seem to be limited to the word "for". This may explain Lord Brightman's definition of the whole phrase as meaning "expended to serve the purposes of the trade, profession or vocation", in *Mallalieu v Drummond*.[51] The only difference between the statutory phrase and Lord Brightman's definition lies in the replacement of the word "for" in the statute with the phrase "to serve", and the definition therefore seems to involve no gloss on the statutory words. However, Lord Brightman then went on to approve Lord Davey's definition in *Strong & Co of Romsey Ltd v Woodifield* as an "elaboration" of his definition - which then reintroduces the gloss initially avoided.

So what is the result of this analysis? From the judicial *dicta* on the issue, it seems to be this: an item of expenditure is prohibited by this subsection unless the whole of the amount claimed had been expended, either solely for the purpose enabling the spender to carry on and earn profits in his or her business, or solely for the object of promoting the business or its profit earning capacity. We might prefer to put it differently from the judicial dicta by saying that an item of expenditure is prohibited by this subsection unless the whole of the amount claimed had been expended solely for (or to serve) the purposes or interests of the business as opposed to any other private or domestic purpose or interest.

The most important word in the statutory test is "exclusively". This is what establishes the singularity concept - that there must only be a business purpose. In *Mallalieu v Drummond*[52] Lord Brightman said that the effect of the word is to preclude a deduction if it appears that the expenditure was not only to serve the purposes of the trade, profession or vocation of the taxpayer but also to serve some other purposes. According to him, such other purposes, if found to exist, will usually be the private purposes of the taxpayer. Thus if at the time of incurring the expenditure, there existed, wholly or partly, some other purpose for the expenditure, such as a personal, private, or domestic purpose, then the whole of the expenditure will be incurred for a dual purpose and the whole of it will be disallowed - and it is immaterial that the business purposes are the predominant ones.[53]

The courts have taken a strict approach to the question whether the

---

[51]   [1983] 2 All ER at page 1099 (emphasis supplied).
[52]   [1983] 2 All ER at page 1099.
[53]   ibid.

requirement for singularity of purpose is satisfied. In so doing, they have fastened onto the word "purpose". The relevant purposes are, in this respect, the purposes of the business, as opposed to the purposes of the taxpayer.[54] The two are different concepts, even though the purposes of the taxpayer (i.e., his or her intentions or objects) are fundamental to the whole statutory test, in that, in order to ascertain whether the expenditure was incurred to serve the purposes of the taxpayer's business, it is necessary to discover the taxpayer's object in making the expenditure.[55] This might require the Commissioners to "look into the taxpayer's mind at the moment when the expenditure is made".[56] In this analysis, it is clear that the purpose of the expenditure is a different concept from the issue of whether a personal benefit accrues to the taxpayer by virtue of the expenditure. It was Romer LJ who said in *Bentleys, Stokes & Lowless v Beeson*[57]:

> And it is quite clear that the purpose must be the sole purpose. The paragraph says so in clear terms. If the activity be undertaken with the object both of promoting business and also with some other purpose, for example, with the object of indulging an independent wish of entertaining a friend or stranger or of supporting a charitable or benevolent object, then the paragraph is not satisfied though in the mind of the actor the business motive may predominate. For the statute so prescribes. Per contra, if in truth the sole object is business promotion, the expenditure is not disqualified because the nature of the activity necessarily involves some other result, or the attainment or furtherance of some other objective, since the latter result or objective is necessarily inherent in the act.

Thus it appears that an inherent or unintended incidental personal or other benefit will not detract from the singularity of the business purpose and the deductibility of the expenditure. This approach was confirmed by the House of Lords in *Mallalieu v Drummond*. Lord Brightman said[58] that the object of the taxpayer in making the expenditure must be distinguished from the effect of the expenditure. He explained that expenditure made exclusively to serve the purpose of the business, may confer a private advantage but that that private advantage will "not necessarily preclude the exclusivity of the business purpose". He gave the example of a medical consultant flying to the South of France to attend to a patient. If a stay in the South of France was a reason, however subordinate, for the trip, no deduction was allowable, whereas if it were not a reason, but only an unavoidable effect, the deduction could be made.[59]

---

[54] Per Lord Brightman in *Mallalieu v Drummond*, at page 1099.
[55] ibid.
[56] ibid. Compare Lord Elwyn-Jones (dissenting, but concurring on this point) at page 1097.
[57] 33 TC at page 504.
[58] [1983] 2 All ER at page 1100.
[59] ibid. Compare Lord Elwyn-Jones (dissenting) at page 1098.

This apparently pragmatic (and sensible) approach was however not entirely apparent in the majority's decision in *Mallalieu v Drummond* itself. This case involved Ann Mallalieu, a barrister, who sought to deduct expenses on clothes bought for wear in court. The clothes were of a type demanded by court etiquette and it was clear that when the clothes were purchased the taxpayer's motive or object was exclusively the need to comply with court etiquette. The Commissioners found as a fact that she had ample other clothing for the purposes of warmth and decency and that the relevant clothes were used only in connection with her work. Nevertheless, they concluded that the expenditure had a dual purpose – the professional one of enabling her to earn profits and the personal one of enabling her to be properly clothed while working. They therefore disallowed her claim to deduct the expenses of cleaning and upkeep of the clothes. The House of Lords upheld this decision. While Lord Brightman admitted that Miss Mallalieu's only conscious motive when buying the clothes was her professional and business requirements,[60] he said that she however needed clothes to travel to work and clothes to wear at work. Therefore it was "inescapable" that one object (although not a conscious motive) was the provision of clothing which she needed as a human being. Referring to the Court of Appeal's decision that the conscious motive was decisive, he rejected the notion that the object of a taxpayer is inevitably limited to the particular conscious motive in mind at the moment of expenditure.[61] Thus, while the motive of which the taxpayer is conscious of is of vital significance, it is not inevitably the only object which the Commissioners are entitled to find to exist. For Miss Mallalieu, the conclusion was that one object of the expenditure was the provision of clothes which she needed as a human being, in the interests of warmth and decency, although this was not a conscious object. Thus there was a duality of purpose.

Lord Elwyn-Jones delivered a brief but sharp dissenting speech. It seems that the main bone of contention between him and the majority lay in the proper weight to be accorded to the taxpayer's conscious motives. Referring to Romer LJ in the *Bentleys* case, he explained that the test as to why the expenditure was incurred is subjective.[62] Applying this test, he was "inevitably" led to the conclusion that the expenditure had been incurred wholly and exclusively for the purposes of the taxpayer's profession. According to him, the other benefits derived from the expenditure (that the clothes also provided the taxpayer with warmth and decency) "were purely incidental to the carrying on of her profession in the compulsory clothing she had to wear".[63]

The majority's decision in this case deserves the criticisms that it has

[60] at page 1103.
[61] at page 1103.
[62] at pages 1097-1098.
[63] at page 1098.

attracted.[64] The rather harsh application of the "dual purpose" rule by the majority adds the possibility of the courts deciding on one's subconscious motives at the time of purchase. Added to the task of also deciding on one's conscious motives, this raises questions. Can one individual profess to know the conscious motives of another? If not, how can a person proceed beyond that rather impossible task to an even more impossible one (if such a comparative exists) of discovering another's subconscious motives and intentions? The fact that such motive is considered to be subconscious indicates that not even the person who is alleged to have it is aware of it. This approach is astonishing.[65] It may of course be explained partly by the "policy" considerations, which may actually have played more than a passing role in the outcome. This is obvious in the question posed by Lord Brightman[66] as to whether, if the deduction were allowed, it would also extend to "other professional persons, such as solicitors accountants, medical practitioners, trades people and persons in all other works of self-employed life, and if not why not".[67] With respect, this is nothing but the old "floodgates" argument, which has been argued unconvincingly in other areas of law.[68] Issues of tax policy such as this should perhaps be left in the hands of the those with the power to levy taxes and who are consequently accountable to the taxpayer at general elections.

To complicate matters, the decision seems not to be all doom and gloom for those who must incur expenditure on business clothing. Lord Brightman went on to explain that the question is always one of fact and degree.[69] He cited the example of a self-employed waiter who would need to wear "tails" as an essential part of the equipment of his trade. In such an instance Lord Brightman said that it would be open to the commissioners to allow the expense of their upkeep on the basis that the money was spent exclusively to serve the purpose of the business. In this respect, it may well be that the statement of Templeman J in *Caillebotte v Quinn*[70] that "the cost of protective clothing worn in the course of carrying on a trade will be deductible, because warmth and decency are incidental to the protection necessary to the carrying on of the trade" is still good law – the emphasis here being on the phrase "protective clothing" – which is quite different from the barristers' regulated clothing involved in *Mallalieu v Drummond*.

In the event, the wisdom to be derived from this case is that the question whether an expense is incurred exclusively for the purposes of the taxpayer's business involves an examination of the state of the taxpayer's mind, both conscious and subconscious, at the time of the expenditure. A non-business conscious or subconscious object would negative a singularity of purpose, but an unavoidable effect would not. This may seem

---

[64] See J F Avery-Jones (1983) BTR 199. Kerridge ((1986) BTR 36) agrees with the outcome, but criticises "the form of the decision".

[65] Avery-Jones ((1983) BTR 199) rightly says that the taxpayer's unconscious motive is "not a meaningful expression", and that all purposes must be conscious.

[66] at page 1102.

[67] ibid.

[68] See generally, A Olowofoyeku, "Suing Judges", at pages 178-201 (1993, Clarendon Press, Oxford).

[69] at page 1103.

[70] (1975) 50 TC 222 at 226.

clear enough, but it is not clear why the fact that Miss Mallalieu was warm and decent while working in her regulated attire was not a mere unavoidable effect as opposed to an object of the expenditure.

Dissection and Apportionment

The harshness of the "wholly and exclusively" rule may be reduced in situations where apportionment is possible. If the expenditure incurred can clearly be divided to represent (i) expenditure that was wholly and exclusively incurred for business purposes, and (ii) expenditure that was incurred for, wholly or partly, a non-business purpose, the Revenue may accept apportionment of that expenditure. For example, the use of a room in one's home for business purposes may permit the apportionment of heating, lighting and other expenses of maintaining the house.

The principle that an item of expenditure can be split seems to have been accepted by both the Revenue and the court in *Copeman v William Flood & Sons Ltd*.[71] In this case, William Flood was a pig dealer. A private company was formed to take over his pig business. The directors and shareholders of this company consisted of him, his wife, their two sons, and their daughter. In the relevant year, the daughter, aged 17, and one of the sons, aged 23, were each paid £2600 as directors' fees. The daughter's duties involved answering telephone calls made to her father's residence by farmers, and the son's duties involved calling on farmers in order to purchase pigs. The company wanted to claim these directors fees as deductions. The Revenue argued that, having regard to the ages and duties of the children, the whole of the payments made to them could not be regarded as disbursements or expenses wholly and exclusively laid out or expended for the purposes of the company's trade. They argued that £78 would be an adequate sum to allow as a deduction in respect of remuneration for the daughter's services and £350 would be adequate in respect of the son's services. The company on the other hand argued that age was not a bar to earning capacity, that the directors' fees were expenses wholly and exclusively laid out for the purposes of their trade, and that it was for the company and not for the Inspector of Taxes to decide how much remuneration it would pay its officers. The General Commissioners decided that they could not interfere with the prerogative of the company in paying such sums as remuneration to the directors as the company think fit. Lawrence J held that it did not follow that, because the sums of money were paid to the directors as remuneration, they were necessarily wholly and exclusively laid out for the purposes of trade.[72] He agreed that the

---

[71] [1941] 1 KB 202; 24 TC 53.
[72] 24 TC at page 56.

Commissioners could not interfere with the prerogative of the company to pay to its directors whatever it thinks fit, but said that they could find "in a proper case" that sums so paid are not wholly and exclusively laid out for the purposes of the trade. Since the Commissioners had not addressed their minds to answering the question whether the expenses were incurred wholly and exclusively for the company's trade, Lawrence J decided to remit the case to the Commissioners, "to find as a fact whether the sums in question were wholly and exclusively laid out for the purpose of the Company's trade, and if they were not, to find how much of such sums was wholly and exclusively laid out for the purposes of the Company's trade."[73]

In the emphasised part of this statement lies the principle of dissection. It is clear that Lawrence J envisaged that at least part of the fees would have been incurred wholly and exclusively for the company's trade. The Revenue acknowledged this by suggesting what they felt were the "adequate" sums to be allowed. It would seem that the principle of dissection that was recognised in this case relates only to quantum (i.e., the question whether the expenses were incurred "wholly" for the purposes of the trade). It is clear that, generally, and objectively, staff salaries and directors' fees are business expenses. Very few businesses (if any) could get away with not paying their staff and officers for their services. Thus the question whether there is a duality of purpose in paying staff salaries will not arise. The labourer is worthy of his or her hire and there is no duality of purpose in paying for that hire. What might raise questions is the amount paid as salaries and fees. This is what the Revenue were challenging in this case – the reason probably being that the family relationship in the case. In cases wherein there is no family or other close relationship, it would be difficult for the Revenue to query the amount of directors fees because that purely a matter for the company concerned. However, where there is a close family connection and some of the fees may actually be more in the nature of pocket money than true fees for services, perhaps the Commissioners are entitled to scrutinise the transaction to see whether the sums should be dissected.[74] So it may well be that the principle of dissection or splitting does not apply to issue of whether an expense was incurred exclusively for the purposes of the trade.[75] Where the issue is whether any part of an item of expenditure was exclusively incurred, that may be an issue of apportionment, rather than dissection. A claim for apportionment may itself betray a duality of purpose[76] and apportionment may not be possible at all in respect of some things (e.g., the cost of a meal).[77]

---

[73]   ibid (emphasis added).

[74]   This approach may of course open up a can of worms - especially in respect of the so-called "fat cat" directors, who earn such huge sums, the justifiability of which many would question.

[75]   See especially the judgment of Templeman J in *Caillebotte v Quinn* (1975) 50 TC 222 - discussed below.

[76]   Templeman J, ibid, at page 227. See also Plowman J in *Murgatroyd v Evans-Jackson*, (1966) 43 TC 581 at 589-590.

[77]   ibid.

Domestic Expenditure

S.74(1)(b) provides that no sum may be deducted in respect of

> any disbursements or expenses of maintenance of the parties, their families or establishments, or any sums expended for any other domestic or private purposes distinct from the purposes of the trade, profession or vocation.

This provision is closely linked with the "wholly and exclusively incurred" test just discussed. We have seen that, in respect of that test, Lord Brightman said in *Mallalieu v Drummond*[78] that, if more than one purpose if found to exist for the expenditure, the other purposes will normally be the private purposes of the taxpayer. Thus it may be that this provision serves no useful purpose of its own, because it is clear that the presence of any of the purposes referred to in the provision would mean that the expense was not incurred "exclusively" for business purposes. It may of course be argued that the usefulness of this provision lies in the way in which it will present a swift and decisive response in any case where the expenditure is clearly of a domestic nature. The answer to this argument would be that s.74(1)(a) would also have provided the same swift and decisive response to such an expense – for the expense would clearly not have been incurred for business purposes at all. Indeed, this much was stated by Pennycuick J in *Prince v Mapp*[79] – "the second limb of [s.74(1)(b)] is more or less automatically satisfied where [s.74(1)(a)] is satisfied, that is to say, a sum which is expended in part for the purposes of a trade and in part for the purposes of a hobby is a sum expended for some other domestic or private purpose distinct from the purposes of the profession." Thus perhaps the correct approach is to treat s.74(1)(a) and s.74(1)(b) as being two aspects of the same principle. However, s.74(1)(b) exists in the statute as a distinct provision in its own right and needs therefore be addressed. It is illustrated in practice in a number of areas, but it must be noted that most of the cases to which we shall refer here are as relevant to the question of exclusivity of purpose as they are to the question whether they are domestic or personal expenses.

1. Food

One eats in order to live, not in order to work.[80] Corporations, partnerships, trusts, and human beings can all carry on a trade – but only humans need to eat to stay alive. All humans need to eat in order to stay

---

[78] [1983] 2 All ER at page 1099.
[79] (1969) 46 TC 169 at 176.
[80] Templeman J in *Caillebotte v Quinn* (1975) 50 TC 222 at 226.

alive, and these facts provide prima facie evidence that eating to stay alive normally has nothing to do with business. Thus the cost of feeding oneself will be a personal, not a business expense. In *Caillebotte v Quinn*[81] the taxpayer was a self employed carpenter, working on sites within a 40-mile radius of his home. He could not go home for lunch while away at work and so had to buy lunches at work. The cost of the lunches were much more than what it would have cost to have lunch at home. Ingeniously, he claimed that the additional cost of eating out was attributable to the need to eat a more substantial meal in order to maintain the energy expended in carrying out physical work, and to keep warm during the winter. The General Commissioners decided to allow a proportion of the costs of the lunches. Templeman J, considering both the exclusivity rule and the rule relating to domestic expenses, held that the Commissioners were wrong, that the cost of eating lunches was not apportionable, and that no part of the cost was deductible. Although this case was decided primarily on the exclusivity issue, it is clear from the first statement on this topic above, that it might very well (and arguably more appropriately) have been decided on the basis that the eating is purely a human thing and as such is an expense of maintaining the eater.

It is not clear however whether it is necessarily the case that the cost of food will not be deductible. Some types of expenditure on food may well not amount to expenditure of maintaining the eater as a living human being. For example, a Sumo wrestler may require a special diet, not to keep from starving and thereby stay alive, but in order to build or maintain his weight. The same goes for a heavyweight boxer who is considered "small" and who therefore has to embark on a special diet to gain more weight and develop his strength. Would the expenditure on these special diets be considered to be over an above what these professionals need as human beings, and therefore wholly and exclusively incurred for the purposes of their professions? The answer is arguably "yes". The contention that they need to eat as human beings would appear too artificial in this type of context. [82]

2. Medical expenses

Medical expenses constitute another example of domestic or personal expenses (or expenses of maintenance of the patient). They are incurred because the taxpayer is ill and the purpose is to cure that illness – they are not incurred because the taxpayer is a business person. The principle can be found in many cases. In *Norman v Golder*[83] the taxpayer, was a shorthand writer who had incurred medical expenses to cure an illness which he claimed to be a direct result of working in unfavourable circumstances. His

---

[81]   (1975) 50 TC 222.

[82]   Note however that in *Ansell v Brown* [2001] STC 1166, Lightman J held (in the context of Schedule E) that the cost of dietary supplements taken by a rugby player to maintain certain levels of fitness and weight were not deductible for Schedule E because the expenses were not incurred "in the performance" of his duties and they were not "necessary" expenses as required by TA 1988, s.198(1). This decision can be explained on the basis of the peculiar wordings of the Schedule E expenses rule.

[83]   (1944) 26 TC 293.

claim to deduct the expenses failed. According to Lord Greene MR[84]:

> It is quite impossible to argue that doctors' bills represent money wholly and exclusively laid out for the purposes of a trade, profession, employment or vocation of the patient. True it is that if you do not get yourself well and so incur expenses to doctors you cannot carry on your trade or profession and if you do not carry on your trade or profession you will not earn an income, and if you do not earn an income the Revenue will not get any tax. The same thing applies to the food you eat and the clothes you wear. But expenses of that kind are not wholly and exclusively laid out for the purposes of the trade, profession or vocation. They are laid out in part for the advantage and benefit of the taxpayer as a living human being ... they are, in my opinion, expenses of maintenance of the party, his family, or a sum expended for a domestic or private purpose, distinct from the purpose of the trade or profession.

This case was followed in *Prince v Mapp*.[85] The taxpayer was an engineering draughtsman who played the guitar professionally and as a hobby. Due to an accident, he had to have an operation in his finger, in order to be able to continue to play the guitar. He is claim to deduct the cost of this operation was disallowed. Pennycuick J said that the expense in this case was not an expense of maintenance of the taxpayer – however, it was incurred at least partly for his private purposes.[86] He referred to the statement of Lord Greene MR (above), but seemed to qualify it somewhat[87]:

> Lord Greene M.R. in that passage lays down in perfectly unqualified terms the proposition that expenses to doctors must always serve a dual purpose and accordingly can never be treated as representing money wholly and exclusively laid out for the purposes of a trade or profession. It may well be that in that passage Lord Greene did not have in mind the sort of medical care which an individual carrying on a trade or profession would not incur for any reason apart from the promotion of his trade or profession. It is quite easy to think of instances in which someone carrying on a trade or profession incurs some injury which is trivial in itself and in respect of which he would never otherwise expend money on medical care but which happens to be of vital importance for the purpose of that particular trade or profession. In such a case I am prepared to assume in favour of the taxpayer here that it would be possible for a taxpayer to incur expense

[84] at page 298.
[85] (1969) 46 TC 169.
[86] at page 176.
[87] at pages 173-174.

which was wholly and exclusively for the purpose of his trade or profession. I say I am prepared to assume. I do not give any decision upon it because on the particular facts of this case it is not necessary for me to do so.

This raises the prospect of medical expenses being deductible, depending on the circumstances and motives of the taxpayer in incurring those expenses. Pennycuick J made it clear that the crucial factor in this case was the fact that, while the doctor's evidence and the Commissioners' findings established that the taxpayer would not have had the operation if he had not wished to continue to play the guitar, the word "professionally" was missing from both. Thus the inference must be that he wished to continue to play as he had done before (partly professionally and as partly a hobby).[88] This at the very least showed a dual purpose. Pennycuick J then said[89]:

> I would mention in passing that if the finding had included the word "professionally" (i.e. if it had read "He would not have undergone it had he not wished to continue to play the guitar professionally") the result would I think have been otherwise. However, that word "professionally" is not there.

In short, if the taxpayer had supplied the missing word in his discussions with his doctors, and had insisted that the word be included in their statement, then he would have been able to deduct the money, because this would have shown that it was not a private or domestic expense. With respect, this would seem to be a questionable approach to the issue, first, in the light of *Norman v Golder*, and also in the light of the judgment of Plowman J in *Murgatroyd v Evans-Jackson*.[90] James Evans-Jackson was a trademark agent who was treated for an illness at a private nursing home. He had chosen private treatment because of the lack of a telephone, and the restricted facilities for visiting, that were involved in NHS hospital treatment. At the private nursing home, he was provided with a room and with all the necessary facilities for carrying on his business. He held conferences with clients there and saw members of his staff every day. He also dealt with correspondence. He claimed to deduct 60% of his total expenses at the nursing home (i.e., nursing home fees and charges for drugs and dressings, treatment, television and telephone) as a business expense in respect of the use of the room as an office. The Revenue claimed that the expenses were of a domestic or private nature and therefore were not allowable. The General Commissioners held that the

---

[88]   at page 176.
[89]   ibid.
[90]   (1966) 43 TC 581.

taxpayer was entitled to the deduction, but they were reversed by the court. Plowman J said[91] that the case was indistinguishable from *Norman v Golder.* He said that even if the taxpayer had claimed the whole expense, it would not be a rational view of the situation to conclude that the whole of his expenses in the nursing home were incurred wholly and exclusively for the purposes of his business.[92] According to Plowman J:

> The whole object of going into the nursing home in the first place was to receive treatment for the injury which he had sustained, and it seems to me that it would offend common sense to say that at any rate one of his motives or purposes for going into the nursing home was not to receive treatment for that injury – treatment that would be enure to his benefit, not merely during the time when he was carrying on his business, but as a living human being.

The implication of this case and *Norman v Golder* is that medical expenses will always have a private or domestic element, regardless of the taxpayer's motives or subjective intentions in seeking medical treatment. This seems to be the better approach to the issue, since it is difficult to see how, except in rare cases, one of the taxpayer's purposes for receiving treatment will not be to be cured of a human ailment. The fact that this will then enable the taxpayer to work in a particular occupation is not relevant, for, as Lord Greene MR said in *Norman v Golder*, the same point can be made about food, clothing, and perhaps, housing.

But as with food, perhaps there may be factual situations wherein medical expenses will be deductible. One example that springs to mind is cosmetic surgery. If a model or film star incurs medical expenses on cosmetic surgery such as silicone implants so as to increase his or her earning capacity, such expenses may well be deductible, for it may be argued that this is not an expense which he or she required as a human being. There would not be the purpose of receiving treatment for an injury which he or she had sustained, thereby introducing a duality of purpose. Whether the courts will accept this kind of analysis remains to be seen.

3. Travelling expenses

The situation in respect of travelling expenses depends on the origin and destination of the journey. This will determine whether the travel is for private or domestic purposes, or whether it is for business purposes. Where the origin or destination of the journey is the taxpayer's home, this will point strongly to a domestic purpose, and it will be conclusive against the

[91]   at page 588.
[92]   at page 590.

taxpayer in many cases. So for example, the cost of travelling from home to work will not be deductible, because it is merely a living expense, incurred because a person chooses to live at a distance from where he or she works. Such expenses are not incurred because the traveller is a trader or professional person. One of the leading cases is *Newsom v Robertson*.[93] Mr Newsom was a barrister who had his chambers at Lincoln's Inn in London, and his home in Whipsnade, Bedfordshire. He practiced his profession at his chambers, but often worked at home – particularly at evenings and weekends. During vacations he seldom went to London, but did most of the work at home. He claimed to deduct the expenses of travelling from his home to his chambers. The Special Commissioners held that the expenses were not deductible during term time, but were deductible during vacations. The Court of Appeal held that the expenses were not deductible at any time. Somervell LJ[94] doubted whether it was helpful to consider the journeys separately – rather, what had to be considered was "the expenses of going to and fro", and it would be impossible to hold that one was deductible and the other not. According to him, Whipsnade as a location had nothing to do with Mr Newsom's practice – he could have had his home anywhere. The taxpayer's purpose in making the journeys was to get home in the evenings or at weekends, and the fact that he intended to and did do professional work when he got there did not even make this a subsidiary purpose of his profession.[95] Romer LJ concurring said[96] that it was "almost impossible" to suggest that, when the taxpayer travelled to Whipsnade in the evenings or at week ends, he did so for the purpose of enabling him to carry on and earn profits in his profession – how much more to say that he did it exclusively for that purpose. He said[97] that not even the journey to work in the morning can be said to be undertaken in order to enable the traveller to exercise his profession. Rather, such a journey is undertaken for the purpose of "neutralising the effect of his departure from his place of business, for private purposes, on the previous evening". Thus, the object of the journeys between home and work "is not to enable man to do his work, but to live away from it". It is however in the judgment of Denning LJ that the applicable test in such cases is to be found. Denning LJ said[98] that one must draw a distinction between living expenses and business expenses. In order to determine where to put a travelling expense, one must determine the base from which the trade, profession or vocation is carried on. According to Denning LJ[99], in the case of a tradesman, the base of his trading operation is his shop, but in the case of a barrister, it is his chambers

Once he gets to his chambers, the cost of travelling to the various courts is incurred wholly and exclusively for the purposes of his profession. But

[93] [1952] 2 All ER 728.
[94] [1952] 2 All ER 728 at 730.
[95] ibid.
[96] at pages 732-733.
[97] at page 732.
[98] at page 731.
[99] ibid.

it is different with the cost of travelling from his home to his chambers and back. That is incurred because he lives at a distance from his base. It is incurred for the purposes of his living there and not for the purposes of his profession, or at any rate not wholly or exclusively; and this is so, whether he has a choice in the matter or not. It is a living expense as distinct from a business expense.

This decision was followed in *Sargent v Barnes*.[100] The taxpayer, a dentist, travelled some 12 miles from home to his surgery. He had a laboratory about one mile from home, at which he called in the mornings (on the way too the surgery) to collect completed work and at evenings (on the way home) to deliver work. He claimed to have two bases of operation i.e., the laboratory, and the surgery. His claim to deduct the cost of travelling between the laboratory and the surgery failed. Oliver J said[101] that what the court is concerned with is not simply why the traveller took a particular route (although that may be of the highest relevance in considering the deductibility of any additional expense caused by a deviation) but why he incurred the expense of the petrol, oil, wear and tear and depreciation in relation to this particular journey. In the present case, the expense was incurred, if not exclusively then at least in part, for the purpose of enabling the taxpayer to get from his private residence to the surgery where his profession was carried on, and the fact that it served the purpose also of enabling him to stop at an intermediate point to carry out there an activity exclusively referable to the business could not, convert a dual purpose into a single purpose.

It is obvious that the question of what constitutes a trader's base of operations is a question of fact, and that, in some cases, a person's home can also be a base of operations. This would be the case in respect of doctors who have their surgeries in their residences, and would "normally" be the case where the nature of the job is truly "itinerant".[102] It would also be the case in respect of a "circuteer" – the barrister who has his home near London, but spends most of his time on the circuit, hardly ever appearing at his chambers in London.[103]

Where a trader's home is clearly his or her base of operations, the principle propounded by Denning LJ in *Newsom v Robertson* comes into play, as was the case in *Horton v Young*,[104] where the taxpayer, a self-employed bricklayer, was allowed to deduct the cost of travelling between his home and various building sites where he worked for short durations. In this case the taxpayer's home, where he kept his tools and did his office work, was held to be his base of operations. The Revenue claimed that his base of operations was the building sites where he worked, which meant that the base shifted as he moved from one site to the next. Lord Denning MR

---

[100] (1978) 52 TC 335.
[101] at page 344.
[102] See Brightman J in *Horton v Young* (1972) 47 TC 60 at 68.
[103] See Lord Denning MR in *Horton v Young* 47 TC at page 71.
[104] 47 TC 60.

said[105] however that there was only one reasonable inference to draw from the primary facts – "that Mr. Horton's house at Eastbourne was the *locus in quo* of the trade, from which it radiated as a centre. He went from it to the surrounding sites according as his work demanded." Thus, when travelling between this base of operations to the various building sites he was travelling wholly and exclusively for business purposes and in the course of his business. His trade, commenced at his base of operations and was continued at the various building sites.[106]

Horton v Young raises more strongly the possibilities of categorising one's home as a base of operations and enabling travel from that base to other places of work to be deducted. It was even stated clearly there that a "circuteer" barrister can have his home as his base of operations. So what befell Mr Newsom in his case? It seems that, despite the fact that Mr Newsom in *Newsom v Robertson* did complete some of his work at home, maintained a study at home for that purpose, and spent most of his time working at home during vacations, he did not do enough to convert his home into his base of operations. While this may have been true of term time, it is not clear why he could not have been regarded as having changed his base during vacations – unless the principle is that a person can only have one base of operations, and that this base can never change (a proposition which can hardly be correct).

4. Conference attendance and expenses

Attendance at a conference will normally involve travel, accommodation, subsistence and possibly conference fee expenses. Having examined the case law on food and travel expenses in general, what is the situation with respect to these types of expenses when incurred at conferences? Let us examine some of the cases relating to this specific point. In *Bowden v Russell and Russell*[107], a solicitor attended conferences in Washington and Ottawa. His wife accompanied him on these visits. Although he did put forward genuine business reasons to support his choice of conference, he also admitted an intention to enjoy, together with his wife, the social and holiday opportunities presented by the visits to Washington and Ottawa. The conference and travel expenses were disallowed on the grounds that the taxpayer had dual purposes, and as such the expenses were not incurred exclusively for business purposes. By contrast, in *Edwards v Warmsley, Henshall & Co*[108], a partner in a firm of accountants represented the practice at an international congress of accountants in New York. All the partners of the firm considered that information and contacts deriving from the visit was beneficial to the firm, that some useful contacts had been made, that methods of accounting had been seen which might be adopted by the

---

[105] 47 TC at page 71.

[106] It is interesting to note that Brightman J at first instance did suggest (47 TC at page 68) a possible restriction in terms of ascertaining his "normal area of work". Should the taxpayer's home be situated outside that "normal area", travel to and from that home would not be in the course of business and, consequently, would be disallowed.

[107] [1965] 2 All ER 258; 43 TC 301.

[108] [1968] 1 All ER 1089; 44 TC 431.

firm, and that the firm's prestige had been increased. A claim to deduct the expenses in respect of the partner's return air fare, conference fee, and living expenses during the six days of the congress succeeded.

It is important to appreciate at this point the illustration of the medical consultant, provided by Lord Brightman in *Mallalieu v Drummond*[109] where Lord Brightman was careful to distinguish between object and effect. Thus, it appears that the taxpayer in *Edwards v Warmsley, Henshall & Co*, having incurred the expense with the proper business purpose, might seek on his arrival in New York to indulge in the personal benefits and opportunities of visiting New York. The latter might be regarded as an incidental effect of the exclusive business purpose.

Finally, the distinctions adopted in *Watkis v Ashford Sparkes & Harwood*[110] provide an interesting treatment of the costs of food, drink and accommodation. This case involved a firm of solicitors who wished to deduct (i) the costs of meals during business meetings held at lunchtime and in the evening during which times the solicitors would discuss the firm's business; and (ii) the cost of overnight accommodation, drinks and meals. These expenses were incurred as part of the attendance of the solicitors at the firm's annual conference. It was held that expenses in category (i) were not deductible, but all the expenses incurred in category (ii) were deductible. Nourse J, explained that the expenses of the meals in category (i) were expenses for a dual purpose; they served their private needs and purposes

Just as Miss Mallalieu needed to wear clothes not only when she was in court but also when she was not, so did the taxpayers need food and drink irrespective of whether they were engaged on a business activity or not.[111]

Nourse J further explained that the cost of food, drink and accommodation at the annual conference stood on a different footing. It could not necessarily be said to have been expenditure which met the needs of the partners as human beings. They did not need it, since they had their own homes where they could have spent the night. Thus the whole of the expenditure at the conference (food, drink and accommodation) was deductible as expenditure incurred wholly and exclusively for business purposes.[112]

Rent

Section74(1)(c) prohibits the deduction of rent for "the whole or any part of any dwelling-house or domestic offices", except where such part is used for the purposes of the trade, profession or vocation. Where any part is used

---

[109] supra.
[110] [1985] STC 451.
[111] at page 468.
[112] It is interesting to note Nourse J's statement (at page 469) that, with regard to the costs of the food and drink, "reasonable amounts, are usually allowed in full. I have no reason to think that that practice does not correctly represent the law".

for these purposes, the deduction allowable is restricted to two-thirds of the rent *bona fide* paid for any such dwelling-house or office, unless it appears in any particular case that, in the light of its circumstances, some greater sum ought to be allowed.

Repairs and Improvements

Section 74(1)(d) prohibits the deduction of "any sum expended for repairs of premises occupied, or for the supply, repairs or alterations of any implements, utensils or articles employed, for the purposes of the trade, profession or vocation, beyond the sum actually expended for those purposes". The effect of the last phrase in the provision is to limit the deduction to sums actually expended during the relevant year of assessment and to exclude apportionment of sums subsequently expended but attributable to repairs which may have accrued over a period.[113] Under this provision, the cost of purchasing and replacing tools can be deducted.[114] The provision also covers such things as repairs of plant and machinery[115], and renewals of the same.[116] And, of course, as the subsection clearly shows, it also covers expenditure on the repairs of premises. The last point raises other issues, because s.74(1)(g) prohibits the deduction of "any capital employed in improvements of premises occupied for the purposes of the trade, profession or vocation". The principle underlying these provisions seems to be that expenditure on repairs of premises is income in nature, but expenditure on improvements is capital, which accordingly has to be disallowed. If this be so, it is not clear why there should be a specific provision to disallow what would in any case have been disallowed under general principles. Be that as it may, it becomes necessary to ascertain the difference between the repair of premises and the improvements thereof.

The distinction between repair and improvement is not always easy to explain. Traditionally, the question has often been asked whether what took place was a repair or a "renewal" - a concept which is not in the statutory words but with which many cases have concerned themselves.[117] A variety of approaches have been suggested and, at times, applied by the courts. One of the more attractive approaches is to consider whether the final result produces an increase in value of the asset. For example, expenditure on the same asset, a railway line, may result in an improvement (via an increase in its value) or may be merely a repair (i.e., keeping the

---

[113] Vinelott J in *Brown v Burnley Football and Athletic Co Ltd* (1980) 53 TC 357 at 365.

[114] See Pollock B in *Forder v Andrew Handyside and Co. Ltd* (1876) 1 TC 65 at 69.

[115] See the Lord Justice-Clerk in *Caledonian Railway Co. v Banks* (1880) 1 TC 487 at 494.

[116] ibid. See also Somervell LJ in *IRC v Great Wigston Gas Co* (1946) 29 TC 197 at 207. Here, Somervell LJ rejected the Revenue's argument that their practice of allowing deductions in respect of renewals of plant and machinery was simply an extra-statutory concession. He said that such deductions were, in most cases, clearly authorised by the statute.

[117] Lord Nicholls of Birkenhead said in the Privy Council decision of *Auckland Gas Co Ltd v CIR (New Zealand)* ([2000] BTC 249 a page 253) that these words are not technical expressions with a special meaning, but are rather to bear their "ordinary, everyday meaning" – viz., "repair, or replacement, of a tangible object".

asset in proper working conditions, or maintaining its value or keeping it in its original state). Two cases serve as illustration. In *Rhodesia Railways Ltd v Bechuanaland Protectorate IT Collector*[118] the company had renewed some 74 miles of its railway track by putting down new rails and sleepers in place of ones which were worn, and it claimed the cost as a deduction. At first instance, it was held that the expenditure was of a capital nature, and was not the cost of a repair but of a reconstruction. However, the Privy Council reversed this decision and held that the periodical renewal of the rails and sleepers of a railway was in no sense a reconstruction of the whole railway. The track was simply restored to its previous unworn condition, without any element of improvement. Lord Macmillan said[119] that the expenditure did not result in the creation of any new asset, but that it was incurred to maintain the taxpayer's existing line in a state to earn revenue. On the other hand, in *Highland Railway Co v IRC*[120] the replacement of old track and rail was not deductible because it represented an improvement: the new rail was of a superior kind and represented an increase in the value of the railway line. The Lord President[121] noted that what was involved was not a mere relaying of the line after the old fashion. It was not taking away rails that were worn out or partially worn out, and renewing them in whole or in part along with the whole line. According to him, that would neither alter the character of the line nor would it affect the nature of the heritable property possessed by the company. What was done was to substitute one kind of rail for another, steel rails for iron rails – this amounted to "a material alteration and a very great improvement on the corpus of the heritable estate belonging to the Company" and thus the expenditure was incurred entirely "for the permanent improvement of the property".

Another approach stems from the much quoted statement of Buckley LJ in *Lurcott v Wakely and Wheeler*[122].

"Repair" and "Renew" are not words expressive of a clear contrast. Repair always involves renewal, renewal of a part; of a subordinate part...Repair is restoration by renewal or replacement of subsidiary parts of a whole. Renewal, as distinguished from repair, is reconstruction of the entirety, meaning by the entirety not necessarily the whole but substantially the whole subject matter under discussion.

In applying this *dictum*, Rowlatt J said in *O'Grady v Bullcroft Main Collieries Ltd*[123]:

[118] [1933] AC 368.
[119] at page 374.
[120] (1889) 2 TC 485.
[121] at page 488.
[122] [1911] 1 KB 905 at 923-924.
[123] (1932) 17 TC 93 at 101.

Of course, every repair is a replacement. You repair a roof by putting on new slates instead of the old ones, which you throw away. There is no doubt about that. But the critical matter is – as was pointed out in the passage read from Lord Justice Buckley's judgment in [*Lurcott v Wakely and Wheeler*] – what is the entirety? The slate is not the entirety in the roof. You are repairing the roof by putting in new slates. What is the entirety? If you replace an entirety, it is having a new one and it is not repairing an old one.

Thus since every repair is a replacement of something, and the replacement of an entirely is not repair, the courts face the question of what is to be regarded as an "entirety" (a question posed more than once by Rowlatt J in the passage just quoted), and what is to be regarded as a "part" of an entirety. The pertinence of this quest was pointed out by Lord Carmont in *Lawrie v IRC*[124] who said that the importance of considering an entirety is with a view to determining "the character of the work done", because "what might at first look like a renewal may when applying the matter to a larger unit, be shown to be only a repair." It is also relevant to the question "repair of what?"[125] – which then results in a quest to ascertain "the whole which is said to have been repaired."[126] The answer to these questions is not always clear. To the question "repair of what?", we may answer "repair of the factory", or "repair of the factory's chimney", or "repair of the waterworks" or "repair of the railway line". This would still raise the original question as posed by Rowlatt J in O'Grady – "what is the entirety here?". In other words, does the thing which is presented as the answer to the question "repair of what?" really amount to an entirety or does it amount to merely a part of an entirety?

In this analysis, the same thing can be an entirety in one case, and yet be a part of another entirety in another case. The difficulty inherent in such an analysis was presented by Donovan J in *Phillips v Whieldon Sanitary Potteries Ltd*[127]:

In my judgment, the "premises" for the purpose of [s.74(1)(g)] may sometimes be the whole of the trader's business premises and may sometimes be a specific building forming part of those premises. Thus, if a factory window were blown out and had to be repaired, it would be obviously wrong to argue that as the entirety of the window had been restored it was not a repair to the premises. In such a case the "premises" would be the entire factory, in relation to which the window would be a repair and nothing else. But if, for example,

---

[124] (1952) 34 TC 20 at 26.
[125] See Vinelott J in *Brown v Burnley Football and Athletic Co. Ltd* (1980) 53 TC 357 at 366.
[126] Ibid. In *Auckland Gas Co Ltd v CIR (New Zealand)* [2000] BTC at page 253, Lord Nicholls said that, in order to decide whether work constitutes repair or "replacement", the first step is to identify the object to which the test of repair or replacement is being applied.
[127] (1952) 33 TC 213 at 219.

a retort house in a gasworks was destroyed and had to be rebuilt, one would hardly call that a repair to the gasworks. The size of the retort house would compel one to regard that as the premises for the purpose of [s.74(1)(g)]; and since it had been replaced in full it could not be said to have been repaired. These examples illustrate what I think is the truth, that there is no one line of approach to the problem which is exclusively correct. In some cases it will be right to regard the premises as the entire factory, and in others as some part of the factory. Whichever alternative is the right one to adopt will depend upon the facts of the particular case.

The decided cases offer further proof of the problems. *O'Grady v Bullcroft Main Collieries Ltd* itself involved a factory chimney which had become unsafe, and which was replaced with a new one at an adjacent location. The new chimney was admitted to be an improvement on the old one. Rowlatt J held that the entirety in this case was the chimney itself, not the building to which it was attached. His reasoning was thus[128]:

> What was this? This was a factory chimney to which the gases and fumes, and so on, were led by flues and then went up the chimney. It was unsafe and would not do any more. What they did was simply this: They built a new chimney at a little distance away in another place; they put flues to that chimney and then, when it was finished, they switched the gases from the old flues into the new flues and so up the new chimney. I do not think it is possible to regard that as repairing a subsidiary part of the factory. I think it is simply having a new one. And they had them both. Perhaps they pulled down the old one; perhaps they kept it, because they thought it was an artistic thing to look at. There is no accounting for tastes in manufacturing circles. Anyhow, they simply built a new chimney and started to use that one instead of the old one. I think the chimney is the entirety here and they simply renewed it,

By contrast, in *Samuel Jones & Co (Devonvale) Ltd v IRC*[129] the factory, not the chimney, was the entirety. In this case, the taxpayer company was involved in processing paper. A chimney of its factory was replaced because of its dangerous condition. However, the replacement chimney did not constitute an appreciable improvement over the original one. The company claimed to deduct the costs of removing the old chimney and building the new one. The Commissioners held that the cost of

[128] at page 102.
[129] (1951) 32 TC 513.

replacement of the chimney was capital expenditure but allowed the cost of removing the old chimney, but the court held that the whole cost of replacing the chimney (including the cost of removing the old chimney) was deductible. The Lord President (Cooper)[130] felt that O'Grady was distinguishable because in this case the facts demonstrated beyond a doubt that the chimney in the case was "physically, commercially and functionally an inseparable part of an entirety, which is the factory." He said that it was "quite impossible" to describe this chimney as being the entirety, saying that it was "doubtless an indispensable part of the factory, doubtless an integral part; but none the less a subsidiary part, and one of many subsidiary parts, of a single industrial profit-earning undertaking." In spite of this explanation, it is not really clear why in this case the chimney was inseparable from the factory, but the one in O'Grady was. It may well be significant that, in O'Grady, at the end of the expenditure the taxpayer was left with both the old and the new chimneys, whereas in this case the old was replaced by the new.

In *Rhodesia Railways Ltd v Bechuanaland Protectorate IT Collector* the entirety was the whole of the railway, not the lines and the sleepers themselves. The lines and sleepers were merely subsidiary items of the whole concern. This seems sensible enough. The decision in *Samuel Jones & Co (Devonvale) Ltd v IRC* that the factory was the entirety and the chimney was just a part of that entirety also seems sensible enough. In *Margarett v The Lowestoft Water and Gas Co*[131] a new reservoir, constructed some distance away from an older one which it replaced, was twice the capacity of the old one and, was, in several respects, an improvement on the old one. Finlay J held that this was not expenditure on repair but capital expenditure. According to him[132]:

> Now here the subject matter under discussion seems to me to be the reservoir, and I cannot think that it is material, though it is undoubtedly the fact, that the reservoir is part only of the Respondents' whole physical undertaking. It is a part perfectly clearly divisible from the rest, and it is the part with which we are dealing here.

The reservoir was the entirety because it was clearly "divisible" from the rest of the property. Again, this concept of divisibility or separability appears.

In *Lawrie v IRC*[133] the roof of the taxpayer's building fell into disrepair and reconstruction of the premises was undertaken involving the lengthening and heightening of the building and the construction of a

---

[130] at page 518.
[131] (1935) 19 TC 481.
[132] at page 488.
[133] (1952) 34 TC 20.

new roof. The Special Commissioners held that the cost of the new roof was not deductible. They held that the expenditure was not on the repair of the premises or subsidiary or subordinate parts thereof, but on the reconstruction, alteration, extension and improvement of the building as a whole, involving in particular expenditure on an entirely new and enlarged roof. They also held that the roof was the entirety. Their decision that the expenses were not deductible was upheld by the court. However, the Lord President (Cooper) disagreed with their ruling that the roof was the entirety, holding[134] that the "entirety" to be considered was the building as a whole and not its roof. This was also the opinion of Lord Carmont.[135] In so deciding, both judges founded their analyses on *Samuel Jones & Co (Devonvale) Ltd v IRC.*

Finally, in *Brown v Burnley Football and Athletic Co Ltd*[136] the erection of a new stand at a football ground was not a repair of any larger premises. Vinelott J said[137] that the question, "What is the whole, the entirety, the entity which is said to have been repaired by replacement of part?", cannot be answered by any one yardstick or rule of thumb. Rather, it must "be answered in the light of all the circumstances which it is reasonable to take into account". Presumably in this case the new stand itself was the entirety.[138] This again would be sensible. It is a decision that could be reached by the principle of separability or divisibility, because the seating stands can clearly be separated from the other structures in a football ground.

So the cases seem to point to divisibility being a helpful criterion to decide the question "what is the entirety with which we are concerned?". Rowlatt J did not seem to consider this point in *O'Grady v Bullcroft Main Collieries Ltd*, and in the light of subsequent decisions, it is doubtful whether that decision can now be regarded as correct. However, in approaching this question, one must bear in mind that there is no infallible test, and that the matter is a question of degree. Thus O'Grady may be seen as being correct in the light of its own facts – in particular, when considering that the new chimney did not replace the old in situ, but rather, they both existed at adjacent locations. The fact that both chimneys could exist at the same time may point to the severability of the old chimney from the rest of the factory. On the other hand, new rail lines and sleepers cannot coexist with the ones that they replace – which may mean that they are not severable from the whole line. The same may be said for a window which has to be replaced.

---

[134] at page 25.
[135] at page 26.
[136] (1980) 53 TC 357.
[137] at page 370.
[138] Vinelott J did not make clear what he considered to be the entirety, but since he clearly took the view that the entirety must be identified correctly, it can be presumed that the stand, and not some larger entity, was, in his judgment, the entirety.

Initial repairs

One interesting application of the distinction between repairs and improvements can be seen in the judicial approach to reduced costs of purchase. Generally, if the acquisition costs of an asset are reduced to reflect the works that are needed to put the asset into a usable state, actual and subsequent costs of those works are not deductible. The works and costs represent capital expenditure – they are part of the costs of acquiring a "usable" asset. This principle has been applied from early times,[139] but the most celebrated case on the point is *Law Shipping Co Ltd v IRC*.[140] Here a shipping company bought a second-hand ship at a reduced price at a time when the ship's periodical "Lloyd's survey" was overdue. Substantial amounts were later spent on repairing the ship in order to enable it to pass its Lloyd's survey and to be in a recognised usable condition. The company's claim to deduct the cost of repairing the ship failed. According to the Lord President (Clyde)[141]:

> It is obvious that a ship, on which repairs have been allowed to accumulate, is a less valuable capital asset with which to start business than a ship which has been regularly kept in repair. And it is a fair inference that the sellers would have demanded and obtained a higher price than they actually did, but for the immediate necessity of repairs to which the ship was subject when they put her in the market. The additional gains they had made by postponing repairs were thus counter-balanced by the diminished value of the ship on realisation

Lord Cullen said[142] that the repair costs were in substance equivalent to an addition to the price of the ship.

On the other hand, in *Odeon Associated Theatres Ltd v Jones*[143] a sum of money spent on completing repairs to a cinema that had recently been purchased was allowed as a deductible expense. The cinema was purchased in a state of disrepair because repairs had been impossible to complete owing to war-time restrictions. Salmon LJ[144] distinguished the *Law Shipping* case. First, in that case, the purchase price was substantially less than it would have been had the vessel been in a fit state of repair to pass the Lloyd's survey at the date of purchase. Here however, the purchase price paid by the taxpayers was in no way affected by the fact that the cinema was in disrepair at the date of its acquisition. Secondly, in the Law Shipping case the vessel was not in a state to pass survey at the time of purchase, and in order to obtain a Lloyd's certificate and turn it into a profit-earning asset

---

[139] See *Highland Railway Co v Balderston* (1889) 2 TC 485 - especially the Lord President at pages 487-488.
[140] (1924) 12 TC 621.
[141] at page 626.
[142] at page 628.
[143] [1972] 2 WLR 331; (1971) 48 TC 257.
[144] 48 TC 257 at pages 283-284.

it was necessary to spend a large sum on deferred repairs. Here, the cinema was a profit-earning asset at the date of its acquisition in spite of its state of disrepair. And, thirdly, in the *Law Shipping* case there had been no evidence that on established principles of sound commercial accounting the expenditure could properly be charged by the taxpayer as revenue expenditure. Here however, the commissioners held, on ample evidence, that it was in accordance with the established principles of sound commercial accounting to charge the items to revenue expenditure, and these principles did not conflict with any statute.

Thus the court was able to view the expenditure as merely repair costs of a capital asset rather than as part of the acquisition costs of a capital asset.

Damages and "Losses"

Section 74(1)(e) prohibits the deduction of "any loss not connected with or arising out of the trade, profession or vocation". The first thing to note in respect of this provision is that the concept of "loss" therein is not one which refers to overall trading loss computed in accordance with accountancy practice after taking account of the trader's receipts and expenses over the relevant period or year. The concept of "loss" here refers to some liability or damage or other diminution in the trader's finances, which the trader then seeks to claim as a deduction. This could take the form of a payment of fines, damages or other form of compensation, either in contract or in tort, or it could take the form of fraud or thefts by employees. The principle of this provision is that such a "loss" can only be deducted if it is connected with the trade, or arises out of it – i.e., it must be occasioned or suffered as a consequence of pursuing profits through the exercise of the trade, profession or vocation – it must fall on the trader in his or her professional or trade capacity and not in any other capacity. That causal link appears to be hard to establish, and the cases mostly go against the taxpayer. There is often a fine line between what is allowed and what is not, and, according to Lord Loreburn LC in *Strong & Co of Romsey Ltd v Woodifield*[145] many cases might be put near the line, and no degree of ingenuity can frame a formula so precise and comprehensive as to solve at sight all the cases that may arise. In *IRC v E C Warnes & Co Ltd*[146] Rowlatt J would only go as far as saying that "a loss connected with or arising out of a trade must, at any rate, amount to something in the nature of a loss which is contemplable, and in the nature of a commercial loss." It seems that s.74(1)(e) and s.74(1)(a) "involve essentially the same test for deductibility"[147]. Policy questions can also play a significant part in

---

[145] [1906] AC 448; 5 TC 215 at 220.
[146] (1919) 12 TC 227 at 231.
[147] Finlay J in *Allen v Farquharson Bros* (1932) 17 TC 59 at 64-65; Lightman J in *McKnight (HMIT) v Sheppard* [1996] BTC 355 at 374 (reversed on other grounds, [1997] BTC 328).

deciding which losses should be allowed or disallowed.[148]

One of the leading cases on this issue is *Strong & Co of Romsey Ltd v Woodifield*[149]. Here the taxpayers carried on the business of brewers and innkeepers. Part of their hotel (a chimney) collapsed and injured a guest. The taxpayers paid compensation to the injured guest and then sought to deduct that payment as a loss arising out of their trade. The House of Lords held that the loss was not deductible. It was held that the loss sustained by the taxpayers was not really incidental to their trade as innkeepers, but rather fell upon them in their character not of traders but of householders. According to the Lord Loreburn LC[150]:

> [I]t does not follow that if a loss is in any sense connected with the trade, it must always be allowed as a deduction for it may be only remotely connected with the trade or it may be connected with something else quite as much as or even more than with the trade. I think only such losses can be deducted as are connected with it in the sense that they are really incidental to the trade itself. They cannot be deducted if they are mainly incidental to some other vocation, or fall on the trader in some character other than that of trader. The nature of the trade is to be considered. To give an illustration, losses sustained by a railway company in compensating passengers for accident in travelling might be deducted. On the other hand, if a man kept a grocer's shop, for keeping which a house is necessary, and one of the window shutters fell upon and injured a man walking in the street, the loss arising thereby to the grocer ought not to be deducted.[151]

In practice a wide range of losses have been allowed, even though it is not always possible to agree on or perceive the link between the loss and the carrying on of or capacity of the trade, profession or vocation. Examples include damages for libel published in the course of publishing a newspaper[152], damages for the wrongful dismissal of an employee[153], and legal expenses.[154] One thing that is clear is that the courts will often take a strict view of the question whether the necessary link with the trade exists. This can be seen from the cases involving fraud or thefts by employees. While fraud or theft by strangers may be difficult to link with the trade, if an employee of a trader defrauds the business or steals from the employers, one would have thought that this is a loss that is connected with the trade.

---

[148] See Lord Hoffmann in *McKnight (HMIT) v Sheppard* [1999] BTC 236 at 239-240.

[149] [1906] AC 448; 5 TC 215.

[150] 5 TC at page 219.

[151] The speech delivered by Lord Davey was unique (the rest of their Lordships agreed with the Lord Chancellor) in that it did not focus on the issue of "loss". Lord Davey appeared to support his conclusion by a consideration of the general requirement that the expense (loss, in this instance) must be wholly and exclusively incurred for the purpose of the business.

[152] *Herald and Weekly Times Ltd v Fed. Commr. of Taxation* (1932) 48 CLR 113 (High Court of Australia, approved by Lord Hoffmann in *McKnight (HMIT) v Sheppard* [1999] BTC 236 at 240). Contrast *Fairrie v Hall* (1947) 28 TC 200 (damages for malicious libel by sugar broker not deductible).

[153] *Mitchell v B W Noble Ltd* [1927] 1 KB 719, 11 TC 372.

[154] *McKnight (HMIT) v Sheppard* (supra); Finlay J in *Allen v Farquharson Bros* (1932) 17 TC 59 at 64.

It is unrealistic to say that the loss fell on the trader in the capacity of employer and not in the capacity of trader, for it is arguably the fact that the trader has employed the fraudster to help carry on the business and earn profits that has given the fraudster an opportunity which he would not have had otherwise - access to the trader's money. However the courts have not accepted this type of analysis.

In *Curtis v Oldfield*[155] the managing director of the taxpayer company, who had been in sole control of the company's business, had allowed to pass through the company's books some money matters relating to his private affairs. On his death, it was found that some money was owing to the company from his estate. The debt was valueless because his estate was insolvent, and it was written off as a bad debt in the company's account. Rowlatt J disallowed the claim because it was neither a trading debt (see below) nor a loss that had arisen out of the trade. He said[156] that, in point of law it was the profits of the company's trade, and not of the company itself, that was being assessed to tax. In considering whether these losses arose out of the company's trade, the situation was that "the assets of the Company, moneys which the Company had got and which had got home to the Company, got into the control of the Managing Director of the Company, and he took them out. It seems to me that what has happened is that he has made away with receipts of the Company dehors the trade altogether in virtue of his position as Managing Director in the office and being in a position to do exactly what he likes." However, Rowlatt J suggested that petty thefts by employees may be deductible[157]:

[I]f you have a business in the course of which you have to employ subordinates, and owing to the negligence or the dishonesty of the subordinates some of the receipts of the business do not find their way into the till, or some of the bills are not collected at all ... that may be an expense [or loss] connected with an arising out of the trade in the most complete sense of the word.

This decision was applied in *Bamford v ATA Advertising Ltd.*[158] wherein a director of a company had misappropriated some £15,000, which the company claimed to deduct. Brightman J held that the money was not deductible because it was not a loss "connected with or arising out of" the company's trade. In this case, counsel for the company had argued that there was no logical distinction between petty theft by a subordinate employee and massive defalcation by director. Brightman J rejected that argument[159].

---

[155] (1925) 9 TC 319.
[156] at page 330.
[157] at pages 330-331.
[158] [1972] 3 All ER 535; 48 TC 359.
[159] 48 TC at page 368.

In my view there is a distinction. I can quite see that the commissioners might find as a fact that a £5 note taken from the till by a shop assistant is a loss to the trader which is connected with and arises out of the trade. A large shop has to use tills and to employ assistants with access to those tills. It could not trade in any other way. That, it seems to me, is quite a different case from a director with authority to sign cheques who helps himself to £15,000, which is then lost to the company. In the defaulting director type of case, there seems to me to be no relevant nexus between the loss of the money and the conduct of the company's trade. The loss is not, as in the case of the dishonest shop assistant an incident of the company's trading activities. It arises altogether outside such activities. That, I think, is the true distinction.[160]

With respect, this distinction between petty thefts and massive defalcations is not convincing. If the distinction lies in the amounts involved, that would seem illogical and arbitrary. For example, if a shop assistant takes £5,000 from the till, or if a bank cashier helps himself to huge sums of money from his till, is this a petty theft or a massive defalcation? If the true distinction lies in where the theft occurs, that still seems to be arbitrary. If a shop assistant takes £5 from the till that would be a petty theft that arises out of the trade. What if the money was taken from the safe in the backroom – or from the money bag on the way to make a deposit at the bank? It would make no sense to say in the first case that the loss fell on the trader as a safe-owner, and, in the second case, as a bank depositor. So wherein lies the true distinction, if one does in fact exist? Does it lie in whether the loss occurred when the employee was engaged in the activity of earning profits in the trade? This would cover the case of a check-out assistant or cashier taking money from the till. Would it cover the case of a finance director with the authority to write cheques who then fraudulently writes a cheque to himself? If not, why not? By analogy with Brightman J's own example, a large business or company has to have a finance manager or director with access to the company's money. It could not trade in any other way. It is unconvincing to say that the finance director's duties are not connected with the company's trade. A trader does not just sell goods. He or she or it would need (if the business is successful) an organisation to provide the necessary infrastructure for the carrying on and management of the business. Lack of good management and infrastructure can quickly reduce a profitable business (or one with the potential to be profitable) to nothing, as customers vote with hastily their feet.

---

[160] See also *Roebank Printing Co. Ltd v IRC* (1928) 13 TC 864.

Thus, the distinction being sought to be made here seems completely artificial. A better approach would be that all losses caused by the activities of the trader's employees due to opportunities presented to them by their employment arise out of or are connected with the trade.

Bad Debts

Section 74(1)(j) prohibits deductions in respect of any debts, except a bad debt proved to be such, a debt or part of a debt released by the creditor wholly and exclusively for the purposes of his trade, profession or vocation as part of a relevant arrangement or compromise, and a doubtful debt to the extent estimated to be bad. The last phrase means, in the case of the bankruptcy or insolvency of the debtor, the whole debt except to the extent that any amount may reasonably be expected to be received on the debt. Although not clearly specified in the subsection, it seems that, for a debt to be deductible, it must be a debt of the trade. According to Rowlatt J in *Curtis v Oldfield*[161]:

> When the rule speaks of a bad debt, it means a debt which is a debt that would have come into the balance sheet as a trading debt in the trade that is in question and that is bad. It does not really mean any bad debt which, when it was a good debt, would not have come in to swell the profits.

Business Entertainment

The statutory rules in respect of business entertainment constitute Parliament's reaction to cases such as *Bentley, Stokes and Lowless v Beeson*.[162] S.577(1) provides that no deduction is allowed in respect of expenses incurred in providing business entertainment. S.577(3) includes in this prohibition an allowance given to an employee for business entertainment, except where the amount falls to be charged on the employee as an emolument under Schedule E. S.577(5) defines "business entertainment" to mean entertainment (including hospitality of any kind) provided by a trader or a member of his staff in connection with the trade. However, the definition excludes things provided for bona fide members of the trader's staff, unless its provision for them is also incidental to its provisions for others. S.577(8) extends the prohibition to the provision of gifts, except where the article given incorporates a conspicuous advertisement for the

---

[161] 9 TC at page 330.
[162] [1952] 2 All ER 82; 33 TC 491.

donor and is not food, drink, tobacco, token or voucher exchangeable for goods, and the cost to the donor together with the cost of other gifts to the same person in the same relevant tax period does not exceed £50. This exception would cover things like calendars, diaries, pens and mugs. S.577(9) allows the deduction of gifts made to charities, and s.577(10) allows deductions in respect of trading stock provided by the trader in the ordinary course of the trade for payment, or, with the object of advertising to the public generally, gratuitously. This will cover promotional or complimentary copies of items which the trader sells in his her trade.

Partnerships

Partnerships are not legal persons and so the profits and expenses of a partnership belong to the individual partners. The logical consequence of the partnership's lack of legal personality is that one must look to the individual partners rather than the firm's intentions when considering the purpose of the expenditure incurred by the firm.   For example, in *MacKinlay v Arthur Young McClelland Moores & Co*[163] a partnership (the "firm") sought to deduct expenditure incurred in providing a substantial contribution toward the removal expenses of two of the partners. The partners had moved at the firm's request. The Court of Appeal had held that these expenses were deductible because they were incurred by the firm wholly and exclusively for business purposes,[164] Slade J suggesting that it was "the collective purpose of this notionally distinct entity which has to be ascertained". The House of Lords disagreed with the reasoning of the Court of Appeal. The House confirmed that in ascertaining the purpose of the expenditure, one must look to the intentions and motives of the individual partners. In this particular case, the expenditure had a dual purpose, one of which was the provision of personal and private benefits to the partners as householders. Accordingly the expenditure was disallowed as not being incurred "wholly and exclusively" for business purposes.

---

[163] [1989] STC 898.
[164] [1988] STC 116.

Trading Losses

A trading loss will arise if, in the relevant accounting period, the computation of profits reveals that expenditure and allowances (including adjustments to stock) exceed receipts. If a loss is computed the taxpayer will need to consider whether any relief is available. That some relief should be available has long been acknowledged[165], but the form of the relief has caused some debate. The debate has focused on the issues of (1) whether relief should be confined to allowing the taxpayer to carry forward any loss to set against the future profits of the same trade or business only; (2) whether the relief suggested in (1) should be limited in time, perhaps for six years only; (3) whether the taxpayer should enjoy the ability to carry forward the loss to set against his future profits or income from whatever source; and (4) whether the taxpayer ought to be able to roll back the loss suffered and set it off against previous years trading profits – with or without a time limit.

S James and C Nobes[166] give a number of arguments in favour of losses being allowed to be set against trading profits, the main thrust of which is that this would bring government into a sort of partnership with enterprise, sharing in the profits (through taxation) and losses (through loss-offsets) thereby reducing the risks associated with enterprise.

Following the enactment and development of earlier legislation, provisions now exist (TA 1988 ss.380-401) to facilitate loss relief in the form of (1), (3) and (4) above. Loss relief started life as the ability to set-off trading loss against current trading profit enjoyed by the same taxpayer in distinct and separate trades.[167] This was developed to allow a trader to set off a trading loss against other income (from whatever source) of the same period. Eventually, the situation was reached where business or trade losses could be carried forward to be set-off against trade profits of the same business or trade.[168] This ability to carry forward was also developed and extended to set-off against general income from whatever source.

The issue of whether a taxpayer ought to be allowed to carry back loss caused some concern. In 1951 the Committee on the Taxation of Trading Profits stated that objections of principle can be raised against any suggestion of carrying losses back:

> It would introduce a novel proposition into Income Tax if tax admittedly due for a particular year and correctly representing the taxpayer's capacity to pay for that year could be reclaimed by reference to circumstances arising in a later year.[169]

---

[165] For example, see the Final Report of the Royal Commission on the Taxation of Profits and Income, Cmnd 9474 (1955) at para 486, where the Commission said that any suggestion that a relief for loss should not be available was plainly unacceptable. The same Committee did however refer to the development of loss provisions under Schedule D as a comparatively recent growth.

[166] "The Economics of Taxation", page 61.

[167] Income Tax Act 1805 and 1842.

[168] This was originally subject to a six year limitation period - until the limitation period was removed by the Income Tax Act 1952.

[169] Report of the Committee on the Taxation of Trading Profits, Cmnd 8189 (1951) at para 80.

In 1955 the Radcliffe Commission stated that it would be theoretically unreasonable to allow losses to be carried back and set–off against profits of past years.[170] Despite the theoretical objections, both Committees actually objected to any general ability to carry back losses on practical grounds. It was stated that complicated provisions would be necessary in order to facilitate and achieve "carry back" and that it would cause additional work to the Inland Revenue and to the taxpayer and his advisers. However, one exception and permitted area of carry back was deemed necessary to facilitate the circumstances where, during the last year of the business's operation, the business and the taxpayer suffer a substantial loss with no corresponding general income against which that loss might be set. There was therefore a need to provide an avenue of relief for such a loss. That avenue of relief is now to be found in s.388, TA 1988.

Before we proceed to examine the details of the current provisions dealing with loss relief, it is important to appreciate that some of the provisions overlap, giving the taxpayer a choice as to the order in which the provisions and relief will apply.[171]

The Statutory Provisions for Loss Relief (ss.380-401)

Opening losses

Section 381 allows the trader to make a claim for losses sustained in the first year of the business, or in any of the next three years of assessment, to be carried back and set off against general income for the three years before that in which the loss was sustained. The loss must be first set against the income of earlier years before later years. S.381 is available to individuals (e.g., partners and sole traders) but not to limited companies.

Terminal losses

Section 388 allows a trader to claim for "terminal" losses in his or her trade to be carried back and set off against the profits of that trade for a period of three years preceding the one in which the trade ended. As the phrase "terminal loss" indicates, carry back under s.388 only applies where the trade, profession or vocation has been permanently discontinued.

Set-off against general income

Section 380 allows the taxpayer to carry across losses from his trading activities to be set off against his general income in that year of assessment,

---

[170] Supra.
[171] See *Butt v Haxby* [1983] STC 239; 56 TC 547.

and against general income from the preceding year. Losses must first be set against income of the current year before any unrelieved excess can be set against income of the preceding year. There is also the possibility to elect to set any unrelieved losses against any chargeable gains tax realised in that year. In making such an election, the taxpayer will not enjoy any Capital Gains Tax annual exemption.[172]

Two main restrictions apply to the use of s.380. First, the taxpayer has to make a claim for the relief, within a specified 12 month period[173], and secondly, relief is only available if the business was genuine, i.e., the loss-making business was run on a commercial basis with a reasonable expectation of profit.[174]

Carry forward against subsequent profits of the same trade

Section 385 allows the taxpayer to carry forward any unrelieved loss of his trade, profession or vocation and set that loss against the first available profits of the same trade, profession or vocation without time limit. Where the loss cannot be relieved wholly in this way, the trader can set it against any income received by the business which has already been taxed at source, such as dividend or interest payments.[175] In doing so, a repayment claim may be made. The overriding restriction imposed on section 385, is the requirement that the taxpayer carries on the trade, profession or vocation. Any discontinuance of the activity will remove the relief, except:

1. any technical discontinuance of a partnership through the retirement of one of the partners shall be ignored. The continuing partners will be entitled to carry forward a share of the loss[176]; and

2. if the taxpayer transfers his business to a company in return for a transfer of shares, the taxpayer can carry forward the loss to set off against income derived by him from the company - for example, earned income from a service contract with the company, or unearned income in the form of a return on his shares (dividends).[177]

Relief under s.385 will apply automatically unless the taxpayer makes a claim under s.380. If the latter option is chosen, then any unrelieved loss remaining after the application of s.380 will be dealt with, automatically, under section 385.

---

[172] FA 1991 s.72.
[173] S.380(1).
[174] TA 1988 s.384.
[175] S.385(4).
[176] TA 1988 s.113.
[177] TA 1988 s.386.

Carry forward on transfer of business to company

If a business, a sole trader or partnership, is sold (either through incorporation or take over) to a limited company, any loss sustained by the business in its final year cannot be carried forward into the company. Instead, s.386 allows the former proprietor of the business to set off any loss against any future income that he or she receives from the company (salary, dividends, etc.) provided that, in the relevant year of assessment he or she own shares in the company, and the company continues to trade. As an alternative to s.386, the proprietor could use the carry back provisions of s.388. In more complex situations, s.386 will assist in providing relief for any unabsorbed losses under s.388.

Further Reading

James S and Nobes C, *The Economics of Taxation*.

Kerridge R, *Deductibility of Expenses for Schedule D Income Tax – The "All or Nothing" Rule* [1986] BTR 36.

Avery-Jones J F, *Objective Purpose Comes to the United Kingdom* [1983] BTR 199.

Grout V, *Wholly and Exclusively and Duality of Purpose Pts I & II* [1979] BTR 44–49; 96–111.

chapter nine
Income Tax -
Capital Allowances

In the post-war period in particular, businesses have received tax incentives in an attempt to encourage the acquisition of and investment in capital assets such as plant, machinery and industrial buildings. The tax incentive have taken the form of an allowance to be set-off against the annual profits of the business. Normally, the acquisition costs of the capital asset would only be taken into account on the assets "disposal" under the Capital Gains Tax regime - a large and unnecessary wait. Relying on the Capital Gains Tax regime to accommodate the costs of expenditure would probably result in a disincentive effect with little investment taking place in the development and updating of business machinery and premises. A lack of investment would have consequent adverse effects on the economy.[1]

The "allowance" received under the capital allowances scheme has varied at different times between a 100% initial allowance, and a mixture of initial and writing down allowances, and a reduced percentage writing down allowance only. The latter demanded more patience and planning from the businesses and would not offer immediate tax consequences and benefits.

It became increasingly apparent that the capital allowance system was subject to abuse: businesses would invest in unnecessary or unproductive capital simply to enjoy the tax deductions attributable to those investments. This abuse (and suspected abuse) caused the Government to review the system and announce a three stage reform of the capital allowances system. The (then) Chancellor of the Exchequer, Mr Nigel Lawson, explained that "too much of British investment had been made because the tax allowances made it look profitable rather than because it would be truly productive". In order to encourage "investment decisions based on future market assessments, not future tax assessments", Mr Lawson announced a three stage reform as follows :

---

[1] It is important to note that capital allowances postpone tax rather than permanently reduce it. Such a postponement is useful in the early years when the money can be used for other purposes or in times of inflation when the real value of the eventual payment falls.

In the case of plant and machinery ... the first year allowance will be reduced from 100 per cent to 75 per cent for all such expenditure incurred after today [13 March 1984], and to 50 per cent for expenditure incurred after 31 March next year. After 31 March 1986 there will be no first year allowances, and all expenditure on plant and machinery will qualify for annual allowances on a 25 per cent reducing balance basis ....

... For industrial buildings, I propose that the initial allowance should fall from 75 per cent to 50 per cent from tonight, and be further reduced to 25 per cent from 31 March next year. After 31 March 1986 the initial allowance will be abolished, and expenditure will be written off on an annual 4 per cent straight line basis ....[2]

Since that statement there does appear to have been a change in attitude. For example, first year allowances became available on expenditure on qualifying assets between the period of 1 November 1992 to 31 October 1993 at a rate of 40%. The relief was then increased to 50% for expenditure incurred between 2 July 1997 and 1 July 1998.

The full details of these changes can be found in the Capital Allowances Act 2001. The Capital Allowances Act 2001 is the first piece of legislation to be enacted under the Tax Law Rewrite project. The purpose of the project is to rewrite most of the UK's existing primary direct tax legislation in order to make it clearer and easier to use, without changing or making less certain its general effect. The Capital Allowances Act 2001 (CAA) replaces the 165 sections of the Capital Allowances Act 1990 with 581 sections of simple rewritten rules! The CAA took effect from April 2001. Before we look at those details, we must first consider the meaning of industrial building and plant and machinery.

Industrial Buildings (CAA 2001, Part 3)

Industrial buildings were defined in the 1990 Act[3] and provision for them is now found in Part 3 of the 2001 Act.[4] In essence the definition attempts to equate "industrial" with manufacture and production, but not distribution activities.[5] However, if the storage and distribution of goods is for the purpose of the business, then the building and its use will be classed as "industrial".[6] S.277 excludes a number of buildings − for example,

---

[2]   March 13, 1984. Hansard, HC, Vol 56, Cols 295-296. Mr Lawson still believed that the much amended and reduced capital allowance system would still be more generous than a system of commercial depreciation. Note that an initial allowance has been retained in respect of industrial buildings in particular circumstances, such as Capital expenditure on the construction of a building in an enterprise zone where expenditure on commercial buildings or structures may qualify for a full 100% first year allowance.

[3]   See s.18, CAA 1990

[4]   See especially ss.271 and 274.

[5]   S.274.

[6]   See *Saxone Liley and Skinner (Holdings) Ltd v IRC* [1967] All ER 756.

buildings used as a dwelling, retail shop, hotel, office[7] or showroom do not qualify. A warehouse[8] is not an industrial building — neither is a crematorium.[9] Apportionment is allowed to facilitate part qualifying and part non-qualifying use. Apportionment is subject to a very generous allowance of total costs where the non-qualifying use is insignificant - representing not more than 25% of the total construction costs of the building.

Finally, it is important to appreciate that where an initial allowance still remains, it is only available to the person who incurs the cost of the building; writing down and balancing allowances are available to those who enjoy a relevant interest. A relevant interest means that the person who incurs the expenditure must have an interest in the property at the time of the expenditure. For example, a leaseholder or freeholder who incurs capital expenditure on improvement would be able to enjoy the allowance. Their position as freeholder or leaseholder represents an interest in the property.

Plant and Machinery (CAA, Part 2)

"Plant" and "machinery" have not been traditionally defined by legislation and the Law Tax rewrite avoided any attempt to define "plant". Their meanings have traditionally been determined by the courts and depend on the particular facts of the case. Judicial guidance on this matter contains many contradictions and difficulties. The best advice is to focus on the facts of the case and to consider

> ... whether it can really be supposed that Parliament desired to encourage a particular expenditure out of, in effect, taxpayers' money and ... ultimately, in extreme cases, to say that this is too much to stomach ...[10]

The real difficulty in understanding and distinguishing "plant" involves the need to distinguish "premises and setting" from "plant", in a manner that facilitates the recognition of plant as an integral part of the carrying-on of the business. Such a recognition of the integral nature of plant has appeared in judicial comments as the "functional", "business" or "amenity" test. Some even refer to a very broad "premises" test to support the need for a distinction. The *dictum* of Lindley LJ in *Yarmouth v France* is often cited as the basis for the adopted distinctions:

---

[7] See also *Girobank Plc v Clarke* (HMIT) [1996] BTC 241.
[8] *Sarsfield v Dixons Group plc* [1998] STC 938; BTC 288.
[9] *Bourne v Norwich Crematorium* (1967) 44 TC 164.
[10] Per Lord Wilberforce in *IRC v Scottish and Newcastle Breweries Ltd* [1982] BTC 187 at 190; STC 296. It was suggested that this was destined to become known as the "nausea test". See [1983] BTR 54 at 55.

... in its ordinary sense [plant] ... includes whatever apparatus is used by a business man for carrying on his business – not his stock-in-trade which he buys or makes for sale; but all goods and chattels, fixed or moveable, live or dead, which he keeps for permanent employment in his business.[11]

This definition covers things such as knives and lasts used by shoe manufacturers in their business[12], and law books and law reports used by barristers in their profession.[13] But it appears that we ought to accept (with some caution) that "plant" is not stock-in-trade nor business premises – unless those business premises perform the function of and represent "plant" (integral to the business). The following cases serve to illustrate the distinctions and the difficulties in this area.

IRC v Scottish and Newcastle Breweries Ltd[14]: this case included a claim for costs of metal structures (seagulls in flight) incurred by the owners of a hotel. The purpose of the purchase and erection of these metal structures was to contribute to the creation of an "ambience" or "atmosphere" in the hotel. The Court accepted that the metal structures were plant. The court emphasised that the seagulls performed a functional role in that the creation of ambience or atmosphere was an important function of the trade of successful hoteliers and publicans. It was also stated that the metal structures were not part of the setting in which they did their business – but, the setting offered to customers for them to resort to and enjoy, and hence plant.

In *IRC v Barclay, Curle & Co Ltd*[15], expenditure was incurred on the excavation and concrete work in the construction of a dry dock. The House of Lords accepted that this represented expenditure on plant. Lord Reid explained that although the dry dock was a structure or premises, it was also plant[16]: "The only reason why a structure should also be plant ... is that it fulfils the function of plant in the trader's operations ..."[17]

Similarly in *Cooke (Inspector of Taxes) v Beach Station Caravans Ltd*[18], the "structures" of a swimming pool and a paddling pool in a caravan park were held to be plant. Megarry J emphasised that they were not premises in the sense of "where it's at" (the location of the business activity). They were apparatus in that they were part of the means whereby the trade of a caravan park was carried on.

In *J Lyons & Co Ltd v A-G*[19], the purchase and erection of lamps in a tea

---

[11] [1887] 19 QBD 647 at 658. For an interesting debate on the conflict between the functional and the business test see the debate in *Gray v Seymours Garden Centre* [1993] 2 All ER 809 (noted [1994] BTR 5).

[12] *Hinton v Maden and Ireland* (1959) 38 TC 390.

[13] In *Munby v Furlong* ([1977] Ch 359; 2 All ER 953) it was held (overruling Rowlatt J in *Daphne v Shaw* (1926) 11 TC 256) that a barrister's law books and reports constituted plant.

[14] Supra.

[15] [1969] 1 WLR 675.

[16] This case inspired the advice that one should "always re-decorate one's walls and ceilings with loose chattels" (1983) BTR 54 at 56.

[17] Ibid. at 679.

[18] [1974] STC 402.

[19] [1944] Ch 281.

shop were not plant in that they performed a general function of the provision of light and not a specific trade function in relation to the particular needs and conduct of that trade.

In *Wimpy International Ltd v Warland*[20], Wimpy failed in its claim that expenditure on such items as shop fronts, floors, suspended ceilings, lights and wall finishes represented expenditure on plant. The court emphasised that the fact that different things might perform the same functions of creating atmosphere was irrelevant: what matters is that one thing may function as part of the premises and the other as plant.

Thus it was concluded that

... something which becomes part of the premises instead of merely embellishing them, was not plant, except in the rare case where the premises are themselves plant.[21]

Capital Allowances: The Details

1. Plant and Machinery (CAA 2001, Part 2)

Capital allowances for plant and machinery are available for those who carry on a "qualifying activity" and incur qualifying expenditure.[22] A list of qualifying activities is provided in s.15(1), and includes the carrying on of a trade, profession or vocation, employment or office, an ordinary Schedule A business, a furnished holiday lettings business, the management of an investment company, etc. By s.11(4) the general rule is that expenditure is qualifying expenditure if it is capital expenditure on the provision of plant or machinery wholly or partly for the purposes of a qualifying activity, and the person incurring the expenditure owns the plant or machinery as a result of incurring the expenditure[23]. Chapter 3 of Part 2 (especially s.21 and s.22) contains detailed listings of things that qualify and those which do not. For example, s.21 excludes expenditure on the provision of a "building". Building is defined to include assets which are incorporated in a building, and a number of items are listed as being treated as buildings (e.g., walls, floors, ceilings, doors, waste disposal systems, fire safety systems). S.22 contains a list of several other items which are not treated as qualifying for allowance. There is a long list of exceptions (i.e., expenditure unaffected by ss. 21 and 22) in s.23. Thus to determine whether expenditure on an item is disqualified, sections 21 − 23 have to examined closely.

[20] [1989] STC 273.
[21] Supra at 279, per Fox LJ.
[22] CAA 2001, s.11(1).
[23] Emphasis added.

The Schedule E taxpayer is required to establish that the expenditure on the plant and machinery took place because it was "necessarily" provided for use in the performance of the duties of the Schedule E taxpayer.[24] This additional requirement of the Schedule E taxpayer can, once again, prove excessively onerous.[25]

To accord with accountancy practice, expenditure is deemed to have been incurred on the date on which the obligation to pay becomes unconditional[26] even though the sum does may not be due until a later date.[27] Exceptions apply if the date of payment falls four months after the obligation to pay has become unconditional – the due date of payment will then be used in this instance.[28]

Having determined the timing of the expenditure, we need to consider next the tax period in which the allowance may be claimed. For the corporation tax payer, the relevant period is the appropriate accounting year, while for the purposes of income tax, it is the "period of account".[29]

The Allowances

First year allowances

Previously a first year allowance together with a writing down allowance was permitted. We noted in the introduction the concern that was caused by the possible abuse of, in particular, the first year allowance. First year allowances were removed for expenditure incurred after 31 March 1986, but allowances were reintroduced for expenditure incurred on qualifying assets between 1 November 1992 and 31 October 1993 at 40% of the costs of the qualifying asset.

First year allowances next became available at 50% for expenditure incurred between 2 July 1997 and 1 July 1998 for small and medium sized companies. The Finance Act 1998 extended the period to 1 July 1999, whilst reducing the first year allowance to 40% except for capital expenditure on British qualifying films where the first year allowance was 100%. In March 1999 the Chancellor announced that the 40% first year capital allowances would be extended for a further year and that the British Film Industry would continue to qualify for greater relief. In the Budget 2001, the Chancellor announced the introduction of a new scheme for 100% first year capital allowances for investments by businesses in designated energy-saving equipment. This scheme enables a business to write off immediately the whole of its capital on designated energy-saving plant and machinery against its taxable profits. The CAA 2001 now lists the

---

[24] See s.36 (2). This requirement is subject to the provisions of s.80, which relates to vehicles provided for the purpose of an office or employment.
[25] See for example *White v Higginbotham* [1983] STC 143 where the provision of a projector to a vicar was not "necessarily" incurred for the performance of his duties.
[26] S.5(1).
[27] S.5(2).
[28] S.5(5).
[29] S.6(1).

available first year allowances in s.39 (subject to some general exclusions in s.46). The list includes expenditure incurred for by small or medium sized enterprises, expenditure on energy-saving plant and machinery, and expenditure on ICT (Information and Communications Technology) by small enterprises.

First year allowances are made for the chargeable period in which the first year qualifying expenditure is incurred[30] in form of a percentage of the qualifying expenditure (according to a table in s.52(3)).

Writing down allowances

The writing down allowance has been retained and this allows the taxpayer to progressively write-off the cost of the plant and machinery. The details are below:

The basic allowance – the writing down allowance is an allowance of 25% (on a reducing balance basis) of the "available qualifying expenditure" (expenditure minus any other allowances) on the plant and machinery[31]. The allowance will apply once the expenditure has been incurred, irrespective of whether the asset is in use, on assets wholly and exclusively purchased for the purposes of the trade, profession or vocation. Apportionment of the allowance on terms that are just and reasonable is permitted to recognise non-business purpose and use.

There is an exception to the 25% writing down allowance in the case of long-life assets (machinery and plant with a "useful economic life" of 25 years or more)[32]. Here the writing down allowance is 6% where a person incurs expenditure of more than £100,000 on such assets and they were acquired on or after 26 November 1996.[33]

Pooling – it is normal for a trade to acquire a number of items of plant and machinery. It then becomes convenient, and possible, to create a "pool" of plant and machinery. Pooling is generally required by s.53(1).[34] The writing down allowance of 25% will then be applied to the value of the "pool" rather than the value of individual items.

Disposal – if an item of plant or machinery is disposed of, provision must be made to ensure that the disposal consideration or value is taken into account.[35] It is most important that the allowance enjoyed by the business equate with the actual cost to the business of that item of plant or machinery. "Disposal" is given a wide meaning to include a disposal by sale, a disposal by extinction (destruction), and a disposal through the loss of possession ("loss" or theft).[36] Sale consideration, insurance monies or

---

[30] S.52(2).
[31] S.56. See also ss.55 and 57.
[32] S.91.
[33] See ss.99-102.
[34] By s.53(2), if a person carries on more than one qualifying activity, expenditure relating to different activities must not be allocated to the same pool.
[35] See ss.55-56.
[36] S.61(1).

deemed market value will represent the sum that must be taken into account.[37]

Balancing allowances and charges – no writing-down allowance is available in the year that the business ceases or terminates. Proceeds from the sale of the plant and machinery are deducted from the "available qualifying expenditure". If a surplus of "qualifying expenditure" remains, that surplus will be converted into a "balancing allowance" to be deducted from the taxpayer's profits and income. Conversely, if the proceeds of sale of the plant and machinery exceed the qualifying expenditure, the excess is treated as a "balancing charge" and becomes a taxable receipt of the business[38] – this process is known as the "clawback" of capital allowances.

Short-life assets[39] – it is possible for the taxpayer to elect that certain short life assets should not join a general pool of plant and machinery. It is also possible to enjoy a pool of short life assets. A short life asset is one that is expected to be disposed of within five years. Any election in relation to those assets must be made within two years from the date of their acquisition.

The purpose of this permitted de-pooling election is to enable the taxpayer to realise the balancing allowance on short life assets at an earlier time than would normally be available. If those assets were part of a general pool, it normally results in 80% of the cost being written off over eight years.

2. Industrial Buildings (CAA 2001, Part 3)

Capital allowances are available for the construction of an industrial building.[40] The base allowance is a writing-down allowance at a rate of 4% of the cost price of the industrial building. This 4% allowance is available for each year the taxpayer uses the building for industrial purposes[41] up to a maximum of 25 years. The entire expenditure is deemed to have been written-off after 25 years.[42] Note that only the expenditure on the building or structure qualifies, the cost of buying the land on which the building or structure stands is specifically excluded.[43]

A balancing allowance or balancing charge will arise if the building or interest in the building is sold (or demolished, destroyed or relevant use ceases) within the 25-year period.[44] The balancing allowance or charge is computed involving a comparison of the disposal expenditure with the outstanding qualifying expenditure. It is important to appreciate that a

---

[37]   See s.61(2) – s.63.
[38]   See generally s.55.
[39]   See ss.83-89.
[40]   S.271.
[41]   s.310(1)(b).
[42]   S.311.
[43]   s.272.
[44]   See ss.314-315.

balancing charge will not recover more than the allowances given, thus an excessive disposal consideration will give rise to the potential of Capital Gains Tax. This represents an attempt to ensure that the capital allowances given correspond to the actual depreciation suffered by the taxpayer.

The purchaser of a second hand industrial building, may also be entitled to a writing-down allowance. This entitlement depends on the sale to the purchaser falling within the 25-year period. That purchaser will then be entitled to an allowance (not confined to the 4% rate) based upon the residue of expenditure. The residue of expenditure represents any unrelieved expenditure of the vendor plus any balancing charge (or minus a balancing allowance).

Special rules apply to (1) hotel buildings and extensions; and (2) Enterprise Zones. Although hotels do not technically fall within the definition of industrial buildings[45], specific provisions have been introduced to permit expenditure on the construction or improvement of "qualifying hotels"[46] to be written-off on an annual writing-down allowance of 4%.

In order to stimulate development in declared Enterprise Zones, 100% initial allowances are available for capital expenditure on industrial buildings, hotels and commercial buildings in those zones.[47] The 100% initial allowance is not mandatory: an election can be made to enjoy a reduced percentage initial allowance with the balance being written-off annually at 25% of the cost on a straight line method of provision.[48]

3. Other Allowances

Other specific items and areas of expenditure are eligible for capital allowances and charges. These include expenditure incurred on the construction, wholly or partly, of agricultural or forestry buildings;[49] expenditure incurred on the construction of property for letting as assured tenancies;[50] capital expenditure on scientific research;[51] and expenditure incurred in the acquisition of patents and "know-how".[52]

Assessment of the changes and reform

We mentioned at the beginning of this chapter, that Mr Nigel Lawson as Chancellor sought reform of the capital allowance system in a direction that would encourage a balanced approach to investment. He, and others, were concerned that the "old" system of capital allowance was far too

---

[45] S.277.
[46] See s.279.
[47] S.306.
[48] See ss.306 and 310.
[49] Part 4, CAA 2001.
[50] Part 10, CAA 2001.
[51] Part 6, CAA 2001.
[52] Parts 7 and 8, CAA 2001.

generous and had resulted in low-yielding, and even loss-making, investment at the expense of jobs. Following the changes introduced there was some concern that the reforms may have swung the pendulum too far: that there was no longer sufficient encouragement for investment. During the 1990s there were various campaigns seeking a more generous treatment of investment. These included campaigns by the CBI, and by employer's federations in engineering, motor manufacturing and in metal trades. They were supported in their campaigning by the results of academic papers and research. For example, Devereux concluded that the new system of capital allowances acts as a disincentive to real investment.[53]

It is certainly a difficult task to develop and arrange a system of capital allowances that provides the required balance of sufficient incentives for good investment. Although in the March Budget of 1993, the Chancellor did provide some good news for businesses, the issue of capital allowances and incentives for investment was once again a cause of criticism. The Chancellor announced a number of peripheral and limited changes to capital allowance details.[54] The failure to directly address or consider the possible extension and increase of capital allowances was described as "one by omission".[55]

It also drew the following comments from industry :

> We were disappointed that little emphasis was placed on improving investment in high technology. This Budget fell short of directly encouraging UK companies to invest and to meet the anticipated recovery.[56]

and,

> This Budget does nothing to bring about the massive switch from consumption to investment which is essential for lasting recovery.[57]

The debate is certain to continue. The 2001 Budget made advances in respect of the Green Technology Challenge through the capital allowances mentioned earlier. It also extended allowances for the Film Industry. The temporary re-introduction of a first year allowance rate of 40% in 1992-93 and 50% for small/medium sized companies and unincorporated associations in 1997-98 provides some encouragement to those calling for greater assistance to businesses, particularly the small and medium sized enterprises. So far, things seem to be improving.

---

[53] M Devereux. "Corporation Tax: The Effect of 1984 Reforms on the Incentive to Invest", (1988) *Fiscal Studies*, 9(1), 62.
[54] Those changes relate to the ability of a connected person to elect to treat the sale of industrial buildings as having taken place at their tax written-down value.
[55] Financial Times, March 17, 1993 at page 24.
[56] Spokesperson for the Machine Tool Technologies Association. Reported in *Financial Times*, March 17 1993.
[57] Mr Neil Johnson, Director-General of Engineering Employers' Federation. Reported in *Financial Times*, March 17 1993.

Further Reading

Devereux M: *Corporation Tax: The Effect of 1984 Reforms on the Incentive to Invest* (1988) Fiscal Studies, 9(1), 62.

chapter ten

Income Tax -
Schedule D - Case VI

Schedule D Case VI imposes a charge on any annual profits or gains not falling under any other case of Schedule D, and not charged by virtue of Schedule A or E. [1] This is the general or sweeping-up provision of the Schedular system (see earlier discussion of the doctrine of source). Case VI also catches matters specifically declared by statute to be placed within Case VI - these include income from settlements, profits and gains from furnished lettings, securities transactions, post-cessation receipts and the transfers of assets abroad. [2]

It is the general (or sweeping-up) aspects of Case VI that are of interest. An examination of judicial comments and application of Case VI reveals that it is not as wide nor as all-embracing as it initially appears. As Viscount Dunedin said in *Jones v Leeming*[3]:

> Now, Case VI sweeps up all sorts of annual profits and gains which have not been included in the other five heads, but it has been settled again and again that that does not mean that anything that is a profit or gain falls to be taxed.

The first restriction on Case VI is that it applies to income receipts only and (not capital gains or profits).[4] Thus in *Scott v Ricketts*[5] the Court of Appeal declared that a payment to an estate agent for the agent agreeing to forego claims in a development scheme was a capital sum and therefore not caught nor taxable under Case VI. Similarly in *Earl Haig's Trustee v IRC*[6] a trustee owned some diaries and the copyright attached to those diaries. The trustees permitted the use of the diaries in the production of a bibliography and received a sum of money for doing so. The Court of Appeal held that the sum of money received was as a consequence of a realisation (in part) of a capital asset (the diaries and copyright). The money

---

[1] TA 1988, s.18(3) (it is also a residual provision to those sums not caught by Schedule F, TA 1988 s.20).
[2] See generally, TA 1988, s.103(1), s.660C, and s.761.
[3] (1930) 15 TC 333 at 359; AC 415;
[4] See *Jones v Leeming*, supra.
[5] [1967] 2 All ER 1009.
[6] (1939) 22 TC 725.

was not income and was not therefore assessable under Case VI. The true question has thus been described as being whether the transaction in question is really a sale of property or the performance of services.[7]

A second limitation on the scope of Case VI emanates from the words "annual profits or gains".[8] The term "profits or gains" is used elsewhere in Schedule D and the implication is that the words must be consistent in their meaning and application and that the activities that present or create the profit or gain must be analogous. Technically the requirement is that the "profit and gains" are of the same kind (*ejusdem generis*) as "profit and gains" taxed elsewhere under Schedule D. In *Jones v Leeming*[9] Viscount Dunedin cited with approval the dictum of Blackburn J in *AG v Black*[10] that "profits and gains in Case VI must mean profits and gains ejusdem generis with the profits and gains specified in the preceding five Cases".

This requirement has invited the conclusion that the profit or gain must be derived from an activity analogous to an "adventure in the nature of a trade or profession"[11]. This means that Case VI will usually apply to casual earnings (normally from the performance of services) but not gifts[12] nor betting winnings and receipts[13]. For example, in *Hobbs v Hussey*[14] a solicitor's clerk wrote and published his memoirs in *The People* newspaper. This was not the clerk's profession or trade, merely a "casual" activity. The clerk also assigned the copyright of the article to the newspaper. The Court held that the payment received by the clerk was in return for the performance of "casual" services and therefore assessable under Case VI. Although the performance of the services also involved the sale of property (the copyright), Lawrence J emphasised that the essence of the performance was the revenue nature of the receipt which was "the fruit of the individual's capacity" but was not "the capital itself".[15]

In some instances the distinction between an "adventure in the nature of trade" (Schedule D Case I) and an analogous activity (Schedule D Case VI) is difficult to determine. For example, in *Jones v Leeming* the taxpayer was party to a scheme whereby he participated in the acquisition and sale of rubber estates for a profit. The House of Lords concluded that the profit was not assessable under Case VI because it was not a profit within Schedule D. At an earlier stage the Court of Appeal had pointed out the difficulty (if not illogical approach) of the ejusdem generis application. Lawrence LJ suggested that if an isolated transaction such as this is not an adventure in the nature of a trade (Case I) then it is difficult to conclude

---

7 Lawrence J in *Hobbs v Hussey* (1942) 24 TC 153 at 156; 1 KB 491.
8 The term "annual" does not imply that the profit or gain must recur, simply that the "profit or gain" must fall within and be assessed in a year of assessment (see Rowlatt J in *Ryall v Hoare* [1923] 2 KB 447 at 455).
9 15 TC at page 359.
10 (1871) LR 6 Exch. 308 at 309; 8 TC 521 at 525.
11 This analogy is necessary because "profits and gains" are related in Schedule D Cases I and II to "adventures in the nature of a trade" or to a profession. The ejusdem generis approach demands such an analogy and application.
12 In *Scott v Ricketts* [1967] 2 All ER 1009, Lord Denning MR confirmed that "profits and gains" does not include gratuitous payments.
13 See *Graham v Greene* [1925] 2 KB 37.
14 Supra.
15 24 TC at page 156.

that it is a transaction *ejusdem generis* with such a transaction (Case VI):

> All the elements which would go to make such a transaction an
> adventure in the nature of trade would, in my opinion, be required
> to make it a transaction ejusdem generis with such an adventure. It
> seems to me that in the case of an isolated transaction of purchase and
> resale of property there is really no middle course open. It is either
> an adventure in the nature of trade, or else it is simply a case of sale
> and resale of property. If in such transaction as we have here the idea
> of an adventure in the nature of trade is negatived, I find it difficult
> to visualise any source of income, or to appreciate how such a
> transaction can properly be said to have been entered into for the
> purpose of producing income or revenue.[16]

The logical conclusion would be that Case VI is redundant in that *ejusdem
generis* activities must demonstrate the characteristics of trade and would
therefore be "trade" and assessable under Case I. Perhaps a more generous
approach to the interpretation of Case VI is required - especially if it is to
adequately perform a role as a "sweeping-up" or anti-avoidance provision
for casual earnings.

Finally, it should be noted that there are no rules for allowable
deductions under Schedule D, Case VI. Deductibility of expenses is merely
implied from the fact that the charge is on "profits" and not "gross
receipts".[17] Case VI losses can only be set against other Case VI income of
the same tax period or of subsequent tax periods.[18]

---

[16]   15 TC at pages 353-354.
[17]   TA 1988 s.69(1) provides that tax under Case VI "shall be computed on the full amount of the profits or gains arising in the year of assessment".
[18]   TA 1988 s.392(1).

chapter eleven

Income Tax -
Schedule D - Case III
The Taxation of Pure Income Profit

The uncertainties of life in modern societies often lead the astute to endeavour to lay aside some money, either to save for the proverbial rainy day or, to provide some financial independence or security in respect of the inevitable retirement. In such cases it often makes sense to keep the money, not in current banking accounts which return no profit but rather attract charges, but, for the security conscious, in interest-yielding building society/bank accounts or government Treasury Bills; or, for the more adventurous and daring, in various high profit investments. Whichever way the money is kept, it may yield some financial return, in which event there will be the inevitable income tax implications. The financial return on a person's investment may take one of several forms – interest, annuities, discount, rent, dividends, etc. Some of these forms of return will normally be pure profit (in the sense that the financial return is, in its entirety, a profit). This chapter is concerned with the principles that govern the taxation of such "pure profit" income under Case III of Schedule D. While rent and dividends can be regarded as annual investment yields, for reasons that will presently appear, they will not feature in this discussion, either because they are not pure profit (rent) or because, for one reason or another, they do not fall within the technical definition of annual payments (dividends[1]), or because they are specifically excluded from the Case II charge (rent[2]).

The principal charging provision on pure income profit for income tax purposes is s.18(3) of the ICTA 1988 which charges tax under Case III of Schedule D in respect of

---

[1] See Viscount Simon LC in *Canadian Eagle Oil Co. Ltd. v R* [1945] 2 All ER 499 at 504.
[2] See s.18(3) and s.15 ICTA 1988.

a.   any interest of money, whether yearly or otherwise, or any annuity or other annual payment, whether such payment is payable within or out of the United Kingdom ... but not including any payment chargeable under Schedule A, and

b.   all discounts, and

c.   income from securities which is payable out of the public revenue of the United Kingdom or Northern Ireland.

For the purposes of corporation tax, s.18(3A) provides for a different charge under Case III. In this respect, the subsection charges tax under Case III in respect of

a.   profits and gains which, as profits and gains arising from loan relationships, are to be treated as chargeable under this Case by virtue of Chapter II of Part IV of the FA 1996.[3]

b.   any annuity or other annual payment which

i.   is payable ... in respect of anything other than a loan relationship; and

ii. is not a payment chargeable under Schedule A;

c.   any discount arising otherwise than in respect of a loan relationship.

The discussions in this chapter will focus mainly on annuities and other annual payments, while interest and discounts are examined in outline only.

Interest of Money

The question whether a particular sum of money amounts to "interest of money" is a question of law.[4] The answer is dependent, not on the form of words used by the parties to a transaction, but rather, "the question must always be one of the true nature of the payment".[5] However, as is typical of the Taxes Act, the statutory definition of "interest" is not particularly illuminating. S.832(1) of the ICTA 1988 provides that interest "means both annual or yearly interest and interest other than annual or yearly interest". This strange definition, which at least one judge has found himself reading "with disappointment"[6], by simply saying that "'interest', in short, means 'interest'"[7] begs the question "what is interest?". Fortunately, there is no

---

[3]   Case V of Schedule D does not include tax in respect of any income falling under this provision.

[4]   Megarry J in *Re Euro Hotel (Belgravia) Ltd* [1975] 3 All ER 1075 at 1083.

[5]   Megarry J, ibid.

[6]   Megarry J in *Re Euro Hotel (Belgravia) Ltd* [1975] 3 All ER 1075 at 1081.

[7]   ibid.

shortage of judicial definitions.

It seems that, while the meaning of interest is a question of law, there is no special or technical meaning to be attributed for income tax purposes to the word. In *Re Euro Hotel (Belgravia) Ltd*[8], Megarry J commenced his analysis of the word with a reference to the Shorter Oxford Dictionary definition which defined interest as "money paid for the use of money lent (the principal), or for forbearance of a debt, according to a fixed ratio (rate per cent)".[9] Rowlatt J presented a similar answer to this question in *Bennett v Ogston*[10], saying that interest is a "payment by time for the use of money".[11] In *Re Euro Hotel (Belgravia) Ltd*[12] itself, Megarry J referred with approval to a definition given by Rand J of the Supreme Court of Canada in *Re Saskatchewan Farm Security Act 1944*, Section 6[13], that, "interest is, in general terms, the return or consideration or compensation for the use or retention by one person of a sum of money belonging to, in a colloquial sense, or owed to, another". This form of words has also been used in the USA. In *Old Colony R. Co v Comm*[14] the US Supreme Court said that "the usual import of the term is the amount which one has contracted to pay for the use of borrowed money" and in *Lloyd v CIR* O'Connell J said that it is "compensation for the use or forbearance of money."[15]

Thus the essence of interest is that it is a payment which becomes due because the creditor has not had his money at the due date.[16] It may be regarded either as representing the profit which the creditor might have made if he had had the use of his money, or the loss that he suffered because he did not have that use. The general idea is that the creditor is entitled to compensation for the deprivation.[17]

It seems that, as a general rule, there are two specific requirements that must be satisfied for a payment to amount to "interest of money". These were outlined by Megarry J in *Re Euro Hotel (Belgravia) Ltd*[18].

First, there must be a sum of money by reference to which the payment which is said to be interest is to be ascertained ... Secondly, those sums of money must be sums that are due to the person entitled to the alleged interest.

[8]   [1975] 3 All ER at page 1083.
[9]   Emphasis supplied.
[10] (1930) 15 TC 374 at 379.
[11] Compare Farwell J in the non-tax case of *Bond v Barrow Haematite Steel Co* [1902] 1 Ch 353 at 363: "Interest is compensation for delay in payment".
[12] [1975] 3 All ER 1075 at 1084.
[13] [1947] 3 DLR 689 at 703.
[14] 76 L.ed. 484.
[15] 154 F.2d 643 at 646. See also *Nicodemisen v The Dartmouth*, 157 F. Supp. 339 at 334, "damages for delay in the payment of money"; *Columbia Auto Loan v District of Columbia*, 78 A.2d. 857 at 860, "consideration paid for the use of money or for forbearance in demanding it when due".
[16] Lord Wright in *Riches v Westminster Bank Ltd*. [1947] 1 All ER 469 at 472.
[17] Lord Wright, ibid.
[18] [1975] 3 All ER 1075 at 1084.

According to Megarry J, these two requirements are not exhaustive in every case, nor are they inescapable.[19] Thus for example, a payment does not cease to be interest of money "if A lends money to B and stipulates that the interest should be paid not to him but to X".[20]

From the above authorities, we may derive a number of propositions. First, there must be a principal sum by reference to which the interest is calculated. In this respect, Rand J of the Supreme Court of Canada said in *Re Saskatchewan*[21] that "the definition" and "the obligation" of interest assumes that it is referable to "a principal in money or an obligation to pay money." According to him, without this "relational structure" in fact, no obligation to pay money can be an obligation to pay interest - regardless of the basis of calculating the amount.[22] In the same case, Kellock J said that there can be no such thing as interest "on principal which is non-existent".[23] Secondly, the principal sum must be owed to, or "belong" (in the colloquial sense) to a creditor.[24] Thirdly, the payment alleged to be interest must be for the use of that principal sum[25] as compensation calculated by time, for delay in payment.[26] Fourthly, the payment must be due to the creditor or the creditor's nominee.[27]

It had once been thought that, in cases of an award of damages with interest by a court, that "interest" is really "damages" and therefore does not fall within the charge to income tax. This was the approach taken by Wright J in *Re National Bank of Wales Ltd*.[28] This approach was rejected by the House of Lords in *Riches v Westminster Bank Ltd*.[29] The appellant in this case had entered into an agreement with R under which he introduced R to a transaction involving the purchase of certain shares. The agreement provided for R to pay to the appellant 50% of any profit which R might make on resale of the shares. R bought the shares and sold them at a profit, but fraudulently understated the amount of profits made on the sale. On the death of R, the appellant discovered the true extent of the profits, and commenced an action against the respondents as judicial trustee of R's will, claiming an account of the profits of the resale of the said shares, and payment of the difference between the amount already paid by R and the amount due on the true profits.

The judge gave judgment for the appellant in the sum of £36,225 (the correct amount due to the appellant from R on the resale of the shares), and added a sum of £10,028 in exercise of his discretion to award interest under s.3 of the Law Reform (Miscellaneous Provisions) Act 1934. The

[19]   ibid.
[20]   ibid.
[21]   [1947] 3ALR at 703.
[22]   ibid.
[23]   [1947] 3 DLR 689 at 707.
[24]   Rand J in *Re Saskatchewan* ([1947] 3 DLR 689 at page 703); Megarry J in *Re Euro Hotel (Belgravia) Ltd* ([1975] 3 All ER 1075 at 1084-1085).
[25]   Rowlatt J in *Bennett v Ogston* (15 TC 374 at 379); Megarry J in *Re Euro Hotel (Belgravia) Ltd* ([1975] 3 All ER 1075 at 1085).
[26]   Megarry J in *Re Euro Hotel (Belgravia) Ltd*, [1975] 3 All ER 1075 at 1085.
[27]   Megarry J in *Re Euro Hotel (Belgravia) Ltd*, [1975] 3 All ER 1075 at 1084.
[28]   [1899] 2 Ch 629.
[29]   [1947] 1 All ER 469.

respondent paid the amount due under the judgment, but deducted the £5,014, representing income tax due on the interest payment of £10,028 awarded by the judge. The appellant claimed that the tax was not due, because although the £10,028 was called "interest" in the judgment, it was, in reality, damages. The House of Lords upheld decisions of the lower courts in favour of the respondent.

According to Viscount Simon, there is no essential incompatibility between the two conceptions (interest and damages).[30] He said that the observations of Wright J in *Re National Bank of Wales* (above) were wrong[31], and that if damages are increased by adding interest to a principal sum, that does not prove that such interest is not liable to tax.[32]

Viscount Simon then referred to the argument of counsel for the appellant that the added sum was not in the nature of interest as used in the Income Tax Acts because that added sum only came into existence when the judgment was given, and that, from that moment, it had no accretions under the order awarding it, and thus responded[33]:

> I see no reason why, when the Judge orders payment of interest from a past date on the amount of the main sum awarded (or on a part of it), this supplemental payment, the size of which grows from day to day by taking a fraction of so much per cent. per annum of the amount of which interest is ordered, and by the payment of which further growth is stopped, should not be treated as interest attracting Income Tax. It is not capital. It is rather the accumulated fruit of a tree which the tree produces regularly until payment.

Lord Wright described as "artificial" the contention that money awarded as damages for the detention of money is not interest and has not the quality of interest.[34] Such a contention was also erroneous because interest was in essence a payment that was due because the creditor did not get his money when it was due. From that point of view, it was immaterial whether the money was due under a contract, or under a statutory provision, or whether it was due for any other reason in law.[35] According to Lord Wright[36]:

> In either case the money was due to him and was not paid or, in other words, was withheld from him by the debtor after the time when payment should have been made, in breach of his legal rights, and interest was a compensation, whether the compensation was

---

[30] at page 470. Compare Lord Wright at page 473 - "there is no incompatibility ... between interest proper and interest by way of damages".
[31] at page 471. Compare Lord Wright at page 473.
[32] at page 471.
[33] ibid.
[34] at page 472.
[35] ibid.
[36] ibid.

liquidated under an agreement or statute, as for instance under Section 57 of the Bills of Exchange Act, 1882, or was unliquidated and claimable under the Act as in the present case. The essential quality of the claim for compensation is the same, and the compensation is properly described as interest.

In rejecting the argument that the sum in question "could not be interest at all because interest implies a recurrence of periodical accretions, whereas this sum came into existence uno flatu by the judgment of the court and was fixed once for all", Lord Wright said that the payment in truth represented the "total of the periodical accretions of interest during the whole time in which the payment of the debt was withheld".[37]

Lord Simonds for his part also viewed the alleged distinction between interest and damages as fallacious, because it assumes an incompatibility between the ideas of interest and damages, for which there was no justification.[38] According to him, this confuses the character of the payment with the authority under which it is paid. In fact, its "essential character" may be the same regardless of whether it is paid under a contract, a statute, or a court's judgment.[39] Regardless of whether it is called "interest" or "damages in the nature of interest" or even just "damages", the real question remains the same – "what is its intrinsic character?" In Lord Simonds' view, one may well be misled in the consideration of this question by a description due to the authority by which the payment is made.[40]

The result then is that a payment does not cease to be "interest" merely because it emerges and is fixed in one instant by a court, or, because the principal sum by reference to which it is calculated is due, not in contract, but under statute, or, because the liability to pay the interest itself is not contractual but is based on a court order.

Tax on Interest

The general statutory scheme in respect of payments under Sch. D Case III is the deduction of income tax at source by the payer under ICTA 1988 s.348 and s.349 (concerning which we shall say more later), so that the payee or recipient receives the payments net of tax. However, by virtue of s.348(1) and s.349(1), payments of interest are excluded from these deduction rules. Thus the general rule is that interest is to be paid gross, and the recipient will be assessed directly under Case III.[41] There are exceptions however. S.349(2) requires the payer to deduct income tax at

---

[37] at page 474.
[38] at page 476.
[39] ibid.
[40] ibid.

the lower rate[42] from any payment of *yearly* interest[43], and account for such deduction to the revenue, where the payment is chargeable under Sch. D Case III and is paid

a. by a company (excluding building societies) or local authority, otherwise than in a fiduciary or representative capacity (i.e., paid on their own behalf); or,

b. by or on behalf of a mixed partnership (i.e., one having a company in it); or,

c. to any person whose usual place of abode is not in the United Kingdom.

Section 349(3) provides exceptions to the deduction requirements of s.349(2). This would mean in some cases that the payment of interest is to be gross, and, in some other cases, special deduction rules apply.

The exceptions apply in the following situations:

a. interest payable on an advance from a bank, if at the time when the interest is paid the person beneficially entitled to the interest is within the charge to corporation tax as respects the interest (i.e., interest which is paid to a bank by a customer who has borrowed money from the bank, if the bank would be liable to corporation tax in respect of the interest). This type of interest is paid gross;

b. interest paid by a bank in the ordinary course of its business. Note in this respect s.480A which applies to interest paid by a "deposit taker" requiring a deduction of tax at source in certain situations (e.g., if the payee is an individual who is resident in the United Kingdom)[44];

c. a payment to which s.124 applies (interest on quoted Eurobonds);

d. a payment to which s.369 applies (mortgage interest payable under deduction of tax);

e. payments which are "relevant payments" for the purposes of Chapter VIIA of Part IV (paying and collecting agents);

f. cases to which the deduction rules under s.480A apply;

g. cases to which the deduction rules under s.480A would apply, but for s.480B;

h. cases to which the deduction rules under s.480A would apply, but for s.481(5)(k).

---

[41] It has been noted that the tax on interest leads to a "double taxation of savings" (the income is taxed when earned, and then the interest gained from saving it is taxed again) - see S James and C Nobes, "The Economics of Taxation", page 56 et. seq.

[42] see TA 1988, sections 1A, 3, and 4.

[43] Emphasis added.

[44] See s.481 for definitions and requirements.

Because the deduction requirement under s.349(2) applies to yearly interest, a distinction is drawn between short interest which is paid gross, and yearly interest. It seems in this respect that "yearly" does not have any special or technical meaning for tax purposes, and that time is of the essence. As Esher MR said in *Goslings and Sharpe v Blake (Surveyor of Taxes)*[45], "yearly interest of money" cannot be interest for less than a year in ordinary English. In Goslings, it was held that interest received by a banker on loans for a specified time that was less than a year is not yearly interest and is not subject to deduction of tax. More recently, the issue was addressed again by the Court of Appeal in *Cairns v McDiarmid*, where Kerr LJ said[46]:

> [T]he authorities show that the answer depends on the true intention of the parties. A bank loan for a fixed period of less than a year does not carry "yearly" (or annual) interest merely because the rate of interest is expressed as a percentage by reference to the period of a year ... On the other hand, a loan on a mortgage which is nominally repayable after six months and which carries interest at a rate per annum will qualify as carrying annual interest because the true intention of the parties is that it should be a long-term loan, beyond a year and indeed probably over many years.

Sir John Donaldson MR concurring, said[47]:

> It is well settled that the difference between what is annual and what is short interest depends upon the intention of the parties ... because it is possible to have a short term and indeed a very short term investment, e.g. over-night deposits, and such an investment does not involve any annual interest, regardless of whether the interest is calculated at an annual rate. On the facts found by the Commissioners, the loan to Mr Cairns was never intended to last for more than a few days, albeit he was entitled to postpone repayment for two years. In fact, as was always intended, his liability was discharged within the week.

Discounts

As seen earlier, "discounts" fall within the charge to tax under Case III. For the purposes of income tax, the charge is in respect of "all discounts", and for the purposes of corporation tax, the charge is in respect of "any discount ...". Most people who have shopped for goods have on occasion

[45] (1889) 2 TC 450 at 452.
[46] (1982) 56 TC 556 at 582.
[47] 56 TC at page 581.

been given a "discount" (in the form of reduced prices) by their vendors, either as a reward for customer loyalty, or as an inducement to pay cash rather than by cheque or credit card, or as a promotional tool. While these are, in common usage, "discounts" they are not the type of discount taxable under Sch. D Case III, otherwise those who buy goods at the summer or winter sales might find themselves faced with a tax bill for the privilege. As Rowlatt J said in *Brown v National Provident Institution*[48]:

> [I]t is clear that it is not every difference in amount between a sum payable in future of the same sum represented by cash down which is an annual profit or gain by way of discount even though popularly the word "discount" may be used to describe it ... [T]he difference between the cash and the credit prices of an article bought is commonly described as discount for ready money allowed by the seller but it is not taxable as income under case 3.

So what is a discount for the purposes of Case III? As in other situations wherein a statutory definition is lacking, it seems that, while many of transactions which may be described as a discount in colloquial usage will not fall within Case III, the term "discount" itself is not given a special or technical meaning for tax purposes. However, like interest, its context under Case III seems to be that of banking and similar commercial transactions,[49] as opposed to simple merchandising transactions. Thus, in spite of the use of the terms "all discounts" or "any discount" in the legislation, the Case III charge is really on "profits arising from discounts received on discounting transactions".[50] This is, in practical terms, the sensible construction to be given to those words,[51] and thus the first question is whether the profit in question was a profit arising from a discount received on a discounting transaction.[52] The second question (with respect to income tax) is whether the profit in question was "an annual profit or gain" within s.18(3).[53]

So what is a discount in the context of "discounting transactions"? As earlier indicated, there is no special meaning for tax purposes. So we see Fox LJ referring in *Ditchfield v Sharp*[54] to a dictionary which defines discount as (*inter alia*)

> [A] deduction ... made for payment before it is due, of a bill of account ... the deduction made from the amount of a bill of exchange

---

[48]   [1919] 2 KB 497 at 506.
[49]   Fox LJ in *Ditchfield v Sharp* [1983] BTC 360 at 363.
[50]   Walton J in *Ditchfield v Trustees of the Orwell Share Settlement* [1982] BTC 39 at 41; statement approved by Fox LJ in *Ditchfield v Sharp* ([1983] BTC 360 at 363; STC 590 at 593).
[51]   Fox LJ in *Ditchfield v Sharp* [1983] BTC 360 at 363.
[52]   Ibid.
[53]   Ibid.
[54]   [1983] BTC 360 at 363.

or promissory note by one who gives value for it before it is due.[55]

It seems that a discount in this context is similar in character to interest but is different in respect of when it is paid. In essence, a discount can be described as a form of interest – but one which is paid at the beginning of the transaction rather than during its course or at its end. A number of American cases illustrate this point. In *Planters' and Merchants' Bank v Goetter*[56], it was held that a discount is "the taking out of the principal sum, and the retention by the lender, at the time of the loan, of the interest charged for the use of the loan". In *State v Boatmen's Sav. Inst.*[57], it was held that discount means "the interest reserved from a sum of money lent at the time of making the loan."

Thus it seems that the true distinction (apart from the issue of payment by reference to time) between interest and the kind of discount that is chargeable under Case III is that, in respect of the latter, the consideration for the loan is paid in advance. According to Lord Sumner in *Brown v National Provident Institution*[58] there are two economic elements present in discounts "one the value of the usufruct forgone, as measured by interim interest, and the other the risk that the money will never be repaid at all".

We have seen the distinction between discounts and interest. It is also essential to distinguish a discount from a premium (which is normally treated as a capital sum). There is no general rule that any sum which a lender receives over and above the amount which he lends ought to be treated as income.[59] Therefore the question sometimes arises whether an amount received by a lender in excess of the loan represents a discount, or a premium, i.e., a sum payable on the return of money lent, in excess of the loan, but which is not interest because it is not paid by reference to time (e.g., a fixed sum of £500 payable on any loan above £25,000). The line between discounts and premiums is, in substance, a "slender one."[60] In *Lomax v Peter Dixon*[61], it was held that where no interest is payable as such, the transaction will normally, if not always, be a discount. This will also be the situation where the interest is inadequate.[62] Where a proper rate of interest is charged however, the extra sum demanded in addition will be a premium. The point was made in this case that the true nature of the "discount" or the premium, as the case may be, is to be ascertained from all the circumstances of the case and that, apart from any matter of law

---

[55] The receiver of the bill is the one who gives the discount. One common form of discount is government Treasury Bills, whereby members of the public purchase the bills for less than the redemption value (in effect lending the government money for a period) and redeem the bill on maturity for its redemption value. What is taxed here is the difference between what was given for the bill and what was finally received on the bill's maturity.

[56] 19 So. 54 at 55.

[57] 48 Mo. 189 at 191. See *First National Bank v Childs*, 133 Mass. 248 at 252: "discount is interest, either paid in advance, or reserved in the note"; *Eastin v Third National Bank of Cincinnati*, 42 SW 1115 at 1116: "discount is the interest reserved from the amount lent at the time of making the loan".

[58] (1921) 8 TC 57 at 96.

[59] Per Lord Greene MR in *Lomax v Peter Dixon* (1943) 25 TC 353 at 363.

[60] Per Fox LJ in *Ditchfield v Sharp* [1983] BTC 360 at 363.

[61] (1943) 25 TC 353.

which may bear upon the question (such as the interpretation of the contract), the question will fall to be determined as a matter of fact by Commissioners.[63] Lord Greene MR identified the matters which ought to be considered in deciding the true nature of the "discount" or premium (in so far as it is not conclusively determined by the contract). First, the terms of the loan and the rate of interest expressly stipulated for it, and, secondly, the nature of the capital risk and the extent to which, if at all, the parties expressly took or may reasonably be supposed to have taken the capital risk into account in fixing the terms of the contract.[64]

Annuities and Other Annual Payments

The term "annuity" generally refers to income which is payable year by year. It was more particularly described by Watson B in *Foley v Fletcher*[65] when he said that an annuity exists "where an income is purchased with a sum of money, and the capital has gone and has ceased to exist, the principal having been converted into an annuity". A similar idea was expressed by Matthew LJ in *Secretary of State for India v Scoble* when he said[66]:

> "Annuity," in the ordinary sense of the expression, means the purchase of an income. It generally involves the conversion of capital into income, and, reasonably enough, where the buyer places himself in that position, the Act of Parliament taxes him; he is taken at his word, he has got an income secured in the way I have mentioned.

These statements obviously refer to one common kind of annuity – purchased annuities. It should however be noted that not all annuities are purchased (e.g., annuities under a will or trust). These do not cease to be annuities simply because they are not purchased. In this context, a more appropriate definition is found in the American case of *Commonwealth v Beisel*[67] that, generally, annuity designates a right, bequeathed, donated, or purchased, to receive fixed, periodical, but not necessarily annual, payments for life or number of years, and that its determining characteristic is that the annuitant has interest only in the payments themselves, not in the principal fund or source from which they are derived.

Thus the essence of annuities is that they are rights to recurrent or periodic payments of income. The source of the payment or of the right to the payment is not always important. Some other points need to be noted. First, for the purposes of Case III the precise boundary between

---

[62]   See Lord Greene MR at page 367.
[63]   ibid.
[64]   ibid.
[65]   (1858) 157 E.R. 678 at 684.
[66]   (1903) 4 TC 618 at page 622.
[67]   13 A.2d 419 at 421. See also *Schloesser v Schloesser*, 70 NE.2d. 346 at 350; *Everett v Comm. of Corporations and Taxation*, 59 NE.2d. 186 at 187-188.

annuities and what is described in the statute as "other annual payments" is yet to be fixed, but this of itself is of no serious consequence as similar principles apply to both types of payment. Secondly, the category of what constitutes an "other annual payment" is "quite a limited one".[68] Thirdly, neither the Taxes Act nor the courts have attempted to define the term "other annual payment", for the simple reason that, "apart from some broad principles", a precise definition is not possible.[69] Hence we must examine the characteristics which a payment must have in order to fall into this category.

Characteristics of "Annual Payments"

The characteristics of an annual payment were listed by Jenkins LJ in *IRC v Whitworth Park Coal Co Ltd.*[70]

1. The ejusdem generis rule applies: i.e., not all recurrent payments are annual payments for the purposes of Sch. D Case III. For a payment to qualify as an annual payment, it must be ejusdem generis with (i.e., of the same type as) the specific instances given in the shape of interest of money and annuities.[71] Most of the other characteristics to be discussed are actually reflections of this requirement.

2. A binding obligation is required: voluntary payments cannot be annual payments (at best, they will be gifts). Thus, in order to be an annual payment, a payment must fall to be made under a legally enforceable obligation, as distinct from mere voluntary payments.[72] The essence of annual payments is that the payer is thereby alienating a slice of his or her income. According to Lord Upjohn in *Campbell v IRC*, "the payer is regarded as having parted with that part of his income which ... he pays away. The income that he pays away is that of the payee".[73] Thus, if the payments are not made under a binding legal obligation, the payer can hardly be said to have alienated or "parted with" any part of his income. The income is still his, to do with it as he likes, and if he chooses to give it away to someone else on a periodical basis, that is entirely a matter for him. Thus for example, dividends paid by a company are not annual payments since there is no obligation to pay them and their distribution depends in every instance upon a declaration by the company.[74]

For the purposes of the required obligation, a will, a trust, or a contract will suffice. Furthermore, according to Jenkins LJ, the fact that the obligation to pay is imposed by an order of court and does not arise by virtue of a contract does not exclude the payment from Case III. Thus a

---

[68] Sir Wilfred Greene MR in *Re Hanbury (deceased); Comiskey v Hanbury* (1939) 38 TC 588 at 590; compare Lord Radcliffe in *Whitworth Park Coal Co v IRC* [1959] 3 All ER 703 at 715.

[69] Lord Upjohn in *Campbell V IRC* [1968] 3 All ER at 602.

[70] [1958] 2 All ER 91 at 102-104.

[71] Jenkins LJ, referring to Hamilton J in *Hill v Gregory* (1912) 6 TC 39 at 47; see also Watson B in *Foley v Fletcher* (1858) 157 E.R. at 685; Scrutton LJ in *Howe v IRC*, (1919) 7 TC 289 at 303.

[72] Jenkins LJ, referring to Lord Sterndale MR in *Smith v Smith* [1923] P. 191 at 197.

[73] [1968] 3 All ER at page 603.

court order will also suffice.

3. *Recurrence:* like interest and annuities, the payment must possess the essential quality of recurrence implied by the description "annual".[75] In this respect, the word "annual" does not admit of any significant interpretation.[76] To the courts, it simply means "recurrent" – a necessary but inconclusive factor.[77] In other words, "annual" means that the payment must be "of a recurring character".[78] This requirement has been given a broad interpretation in the authorities. Thus Warrington LJ said in *Smith v Smith*[79] that the fact that a payment is to be made weekly does not prevent it from being annual, provided that the weekly payments may continue beyond the year.[80] Furthermore, according to Lord Macmillan in *Moss Empires Ltd v IRC*[81] the fact that payments are contingent and variable in amount does not affect the character of the payments as annual payments. Therefore the element of recurrence is satisfied if the payment is capable of being recurrent[82], even if it never recurs in fact.[83] In *Moss Empires* itself, the taxpayer company, by agreement, undertook to another company, to make available to that company a sufficient sum to enable it to pay, for each of the next five years, a fixed rate of dividends less income tax at the current rate, if its profits fell below a certain level. In each of the five years covered by the agreement, the taxpayers were called upon to make payments under their obligation. The payments thus made by the taxpayer varied significantly from year to year. It was argued for the taxpayers that the payments were not annual payments because they were casual, independent, not necessarily recurrent, and throughout subject to a contingency. While this argument had commended itself to Lord Moncrieff (dissenting) in the Court of Session, the House of Lords did not accept it. Lord Macmillan said[84] that there was a continuing obligation, extending over each and all of the five years, to make the payments. Thus the payments were still annual payments even though they were contingent and variable.

4. *Pure income profit:* it is necessary for the payments to be pure income profit in the hands of the recipient. Viscount Simonds said in *Whitworth Park Coal Co v IRC* [85] that this requirement exists because no deductions are permitted under Case III. Lord Radcliffe explained in *Whitworth Park Coal Co v IRC* [86], that it is inconsistent with the scheme of deduction at source

---

[74] Per Viscount Simon, LC in *Canadian Eagle Oil Co. Ltd v R* [1945] 2 All ER 499 at 504.

[75] See Lord Maugham in *Moss Empires Ltd. v IRC* [1937] 3 All ER 381 at 386.

[76] Lord Radcliffe in *Whitworth Park Coal Co v IRC* [1959] 3 All ER 703 at 715.

[77] ibid.

[78] Viscount Simonds in *Whitworth Park Coal Co v IRC* [1959] 3 All ER 703 at 712.

[79] [1923] P. 191 at 201.

[80] Compare Lord Sterndale MR (at page 196) - an obligation which cannot exceed twelve months cannot create an annual payment.

[81] [1937] 3 All ER 381 at 385.

[82] Lord Maugham in *Moss Empires* [1937] 3 All ER, at page 386).

[83] See Lord Greene MR in *Asher v London Film Productions Ltd.* [1944] KB 133 at 140 - "You can have an annual payment ... even though it happens by some accident or other to fall due in one year only. The question is, has it the necessary periodical or recurrent quality?"

[84] [1937] 3 All ER at page 385.

[85] [1959] 3 All ER 703 at 712.

[86] [1959] 3 All ER at page 715.

that Case III of Sch. D should contain payments that are gross in the hands of the recipient and which are not his pure income. Lord Upjohn further explained in *Campbell v IRC* [87] that it is well settled that tax cannot be deducted by the payer in respect of payments which in the hands of the recipients are gross receipts for advice or services or goods supplied which merely form an element in discovering what the profits of the recipients are. The sum of these statements seems to be that, in order for a payment to be an annual payment for the purposes of Case III, it must be of such a nature that it is taxable in its entirety in the hands of the recipient.

It is obvious that there are some "annual" payments which, by their very nature and quality, cannot possibly be treated as the pure profit income of the recipient (the proper response to them being to treat them as an element to be taken into account in discovering what the profits of the recipient are), or, which themselves contain payments of such nature. Such payments will not fall within Case III. [88] This then raises questions as to the proper distinction between those "annual payments" which are the pure income profit of the recipient, and those which are not. Lord Donovan provided an answer in *Campbell v IRC* [89].

> One must determine, in the light of all the relevant facts, whether the payment is a taxable receipt in the hands of the recipient without any deduction for expense or the like. Whether it is, in other words, "pure income" or "pure profit income" in his hands, as these expressions have been used in the decided cases. If so it will be an annual payment under Case III. If, on the other hand, it is simply gross revenue in the recipient's hands, out of which a taxable income will emerge only after his outgoings have been deducted, then the payment is not such an annual payment.

This test shows for example that, even in the absence of a specific exclusion from the charge under Case III of payments of rent, rent will not fall under Case III, because the rent will only be gross sum revenue (and therefore subject to deduction of expenses) in the hands of the lessor. By the same token, a trading receipt will not be an annual payment. The point is illustrated by *Howe v IRC* [90]. The taxpayer had paid the premiums due in respect of his life insurance policies by the means of payments made under a deed of covenant to pay the same. He claimed to deduct the premiums so paid in computing his total income for super tax purposes, on the grounds that they were annual payments. It was held that such deduction was not allowable. Warrington LJ pointed out [91] that although the payments would go to swell the profits and gains arising or accruing

---

[87]   [1968] 3 All ER at page 602.
[88]   See generally, Sir Wilfred Greene MR in re *Hanbury (deceased); Comiskey v Hanbury* (1939) 38 TC 588 at 590.
[89]   [1968] 3 All ER 588 at 606.
[90]   (1919) 7 TC 289.
[91]   at page 300.

to the insurance company on which income tax is chargeable, the tax is not charged on the premiums themselves. Thus, it was clear that the payments were not pure income in the hands of the insurance company, since they would only be trading receipts, to be taxed in its hands only after deducting allowable expenditure. And, according to Scrutton LJ[92]:

> It is not all payments made every year from which income tax can be deducted. For instance, if a man agrees to pay a motor garage £500 a year for five years for the hire of and upkeep of a car, no one suggests that the person paying can deduct income tax from each yearly payment. So also, if he contracted with a butcher for an annual sum to supply all his meat for a year. The annual instalment would not be subject to tax as a whole in the hands of the payee, but only that part of it which was profits.

For the same reason that trading receipts cannot be annual payments within Case III (the need to deduct expenses before arriving at a profit figure) receipts of an individual's profession will not be annual payments. In *Jones v Wright*[93] the taxpayer was a solicitor, who as trustee of certain trusts was entitled under relevant charging clauses to be paid all the usual professional and other charges for any business done for the trusts. He subsequently arranged with his fellow trustees and with the beneficiaries to retain a percentage of the trust income per annum, as an alternative to charging the usual professional fees. The question was whether these retained profits were annual payments, or whether they were receipts of the taxpayer's profession chargeable under Sch. D Case II. Rowlatt J held that they were receipts of the taxpayer's profession. Referring to *Howe v IRC*, Rowlatt J said[94] that, for a payment out of profits or gains to fall within the principles of Case III, it had to have been paid "by way of a division of profits" (i.e., a payment whereby the payer was alienating a slice of his or her profits, the "divided" part of those profits then becoming the income of the recipient).[95]

According to Rowlatt J, if the relevant payment "is a payment by way of a spending of profits, as in the case put by Lord Justice Scrutton, of a lump sum per annum, say for the use of a motor garage, or something of that sort, it is not division of those profits, but it is a spending which creates a new profit, which is taxable in the hands of the recipient." The implication is that a payment which is a division of profits is pure profit in the hands of the recipient and will fall within Case III (not being receipts of the profession). On the other hand, a payment which is not a division

---

[92]   at page 303.
[93]   (1927) 13 TC 221.
[94]   13 TC at page 226.
[95]   It does not seem that the "division of profits" principle is seeking to create a new criterion for annual payments. Rather, it seems to be linked with the concept of "pure income profit".

of an existing profit but is rather the spending of that profit in return for goods or services (the owner's prerogative), results in a new profit being created. That new profit would have had a cost borne by the recipient, in respect of which the recipient might be entitled to a deduction or allowance, before arriving at a taxable figure. This therefore could not be an annual payment since it is not, in its entirety, a profit.

The principle with respect to trading and professional receipts is clear enough. What is not so straightforward is the response to the proposition that, when a payment is made subject to a counter-stipulation, or in return for consideration, or is not "pure bounty", then it is not pure profit in the hands of the person who is subject to the counter-stipulation or who has to give the consideration. This proposition apparently has some support in the cases. One of the cases often referred to in support thereof is *IRC v National Book League*.[96] The League was a charitable company limited by guarantee, which had the object of promoting and encouraging by all suitable means the habit of reading and the wider distribution of books. It provided certain facilities to its members, including a reading room, a drawing room, and a licensed bar and restaurant. It proposed to increase the subscriptions paid by members from a certain date, but invited members renewing their subscriptions to enter into deeds of covenant with the league "to remain members and to pay their annual subscription at the existing rates for at least seven years". The advantage of such a covenant to members was that they would escape any increases in subscription rates during the seven years. About 2,800 members entered into the covenants. The league claimed to recover tax on the gross sums named in the deeds, on the basis that the sums were annual payments. The Court of Appeal rejected the claim. In deciding whether the covenanted payments were, in these circumstances, pure income profit in the League's hands, Lord Evershed MR said[97] that the question was, "looking at the substance and reality of the matter can it be said that those who entered into these covenants have paid the sums covenanted without conditions or counter stipulations"? He answered this question in the negative. In this case, there was "in a real sense", a condition or counter stipulation on the part of the league against which the covenant was entered into.[98] It therefore followed that the payments under the covenants were not pure income profit. Morris LJ, concurring, proffered the following analysis of the issue[99].

The question arises whether the payments can be said to be pure gifts to the charity. In the terms of a phrase which has been used, can the payments be said to be pure income profit in the hands of the charity? If the payments were made in such circumstances that the

[96]   [1957] 2 All ER 644.
[97]   [1957] 2 All ER 644.
[98]   [1957] 2 All ER 644 at 650.
[99]   ibid.

League was obliged to afford to the covenantors such amenities and such benefits of membership as would at any particular time be offered to all members, and if those amenities and benefits were appreciable and not negligible, then I do not think that the payments were pure income profit in the hands of the charity.

While this case is often referred to as laying down a rule that anything given in return for the payments would be fatal to their being annual payments, it should be noted that this case may not have been trying to lay down such a general principle at all. Morris LJ in the statement above seemed to imply that a payment could still be a "pure gift" if the benefit given in return was not "appreciable" or if it was "negligible". Lord Evershed MR[100] specifically disclaimed laying down any general principle that, "whenever a covenantor in favour of a charity is allowed certain privileges, it therefore follows that he can no longer say that he has paid without conditions or counter stipulations." The proper test, according to him, is whether in all the circumstances, and looking at "the substance and reality of the matter", the covenantor can be treated as being a "donor of the covenanted sums" to the charity.[101] It is noteworthy also that Lord Evershed MR did indicate that the question "whether particular advantages or promises can be dismissed on the principle of de minimis non curat lex" was relevant.[102] This particular question is a question of law.[103]

Although Morris LJ seemed to focus on the facilities offered by the league to its members in general, Lord Evershed MR seemed to be more concerned with the peculiar advantages enjoyed by those who paid their subscriptions by way of the covenant, rather than by any other means. He pointed out[104] that, first, they would be able to continue to be members at the lower subscription rates, and they had a promise or assurance that, whatever may happen to other persons' subscription rates, their own rates would not be raised for seven years. Secondly, they would have the advantage that, while paying the lower, pre-existing rates, they would still continue to enjoy, like other members who paid the higher rates, the full range of club amenities. Given these factors, it is easy to see why it was decided that the covenanted subscriptions were not pure income profit (or "pure gifts") in the hands of the league.

Another case applying the "counter stipulation" principle is *Taw and Torridge Festival Society Ltd v IRC*.[105] Like *IRC v National Book League*, this case involved a company limited by guarantee, established for charitable purposes. Its main object was the management of the North Devon

---

[100] at page 650.
[101] ibid.
[102] at page 651.
[103] ibid.
[104] ibid.
[105] (1959) 38 TC 603.

Festival of the Arts. The society had received payments under deeds of covenant, offering seats at reduced rates for all concerts, recitals, ballets and plays, as a privilege to the covenantors. The Commissioners held that the sums were not annual payments. On appeal to the High Court, Wynn–Parry J said[106], following *IRC v National Book League*, that the question was whether the payments "are properly to be regarded as annual payments within the Income Tax Acts or whether, upon the true view, they have been made subject to conditions and counter-stipulations, in which case they would be robbed of the character of being annual payments." He felt that the case fell squarely within the *IRC v National Book League* decision, and he was, on the facts of this case, unable to apply the de minimis rule to ignore the counter stipulation.[107] According to him, while the offer of one seat at a reduced rate for every concert, recital or ballet or play may at first appear insubstantial, Morris LJ had indicated in *IRC v National Book League* that what he had to consider was the benefit to members.[108] In considering this, he would then find that "an enthusiastic member choosing to attend the ballets and plays over a year" would be able to obtain a rebate amounting to about 25% of the covenanted subscription. Thus, while he had "a very great sympathy" with the society, he could not apply the de minimis rule. Wynn–Parry J agreed that the de minimis issue was a question of law, but added that, in applying it, one must use common sense. This indicated that he could not shut his eyes to the circumstance that experienced special commissioners, in considering this very question, had come to the same view.[109] In the event, the payments under the covenants were not pure income profit.

A more recent example is *Essex County Council v Ellam*.[110] The council arranged for S's son to attend a special school. The school normally looked to local authorities to pay the fees of any child on the usual termly basis, leaving it to the authorities to make any appropriate arrangements for the child's parents to reimburse or contribute to the fees for the child's terms. S then signed an agreement to reimburse the council any amount paid in respect of the fees of his son. Later S executed a deed of covenant to make payments to the council in respect of the said fees. A claim that the payments under the covenant were pure income profit was rejected. Dillon LJ said[111] that it was impossible to regard the payments by S under the deed as pure income of the council without regard to the obligation which the council undertook to pay the fees of S's son. One goes to cancel the other. He said however[112] that the payments would clearly have been the pure income of the council if they had not been earmarked as they were for the particular purpose for which they were earmarked.

In spite of cases like this however, it can be regarded as established that

---

[106] at page 608.
[107] at page 609.
[108] ibid.
[109] ibid.
[110] [1989] STC 317.
[111] at page 322.
[112] [1968] 3 All ER at page 593.

the question whether or not there existed some counter stipulation or whether consideration was given, is not decisive. This point was made quite clearly in *Campbell v IRC* where the House of Lords in disapproved of certain statements of Lord Greene MR in *IRC v National Book League* (above). Viscount Dilhorne described as wrong any notion that any sum paid subject to a condition or counter stipulation will not qualify as an annual payment within Case III[113] while Lord Guest said that this would be a construction of "annual payments" which was too narrow and for which there was "no ground or reason or authority."[114] Viscount Dilhorne was of the opinion that the decision in *IRC v National Book League* could not be justified on the ground that there was a condition or counter stipulation that, during the period of the covenants, the covenantors would be exempt from any increase of subscription.[115] He pointed out that the charge under Case III itself[116] indicated that the amounts charged may be payable as an "obligation by virtue of any contract".[117] Thus, if an annual payment payable by virtue of a contract comes within the relevant statutory provisions, it must follow that the fact that there is consideration for the promise to pay, whether or not in the form of a condition or counter stipulation, does not necessarily exclude the annual payments from the scope of Case III.[118] Lord Hodson took the view that the decision in *IRC v National Book League* could be supported on the broad grounds that the payments in that case were in the nature of annual subscriptions to a club.[119] He however said that Lord Evershed MR, in taking the point about "conditions and counter stipulations", used language which went too far.[120] He rejected the Crown's argument that payments are disqualified unless they are made as "pure bounty".[121]

With regard to what might be considered the correct test, Lord Donovan said[122] that:

> [O]ne cannot resolve the problem whether a payment is an annual payment within Case III simply by asking the questions "Must the payee give or do something in return?" or "Did the payer make some counter stipulation or receive some counter benefit?"; or "Was it pure bounty on his part?"

---

[113] ibid, at page 600.
[114] ibid, at page 594.
[115] see ICTA 1988, s.18(3).
[116] Lord Donovan said (at page 605) that the statements about counter stipulations "contradict the charging words of Case III of Sch. D itself which envisage that an annual payment may be payable 'by virtue of any contract' and that, therefore, the recipient may have to give or do something in return for the payment, which will not in such circumstances be 'pure bounty' in his hands."
[117] [1968] 3 All ER at page 594.
[118] at page 599.
[119] ibid.
[120] ibid; compare Lord Upjohn at page 602.
[121] [1968] 3 All ER 588 at page 606.
[122] ibid.

The question is not whether there was a counter stipulation in respect of a payment but simply whether any sum can be claimed as an expense of earning the payment.[123] Viscount Dilhorne explained further[124]:

> [T]he fact that there is consideration for the promise to pay, whether or not in the form of a condition or counter-stipulation, does not necessarily exclude the annual payment from the scope of [Case III]. If however, the consideration or counter-stipulation relates to the provision of goods or services and so deprives the payments of the character of "pure income profit", it will have that effect.

Thus, the real question (although there may be exceptions) is whether the payment is being made in return for goods and services.[125] The test makes it necessary to decide each case on its own facts.[126]

Apart from the *dicta* in *Campbell v IRC*, the proposition that the presence of consideration or counter stipulations is not necessarily fatal to a payment being pure income also has support in direct decisions. In *Delage v Nugget Polish Co Ltd*.[127] the defendants became entitled, by virtue of an agreement with the plaintiffs, to use a trade secret for the making of "blacking". This was to be in return for payments, for a period of forty years, of an annual sum of money calculated as a percentage of the gross receipts on the sale of the said blacking, and brown polish. It was held that the payments under the agreement were annual payments.[128] Furthermore, annuitants under purchased annuity schemes do give consideration (cash) for the annuities that they receive, but these are still within Case III.

Nevertheless, the effect of a counter stipulation or the provision of consideration cannot always be predicted with certainty. This creates problems for bodies which need to attract funding by donations/deeds of covenant, and which may need to provide some incentive (in the form of benefits) to attract such funds. In this respect statute has now stepped in to assist certain charities in this situation. If the sole or main purpose of a charity is the preservation of property, or the conservation of wildlife, for the public benefit, such a charity is permitted by s.59 FA 1989 to provide consideration (in the form of viewing rights) to persons from whom it receives annual payments.

In addition to the aforementioned characteristics of annual payments outlined by Jenkins LJ in *IRC v Whitworth Park Coal Co Ltd* two other factors emerge from the cases.

---

[123] ibid.
[124] at page 594.
[125] Lord Donovan, at page 605, and 607.
[126] Lord Donovan at page 607.
[127] (1905) 92 LT 682.
[128] See also *Asher v London Film Productions Ltd* [1944] KB 133.

Character of Income

First, the payment must "have the character of income in the hands of the recipient".[129] What this means is that the payment must be of an income (and not capital) nature. This is clear from the requirement that payments have to be the recipient's pure "income" profit. This requirement formed one of the grounds of the decision in *Campbell v IRC* itself. Here, a charitable trust which had been established for the purpose of acquiring a business, received sums under a deed of covenant from the company ("Tutors") which owned the business. The payments under the covenant were subject to an understanding (held by the courts to involve a legally enforceable obligation) that the trustees would use the sums received under the covenant for the purpose of purchasing Tutors' business. The payments under the covenant were held not to be annual payments. Viscount Dilhorne said[130] that the payments had not the quality and nature of income in the hands of the trustees and Lord Hodson said that the payments were "instalments of capital"[131] but it was Lord Donovan's analysis that was most illuminating. According to him[132]:

> The covenant itself is simply to pay an annual sum to the trustees, the amount of which is measured by Tutors' profits. Familiarity with deeds of covenant of this sort fosters an initial assumption, perhaps, that what is being provided is an annual income; but if Tutors had specifically desired to provide the trustees with a capital sum payable by seven yearly instalments the deed of covenant as drafted would have served that purpose equally well ... Tutors wanted the trustees to buy Tutors' business and to do so with money which Tutors would themselves provide. They came to a clear understanding with the trustees that the trustees would use the money so provided for this purpose and for no other; and I agree with your Lordships that in the circumstances of this case the understanding would have been enforceable in contract. One therefore has a case where a person wishing to sell an asset provides the prospective purchaser with the purchase price. That seems to me as clear a case of a gift of capital as one could want.

Thus, in spite of the recurrent nature of the payments, and in spite of the method whereby they were calculated (measured by profits) the payments, being linked to an obligation to purchase assets, had the character of capital in the hands of the recipient. The House of Lords was not in this case

---

[129] Per Viscount Dilhorne in *Campbell v IRC* [1968] 3 All ER 588 at 592; compare Warrington LJ in *Howe v IRC*, 7 TC at page 300.
[130] at page 595.
[131] at page 598.
[132] at pages 604-605.

attempting to lay down any general principle that payments applied to the purchase of assets are necessarily therefore capital payments. Lord Donovan himself expressly disclaimed any such notion[133] and Lord Upjohn[134] was careful to avoid laying down any general principle. However, in spite of these disclaimers, it can be taken as established that where recurrent payments clearly represent instalments of the purchase price of a capital asset they will be capital instalments and not annual payments.[135] This is illustrated by *IRC v Ramsay*.[136] The taxpayer agreed to buy a dental practice for £15,000, of which £5000 was to be paid at once, the balance being paid by ten yearly instalments of a sum equal to 25% of the net profits of the practice for each year. If the amounts so paid over during the ten years were, in the aggregate, more or less than the balance of the primary purchase price, that price was to be treated as correspondingly increased or diminished. No interest was payable on any outstanding balance. The taxpayer claimed that the practice was sold, not for a fixed capital sum, but for a down payment and further annual sums of the nature of income payments. He argued that the description given to such payments in the agreement was immaterial, and therefore claimed to deduct the instalments in computing his income for surtax purposes. It was held that the instalments were capital payments, and not annual payments, and therefore the deductions sought were not permissible. According to Lord Wright MR[137]:

> [T]his is not the case of an annuity, or a series of annual payments. It is a case in which a capital lump sum has been stipulated as the price of a piece of property, and it is none the less so because the payment of that sum is to be made by instalments, instalments at certain specific periods, no doubt, but not instalments of a fixed price. It is none the less, in my judgment, a capital sum because in the working out of the transaction, and in the discharge of that capital sum, the Vendor according to the terms of the agreement may have to be content with a lesser amount than the £15,000. The £15,000 is not an otiose figure; it is a figure which permeates the whole of the contract, and upon which the whole contract depends. That being so, I think that the [instalment] in question was a sum in the nature of capital.

This case highlights some of the problems of determining whether periodic payments linked to disposals of property are capital or income. The arguments proceeded on an "all or nothing" basis - i.e., either the

---

[133]   at page 605.
[134]   at page 603.
[135]   See for example Channell B in *Foley v Fletcher* - "I am of opinion that the words ... annual payments do not include those payments which are in respect of the purchase money of an estate, and are in the nature of capital and not of income." (1858) 157 E.R. at 686.
[136]   (1935) 20 TC 79.
[137]   20 TC at page 98.

whole of the relevant instalment was an annual payment (income), or the whole of if was an instalment of the purchase price of an asset (capital). This wholistic approach to the question is bound to lead to difficulties in some situations. Happily, it is not a universal principle and can give way when necessary. Thus, if a payment is part income and part capital it can be dissected for income tax purposes. Authority for this proposition can be found in *Secretary of State for India v Scoble*.[138] In this case, the East India Company contracted with the Great India Peninsular Railway Company to purchase the railway and works. The agreement gave the East India Company the option, instead of paying the purchase price by a lump sum, to pay by "an annuity to be reckoned" from a certain date. In such a case, the rate of interest which was to be used for calculating the "annuity" was prescribed. The British Government, which succeeded to the obligations of the East India Company, gave notice to exercise the option of paying an annuity. The Secretary of State deducted income tax from the first two instalments, and the plaintiffs, as the annuity trustees brought an action to recover the tax deducted from so much of the payments as represented capital. Phillimore J decided in favour of the Secretary of State. The Court of Appeal (in a judgment which was upheld by the House of Lords) reversed that judgment. It was held that the payments under the contract were not pure "annuities", but contained a capital element – viz, part of the purchase price of the railway and works. It was common ground that the parts of the payments which represented interest were taxable. The real question in the case, according to Vaughan Williams LJ[139] was "is Income Tax payable upon that portion of the annual payment which you can discover from the very terms of the contract is a mere payment of an instalment necessary to complete the payment of an existing debt?" The question was answered in the negative. Stirling LJ[140], referring with approval to the judgment of the Divisional Court in *Nizam Guaranteed Stock Railway Company v Wyatt*[141] said that the mere fact that a sum is designated as an annuity is not conclusive, but that "the real nature of the transaction" must be looked at. According to him, the real nature of the transaction in this case was that the so called "annuities" were simply annual payments of equal amount, being instalments of a debt, and were made up partly of principal, partly of interest.[142]. Following *Foley v Fletcher*[143], the word "annuity," under these circumstances, is not to be read in such a way as to make capital taxable.

The Secretary of State had argued against this type of dissection on the grounds that, if that dissection was to be permitted in this type of case, then in the case of every terminable annuity which has been purchased for value, each annual payment of that annuity would have to be dissected into

[138] [1903] AC 299; 4 TC 618.
[139] 4 TC 618 at 619.
[140] at page 621.
[141] (1890) 2 TC 584.
[142] 4 TC at page 621.
[143] 157 E.R. 678.

capital and interest and only the portion which represents interest ought to be taxed. Stirling LJ in response to this argument said[144]:

> Those are cases of purchase of annuities, where investment has been made in that form of property, and the legislature in so many words has said that that is to be taxed; and it is recognised in this very case throughout that an annuity of that kind is taxable. And I in no way depart from that. ... it is a different matter where it appears, on the face of the transaction, that the so-called annuity is not a thing of that kind, but simply represents instalments of an existing debt. It matters not, it appears to me, whether the debt be one which is a purchase arising from a sale, or be in the case of the repayment of a loan.

So two main principles come out of *Secretary of State for India v Scoble*. First, the terminology employed by the parties is not conclusive (rather, the court has to examine the real nature of the transaction), and, secondly, a payment which, when properly analysed, partly represents income and partly represents capital will be dissected for income tax purposes. Both issues came up again in *Vestey v IRC*.[145] Here, a block of shares were estimated by accountants to worth £2 million. This price assumed an immediate payment in full by the purchaser. However, the parties were contemplating a sale of the shares on the term that the taxpayer should receive an annual sum over a long period of years. In this wise, the accountants considered that, in respect of this "unusual arrangement", allowance must be made for "the interest factor". Assuming a net interest rate of 2%, it was recommended that the shares be sold in return for "an annual payment of £44,000 extending over 125 years". Consequently, the shares were sold "in consideration of the sum of £5.5 millions payable by instalments of £44,000 per annum over 125 years". The sale was expressed to be "without interest". The Revenue claimed that, since the payments of £44,000 were annuities, they were taxable as the taxpayer's income. The taxpayer on the other hand contended that the payments were capital sums, being instalments of the price payable for the shares. The Special Commissioners held that the payments of £44,000 (other than the first) contained an interest element which was taxable. The taxpayer appealed, and the Revenue cross-appealed. Cross J, after reviewing the existing case law, including *Secretary of State for India v Scoble*, held that the amounts of the instalments should be dissected into capital and interest. Reiterating that the use of terminology by the parties is inconclusive, he said that "if the Crown cannot say that there is any magic in the use of the word 'annuity', why should the taxpayer be able to say that there is any magic in the use

---

[144] 4 TC at page 622.
[145] [1961] 3 All ER 978.

of the words 'purchase price'?".[146]

Cross J was of the opinion in this case that the authorities on the point were in "a somewhat confused state".[147] However, *Secretary of State for India v Scoble* seemed to have been clear enough, so where did the confusion lie? The apparent confusion lay in dicta. In *Foley v Fletcher*[148], Pollock CB had said that "if the plaintiff had sold her estate for an annuity, so calling it, the annuity would have been liable to Income Tax. But she sold it for a sum which is payable by instalments, which, is therefore, not chargeable." There is nothing wrong with the second part of the statement. However, the first part might have been problematic if it had not been disregarded by the Court of Appeal in *Secretary of State for India v Scoble*. If that part of the the the statement was purporting to state that the label attached to the transactions by the parties is conclusive, then it is clear that such a view can no longer be sustained.

More troublesome is dicta from the Court of Appeal in more recent cases. First, a statement in the judgment of Romer LJ in *IRC v Ramsay*[149].

> If a man had some property which he wishes to sell on terms which will result in his receiving for the next twenty years an annual sum of £500, he can do it in either of two methods. He can either sell his property in consideration of a payment by the purchaser to him of an annuity of £500 for the next twenty years, or he can sell his property to the purchaser for £10,000, the £10,000 to be paid by equal instalments of £500 over the next twenty years. If he adopts the former of the two methods, then the sums of £500 received by him each year are exigible to Income Tax. If he adopts the second method, then the sums of £500 received by him in each year are not liable to Income Tax, and they do not become liable to Income Tax by it being said that in substance the transaction is the same as though he had sold for an annuity. The vendor has the power of choosing which of the two methods he will adopt, and he can adopt the second method if he thinks fit, for the purpose of avoiding having to pay Income Tax on the £500 a year. The question which method has been adopted must be a question of the proper construction to be placed upon the documents by which the transaction is carried out.

Secondly, a statement in the judgment of Lord Greene MR in *IRC v Wesleyan and General Assurance Society*[150].

---

[146] [1961] 3 All ER 978 at 986.
[147] at page 982.
[148] 157 E.R. 678.
[149] 20 TC at page 98.
[150] [1946] 2 All ER 749 at 751.

In dealing with Income Tax questions it frequently happens that there are two methods at least of achieving a particular financial result. If one of those methods is adopted, tax will be payable. If the other method is adopted, tax will not be payable. It is sufficient to refer to the quite common case where property is sold for a lump sum payable by instalments. If a piece of property is sold for £1,000 and the purchase price is to be paid in ten instalments of £100 each, no tax is payable. If, on the other hand, the property is sold in consideration of an annuity of £100 a year for ten years, tax is payable. The net result from the financial point of view is precisely the same in each case, but one method of achieving it attracts tax and the other method does not.

As indicated earlier, Cross J in *Vestey v IRC* took the view that the authorities were in a confused state. According to him[151], if Romer LJ was right in *IRC v Ramsay*, it would follow that the whole of the £5.5 million of the *Vestey v IRC* transaction could properly be regarded as the purchase price of the shares. With all respect to Cross J, that conclusion does not follow at all. Romer LJ's statement can be seen as dealing only with a situation where there was clearly no element of interest in the instalments of £500. If the facts establish that the parties contemplated a real element of interest (as they quite clearly did not in *IRC v Ramsay*, but they quite clearly did in *Vestey v IRC*), the court would have to accept that as evidence of the real intention of the parties. It is arguable that the statement of Romer LJ does not deal with this type of situation at all, and that therefore it is correct in what it purports to deal with. Cross J said in *Vestey v IRC*[152] that the £10,000 in Romer LJ's example must clearly have been far more than the value of the property at the date of the supposed sale, and that if it had been worth £10,000, the annuity would have been far more than £500 a year. With respect, this seems to be nothing more than conjecture and there is nothing to indicate that this will be the case (other than an assumption that people will always desire to receive interest on instalmental payments). Modern commerce (e.g., the "zero percent interest for two years" often offered by dealers in furniture and other household goods) proves that such an assumption is often false, even in the context of pure commercial transactions. In short, if the statement of Romer LJ is restricted to its proper context, there is nothing wrong with it or confusing about it. Viewed in any other context, it is merely *obiter* and can admit of exceptions.

Much the same can be said of the statement of Lord Greene MR in *IRC v Wesleyan and General Assurance Society*. It is clear that this statement was also

---

[151] [1961] 3 All ER at page 985.
[152] ibid.

obiter, and was made in a different context. The context was that of a discussion of the doctrine of "form and substance" in which the court was invited to convert, by judicial construction, transactions which were actually loans, into payments of an annuity, so that the Revenue could charge tax on the payments. This invitation was rejected by Lord Greene MR[153] on the basis that this was not the function of the court, especially since the principle of the "substance of the transaction" had been "exploded" in *IRC v Duke of Westminster*.[154] Thus, again, the statement under discussion seems to be correct when viewed in its proper context, and again, it clearly can admit of exceptions.

In sum, the state of the authorities seems to be that the courts will examine the true nature of the parties' transactions to determine whether periodical payments connected to a sale of an asset are really payments of instalments of the purchase price (in which case they are capital and not liable to tax under Case III); or whether there really has been a purchase of an annuity (in which case the payments are income and liable to tax under Case III); or, whether they contain a mixture of instalments of purchase price and sums representing interest on the purchase price (in which case the payments are dissected).

Income of the recipient

Secondly, the payment must "form part of the income of the recipient".[155] This, although related to the income/capital discussion above, concerns a different issue. It is concerned with the question whether a payment is really the income of the recipient or whether it is the income of someone else (i.e., who "owns" the income?). This was another ground for the decision in *Campbell v IRC*. Viscount Dilhorne raised (without answering) the question "whether the payments made by Tutors to the trustees on the clear understanding that they would be used to buy Tutors' business and so returned to Tutors can properly be regarded as ever belonging to the trustees in a real sense at all".[156] Lord Guest answered this question in the negative. Approving the Crown's argument that "there must be a transfer of title to the income", Lord Guest said[157]:

> If *unico contextu* with the alleged transfer there is a contract to pay it back on the purchase of the business, then there is no transfer of title

---

[153] [1946] 2 All ER at page 751.
[154] [1936] AC 1.
[155] Viscount Dilhorne in *Campbell v IRC* [1968] 3 All ER at 588 at 592; compare Lord Upjohn at 603.
[156] at page 595.
[157] at page 601.

to the income and, therefore, no annual payment.

Conclusion

In sum, the words "other annual payments" under Sch. D case III can be said to refer to payments similar in character to interest of money and annuities, made under a binding legal obligation, having the quality of recurrence, which are the income of the recipient, and which constitute pure profit in his or her hands.

Having examined the meanings of the different types of income charged under Case III, we will now proceed to examine the machinery of collection under the Case.

Deduction of Tax at Source

As has been noted earlier, the scheme of Sch. D Case III is the deduction of income tax by the payer before making the payment. The rationale for such deductions was given by Lord Upjohn in *Campbell v IRC*[158].

> For the purposes of income tax the payer is regarded as having parted with that part of his income which by covenant or contract he pays away. The income that he pays away is that of the payee and so he is entitled to deduct tax on paying it.

The machinery for the deduction is contained within ss.348 and 349 ICTA 1988. Both sections apply to different types of payment and the consequences attendant upon their application are significantly different – all we will say about this now is that s.348 is far more beneficial to the taxpayer than s.349.

First, we need to identify the types of payment to which each of the sections applies. S.348 applies "where any annuity or other annual payment charged with tax under Case III of Schedule D, not being interest, is paid wholly out of profits or gains brought into charge to income tax".[159] The section extends to royalties and other sums paid in respect of the user of a patent.[160] On the other hand s.349 applies where the payments are "not payable or not wholly payable out of profits or gains brought into charge to income tax".[161] Hereafter, we will refer to the phrase "profits or gains brought into charge to income tax" as "taxed income", and to profits or

---

[158] [1968] 3 All ER 603.
[159] See s.348(1) (emphasis added). For a critical view of this provision see J Tiley [1981] BTR 263.
[160] S.348(2).
[161] See s.349(1).

gains which do not fall within that description as "untaxed income".

If s.348 applies only in respect of payments made wholly out of taxed income and s.349 applies in respect of payments not so made, the question then arises as to how the source of any particular payment is to be decided. The first point to note here is that the mere fact that accounts are kept in some particular way ought not to alter the rights of the Revenue, and ought not to militate against the rights of the taxpayer,[162] i.e., the particular form adopted by a taxpayer in his accounts should neither assist nor injure him.

The question of how the source of a payment is to be determined was answered by Lord Wilberforce in *IRC v Plummer*[163].

> The general rule, in the case of an individual at least, is that what is significant when one is considering the application of the statutory rule, is not the actual source out of which the money is paid, nor even the way in which the taxpayer for his own purposes keeps his accounts, if indeed he keeps any, but the status of a notional account between himself and the revenue. He is entitled, in respect of any tax year, to set down on one side his taxed income and on the other the amount of the annual payments he has made and if the latter is equal to or less than the former, to claim the benefit of [s.348].

What this statement means is simply that if the payer has income out of which the annual payment could have been made, s.348 applies rather than s.349, even if the payment is actually made out of capital. All that we are concerned with is whether the payer had sufficient taxed income to cover the payment, and not, for example, whether he made the payment straight out of his salary or out of funds borrowed from Australia.

Example

Launcelot is a barrister who earns at least £100,000 every year from his profession. He has an obligation under a covenant to make payments of £2,000 every month to his favourite charity for the next six years. Last year, he made a cash purchase of some farmland at an auction, and so was a little short of cash. He had to sell some shares in order to meet his obligations under the covenant.

Although Launcelot's payments for last year were actually made out of the proceeds of the sale of the shares, and not out of his earnings as a barrister, they will still be covered by s.348. He earned enough from his profession (at least £100,000) to cover his obligations under

---

[162] Per Lord Hanworth MR in *Central London Railway Co. v IRC* (1934) 20 TC 102 at 134.
[163] [1980] AC 896 at 909.

the covenant ($\pounds 24,000$) and the fact that the payment was in real life made from another source is irrelevant.

If, however, the payer has deliberately restricted himself for other legal reasons to pay out of capital, then the general rule stated by Lord Wilberforce is overridden and s.349 will apply. The point was made by Romer LJ in *Central London Railway Co v IRC*[164] that although the form in which accounts are kept is not conclusive, yet it may be that a particular form has been adopted for the purpose of definitely deciding and recording the fact that a decision has been made, that a certain payment is to be made out of capital. Such a form of account, which debits the payment to capital, may have been adopted for the purpose of making it clear that revenue is set free for other purposes. According to Romer LJ[165]:

> [W]here, not for the purposes of convenience or for the purposes of giving effect to the payer's own notions of account keeping, but for the purpose of definitely deciding and of recording the fact that a decision has been come to that a certain payment of interest is to be paid out of capital and not out of interest, then the account is not only of great importance but, in the absence of evidence to the contrary, is conclusive upon the matter.

This principle was applied in *Chancery Lane Safe Deposit and Officers Co Ltd v IRC*.[166] The company borrowed some money to finance building works. On the advice of its auditors, the company, in order to give a fair view of its affairs, charged part of the interest payments on the loans to capital (the company's taxable profits exceeded the amount of the interest payments and so it could have paid out of taxable profits). The Revenue claimed that the interest payments were paid out of capital and not out of profits or gains brought into charge to income tax. The company on the other hand claimed that the allocations to capital were mere book keeping entries irrelevant for tax purposes, and that the interest payments were made out of profits brought into charge to income tax. It was held by a majority of the House of Lords (Lords Reid and Upjohn dissenting) that the payments must be treated as having been made out of capital. There was a deliberate choosing of attribution to capital rather than to revenue. It was not a matter of method of domestic bookkeeping. The accounts merely evidenced the fact that a decision was taken, was acted upon, and was maintained. The company's definite attribution precluded an entirely

---

[164] (1934) 20 TC 102 at 141.
[165] ibid.
[166] (1965) 43 TC 83.

inconsistent attribution for tax purposes. Lord Morris of Borth-y-Gest said[167]:

> If a company makes and adheres to a decision that a payment should be out of capital and orders all its affairs on that basis, it would be strange if it could assert that the payment should be deemed to be one payable out of profits or gains. An attribution of a yearly payment to profits or gains brought into charge to tax can only be in reference to the year in which the payment is made. If a payment is attributed to capital, the practical result follows that the sum available or carried forward as available for distribution by way of dividends is increased. If a sum is so carried forward it does not, of course, follow that distribution by way of dividends will take place, nor does it follow that, if there are dividends, there will be deductions of tax. It would seem incongruous, however, if a company, having decided (which means the same as "definitely" decided) to charge a payment to capital and having regulated its proceedings on that basis, could say that the payment was not to be deemed to be charged to capital. This does not mean that in any ordinary case a company, in seeking vis-a-vis the Revenue to make an attribution of an annual payment, is fettered merely because of some form of entry that it has made in books or accounts. It merely means that what was in fact and in reality a payment out of capital cannot be paraded in the guise of a payment out of revenue. That would be more than departing from documents or accounts: it would be departing from fact: it would be a distortion of history.

The gist of this decision is that, a deliberate decision to pay out of capital, which has practical consequences in the real world, or which affects the interests of persons other than the decision maker, cannot thereafter be interpreted differently. If Mr. X decides to make a particular payment out of his savings, or from proceeds of the sale of his car, that is his own business (as long as his taxed income is sufficient to cover his liability to make annual payments in the relevant year). The method so chosen may just have been the most convenient means of making the payment at that particular time – a case of simple domestic bookkeeping, and he has not committed himself, for any defined period, to continue making the payments in that fashion. The same result will ensue if the Managing Director of X Ltd. decided to make this month's royalty payment from the proceeds of a sale of equipment, simply because the cash was available

---

[167] at page 115.

there and then. That is again a case of domestic bookkeeping. If however the same X Ltd. passed a resolution to make all future payments of particular royalties by realising investments, this, because of all the consequences that will invariably flow therefrom, may lead to a different result, and X Ltd. may not be able to claim that the payments are from income. As Lord Morris noted in the *Chancery Lane* case[168], a payment cannot in one and the same year be debited to capital, with the result that the dividend fund is enhanced, and also notionally be treated as debited to revenue so as to enable tax which is deducted to be retained. "That would require the sum in one year to render two incompatible and inconsistent services. The money must speak either as a payment out of capital or as a payment out of income".

We will now examine the effects of the application, first, of s.348, and secondly, that of s.349.

Payments under section 348

When s.348 applies[169], the payer is entitled (but not obliged) to deduct (and retain) a sum representing the amount of income tax on the payment[170], the recipient shall allow such deduction to be made[171], and the payer shall be discharged of his obligation to make the payment.[172] This in effect means that the payment is deductible in the hands of the payer. As has been noted earlier, the payment is an alienated slice of the payer's income, and since it represents the income of someone else (i.e., the recipient) and not of the payer, it follows that the payer is not liable to tax on that slice of income.

Example

Natalia undertakes to pay a gross sum of £1,000 every year to "Save the Elephant", a registered charity. Assuming a basic rate of 22%, if s.348 applies, Natalia is entitled to deduct tax of £220 and to pay the balance of £780 to the charity.

The annual payment is part of the recipient's total income in the year when the payment becomes due and if the deduction is made, the recipient is treated as having received the gross sum, and as having paid tax on it at basic rate (s.348(1)(d)). Thus in the example above, "Save the Elephant" will be treated as having received £1,000, and having paid tax of £220 on that sum.

If the recipient is only a basic rate tax payer then there is nothing more to be done in respect of the payment. If, on the other hand, the

---

[168] 43 TC at page 117.

[169] It does not apply to payments to which s.687 applies, or to payments that are "relevant payments" for the purposes of Chapter VIIA of Part IV of the Act, or to qualifying donations to charity (see s.348(3)). Donations to charity now have their own specific provisions for deduction of tax (see s.25 FA 1990; s.41 FA 2000).

[170] S.348(1)(b). The deduction will normally be at the basic rate, except in the case of interest, where the deduction will be at the lower rate (see s.4 and s.1A ICTA 1988).

[171] S.106(1) TMA 1970 imposes a penalty for refusing to permit deduction.

[172] S.348(1)(c).

recipient is a higher rate tax payer then he has to pay the difference between the tax paid at basic rate and that which would have been due at the higher rate. If the recipient's marginal rate is zero (e.g., charities, and individuals who either have no income or whose income fall below the personal allowance) then a refund of tax may be claimable from the Revenue.

Payments under section 349

When s.349 applies, the payer is obliged to deduct the amount of income tax from the payment (s.349(1)). [173] Where only part of the payment was not made out of taxed income, the tax, in effect, only has to be deducted from that part. The person by or through whom the payment was made, is obliged to deliver an account of the payment to the inspector, and is liable to tax at the applicable rate on the whole of the payment, or on so much of it as is not made out of taxed income (s.350(1)).

S.349(1) does not apply to payments to which s.687 applies, or to payments that are "relevant payments" for the purposes of Chapter VIIA of Part IV of the Act, or to qualifying donations to charity.

Payments without Deduction of Tax

We have just discussed the requirement for deduction of tax under s.349. What if the parties wish to dispense with the deduction of tax? This section examines the various ways in which such a wish may possibly be achieved.

Agreements for non-deduction

One obvious method of implementing a wish to dispense with the deduction of tax is for the parties to enter into an agreement to that effect. However, an obstacle to this course of action exists in s.106(2) TMA 1970, which provides that, every agreement for the payment of interest, rent or other annual payment in full without allowing deduction of income tax shall be void. A number of points should be noted with respect to this provision. First, the provision applies only to agreements. It does not for example apply to trustees. In *Re Goodson's Settlement*[174] the settlor directed trustees to pay annuities to his wife, and directed that the annuities should be enjoyed free of income tax. It was held that the settlor did not by the

---

[173] Note that ESC A16 gives relief from this requirement where payments are made in a later year out of untaxed income but could have been paid out of taxed income in the year in which they were due.
[174] [1943] Ch 101.

settlement create any agreement with the trustees or anybody else. Thus the provisions of (what is now) s.106(2) TMA 1970 did not apply (see below however, for the effect of a "free of tax" stipulation). Secondly, the provision invalidates only the part of the agreement relating to non-deduction of tax and not the whole agreement. It follows that where there is such a provision in an agreement, the payer is still entitled, or obliged to deduct tax depending on whether s.348 or s.349 applies.[175]

The use of formulae

The provisions of s.106(2) TMA 1970 can be circumvented by the use of certain formulae. If the parties wish to ensure that a fixed sum is paid each year to the recipient irrespective of fluctuations in tax rates, such a wish can be implemented by the means of the common formula - to pay such sum as after the deduction of income tax at the basic rate for the time being in force will leave £x. Such a formula was approved in *Booth v Booth*[176] as not being contrary to s.106(2). All that it means is that the amount so specified is net of income tax. The payer is thus left with the responsibility for handling the tax affairs in respect of the gross sum. However, while circumventing s.106(2) TMA 1970, this is only a partial solution to the problem of non-deduction of tax. The recipient is relieved of the responsibility of bothering about tax deductions, but the payer is not. In fact, the payer is in a situation which is not much different from what it would have been if the formula had not been used at all.

Payments "free of tax"

It is actually possible to stipulate that a payment be made "free of tax". A provision to pay £x "free of tax" does not fall foul of s.106(2) because of the decision of the House of Lords in *Ferguson v IRC*[177] that the effect of such a provision is an undertaking to pay such sum as after deduction of income tax leaves £x. In *Ferguson*, a husband and wife entered into a deed of separation whereby the husband agreed to pay the wife the sum of £35 free of income tax. During the relevant periods, the husband lived abroad and had no UK income and thus the revenue sought to tax the wife on the £35. It was held that the sum had already borne tax because the agreement was to pay a gross sum which, after deduction of tax, leaves £35, and that therefore the tax sought was not claimable.

---

[175] See Scrutton J in *Blount v Blount* [1916] 1 KB 230 at 237-238.
[176] [1922] 1 KB 66.
[177] [1970] AC 412.

A "free of tax" stipulation attracts a number of consequences. Generally, it operates to ensure that the recipient in any event ends up with the specified amount, no more and no less. Thus if the recipient obtains any repayment of tax from the Revenue, he is obliged to return such repayment to the payer. This is the rule in *Re Pettit*.[178] In this case a testator provided an annuity "free of tax" by his will. The sums were paid wholly out of taxed income, and the annuitant received some repayment from the revenue. It was held that the annuitant must return a proportion of that repayment to the trustees as the annuity bore to the annuitant's total income. A further consequence is that if the recipient is liable to higher rate tax, the payer is obliged to satisfy this liability too. This is the rule in *Re Reckitt*.[179]

The result is that the obligation of the payer varies with the marginal rate of the payee and this can present some accounting problems. Apart from this fact, just as with the case of the use of formulae (above), a "free of tax" stipulation does not actually provide a solution to the non-deduction problem. While it relieves the recipient of all responsibility for tax, it imposes on the payer a far higher burden than he would normally have had to bear. As such, except this is precisely what the parties want, such a provision is counter productive. The inevitable conclusion therefore is that there is no practical way of implementing a non-deduction of tax.

Failure to Deduct Tax

The payer and the recipient

In cases of a failure by the payer to deduct the tax which he is entitled or obliged to deduct there is no obligation on the recipient to refund the over payment – at least as long as the payer failed to make the deduction under a mistake of law (e.g., thinking that no deduction is necessary because the recipient is a charity). An action will not lie against the recipient for recovery of the sum, and the payer is not entitled to withhold later payments.[180] Where the payment is one of a series within the same tax year, and some instalments remain to be paid, the payer may not make good his loss by making the deduction from one of the later payments.[181]

Exception may be made, where the failure to deduct was due to a mistake fact, in which case recovery is possible[182] (e.g., where the mistake is one of calculation); and where the applicable rate of tax increases after the payment, the excess can be recovered (s.821 ICTA 1988).

---

[178] [1902] 2 Ch 765.
[179] [1932] 2 Ch 144.
[180] Re Hatch [1919] 1 Ch 351; *Warren v Warren* (1895) 72 LT 628.
[181] *Johnson v Johnson* [1946] 1 All ER 573 (explaining *Taylor v Taylor*, [1937] 3 All ER 571).
[182] *Turvey v Dentons* [1953] 1 QB 218.

The parties and the Revenue

The first point to note here is that there is no penalty for non-deduction. If the payment is made under s.348, failure to deduct tax will not generally be of any concern to the Revenue, since they will have got the tax already, or will still get it (in both cases, from the payer). However, since any deduction which is made is to be treated as income tax paid by the recipient (s.348(1)(d)), it follows that, in cases of non-deduction, no tax can be treated as having been paid. The Revenue take the view that the recipient cannot make a repayment claim, but give concessionary relief in respect of maintenance payments.[183]

If the payment is made under s.349 the Revenue will simply assess the payer, who in any case is liable under s.350(1), to the appropriate rate of tax on the payment. The result is that the payer has nothing to gain by not deducting the tax.

The Effect of Section 347A

The FA 1988 introduced certain rules in respect of the income tax treatment of annual payments, the effect of which was to take most of them out of the tax system. The relevant provision is now in s.347A, ICTA 1988, which provides that any annual payment made after 14 March 1988 by an individual, which would otherwise have fallen within Case III of Sch. D, shall not be a charge on the payer's income, that no deduction can be made on account of the payment, and that the payment is not the income of the recipient or of any other person. This means that, as a general rule, new arrangements for annual payments (e.g., covenants) by individuals have no income tax consequences whatsoever. Thus, for example, the covenants which parents used to make in favour of their children who were attending university will no longer be effective as a means of getting the Revenue to "subsidise" university education.

This is the general rule, but s.347A(2) provides exceptions for payments of interest, payments made for *bona fide* commercial reasons in connection with an individual's trade, profession or vocation etc. (e.g., partnership retirement annuities), and payments which fall within s.125(1) (i.e., purchased annuities paid wholly or partly out of capital).[184] These still fall within the Case III provisions. Payments made in pursuance of an existing obligation were exempted from this rule by s.36(3) FA 1988. "Existing obligation" for these purposes is defined by s.36(4), and generally refers to obligations incurred before 15 March 1988.

---

[183] Under ESC A52. This concession is classified obsolescent.

[184] The original provisions included covenanted payments to charity. The FA 2000 (s.41) repealed the provision relating to covenanted payments to charity in respect of payments falling to be made after 5 April 2000 by individuals or after 31 March 2000 by companies. This provision is part of the general schemes for giving tax relief for donations to charities (see e.g., s.25 FA 1990).

Section 347A of the Taxes Act 1988 (annual payments not a charge on the income of the payer) applies to a payment which is treated by virtue of Chapter IA of Part XV of the Taxes Act 1988 as income of the payer notwithstanding that it is made in pursuance of an obligation which is an existing obligation within the meaning of section 36(3) of the Finance Act 1988.

What this means is that, payments which are treated as the income of the settlor under the anti-avoidance rules of part XV (see below) now fall within the exclusions in s.347A. Generally, an annual payment will be ineffective for tax purposes under part XV, and the payments will be treated as the income of the payer (s.660A) unless the income arises from property in which the settlor has no interest (see exceptions in s.660A(8) and s.660A (9). By this token, even covenants entered into before 15 March 1988 would seem now to be ineffective unless they fall within an exception to the s.660A provisions. The result is that the only exceptions now are, those within s.347A itself, and those excluded from the operation of s.660A.

S.347A applies only to payments made by individuals (references to an individual in s.347A(2) include references to a Scottish partnership in which at least one partner is an individual[185]). Thus payments made by other entities, such as companies or trusts, and payments under wills, are not affected, and are still subject to the normal Case III provisions.

Anti-Avoidance Provisions

A discussion of the taxation of pure income profit will not be complete without a mention of the anti-avoidance provisions contained in Part XV ICTA 1988, and which generally apply in respect of "settlements". Annual payments within Case III will generally come within the scope of these provisions because of the wide meaning given to "settlement". S.660(G)(1) defines a settlement as including any disposition, trust, covenant, agreement or arrangement, or transfer of assets. Most annual payments are made under trusts, covenants, or agreements, and any payment not made under these will definitely be made under an "arrangement" or a "disposition". The Part XV provisions are discussed in more detail in the next chapter. However, it is useful to note here the general principle in s 660A(1) to the effect that (with certain exceptions) any income arising under a settlement during the life of the settlor will be treated as the income of the settlor unless the settlor has no interest in the property from

---

[185] See s.347A(6).

which the income arises.

Further Reading

Wosner J, *The Meaning of Annual Payment* – I [1989] BTR 265.

Robson MH, *The Meaning of Annual Payment* - *II* [1989] BTR 270.

Stebbings C, *The Taxation of Mortgage Interest at Source in the Nineteenth Century* [1989] BTR 348.

Stopforth D, *Charitable Covenants by Individuals* - *a History of the Background to their Tax Treatment and their Cost to the Exchequer* [1986] BTR 101.

chapter twelve
Income Tax -
Taxation of Trusts and Settlements

Individuals, partnerships, and corporations are generally taxable on their income, whether arising from employments, trades, or investments. The taxation of the income arising or accruing to these persons or entities are covered in various sections of this book. There remains however yet another entity which is capable of making profits and receiving income. This entity is the trust.

Trusts can often serve as convenient mechanisms for splitting, accumulating, or distributing income. The planning opportunities inherent in this method of handling income are evident. For example, a taxpayer with income-yielding properties may settle the property with a direction to the trustees to accumulate the income arising therefrom. On one view of the matter, without more, tax could be saved – the income accrues to the trustees and therefore the settlor will not be liable to tax on it. Since it does not "really" belong to the trustees, they might also not be liable to tax on it. The income will accumulate tax-free, until one day, when it has been capitalised, it will be distributed free of income tax to one or more beneficiaries. In another scenario, an individual with a high marginal rate may settle income or income-producing assets on trust for beneficiaries who are not taxpayers or who have lower marginal rates. This would not only take advantage of the beneficiaries' lower rates, it would also take advantage of their personal reliefs.

Not surprisingly, this state of affairs is largely a dream because, under the UK tax system, trustees are "persons", trusts are taxable entities in their own right, just like individuals and corporations, and, the income accruing to trustees is taxable in their hands. Lest this be seen as presenting another opportunity for total avoidance of UK tax (e.g., by appointing foreign trustees), although any income arising from the trust property would normally accrue to the trustees only, it is not the rule that the trustees alone are to attract the attention of the tax collector. According to Viscount Cave LC in *Williams v Singer*[1], such a principle would lead to "strange" results, because[2]:

> If the legal ownership alone is to be considered, a beneficial owner in moderate circumstances may lose his right to exemption or abatement by reason of the fact that he has wealthy trustees, or a wealthy beneficiary may escape Super-tax by appointing a number of trustees in less affluent circumstances. Indeed ... a beneficiary domiciled in this country may altogether avoid the tax on his foreign income spent abroad by the simple expedient of appointing one or more foreign trustees.

Thus, the taxation of trust income falls into a three-tier system. In some cases, income tax is charged on the trustee. In cases where a trustee is chargeable with the tax, the statutes recognise the fact that he is a trustee for others, and he is taxed on behalf of his beneficiaries, who will accordingly be entitled to any exemption or abatement which the income tax statutes allow.[3] In other instances, the tax is charged on the beneficiary, who will normally be given credit for any tax already borne by the trustees in respect of the income that is to be taxed. Finally, in certain situations (see the anti-avoidance rules in respect of "settlements" later in this chapter), tax is charged on the settlor.

The question why we should tax trusts is easy enough to answer. As seen above, the tax planning opportunities that would be created if trusts were not taxed would be enormous. This factor has been seen to be inherent in the history of trusts. For example, according to Mayson[4]:

> The lineal ancestor of the trust, the use, was itself developed in order to avoid taxation - the feudal dues of the Crown. It is a tribute to the ingenuity of many that some 450 years after the enactment of the Statute of Uses the trust is still an appropriate vehicle for the avoidance of one's fiscal burden.

Thus we should tax trusts in order to avoid the shortfall in tax revenue that would be the inevitable result of not taxing them. If an anti-avoidance motive is thought to be insufficient justification, then there is the added justification that if trusts, like other legal entities, can trade, invest, and

---

[1]   [1921] 1 AC 65; (1920) 7TC 387.
[2]   7 TC at 411.
[3]   See Viscount Cave LC in *Williams v Singer* 7 TC at 411 - 412.
[4]   Mayson on Revenue Law (1993) 14th edn., page 431.

otherwise earn income, then there is no reason why, unlike other legal entities, they should escape tax on those activities. That trusts are administered solely for the benefit of others (the beneficiaries) does not lead to a different result, since on one view of the matter, companies can also be said to be run solely for the benefit of others (the shareholders) – but this has never been seen as a reason why companies should not be taxed.

The question how we should tax trusts is more involved, and we will discuss it under a number of subheadings.

Taxing Trusts like Individuals

For one, we could simply treat them like individuals and tax them accordingly. This would apparently present a simple and straightforward solution. The "rate applicable to trusts" (chargeable generally in respect of accumulation or discretionary trusts) would go. Trusts would suffer tax on trust income at the starting/lower, basic, and higher rates, just like individuals, and that would be it. This would remove the distortions in fiscal matters caused by trusts and discourage the use of trusts solely for tax planning purposes. However attractive this solution may seem, a closer examination reveals problems.

First, it is obvious that trusts are not individuals and therefore there is no analogy that can be drawn between the two. Any attempt to treat them on an equal basis rests on shaky foundations which will quickly unravel. For example, if we are to treat trusts as we treat individuals, do we allocate "personal reliefs" to them as well? If not, why not? It may be argued that since personal reliefs are only allocated to "individuals", trustees should not receive them. This begs the question why personal reliefs should be allocated only to individuals, but it also undermines the principle of treating trusts like individuals. In this respect, it is useful to note that, while under the ICTA 1988 trustees do not enjoy the "personal allowance" given to individuals under s.257, the Capital Gains Tax legislation generally allows trustees to claim half of the annual exemption available to individuals.[5] In respect of certain types of trust, the trustees can claim the full exemption.[6] The allocation of this exemption (or part of it) to trustees is not due to the fact that trustees are taxed like individuals under the Capital Gains Tax legislation. The legislation recognises the difference between trusts and individuals quite clearly, and there are specific provisions for taxing trustees. However, the annual exemption allocated to trustees can be defended by pointing out that the exemption is simply

---

[5]   TCGA 1992, Sch. 1 para. 2.
[6]   TCGA 1992, Sch. 1, para. 1.

referred to in the statute as an "annual exempt amount"[7] – which is not as clearly linked to individuals as the "personal allowance" of the income tax legislation. This answer itself raises a number of other questions, but at the least, it would be supportive of the argument that to treat trustees like individuals for income tax purposes should involve allocating personal reliefs to them too. However, this might lead to distortions if beneficiaries are to receive credit for the tax paid by the trustees (see below). In any event, if it is thought that trustees should also be entitled to personal reliefs, then at what level should this be? Should the trustees' "personal allowance" be the same as that of an individual[8], or should it be less, or indeed, more? Arguments can be advanced in favour of each option.

Secondly, this solution does not address the issue of income-splitting. A high earner with income-yielding assets could still save a considerable amount of tax by settling those assets on trust for others. The effect of this would still be as described above – the settlor would then be taking advantage of the trustees' marginal rates (from the starting/lower, to basic to higher rates) instead of paying higher rate tax on the whole. If trusts had personal reliefs, the settlor (who would have exhausted his or hers) would also be taking advantage of these. Thus, unless other rules are in place to combat avoidance, trusts would still be valuable devices for tax planning.

Thirdly, what would be done with the beneficiaries when they finally receive distributions from the trustees? Would they still be taxable on the distributions, or would the trustees have exhausted all the tax liabilities? If the beneficiaries are to receive a tax credit in respect of tax paid by the trustees, what would the tax credit amount to? Would the beneficiaries then be entitled to refunds of tax if they are non-taxpayers, and if so, at what rate would the refunds be calculated? If beneficiaries are basic rate tax payers would they be entitled to a refund in respect of any higher rate tax paid by the trustees? If the trustees had claimed any "personal reliefs", how would this be reflected in the tax credits given to beneficiaries?

Thus this approach to taxing trusts raises difficult questions and would be extremely problematic to implement. In order to recognise fully the nature of trusts, it would need to be underpinned by intricate provisions relating to settlors and beneficiaries, and perhaps, some provisions dealing with undistributed income. The result would be a situation which is as complicated as the present one.

---

[7]   TCGA 1992, s 3.
[8]   see ICTA 1988, s. 257.

Taxing Trusts at a Flat Rate

A second possible approach to the issue of how we should tax trusts would be to recognise the differences between trusts and individual, charge trusts only at a flat rate (e.g., the basic rate) and give tax credits to beneficiaries in respect of the tax already paid by trustees. The beneficiaries would then resolve any remaining tax liabilities or any tax refunds with the Revenue. This approach would also however raise the planning opportunities already referred to – and provision would need to be made in respect of undistributed income.

Disregarding Trusts for Tax Purposes

A third possible approach would be to ignore trusts completely for tax purposes, and treat any income accruing to trustees as income accruing to the settlor. This would arguably be the simplest and most effective approach of all. All trusts would be ineffective for tax purposes, and for these purposes only, the settled property and the income thereof would be deemed to still belong to the settlor. There would be no tax on trustees or beneficiaries, and whether trust income is accumulated or distributed would be inconsequential. The problem with this approach would be in respect of cases where the settlor is dead and the settlor's death has not terminated the trust. In such cases, income received by the trustees after the settlor's estate has been administered may escape tax altogether.

The Current Approach

The approach currently adopted by the ICTA 1988 to taxing trusts is a curious caricature involving a blend of aspects of the second and third approaches just discussed. Trust law is generally thought to be complex, and the law relating to the taxation of income from trusts and settlements is no less complex. The complexity arises out of the problems inherent in different approaches to taxing trusts, some of which have been highlighted above. These problems and the need to avoid a loss of tax revenue have led to intricate provisions which have the effect of reducing (but not eliminating) the attractiveness of trusts as devices for tax planning. Recent years have witnessed moves to simplify the applicable rules (particularly those relating to the taxation of "settlements"), but these have probably not gone far enough. The discussion that follows attempts to present the principles in a clear and accessible way.

"Trust"

The first question that we address our minds to is what the tax legislation means when it refers to a trust. Not surprisingly, we find that the word "trust" is not defined in the Taxes Act. This omission (which is typical of the Act) may be due to the fact that "trust" does not appear to have any special meaning for tax purposes. As is inevitably the case in such situations, it would appear that its plain and ordinary meaning under the general law would suffice. Trust law texts are often shy of giving a definition and, perhaps it is impossible to produce a universally acceptable and all-encompassing definition. Thus, we will not attempt to give such a definition here. We can however take as a starting point one of the definitions in the *Concise Oxford English Dictionary*, which defines trust as (*inter alia*) "a confidence placed in a person by making that person the nominal owner of property to be used for another's benefit".[9] A trust can also be seen as the entity in which the property is placed, or, the vehicle whereby the person in whom the confidence is placed is able to become the nominal owner of the property in question. The Inland Revenue in one of their booklets ("Trusts, An Introduction") defines a trust as "an obligation binding a person or a company (a trustee) to deal with property in a particular way, for the benefit of one or more beneficiaries."[10] An American court has described a trust in its "most enlarged sense" in which it is used in English jurisprudence as "an equitable right, title or interest in property, real or personal, distinct from the legal ownership thereof".[11] Finally, we will refer to another American case[12], where it was said:

> Generally a trust may be said to exist where the legal estate is in one person and the equitable estate is in another, or where there are rights, titles and interests in property distinct from the legal ownership thereof.

These are all different aspects of the same broad principle – that the legal owner of property is not the person with the beneficial interest in the property, but is rather obliged to manage the property for and on behalf of others (who therefore have an equitable interest in the property). In terms of the taxation of trust income, the term "trust" is often used in the sense of the entity or structure in which the confidence referred to in the definitions above is reposed, or on which the obligation to deal with property for another's benefit is imposed. Obviously the entity is unable manifest itself in the real world and therefore has to be represented by others. It also has to carry out its functions and discharge its obligations

9   9th Ed., 1995, page 1498.
10   IR booklet IR152, page 1
11   *Jones v Byrne*, 149 F. 457 at 463.
12   *Merchants Nat. Bank of Aurora v Frazier*, 67 NE.2d. 611 at 617.

through those representatives. Normally, those representatives would be the trustees. One of their first duties in respect of taxes would be to inform the Revenue of the fact that a trust has been created and that they are the trustees thereof.[13] This then raises the question "who is a trustee"?

Trustee

Again, there is no specific definition of "trustee" for income tax purposes – and again, this word is not a term of art and does not generally have any special meaning for income tax purposes.[14] The *Concise Oxford English Dictionary* defines "trustee" as "a person or member of a board given control or powers of administration of property in trust with a legal obligation to administer it solely for the purposes specified".[15] The American case of *Jones v Bryce*[16] again refers to its "widest meaning" – "a person in whom some estate, interest, or power in or affecting property of any given description is vested for the benefit of another". The Revenue booklet IR152[17] seems to accept that there is no special or technical meaning to be attributed for income tax purposes to "trustee", since it simply repeats the position under the general law.

> The trustees are the legal owners of the trust property. They are under a legally binding obligation to handle the property of the trust in a particular way and for a particular purpose ... The trust can continue even though there may be changes in the people who are its trustees, but there must normally be at least one trustee.

Finally, in *Williams v Singer*[18] Lord Phillimore said

> The very essence of the position of a trustee is that he is a person who at law has all the rights of an owner, but who has nevertheless the obligation, which he has undertaken by accepting the trust, of using his powers as legal owner for the benefit of some person not himself or some object not his own.

The Charge on Trustees

There is no specific provision in the Taxes Act which charges trustees, qua

---

[13] See IR152, page 3.
[14] See however s.69(1) TCGA 1992 which provides that the trustees of a settlement shall be treated as being "... a single and continuing body of persons (distinct from the persons who may from time to time be the trustees) ..."
[15] 9th Ed., 1995, page 1498. Compare IR152, page 2.
[16] 149 F. At page 463; see also *Caruso v Caruso*, 134 A. 771 at 775; *Kaehn v St. Pauls Co-op. Assoc.*, 194 NW 112.
[17] IR152, page 2.
[18] 7 TC 387 at 416.

trustees, to tax on income accruing to them. However, the Act does contain specific provisions charging people who receive income. Thus, s.21(1) ICTA 1988 provides that income tax under Schedule A shall be charged on and paid by the persons receiving or entitled to the income. S.59(1) charges income tax under Schedule D on the persons receiving or entitled to the income. S.231(1) gives a tax credit in respect of qualifying distributions under Schedule F to the persons receiving the distributions. Since it is the trustees who are normally in receipt of trust income, such provisions apply to charge them to income tax in respect of the income which they have received. The principle that trustees are charged by virtue of the fact that they receive income is exemplified in the speech of Viscount Cave LC in *Williams v Singer*, where he said[19]:

> [I]f the Income Tax Acts are examined, it will be found that the person charged with the tax is neither the trustee nor the beneficiary as such, but the person in actual receipt and control of the income which it is sought to reach. The object of the Acts is to secure for the State a proportion of the profits chargeable, and this end is attained (speaking generally) by the simple and effective expedient of taxing the profits where they are found. If the beneficiary receives them he is liable to be assessed upon them. If the trustee receives and controls them he is primarily so liable.

The point was reiterated in *Reid's Trustees v IRC*[20] where trustees were held assessable under Schedule D because they received the income. The Lord President (Clyde)[21] rejected the argument that the only "person" to whom income could arise or accrue within the meaning of the Act is a person who is beneficially entitled to the income in his own right. In his view, trustees are the proper persons to be assessed in all cases in which the income of the trust estate received by them, or to which they are entitled, is not tax-deducted at source.[22] And, in the case of trust income which is tax-deducted at source, they could not be heard to ask repayment of the tax on the plea that the income did not arise or accrue to them but to others, whether such others were income-beneficiaries or capital-beneficiaries.[23]

The Scope of the Charge

Trust income accrues to trustees jointly, and they are liable to tax on it

---

[19]   7 TC at 411.
[20]   (1929) 14 TC 512.
[21]   at page 523.
[22]   For a similar principle in the USA, see *Brandon v State Revenue Commission*, 186 SE 872 – liability rests on the person "by whom the income is received or receivable"; compare *Commr. of Corporations and Taxation v Williston*, 54 NE.2d. 43 – liability attaches to the "ownership of the income".
[23]   at page 524 (emphasis added).

jointly, not jointly and severally.[24] It has already been seen in a statement referred to at the beginning of this chapter that trustees are charged on behalf of their beneficiaries.[25] This means that their personal circumstances are not relevant to the charges imposed on them in their capacities as trustees. There are a number of points to note in this respect, which are discussed immediately below.

Individuals

Although trustees in their official capacities are "persons", they are not "individuals".[26] This has certain consequences. First, because personal reliefs are generally available only to individuals, the trustees cannot claim any personal reliefs[27], although they may claim reliefs available to "persons", (e.g. loss relief) and, they may claim deductible expenses in respect of a trade carried on by the trust. Secondly, the trustees are not charged at rates lower than the basic rate because these apply only to individuals.[28] Thirdly, the trustees are not liable to higher rate tax because, by virtue of s.1(2)(b) ICTA 1988, this rate of tax is charged only on individuals. This particular point makes trusts still appear to be profitable devices for tax planning by high income earners whereby they may dump their income-producing assets in trusts, and leave the income thereof to accumulate. The attractiveness of this has been reduced by the introduction of a different rate of tax (the "rate applicable to trusts") in respect of certain types of trust (see below).

Trust Expenses

In calculating the taxable income of the trust for basic rate tax purposes, no deduction can be made for trust expenses of administration. In *Aikin v MacDonald's Trustees*[29] the trustees had an interest in certain tea estates in India. They received remittances representing profits from those estates. This income was subject to charge under Schedule D Case V and the trustees sought to deduct certain expenses incurred in this country in connection with the management of the trust. The Lord President, rejecting the claim, said[30]:

---

[24] *Dawson v IRC* [1989] STC 473; [1989] BTC 200 (HL); note that the effect of this particular decision (as far as the residence of trustees is concerned) has been reversed by FA 1989, s.110.

[25] Viscount Cave LC in *Williams v Singer* (7 TC at pages 411-412).

[26] See for example Viscount Sumner in *Baker v Archer-Shee*, (1927) 11 TC 749 at 767.

[27] See for example Lord Johnston in *Fry v Shiels* (1914) 6 TC 583 at 588: "I think that the question before us is solved at once when one observes that Section 19, which gives this relief commences not with the usual words, 'Any person' which may be held to include not merely a plurality of persons but a body, whether trustees or a corporation, regular or irregular, but that the word 'individual' is used; and I think it is used with a clear intention, and that intention is one which squares with the object of the provision. That object I conceive to be to relieve a man who by his own exertions and his own daily work makes an Income."

[28] See s.1(2)(aa) ICTA 1988.

[29] (1894) 3 TC 306.

[30] at page 308.

It seems to me that all the authorised deductions and charges occur at an earlier stage than that at which these expenses have been incurred. When the net sum was placed in the hands of the trustees, it had passed through all the vicissitudes which entitled anyone to make deductions. It had come home, and was in their hands for them to apply to their uses. The fact that their uses are trust uses does not seem to me to make any difference in the present question ... It seems to me that the expenses which are authorised to be deducted are expenses excluded by the terms of the present claim, because the words of the present claim are quite explicit that these expenses have been incurred in this country in connexion with the management of the trust, and they are not expenses at all specifically relating to the investment in question, except in this sense, that the income of the investment in question constitutes the bulk of the trust estate.

The *ratio* of this decision is that, the deduction sought was not permissible under Schedule D because it had not (as required by the Schedule D deduction rules) been incurred wholly and exclusively in earning the profit in question, but had rather been incurred after the income was earned. According to Lord Adam[31], the expenses looked very much like sums "expended in any domestic or private purposes, as distinct from the purposes of the manufacture, adventure, or concern". Lord McLaren said[32] that the only kind of deductions allowed is expenditure incurred in earning the profits, and, "that there is no deduction under any circumstances allowable for expenditure incurred in managing profits which have been already earned and reduced into money pounds, shillings, and pence". Lord Kinnear said[33] that this was not a deduction of money laid out or expended for the purpose of the trade or concern at all, but merely a deduction from the cost of distributing net income after it had come into this country.

However, even though the case did not purport to lay down any general principle in respect of trust expenses of administration generally, its practical effect is that such expenses will not ever be deductible for basic rate tax purposes, simply because they could never be expenses of earning the relevant income.

Trustees not Receiving Income

The principle that trustees are charged to tax because they receive income may have a corollary – that, if the trustees do not receive the income, but

---

[31]   at 308-309. Compare Lord McLaren at page 309.
[32]   at page 309.
[33]   at page 310.

the income rather "accrues directly" to a beneficiary, the trustees are not liable to tax on the income. Some authority for this proposition can be found in *Williams v Singer*[34]. The trustees in the case were resident in the United Kingdom but the trust income in question was derived from shares in an American company. The trustees were the registered owners of the shares, and they gave instructions to the Bank of British North America, in New York, to collect and receive the dividends on the shares and to credit them to the account of the beneficiary at the said bank in New York. No part of the dividends was at any time remitted to, or received in this country, and the beneficiary was at all material times resident and domiciled outside the United Kingdom. Since the beneficiary (being non domiciled and not having remitted any income to the United Kingdom) could not be taxed on the income, the Revenue sought to tax the trustees. The Revenue relied on the first general rule in s.100 of the Income Tax Act 1842 which, like s.21(1) of the ICTA 1988, charged tax on the persons "receiving or entitled unto" such profits, and argued that, since the income in the case "accrued" to the trustees as the legal holders of the investments, and the trustees were the persons legally entitled "to receive" the income, they were the persons chargeable under the Act. The Revenue claimed that they were entitled to look to those trustees for the tax and were neither bound nor entitled to look beyond the legal ownership. It was held that the trustees were not liable to tax on the income, because they had received no part of it. Viscount Cave LC said[35] that the trustees, who had directed the trust income to be paid to the beneficiaries, and who had themselves received no part of it, were not assessable to tax in respect of such income. Lord Phillimore said[36] that, the trustees in this case merely existed in order to preserve the settlement. Their duty so long as the beneficiary remained alive was to see that the dividends reached her. Although they in law were entitled to the dividends, the person "entitled" within the meaning of the relevant statutory provisions, and the person to whom they "belonged" within the meaning of the provisions was the beneficiary.

This case indicates that the person "entitled" to receive income is not necessarily the person in whom the legal title vests. In cases in which a trustee has directed income to be forwarded directly to a beneficiary or to an agent of the beneficiary, the trustee has the duty under s.76(1) TMA 1970 to make a return of the name, address and profits of the person to whom the payment was directed to be made.

---

[34] [1921] 1 AC 65; 7 TC 387.
[35] 7 TC, at page 412.
[36] at page 418.

The Extent of Trustees' Liability

Much has been said about the correct interpretation of the authorities (especially *Williams v Singer* and some cases referring to it) in the context of the extent of the liability of trustees to income tax. Whiteman and Wheatcroft took *Williams v Singer* to establish the principle that "income of a trust which is paid directly to a beneficiary without passing through the hands of a trustee is not assessable on the trustee."[37] They also stated that the fact that income accrues to a beneficiary in whose hands it is not liable to tax may constitute a good answer to an assessment on the trustees.[38] The authors then referred[39] to *dicta* in *Baker v Archer-Shee*[40] suggesting that a trustee may not be assessable in respect of income to which a beneficiary is absolutely entitled, even if not paid to the beneficiary, and stated that these dicta were "disregarded" in *Reid's Trustees v IRC* (above). Their conclusion was that, in view of this, and of the wordings of the relevant statutory provisions, their interpretation was correct. Mayson (referring to *Williams v Singer* (above) and *Corbett v IRC*[41]) said that "income which is not received by [the trustees] but is paid directly to a beneficiary, or which they do receive but which they have a duty to pay to a beneficiary is not their income for income tax purposes".[42] Tiley and Collison, referring to *Williams v Singer*, state that "since the trustee is assessable simply because income accrues to him, it follows that where income accrues not to him but directly to the beneficiary, the trustee is not assessable."[43] They further state (referring to *Reid's Trustees v IRC*) that where trustees receive income they may not be assessable if the income accrues beneficially to a cestui que trust in whose hands it is not liable to income tax.[44] According to them, this is a "second interpretation" of *Williams v Singer*, which can only apply where "the link between the income and the beneficiary is established".[45] Finally, Shipwright and Keeling[46] (referring to *Williams v Singer*, *Reid's Trustees v IRC* and *Dawson v IRC*[47]) list three possible bases on which trustees may be assessed to income tax. First, trustees are liable in respect of trust income except where they have not received it, but it has rather gone directly to the beneficiary; secondly, trustees are liable except in cases where the beneficiary entitled to the trust income is not a UK taxpayer; thirdly, trustees are liable except in cases where a beneficiary is absolutely entitled to the income (in this case, entitlement is determined according to trust law principles). They prefer the third approach, saying that this is an extension of the "actual receipt and control" test.

---

[37] Whiteman and Wheatcroft on Income Tax, 2nd ed. para 17-02.
[38] ibid.
[39] ibid.
[40] [1927] AC 844; 11 TC 749.
[41] [1937] 4 All ER 700; [1931] 1 KB 567.
[42] Mayson on Revenue Law, 14th edn., page 454.
[43] Simon's Tiley and Collison: UK Tax Guide, 2000-2001, para 11:03 (Butterworths).
[44] ibid, para 11:04.
[45] ibid.
[46] A Shipwright and E Keeling, Textbook on Revenue Law, 2nd. Edn. 1998, pages 395-396.
[47] [1988] 3 All ER 573; [1988] STC 684 (CA).

Let us examine the relevant *dicta* in the cases. In *Corbett v IRC* [48] Sir Wilfred Greene MR said:

> [W]here trustees are in receipt of income which it is their duty to pay over to beneficiaries, either with or without deduction of something for the trustees' expenses on the way, that income is, at its very inception, the beneficiaries' income. It is perfectly true that for assessment purposes the trustees may fall to be assessed, but the income is the beneficiaries' income from the very first ...[49]

Later in the same case, Sir Wilfred Greene MR said that, although the trustees hands were the hands to receive the income, and although the trustees, after receiving the income, might have to pay expenses out of it with the effect that the beneficiaries only received a net sum, the income when it came into the hands of the trustees was the beneficiaries' income and any tax which it had borne before reaching the trustees was the beneficiaries' tax.[50]

In *Baker v Archer-Shee* Lord Carson[51] approved the statement of Lord Hanworth MR in the Court of Appeal that, in respect of sums placed in the hands of trustees for the purpose of paying them over to beneficiaries, one may eliminate the trustees for income tax purposes, since the income is that of the beneficiaries, not the trustees. In the same case, Viscount Sumner[52] said that the court had to consider whether the income of a trust fund "belongs" to the beneficiary "so that the beneficiary is chargeable as if it arose to him directly as his".

These *dicta* seem clear enough. However, as noted above, *Reid's Trustees v IRC*[53] seemed to throw a spanner in the works. The facts of this case are relevant. The testator held some 5% War Loan, the interest on which was payable without deduction of income tax. According to the testator's settlement his wife and daughter were each to have the life rent of £20,000, and his son was to have another sum of £20,000 absolutely. If the daughter died leaving children they were to have her £20,000 among them; if she died leaving no children her £20,000 was to go to the testator's son or his heirs. The residue of the estate was to be divided into three equal shares, of which one was to go to the son absolutely and the other two were to be held for the wife and daughter in the same way as the respective provisions of £20,000 each. Shortly after the testator's death, the trustees received some interest in respect of the War Loans, and were assessed to income tax thereupon. The trustees argued that, on the basis of *Williams v Singer* and *Baker v Archer-Shee*, they were not liable to the tax and

---

[48] [1937] 4 All ER 700 at 705.
[49] Emphasis added.
[50] [1937] 4 All ER 700 at 707.
[51] 11 TC 749 at 782.
[52] 11 TC 749 at 766.
[53] (1929) 14 TC 512.

that they would be liable only when acting for incapacitated or non-resident beneficiaries. It was also their argument that the only "person" to whom income could "accrue" under the Income Tax Acts was a person beneficially entitled to the income in his or her own right. The General Commissioners held that the trustees were liable in respect of two-thirds of the income (i.e., the part referable to the testator's wife and daughter), but that they were not liable in respect of the one-third which was referable to the testator's son, since their sole duty was to pay the amount to him as his income.

The Court of Session held that the trustees were liable in respect of the whole of the interest, because they were the persons "receiving or entitled to" the income.

Much was said in the judgments about the effects of *Williams v Singer* and *Baker v Archer-Shee*. The Lord President (Clyde) said[54] that, notwithstanding the apparently imperative terms of the relevant statutory provision, the decision in *Williams v Singer* negatived the view that trustees receiving or entitled to the income under Case V of Schedule D are necessarily the persons liable to income tax in respect of such income. He said that, in both *Williams v Singer* and *Baker v Archer-Shee*, there were *dicta* "enunciated without apparent qualification, which point to the complete elimination of trustees in the matter of assessability to Income Tax",[55] but he felt that such a consequence was not "really contemplated by the decisions pronounced nor in the judgments by which those decisions were supported."[56] According to him, it was recognised that there are many cases in which trustees are assessable, "albeit as trustees having no beneficial right of their own to the income."[57] Lord Clyde said[58] that trustees are the proper persons to be assessed "in all cases in which the income of the trust estate received by them, or to which they are entitled, is not tax-deducted at source". Where the tax has been deducted at source, the trustees cannot request a repayment on the plea that the income did not arise or accrue to them but to others. The effect of the two cases is, according to him, that while trustees who receive or are entitled to income cannot now be regarded as "assessable and liable *prima instantia* for the tax in all cases", they would be so liable in "a great many" cases.[59] Thus the conclusion:

[T]rustees, albeit only the representatives of ulterior beneficial interests, are assessable generally in respect of the trust income ... but that – just because they represent those beneficial interests – they may have a good answer to a particular assessment, as regards some share or part of the income assessed, on the ground that such share or part arises or accrues beneficially to a cestui que trust in whose hands it

[54]   14 TC at page 522.
[55]   at page 524.
[56]   ibid.
[57]   ibid.
[58]   ibid.
[59]   at pages 524-525.

is not liable to Income Tax, e.g., a foreigner under Case V, Rules 1 and 3.

Lord Sands was able to distinguish both *Williams v Singer* and *Baker v Archer-Shee*. First, none of the beneficiaries had any interest or claim to the specific sum of interest, other than as part of the general estate in which they were interested. Thus, the trustees were the persons entitled to or receiving the income represented by the interest in question and were liable to tax in respect thereof.[60] Secondly, the two cases were not really applicable. *Williams v Singer* simply involved the question whether substance was to be preferred to theory.[61] The substance was that the income never came into the coffers of the trustees, and they never touched or handled it. The theory was that, since they were the owners of the securities, and it was by their own mandate, which presumably they might have recalled, that payment was made directly to the beneficiary, it was open to argument that theoretically the income must be held to have been received by them. In this respect:

> [I]t was found that the substance of the matter and not any mere theory was to be regarded. That was all that was determined by the judgment in *Williams v Singer*. It was not held, and the decision does not involve, that when a body of trustees receive income of the trust estate not taxed at the source and proceed to distribute it among beneficiaries, they are not assessable to Income Tax and are bound to pay over the income to the beneficiaries without deduction, leaving it to the Revenue to pursue the beneficiaries.[62]

As far as *Baker v Archer-Shee* was concerned, Lord Sands felt that the question was simply whether substance was to be preferred to form. His interpretation of the case was as follows. There was a life interest in a foreign trust estate, consisting partly of stocks and shares. The matter turned upon the question whether the trust income arose from "stocks, shares or rents", or from "other possessions". The substance of the matter was that the thing from which the income arose was dividends on stocks and shares. The form of the matter was that, technically the source of the income was not stocks and shares but a beneficial interest in a trust estate. The House of Lords decided in favour of the substance, and "this was the sole subject matter of decision in the case."[63]

---

[60] 14 TC at page 526.
[61] at page 527.
[62] ibid.
[63] at page 528.

Lord Morison said[64] that neither *Williams v Singer* nor *Baker v Archer-Shee* raised any question as to the person chargeable to tax. Rather, they related solely to the ascertainment of the income from foreign investments chargeable under Cases IV and V of Schedule D. Both Lord Morison[65] and Lord Blackburn[66] said that the trustees were the ones "entitled" to the income – a view concurred in by Lord Clyde[67] and Lord Sands.[68]

Can all these *dicta* and decisions be reconciled? One thing to be noted from the statements of Sir Wilfred Greene MR in *Corbett v IRC* is that, although he was clear that income which trustees are obliged to hand over to a beneficiary (i.e., income to which a beneficiary is absolutely entitled) "belongs" to the beneficiary, it does appear from the statements that, in such cases, the trustees are necessarily not liable to income tax on such income. On the contrary, he made it clear that the trustees "may fall to be assessed". On the other hand, clearly, the statements of both Lord Carson and Viscount Sumner in *Baker v Archer-Shee* imply that, in cases wherein a beneficiary is absolutely entitled to the trust income, only the beneficiary is liable to tax thereon.

A connecting thread in all these disparate statements may be *Dawson v IRC*[69] where Dillon LJ pointed out[70] that it was the beneficiary in *Williams v Singer* who was "in receipt and control" of the trust income. In the same case, Nicholls LJ said[71] that, in cases where the beneficiary has "an absolute, vested interest" in trust income, "nice questions" might arise as to whether there was any income accruing to the trustees, as distinct from, or in addition to, the beneficiary, and in respect of whether the trustees, as distinct from, or in addition to the beneficiary, received or were entitled to the income.

The connecting thread seems to lie in the concepts of receipt (and control), and entitlement. Therefore it may be argued that the real distinction between *Reid's Trustees v IRC* and the combination of *Williams v Singer* and *Baker v Archer-Shee* lies in the fact that, while in Reid's Trustees v IRC, the trustees were the ones who in fact received the income and who also were the ones held by the court to be "entitled to" the income (i.e., both elements of receipt and entitlement were satisfied), in *Williams v Singer* and *Baker v Archer-Shee*, the beneficiaries were the ones who in fact received the income, and who were held by the court to be "entitled to" the income. *Baker v Archer-Shee* was not even about the liability of trustees at all.

The "nice questions" referred to by Nicholls LJ in *Dawson v IRC* still remain. These revolve around the meanings of "receive" and "entitled to". First, "receive". This can refer either to actual (i.e., *de facto*) receipt of income, or to constructive (theoretical) receipt of income. This was the

---

64   14 TC at page 531.
65   at page 530.
66   at page 529.
67   at page 522.
68   at page 526.
69   [1988] 3 All ER 753.
70   at page 759.
71   at page 757.

distinction referred to by Lord Sands in *Reid's Trustees v IRC* (above) when he said that "the income never came into the coffers of the trustees, they never touched or handled it. But they were the owners of the securities, and it was by their own mandate, which presumably they might have recalled, that payment was made directly to the beneficiary. It was, therefore, open to argument that theoretically the income must be held to have been received by them." As Lord Sands pointed out, the constructive receipt option was rejected by the House of Lords in *Williams v Singer*. Thus, "receive" for these purposes must mean "receive in fact", or "actually receive".

The issue of entitlement (i.e., who is "entitled to" income) is not as easily settled. It may be related to the question of who the income "belongs" to, but even that is not without its difficulties. In *Williams v Singer*, the Revenue argued for a construction of entitlement which was based solely on legal title. If such an argument were to succeed, the question who is entitled to trust income would attract a swift and decisive response – the trustees – since legal title in the trust property, and thus the trust income, resides in them. However, this argument was not accepted in the case. As indicated earlier, the approach of Lord Phillimore[72] to the issue was that the trustees in the case merely existed in order to preserve the settlement, and their duty so long as the beneficiary remained alive was to see that the dividends reached her. Thus, although they in law were entitled to the dividends, the person "entitled" within the meaning of the relevant statutory provisions, and the person to whom they "belonged" within the meaning of the provisions was the beneficiary. This indicates that entitlement in equity may be more important than entitlement in law. This view is also evident in the speeches in *Baker v Archer-Shee*.[73] On this view of the matter, the beneficiary who is absolutely entitled to trust income would always be the person "entitled to" the trust income under the tax statutes, and trustees would only be "entitled to" trust income if there is no beneficiary with an absolute entitlement.

However, the Court of Session in *Reid's Trustees v IRC*[74] seemed to define entitlement to mean entitlement in law (which would support the Revenue's argument in *Williams v Singer*). This may indicate that the Court of Session, in taking this approach, was wrong in this aspect of its decision in *Reid's Trustees v IRC*. However, since the trustees in that case had actually been in receipt of the income, the decision itself (that they were assessable in respect of the whole of it) may have been correct on the basis that the person receiving the income was liable to tax on it. It may also be that the decision that the trustees were entitled to the income may be supported on an alternative basis – Lord Sand's view that none of the beneficiaries

[72] 7 TC 387, at page 418.
[73] See for example, Lord Wrenbury, 11 TC 749 at page 779.
[74] See for example Lord President Clyde at page 522.

(under the terms of the settlement) had "any interest or claim to the specific sum of interest" – in which case the trustees would be the only ones who could have been entitled to the income.

The final issue that arises from these cases involves those situations wherein the person receiving the income is different from the person "entitled to" it. In *Williams v Singer* and *Baker v Archer-Shee*, the persons receiving the income (the beneficiaries) were also the persons entitled to it. The same was true (on one interpretation – the one that looks to the terms of the settlement rather than legal entitlement) of *Reid's Trustees v IRC*. It may thus be said that all these cases were correctly decided. As seen earlier, one interpretation of the dicta in some of the cases is that, in cases where the receiver of the income is different from the person entitled to it, the receiver (i.e., the trustees in most cases) would not be liable to tax. This is just another way of saying that, where a beneficiary is absolutely entitled to the trust income, the trustees will not be liable to tax on that income, whether or not the trustees receive it. This approach was not accepted by the Court of Session in *Reid's Trustees v IRC*, but seems to be accepted in other cases. If it is agreed that the receiver of the income was also the person entitled to it in the three cases just referred to, the result would be that anything said about this present point in all of those cases was obiter dicta. If this is so, then it does not matter whether or not the Court of Session in *Reid's Trustees v IRC* "disregarded" the *dicta* in *Baker v Archer-Shee*. Presumably, *obiter dicta* from the House of Lords is to be preferred to conflicting *obiter dicta* from the Court of Session.

Therefore we may say that the following principles are established:

a. where trustees do not in fact receive income, they are not liable to tax on it;

b. if someone other than the trustees is entitled to the trust income, then, that person, rather than the trustees, is liable to tax on it – and this regardless of who is in actual receipt of the income.

These propositions more or less sum up the academic comment referred to at the beginning of this section. They however still raise questions. First, in respect of proposition (a) what would be the case if the trustees are entitled to the trust income (for example in the case of a discretionary trust), but yet direct trust income to be paid directly to a discretionary beneficiary? Would *Williams v Singer* and the *dicta* in *Baker v Archer-Shee* apply? That is arguably the case, but it is not the inevitable conclusion because both *Williams v Singer* and *Baker v Archer-Shee* involved cases where the beneficiary had a vested interest and it could be argued that they did not contemplate this type of scenario at all. If the trustees were to escape tax in these circumstances, might this be an effective way to avoid "the rate applicable to trusts" in respect of discretionary trusts? (see below). In respect of proposition (b) where the trustees receive the income, but the person entitled to it is a beneficiary, is there a rule that the liability of the beneficiary is exclusive? The *dicta* of Lord Carson and Viscount Sumner in *Baker v Archer-Shee* (above) indicate that this would be the case. However, in the context of statutory provisions charging the persons "receiving or entitled to" income, why should the Revenue not be able to assess either?

In sum, although the extent of the liability of trustees may be summarised in the two propositions above, it is clear that this area of the law is not free from uncertainty. This is an area where the law is in dire need of some clarification.

The "Rate Applicable to Trusts"

As seen earlier, because trustees (not being individuals) are not liable to higher rate tax, trusts provide planning opportunities for those in higher income brackets, whereby income-yielding assets could be settled, the income taxed at the trustee's (basic) rate, left to accumulate, and finally be distributed as capital. The attraction of such planning has been reduced (but not eliminated) by the imposition of a special tax rate on the income of certain trusts. This special rate is known as the "rate applicable to trusts", and, in the case of Schedule F type income, the "Schedule F trust rate". S.686(1A) of the ICTA 1988 (as amended by s.54(3) of the FA 1997) provides that the rate applicable to trusts, in relation to any year of assessment for which income tax is charged, shall be 34% (and the Schedule F trust rate is 25%) or such other rate as Parliament may determine. The rate applicable to trusts currently in force still amounts to a few percent below the higher rate of tax and the Schedule F trust rate is significantly lower than the Schedule F upper rate. This means that it may still be profitable for people with high incomes who possess income-yielding properties to settle such properties on trusts which will attract the rate applicable to trusts. In the discussion that follows, unless the context otherwise indicates, the term "the rate applicable to trusts" is used so as to include the Schedule F trust rate.

S.686(2) specifies the situation in which the rate applicable to trusts applies. The first condition is that the trust income is income which is to be accumulated or which is payable at the discretion of the trustees or any other person (whether or not the trustees have the power to accumulate the income).[75] The second condition is that the income is not, before being distributed, either the income of any person other than the trustees, or treated as the income of a settlor for any of the purposes of the Income Tax Acts.[76] In short, the rate applicable to trusts applies to accumulation and discretionary trusts in circumstances wherein the income, while remaining with the trustees, is treated only as that of the trustees. Exception is made in respect of income arising under trusts established for charitable purposes only, and to income from investments, deposits or other property held for the purposes of certain specified retirement benefit schemes and personal pension schemes.[77] With respect to the latter exemption, although the word "property" can have a wide meaning, it has been held that it is to be construed in this context ejusdem generis with the words that precede it ("investments" and "deposits").[78] Thus construed, it "connotes some asset held by the trustees which (like investments and deposits) produces income".[79] Thus, the exemption is restricted to the "fruits of ownership", and does not extend to the fruits of other activities. By this token, income derived by trustees from an activity which was subsequently held to be a trading activity was not exempt under this provision.[80]

It has been seen that one of the conditions for the rate applicable to trusts is that the trust income is income which is to be accumulated or which is payable at the discretion of the trustees. For these purposes, it is not necessary for the trustees to be under a duty to accumulate. It suffices that they have a power to accumulate the income. This is illustrated by *IRC v Berrill*[81] in which the trustees of a settlement were directed to hold the income for the settlor's son. The trustees had an overriding power, during the beneficiary's life, or for 21 years, whichever was the shorter, to accumulate the whole or part of the trust income and to hold such accumulations as an accretion to capital. The trustees having exercised the power to accumulate, the Revenue assessed them to tax at the additional rate (now the rate applicable to trusts). The taxpayers argued that, the language of [s.686(2)] which describes the income arising to trustees which is to be subject to additional rate tax, is wholly inapt to include income arising to trustees to which a beneficiary is entitled subject to a power of accumulation. This is because the opening words of [s.686(2)(a)], "income which is to be accumulated", are apt to describe only income which trustees are under a positive duty to accumulate. They also argued that the words "before being distributed" in [s.686(2)(b)] were apt to exclude and must have been intended to exclude from subsection (2) a trust under which income when it arises to trustees is income to which a

---

[75] S.686(2)(a).
[76] S.686(2)(b).
[77] S.686(2)(c).
[78] Lightman J in *Clarke (HMIT) v British Telecom Pension-Scheme Trustees* [1998] BTC 362 at 404.
[79] ibid.
[80] ibid.
[81] (1981) 55 TC 429; [1981] STC 784.

beneficiary is entitled subject to the exercise of a power to accumulate it. They contended that the relevant contrast was between income which, when it arises, is income to which a beneficiary is entitled (albeit subject to a power to accumulate it) and income which will become the income of a beneficiary only when it is distributed in pursuance of some discretion vested in the trustees or in some other person. Vinelott J, whilst of the view that the argument was "formidable"[82] held that the trustees were indeed assessable at the additional rate. According to him,[83] the words "income … which is payable at the discretion of the trustees" were as easily applied to income which trustees have power to withhold from a beneficiary entitled in default of the exercise of the power, as they were to income which they have power to apply or which they are bound to apply pursuant to a mandatory discretionary trust. He said that, while it is true that the words "whether or not the trustees have power to accumulate it" do not fit naturally the case where the discretion consists of a power to withhold income by accumulating it, that inelegance of expression did not afford a ground for departing from what appeared to be the plain intention of the legislature. He accepted the Revenue's argument that the purpose of [s.686 (2)(a)] is to describe in general terms the income to which subsection (2) is intended to apply, and that the rest of the subsection contain particular savings or exceptions from that general description.[84]

The rate applicable to trusts also applies in situations where infant beneficiaries have contingent interests and s.31 Trustee Act 1925 applies, whereby the trustees may apply the income for their maintenance. Finally, the trustees of a discretionary trust may be subject to a further charge to tax under s.687 when they make a distribution of income to a beneficiary. This charge will arise where the rate of income tax is higher in the year of distribution than it was in the year when the income arose to the trustees. The section applies where in any year of assessment trustees make a payment to any person "in the exercise of a discretion" (whether the discretion is exercisable by them or by another person) in circumstances wherein the income is, by virtue of the payment only, the income of the recipient for all the purposes of the Income Tax Acts, or, is treated as the income of the settlor by s.660B.[85] By virtue of s.687(2), the amount paid will be treated as a net amount corresponding to a gross amount from which tax has been deducted at the rate applicable to trusts for the year in which the payment is made. The tax which is deemed to have been deducted will be treated as tax paid by the recipient (or where appropriate, by the settlor), and will be treated as income tax assessable on the trustees. The trustees will be entitled to credit for the tax already borne by them at the time when the income arose, and to some other specified deductions.[86]

---

[82] 55 TC at 441.
[83] at page 443.
[84] ibid.
[85] s.687(1).
[86] See generally, s.687(3).

Obviously, if there is no difference between the tax rates applicable in the year in which the income arose and those applicable in the year in which the payment was made, the section would have no real bite. Thus it is only of real importance when tax rates are increasing.

The Charge on Beneficiaries

Trust income which has accrued to trustees would normally have suffered tax either by deduction at source before payment to the trustees, or in the hands of the trustees. Thereafter, either there will be beneficiaries entitled to the income, or the trustees will exercise a discretion to accumulate, or distribute the income among beneficiaries. The taxability of a beneficiary depends on whether or not he or she has a vested right in the trust income.

Vested rights

As has been pointed out in the discussion on the extent of the liability of trustees, income to which a beneficiary is entitled forms part of his total income, whether or not he receives it from the trustee. This is because the income "belongs" to the beneficiary, not to the trustee. The leading case is *Baker v Archer-Shee*.[87] In this case, Lady Archer-Shee had a life interest, under her father's will, in a trust estate held by trustees in the United States. The trust fund consisted of foreign stocks and shares. The dividends, as they accrued, were placed to the credit of Lady Archer-Shee's bank account in New York and were not remitted to this country. The question was whether these dividends fell to be assessed as part of the income of her husband, who was resident in the United Kingdom. The House of Lords held (Viscount Sumner and Lord Blanesburgh dissenting) that, Lady Archer-Shee was entitled to the stocks and shares which formed the trust fund, and to the income thereof, during her life. Therefore her husband was rightly assessed whether the income was remitted here or not. According to Lord Wrenbury[88], the question was not what the trustees had thought proper to hand over and had handed over (which is a question of fact) but what, under her father's will, Lady Archer-Shee was entitled to (which is a question of law). Even though the trustees had a first charge upon the trust funds for their costs, charges and expenses, the fund still belonged to the beneficiary. Lord Carson concurring, said[89]:

---

[87]   (1927) 11 TC 749.
[88]   at pages 778-779.
[89]   at page 782.

In my opinion upon the construction of the will of [Lady Archer-Shee's father] once the residue had become specifically ascertained, the Respondent's wife was sole beneficial owner of the interest and dividends of all the securities, stocks and shares forming part of the trust fund therein settled and was entitled to receive and did receive such interest and dividends. This, I think, follows from the decision of this House in *Williams v Singer* ... and in my opinion the Master of the Rolls correctly stated the law when he said that "when you are considering sums which are placed in the hands of trustees for the purpose of paying income to beneficiaries, for the purposes of the Income Tax Acts you may eliminate the trustees. The income is the income of the beneficiaries; the income does not belong to the trustees".

The decision of the majority in this case was based on the assumption that American law on the rights of Lady Archer-Shee under the trust was the same as English law. Subsequently, in *Garland v Archer-Shee*,[90] expert evidence on American law showed that it was different from English law, and that the assumption of the majority in *Baker v Archer-Shee* was incorrect. The case was finally resolved in favour of the taxpayers (to the extent that liability was based on amounts actually remitted to the UK). In spite of this development (i.e., a determination based on expert evidence as to the differences between English and American law), the main principle in *Baker v Archer-Shee* remains valid. The principle therein established is that, when a beneficiary is entitled to trust income as it arises, such a beneficiary is taxable on that income as it arises, because it is his income. Thus there is liability even on undistributed income. As seen earlier, dicta by Lord Carson and Viscount Sumner in the case seem to indicate that the beneficiary's liability is exclusive in such cases. The rate applicable to trusts will not apply even if the income is accumulated because the income "before distribution" belongs to someone other than the trustees, i.e., the beneficiary.

This principle can apply only where certain conditions are fulfilled. First, it is necessary that the beneficiary has a vested interest, and, secondly, it is necessary that the beneficiary's vested interest is not liable to be divested, i.e. it is indefeasible. Thus for example the rule will not apply where the beneficiary's interest is contingent, or where the interest can be divested. This latter point is illustrated by *Cornwell v Barry*[91] in which funds were held in trust for settlor's grandchildren then living, or born during the eight year life of the settlement, for their, his or her absolute use and

---

[90]   [1931] AC 212; 15 TC 693 (HL).
[91]   (1955) 36 TC 268.

benefit. During the period, there was only one child. A claim was made in respect of personal reliefs and allowances on behalf of the child, on the ground that, as he was the only child living, the trustee was required during those years to hold the income as and when received upon trust for the child absolutely. It was held that, the child's interest, if vested, was liable to be divested. His interest was defeasible because more children could have been born during those eight years, and thus the claim failed. Harman J said[92] that any child either in existence when the deed was made or coming into existence during the eight years thereafter was an object of the trust. He rejected the argument of the taxpayer that, so long as there is only one child who fulfils any of those qualifications, he is entitled to the whole income as and when received, and it is indefeasibly his. This, according to Harman J, would be an entirely mistaken view of the trust, because:

> [T]he Trustee is to look not only at the child in existence but any child who may come into existence, and during the eight years he is not bound, as I see it, to make any application of the money at all. He would if he were a reasonable man, but he is not bound to. It is quite true that the trust is for the absolute use and benefit of these children, but it is in such shares and in such manner as the Trustee thinks fit. Consequently, he has the eight years in which to make up his mind. He may during that time divide it into shares or give it all to one or other of the objects of the trust, and even if at any time during the eight years there were no object of the trust, he would still, in my view, have to hold the money in case, before the end of the period, an object should come into being. Consequently, though it may well be, and I think is, the fact that [the child] being in existence had got a vested interest in this money, it was an interest which was liable to be divested if another object of the trust came into existence during the eight years. It is not until the end of this time that you could say: The class is closed; the object is achieved; and the money, if there be any unapplied, vests absolutely in any of the persons who were objects of the trust, and whether then dead or then living matters not.[93]

Grossing up

The income to which the beneficiary is entitled would have suffered tax in the trustee's hands. In order to ascertain the amount which will enter

---

[92] at page 274.
[93] ibid. See also *Stanley v IRC*, 26 TC 12; [1944] 1 All ER 230.

into computation for the beneficiary's total income, the income would fall to be grossed up in order to reflect basic rate tax paid by the trustees. Depending on the beneficiary's circumstances, he may either be liable to higher rate tax on the trust income, or be entitled to a refund. The formula for grossing up the income is as follows:

$$Z = Y \times \frac{100}{100 - R}$$

Where;

R = the rate of tax

Y = the amount of the payment

Z = the gross sum

It should be noted that the gross amount so calculated will not necessarily be the same as the income accruing to the trustees. This is due to the decision of the Court of Session in *Macfarlane v IRC*[94] where it was held that, although trust expenses are not deductible in the trustees' hands in computing the trustee's income, they are deductible in the trustees' hands in computing the beneficiary's income. In this case the taxpayer had made a claim to the Revenue for repayment of income tax on the basis that the whole of the income of the trust estates was his income, without any deduction in either case in respect of the expenses of management of the estates (i.e., that he was liable to income tax in respect of the part of the income of the trust estate which was expended upon the administration of the trust, so as to yield a higher repayment of tax). The Revenue argued that the taxpayer's income was only the net income remaining after deduction of the expenses of management of the trust estates. The Revenue's argument was upheld. Lord Sands said[95] that the primary aspect of the matter was not one of abatement or exemption but of initial liability. He said that the argument of the taxpayer involved the contention that he was liable to income tax in respect of income which he did not handle and could not under any arrangement handle, which was not expended under any authority conferred by him, and over the expenditure of which he had no control. Lord Blackburn said[96] that, on the true construction of the trust deed, the income to which the beneficiary was entitled was no more than the amount of the income of the trust funds which may be available after the expenses of the trust had been paid.[97]

---

[94] (1929) 14 TC 532.
[95] at page 540.
[96] ibid.
[97] See also *Elizabeth Murray v IRC* (1926) 11 TC 133.

Thus a beneficiary is worse off and ends up with a lower tax credit, as the following example shows.

The trustees receive income amounting to £100. They incur £20 expenses in managing the trust. Since this £20 is not deductible in their hands in computing their own tax liability, they pay tax on the full £100. Assuming a basic rate of 22%, they pay £22 in tax, and have £78 left for distribution. Because the £20 is deductible in their hands in computing the beneficiary's income, they deduct it, and have £58 left for distribution to the beneficiary. This amount is grossed up at the basic rate:

$$\frac{58 \times 100}{78} = £74.36$$

The tax credit is: £74.36 - £58 = £16.36

Since the total income coming into the trust has suffered £22 in tax, a tax credit of just £16.36 leaves the taxpayer out of pocket.

Annuities

Where the beneficiary is entitled to an annuity under a trust, he is not entitled to the trust income as it arises, and the rule in *Baker v Archer-Shee* does not apply. The annuity will fall to be taxed under Case III of Schedule D. The Finance Act 1988 provisions, which render annual payments by individuals ineffective do not apply to take the payments out of the tax scheme because the trustees are not "individuals".

No vested rights

Typical cases in which beneficiaries do not have vested interests in trust income involve discretionary and accumulation trusts. A beneficiary under a discretionary or accumulation trust cannot be taxed unless he receives the income, since he is not entitled to anything. If and when a payment is made to the beneficiary, the income would fall to be classified as an annual payment under Schedule D Case III.

Contingent rights: Trustee Act 1925, Section 31

Where beneficiaries have contingent rights to income, the rule in *Baker v Archer-Shee* cannot apply simply because the contingency which will entitle them to income may never happen. This will be the case where s.31 of the Trustee Act 1925 applies. S.31 relates to trusts for infant beneficiaries. In subsection (1), it provides that, where any property is held by trustees in trust for any person, whether that person's interest is vested or contingent, the trustees may (at their sole discretion), during the infancy of such person, pay or apply the whole or part of the income produced by the trust property for his maintenance, education or benefit. The trustees have the discretion regardless of whether any other fund exists for the same purpose, and regardless of whether there is any person bound by law to provide for the infant beneficiary's maintenance or education.[98] The trustees are obliged by s.31(2) to accumulate the residue of the income during the beneficiary's infancy. The power to apply the income for the infant's education, maintenance or benefit is subject to any prior interests or charges affecting the settled property.[99] The effect of s.31 of the Trustee Act 1925 is to convert trusts in which an infant has an interest (which interest is not dependent on that of an adult) into an accumulation and maintenance trust in the sense that any income which is not spent on the maintenance or education of the infant must be accumulated.

If the beneficiary, on attaining the age of 18, does not have a vested interest in the income, the trustees are directed to pay the income from the trust property and the income from any accretions thereto to the beneficiary, until he dies, or his interest fails, or he attains a vested interest in the income.[100] This means that if a beneficiary only had a contingent interest during his infancy, he will, on attaining the age of 18, be entitled only to the income from the accretions and not to the accretions themselves. On the other hand, if the beneficiary attains the age of 18 years or marries under that age, and the beneficiary had a vested interest in the income until either event, then the trustees are to hold all accumulations in trust for that beneficiary absolutely.[101] The same principle applies where, on attaining the age of 18 or on marriage below that age, the beneficiary becomes entitled to the settled property from which the income arises.[102] In any other case (for example where a beneficiary dies below 18 years), the trustees must hold the accumulations as an accretion to the capital of the settled property.

A number of things follow from these provisions. First, even in cases where an infant beneficiary has a vested interest in trust income, he will not be liable to income tax on any undistributed income. The income is not his own because, although he has a vested interest, his right to receive

---

[98]   Trustee Act 1925, s.31(1)(a) and s.31(1)(b).
[99]   S.31(1).
[100]   S.31(1)(ii).
[101]   S.31(2)(i)(a).
[102]   S.31(2)(i)(b).

income is contingent or subject to being divested if he fails to attain majority. This is because by virtue of s.31(2), the accumulations will be added to capital in that event, and will not go to his estate. If he eventually reaches 18 and the accumulations are paid to him, they will by then have become capital in nature. The leading case is *Stanley v IRC*.[103] In this case an infant had vested interests in certain estates under his father's will. The trustees accumulated the surplus income which was not applied for his maintenance, and when he attained majority, he became absolutely entitled to those accumulations. The Revenue sought to tax him for the years of his infancy. The real question concerned the precise interest in surplus income which an infant having a vested interest enjoys during his infancy by virtue of the provisions in s.31. The Revenue's contention was that the infant had a vested interest in the surplus income as it accrued and that there was nothing in s.31 which deprived him of that interest during infancy. Rather, all that the section did was to divest him of his title to the accumulations of surplus income if he died before attaining his majority. In other words, an infant has a vested interest in the accumulations, which interest is defeasible in the event of his dying before majority. The Court of Appeal rejected these arguments and held that the income was not the infant's income at the time that he should have been assessed to tax on it. The reason for this was that, s.31 of the Trustee Act 1925, if he had not attained majority, the accumulations would never have been his, but would have been added to capital which would go to the remainderman. Lord Greene MR said[104]:

> The infant does not during infancy enjoy the surplus income. It is not his in any real sense. The title to it is held in suspense to await the event and if he dies under [the age of 18] his interest in it (whether or not it be truly described as a vested interest) is destroyed. He is in fact for all practical purposes in precisely the same position if his interest in surplus income were contingent. If he attains [the age of 18] he takes the accumulations, if he dies under [the age of 18] he does not ... We are disposed to think that the effect of the Section is better described not as leaving the interest of the infant as a vested interest subject to defeasance, but as engrafting upon the vested interest originally conferred on the infant by the settlement or other disposition a qualifying trust of a special nature which confers on the infant a title to the accumulations if and only if he attains [the age of 18] or marries. The words in Sub-section (2)(i)(a), if "his interest ... during his infancy or until his marriage is a vested interest", and the corresponding words in Subsection (2)(ii), "notwithstanding that

---

[103] (1944) 26 TC 12; [1944] 1 All ER 230.
[104] 26 TC at page 19.

such person had a vested interest in such income", appear to us to refer to the nature of the interest conferred upon the infant by the settlement or other disposition, and not to affirm that the interest of the infant in the surplus income remains a vested interest notwithstanding the alteration in his rights effected by the Section. If this view is right, the interest of the Appellant in the surplus income during his minority was a contingent.

Thus, the effect of s.31 of the Trustee Act 1925 is to make the infant's interest in the surplus income accruing during his infancy a contingent interest only – it prevents an infant from having an indefeasible vested interest in the income of the trust fund (i.e., until something is paid, nothing is an infant's income, no matter what his interest is in the trust property). However, if an infant who does not have a vested interest in the settled property receives income from the trustees, or if amounts are applied for his education, maintenance or benefit, then the infant becomes liable to tax on those payments. S.687 will apply, and the amount of the payment (grossed up at the rate applicable to trusts) will enter into the computation of his total income.

In cases wherein a beneficiary has an interest in income which interest is contingent upon his attaining an age in excess of 18, (e.g., "to S when he is 30 years old"), s.31(1)(ii) provides that the trustees should pay the income (from the trust fund and from the accretions to the fund) to him on attaining 18. This means that, on attaining majority, the beneficiary obtains an indefeasible vested right in the income and he will be liable to tax in respect of that income whether or not he receives it. This is illustrated by *IRC v Hamilton-Russell*.[105] The trustees in this case were directed to hold funds and income for the beneficiary upon his attaining 21. The beneficiary attained 21 in 1928, became the sole beneficiary under the settlement, and thereupon became entitled to call for the transfer of all the trust funds and the accumulations thereof to himself. He did not do so, but allowed the trustees to receive the income from the trust fund and the accumulation fund, and to continue investing the income, until early in 1939. The beneficiary's executors argued that, although as the sole beneficiary under those trusts, he could have legally determined them, he did not in fact do so. Consequently the income did not become his, but was accumulated under the trusts, and turned into capital before the trusts were determined. The Court of Appeal however held that the income belonged to the beneficiary as from the time when he attained 21 and was assessable to income tax. Luxmoore LJ said[106] that the trust became unenforceable as soon as the specified event occurred. The trustees could

---

[105] (1943) 25 TC 200; [1943] 1 All ER 474.
[106] 25 TC at page 208.

at any time after the happening of that event, even though asked by the beneficiary to continue the accumulations, have refused to do so, and, in the same way, the beneficiary could, contrary to the wishes of the trustees, have insisted on a transfer to himself of the whole of the trust funds. According to Luxmoore LJ, the reason why the trusts then became unenforceable and ineffective was because the funds were "at home" and belonged solely to the beneficiary for his own absolute use and benefit. The capital and income were his and no one else was interested in them: if the income was left in the hands of the trustees, and they invested it, they only did so by the sufferance of the beneficiary whose income it was.

Payments out of Capital

The general rule in respect of payments out of capital is that, when trust income has been capitalised, it retains that character when paid out to the beneficiaries, and is not liable to income tax. However, where the trustees have to pay an annuity, with power to supplement the payments with payment out of capital, the situation may be different, and payments made out of capital in such cases may be income in the recipient's hands. The principle is that the situation depends on the rights of the recipient, not the source of the payments. In *Brodie's Will Trustees v IRC*[107] the testator directed the trustees to pay the income from certain trust property to his widow during her life. He wished that the payments would not be less than £4,000 per annum and therefore directed that, should trust income be deficient in any year to pay this sum, recourse should be had to capital to make up the deficiency. During a number of tax years, the trustees made payments to the widow of varying amounts out of the capital of the estate, in order to make up that sum each year. It was held that the payments were income in the hands of the widow and were taxable under Case III of Schedule D, even though they were paid out of capital. Finlay J said[108]:

> [I]f payments out of capital are made, and made in such a form that they come into the hands of the beneficiaries as income, it seems to me that they are income, and not the less income because the source from which they came was in the hand, not of the person receiving them, but in the hands of somebody else, capital.

According to Finlay J,[109] if the capital belonged to the beneficiary, or if he was beneficially entitled to both the income and capital of the trust, then the payments out of capital would have been capital in his hands. Another

[107] 17 TC 432.
[108] at page 439.
[109] 17 TC 432 at 439.

relevant case is *Cunard's Trustees v IRC*.[110] Trustees held a fund on trust to pay the income thereof to the testatrix's sister. The will further provided that, if in any year the income of the trust fund was insufficient to enable the sister to live at the testatrix's residence in the same degree of comfort as during the testatrix's lifetime, the trustees were empowered to resort to the capital of the testatrix's residuary estate to make up any deficiency in the trust income. The trustees paid sums out of capital to the sister in two years of assessment. The Court of Appeal held that the payments were income in the hands of the beneficiary. Lord Green MR said[111] that the sister's title to the income arose when the trustees exercised their discretion in her favour and not before, and that, at that moment a new source of income came into existence. The fact that they were made out of capital was irrelevant. The payments were to be made "by way of addition to the income" in order to enable the sister to live in the same degree of comfort as before. The testatrix was in fact providing for a defined standard of life for her sister, that provision being made in part out of income and in part (at the discretion of the trustees) out of capital. According to Lord Greene MR, the purpose of the payments was an income purpose and nothing else[112] and the payments were therefore income.

This type of reasoning led the Revenue to argue in *Stevenson v Wishart*[113] that any payment out of capital, which is made for an income purpose, is income in the beneficiary's hands. In this case, properties were transferred by the settlor into discretionary trusts on behalf of (*inter alia*) his mother-in-law (Mrs H). The trustees made a series of payments totalling £109,000 out of the capital of the fund to meet Mrs H's medical and nursing home expenses before her death. The Revenue claimed that, the payments, being recurrent sums paid out of capital for the maintenance of a beneficiary, were for an "income purpose" and therefore constituted the income of the beneficiary for tax purposes. The argument was rejected. The Court of Appeal held that, although payments by trustees out of capital could be income in the beneficiary's hands, it was not sufficient that the payments were either periodic, for educational purposes, or for personal maintenance. The payments involved in this case, although recurrent, were of substantial amounts that were outside normal income resources, did not create an income interest, and were of capital nature. Fox LJ said[114]:

> [T]here is nothing in the present case which indicates that the payments were of an income nature except their recurrence. I do not think that is sufficient. The trustees were disposing of capital in

---

[110] (1945) 27 TC 122; [1946] 1 All ER 159.
[111] 27 TC at page 132.
[112] at page 133.
[113] (1987) 59 TC 720; [1987] STC 266; [1987] 1 WLR 1204.
[114] at page 765.

exercise of a power over capital. They did not create a recurring interest in property. If, in exercise of a power over capital, they chose to make at their discretion regular payments of capital to deal with the specific problems of [Mrs H's] last years rather than release a single sum to her of a large amount that does not seem to me to create an income interest. Their power was to capital what they appointed remained capital.

It is thus clear that neither regularity nor recurrence is a conclusive factor, and the courts have to look at the whole set of circumstances.

Settlements

We have seen earlier in this chapter the opportunities presented by trusts. A person who wishes or who is obliged to provide another person with an income, or with a source of income may do so in one of many ways. First he may simply transfer the sum of money, either in a lump sum or periodically, and without any legal formalities. This is a simple transfer of assets. Each such transfer is entirely voluntary and is in law nothing more than a mere gift. Secondly, he may execute a deed or other type of legal instrument transferring part of his income. This may be referred to as an income settlement – it enables the donor to retain the source from which the income flows (the tree), while giving away the income itself (the fruit). While the execution of the instrument transferring the money may have been voluntary, a legal obligation may arise under the instrument, and the payments thereunder may be legally due. Thirdly, he may transfer income-producing capital assets to trustees to pay the income generated thereby for the benefit of the objects. This is known as a capital settlement, because the donor gives away the capital out of which the income is to be made (the tree – and by the same token, the fruit which it produces). The first method (voluntary gifts) would not normally be tax efficient, and would in most cases attract no income tax consequences. Little planning can be achieved in this way. On the other hand, income and capital settlements inherently contain tax planning opportunities, especially for those in large income brackets. Income or capital may be settled for one's spouse, children or grand children (who one would normally be obliged to maintain) to take advantage of their personal reliefs and/or low tax rates, and to reduce one's total income from high tax brackets to lower ones.

The tax system's response to the planning opportunities has been two-fold. First, to introduce a different rate of tax (the rate applicable to trusts and the Schedule F trust rate) for certain types of trusts (see above), and, secondly, to introduce anti-avoidance legislation in Part XV of the ICTA 1988, in respect of arrangements described as "settlements". All the three methods of parting with one's income or property described above may well fall within the scope of these anti-avoidance provisions. The Finance Act 1988 rendered income settlements largely ineffective by disallowing the deduction of annual payments made by individuals, and so the real choice now for new arrangements is whether or not to settle capital. The discussion that follows analyses the anti-avoidance provisions relating to the taxation of settlements.

Definition

Section 660(G)(1) ICTA 1988 defines settlement to include any disposition, trust, covenant, agreement, arrangement, or transfer of assets. This is a very wide definition, which would cover almost all types of transaction that a person may engage in – including the type of voluntary gifts referred to above. A number of cases provide illustrations. In *Thomas v Marshall*[115] a father opened Post Office Savings Bank accounts for his children, and transferred certain sums into those accounts by way of absolute and unconditional gifts. He also gave each child £1,000 in 3% bonds. The interest on the bank accounts and on the bonds were treated by the Revenue as his income for tax purposes. The taxpayer, while conceding that each of the relevant gifts might be described as a transfer of assets, if the phrase were to be given its ordinary meaning, argued that, since the word "settlement" was the only word used in the charging provision, it was "the dominant word", and a transaction does not come within the provision unless it was "something in the nature of a settlement". Thus, a transaction which might ordinarily be described as a transfer of assets did not come within the section unless, either it was accompanied by some restraint on alienation, such as would subject the transferee to some action at law or in equity if be attempted to alienate the subject of the gift, or, the income and the capital of the subject of the gift were given to different persons, or, the legal title and the equitable interest in the subject of the gift were conferred on different persons. The House of Lords however held that there was nothing in the context which should lead the courts to give the words "transfer of assets" any meaning other than that which they ordinarily bore, or to infuse into them some flavour of the meaning ordinarily given to the word "settlement".[116] Thus, the absolute gifts to the children were settlements. Similarly, in *Hoods-Barrs v*

---

[115] (1953) 34 TC 178; [1953] AC 543.
[116] See Lord Morton of Henryton at page 202.

IRC[117] the taxpayer transferred a block of shares to each of his two infant and unmarried daughters. It was held that, these as transfers of assets, were settlements and that he was liable to tax on the dividends. The argument that the phrase "transfer of assets" cannot include an absolute gift by a parent to a child was rejected by the Court of Appeal.

These cases illustrate the width of the definition given to the word "settlement" and the willingness of the courts to give certain words in the definition (particularly, "transfer of assets") their ordinary (and wide) meanings. It has even been held that transfers of money can be settlements if made under compulsion (e.g., under a court order).[118] However, according to Nourse J in $IRC \, v \, Levy$[119], it has long been recognised that Parliament cannot have intended the definition of "settlement" to extend as widely as a literal reading of it might suggest. Thus, the courts have imposed a limitation on the meaning of settlement. This judicial gloss on the statutory words takes the form of a requirement of "bounty" in a transaction in order for it to constitute a settlement. This requirement seems to have developed from a principle that, in order for a transaction to be excluded from the ambit of the settlement provisions, it must be a bona fide commercial transaction.[120] This concept was then extended by Plowman J in $IRC \, v \, Leiner$[121] into a statement that some element of bounty is necessary and that a *bona fide* commercial transaction is excluded. This analysis was accepted by Lawrence J in *Bulmer v IRC*.[122] The definitive statement of the bounty principle is however to be found in the decision of the House of Lords in $IRC \, v \, Plummer$[123]. In this case, a charity paid £2,480 to the taxpayer in return for a covenant by the taxpayer to pay it a sum of £500 each year for five years. The purpose of the scheme was to enable the taxpayer to deduct the payments and so reduce his total income for surtax purposes. The Revenue claimed that, far from being annual payments, the scheme was a settlement and the payments remained the income of the taxpayer. It was held that, because the transaction contained no element of bounty, it was not a settlement.[124] According to Lord Wilberforce[125]:

[I]t can, I think, fairly be seen that all of these provisions [in Part XV], have a common character. They are designed to bring within the net of taxation dispositions of various kinds, in favour of a settlor's spouse, or children, or of charities, cases, in popular terminology, in which a taxpayer gives away a portion of his income, or of his assets, to such

---

[117] 27 TC 385.
[118] See *Yates v Starkey* (1950) 32 TC 38, *Harvey v Sivyer* [1985] 2 All ER 1054; (1985) 58 TC 569.
[119] (1982) 56 TC 68 at 86.
[120] See *Copeman v Coleman* [1939] 3 All ER 224.
[121] (1964) 41 TC 589 at 596.
[122] [1966] 3 All ER 801 at 809-811.
[123] (1979) 54 TC 1; [1980] AC 896.
[124] Note that the effect of this decision has now been reversed with respect to reverse annuity schemes (see ICTA 1988 s.125).
[125] 54 TC at page 43.

persons, or for such periods, or subject to such conditions, that Parliament considers it right to continue to treat such income, or income of the assets, as still the settlor's income. These sections, in other words, though drafted in wide, and increasingly wider language, are nevertheless dealing with a limited field - one far narrower than the field of the totality of dispositions, or arrangements, or agreements, which a man may make in the course of his life. Is there then any common description which can be applied to this? The courts which, inevitably, have had to face this problem, have selected the element of "bounty" as a necessary common characteristic of all the "settlements" which Parliament has in mind. The decisions are tentative, but all point in this direction.

The requirement of bounty is said not to be a word of definition[126] – rather, it is a judicial gloss on the statute which is "descriptive of those classes of cases which are caught by the section in contrast to those which are not".[127] Although it is "a conception admittedly not without its difficulty"[128] it has been applied consistently by the courts. However, Lord Roskill has warned that, because it is a judicial gloss on the statutory words, the courts must be extremely careful not to interpret this descriptive word too rigidly. Lord Roskill then went to state the sense behind the requirement of bounty[129]:

> What the cases have sought to do is to distinguish between those cases where the recipient has in return for that benefit which he has received accepted some obligation which he has to perform, either before receiving the benefit or at some stated time thereafter, and those cases where the recipient benefits without any assumption by him of any correlative obligation.

This indicates that the idea of bounty is closely linked to the presence or otherwise of a correlative obligation (or consideration) of the part of the recipient. However, it seems that this is not conclusive and that the principle of the exclusion of *bona fide* commercial transactions may be more determinative of the bounty issue than the mere presence or absence of a correlative obligation. Thus, in *IRC v Levy*,[130] where the taxpayer made an interest-free loan to a company of which he was the sole beneficial shareholder, it was held that there was no settlement as there was no element of bounty (even though the company got something - the use of

---

[126] Lord Roskill in *Chinn v Collins* [1981] 1 All ER 189 at 200.
[127] Lord Roskill, ibid.
[128] See Lord Wilberforce in *Chinn v Collins* [1981] 1 All ER 189 at 194.
[129] [1981] 1 All ER at 200.
[130] (1982) 56 TC 68; [1982] STC 442.

the money – for nothing). Nourse J said[131]:

> Before a disposition, trust, covenant, agreement or arrangement can
> be a settlement within [s.660(G)(1)] it must contain an element of
> bounty. For that purpose a derivative bounty of the kind conferred
> by the exercise of a special power of appointment may be enough.
> On the other hand, a commercial transaction devoid of any element
> of bounty is not within the definition. The absence of any correlative
> obligation on the part of him who is on the receiving end of the
> transaction may be material, but is not conclusive in determining
> whether it contains an element of bounty or not.

The decisions on "bounty" are not necessarily inconsistent with those
which held payments made under compulsion to be settlements. Cases
such as *Yates v Starkey* (above) and *Harvey v Sivyer* (above) involved payments
by parents to their own children under court orders. Nourse J suggested
in *Harvey v Sivyer*[132] that it may well be that the natural relationship between
parent and young child is one of such deep affection and concern that
there must always be an element of bounty by the parent, even where the
provision is on the face of things made under compulsion.

"Settlor"

Section 660(G)(1) provides that a settlor is any person by whom the
settlement was made. S.660(G)(2) further provides that a person shall be
deemed to have made a settlement if he has made or entered into it
directly or indirectly, and in particular, if he has provided or undertaken to
provide funds directly or indirectly for the purpose of the settlement or has
made with any person a reciprocal arrangement for that other person to
make or enter into the settlement. The word "purpose" in this definition
does not import any mental element, as *IRC v Mills*[133] shows. The taxpayer
in this case was an actress. When she was 14 years old, her father, in order
to make sure that her earnings were "legally protected", incorporated a
company and settled the shares on trust for her absolutely on attaining the
age of 25. She then signed a service contract with the company giving it
the right to her exclusive services for five years at a salary of £400 a year.
The bulk of the company's profits in respect of her films was distributed
to the trustees as dividends. The trustees accumulated the income. It was
held that, the incorporation of the company, the issue and settlement of
the shares therein, and the service agreement, were an arrangement which

---

[131] 56 TC at page 87.
[132] 58 TC at 577.
[133] (1975) 49 TC 367; [1975] AC 38.

constituted a settlement. The taxpayer was the settlor, since it was her services that provided the company with funds from which to pay dividends to the trust – she had thereby indirectly provided income for the purposes of the settlement. Viscount Dilhorne said[134]:

> I do not agree with Lord Denning M.R. that the word 'purpose' in this section connotes a mental element or with Buckley L.J. that there must be a motivating intention. I do not myself think that it assists to consider whether the question he posed is to be answered objectively or subjectively. I do not consider it incumbent, in order to establish that a person is a settlor as having provided funds for the purpose of a settlement, to show that there was any element of mens rea. Where it is shown that funds have been provided for a settlement a very strong inference is to be drawn that they were provided for that purpose, an inference which will be rebutted if it is established that they were provided for another purpose.

It is possible to have more than one settlor for a settlement. For example, in *IRC v Mills* the taxpayer's father was also a settlor because he had made the settlement.[135] However, where there is more than one settlor, then s.660E(1) provides that the provisions shall apply to each settlor as if he were the only settlor, whereby references to property comprised in a settlement would only include property originating from that settlor[136], and references to income arising under the settlement would include only income originating from that settlor.[137]

The Basic Charge

Section 660A(1) provides that income arising under a settlement during the life of the settlor shall be treated for all purposes of the Income Tax Acts as the income of the settlor and not as the income of any other person, unless the income arises from property in which the settlor has no interest.[138] From this basic charge, s.660A(9) excludes income consisting of annual payments made by an individual for *bona fide* commercial reasons in connection with his trade, profession or vocation, and qualifying donations to charity (under FA 1990, s.25). By virtue of s.660C(1), the tax charged under this Chapter will generally be charged under Sch. D Case VI. The settlor is entitled to the same deductions and reliefs as he would have if the income taxed here had been received by him (s.660C(2)). The income is

---

[134] at page 408.
[135] See Viscount Dilhorne at page 409.
[136] s.660E(2)(a).
[137] s.660E(2)(b).
[138] For a discussion on a predecessor of this charge, see R Burgess [1971] BTR 278.

treated (subject to s.833(3)) as the highest part of the settlor's income (s.660C(3)). The settlor is entitled to reclaim tax paid under this provision from the trustee or any other person to whom the income is payable (s.660D(1)). Where there are two or more settlors, s.660E provides for apportionments to be made.

Retaining Interest

We have seen that the general charge under Part XV does not apply in respect of income arising from property in which the settlor has no interest. In what circumstances does a person retain an interest in property for these purposes? S.660A(2) provides (subject to the rest of the section) that, a settlor shall be regarded as having interest in property, if that property, or any derived property is, or will or may become payable to or applicable for the benefit of the settlor or the settlor's spouse in any circumstances whatsoever. "Derived property" is defined by s.660A(10) as being, in relation to any property, income from that property or any other property directly or indirectly representing proceeds of, or of income from, that property or income therefrom.

However, there are some permitted interests and, by virtue of s.660A(4), the settlor will not be regarded as having an interest in property if the property can only be payable to or applied for the benefit of the settlor or the settlor's spouse in the event of:

a.   the bankruptcy of any person who is or may become beneficially entitled to the property or any derived property, or

b.   an assignment of or charge on the property or any derived property being made or given by some such person, or

c.   in the case of a marriage settlement, the death of both parties to the marriage and of all or any of the children of the marriage, or

d.   the death of a child of the settlor who had become beneficially entitled to the property or any derived property at an age not exceeding 25.

Section 660A(5) also provides another exception – that, a settlor will not be regarded as having an interest in property if and so long as some person is alive and under the age of 25, during whose life the property concerned or any derived property cannot be payable to the settlor or the settlor's spouse, except in the event of that person becoming bankrupt or assigning or charging his interest in the property or any derived property.

For these purposes, the "spouse" of the settlor does not include a person to whom the settlor is not married but who he may later marry.[139] The term also does not include a spouse from whom the settlor is separated, under a court order, or under a separation agreement, or in such circumstances that the separation is likely to be permanent.[140] Finally, it does not include the widow or widower of the settlor.[141]

The principle relating to retaining an interest is probably the only reason why outright gifts to people who are not spouses or unmarried infant children of the settlor will not fall within the settlement provisions.

Gifts between Spouses

We have referred earlier to the suggestion of Nourse J in *Harvey v Sivyer* that the natural relationship between parent and young child is one of such deep affection and concern that there must always be an element of bounty by the parent. It may well be thought that the same goes for the natural relationship between spouses (at least, those who are not estranged). In order to prevent the situation which may otherwise arise that gifts between spouses will invariably be treated as settlements, these anti-avoidance provisions provide some relief for transfers of property between married couples. S.660A(6) provides that the reference in s.660A(1) to a settlement does not include an outright gift by one spouse to the other, of the property from which the income arises, unless either the gift does not carry a right to the whole of that income, or the property given is wholly or substantially a right to income. "Outright gift" is defined by exclusion. For these purposes, a gift is not an outright gift if it is subject to conditions, or if the property given or any derived property is or will or may become payable to or applicable for the benefit of the donor in any circumstances whatsoever. Some of these terms were examined in the case of *Scrutton v Young*.[142] In this case, a company, of which the taxpayers were the only shareholders and directors, resolved at an extraordinary meeting to create some preference shares which were eventually allotted to the taxpayers' wives. The preference shares carried the right to 30% of the net profits of the company in any year in which the company resolved to distribute profits. They also carried the right to attend and speak but not to vote at general meetings of the company. The preference shareholders were only entitled on liquidation of the company to repayment of the sums subscribed for their shares. Subsequently, the company resolved to distribute some profits, and paid substantial sums as dividends on the preference shares for three successive years of assessment. It appears that the

---

[139] S. 660(3)(a).
[140] S. 660(3)(b).
[141] S. 660(3)(c).
[142] [1996] BTC 322.

transactions were entered into in order to take advantage of new rules on the separate assessment of wives. The questions arose whether the creation of a new class of preference shareholder and the allotment of shares to the taxpayers' wives constituted an "arrangement" and were therefore "settlements", and, if so, whether income arising under the settlements were to be treated as the income of the settlors. The question also arose whether the preference shares taken by each wife were gifts wholly or substantially a right to income. These questions were all answered in the affirmative. The allotment of preference shares was within the definition of settlement "as being an arrangement or disposition containing the necessary element of bounty".[143] With respect to the question whether the preference shares were wholly or substantially a right to income, Sir John Vinelott said[144]:

> It seems to me that the answer to that question must be in the affirmative. The preference shares entitled the holders to a preferential dividend if the taxpayers (the only directors and the holders of all the ordinary shares) determined to distribute the whole or part of the profits arising in any given year. Apart from that right to income, the only rights conferred on the preference shareholders were the right to repayment of the nominal sum paid on the allotment of the shares and the right to attend and be heard, but not to vote at, general meetings of the company. As a matter of strict legal principle, the preference shares were assets distinct from the income derived from them, but in reality they could never have been realised. The income was dependent upon the taxpayers determining to distribute part of the profits of the company.

Section 660A(7) excludes from the scope of the meaning of settlement an irrevocable allocation of pension rights by one spouse to another in accordance with the terms of a relevant statutory scheme. S.660A(8) also excludes income arising under a settlement made by one party to a marriage by way of provision for the other, either after the dissolution of the marriage, or while they are separated under an order of a court, or under a separation agreement or in such circumstances that the separation is likely to be permanent.

---

[143] Sir John Vinelott at page 333.
[144] ibid.

Unmarried Minor Children of the Settlor

The lenient treatment given to spouses does not extend to unmarried young children of the settlor. Thus, there is a residual charge in respect of income paid to an unmarried minor child of the settlor during the settlor's life. Where income arising under a settlement has not been treated as the settlor's income under s.660A, and it is then paid to an unmarried minor child of the settlor or otherwise falls to be treated as income of an unmarried child of the settlor during the settlor's life, such income is treated for all the purposes of the Income Tax Acts as the income of the settlor and not as the income of any other person.[145] An exemption is provided in s.660B(5) in respect of income paid to a child in a year in which the aggregate amount paid to that child does not exceed £100.

For the purposes of this residual charge, "child" is defined to include a step child and an illegitimate child.[146] "Minor" means a person under the age of 18, and references to "payments" include payments in money or moneys' worth.[147]

The provision is widened to cover possible payments out of capital (in cases where trust income has been accumulated), for which purpose s.660B(2) provides that, where income arising under a settlement is retained or accumulated by the trustees, any payment whatsoever made thereafter by virtue or in consequence of the settlement to an unmarried minor child of the settlor shall be treated as a payment of income to the extent that there is available retained or accumulated income. For this purpose s.660B(3) deems that there is available retained or accumulated income if the aggregate of the income which has arisen under the settlement since it was made is more than the aggregate of any income so arising, which has been:

a.   treated as the income of the settlor, or

b.   paid (whether as income or capital) to or for the benefit of, or otherwise treated as the income of, a beneficiary other than an unmarried minor child of the settlor, or

bb. treated as the income of an unmarried minor child of the settlor, and subject to tax in any of the years 1995-96, 1996-97, or 1997-98, or

c.   applied in defraying any of the trustees' expenses which were properly chargeable to income, or would have so been but for any express provision of the trust.

---

[145] s.660B(1).
[146] s.660B(6)(a)
[147] s.660B(6)(c)

Capital Sums paid to the Settlor

Section 677(1) provides that any capital sum paid to the settlor by the trustees of a settlement shall be treated as the settlor's income, to the extent that it falls within the amount of available income of the year of payment and up to the next ten years. Any sum which is treated as the settlor's income under this section is grossed up at the rate applicable to trusts[148] in order to ascertain the amount that would enter into the calculation of his total income. Tax is charged under Schedule D Case VI, and credit is given for tax at the rate applicable to trusts, or the tax charged on the grossed up sum, which ever is less.[149] The provisions apply equally to capital sums received by the settlor from a body corporate connected with the settlement.[150]

By s.677(9), "capital sum" means any sum paid by way of loan or repayment of a loan, and any other sum paid otherwise than as income, which is not paid for full consideration in money or money's worth. The definition excludes sums which could not have become payable except in one of the events mentioned in s.673(3), but, a sum paid to the settlor includes sums paid to the settlor's spouse, or to the settlor or the settlor's spouse jointly with another person.[151] Also included within the scope of sums paid to the settlor are sums paid by the trustees to a third party at the settlor's direction, or by virtue of assignment by the settlor of his right to receive it, if the assignment was on or after 6 April 1981; and, any sum which is otherwise paid or applied by the trustees for the benefit of the settlor.

For the purposes of s.677(1), s.677(2) provides that, "available income", in respect of a capital sum paid in a year, is the aggregate of the income arising in the year and the income of previous years, to the extent that such income has not been distributed. Thus the concept is linked to income which the trustees have accumulated. Certain deductions from these sums are available in arriving at the amount of available income – e.g., sums which have already been treated as the income of the settlor for tax purposes, and, an amount equal to tax at the rate applicable to trusts on the aggregate of undistributed income which has already been treated as the settlor's income.[152]

Where the capital sum paid to the settlor was paid to by way of a loan, and he repays the whole of the loan, no part of it shall be treated as his income for any year subsequent to the year of repayment.[153]

The moral of the anti-avoidance provisions is that, the settlor should create a capital settlement in which he has completely divested himself of all interest in the settled property. He should also ensure that neither

[148] S.677(6)
[149] S.677(7).
[150] s.678.
[151] S.677(9)(b).
[152] See generally, s.677(2).
[153] S.677(4).

himself, nor his spouse, nor any of his unmarried infant children can or do receive any money from the trustees of that settlement.

Further Reading

Stopforth D, *The First Attack on Settlements Used for Income Tax Avoidance* [1991] BTR 86.

Stopforth D, *Settlements and the Avoidance of Tax on Income - the Period to 1920* [1990] BTR 225.

McCall C, *Accumulation and Maintenance Trusts: Further Points* [1977] BTR 79.

Sheridan D, *Discretionary Trusts and the Proposed Treaty with the United States* [1977] BTR 48.

Sandford CT, Willis JRM & Ironside DJ, *Trusts under an Accessions Tax* [1972] BTR 333.

chapter thirteen

Capital Gains Tax - Chargeable Persons and Activities

From the introduction of direct taxation in the late 18th century until 1962, profits or gains of a capital nature fell largely outside the direct taxation schemes. The "all or nothing" principle governing the taxation of a particular gain, depending on whether it was a gain of an income nature, or a capital gain, meant that the question of whether a particular payment was income or capital in the hands of the recipient was of paramount importance. If the payment was of an income nature, it was taxable in its entirety (with due allowance for various statutory reliefs) at what used to be very high rates. If, on the other hand, the payment was of a capital nature, no part of it was taxable. This understandably encouraged a thriving tax avoidance industry, and led to artificial attempts to convert what in a straightforward transaction would have been income, into capital.

However, the feeling eventually began to take root that there was no sound reason why capital profits should not be taxed. Apart from the argument that the absence of a tax on capital gains contributes to the course of inflation,[1] there was the view that the question whether a particular profit should be taxed at all should not depend on whether it happened to have been labelled income or capital (especially when the assignment of such label was sometimes a "spin of a coin" affair). A profit is a profit, regardless of its nature, and if one type of profit were to be taxed, the same should apply to other types. A simple example suffices. Let us suppose that, X and Y each had a sum of £500,000 to invest. X sets up a business with his money, or puts it into high interest accounts. The profits of either option would attract tax. Suppose that, Y, on the other hand, buys a nice country estate with his money, lives in it for a few years, and then sells it at a huge profit. This profit, being capital in nature, would escape tax. To anyone who was not already indoctrinated on the "income/capital" divide, this result might seem rather odd.[2] Apart from this type of scenario, there was the point that, most people, poor and rich, earned some sort of

---

[1] See for example, The Royal Commission on the Taxation of Profits and Income, 1955 Cmd. 9474, paras. 104 (the Commission did not endorse this argument).

[2] Note that, even today, Y would still escape tax - not because his profit was capital, but because of the relief given in respect of an individual's only or main residence.

income, and were taxed on it, while only the rich and propertied classes were likely to engage in large capital transactions yielding capital profits. Therefore the exemption of capital profits from direct taxation was unfair, as it was just a disguised means of protecting the rich.[3]

Eventually, a limited scheme was introduced in 1962, in which short-term capital gains were taxed as income under Schedule D case VII.[4] Soon afterward, capital gains tax (CGT) was introduced (by the Finance Act 1965) to tax all capital gains other than short-term capital gains. According to Purchas LJ in *Kirby v Thorn EMI Plc*,[5] the purpose of the tax was:

> ... to provide that part of the wealth gained or, according to how one views it, the protection afforded against erosion by inflation as a result of appreciation in the value of assets without any effort on the part of the owner should be taxed so as to divert part of the gain achieved, or loss avoided, to the benefit of the Crown.

True to the principle that "tax is much more easily opposed, ridiculed and guyed than it is proposed, imposed or justified"[6] capital gains tax attracted the criticism of impeding the movement of capital, hindering economic growth, penalising savings and inhibiting personal endeavour.[7] These criticisms obviously did not lead to the abandonment of the tax, although the charge on short-term capital gains under Schedule D case VII was finally abolished in 1971. In 1979, the Capital Gains Tax Act consolidated the capital gains tax legislation not relating exclusively to companies, and in 1992, the Taxation of Chargeable Gains Act (TCGA) consolidated all the capital gains tax legislation. Significant changes to the exemptions and reliefs available were made by the Finance Act 1998.[8]

The TCGA 1992 is now the basic legislation for capital gains tax and, unless otherwise stated, all references to statutory provisions in the following discussions are references to this Act.

The Scope of the Charge

Section 1 of the TCGA 1992 provides that tax shall be charged under the Act in respect of capital gains, that is to say, chargeable gains, accruing to a person on the disposal of assets. Within this phrase is encapsulated all the prerequisites for a charge to capital gains tax, namely:

---

[3] See generally, the Memorandum of Dissent to the Royal Commission's report, para. 35.
[4] The Royal Commission on the Taxation of Profits and Income recommended against taxing capital gains as income (1955 Cmd. 9474, paras. 94 - 108).
[5] [1988] 2 All ER 947 at 957.
[6] H.H. Monroe: "Intolerable Inquisition? Reflections on the Law of Tax", 18 (1981, Stevens & Sons, London).
[7] R.A. Toby: "The Theory and Practice of Income Tax", 71 (1978, Sweet & Maxwell, London).
[8] These are discussed in Chapter 16.

1. a chargeable person;
2. an asset;
3. a disposal of the asset by the chargeable person;
4. a chargeable gain derived from such disposal.[9]

The discussion that follows will examine the law relating to the taxation of chargeable capital gains under these four broad headings.

Chargeable Persons

General

As seen above, s.1(1) charges tax on capital gains accruing to a person on the disposal of assets. The use of the word "person" rather than "individual" here is to be noted. This indicates that capital gains are taxed not only in respect of individuals but also in respect of other legal persons, e.g., trustees and personal representatives. Companies are not subject to capital gains tax, but their chargeable gains (computed on normal capital gains tax principles)[10] are subject to corporation tax, at the usual corporation tax rates (s.1(2)). An unincorporated association is a "person" for capital gains tax purposes. Accordingly it is an entity of assessment and is liable to tax on its chargeable gains.[11]

With respect to the question of whether a particular person is a "chargeable person" for capital gains tax purposes, s.2(1) TCGA 1992 provides that a person shall be chargeable to capital gains tax in respect of chargeable gains accruing to him in a year of assessment during any part of which he is resident in the United Kingdom, or during which he is ordinarily resident in the United Kingdom. This means that, unlike income tax in which the connecting factor that brings a person within the scope of United Kingdom tax is residence, as far as capital gains tax concerned ordinary residence is also such a connecting factor.

Residence and ordinary residence have the same meaning as in the Income Tax Acts (see s.9(1)), and in this respect the six-month rule of residence is similarly applicable here. S.9(3) provides that an individual who is in the United Kingdom for some temporary purpose only and not with a view to establishing his residence there will be charged to capital gains tax only if he is in the United Kingdom for more than six months in the relevant tax year. Concessionary relief is available in respect of the

---

[9] Compare Purchas LJ in *Kirby v Thorn EMI Plc* ([1988] 2 All ER 947 at 958) - "A chargeable gain, therefore, imports the following elements: (1) the acquisition of the asset; (2) an increase in the capital value of the asset whilst in the ownership of the person to be charged; (3) a disposal of the asset giving rise to a realisation of the gain which has accrued during the period of ownership"

[10] See s.8.

[11] *Frampton v IRC* [1985] STC 186 (Peter Gibson J).

dates of commencement and cessation of residence. ESC D2 provides that a person who is treated as resident in the United Kingdom for any year of assessment from the date of his arrival here, but who has not been regarded at any time during the five years immediately preceding such arrival as resident or ordinarily resident here, will be charged to CGT only in respect of the chargeable gains accruing to him from disposals made after his arrival in the United Kingdom. The concession also provides that when a person leaves the United Kingdom and is treated on his departure as not resident and not ordinarily resident in the United Kingdom, he will not be charged to CGT on gains accruing to him from disposals made after the date of his departure. This only applies if the individual concerned was not resident and not ordinarily resident in the United Kingdom for the whole of at least four out of the seven years of assessment immediately preceding the year of assessment in which he or she left the United Kingdom.

This concession does not extend to gains on the disposal of United Kingdom assets used in or for the purposes of a United Kingdom trade, profession or vocation carried on by a person through a branch or agency, at any time between the date of his departure from the United Kingdom and the end of the year of assessment during which such departure took place. Neither does it extend to trustees of a settlement, nor to settlors in relation to gains within a settlement on which they would be chargeable. It is likely that this last point was included to prevent the concession being used as a means of avoiding tax on trust gains.

Branch or agency

Where a person is neither resident nor ordinarily resident in the United Kingdom, but he carries on a trade in the UK through a branch or agency, he will be chargeable to capital gains tax on gains accruing on the disposal of assets situated in the UK, used at, or before the time when the capital gain accrued, in or for the purposes of the trade, or used or held for the purposes of the branch or agency (s.10(1)). For this purpose "branch or agency" means any factorship, agency, receivership, branch or management, but the term does not include general agents and brokers (s.10(6)).

Non-domiciled persons

An individual who is resident or ordinarily resident but not domiciled in the United Kingdom is only chargeable on gains accruing on the disposal of foreign assets on a remittance basis, i.e., only on sums received in the United Kingdom (s.12(1)). For the purposes of this provision, s.12(2) provides that there shall be treated as received in the United Kingdom in respect of any gain, all amounts paid, used, or enjoyed in, or in any manner or form transmitted or brought into the United Kingdom. The subsection furthermore provides that the elaborate provisions of s.65 (6) – (9) of the ICTA 1988 on the question when a person is deemed to have received a sum of money in the United Kingdom apply here as well. Those provisions, applied in the context of capital gains tax, mean that the following will be taken as sums received in the United Kingdom:

1. Any sum applied outside the United Kingdom by a person resident or ordinarily resident in the United Kingdom, in or towards the satisfaction of:
    a.   any debt for money lent to him in the United Kingdom or for interest on money so lent;[12]
    b.   any debt for money lent to him outside the United Kingdom and received in or brought into the United Kingdom;[13]
    c.   any debt incurred for satisfying in whole or in part a debt falling within paragraph (a) or (b) above.[14]

2. Money borrowed abroad by a person who is ordinarily resident in the United Kingdom, which the person then receives or brings into the United Kingdom, in cases in which the debt for that money is wholly or partly satisfied before it was brought into or received in the United Kingdom.[15]

Assets

What is an asset?

It has been seen that capital gains tax is chargeable on a gain accruing on a disposal of assets. The term "assets" is defined by s.21(1) as all forms of property, whether situated in the UK or not, including:

a. options, debts and incorporeal property generally; and
b. any currency other than sterling; and
c. any form of property created by the person disposing of it [e.g., paintings, copyrights], or otherwise coming to be owned without being

---

[12]   S.65(6)(a) ICTA 1988.
[13]   S.65(6)(b) ICTA 1988.
[14]   S.65(6)(c) ICTA 1988.
[15]   S.65(7) ICTA 1988. See also subsections (8) and (9) of s.65.

acquired [e.g., goodwill, and property which is found].

It is clear from the wide definition that the term extends far beyond merely physical property, and that it possesses a meaning for capital gains tax purposes which is different from its usage in colloquial terms. A number of cases illustrate the way in which intangible property may constitute assets for capital gains tax purposes. In *O'Brien (HMIT) v Benson's Hosiery (Holdings) Ltd*,[16] the sales director of the taxpayer company, who was employed under a seven year service agreement, obtained a release from the agreement when it had about five years left to run, in consideration of a payment of £50,000 to the company. It was held that the employer's rights under the service agreement were an asset for capital gains tax purposes, even though contracts of personal service were not assignable. Lord Russell said:[17]

> It was contended for the taxpayer that the rights of an employer under a contract of service were not "property" or an "asset" of the employer because they cannot be turned to account by transfer or assignment to another. But in my opinion this contention supposes a restricted view of the scheme of the imposition of the capital gains tax which the statutory language does not permit. If, as here, the employer is able to extract from the employee a substantial sum as a term of releasing him from his obligations to serve, the rights of the employer appear to me to bear quite sufficiently the mark of an asset of the employer, something which he can turn to account, notwithstanding that his ability to turn it to account is by a type of disposal limited by the nature of the asset.

Marren (HMIT) v Ingles[18] is another illustrative case. The taxpayer sold shares in a private company in consideration of an immediate payment of £750 per share, plus the right to receive a further payment if the market value of the shares on flotation of the company exceeded £750. When the flotation took place, the taxpayer received a further £2,825 per share. It was held that the contingent right to further payment was an asset and, because a capital sum was derived from it, there was a disposal of that asset and a capital gains tax liability.

Still on intangible property, a technical point arose in *Zim Properties Ltd v Procter (HMIT)*[19] concerning whether an intangible right had to be capable of being described as "property" in order for it to be an asset. The taxpayer company had brought an action in negligence against its solicitors. The

---

[16] [1980] AC 562.
[17] At page 573.
[18] [1980] 3 All ER 95; STC 500; applied in *Marson (HMIT) v Marriage*[1980]STC 177 - a right to future payment under an agreement was a chose in action and therefore a chargeable asset.
[19] [1985] STC 90.

action had eventually been compromised, and a sum of £69,000 had been paid to the taxpayer in compensation. Warner J, after "considerable hesitation", came to the conclusion that even if the right to sue the solicitor was not a form of "property" it was nonetheless an asset for capital gains tax purposes. This was based on the decision of the House of Lords in *O'Brien v Benson's Hosiery (Holdings) Ltd* (above), the *ratio* of which, Warner J felt, was that the rights in that case were assets because they could be turned to account. He said that the House of Lords in *O'Brien* treated as virtually irrelevant the use of the word 'property' in what is now s.21(1). Warner J then concluded[20] that it would be inconsistent with the decision in *O'Brien* "to hold that a right to bring an action to seek to enforce a claim that was not frivolous or vexatious, which right could be turned to account by negotiating a compromise yielding a substantial capital sum, could not be an 'asset' within the meaning of that term in the capital gains tax legislation". He accepted that not every right to a payment was an asset for capital gains tax purposes.[21] One example of a right that would not be an asset was the right of a seller of property to payment of its price. The relevant asset then, is the property itself. What this showed however was "no more than that the interpretation of the capital gains tax legislation requires, as does the interpretation of any legislation, the exercise of common sense, rather than just the brute application of verbal formulae".[22]

Thus, an intangible right must be capable of being turned into pecuniary account, and if it is a right of action, then the claim must not be frivolous or vexatious. Furthermore, in order for a "right" to be an asset, it must be legally enforceable and capable of being owned. This principle is illustrated by *Kirby (HMIT) v Thorn EMI plc*.[23] Thorn EMI plc (Thorn) agreed to sell three subsidiaries to an American company, General Electric. Thorn, in consideration of a capital sum, entered into a restrictive covenant that no company in the Thorn group would engage in the trade carried on by the three subsidiaries, for a period of five years. The Revenue argued that the right to engage in a commercial activity was an asset, and thus, the payment for restricting the commercial activities was liable to capital gains tax. The Court of Appeal disagreed, and held that the right of freedom to trade and compete in the market place was not an asset for capital gains tax purposes. According to Nicholls LJ:[24]

> ... the liberty or freedom to trade, enjoyed by everyone, is not a form of "property" within the meaning of [s.21]. This liberty, or freedom, is a "right" if that word is given a very wide meaning, as when we speak of a person's "rights" in a free society. But in [s.21] the words used are "assets" and "property". "Property" is not a term of art, but

---

[20] At page 106.

[21] At page 108.

[22] Ibid. For other examples see *Welbeck Securities Ltd. v Powlson* (HMIT) [1987] STC 468 (an option to acquire an interest in a property development); *Golding (HMIT) v Kaufman* [1985] STC 152 (a 'put' option).

[23] [1988] 2 All ER 947; [1987] STC 621.

[24] At page 627.

takes its meaning from its context and from its collocation in the documents of Acts of Parliament in which it is found and from the mischief with which the Act or document is intended to deal ... The context in the instant case is a taxing Act which is concerned with assets and with disposals and acquisitions, gains and losses. I can see no reason to doubt that in [s.21] "property" bears the meaning of that which is capable of being owned, in the normal legal sense, and that it does not bear the extended meaning that would be needed if it were to include a person's freedom to trade.

However, the Court of Appeal held that the sum was taxable as a capital sum derived from Thorn's goodwill. Even though Thorn itself was not carrying on the trades of the three companies, it could have goodwill in respect of those trades. The company had received payment for agreeing not to exploit that goodwill for a period, and as the question of goodwill had not been canvassed before the Commissioners, the case would be remitted to them for further consideration of evidence and arguments on it.

Underlying assets and ESC D33

Applying the strict position following *Zim Properties* may put some taxpayers at a severe disadvantage. For example, suppose that a taxpayer's property is destroyed as a result of a third party's negligence. It follows from *Zim* that the taxpayer's right to take court action against the third party is an asset for capital gains tax purposes and that the settlement of the action, either in or out of court, is a disposal of that asset. The taxpayer is going to be in a far worse position than he would have been had he sold the asset before it was destroyed. This is for two reasons:

a. If the right to take legal action arose on or after 10 March 1981, the asset will be deemed to have been acquired for no cost. Had the relevant asset been the property itself, the gain would have been computed by deducting the acquisition cost and allowable expenditure from the proceeds.

b. Exemptions and reliefs that could have applied to the property itself may not apply to the right to take legal action. Taper relief, main residence relief and, for a limited period, retirement relief are particularly relevant here.[25]

---

[25] These are discussed later in the context of exemptions and reliefs.

The Revenue have mitigated the harshness of this rule by introducing ESC D33 which specifically relates to capital gains tax on compensation and damages following *Zim Properties*. The concession operates by relating the right of action to an underlying asset. The following extracts from paragraphs 9, 10 and 11 outline the main substance of the concession:

> Where the right of action arises by reason of the total or partial loss or destruction of or damage to a form of property which is an asset for capital gains tax purposes, or because the claimant suffered some loss or disadvantage in connection with such a form of property, any gain or loss on the disposal of the right of action may by concession be computed as if the compensation derived from that asset and not from the right of action.
>
> If the relief was or would have been available on the dipsosal of the relevant underlying asset, it will be available on the disposal of the right of action.
>
> Where the action does not concern loss of or damage to or loss in connection with a form of property which is an asset for capital gains tax purposes, the approach in paragraph 9 above of treating the compensation as deriving from the asset itself is not appropriate. In these circumstances, any gain accruing on the disposal of the right of action will be exempt from capital gains tax.

The effect of this is that, in the example given above, the taxpayer will not be disadvantaged by the rule in *Zim Properties*. He will be able to deduct the acquisition cost of the property and will be allowed to claim any exemptions and reliefs that would have been available to him on the disposal of the property itself. However, it should be noted that these reliefs are by concession and that the strict legal position remains that set out in *Zim Properties*.

Non-chargeable assets

Assets are either chargeable or non-chargeable and, unless otherwise specifically stated, all assets are chargeable. Some specifically identified non-chargeable assets are:

1. s.263: motor cars – these are described as mechanically propelled road vehicles constructed or adapted for the carriage of passengers, except vehicles of a type not commonly used as a private vehicle and unsuitable to be so used.
2. s.204(1): the rights of an insurer under a policy of insurance.
3. s.45(1): tangible movable property (chattels) which are wasting assets, subject to certain exceptions.
4. s.251(1): debts, except debts on a security.

No chargeable gain or allowable loss accrues on the disposal of non-chargeable assets.

Disposals

A charge to capital gains tax arises when an asset is disposed of. Apart from express provisions, there cannot be a disposal unless the disponor had an asset of which he could dispose, since according to Nicholls LJ in *Kirby (HMIT) v Thorn EMI plc*,[26] the Act presupposes that, "immediately prior to the disposal, there was an asset, and that the disponor owned it". Although disposals are central to the theme of the capital gains tax legislation, the term is not defined in the Act. However, there have been some relevant dicta. In *Kirby (HMIT) v Thorn EMI plc* [27] for example, Nicholls LJ said that what is envisaged by the term is a transfer of an asset (i.e., of ownership of an asset) as widely defined, by one person to another; and in *Welbeck Securities Ltd v Powlson (HMIT)*[28] Slade LJ accepted the submission that the word "disposal", as used in s.1 itself is not apt to include the mere release of an option, which is accompanied by no corresponding acquisition of the right in question, but has the effect of extinguishing it.[29]

There are several types of disposal known to the capital gains tax regime. For example, there may be actual disposals, deemed disposals, total disposals (disposing of all interests in an asset), part disposals (disposing of some interests in an asset while retaining other interests, or creating a new interest in the asset by the disposal), and, disposals of part (disposing of all interests in a part of the asset - e.g., by selling half of it). An actual disposal is one which has taken place in fact. Most disposals for capital gains tax purposes will be of this nature. However, there are some situations where no disposal may have taken place in fact, but the legislation nevertheless deems one to have occurred. We first examine here the general concept of deemed disposals. Part disposals are discussed later in this chapter.

---

[26] [1988] 2 All ER 947 at 951.
[27] ibid.
[28] [1987] STC 468 at 473.
[29] However, such a release in return for payment will be a deemed disposal under s.22(1).

Deemed Disposals

When a statute requires that something be deemed to have happened, one is required to implement a fiction. The capital gains tax legislation contains many instances of deemed disposals, and it is therefore helpful to make some general observations about the proper approach to deeming provisions. With respect to deeming provisions in general, Lord Asquith said in *East End Dwellings Co Ltd v Finsbury Borough Council*:[30]

> If you are bidden to treat an imaginary state of affairs as real you must surely, unless prohibited from doing so, also imagine as real the consequences and incidents which, if the putative state of affairs had in fact existed, must inevitably have flowed or accompanied it ... The statute says that you must imagine a certain state if affairs; it does not say that having done so, you must cause or permit your imagination to boggle when it comes to the inevitable corollaries of that state of affairs.[31]

With particular reference to deeming provisions in taxing statutes, Nourse J said in *IRC v Metrolands (Property Finance) Ltd*:[32]

> When considering the extent to which a deeming provision should be applied, the court is entitled and bound to ascertain for what purposes and between what persons the statutory fiction is to be resorted to ... it will not always be clear what those purposes are ... If the application of the provision would lead to an unjust, anomalous or absurd result then, unless its application would clearly be within the purpose of the fiction, it should not be applied. If on the other hand, its application would not lead to any such result then, unless that would clearly be outside the purposes of the fiction, it should be applied.

And, finally, Peter Gibson J said in *Marshall (HMIT) v Kerr*:

> But I do not read the authorities as requiring in the case of a deeming provision the abandonment of what is sometimes called the golden rule of construction, that is to say that in construing a statute the grammatical and ordinary sense of the words is to be adhered to,

---

[30]   [1952] AC 109 at 132-133.
[31]   Compare Peter Gibson J in *Marshall (HMIT) v Kerr* [1993] BTC 194 at 200.
[32]   [1981] 1 WLR 637 at 646.

unless that would lead to some absurdity or some inconsistency, in which case the grammatical and ordinary sense of the words may be modified so as to avoid that absurdity and inconsistency but no further.[33]

With these observations in mind we will now examine the various incidents of deemed disposals in the capital gains tax legislation.

Capital sums

Section 22(1) provides that there is a disposal of assets by their owner where any capital sum is derived from the assets, notwithstanding that no asset is acquired by the person paying the capital sum.[34] In *Marren (HMIT) v Ingles*[35] the House of Lords considered the meaning of the words "notwithstanding that no asset is acquired by the person paying the capital sum". The taxpayer argued that they introduced a condition of a limiting character, with the result that, if an asset is acquired, the subsection does not apply. Slade J at first instance accepted this contention, but the House of Lords disagreed. Lord Wilberforce said:[36]

> In my understanding they are evidently words not of limitation but of extension, the purpose of which is to apply the subsection (so as to establish a "disposal") to cases to which it would not otherwise apply and in which a 'disposal' would not naturally be thought to exist. In other words they mean, in my opinion, 'whether or not an asset is acquired' ...

The charge in s.22(1) fastens on the receipt of a capital sum derived from an asset, including an asset which then becomes destroyed, or which has previously been destroyed, or which has ceased to exist as a distinct asset and which cannot therefore be said to have been disposed of in the ordinary sense of the word.[37]

There are several examples of the general operation of this provision and we will examine some of them in outline.

a. In *O'Brien (HMIT) v Benson's Hosiery*, (above) the company derived a capital sum from releasing an employee from his service agreement, and

---

[33] [1993] BTC 194 at 199.
[34] The term "capital sum" in this section means any money or money's worth which is not excluded from the consideration taken into account in the computation of the gain (s.22(3)).
[35] [1980] 3 All ER 95.
[36] At page 98.
[37] See Vinelott J in *Golding (HMIT) v Kaufman* [1985] STC 152 at 162-163.

this was a disposal of the company's rights under the agreement.

b. In *Marren (HMIT) v Ingles*, (above) the taxpayer derived a capital sum from his right to receive payment, and was taxable although the payer acquired no asset.

c. In *Zim Properties v Procter (HMIT)*, (above) the company received a sum in compromise of a negligence claim against its solicitors.

d. In *Davenport (HMIT) v Chilver*[38] a right to compensation in respect of expropriated property in the USSR, conferred by the Foreign Compensation (Union of Soviet Socialist Republics) Order 1969 was an asset, and the compensation payment itself was a capital sum derived from that asset, resulting in a deemed disposal thereof.

A number of examples involve options. In *Welbeck Securities Ltd v Powlson (HMIT)*[39] the company had been paid £2m for agreeing to release and abandon an option to acquire an interest in a property development in the City of London. It was held that the company had derived a capital sum from an asset (the option) and had therefore disposed of the asset, making a chargeable gain. The date of the disposal was the date when the capital sum has received. *Golding (HMIT) v Kaufman*[40] involved a taxpayer who had options entitling him to require a company to purchase his shareholding in another company. The taxpayer was paid £5,000 in consideration for his abandonment of the options. The question arose whether this was a capital sum derived from an asset, and thus a disposal liable to capital gains tax. Another question that arose in the case was whether the taxpayer had 'abandoned' the options for the purposes of a provision which stated that the abandonment of an option by a person shall not constitute a disposal of an asset by that person (see s.144(4)). Vinelott J held that the £5,000 was taxable as a capital sum derived from an asset. He also held that the effect of the provision referred to above (s.144(1)) was to qualify the operation of s.24(1) (thereby restricting losses). It does not operate to qualify s.22(1), and thus the charge still attached.

Apart from the generality of the provisions however, s.22(1) also provides particular instances of situations to which it relates:

a. capital sums received by way of compensation for any kind of damage or injury to assets or for the loss, destruction or dissipation of assets, or for any depreciation or risk of depreciation of an asset;

b. capital sums received under an insurance policy with respect to the risk of any kind of damage or injury to, or the loss or depreciation

[38] [1983] STC 426.
[39] [1987] STC 468.
[40] [1985] STC 152.

of, assets;

c. capital sums received in return for forfeiture or surrender of rights, or for refraining form exercising rights. There are several examples of this particular situation in the cases, many of which we have discussed above (e.g., *O'Brien (HMIT) v Benson's Hosiery*);

d. capital sums received as consideration for use or exploitation of assets (e.g., for the right to exploit a copyright).

Causation

A vital factor in the principle which treats the derivation of a capital sum from an asset as a disposal is causation. If the capital sum concerned is caused by something other than the asset, then it is not "derived from" the asset. Thus in *Drummond (HMIT) v Brown*,[41] a payment of statutory compensation for the termination of a lease was not derived from the lease, but from the statute. It followed that it was not a capital sum derived from an asset and neither was it (on the facts of the case) compensation for the loss of an asset (because the lease had come to an end by the effluxion of time and the taxpayer was not entitled to security of tenure). Fox LJ said[42] that the payment was simply a sum which Parliament said should be paid.[43] It was therefore not chargeable.

It is to be noted however that there is no general principle that compensation awarded by statute is outside s.22(1).[44] One must look in each case to see whether the capital sum is "derived" from the asset, or from something else. When examining the issue of causation the important thing to look for is the real, rather than the immediate, source of the capital sum.[45] It thus follows that the fact that the immediate source of a capital sum is a statutory provision does not necessarily mean that the sum is not derived from an asset. This principle can be seen in *Pennine Raceway Ltd. v Kirklees Metropolitan Council (no. 2)*.[46] The company had obtained a licence from the owner of an airfield to use the field for the purposes of drag motor racing. The drag racing was covered by existing planning permission with respect to the field. Permission to use the field for drag racing was subsequently revoked by Kirklees Metropolitan Council, the revocation being confirmed by the Secretary of State for the Environment. The company then made an application for planning permission but was refused. The company later received compensation under s.164 of the Town and Country Planning Act 1971, for loss of income and other costs

---

[41] [1984] STC 321.

[42] At page 324.

[43] See also *Davis (HMIT) v Powell* ([1977] STC 32) where it was held that compensation paid to a tenant under s.34(1) of the Agricultural Holdings Act 1948 was not derived from an asset (the lease). It was simply a sum which Parliament said shall be paid.

[44] Per Croom-Johnson LJ in *Pennine Raceway Ltd. v Kirklees Metropolitan Council* (no. 2) [1989] BTC 42 at 51; [1989] STC 122.

[45] Ibid. referring with approval to Warner J in *Zim Properties Ltd. v Procter* [1985] STC 90 at 107.

[46] [1989] BTC 42.

incurred as a result of the revocation of the original planning permission. The question was whether the compensation received was a capital sum derived from an asset under s.22(1). The Court of Appeal held that it was.

Croom-Johnson LJ said[47] that, first, the payment would be a capital sum received by way of compensation for (i) any kind of damage or injury to the asset, or (ii) any depreciation of the asset. Even if there had been no damage or injury to the licence which (as a licence) was still in existence although useless, it could not be said that there had not been a depreciation of the licence, which had granted to the company "sole rights to promote motor and motor cycle events on the Airfield". Counsel had submitted that the payment was simply compensation payable by the council under the statutory requirement laid down by the Town and Country Planning Act 1971, and was derived from the statutory obligation, not from any event in s.22(1). In response to this submission, Croom-Johnson LJ adopted the approach of Warner J in *Zim Properties Ltd. v Procter* (referred to above) – it would be a mistake to say that the asset from which a capital sum is derived must always be the asset that constitutes its immediate source. One has to look for the real source. Croom-Johnson LJ concluded:[48]

> In the present case Pennine had an asset, which was the licence, and that licence depreciated in value when the planning permission was revoked. For that depreciation they are entitled to a capital sum by way of compensation, and their right to the compensation is given by the Town and Country Planning Act 1971, s.164(1) because their asset ... has sustained loss or damage which is directly attributable to the revocation of the permission. It is clear that the capital sum is "derived" from the asset.

Stuart-Smith LJ[49] rejected the submission of counsel that the capital sum had to be consideration for a bargain:

> But it is perfectly clear that both para. (a) and (b) envisage capital sums that do not result from any bargain. Compensation is normally awarded by a court or other Tribunal. Sums received under a policy of insurance are not paid in consideration of the loss or damage to the asset in the sense that there is any bargain for the disposal in that way.

Another question of vital importance was raised in *Pennine*. This concerned

---

[47] ibid at 50.
[48] At page 51.
[49] At page 57.

whether or not the general words of s.22(1) (i.e., "a capital sum ... derived from assets") govern the particular words of paragraphs (a) to (d). Two views were to be found in the case law. First, Nourse J in *Davenport (HMIT) v Chilver*[50] had held that the particular words in paragraphs (a) to (d) stood on their own feet. They were to be construed independently of the opening general words, and if necessary, they were to prevail over the general words. On the other hand, Warner J in *Zim Properties Ltd. v Procter (HMIT)*[51] held that paragraphs (a) to (d) were particular instances of the application of the principle enacted by the general words. Consequently, a case cannot come within any of those paragraphs if it cannot come within the general words.

While holding that the issue did not arise for decision in the present case, two members of the court expressed preferences. Stuart-Smith LJ[52] was content to assume that the narrower construction favoured by Warner J in *Zim Properties Ltd v Procter* was correct. Ralph Gibson LJ on the other hand was inclined to agree with Nourse J in *Davenport v Chilver*.

This divergence of opinion, both at first instance, and in the Court of Appeal, leaves the situation confused. However, when the actual wording of s.22(1) is examined it is, with all respect to Nourse J and Ralph Gibson LJ, difficult to see how the words in paras. (a) to (d) can stand on their own feet. After the general words "where any capital sum is derived from assets" the words immediately preceding paras. (a) to (d) are "and this subsection applies in particular to ...". This indicates that the subsequent words are meant to be particular instances of those preceding that statement. This is in consonance with the *ejusdem generis* rule – where general words are followed by particular words, the particular words ought to be taken as limited in scope to matters of the same kind as the general words. Thus it seems that the approach of Warner J in *Zim Properties v Procter* is to be preferred.

Value shifting

Section 29 treats certain types of transactions as disposals of asset, notwithstanding that no consideration passes, and, in such cases, also treats the consideration or added consideration that could have been obtained if the parties were dealing at arm's length as the market value of the asset:

a. Section 29(2) provides that where a person having control of a company exercises his control so that value passes out of his shares in the company or out of his rights over the company and passes into other shares in, or rights over the company, there is a disposal of the shares or

---

[50] [1983] STC 426 at 439.
[51] [1985] STC 90 at 106.
[52] [1989] BTC at 56.

the rights out of which the value passes. This provision also applies in cases where the value passes out of shares of a person connected with the person who has control of the company, in the way described above.

b. Section 29(4) provides that where after a transaction which results in the owner of the land or any other property becoming the lessee thereof, there is any adjustment of the rights and liabilities under the lease, in a manner which is favourable to the lessor, this is treated as a disposal by the lessee (i.e., the owner), of an interest in the property.

c. Section 29(5) provides that where a person extinguishes or abrogates in whole or in part, any right or restriction held by him over an asset, this is a disposal of the right or restriction.

Satisfaction of debt

Section 251(2) provides that the satisfaction of a debt or part thereof shall be treated as a disposal of the debt by the creditor at the time when the debt is satisfied. Note however that, with the exception of debts on securities, debts are not chargeable assets (s. 251(1)).

Appropriation into trading stock

Where a person appropriates an asset which was not originally acquired as trading stock into his trading stock, this will be treated as a disposal of the asset for its market value, if a chargeable gain or allowable loss would have accrued to him on its disposal for its market value (s.161(1)). However, by virtue of s.161(3), a trader who is taxable under Case I of Schedule D can elect to have the market value of the asset computed for income tax purposes, as being reduced by the amount of the chargeable gain, or increased by the amount of the allowable loss that would have accrued on this deemed disposal. The effect of this is to convert what would have been an immediate liability to capital gains tax into a deferred income tax liability.

Examples

Vladimir bought an asset at a cost of £100. He appropriated this asset into his trading stock when it was worth £150. This will normally be treated as a disposal of the asset for a consideration of £150 under s.161(1), leading to a gain of £50.

If Vladimir makes an election under s.161(3), he will be treated for income tax purposes as having acquired the asset as part of his trading stock at a price of £100 (instead of its current market value of £150). When he eventually sells it as part of his trading stock, the profit on the sale will reflect the £50 gain which the asset was carrying at the time of its appropriation into trading stock.

Termination of life interest

When a person entitled to an interest in possession in settled property dies, the assets forming part of the settled property, and which still remain in the settlement, will be deemed to have been disposed of and immediately re-acquired by the trustee at its market value (s.72(1)). However, no chargeable gain accrues on this disposal.

Beneficiary becoming absolutely entitled against trustee

S.71(1) provides that when a person becomes absolutely entitled to any settled property as against the trustee, all the assets forming part of the settled property to which he becomes entitled will be deemed to be have been disposed of by the trustee, and immediately reacquired by him in his capacity as trustee, at market value. Such assets are deemed to be vested in the beneficiary, the acts of trustee are deemed to be on the behalf of the beneficiary (s.60(1)). Transfers between them are therefore disregarded accordingly.

Assets lost or destroyed

The occasion of the entire loss, destruction, dissipation or extinction of an asset constitutes a disposal of the asset, whether or not compensation is received in respect of it (s.24(1)). If any compensation or insurance payment is received for such loss or destruction, and this is applied for the purposes of replacing the asset within one year of receipt or such longer period as the inspector may allow, the taxpayer can "roll over"[53] any gain on the old asset onto the new asset (s.23(4)). For the purposes of this provision the fact that an asset has ceased to be of any value does not indicate that it has been "dissipated" or "lost".[54]

Assets becoming of negligible value

Section 24(2) provides that, where the owner of an asset which has become of negligible value makes a claim to that effect, the owner will be deemed to have sold and immediately re-acquired the asset for the amount specified in the claim. This means that the owner of the asset will have incurred an allowable loss. S. 24(2)(a) indicates that the time of the deemed disposal is the time when the claim was made, or, if certain conditions are fulfilled, any earlier time specified in the claim. The strict view used to be that the period of this notional disposal is the date on which the inspector was satisfied that the asset had become of negligible value. However, in *Williams (HMIT) v Bullivant*[55] Vinelott J preferred the view relating the notional disposal back to the date when the owner made the claim – a view which (with some exceptions) has now been given statutory effect.

The timing of the notional disposal is important because of the fact that losses can only be carried forward. Thus since the application of the provision will invariably lead to a loss, the claim should be made as early as possible. *Williams (HMIT) v Bullivant* itself is illustrative of the point. The taxpayers owned shares which, by the end of February 1974, had become of negligible value. They only made a claim in 1978. In the meantime, the taxpayers had made chargeable gains back in 1974. It was held that the notional disposal (and losses) could not be related back to any time before the claim was made. Thus they could not set the notional loss against the gains made in 1974.

While the principle that the disposal is deemed to take place when the claim was made is better than that which deemed it to take place when the inspector became satisfied, it could itself lead to problems. These problems were highlighted in *Larner v Warrington (HMIT)*[56], in which Nicholls J applied the *Williams v Bullivant* test, but with apparent misgivings. His reservations are telling:

> I have to confess that on the basis of [*Williams v Bullivant*], that on the inspector allowing the claim [s.24(2)] takes effect as if the claimant had sold the asset when the claim was made and not on the happening of the event giving rise to the claim, [s.24(2)] does seem to me to be capable of working considerable hardship to taxpayers. If a chargeable gain accrues to a taxpayer in a year of assessment and within the same year an asset of his becomes of negligible value, one might have expected that on the latter fact being satisfactorily established following a claim duly made under the subsection, the loss on the notional sale could have been deducted from that chargeable gain even though the claim was not actually made before the close of the year of assessment. As it is, a well-advised taxpayer by making his claim within that year will be able to obtain an advantage

---

[53]   Roll over relief is a mechanism whereby liability to capital gains tax is deferred. We will look at this in more detail in the chapter on disposal consideration.
[54]   Nicholls J in *Larner v Warrington (HMIT)* [1985] STC 442 at 449-450.
[55]   [1983] STC 107.
[56]   [1985] STC 442, at 449.

of which the less well-informed taxpayer, as a matter of strict law, may be deprived. I say 'as a matter of strict law' because that is the effect of the decision in *Williams (Inspector of Taxes) v Bullivant*. In practice the Revenue tempers the wind to the shorn lamb by permitting retrospection for a period of two years. But the existence of this extra–statutory concession serves to underline the unattractive consequences which in law may flow from [s.24(2)] as construed in *Williams (Inspector of Taxes) v Bullivant*. Of course, the loss arising from the notional sale can be deducted from any gains accruing not only in the year of assessment in which the claim is made but also in subsequent years. But this will provide cold comfort indeed to a taxpayer ... who has no such gains and is unlikely to have any such gains in the foreseeable future.

Nicholls J referred in the passage quoted to the Revenue tempering "the wind to the shorn lamb" by permitting retrospection. This concessionary relief was contained in ESC D28 in the following terms:

Where an asset has become of negligible value [TCGA 1992, s.24(2)] allows the owner to claim to be treated as though the asset had been sold and immediately reacquired at the specified value. If the claim is accepted, this will normally give rise to an allowable loss.

In strictness [s.24(2)] requires the deemed sale and reacquisition to be treated as taking place when the claim is made. In practice the Inland Revenue are prepared to accept that a claim by the owner to be treated as having sold and reacquired the asset at a particular date may be made not later than 24 months after the end of the tax year (or accounting period in the case of a company) in which that date fell, provided that the asset is of negligible value both when the claim is made and at that earlier date (whether or not it had first become of negligible value before that earlier date).

This has now been given statutory effect in s 24(2)(b). This subsection allows an earlier time to be specified in the claim, if the asset had become of negligible value at that earlier time, and, (for CGT purposes) if that earlier time is not more than two years before the beginning of the year of assessment in which the claim is made, or, (for corporation tax purposes) if that earlier time is on or after the first day of the earliest accounting period ending not more than two years before the time of the claim.

Assets held on 6 April 1965

Schedule 2 para. 17(1) provides that, on an election by the person making the disposal, assets held by him on 6 April 1965 will be deemed to have been sold and immediately reacquired by him at market value on that date. The rules applicable to assets held on 6 April 1965 are discussed in more detail below.[57]

Assets held on 31 March 1982

Section 35(2) provides, with respect to disposals on or after 6 April 1988, that assets held on 31 March 1982 will be deemed to have been sold and immediately reacquired by their owner at their market value on that date. This provision and the exceptions thereto are discussed in more detail below.[58]

Charities

Section 256(2) provides that if property which is held on charitable trusts ceases to be so held, the trustees shall be treated as having disposed of it and immediately reacquired it at the market value, and any gain on the disposal will be treated as not accruing to a charity.

Part Disposals

Section 21(2)(a) provides that references to a disposal of an asset include reference to a part disposal of an asset. The term "part disposal" is defined by s.21(2)(b). It includes situations where:

i.   an interest or right in or over the asset is created by the disposal;
ii. an interest or right subsists before the disposal;
iii. on a disposal, any description of the property derived from the asset remains undisposed of.

A part disposal of an asset is treated as a disposal of the asset, not as a disposal of part of the asset.[59] Examples of part disposals are the grant of an easement over land, and the creation of a leasehold interest. In both of these examples an interest over the asset is created by the disposal, and some description of property derived from the asset (namely, that part which is retained by the owner - e.g., the freehold) would remain undisposed of.

---

[57] See Chapter 16
[58] Ibid.

Part disposals always lead to apportionments. The disposal consideration is not apportioned since it only relates to the part disposed of, but in order to determine the gain attributable to the part disposal, the acquisition cost and other allowable expenditure will be apportioned (s.42(1)). The formula for such apportionment is given by s.42(2):

$$\frac{A}{A + B} \times C$$

Where:

A = the value or consideration for the disposal

B = the market value of the undisposed part

C = the total allowable expenditure on the asset

The amount arrived at, i.e., the expenditure which is attributable to the part that has been disposed of, is deducted from the disposal consideration to arrive at the amount of the gain that is chargeable. The remainder will be the amount of allowable expenditure which is attributable to the undisposed property. Any expenditure which, on the facts, is wholly attributable to the part which has been disposed of is not apportioned (s.42(4)).

Example:

Sharm bought some freehold property for £100,000. She soon after spent £25,000 on improvements. One year later, she granted an easement over the property to a local company in return for a payment of £5,000. As a result of the easement, the property is now worth £110,000.

The allowable expenditure on this part disposal would be:

$$\frac{£5,000}{£5,000 + £110,000} \times £125,000 = £5,434.78$$

---

[59] Sir John Vinelott in *Watton (HMIT) v Tippett* [1996] BTC 25 at 32.

Thus the allowable expenditure attributable to the part disposal (the easement) amounts to £5,434.78

Assuming that the indexation allowance is nil the gain/loss would be:

$$£5,000 - £5,434.78 = £-434.78$$

This indicates that the transaction of granting the easement has resulted in Sharm incurring a capital gains tax loss of £434.78.

The expenditure which is attributable to the part of the property which remains undisposed of after the easement (the freehold) would be:

$$£125,000 - £5,434.78 = £119,565.22$$

Leases

The payment of a premium on the grant of a lease is a part disposal of the freehold or other asset out of which the lease is granted (Sch. 8 para. 2(1)). In applying the provisions of s.42 (above) to this part disposal, the property which remains undisposed of includes a right to any rent or other payments, other than a premium, payable under the lease. Such a right falls to be valued as at the time of the part disposal (Sch. 8 para. 2(2)).

As part disposals, leases are subject to a special regime under Schedule 8. By Sch. 8 para 5(1) premiums which have been taxed under s 34 of the ICTA 1988 are exempt from capital gains tax.

Small part disposals of land

Special provisions apply to small part disposals of land. S.242(1) applies to a transfer of land forming part of a holding of land, where the consideration for the transfer does not exceed one-fifth of the market value of the holding immediately before the transfer, and the transfer is not one which is treated by s.58 (husband and wife) or s.171(1) (transfers within a group) as giving rise to neither a gain nor a loss. S.242(3) provides further requirements, that the consideration for the relevant transfer should not exceed £20,000, and that the consideration for all disposals of the land made by the transferor in the relevant year should not exceed £20,000.

If these conditions are satisfied, s.242(2) provides (subject to timing requirements in s 242(2A)) that, if the transferor so elects, the transfer will not be treated as a disposal, but the consideration for it will be deducted from the allowable expenditure attributable to the whole holding when the holding is subsequently disposed of. This means that the tax is deferred until the future disposal of the holding.

Death and Capital Gains Tax

Section 62(1)(a) provides that the assets of which a deceased person was competent to dispose should be deemed to be acquired on his death by the personal representatives, or any other person on whom they devolve, at their market value on the date of death. However, s.62(1)(b) provides that these assets shall not be deemed to be disposed of by the deceased at his death, meaning that there is an acquisition with no disposal, and no CGT liability. The death extinguishes all accrued capital gains. The assets which a deceased person was competent to dispose of are defined by s.62(10) as those of his assets which he could, if of full age and capacity, have disposed of by will.

Sale of assets by personal representatives

As seen above, by s.62(1)(a), the personal representatives of a deceased person acquire the deceased's assets at their market value on death. When they dispose of the assets (otherwise than to legatees) they may be liable to CGT on gains accruing since the date of death. For these purposes s.62(3) provides that "personal representatives" shall be treated as a single and continuing body of persons (distinct from the persons who may from time to time fill the posts), and that body shall be treated as having the deceased's residence, ordinary residence and domicile at the date of death. Thus, if the deceased was not resident and not ordinarily resident in the United Kingdom at death, there will be no CGT liability on personal representatives, even if they are resident.

Where CGT is due, s.65(1) provides that it may be assessed and charged on and in the name of any one or more of the personal representatives. The personal representatives are not to be treated as an individual (s.65(2)) and thus they will only be liable to basic rate tax (s.4(1) and (2)). However, personal representatives are entitled to a full annual exemption for the year of death, and the next two years (s.3(7)).

Disposals to legatees

Section 62(4) provides that, on a person acquiring an asset as legatee, no chargeable gain shall accrue to the personal representatives, and the legatee shall be treated as if the personal representatives' acquisition of the asset had been his own. This means that the legatee is treated as having acquired the asset at the time when the personal representatives acquired it (the date of the deceased's death), and that legatee's base cost for CGT purposes is the market value of the asset at the date of the deceased's death. Similar provisions apply in respect of instruments of variation. S.62(6) applies where, within the period of two years after a person's death, any of the dispositions (however effected) of the property of which he was competent to dispose are varied, or the benefit conferred by any of those dispositions is disclaimed. Such variation must be made by an instrument in writing made by the persons or any of the persons who benefit or who would benefit under the dispositions. If these conditions are fulfilled, and the persons making the instrument so elect, the variation or disclaimer shall not constitute a disposal, and the provisions of s.62 shall apply as if the variation had been made by the deceased, or as the case may be, as if the disclaimed benefit had never been conferred.[60]

Harman J (at first instance) said in *Marshall (HMIT) v Kerr* [61] that this subsection applied as if the variations were effected by the deceased so that the legatee taking them, and the personal representatives assenting to their vesting, were to be treated as if the deceased by his will had made the provision which was in the instrument of variation. This sufficiently takes out of any tax net and any computations any difference in value between the date of death and the date of the instrument. The main consequences are that the legatee's acquisition date is the date of death, and the value at which the legatee acquired the asset is the value of the asset at the date of death.[62] Lord Browne-Wilkinson in the House of Lords said[63] that the interests of a beneficiary which in fact arose under the dispositions made by the instrument of variation ("the varied beneficiary") were to be treated as though they had been contained in the will of the deceased. Thus, assets which the deceased was competent to dispose of at the death, which are not sold in due course of administration, but which are vested in the varied beneficiary, are deemed to have been acquired by the varied beneficiary as legatee under the will. However, Lord Browne-Wilkinson stressed[64] that not all assets vested in the varied beneficiary were to be deemed to have been acquired from the deceased, and that such deeming

---

[60] According to Lord Browne-Wilkinson in *Marshall (HMIT) v Kerr* ([1994] BTC 258 at 270) this consequence operates only for the purposes of the section and does not directly apply to any other section.

[61] [1991]BTC 438 at 449; STC 686 (decision reversed by the Court of Appeal, but restored by the House of Lords ([1994] BTC 258)).

[62] See also Peter Gibson J in the Court of Appeal ([1993] BTC 194 at 200-201).

[63] [1994] BTC at page 270.

only applied to assets of which the deceased was competent to dispose at his death. According to him, other assets, whether cash representing the proceeds of sales made by the personal representatives or property purchased by the personal representatives in the course of administration, fell to be treated as though the varied beneficiary's acquisition was the personal representative's acquisition, i.e., as being made at the time, and from the person from whom the personal representatives in fact acquired such cash or property in the course of administration. He said that there was nothing in [s.62(6)] which required one to assume that *all* the assets vested in the varied beneficiary as "legatee" were to be treated as acquired from the deceased at the date of death.[65] Lord Browne-Wilkinson said that still less was there anything which required one to ignore the process of administration of the estate. He concluded the matter thus:

> Assets acquired by the personal representatives after the death are not deemed to have been acquired by them (and hence by the varied beneficiary as legatee) at any time or cost or from any person other than the time, cost and person at which, and from whom, they were in fact acquired. For the purposes of calculating the capital gains tax liability of the varied beneficiary on any future disposal by him of such assets, the acts done by the personal representatives in the course of administration remain relevant and indeed decisive. I cannot therefore see any ground for holding that, once assets are vested in the varied beneficiary, the effect of [subsection (6)] is retrospectively to wipe out the process of administration and deem all the assets vested in the varied beneficiary as having been acquired by him at the date of death from the deceased.[66]

"Legatee" is defined by s.64(2) as including any person taking under a testamentary disposition (e.g. a will) or an intestacy or partial intestacy, whether he takes beneficially or as trustee. A person taking a gift by way of *donatio mortis causa* is treated as a legatee, and his acquisition is treated as made at the time of the donor's death, but s.62(5) exempts from CGT gifts made by way of *donatio mortis causa*.

By virtue of s.64(1), a legatee is entitled to deduct the cost of transferring assets to him by the personal representatives in computing his gains for CGT purposes.

---

[64] At page 271.
[65] Ibid (emphasis supplied).
[66] At pages 271-272.

Settled Property

Definition

Section 68 defines settled property as property held in trust, other than property to which s.60 applies. S.97(7) stipulates that "settlement" and "settlor" have the same meaning as under s.660G(1) & (2) of the ICTA 1988. According to s.660(G)(1) of the ICTA 1988, "settlement" includes any disposition, trust, covenant, agreement or arrangement or transfer of assets, and "settlor", in relation to a settlement, means any person by whom the settlement was made. By virtue of s.660(G)(2) a person is deemed to have made a settlement if he has made or entered into the settlement directly or indirectly, and, in particular, if he has provided or undertaken to provide funds directly or indirectly for the purposes of the settlement, or has made with any other person a reciprocal arrangement for that other person to make or enter into the settlement. S.97(7) TCGA 1992 further provides that "settlor" includes, in the case of a settlement arising under a will or intestacy, the testator or intestate, and that "settled property" shall be construed accordingly.

Section 60 relates to nominees and bare trustees. S.60(1) provides that assets held for another as nominee or bare trustee (i.e., for a person absolutely entitled as against the trustee) are treated as if they are vested in the person for whom the assets are held, i.e. the beneficiary. In such a case, the acts of the nominee or trustee in relation to those assets are treated as the act of the beneficiary.

Trustees

Section 69(1) provides that the trustees of a settlement shall be treated as a single and continuing body of persons, and that body shall be treated as being resident and ordinarily resident in the United Kingdom unless:

a. the general administration of the trust is ordinarily carried on outside the U.K.; and

b. the trustees, or a majority of them, for the time being are not resident or ordinarily resident in the UK.

Note that trustees in that capacity are, by s.286(3), connected with:

a. the settlor;
b. any person who is connected with the settlor; and
c. a body corporate connected with the settlement.

Disposals

With particular respect to settlements, a number of activities are disposals for the purposes of CGT. The discussion that follows examines the instances and CGT consequences of actual and deemed disposals relating to settlements.

Creation of the settlement

A creation of a settlement will usually involve an actual disposal of assets by the settlor. By s.70, a gift into a settlement is also treated as a disposal of the entire property thereby becoming settled property, notwithstanding that the transferor has some interest as a beneficiary under the settlement, and notwithstanding that he is a trustee, or the sole trustee, of the settlement. For these purposes the term "gift" is to be taken according to its ordinary meaning – a voluntary transfer of property to the trustees, without any corresponding consideration from the trustees.[67] However the term "gift in settlement" seems to be related to the beneficial interests created, not to the legal transfer of title. This is also to be taken in accordance with its ordinary meaning.[68] The creation of a settlement will be subject to a market value consideration under s.17 (i.e., the assets will be deemed to have been disposed of for a consideration equal to their market value). If the assets are chargeable, a gain or a loss will result.

Actual disposals by trustees

If trustees sell assets (to unconnected persons) this will attract the normal CGT consequences.

---

[67] See Buckley LJ in *Berry v Warnett (HMIT)* [1980] STC 631 at 644-647 – approved by Lord Roskill in the House of Lords ([1982] STC 396 at 401).
[68] Lord Wilberforce in *Berry v Warnett (HMIT)* [1982] STC 396 at 399.

Exit charge (assets leaving the settlement)

By virtue of s.71(1), where a person becomes absolutely entitled to any settled property as against the trustee, all the assets forming part of the settled property to which he becomes so entitled are deemed to have been disposed of and immediately reacquired by the trustee as a bare trustee (s.60(1)) for a consideration equal to the market value. The implications of this are:

a. there is a charge to CGT imposed on the trustees on the gain accruing on the assets during their period of ownership;

b. the subsequent acts of the trustee in relation to the property are attributed to the beneficiary by s.60(1).

In this respect, the words "absolutely entitled against the trustee" do not presuppose that the beneficiary has to be beneficially entitled to the property. In *Hoare Trustees v Gardner (HMIT)*[69] Brightman J said that if "absolutely entitled" is confined to absolutely entitled in a beneficial sense, then the words "as against the trustee" are meaningless, because they add nothing to the expression. An absolute beneficial owner of property held in trust is absolutely entitled as against the whole world, and not merely as against his trustee: he cannot have absolute beneficial ownership as against some persons and not others. According to Brightman J, the description of a person as being "absolutely entitled as against the trustee" carries the implication that the expression is being used in the sense that that person is not necessarily absolutely entitled as against everyone else. Brightman J gave the following examples:

> If property is held by T, the trustee, in trust for L for life with remainder to R, R, if living at L's death, would then be absolutely entitled to that property as against T. If R were dead, one would think that R's executor would similarly be absolutely entitled to that property as against T, even if the executor is not beneficially entitled. If R's estate is fully administered and there has been an assent in favour of the trustees of R's will, one would think that the trustees of R's will had become absolutely entitled to the property as against T or as against R's executor, as the case might be. If R, in the lifetime of L, assigned his remainder interest to X, on L's death X would become absolutely entitled to the property as against T. The answer should be the same whether X is a person who became beneficially

[69] [1978] STC 89 at 108.

entitled by virtue of the assignment or whether he is the trustee of some new settlement. The absolute entitlement of the propositus as against T, the trustee, would appear to be reasonably clear in those cases as a matter of simple language. There is no particular reason to equate absolute entitlement with beneficial ownership in such cases, but rather with the ability to give a good discharge.[70]

Where a person becomes absolutely entitled on the death of a person entitled to an interest in possession in the settled property, s.73(1) provides that no chargeable gain shall accrue on the disposal. For example, if trust property is held in the following terms: "To A for life, and then to B" - on A's death, B becomes absolutely entitled to the settled property. He takes the assets at their market value on A's death, but no CGT is payable by the trustees.

Note that for the purposes of the exit charge, it is possible for persons acting in their capacity as trustees of a new settlement to become absolutely entitled to assets against themselves as trustees of an existing settlement.[71] With regard to the timing of when a person can be treated as having become absolutely entitled as against the trustee, Blackburne J held in *Figg v Clarke (HMIT)*[72] that, where a person suffered an injury disabling him from having further issue, the impossibility of his having more children should be ignored, and his children became absolutely entitled against the trustees at the date of his death, and not at the date of the injury.

Termination of life interests

By s.72(1), if an interest in possession terminates on the death of the person entitled thereto, and the property continues to be settled property, the trustees are deemed to have disposed of, and immediately reacquired the assets at market value, but no chargeable gain shall accrue on the disposal. The effect of this is to re-base the assets to their market value on the death.

Disposals of interests by beneficiaries

Section 76(1) provides that no chargeable gain arises to a beneficiary where he disposes of an interest under a settlement, provided that he or someone before him did not acquire his interest for a consideration in

---

[70] Ibid.
[71] Hoffman J in *Swires (HMIT) v Renton* [1991] BTC 362 at 371; STC 490.
[72] [1997] BTC 157.

money or money's worth (other than another interest under the settlement).

Timing of Disposals

The timing of a particular disposal depends much on the type of disposal, and on whether or not it is a deemed disposal. Some general principles apply:

Capital sums

Section 22(2) provides that when a capital sum is derived from an asset under s.22(1), the time of the disposal shall be the time when the capital sum was received.

Contracts

Section 28(1) provides, subject to s.22(2) above, that, when an asset is disposed of and acquired under a contract, the time at which the disposal and acquisition is made is the time when the contract is made, and not, if different, the time at which the asset is conveyed or transferred. However, s.28(2) provides that, where the contract is conditional, the time of the disposal/acquisition is the time when that the condition is satisfied.

Hire-purchase transactions

By virtue of s.27, a hire-purchase transaction will treated as an entire disposal of the asset which is the subject matter of the transaction at the beginning of the period for which the hire-purchaser obtains the use and enjoyment of the asset. The section extends to any transaction whereby the use and enjoyment of an asset is passed, but the transfer of the title and consideration is deferred. This provision is illustrated by *Lyon (HMIT) v Pettigrew*.[73] Certain taxis, together with their licences to ply for hire, were sold under contracts providing that the purchase price was payable in instalments spread over 150 weeks. The contracts also provided that the consideration for the licences was to be severed from the consideration for the sale of the taxis, with the property in the taxis passing immediately to the purchaser, and the property in the licences passing when all instalments

---

[73] [1985] STC 369.

had been paid. The taxpayer contended that the contracts were conditional and that the time of disposal was the time when all the instalments are paid. It was held that the contracts were not conditional, that the licences could not be severed from the taxis, and that (what is now) s.27 applied. Thus, the time of the disposal was when the purchaser first obtained the use of the taxis. Walton J said:[74]

> The words "contract is conditional" have traditionally, I think, been used to cover really only two types of case. One is a "subject to contract" contract, where there is really no contract at all anyway, and the other is where all the liabilities under the contract are conditional on a certain event. It would, for example, be possible for a hotelier to make a booking with a tour operator conditionally on the next Olympic Games being held in London. Then, until it had been decided that the next Olympic Games were going to be held in London, there would be no effective contract: the whole contract would be conditional, the whole liabilities and duties between the parties would only arise when the condition was fulfilled. But it is quite clear that the present contract is not in the slightest like that.

With respect to the present contract Walton J said that, if there be only one contract, he could not see how the postponement of the carrying out of one part of one contract until the fulfillment of the consideration by the other party could in any way be properly described as a "condition" of the contract, as distinct from a perfectly ordinary part or term of the contract.

Tax Rates

The normal rate of CGT is equal to the lower rate of income tax for the relevant year (s.4(1)). Where an individual has no income for a year of assessment, or where his total income for the year is less than the starting rate limit, then the individual is chargeable at the starting rate to the extent that the sum of his income and chargeable gains fall within the starting rate limit (s 4(1B)). If an individual is a higher rate tax payer he is charged to CGT at the higher rate (s.4(2)). If the taxpayer is a basic rate tax payer, but his chargeable gains exceed the unused part of his income tax basic rate band, CGT on the excess is charged at the higher rate (s.4(3)).

By virtue of s.5, trustees of discretionary and accumulation trusts are liable to CGT at the rate applicable to trusts for the relevant year.

---

[74] At page 380.

Further Reading

Kerridge R, *Capital Gains Tax - What Next?* [1990] BTR 68.

Bracewell-Milnes B, *The Meade Report and the Taxation of Capital* [1979] BTR 25.

Evans C and Sandford C, *Capital Gains Tax - The Unprincipled Tax?* [1999] BTR No. 5 387.

Hardwick MJ, *Dividend Stripping and Value Shifting* [1999] BTR No. 5 380.

chapter fourteen

Capital Gains Tax
- Disposal Consideration

So far, we have examined three of the four main questions relevant to the capital gains tax charge, namely, what constitutes a chargeable person, what constitutes an asset, and what constitutes a disposal of an asset. The final question concerns what constitutes a chargeable gain. This will involve detailed examination of the principles applicable to the calculation of a chargeable gain or allowable loss. The rest of our discussions on capital gains tax will be devoted to this question. Broadly speaking, a capital gains tax gain or loss is (due allowance being made for all exemptions and reliefs) computed by deducting allowable expenditure on an asset from the consideration received for its disposal. This chapter is concerned with the matters that are taken into account in arriving the at the amount which a person is taken to have received in return for the disposal of an asset.

In general, the value or consideration for a disposal is the actual value or consideration that passed between the disponor and the disponee. There are potential problems here however. First, there are times when no real consideration passes at all. In this type of case the parties would, if left to themselves, be able to manufacture losses or very low profits at will. Secondly, in some cases in which some consideration actually passes, the consideration is either far below the market value of the asset, or much higher than such market value. Furthermore, there are cases in which consideration is given which cannot be valued, e.g., love and affection or friendship. Finally, there are those cases in which there is no disposal in the real world, but which fall within the instances of statutory deemed disposals, and for which a value has to be fixed as the consideration for the disposal.

In cases where real consideration passes in a bargain at arm's length there is no need for statutory intervention. In the other situations outlined above the statute has to intervene to counter the obvious planning opportunities. Thus there are various provisions adjusting the disposal consideration (if any). In some instances, a market value is substituted, and in others the disposal is treated as having been for a no-gain/no-loss consideration.

Market Value

Transactions not at arm's length : section 17

Section 17(1)(a) provides that a person's acquisition or disposal of an asset shall be deemed to be for a consideration equal to the market value of the asset where he acquires or disposes of the asset otherwise than by way of a bargain at arm's length - particularly, where the acquisition or disposal is by way of:

a. a gift;

b. a transfer into a settlement by a settlor;

c. a distribution from a company in respect of its shares.

The typical situations in which this rule will apply concern gifts[1] and transfers at an undervalue. There are however a number of other situations in which it has been applied. In *Davenport (HMIT) v Chilver*[2] for example, Nourse J held that, a right to compensation, conferred by a statutory instrument, on a taxpayer who had nothing beforehand, was an asset acquired by the taxpayer otherwise than by way of a bargain made at arm's length. The right was therefore to be deemed to have been acquired by the taxpayer for a consideration equal to its market value. The argument that, in this case the market value must be the actual amount received, giving rise to neither a gain nor a loss, seemed to appeal to Nourse J, who then suggested[3] that the proper course would be for the Crown to proceed on the footing that there had been neither a gain nor a loss in the value of the taxpayer's right during the material period.[4]

This market value rule was also applied in *Zim Properties Ltd v Procter (HMIT)*[5] where Warner J held that the taxpayer's right to bring an action against its solicitors for negligence was an asset acquired at the time of the solicitors' allegedly negligent act. Such an acquisition was not by way of a bargain at arm's length, and thus the right must be deemed to have been

---

[1]   See e.g., *Turner v Follett (HMIT)* [1973] STC 148 - gifts by the taxpayer to his children were treated as disposals at market value.

[2]   [1983] STC 426.

[3]   At page 442.

[4]   Nourse J said however that, if asked to do, so he would remit the case to the Commissioners to calculate the market value.

[5]   [1985] STC 90.

acquired for a consideration equal to its market value, if any.

Section 17(1)(b) extends this market value rule to situations in which a person acquires or disposes of an asset wholly or partly for a consideration that cannot be valued. The effect of this provision is illustrated by *Fielder (HMIT) v Vedlynn Ltd.*[6] The taxpayer company sold some shares in some of its subsidiaries in return for a sum (which was acknowledged to be the market value of the shares), and some guarantees by the purchaser, that the subsidiaries of the taxpayer into which it was buying would discharge their obligations to the taxpayer. The special commissioner decided that, although the guarantees formed part of the consideration for the sale of the shares, they did not add any monetary value to the sums that had been paid. Harman J, dismissing the Revenue's appeal from the decision of the special commissioner, said:[7]

> The consideration was in part the guarantee by [the purchaser]. It seems to be that ... one would certainly require some prima facie case that the guarantees had a separate monetary value, or were capable of having such value, perhaps because one could find a market in which a comparable guarantee had been sold or some accustomed way of dealing in guarantees so they could be said to be capable of valuation. If that is not so a consideration has passed which cannot be valued and it falls clearly within [s.17(1)(b)]. Therefore one is thrown back on the market value of the assets (the shares). It is agreed that the shares passed at full market value at the cash price. Upon that basis again it seems to me that the special commissioner was entitled to reach the conclusion he did.

Connected persons: section 18

Section 18(2) treats transactions between connected persons as transactions other than by way of a bargain at arm's length. This means that the market value rule of s.17 automatically applies.

Section 286 deals with four situations involving connected persons: individuals, trustees, partners and companies. These are considered below.

1. *Individuals*

By virtue of s.286(2), an individual is connected with:

i. his or her spouse – thus where in divorce proceedings property is

---

[6] [1992] BTC 347.
[7] At page 361.

transferred by a husband to his wife under a consent order, this is to be taken as a disposal by the husband at market value.[8] Note that, although husbands and wives are connected with each other, ss.17 and 18 do not apply to them if they are living together. S.58 instead applies roll over relief, to ensure a "no gain/no loss" situation. On the other hand where the husband and wife are not living together, tax is chargeable;[9]

ii. his/her relatives – a relative is defined in s.286(8) as a brother, sister, ancestor or lineal descendant, and their spouses;

iii. his/her spouse's relatives, and their spouses.

2. Trustees

Section 286(3) provides that a trustee is connected (in his capacity as trustee) with the settlor, anyone connected with the settlor, and with any body corporate connected with the settlement.

3. Partners

Section 286(4) provides that, except for acquisitions and disposals of partnership assets pursuant to *bona fide* commercial arrangements, partners are connected with each other, and with each other's spouses and relatives.

4. Companies

By virtue of s.286(6) a company is connected with another person if it is controlled by that person, either alone, or in conjunction with persons who are connected with him.

Value shifting

This has been discussed in the preceding chapter in our examination of deemed disposals.

Appropriations to and from trading stock

This has also been discussed earlier.

Market value – definition

Section 272(1) provides that "market value", in relation to an asset, means the price which that asset might reasonably be expected to fetch on a sale

---

[8]   *Apsden (HMIT) v Hildesley* [1982] STC 206.
[9]   Ibid.

on the open market. No reduction can be made on this price on the basis of any assumption that the whole of the assets are to be sold at the same time (s.272(2)). It may be that, in some situations in which some consideration had actually been given and in which there is no other evidence as to the market value, the consideration that actually passed will be taken as the best evidence of market value,[10] particularly where the so-called market value is wholly hypothetical.[11]

No Gain/No Loss (Hold and Roll Over Relief)

In a number of situations the statute provides for a disposal or acquisition to be valued at a consideration which will ensure that neither a gain nor a loss accrues to the disponor. In such cases, any gain is either held over or rolled over. Hold over relief applies to gifts of assets, or disposals otherwise than at arm's length, whereas roll over relief applies to replacement of assets. Basically, hold over relief involves the same asset and different taxpayers, whereas roll over relief involves the same taxpayer and different assets. The effect of both reliefs is that the first disposal takes a place so that no gain or no loss accrues. The gain that is held or rolled over becomes taxable on the second disposal. This second disposal will either be one by a different taxpayer of the same asset or one by the same taxpayer of a different asset, depending on which relief applies.

Examples

Pat bought a factory for £50,000. His business expands and he needs larger premises. He sells the factory for £70,000 and buys a new one for £130,000. Ten years later, he sells the new factory for £200,000. This is a case of roll over relief (same taxpayer, different assets) and, ignoring any other reliefs, the position is as follows: the £20,000 gain on the sale of the first factory is rolled over into the acquisition cost of the second factory. This works by reducing the cost of the second factory by the amount of the rolled over gain. The acquisition cost of the second factory is therefore taken to be £110,000. This means that, on the sale of the second factory, the gain is £90,000. The net effect of the relief is therefore to reduce the gain on the sale of the second asset by the amount of the gain rolled over from the sale of the first asset. If Pat wished to, he could roll over this gain into the purchase of a third factory.

---

[10] See Sir John Vinelott in *Whitehouse v Ellam (HMIT)* [1995] BTC 284 at 290.
[11] Sir John Vinelott said in *Whitehouse v Ellam (HMIT)*, ibid - "I do not see how any other method of valuation can possibly have had the result of displacing what was actually received in favour some wholly hypothetical value ...".

Maureen gives half the shares in her personal company to her sister, Kathy. The shares were worth £50,000 when Maureen acquired them, but are now worth £80,000. This is a gift of business assets other than at arm's length (see below). It is a case of hold over relief (same asset, different taxpayers) and, ignoring any other reliefs, the position is as follows: Maureen is treated as having disposed of the shares so that neither a gain nor a loss is made. The gain to be held over is £30,000. Maureen's chargeable gain and Kathy's acquisition cost are each reduced by this amount. If Kathy later disposes of the shares, this will have the effect of increasing her chargeable gain by £30,000.

Details of some of the more important circumstances of disposals at no gain/no loss are given below.

Gifts to charity

Section 257(1) and (2) provide, in respect of gifts to charities (and certain other national bodies listed in Schedule 3 of the Inheritance Tax Act 1984) that, if the disposal is not one to which s 151A(1) applies (venture capital trusts), the disposal and acquisition shall be treated as being for such a consideration as would ensure that neither a gain nor a loss accrues. When the charity later disposes of the asset, the acquisition of the person who made the gift to it is treated as its own acquisition.

Replacement of lost or destroyed assets

Section 23(4) applies if an asset is lost or destroyed, and the insurance compensation received in respect of such loss or destruction is applied for the purpose of replacing the asset within one year of receipt, or such longer period as the inspector may allow. On a claim by the owner, he will be treated as having disposed of the old asset for a consideration which will secure that neither a gain nor a loss accrues to him, and as having acquired the new asset for a consideration reduced by the rolled over gain.

Where a building is destroyed or irreparably damaged, and a capital sum received by way of compensation for the destruction or damage (or under an insurance policy in respect thereof) is wholly or partly applied in constructing or otherwise acquiring a replacement building elsewhere, both the original and the replacement buildings shall, for the purposes of a claim under s.23(4), be treated as distinct assets separate from the land on which they stand, and the old building shall be treated as lost or destroyed (s 23(6)). All necessary apportionments of any consideration or expenditure will be made in such manner as is just and reasonable (s.23(7)).

Replacement of business assets

Section 152(1) provides roll over relief in cases wherein the consideration received for the disposal of assets or of an interest in assets ("the old assets") used solely, throughout the period of ownership, for the purposes of a person's trade, is applied in acquiring other assets or interests in other assets ("the new assets"), which on acquisition are taken into use solely for the purposes of the trade. In such cases, if the trader makes a claim with respect to the consideration which has been so applied, he will be treated as having disposed of the old assets for a no gain/no loss consideration. The acquisition cost of the new assets will then be reduced by the amount by which the actual consideration exceeds the "no gain/no loss" value (the held over gain). These provisions do not affect the treatment of the other parties to the transactions involving the old and the new assets.

Section 152(3) provides that, in order to qualify for the relief, the taxpayer must acquire the news assets — or enter into an unconditional contract to acquire them — during the period beginning twelve months before and ending three years after the disposal of the old assets. The Revenue has a discretion to extend this period.

Where there is a part disposal of a single asset which was acquired for an unapportioned consideration, it cannot be said that the part disposal is a disposal of "old assets", or that the retained part constitutes "new assets", or, that the consideration arising from the part disposal was applied in the acquisition of "other assets".[12] Thus, roll over relief will not apply in such cases. This is because a part disposal of an asset is to be treated as a disposal of the asset, not as a disposal of part of the asset (for example, the grant of a lease of a house is a part disposal of the house but not a disposal of part of the house).[13] However, a part disposal of an asset may involve a disposal of a severable part. Thus, if for example, a taxpayer were to buy from the same vendor two adjacent properties under two separate but contemporaneous contracts, there would be no reason in principle why the sale of one should not be treated as the sale of old assets, and why the retained part should not be treated as new assets for the purposes of s.152.[14] According to Sir John Vinelott in *Watton (HMIT) v Tippett*[15] the description of assets as "old" and "new" is functional and not temporal, and thus, it may be that the result would be the same if the two properties were acquired under the same contract and at a time when they were not physically separated, provided that they could be treated as separate assets and, that

---

[12] Sir John Vinelott in *Watton (HMIT) v Tippett* [1996] BTC 25.
[13] Sir John Vinelott at page 32.
[14] At page 33.
[15] Ibid.

the consideration was apportioned between them at the time of sale.[16] This was upheld by the Court of Appeal, although Peter Gibson LJ did express some reservations about reaching this conclusion:[17]

> I readily see the good sense of a policy allowing the taxpayer trader roll-over relief whatever the sequence of acquisition and disposal, but I cannot disguise my unease at the distortion of the language of s.115(1) with its central condition that the consideration obtained for the disposal of the old assets should be "applied" in acquiring the new assets. If the draftsman only had intended that the consideration on the disposal of the old assets should be matched by the cost of the acquisition of the new assets, he could have said so. However, in the absence of argument from the Crown on the word "applied", I will proceed on the assumption common to both sides that there must merely be a disposal by the taxpayer of old assets and the acquisition by him of new assets.

For the purposes of roll over relief on replacement of business assets, when the proceeds of the sale are used to enhance the value of other assets, concessionary relief is available in ESC D22 which treats the expenditure as expenditure incurred on acquiring new assets, if:

a. the other assets are used only for the purposes of the trade; and

b. on completion of the work on which the expenditure was incurred, the assets are immediately taken into use and used only for the purposes of the trade.

Furthermore, where the trader uses the proceeds from the disposal of the old asset to acquire a further interest in another asset which is already in use for the purposes of the trade, ESC D25 applies to treat that further interest as a "new asset" which is taken into use for the purposes of the trade.

A final concession with respect to this provision is in ESC D16 which provides that, where a person sells a business or a business asset and, for purely commercial reasons, subsequently repurchases the same asset, that asset will be regarded as a new asset.

Section 152(1) stipulates that, in order for this relief to be available, the new asset must be taken into use for the purposes of the taxpayer's business

---

[16] Ibid.
[17] [1997] STC 893.

at the time when it is acquired. This requirement has been applied strictly by the courts. So for example, Knox J held in *Campbell Connelly and Co Ltd v Barnett (HMIT)*[18] that, when a new asset is acquired in January, but is only taken into use for the taxpayer's business in September, the provision is not satisfied. Even if the taxpayer was anxious to take the asset into use immediately on its acquisition, if the taxpayer was in fact unable to do, then its intention is irrelevant. What matters is what actually happened.

The principle that an asset must be taken into use at the time when it is acquired makes the timing of an acquisition very important, especially in respect of disposals under a contract. S.28 provides that where an asset is disposed of and acquired under a contract, the time of the disposal and acquisition is the time when the contract was made, and not, if different, the time when the asset is conveyed or transferred. This would have meant that, in cases where assets were disposed of under contract but the time of delivery was much later than the date of the contract, claims for relief under s.152 would have failed automatically. However Knox J accepted in *Campbell Connelly and Co Ltd v Barnett* that the timing provision in s.28 was not intended to apply here. According to him, there seems to be "enough internal evidence in [s.152] to lead to the conclusion that the acquisitions being aimed at are complete acquisitions, not ones which still lie in contract".[19]

In order to temper the rigours of the requirement that the new asset be taken into use immediately, ESC D24 gives a measure of relief in certain cases in which the new asset is not taken into use immediately, by treating the new asset as having nevertheless qualified for the relief given by s.152. There are a number of conditions before this concession will be available:

i.   the owner proposes to incur capital expenditure for the purposes of enhancing the value of the new asset; and

ii. any work arising from such capital expenditure begins as soon as possible after acquisition, and is completed within a reasonable time; and

iii. on completion of the work the asset is taken into use for the purpose of the trade and for no other purpose; and

iv. the asset is not let or used for any non-trading purpose in the period between acquisition and the time it is taken into use for the purposes of the trade.

The concession extends to cases where a person acquires land with a

---

[18] [1992] BTC 164; STC 316 (upheld by the Court of Appeal, [1994] BTC 12).
[19] ibid at 172.

building on it, or with the intention to construct a building on it. In such cases the land will qualify for relief provided that:

i. the building itself qualifies for relief; and

ii. the land is not let or used for any non-trading purpose in the period between its acquisition and the time that both it and the building are taken into use for the purposes of the trade.

The assets in respect of which a claim is made must be one of those specified in s.155 which lists six Classes of asset. Class 1 is divided into two "Heads" - A and B. Head A covers (subject to restrictions in s.156) any building or part of a building, any permanent or semi-permanent structure in the nature of a building occupied (as well as used) only for the purposes of a person's trade, and any land occupied (as well as used) only for the purposes of the trade. Head B covers fixed plant or machinery which does not form part of a building or of a permanent or semi-permanent structure in the nature of a building. Class 2 concerns ships, aircraft and hovercraft. Class 3 concerns satellites, space stations and spacecraft (including launch vehicles). Class 4 concerns goodwill, Class 5 concerns milk quotas and potato quotas, and Class 6 concerns ewe and suckler cow premium quotas.

Class 1 has attracted some attention in the cases. First, with respect to land, case law indicates that the requirement that the land be occupied and used for the purposes of the trade, is to be taken strictly. This approach is illustrated by *Temperley (HMIT) v Visibell Ltd.*[20] The taxpayer company purchased some land on which it intended to build a factory specially designed for its trade of the forming and printing of plastic guide-cards, and some offices. Planning permission was obtained for the construction, but during negotiations on the commencement of building works, and as a result of observations on visits to the site, it became apparent that the adverse conditions on the site would necessitate considerable expenditure before production could be commenced. A more suitable site was therefore acquired, and the old one was disposed of. The company claimed roll over relief. Relief was denied on the grounds that the old site had not been occupied as well as used for the company's trade. Mere visits to the site, coupled with an intention to build, and an application for planning permission, were not enough, and could not constitute use and occupation for the purposes of the company's trade.

When the land has actually been occupied as well as used for the

---

[20] [1974] STC 64.

purposes of the taxpayer's trade, it is essential that it was used only for those purposes. In *Anderton (HMIT) v Lamb*[21] Goulding J applied a strict interpretation of the phrase "land occupied (as well as used) only for the purposes of the trade" in Head A. He held that buildings occupied partly for use as homes could not qualify for relief because they were not occupied as well as used only for the purposes of the trade.

Secondly, with respect to plant, Nourse J held in *Williams v Evans (HMIT)*[22] that the phrase "fixed plant and machinery" under Head B meant "fixed plant" and "fixed machinery". So when the taxpayer sold earth-moving machines and used the proceeds to buy new earth-moving machines, this transaction was not eligible for roll over relief because the earth-moving machines were not fixed machinery but movable machinery. Thus the gain on the sale of the old machines was chargeable. According to Nourse J:[23]

> ... head B is referring to fixed plant which does not form part of a building etc and to machinery which does not form part of a building etc. On that footing I think it would be unnatural to read "fixed" as qualifying only plant and not machinery as well, because it would be rather strange, if not actually ridiculous, for the provision to contemplate that movable machinery might form part of a building. On the other hand it is perfectly natural for it to contemplate that fixed machinery might form part of a building.

There are a number of statutory restrictions with respect to this relief. By virtue of s.152(5), the section will not apply unless the acquisition of the new asset was made for the purpose of its use in the trade, and not wholly or partly for the purpose of realising a gain from the disposal of the new asset or of an interest in it. Also, if the old assets were not used for the purposes of the trade throughout the period of ownership, s.152(7) requires apportionment of the consideration in order to determine the part which represents use for trade purposes. Only this part will qualify for relief. Finally, "period of ownership" in the section does not include any period before 31 March 1982.[24]

The question of whether the improvements were completed within a reasonable time was considered in *Steibelt (Inspector of Taxes) v Paling.*[25] In this case, the taxpayer had sold his public house in 1986. In 1988, he used some of the proceeds to buy a barge which he intended to convert for use as a wine bar and restaurant. Between 1989 and 1994 he spent an amount in

---

[21]   [1981] STC 43.
[22]   [1982] STC 498.
[23]   At page 503.
[24]   See s.152(9); cf *Richart (HMIT) v Lyon* ([1989] STC 665), in which the Court of Appeal held that "period of ownership" in the predecessor of s.152 included a period before 6th April 1965.
[25]   [1999] STC 594.

excess of the proceeds of sale on converting the barge before starting trading in 1995. The General Commissioners held that the taxpayer was entitled to the relief following ESC D24. The Revenue appealed to the High Court. Sir Richard Scott VC. allowed the appeal for three reasons. Firstly, it was not open to the Commissioners to exercise discretion under s.152(3) to extend the time limit. This discretion was exercisable by the Revenue and, although it was subject to judicial review, the Commissioners could not substitute their own judgment on appeal. Secondly, the Commissioners could not substitute their view for the Revenue's as to whether the requirements of ESC D24 had been complied with. Thirdly, no reasonable body of Commissioners could have reached the conclusion that the work on the barge was begun as soon as possible and was completed within a reasonable time.

Replacement of compulsorily acquired land

Section 247 provides roll over relief in cases of compulsory acquisition of land. The conditions for the relief are specified in s.247(1):

a. land is disposed of by a landowner to an authority exercising or having compulsory powers;

b. the landowner did not take any steps, by advertising or otherwise, to dispose of the land or to make his willingness to dispose of it known to the authority or others; and

c. the consideration for the disposal is applied by the landowner in acquiring other land.

If these conditions are satisfied and the landowner makes a claim, s.247(2) provides, in cases where the whole of the consideration for the old land was applied in acquiring the new land, that he will be treated as having disposed the old land for a no gain/no loss consideration, and having acquired the new land for a consideration reduced by the held over gain. If only a part of the consideration was applied for the purpose of acquiring the new land, then if the part of the consideration which was not so applied is less than the amount of the gain, there will be an apportionment, if the landowner so claims (s.247(3)).

These provisions do not affect the tax treatment of the authority which acquired the old land or the other party to the transaction involving the acquisition of the new land (s.247(4)). There is a further restriction in s.248

which provides that these provisions do not apply to private residences qualifying for the "main residence" relief.

Gifts of business assets

Section 165(1) provides that, if an individual makes a disposal, otherwise than by way of a bargain at arm's length, of certain qualifying assets, then on a claim by both the transferor and transferee, the chargeable gain on the disposal, and the acquisition cost of the transferee, will be reduced by the held over gain. The qualifying assets are described in s.165(2). An asset qualifies if:

a. it is an asset or an interest in an asset, used either for the purposes of a trade, profession or vocation, carried on by the transferor, or his personal company, or a member of a trading group of which the transferor's personal company is the holding company; or

b. the asset consists of shares or securities of a trading company or of the holding company of a trading group, and the shares are unlisted, or the company is the transferor's personal company.

For definitions, s.165(8) refers to definitions contained in Schedule 6, para.1.

a. *Personal Company*, in relation to an individual, means a company in which the individual himself can exercise not less than 5% of the voting rights (Sch. 6 (1)(2)).

b. *Trading company* means any company whose business consists wholly or mainly of the carrying on of a trade or trades (Sch. 6(1)(2)).

c. *Trading group* means a group of companies the business of whose members, taken together, consists wholly or mainly of the carrying on of a trade or trades (Sch. 6(1)(2)).

Husband and wife

Section 58(1) provides that, if in any year in which they are living together, a husband and wife dispose of assets to one another, the transaction will be treated as if the asset was acquired for such consideration as would secure that neither a gain nor a loss would accrue to the disponor. By virtue of s.58(2)(a) this provision does not apply if the asset, before disposal, formed part of the trading stock of the disponor, or if it was acquired as trading stock by the disponee. S.58(2)(b) also excepts any disposal by way of *donatio mortis causa* from the operation of the provision.

Concerning the question when a husband and wife will be taken as living together, s.288(3) stipulates that the matter shall be construed in accordance with s.282 of the ICTA 1988. According to s.282 ICTA 1988, a husband and wife shall be treated as living together unless they are separated under an order of a court of competent jurisdiction, or by deed of separation, or they are in fact separated in such circumstances that the separation is likely to be permanent.

Example

Victor inherited a painting that was valued at £50,000 but which is now valued at £90,000. He gives the painting to his wife, Margaret. She then sells the painting when it is worth £100,000. Margaret is deemed to acquire the painting for £50,000 so that Victor has disposed of it at neither a gain nor a loss. The £40,000 gain is held over until Margaret sells the painting, when she makes a gain of £50,000.

The effect of this arrangement is very similar to hold over relief and it is convenient to consider it here for this reason. However, note that s.58 is not expressed as a relief and does not allow the taxpayers to make an election. In the example above, Victor does not have the option of paying tax on the £40,000 gain when he gives the picture to Margaret, so leaving her only to pay tax on the £10,000. This means that there is no scope for the parties to cream off the annual exemption each year by passing the asset back and forth between them. On the other hand, the arrangement has the advantage of allowing a spouse who has exhausted the annual exemption to give an asset to the other spouse who has not, so allowing spouses to make efficient use of the annual exemption.

Company reorganisations

There are a number of provisions which govern the CGT consequences of company reorganisations. First, s.127 provides that a reorganisation of a company's share capital shall not be treated as involving any disposal of the original shares or any part of it, or as involving any acquisition of the new holding. Rather, the original and new shares, each taken as a single asset, shall be treated as the same asset acquired as the original shares were acquired. Secondly, s.135(1) extends this principle to situations where a company exchanges its shares or debentures for shares or debentures in another company. In such cases s.135(3) provides that s.127 shall apply (with any necessary adaptations) as if the two companies were the same company and the exchange were a reorganisation of its share capital. Thirdly, in cases involving disposals by one member of a group of companies to another member of the group, s.171(1) provides that both members shall be treated, for the purposes of corporation tax on chargeable gains, as if the asset acquired by the disponee were acquired for a consideration of such amount as would secure that neither a gain nor a loss would accrue to the disponor. However, by s.171(3), this provision does not apply to a transaction treated by sections 127 and 135 as not involving a disposal by the disponor company. This means that disposals between members of the same group take place at a "no gain/no loss" consideration except where the disposal involves an exchange of the shares of one company in the group for the shares of another company in the group.

The policies underlying these provisions have been explored in the cases. According to Hoffman J in *Westcott (HMIT) v Woolcombers Ltd*[26], the policy of (what is now) s.171(1) is:

> ... to recognise that in the case of transactions between members of a group of companies, the legal theory that each company is a separate entity does not accord with economic reality. It gives effect to that policy by, broadly speaking, ignoring transactions within the group, computing the gain as the difference between the consideration given when an asset was acquired by the group and the consideration received when it left the group and charging the tax on upon whichever company made the outward disposal.[27]

In the light of s.171(3), this policy seems to have now been abandoned in respect of inter-group share exchanges. While s.171 is aimed at transactions within a group, s.127 and s.135 are directed at the position of a shareholder who is as likely to be a private individual as a company, and the underlying philosophy is to "secure that shareholders in companies which are involved in reorganisations of share capital or which are the subject of amalgamations or takeovers do not incur chargeable gains on disposals over which they have little or no control. Only when they later dispose of the new shares will a chargeable gain arise."[28]

The courts have had the opportunity to examine these provisions. Since s.171(1) no longer applies to group reorganisations, we will examine the cases in the context of sections 127 and 135. In *Westcott   (HMIT) v*

---

[26] [1986] BTC 130 at 138 (approved by Lord Keith in *NAP Holdings UK Ltd v Whittles (HMIT)*).

[27] Compare *NAP Holdings UK Ltd v Whittles (HMIT)* [1994] BTC 450; Lord Keith of Kinkel at page 458, and Lord Jauncey of Tullichettle at page 459.

[28] ibid. Lord Jauncey of Tullichettle at page 459.

Woolcombers Ltd[29] Fox LJ said[30] that the combined effect of these provisions is to impose two fictions. The first is the "no disposal fiction". This is the consequence of the words "... shall not be treated as involving any disposal of the original shares or any acquisition of the new holding ..." He said that those words seem to assume that a share reorganisation or reduction can give rise to a disposal, and the provision is artificially displacing that assumption. The second fiction is the "composite single asset fiction". This is the consequence of the words "... the original shares (taken as a single asset) and the new holdings (taken as a single asset) shall be treated as the same asset acquired as the original shares were acquired". These fictions are however only applicable to a case which is within s.135 "with any necessary adaptations". Fox LJ said[31] that cases to which s.127 apply can be described as the "one company situation". Here, the shareholder starts and finishes with shares in the same company. They may, wholly or in part, be shares of a different nature to those originally held, but he remains a shareholder in the same company. Cases to which s.135 apply can be described as the "two companies situation". Here the shareholder starts with shares in one company and ends with shares in a different company.

According to Fox LJ[32] there is no difficulty in applying the two fictions to the "one company situation". The purpose of s.127 is to exclude any claim for capital gains tax on the reorganisation or reduction of the company's share capital. This is achieved in effect by treating the new shareholding as if it were the original shareholding. However the matter is not so straightforward in the "two companies situation". Some adaptations of the provisions of s.127, which were designed for the one company situation, will be required here. The "composite single asset fiction" cannot be applied fully, and s.135 does not require that the exchange be disregarded. The requirement is that it be treated as a reorganisation. In this respect, Fox LJ noted that shares in the hands of one person cannot be treated as the same asset as other shares in the hands of another person. The position of the company which transfers the original shares is different. The original asset and the new asset cannot be treated as the same asset in the hands of such a transferor.

In order to determine the adaptations necessary for the two companies situation, Fox LJ went on to consider the purpose of s.135. The section is concerned to ensure that where a shareholder in company A exchanges that shareholding for an issue of shares in company B, the shareholder is not taxed on that transaction. The shareholder in company A is treated as continuing to own the same asset, but company B cannot be treated as owning the shares which it has issued in consequence of the exchange. Furthermore, company B has become the owner of the shares in company

---

[29]   [1987] STC 600; 60 TC 575.
[30]   At page 603.
[31]   Ibid.
[32]   At page 604.

A and so the composite single asset fiction cannot operate in relation to company B. If one of the fictions cannot be applied to company B, neither can the other. The position with the fictions is that they are both part of a single hypothesis and go together. The purpose of this hypothesis is to relieve the shareholder in a one company situation, and the transferor in a two companies situation from liability to tax. Thus the proper solution in the two companies situation is to limit the fictions to the tax consequences of the transaction to the owner of the original shares.[33] This decision was approved by the House of Lords in *NAP Holdings UK Ltd v Whittles (HMIT).*[34] Lord Keith of Kinkel said[35]:

> It is plain that [s.127] can apply only to the tax position of a shareholder who as a result of a company reorganisation disposes of his original holding in it and receives in exchange, a new holding in it. It cannot affect the company which is the subject of the reorganisation ... I am of the opinion that [s.135] is likewise intended to affect only the tax position of the shareholder who disposes of his shares in one company in exchange for shares in another company, and not the tax position of that other company.

Partnerships

Section 59(a) provides that, where two or more persons carry on a trade or business in partnership, they are to be charged and assessed on gains accruing on the disposal of partnership assets, separately. The principle extends to Scotland (ibid). By s.59(b), partnership dealings are treated as made by the partners and not by the firm as such. The approach of the revenue to CGT and partnerships is detailed in an important and lengthy statement of practice (D12, of 17 January 1975). Many of the principles discussed below are derived from this statement of practice.

Partnership assets

Each partner is regarded as owning a fractional share of each of the partnership assets and it is this fractional share that the partner disposes of when a partnership asset is sold. Thus when an asset is disposed of by the partnership to an outsider, each of the partners will be treated as having disposed of his fractional share of the asset. The same principle applies in respect of part disposals of partnership assets. In these cases each partner

---

[33] The effect of this decision has subsequently been reversed in part by s.171(3).
[34] [1994] BTC 450 (Lord Lloyd of Berwick dissenting).
[35] At page 458.

will be treated as having made a part disposal of his fractional share.

In computing the gains or losses on the disposal, the consideration received for the disposal is allocated between the partners in the ratio of their shares in asset surpluses at the time of the disposal. In the absence of any surplus sharing provision, regard is had in the first instance to the actual destination of the surplus as shown in the partnership accounts, or to the ordinary profit-sharing ratio. When a new partnership asset is acquired, the expenditure on the acquisition is allocated between the partners in similar fashion at the time of the acquisition.

Dealings between partners

It is important here to note that by s.286(4) partners are connected with:

i.   each other;
ii.   each other's spouses; and
iii.   each other's relatives.

The only exception to this is with respect to "acquisitions or disposals of partnership assets pursuant to bona fide commercial arrangements". Thus, in many instances dealing between partners will be subject to the market value rule in s.17.

Changes in profit sharing ratios

A change in the profit sharing ratios, including one occurring when a partner joins or leaves the firm is a disposal by some partners of a fraction of their interests in partnership assets, and a corresponding acquisition by other partners. More specifically, a partner who reduces or gives up his share in asset surpluses will be treated as disposing of part or the whole of his share in each of the partnership assets, and a partner who increases his share will be treated as making a similar acquisition. Where no adjustment is made through the partnership accounts, the disposal is treated by the Revenue practice statement as being at a consideration equal to the disposing partner's CGT cost, and thus there will be neither a gain nor loss at that point. It results in a reduction of the base cost of the partner whose share is reduced, and an increase for one whose share is increased.

General Notes on Consideration

Deferred payments

There is no discount for deferment of the consideration for the disposal of an asset. S.48 provides that the disposal consideration shall be brought into account without any discount for the   postponement of the right to receive any part of it, and without regard in the first instance to a risk of any part of the consideration being irrecoverable, or to the right to receive any part of the consideration being contingent. However, if any part of the consideration brought into account subsequently proves to be irrecoverable, any necessary adjustment will be made. These provisions have the potential to result in transactions being treated for CGT purposes in a way that departs from economic or commercial reality.[36] One problem is "acceleration" (that something which has not yet been paid is deemed to have been paid). In this respect, Lloyd J said in *Goodbrand (HMIT) v Loffland Bros North Sea Inc*[37]:

> [I]f a disposal is in whole or in part for deferred consideration, that element of business reality is ignored at the outset, and tax is payable on the false assumption that there is no postponement, and on the assumption (which may or may not turn out to be false) that the whole amount is in fact paid. If, however, some part is contingent, and the contingency is not satisfied, or if the debtor defaults on some part of the price, an adjustment is to be made to reflect the non-payment. No adjustment, however, is to be made to counteract the deemed acceleration of the deferred instalments which are in fact paid. This led Lord Wilberforce [in *Marren (HMIT) v Ingles*] to apply the epithet 'draconian' to this provision.

Acceleration produces an "anomaly" – that the consideration deemed to be paid is worth more than its real financial value because of there being no discount for postponement.[38] According to Lloyd J,[39] the phrase "subsequently shown to be irrecoverable ..." covers both the risk of part of the consideration being irrecoverable on the default of the debtor and the possibility that the right to receive part of it may be contingent, and the contingency may not be satisfied. However, the section is only concerned with acceleration (for which there is no discount or adjustment) and, with presuming that all the consideration will be received (for which an adjustment can be allowed if it is not received).[40] Consideration may be shown to be irrecoverable for this purpose, only if, although due, it is not

---

[36]   See generally *Goodbrand (HMIT) v Loffland Bros North Sea Inc* [1997] BTC 100.
[37]   [1997] BTC 100 at page 105.
[38]   Lloyd J at 107.
[39]   [1997] BTC 100 at 107.
[40]   Ibid.

received (presumably because of the default of the debtor), or if the right to receive it is subject to a contingency which, in the event, is not satisfied.[41] Thus, Lloyd J rejected the taxpayer's argument that, where an asset is disposed of for a cash sum payable in foreign currency, and the sterling value of the proceeds when received is less than its value at the time of the disposal, the difference is "irrecoverable", and an adjustment falls to be made under this provision. According to him, the section was not directed at changes in exchange rates or other changes in valuation after the original valuation. The taxpayer had anticipated receiving and did receive the full amount of the original consideration, no part of which became or proved to be irrecoverable – and this was the case regardless of the fact that the depreciation of sterling during the payment period resulted in the amount received at the end being worth less than it was at the beginning.[42]

The Court of Appeal agreed that s.48 did not apply and dismissed the taxpayer's appeal.[43] According to Millett LJ:

> In my judgment, the taxpayer's argument, like the decision of the special commissioners, suffers from two fallacies. First, it treats the tax computation as if it involved an actual conversion of dollars into sterling, whereas what is involved is merely a valuation exercise. Secondly, it assumes that, because the tax computation is carried out by reference to the sterling value of the consideration in money's worth, it is this sterling value and not the consideration itself which has to be brought into account and which may prove to be irrecoverable. Close examination of the section shows that this is not the case.[44]

Relief for instalmental payments

Section 280 gives some relief where consideration is payable instalmentally for more than eighteen months from the disposal. At the option of the person making the disposal, the tax on a chargeable gain accruing on the disposal may be paid by such instalments as the Board may allow, over a period not exceeding eight years, and ending not later than the time when the last of the instalments of the disposal consideration is due.

Options

Following s.144(1), the grant of an option is the disposal of an asset. However, this position is subject to change if the option is exercised.

---

[41] At page 108.
[42] See pages 107-108.
[43] [1998] BTC 297; STC 930.
[44] [1998] BTC at page 301.

Following s.144(3) the exercise of the option does not constitute a disposal of an asset.

If the option is exercised, s.144(2) provides that the consideration for the option is part of the consideration for the sale. In this case, s.144(3) also provides that the acquisition of the option and the transaction entered into by the person exercising his right under the option shall be treated as a single transaction.

Section 144(4) provides that the abandonment of an option shall only constitute the disposal of an asset in three specific cases:

a. the abandonment of a quoted option to subscribe for shares in a company;

b. the abandonment of a traded option or financial option;

c. the abandonment of an option to acquire assets exercisable by a person intending to use them, if acquired, for the purpose of a trade carried on by him.

In all other cases, the abandonment of an option does not constitute the disposal of an asset.

In the case of options, it is important to bear in mind that it is difficult to reach a final tax position until it is known whether or not the option has been exercised.

Example

Peter owns a piece of sought-after development land, which Paul wishes to buy. Paul pays Peter £10,000 for an option to buy the land for £1m within the next month. Paul intends to use this time to raise the capital that he will need to develop the land. At this point, Peter has disposed of an asset – the option – to Paul and has made a chargeable gain of £10,000.

Suppose that Paul exercises the option. The combined effect of s.144, subsections (2) and (3) is that the money Peter receives for the option is taken to be part of the consideration for the land and that Paul's purchase of the option and purchase of the land are taken to be the same transaction. The effect of this is the same as if Paul had bought the land from Peter for £1,010,000.

On the other hand, suppose that Paul cannot raise the capital and so abandons the option.   Peter has made a £10,000 chargeable gain because of s.144(1), but the effect of s.144(4) is that Paul does not have a corresponding allowable loss.

Further Reading

Venables R, *Capital Gains Tax on Gifts - A Critique* [1989] BTR 333.

chapter fifteen

Capital Gains Tax - Acquistion Cost and Allowable Expenditure

The factors discussed in the preceding chapter are taken into account in the determination of the amount of the consideration which a person who has disposed of an asset will be taken to have received in return for the asset. The amount so determined will invariably be gross in the hands of the disponor, and, since the TCGA charges tax only on gains, there will be a need to deduct expenses from the gross receipts. The types of expenditure which can be so deducted are specified in s.38 and are the subject of this chapter.

Acquisition Cost

Expenditure which is deductible as the acquisition cost of an asset is described in s.38(1)(a) as the consideration given wholly and exclusively for the acquisition of the asset. This refers to the amount of the consideration if it is in money, or its value in money's worth, if it is not in money.[1] As far as possible, the matter should be determined according to normal business principles.[2] The acquisition cost will normally be the actual price paid for the asset.[3] Where non-monetary consideration is given, the value of the consideration will normally be the market value except if the transaction was by way of a bargain made at arm's length. In the latter type of case, the value of the non-monetary consideration will be that which was placed on it by the parties, which need not be the market value. This principle is established by *Stanton (HMIT) v Drayton Commercial Investment Ltd.*[4] where assets were acquired at a consideration fixed at nearly £4m, to be satisfied by a share issue (about 2.5m shares at £1.60 each). It was held that, since the transaction was a *bona fide* one made

[1] See Lord Fraser in *Stanton (HMIT) v Drayton Commercial Investment Ltd.*, [1982] STC 585 at 588.
[2] Lord Wilberforce in *Aberdeen Construction Group Ltd v IRC* ([1978] 1 All ER 962 at 966; 52 TC 281 at 296).
[3] See Carnwath J in *Garner (HMIT) v Pounds Shipowners & Shipbreakers Ltd* ([1997] BTC 223 at 230); "... in the case of an arm's length disposal for a monetary consideration such consideration is the starting point for the computation of the gain."
[4] [1982] STC 585.
[5] [1980] STC 578.

at arm's length, the acquisition cost was that fixed by the parties, and not the market value of the shares (£1.25 each on flotation, totalling £3,125,000). It has also been held in *E V Booth (Holdings) Ltd v Buckwell (HMIT)*[5] that where parties to a transaction had, as a result of negotiations between them, provided for a certain consideration for the disposal, they cannot subsequently seek to change it for tax purposes.

In those situations wherein a market value is specified by the Act (e.g., in cases where the transaction is not by way of a bargain at arm's length under s.17(1)), the acquisition cost will be the market value. This will be the case even in the case of an acquisition which is not matched by a corresponding disposal. In *Harrison (HMIT) v Nairn Williamson Ltd*[6] the Court of Appeal held that, in computing the acquisition cost of the taxpayer, the market value rule (in respect of transactions not by way of a bargain at arm's length) applies not only to transactions where there was an acquisition and a disposal (i.e., where the acquisition is the consequence of a disposal), but extends to cases where there was an acquisition by the taxpayer without a corresponding disposal by the person from whom the asset was acquired (as in for example, an original subscription for stocks or shares in a company). According to Buckley LJ,[7] where there are both an acquisition and a disposal, the subsection will apply to both the acquirer and the disponor; where there is only an acquisition it will apply only to the acquirer, there being no disposal to be affected.

By virtue of s.38(1)(a) where an asset was not acquired (e.g., goodwill and paintings) the allowable expenditure will be "any expenditure wholly or exclusively incurred ... in providing the asset". Thus in the case of paintings created by the disponor for example, the costs of the canvas, the brush, the oil paint, etc., used for the painting, will be deductible as part of the acquisition costs.

Incidental Costs of Acquisition

In many cases, the purchase price of an asset will not be the only costs that will have been incurred in acquiring the asset. There are sometimes fees and commissions to be paid, and there may well be sundry petty expenses. The CGT regime recognises the existence of these expenses and attempts to relieve them. In this respect s.38(1)(a) provides for the deductibility of the incidental costs of acquiring an asset. This are defined in s.38(2) as expenditure wholly and exclusively incurred for the purposes of the acquisition, being fees, money paid to a surveyor or valuer, auctioneer or accountant, agent or legal adviser, and costs of transfer or conveyance

---

[6]   [1978] STC 67.
[7]   At page 71.
[8]   [1986] STC 89 at 94.

including stamp duties, together with the advertising costs to find a seller. Apart from the items specifically enumerated in the subsection, the provisions should be wide enough to include items such as fees paid to the Lands Registry.

Enhancement Expenditure

Most people who have held an asset for more than a brief period would as a matter of course have spent money on maintenance, repair, improvements and other similar matters, either for the purpose of maintaining or increasing the value of the asset, or for the purpose of keeping it from being run down. If such expenditure serves to increase the value of the asset beyond what it would have been without the expenditure, this will inevitably lead to a higher profit figure which will be to the benefit of the Revenue. If while so benefiting the Revenue the taxpayer is unable to claim the expenditure as a deduction, the result will be a grossly unfair tax situation. The tax legislation therefore tries to provide relief for people who have incurred expenditure in this way. The relief so provided is not an open invitation to taxpayers to spend money freely on their assets. While all the types of expenditure just mentioned may well be legitimate items of expenditure in the views of asset owners, the CGT legislation is somewhat selective about the ones that will be relieved.

The relieving provision is found in s.38(1)(b) which provides for the deductibility of the expenditure wholly and exclusively incurred in enhancing the value of the asset, which is reflected in the state or nature of the asset at the time of the disposal. With regard to disposals under a contract, even though s.28(1) provides that the "time of disposal" is the time when the contract was entered into, for the purposes of s.38(1)(b) (particularly with regard to the question whether the expenditure is reflected in the state of the asset at the time of disposal) the timing may be more flexible. Nicholls J said in *Chaney v Watkis (HMIT)*[8] that the context in which the phrase "at the time of the disposal" is found in [s.38(1)(b)] compels the conclusion that that phrase does not exclude expenditure which is first reflected in the state or nature of the property after the date of the contract, but before completion.

There are a number of restrictions on the deductibility of an item of expenditure under the heading of enhancement expenditure. First, the expense concerned must not be one which is an ordinary incident of the taxpayer's ownership or usage of the asset. Thus it was held by the Court

[9]   [1977] STC 170.

of Appeal in *Emmerson (HMIT) v Computer Time International Ltd*⁹ that a tenant who incurred expenditure in discharging his obligations under a lease, which obligations were an incident of his title, could not claim the expenditure as enhancement expenditure, or as expenditure for establishing, preserving or defending his title to the lease. Explaining the position, Orr LJ said:[10]

> ... in my judgment the phrase "expenditure wholly and exclusively incurred ... in establishing, preserving or defending his title to, or to a right over, the asset" applies to such matters as evicting a squatter or registering a charge over property, but has no application to the performance of a tenant's obligations under a lease.

Furthermore, the expenditure sought to be deducted must actually have been incurred, i.e., it must reduce taxpayer's estate in some quantitative way. Thus for example, it does not include the estimated cost of the taxpayer's own labour. The principle in point here was examined in *Oram v Johnson*.[11] The taxpayer had bought some property which he improved and enlarged by himself. He decided to deduct as enhancement expenditure the cost of his own labour and skill in improving the property, which he estimated at £1700 on the basis of 1,700 hours' work at £1 per hour. It was held that this sum was not deductible. Walton J explained:[12]

> It seems to me that, although one does in general terms talk about expenditure of time and expenditure of effort, ... where the expenditure is to be a "deduction", the primary matter which is thought of by the legislature in [s.38(1)(b)] is something which is passing out from the person who is making the expenditure. That will most normally and naturally be money, accordingly presenting no problems in calculation; but that will not necessarily be the case. I instance the case (it may be fanciful, but I think it is a possible one and tests the principle) of [the taxpayer employing] a bricklayer to do some casual bricklaying about the premises, the remuneration for the bricklayer being three bottles of whisky at the end of the week. It seems to me that that would be expenditure by the taxpayer, because out of his stock he would have to give something away to the person who was laying the bricks, and I do not think that that would present any real problems of valuation or other difficulty.
>
> But when one comes to his own labour, it does not seem to me that that is really capable of being quantified in this sort of way. It is not

[10]   At page 175.
[11]   [1980] 2 All ER 1.
[12]   At pages 5-6.
[13]   [1986] STC 89.

something which diminishes his stock of anything by any precisely ascertainable amount ... I think that the whole group of words, "expenditure", "expended", "expenses", and so on and so forth, in a revenue context, mean primarily money expenditure, and, secondly, expenditure in money's worth, something which diminishes the total assets of the person making the expenditure ...

Contrast this case with *Chaney v Watkis (HMIT)*[13]. The taxpayer owned a house which his mother-in-law occupied as a protected tenant. He wished to dispose of this property and agreed to pay her a sum (which under the agreed formula amounted to £9,400) in return for her vacating the property. This agreement would have the effect of increasing the value of the property because of vacant possession. Between the time of the agreement and the actual completion of the sale of the property, the taxpayer agreed to provide his mother-in-law with rent-free accommodation for life, in return for her releasing him from the obligation to pay the £9,400. He claimed this sum as an allowable deduction in respect of the sale of the property. The Commissioners held that the sum was not allowable because it had not been paid by the taxpayer. Reversing the Commissioners, Nicholls J said:[14]

> ... what one finds in this case is that the debt of £9,400 was never paid. Instead, the taxpayer agreed with Mrs. Williams that in lieu of paying that sum he would provide her for life with rent-free accommodation... I can see no reason in principle why the obligation thus undertaken by the taxpayer is not capable of being valued in money terms. It is not suggested that because of the domestic nature of the arrangement there was not a genuine, legally binding contract for the provision of the rent-free accommodation. That being so, I would have thought that, equally as if this accommodation arrangement had been made at arm's length with a stranger, a figure, albeit of a very approximate nature, could be placed on this agreement as the measure in lump sum terms of the cost of such an agreement ... The obligation to pay £9,400 was the price of obtaining vacant possession of the property. If payment in cash of that sum for that purpose by the taxpayer would have been expenditure wholly and exclusively incurred on the asset by the taxpayer for the purpose of enhancing its value, so must have been payment by the taxpayer for the like purpose made not in cash but by providing money's worth at his expense, regardless of the precise nature of the benefit provided in lieu of money.

[14] At page 94.
[15] At pages 94-95.

There had however been no evidence before the Commissioners quantifying the amount of the expenditure represented by the financial detriment suffered by the taxpayer in undertaking the obligation to provide rent-free accommodation. In this respect Nicholls J said[15] that if the parties had been at arm's length he might have been attracted to the view that, unless evidence to the contrary were forthcoming, it could and should be assumed that the cost of providing the alternative benefit was of the order of £9,400.   But given the relationship between the parties, considerations other than merely financial ones may have influenced the substitution of one arrangement for the other. Nicholls J therefore remitted the case to the Commissioners to determine the value of the obligation.

The questions (a) what can be regarded as "expenditure" for these purposes, and (b) what is meant by "reflected in the state or nature" of the asset, were faced by the Court of Session in *Aberdeen Construction Group Ltd v IRC*[16] The taxpayer company made loans totalling £500,000 to one of its subsidiaries, Rock Fall, the share capital of which it had acquired at a total cost of £114,024. When the subsidiary's business ran into difficulties, the taxpayer company agreed to sell it for £250,000 on the condition (demanded by the purchaser) that the loan of £500,000 was waived. The taxpayer company thus wrote off the loan in its books. One of the questions that arose was whether the making of the loan, or the waiver of the loan, was expenditure incurred on the assets (i.e., the shares) for the purpose of enhancing the value of the assets. The Court of Session answered the question in the negative.[17]

Lord President Emslie[18] outlined the company's contention in this respect. The taxpayer company took the view that the money laid out by way of the loans was "expenditure" wholly and exclusively incurred "on" the share capital for the purpose of enhancing its value. It argued that the words "state or nature" must be applicable to incorporeal property and are wide enough to include every circumstance which can affect the value of such property. It follows that, on the extinction of the loans the "expenditure" was reflected "in the state or nature" of the shares sold, for they were then shares in a debt-free company and, having been worthless, they had acquired the value for which they were eventually sold. Lord President Emslie was unable to accept these arguments. He said[19] that, although it was permissible to suppose that the extinction of the debt owed by Rock Fall enhanced the value of its shares, to describe the making of the loans, or their waiver, as expenditure within the meaning of the section, was quite unacceptable. The making of the loan created rights and obligations, and the waiver constituted an abandonment of the rights; but

[16]   [1977] STC 302.
[17]   The taxpayer's appeal against the judgment of the Court of Session was allowed on other grounds.
[18]   At page 310.
[19]   At pages 310-311.
[20]   [1971] 1 All ER 785; 46 TC 626.

in neither case was there any kind of expenditure with which the section is concerned. In any event, by no reasonable stretch of the imagination was it possible to classify the making of the loans or their waiver, as expenditure wholly and exclusively incurred "on" the shares, and it was impossible to say that either was reflected in the state or nature of the shares which were sold. The waiver of the loans may well have enhanced their value but what the section is looking for is, as the result of relevant expenditure, an identifiable change for the better in the state or nature of the asset, and this must be a change distinct from the enhancement of value.

Preservation of Title

It is not uncommon for a person's title to an asset to be contested, sometimes leading to litigation, or for a person to have to take some other type of action to protect his or her investment in the asset. With respect to the expenses that would necessarily be incurred in such event, s.38(1)(b) further provides for the deductibility of expenses wholly and exclusively incurred in establishing, preserving or defending title to the asset or to a right over it. This will for example cover situations where a person has had to defend his or her claim to an asset against a person who has challenged the title. It should also cover cases where a property owner has to take action against squatters. Other possible situations can be seen in the case law. In *IRC v Richards' Executors*[20] for example, costs incurred by personal representatives in valuing shares and securities for estate duty were held to be deductible because the main purpose was to obtain probate of the will, which established their title to the assets.

On the other hand, where a residuary legatee under a will paid some money to the executor upon which the executor agreed to transfer property to the legatee, the payment could not be classified as expenditure incurred in establishing, preserving or defending the legatee's title to the property. Rather, it was expenditure incurred in acquiring the title. This is because the residuary legatee did not acquire any legal or equitable interest in the estate on the testatrix's death. The time of the agreement to transfer the property was the time when the legatee acquired any title to the property. Thus the payment could not be deducted under s.38(1)(b) (see *Passant v Jackson (HMIT)*).[21]

Incidental Costs of the Disposal

Just as a person who is about to buy an asset may have to incur some

---

[21] [1986] STC 164. However the payment fell to be taken into account as part of the acquisition cost of the asset.
[22] [1996] BTC 114.

additional costs incidental to the cost of acquiring the asset, a person who is about to dispose of an asset is likely to incur some expenditure on the venture. More likely than not, there will be a need to advertise to find a buyer. There may also be a need to have valuation, and there may be commissions to be paid. S.38(1)(c) provides for the deduction of the incidental costs incurred in the disposal of an asset. Such costs are defined in s.38(2) as expenditure wholly and exclusively incurred for the purposes of the disposal, being fees, commission or remuneration paid for the professional services of any surveyor or valuer, auctioneer, accountant, agent or legal adviser, and the costs of transfer or conveyance, including stamp duty. S.38(2)(b) adds to this list the costs of advertising to find a buyer and costs reasonably incurred in making any valuation or apportionment required for the purposes of the computation of the gain, including expenses reasonably incurred in ascertaining market values where required by the Act. The provisions should cover most of the genuine expenses that fall on a seller of property. However, the phrase "expenses reasonably incurred in ascertaining market value where required by this Act" in s.38(2)(b) does not include the costs of appealing to a Special Commissioner against the Revenue's valuation of an asset. In *Couch (HMIT) v Caton's Administrators*[22], the taxpayers, administrators of the estate of a certain Mr Caton, were deemed to have acquired his holding of 14.02% of the issued share capital of an unquoted company on his death for a consideration equal to their then market value. About 7 months after the death, all the issued shares in the company were sold and the taxpayers received £3,269,173 in respect of Mr Caton's shares. The taxpayers appealed to a Special Commissioner against the Revenue's decision on the market value of the shares on Mr Caton's death. The Commissioner having decided that the costs of that appeal were deductible as expenses reasonably incurred in ascertaining the market value of the shares, the Revenue appealed.

Rimer J, allowing the Revenue's appeal, held that the costs referred to in the relevant part of [s.38(2)(b)] included the costs of the initial valuation carried out by the taxpayer in order to determine the value of the relevant shares "so as to enable him to compute the chargeable gain and to comply with his statutory obligations to make the requisite return".[23] With respect to the taxpayers' argument that the relevant words extended beyond the costs of that initial valuation to the costs in cases involving a negotiated valuation with the Revenue, or, if there is none, to the costs of any appeal in so far as it is concerned with the issue of valuation, Rimer J said:[24]

> I do not, however, regard the costs which a taxpayer may subsequently incur in (a) negotiating (whether successfully or not)

23 At page 141.
24 Ibid.
25 Ibid.

the question of value with the Revenue or (b) pursuing an appeal against an assessment, being an appeal which involves a question of the value of the shares, as being costs "incurred in making [a] valuation" of the shares or as being "expenses ... incurred in ascertaining [their] market value". If the valuer retained to produce the initial valuation were to be asked what he was being paid by the taxpayer to do he could quite properly and naturally reply that he was making a valuation of the shares, or was ascertaining their value. If the solicitors, counsel and expert witnesses retained by the taxpayer for the purposes of an appeal against an assessment were to be asked what they were being paid to do it is in my view most unlikely that they would answer that they were making a valuation of the shares or ascertaining their value. They would not so answer because that is not what they were doing. It is more likely that they would answer that they were together playing their respective roles in presenting to the Special Commissioner the taxpayer's case on the question of value. They would so answer because that is what they were doing.

According to Rimer J, this description of the functions of the lawyers and expert witnesses does not involve a mere playing with words. Rather, it reflects a material and relevant difference between their task and that which is performed by the valuer doing the initial valuation. Rimer J said that, at the appeal stage, the only person who could with any accuracy be described as making the relevant valuation, or as making a relevant ascertainment of the market value of the shares, is the Special Commissioner. Thus, the costs incurred by the taxpayers for the purposes of the appeal were nothing more than costs incurred for the purposes of conducting a tax controversy with the Revenue.[25]

This was later upheld by the Court of Appeal.[26] Morritt LJ cited the judgment of Rimer J with approval. He also pointed out the consequences of the administrators' argument in the case of an unsuccessful appeal against the Revenue's valuation:

To construe the paragraph as the Administrators suggest would be a positive deterrent to reaching a sensible agreement with the Revenue as to the quantum of liability. It would give rise to the absurd position that on an appeal against an assessment which had failed the assessment would nevertheless require reduction to take account of such costs of the unsuccessful appeal as had been reasonably incurred. But as appeals to the High Court, the Court of Appeal and the House

[26] [1997] STC 970.
[27] Ibid.

of Lords lie on points of only the factual question whether the costs had been reasonably incurred would, at each stage, have to be remitted to the Commissioners for their determination. So absurd a result may be avoided by adopting the construction advanced by the revenue.[27]

A final point to note with respect to the incidental costs of disposal concerns some restrictions in s.38, which in subsection (3) establishes a general rule (subject to exceptions in s.40) that no payment of interest will be allowable, and in subsection (4) provides that where there is a deemed disposal and re-acquisition, this does not imply that any expenditure is incurred as incidental to the sale and re-acquisition.

Expenditure not Allowable

Expenditure which does not fall within the broad headings discussed above will not qualify for deduction. However, in cases where an item of expenditure *prima facie* falls within those categories, it may still be disallowed, or have its scope restricted by statute. There are several examples of such types of expenditure. The discussion that follows examines some of them in outline.

Payments of interest

Section 38(3) disallows the deduction of payments of interest, subject to the provisions of s.40, which provides for the deduction of interest payments (charged to capital) by companies in certain circumstances. The conditions imposed by s.40(1) are, that the company should have paid the interest on a loan to finance expenditure on the construction of any building, structure or works, being expenditure allowable under s.38 in computing the company's gains on the disposal of the building, structure or work or the disposal of any asset comprising such building, structure or work. If these conditions are satisfied, then the sums allowable under s.38 will include the interest payment, if such payment is referable to a period or part of a period ending on or before the disposal. This relief is subject to s.40(2) which provides that it shall not apply to interest which is a charge on income.

Revenue expenditure

We have seen in our discussions on income tax that expenditure of a capital nature is not deductible for income tax purposes. The corollary of

---

[28] [1992] BTC 76.

this is that expenditure of an income or revenue nature will not be deductible for capital gains tax purposes. For this purpose s.39(1) provides that there shall be excluded from the sums allowable under s.38, any expenditure which is allowable for the purpose of computing the profits of a trade, profession or vocation, or any other income tax profits or gains, and expenditure which would have been so deductible but for an insufficiency of profits.

Extending this further, s.39(2) disallows expenditure on an asset which, if the asset had been used as part of the fixed capital of a trade, would have been allowable for the purposes of computing the profits or losses of that trade.

Capital allowances: restriction of losses

The general rule is that expenditure is deductible even where capital allowances have been granted. S.41(1) provides that the restrictions in s.39 (above) shall not require the exclusion from the sums allowable as a deduction of any expenditure, simply because it is expenditure in respect of which a capital allowance or renewals allowance is made. This provision applies in cases of disposals which turn in a gain. However, where a loss accrues on a disposal, different considerations apply. This is because s.41(1) also provides that the amount of any losses accruing on the disposal of an asset shall be restricted by reference to capital allowances and renewals allowances.

The main restriction is in s.41(2) which provides that, in computing the amount of a loss accruing on a disposal, there is no allowable deduction in respect of any expenditure on which capital or renewal allowances have been given or may be given.

Expenditure reimbursed out of public money

Section 50 disallows the deduction of any expenditure which is to be met directly or indirectly by the Crown, or any Government, Public or Local authority, in the United Kingdom or elsewhere.

Premiums on insurance policy on an asset

Section 205 provides, without prejudice to s.39, that there shall be excluded from the sums allowable as a deduction in the computation of the gain accruing on the disposal of an asset, any premiums or other payments made under a policy of insurance of the risk of any kind of damage or injury to, or loss or depreciation of, the asset.

Wasting Assets

General principles

The allowable expenditure on the disposal of wasting assets is subject to special rules which are examined in this section. For CGT purposes, a wasting asset is an asset with a predictable life not exceeding 50 years (s.44(1)). Thus for example, a lease for a term of less than 50 years is a wasting asset. The following general rules apply with respect to wasting assets (see s. 44(1)):

a. freehold land is never a wasting asset;

b. plant and machinery are always wasting assets;

c. a life interest in settled property shall not be a wasting asset until the life tenant's predictable life expectation (ascertained from actuarial tables approved by the revenue) is 50 years or less.

Since wasting assets will normally be depreciating assets, it is entirely possible, or even likely, that the sale of a wasting asset that is only a few years old will result in a loss or in a very small profit figure. For this and other reasons special rules apply to the computation of the gains/losses on the disposal of wasting assets. S.46(1) provides that any residual or scrap value of the asset is to be deducted from the acquisition cost, and the resulting sum is written off at a uniform rate over the predictable life of the asset. Enhancement expenditure is similarly written off from the time it first becomes reflected in the state of the asset. This increases the amount of any chargeable gain on the disposal.

The formulae for determining the "wasted" expenditure (i.e., a fraction of what would have been the allowable expenditure, which will now be disallowed) are presented by s.46(2).

With respect to the acquisition cost and the incidental costs of acquisition the formula is:

$$\frac{T\ (1)}{L} \quad x \quad (\text{Expenditure} - \text{Scrap Value})$$

Where:

T (1) = the period from acquisition of the asset to its disposal
L   = the predictable life of the asset at the time of acquisition

Which can be translated into:

$$\frac{\text{Period of ownership}}{\text{Predictable life}} \quad \text{x} \quad (\text{Expenditure} - \text{Scrap Value})$$

Example

Emily bought an asset for £350. It had a predictable life of 40 years. She kept it for 10 years, after which she sold it for £450. Its scrap value was £50.

On a normal calculation, the gain on this disposal would have been:

£450 - £350 = £100

Applying the "wasting asset" rules:

S.46(2) calculation for the "wasted" expenditure:

$$\frac{10}{40} \quad \text{x} \quad (£350 - £50) = £75 \text{ ("wasted expenditure")}$$

The gain on the disposal will be:

Disposal consideration	£450
deduct	
Allowable expenditure:	
Acquisition cost	£350
less	
Wasted expenditure	£ 75
	————
Gain	£175

Short leases of land

A lease with an unexpired term of 50 years or less is, in general, a wasting asset (Sch.8 para 1(1)). This is so even if there exists the possibility of the lease being extended under statute, as is shown by *Lewis (Executor of F H Lewis) v Walters (HMIT)*[28]. The taxpayer's lease had 16 years left to run, and when the leasehold interest was disposed of, the Revenue assessed him to capital gains tax on the basis that the lease was a wasting asset. The Leasehold Reform Act 1967 gave tenants the right to extend their lease for a further term of 50 years by notice given to the landlord. Furthermore Sch. 3 para 8(5) of the CGTA 1979 (Sch. 8 para 8(5) TCGA 1992) provided that, where the terms of the lease include provision for the extension of the lease beyond a given date by notice given by the tenant, the paragraph will apply as if the term of the lease extended for as long as it could be extended by the tenant, but subject to any right of the landlord to determine the lease by notice. The taxpayer argued that, on the basis of these provisions, the overall result was that the at the date of disposal the duration of the lease for capital gains tax purposes was not 16 years but 66 years, i.e., the unexpired term of 16 years plus the extension of 50 years under the Leasehold Reform Act 1967. Thus the lease was not a wasting asset because it had a predictable life exceeding 50 years. Rejecting the taxpayer's contentions, Mummery J said[29] that the relevant provisions, read in their ordinary and natural sense, require that the provision for the extension of the lease should be included among the "terms of the lease". The provision for extension relied on by the taxpayer was not in "the terms of the lease". Rather, it was in the Leasehold Reform Act 1967. This term was not implied into the lease by that statute. According to Mummery J,[30] even if the statutory right were to be regarded as a "term of

[28]   [1992] BTC 76
[29]   At page 81.
[30]   At page 82.

the lease" it would not constitute a provision "for the extension of the lease beyond a given date". Close examination of the Leasehold Reform Act reveals that what is envisaged is a new tenancy for a term expiring 50 years after the term date of the existing tenancy. Thus, the new tenancy would not be an "extension of the lease" within the meaning of the provision.

With respect to new tenancies, an Extra-Statutory Concession has been made by an Inland Revenue Press Release of 17 October 1991. This is to the effect that the surrender of a lease before its expiry and the grant of a new lease for a longer term will not be regarded as a disposal or a part disposal of the old lease where all of the following conditions are met:

i.   the transaction is between unconnected parties bargaining at arm's length;

ii. the transaction is not part of or connected with a larger scheme or series of transactions;

iii. a capital sum is not received by the lessee;

iv. the extent of the property in which the lessee has an interest under the new lease does not differ in any way from that to which the old lease related;

v.   the terms of the new lease (other than its duration and the amount of rent payable) do not differ from those of the old lease.

As wasting assets, leases have a special regime. Allowable expenditure for CGT purposes is treated as wasting away over the length of the lease, in accordance with a table contained in Sch. 8 para 1.

Further Reading

Stopforth D, *Events Affecting the Deduction of Trading Losses from Capital Gains* [1992] BTR 384.

Burgess R, *The Capital Gains Tax Expenditure Rules* [1978] BTR 291.

chapter sixteen

Capital Gains Tax
Exemptions and Reliefs

In addition to the issues already discussed there are some further factors which have to be taken into consideration in the computation of the amount on which capital gains tax is charged. In some cases the disposal consideration and/or allowable expenditure fall be apportioned. In other cases there are further deductions which do not fall strictly within the description of allowable expenditure, and finally there are sundry exemptions and reliefs which may be available to the taxpayer. This chapter examines some of the available deductions, exemptions and reliefs.

Losses

Introduction

One of the most important reliefs relates to losses. S.2(2) provides that capital gains tax shall be charged on the total amount of the chargeable gains accruing to a person in the year of assessment, after deducting:

a. any allowable losses accruing to that person in that year of assessment; and

b. unused allowable losses of the previous years.

Capital gains tax losses are generally computed in the same way as gains (s.16(1)), and, except as otherwise expressly provided, all the provisions of the Act which distinguish between chargeable and non-chargeable gains shall also apply to distinguish losses which are allowable from those which are not (s.16(2)). References to an allowable loss are to be so construed.

Loss relief: general

The scope of allowable losses is restricted by s.16. S.16(3) provides that a loss which accrues to a person who is neither resident nor ordinarily resident in the United Kingdom shall not be an allowable loss unless the person would have been chargeable under s.10 (gains made on the disposal of assets used for branch or agency within the United Kingdom) if there had been a gain instead of a loss on the relevant occasion. Furthermore s.16(4) disallows losses incurred by persons who are not domiciled in the United Kingdom, on the disposal of foreign assets. Finally, in order to claim loss relief, the taxpayer must give notice to "an officer of the Board", quantifying the amount of the loss (s 16(2A)).

As seen above, past losses which have not been relieved can be set against current gains (s.2(2)). Current losses cannot be carried backward to set against gains of earlier years (s.2(3)), except on death (s.2(3) & s.62(2)). If a loss occurs on a disposal to a connected person, s.18(3) provides that it will only be deductible from chargeable gains accruing on a disposal to the same person, made at a time when they are connected persons. Exception is made for gifts made into settlements for education, cultural or recreational purposes, for the benefit of persons all, or most of whom are not connected persons.

Loss relief on death

By s.62(2) allowable losses sustained by the deceased in the year of death will first be deducted from chargeable gains accruing in that year, and any excess can be carried back to set off against gains of the three years of assessment preceding the year of death, taking later years before earlier years.

Annual Exemptions

As is the case with the Income Tax Acts, the TCGA allows some chargeable persons a certain amount of tax-free gains every year. This amount varies with the type of chargeable person.

Individuals

Section 3(1) provides that an individual shall not be chargeable to capital gains tax in the respect of so much of his taxable amount for any year of assessment as does not exceed the exempt amount for that year. S.3(2) fixes the annual exempt amount, which varies from year to year (for example, for 2001–02, it was fixed at £7,500 and, for 2002–03, it was fixed at £7,700). By s.3(3), this amount is index-linked. S.3(5) provides that an individual's taxable amount is the amount on which he is assessed under s.2(2), but where the chargeable gains less allowable losses accruing to an individual in a year are less than the exempt amount for that year, no deduction shall be made for that year in respect of losses carried forward from past years.

Personal representatives

Personal representatives have the same annual exemption as an individual in the tax year of the deceased's death and the next two tax years after death (s.3(7)). Thereafter, they have no more annual exemptions.

Trustees

Schedule 1 para. 2(1) and (2) provide that trustees are entitled to half the annual exemption of an individual. If the trust is for a mentally or physically disabled person, Sch. 1 para. 1 provides that the same annual exemption as that of an individual will be available. Where a settlor has created more than one settlement, the annual exemption is either 10% of an individual's exempt amount, or 50% of the individual's exempt amount, divided by the number of settlements, if this would yield a higher figure (Sch 1. para 2(4)).

Indexation Allowance

Introduction

The indexation allowance was introduced by the Finance Act of 1982 to give relief for the effects of the high rates of inflation witnessed in the late

1970s, thereby preventing the taxation of paper gains (i.e., "gains" which were only attributable to the effects of inflation, as opposed to "real" gains).

The relevant legislation is contained in ss.53 - 56 and s.109 TCGA 1992. The system works by linking items of relevant allowable expenditure to rises in the retail prices index (RPI). The allowance is deducted from the unindexed gain or loss (i.e., the gain/loss computed on normal principles). For these purposes "relevant allowable expenditure" means the sums which are deductible by S.38(1)(a) (see s.53(2)). These are, the acquisition costs (including incidental costs of acquisition), enhancement expenditure, and expenditure on preservation of title. The incidental costs of the disposal are not indexed.

Section 53(1A)[1] provides that indexation allowance in respect of changes in the RPT for months after April 1998 shall only be allowed for the purposes of corporation tax. Therefore, for individuals, trustees and personal representatives, indexation ceases to apply after this date. The new taper relief, discussed below, applies to gains after that date.

With respect to assets owned by a person on 31 March 1982, the indexation allowance works by deeming that the asset was disposed of, and immediately reacquired, on that date, at its market value on that date (s.55(1)). This means that, the base cost of an asset which was acquired before 31 March 1982 is, for the purposes of the indexation allowance, taken to be its market value on that date. Where however, the indexation allowance would otherwise be higher (e.g., if there was a fall in the value of the asset between the date of its acquisition and 31 March 1982), then, unless the taxpayer has made an election under s.35(5), the deemed disposal of s.55(1) will not apply (see s.55(2)). The purpose of this exception is to ensure that the taxpayer is not unduly prejudiced by the re-basing provisions of s.55(1).

Calculation

In order to calculate the indexation allowance, the RPI for the month in which expenditure was incurred is compared with that of the month of disposal of the asset. The indexed rise for each item is ascertained separately, and then aggregated to get the total indexation allowance (S.54). The formula to be applied for determining the indexed rise of each item (S.54(1)) is:

$$\frac{RD - RI}{RI} \quad x \quad \text{allowable expenditure}$$

[1] Inserted by s.122(1) FA 1998.

Where:

RD = RPI for the month of disposal

RI = RPI for month of incurring the expenditure or the RPI for March 1982, whichever is the later.

Where the RPI of the month of expenditure exceeds, or is equal to, the RPI for the month of disposal, the indexed rise is nil (S.54(2)(b)). This is because this situation will only occur in cases of zero inflation, or where prices are falling. The indexed rise has to be expressed as a decimal figure, and is rounded to the nearest three decimal places (S.54 (3)).

Application

The indexation allowance is applied by setting it against the unindexed gain. This is the gain calculated on normal CGT principles prior to deduction of the indexation allowance. The provisions for indexation do not apply to a disposal on which a loss accrues (s 53(2A)), thus the indexation allowance cannot be used to increase the amount of a loss. By virtue of s 53(1) the indexation allowance can be used to reduce the amount of a gain which accrues on a disposal, and, if the indexation allowance exceeds or equals the unindexed gain, then the gain is extinguished, and the disposal is taken to be one which, after taking account of the indexation allowance, neither a gain nor a loss accrues.

Example

Melina bought some property in January 1988, for £100,000. She sold it in January 1997 for £250,000. The RPI for January 1988 was 300 and the RPI for January 1997 was 360. She has already used up her annual exemption.

The unindexed gain on this transaction will be:

£250,000 - £100,000 = £150,000

(b) The indexation fraction will be:

$$\frac{RD\ (360)\ -\ RI\ (300)}{RI\ (300)} = 0.2$$

(c) The indexation allowance will be:

0.2 x £150,000 = £30,000

(d) The indexed gain will be:

£150,000 - £30,000 = £120,000

Apportionments

Introduction

In some situations the TCGA grants exemptions and reliefs in the form of an apportionment of the gains made on the disposal of an asset. We will examine two main reliefs given in this way. The first is in respect of assets held on 6 April 1965 (which relief is now largely obsolescent) and the second is in respect of assets held on 31 March 1982.

Assets held on 6 April 1965

CGT is charged only on gains accruing after the 6 April 1965 (Sch. 2 Para. 16(2)). Thus where an asset was acquired before that date, the gross gain on the disposal would fall to be apportioned, and only that part which is referable to the period after 6 April 1965 will be liable to tax. In such cases, Sch.2 para. 16(3) indicates that the gain will be presumed to have grown at a uniform rate, from nothing at the date of acquisition, to its full amount at the date of disposal.[2] The chargeable gain is then calculated by applying the following fraction to the gross gain:

$$\frac{T}{P + T}$$

Where:

T = period between 6th April 1965 and the date of disposal

P = period from acquisition to 6th April 1965

---

[2] By Sch. 2 para 16(6) the gain is deemed to grow from a period not earlier than 6 April 1945.

This translates to the following formula:

$$\text{Gross Gain} \quad x \quad \frac{\text{Period of ownership since 6 April 1965}}{\text{Total period of ownership}}$$

The figure that is arrived at is the chargeable gain.

Example

Sean bought some property in 1960 at a cost of £20,000. He sold this property in 1975 for £60,000. The gross gain on this disposal (assuming all other allowances had been used up) would have been be £40,000. The taxable fraction would, applying the rule under discussion, be:

$$£40,000 \quad x \quad \frac{10}{15} \quad = \quad £26,666$$

The indexation allowance in these cases is to be deducted from the gross gains accruing throughout the whole period of ownership, and not just from the gains accruing since 6 April 1965. Thus, the time-apportionment formula is to be applied to the gain after the indexation allowance is used, making the allowance less valuable – i.e, the indexed gain is the gain that has to be apportioned.[3]

Election for 6 April 1965 value

Sch. 2 para, 17(1), permits the taxpayer to make an election for the value of the asset on 6th April 1965 to be used, instead of the time apportionment formula. If the election is made it applies for all purposes both in relation to the taxpayer and other persons. It is irrevocable (Sch.2 para. 17(4)) and it is given effect by treating the taxpayer as having disposed of and immediately reacquired the asset at its market value on 6 April 1965. This means that the base cost of the asset is now its market value on 6 April 1965, extinguishing all accrued gains on that date. There are restrictions in this respect. The election may not be used to increase a loss, or to convert a gain into a loss. In such circumstances a no gain/no loss

---

[3] See *Smith v Schofield*[1993] BTC 147 (House of Lords, reversing the Court of Appeal).

figure is used (Sch.2 para. 17(2)). However, this no gain/no loss rule will not apply unless the election for the 6 April 1965 value has been made in the first instance. If no such election has been made, the time apportionment rule will still apply, even if the conditions of para. 17(2) are satisfied.[4] Note that the election may be used to reduce or increase a gain and to reduce a loss.

The 6 April 1965 value also becomes the base value of the asset in another case, this time, automatically. Sch. 2 para. 9 (1) and (2) provide for a deemed disposal and re-acquisition at the market value on 6th April 1965 if the consideration for the disposal of an interest in land situated in the United Kingdom, and held on 6 April 1965, exceeds the current value of the asset at the time of disposal (i.e., if the disposal consideration reflected development value). The market value of the land at the date of disposal will fall to be assessed partly on the footing that no material development (defined as "the making of any change in the state, nature, or use of the land"[5]) is permissible or will ever be permissible.[6] In this case, development value includes "hope value", i.e., an increase in the disposal consideration, based on the hope that development permission would be forthcoming.[7]

Assets held on 31 March 1982 (including assets held on 6 April 1965)

The general rule

The Finance Act 1988 introduced new rules applying to disposals which take place on or after 6 April 1988. Relief is given for pre-1982 inflation by re-basing assets held on 31 March 1982 to their market value on that date. S.35 treats the owner as having disposed of the asset, and as having immediately re-acquired it at its market value on 31 March 1982 (see s.35(2)). The effect of this is to extinguish any pre-March 1982 gain. Thus where the asset was acquired before 1965 and was disposed of after 6 April 1988, the 1965 rules (discussed above) will generally be redundant.

Exceptions to the general rule

Although the deemed disposal and reacquisition at 31 March 1982 values will normally be automatic, there are statutory exceptions which may prevent such a deemed disposal in specific cases. By virtue of s.35(3) the re-basing will not apply where:

---

[4] See *Whitaker v Cameron* (HMIT) [1982] STC 665.
[5] Sch. 2 para 13(1).
[6] See Scott J in *Morgan (HMIT) v Gibson* [1989] BTC 272 at 279; STC 568.
[7] See *Morgan (HMIT) v Gibson*, supra.

a. it would increase the amount of a gain or convert a loss into a gain (i.e. the taxpayer should not be unduly prejudiced by re-basing);

b. it would increase the amount of a loss or convert a gain into a loss (i.e. the taxpayer cannot unjustly benefit from re-basing);

c. a no gain/no loss situation would apply on the facts, under the 1965 rules, or under some other specified statutory provisions.

Where the effect of the re-basing would be to substitute a loss for a gain or a gain for a loss, and the re-basing provisions are excluded by s 35(3), then the disposal will be taken to have been made for such consideration as will secure that neither a gain nor a accrues (s.35(4)). Thus the 1988 rules will normally be used only for the purposes of reducing the amount of a loss or reducing the amount of a gain.

Example

Ewing bought a house in 1977 for £100,000. The house is not his main residence. On 31 March 1982 the house was worth £180,000. He sold the house in 1997 for £165,000.

Applying normal principles (assuming that the indexation factor is nil, because of deflationary trends), the sale in 1997 would have resulted in a gain of £65,000.

If house were re-based to the value on 31 March 1982, £180,000 would become the base cost, and there would be a loss of £15,000. This would then be a case in which the re-basing would have the effect of converting a gain of £65,000 into a loss of £15,000. It would fall within the exceptions mentioned in (b) above, and thus the re-basing to the 31 March 1982 value will not apply here.

Instead, s.35(4) will apply to deem the house to have been sold for a no gain/no loss consideration.

Election for 31 March 1982 value

The exceptions to the re-basing rules listed above show the need for taxpayers to keep pre-1982 records. They also show the complexity of tax calculations which would have to be made on alternative bases in order to determine whether the exceptions apply. However, s.35(5) enables a person to make an election for the operation of the exceptions in s.35(3) to be displaced. This means that the relevant asset will just simply be re-based to 31 March 1982 values without any consideration of the likely capital gains tax consequences. By s.35(6) the election must be made before 6 April 1990, or within certain specified periods from the "first relevant disposal" (i.e. a disposal to which s.35 applies). Once made the election is irrevocable.

Other Exemptions and Reliefs

In addition to the reliefs already discussed, there are a number of other sundry exemptions and reliefs in the CGT legislation, in respect of gains which would otherwise have been fully chargeable. Some of the reliefs operate to remove the tax burden completely, while some others are, in effect, partial reliefs. Some of the so-called exemptions are in fact nothing more than measures to ensure that loss relief will not be available in respect of certain transactions which are almost always likely to result in a loss. The discussion that follows examines some of these exemptions and reliefs. Most of them will be discussed in outline only, but a number of them are, because of their relative importance, discussed in greater depth.

Debts

The general rule in S.251(2) is that the satisfaction of a debt is a disposal of the debt at the time when the debt is satisfied. However, S.251(1) provides that no chargeable gain shall accrue on a disposal of a debt, except in the case of a debt on a security. The policy underlying s.251(1) was explained by Templeman LJ in *WT Ramsay Ltd v IRC*[8]:

> An original creditor who lends money repayable by the debtor at any time or on demand by the creditor can never make a capital gain because in the hands of the original creditor the debt can never be worth more than the sum advanced. Such a creditor can, however, make a loss, particularly if the debtor becomes insolvent. The creditor may never recover the whole of the debt or may be forced to sell or may choose to sell the debt for less than the sum advanced. Since capital gains tax is calculated on the amount by which annual chargeable gains exceed chargeable losses it would be illogical to include, in the ambit of tax, assets the disposition of which can result only in a loss and never in a gain. A loan to a corporation may also take the form of a debt in respect of which the original creditor can sustain a loss but cannot earn a capital gain. One example is a bank overdraft repayable on demand. On the other hand there are certain types of loan to a corporation, whether protected by a charge on property or not, which constitute forms of investment and which are

---

[8] (1979) 54 TC 101 at 131.

capable of being realised by the original creditor at any time either at a profit or at a loss depending on the circumstances at the time of disposal ... In order to constitute a coherent system of capital gains taxation it was therefore necessary to exclude the effect of dispositions of debts by owners where the dispositions cannot give rise to a gain but to include dispositions of debts in the form of investments which may result in gains or losses in the same way as dispositions of other investments.

The provision that no chargeable gain accrues on the disposal of a debt relates to the original creditor. It does not affect the original creditor's assignee for value, and an assigned debt is an ordinary asset which is therefore chargeable. According to Templeman LJ in *WT Ramsay Ltd v IRC*[9], even though, for example, the original creditor cannot make a gain on a simple debt, if he assigns the debt for an amount which is lower than the amount of the debt, the assignee will make a gain if he recovers more than the amount for which the debt was assigned to him, or, if he assigns the debt for more than that amount. He would however make a loss if he recovers less than that amount. In the case of an assigned debt, there is no allowable loss if the assignee is connected to the original creditor (S. 251(4)).

The term "debt on a security" is pertinent, but it is not defined in the Act. There is a statutory definition of "security" but no definition of "debt". It has been held however, that a mere contingent liability which may never ripen into a present debt, is not a "debt".[10] The term "security" is defined in s.132(3)(b) by way of inclusion – it includes any loan stock or similar security, of the United Kingdom or foreign government, or of any public or local authority in the United Kingdom or elsewhere, or of any company, and whether secured or unsecured. The context of this definition is the conversion of securities held, in the typical case, as an investment, although this context may not by itself be a reliable guide.[11] The term "security" is itself imprecise and takes its colour from its setting (in this case, investments). The word should not be approached with any preconceptions as to its primary meaning.[12]

In the absence of a statutory definition of "debt on a security", the courts have endeavoured to provide answers to the determination of the distinction between an ordinary debt, and a debt on a security – a question which, according to Lord Wilberforce in *WT Ramsay v IRC*[13], "many learned judges" have found "baffling". Lord Wilberforce said in *WT Ramsay v IRC*[14] that, the legislature seemed to be endeavouring to distinguish

---

[9]   54 TC at 132.
[10]   *Marson (HMIT) v Marriage* [1980]STC 177 (House of Lords).
[11]   Robert Walker J in *Taylor Clark International Ltd v Lewis* (HMIT) [1997] BTC 200 at 209.
[12]   Ibid.
[13]   54 TC 101 at 189.
[14]   Ibid.

between mere debts, which normally (although there were exceptions) did not increase but might decrease in value, on the one hand, and debts with added characteristics which might enable them to be realised or dealt with at a profit, on the other hand.

In *IRC v Cleveley's Investment Trust Co.*[15] Lord Cameron said that "debt on a security" is not a synonym for a secured debt. Lord Migdale provided a more detailed explanation:[16]

> The word "security" has two meanings. It may refer to some property deposited or made over or some obligation entered into by or on behalf of a person in order to secure his fulfilment of an obligation he has undertaken. Or it may refer to a document held by a creditor as evidence or a guarantee of his right to repayment ... I think that the words "the debt on a security" refer to an obligation to pay or repay embodied in a share or stock certificate issued by a government, local authority or company, which is evidence of the ownership of the share or stock and so of the right to receive payment. This reading of this section enables me to give some effect to the words "and whether secured or unsecured". If I take the words "security" and "secured" as meaning the same thing, these last words "and whether secured or unsecured" have no meaning at all. "The debt on a security" means debt evidenced in a document as a security.

What this means is that unsecured debts may be included within the term "debt on a security". This view is reinforced by *Aberdeen Construction Group Ltd v IRC*[17] which involved unsecured loans from the taxpayer company to a subsidiary, which loans were not acknowledged in any document or certificate. Lord Wilberforce said[18] that the use of the words "whether secured or unsecured" in the definition of "security" means that "debt on a security" must include some unsecured debts (repeating Lord Cameron's words that the phrase is not a synonym for a secured debt). But which types of unsecured debt will be included? According to Lord Wilberforce, the only basis on which a distinction can be drawn is between a pure unsecured debt as between the original borrower and lender on the one hand, and a debt (which may be unsecured) which has, if not a marketable character, at least such characteristics as enable it to be dealt in[19], and if necessary, converted into shares or other securities. When this case was in the Court of Session, the Lord President (Lord Emslie) had said[20] that, in order to have a debt on a security one must have "a security" on which

---

[15] (1971) 47 TC 300.
[16] At page 315.
[17] [1980] STC 127.
[18] At page 133.
[19] In *Taylor Clark International Ltd v Lewis* (HMIT) ([1997] BTC at 219) Robert Walker J said that this distinction could not have been intended as a statement of two categories which between them comprehensively covered the whole ground.
[20] [1977] STC 302 at 309.

there is a debt. Referring to the statutory definition of security, he had concluded that, on a proper construction of the subsection, what is in contemplation is the issue of a document or certificate by the debtor institution, which would represent a marketable security as that expression is commonly understood, the nature and character of which would remain constant in all transmissions. However, in *WT Ramsay v IRC*[21] Lord Wilberforce said that documentary evidence is not a necessary condition, saying:

> I am not convinced that a debt, to qualify as a debt on a security, must necessarily be constituted or evidenced by a document. The existence of a document may be an indicative factor, but absence of one is not fatal.

He also doubted[22], on reflection, the usefulness of a test (propounded by him in *Aberdeen Construction Group Ltd v IRC*) enabling the debt to be converted into shares or other securities.

The most recent guidance on this point was given by the Court of Appeal in *Taylor Clark International Ltd v Lewis (Inspector of Taxes)*.[23] In this case, the taxpayer tried to argue that a secured debt was a debt on a security, since he wanted the loss that he had made on the debt to be allowable. The taxpayer's appeal was dismissed. According to Peter Gibson LJ:

> I agree with the submissions of Mr Henderson QC for the Crown that while the existence of proprietary security for a debt should increase the original lender's chances of avoiding a loss, that security does not of itself turn the loan into an asset which is in principle capable of being disposed of at a profit. As he said, Parliament could not have intended that the existence of any security, however inadequate, for any debt, however impermanent, should without more turn the debt into a debt on a security.[24]

From these *dicta*, this much is clear. A "debt on a security" is not necessarily the same thing as a secured debt; it is possible to have unsecured debts which are classed as debts on a security and secured debts which are not. That the debt is evidenced in a document is "indicative" of it being a debt on a security – however, the absence of a document is not fatal. Thus, it seems that the phrase "debt on a security" refers either to debts which are evidenced in a document which constitutes a marketable security, or, which are marketable in character, or, which possess characteristics that enable them to be dealt in.

[21]   54 TC at page 190.
[22]   Ibid.
[23]   [1998] STC 1259.
[24]   Ibid.

Sterling

Section 21(1)(b) provides that sterling is not an asset for CGT purposes. This means that no chargeable gain accrues on the disposal of sterling.

Foreign currency for personal expenditure

A gain accruing on the disposal (e.g., by reconversion into sterling) by an individual of foreign currency acquired for personal expenditure abroad for himself or family, is not chargeable (s.269).

Wasting chattels

Section 45(1) provides that no chargeable gain shall accrue on the disposal of an asset which is tangible movable property and which is a wasting asset. Because of restrictions in s.45(2)(a), this exemption will not apply to cases in which the asset has been used throughout the period of ownership solely for the purposes of the trade, profession or vocation of the person disposing of it, and that person has claimed or could have claimed any capital allowance in respect of the costs of acquiring or enhancing the value of the asset.

Section 45(2)(b) contains a further restriction, in cases where the person making the disposal has incurred any expenditure on the asset which has qualified in full for any capital allowance. This restriction was considered in *Burman (HMIT) v Westminster Press Ltd.*[25] The taxpayer company purchased a printing press and obtained capital allowances in respect of the instalments of the purchase price which it had paid. Five years after its acquisition, the press was sold, never having been brought into use in the company's trade. Because of this, the capital allowances previously obtained were withdrawn retrospectively. A gain was realised on the sale of the press and the revenue sought to tax it. The Revenue rejected the company's claim that the gain was exempt under s.45(1) on the basis that the exemption was negatived by s.45(2)(b), because the asset had qualified in full for capital allowances. The company contended that all the conditions leading to the making of a capital allowance had to be continued to be satisfied at the time of the disposal in question, while the revenue claimed that they only had to be satisfied at some point in time. Knox J upheld the company's argument. According to Knox J, not only the asset, but also the expenditure on it has to qualify for capital allowances, and the conditions must continue to be fulfilled at the time of the disposal. Since the capital allowances given had already been withdrawn retrospectively, they were to be treated as never having been made, and so the exemption applied.

---

[25] [1987] STC 669.

Chattel exemption

Section 262(1) provides that a gain accruing on the disposal of an asset which is tangible movable property will not be chargeable if the amount or value of the consideration for the disposal does not exceed £6,000. Where a chattel is disposed of for more than £6,000, the gain is computed in the normal way, but there is some relief in s.262(2) limiting the gain to five-thirds of the difference between the consideration and £6,000.

> *Example*
>
> Ming bought an ancient Abyssinian hunting knife for £3,000. She later sold it for £8,000, realising a gain of £5,000. Applying the provisions of s.262(2), the chargeable gain will be limited to:
>
> $$\frac{5}{3} \times £8,000 - £6,000\ (£2,000) = £3,333.33$$

Section 262(3) restricts loss relief where a chattel is disposed of for less than £6,000 by deeming it to have been disposed of for £6,000.

> *Example*
>
> Anastasia bought what she thought was a Mayan golden pipe for £14,000. It turned out to be a forgery, and she was only able to sell it for £2,000, incurring an actual loss of £12,000.
>
> By s.262(3), the disposal consideration is deemed to be £6,000, so the loss is limited to:
>
> $$£14,000 - £6,000 = £8,000$$

The proper approach to the predecessor to this provision (s.128(3) CGTA 1979, which set the limit at that time at £2,000) was examined in *Neeley v Ward*[26]. The taxpayer claimed loss relief in respect of some antiques and other chattels which had been stolen from his home, and in respect of which the insurance payments were insufficient to replace the items. There was no evidence that any of the stolen items cost more than £2,000. It was held that the taxpayer was not entitled to loss relief in respect of those items. Nicholls V C held that the effect of s.20(1)(a) of the CGTA 1979 (now s.22(1) of the TCGA 1992) is that a capital sum received by way of compensation for any loss of assets falls to be regarded as an occasion of

---

[26]   [1991] BTC 408; STC 656; affirmed by the Court of Appeal ([1993] BTC 110).

the disposal of that property, but relief for any loss incurred on such deemed disposal was restricted by s.128(3) in cases where the consideration for the disposal was less than £2,000. According to Nicholls V-C[27] the effect of this provision is that there can be no question of an allowable loss [or chargeable gain] in respect of tangible movable property unless the acquisition cost exceeds £2,000 (now £6,000). Although this observation will not always be true, this is a helpful way of looking at the question. This restriction applies only to reduce the amount of the allowable loss claimable if the asset is disposed of for less than the specified sum. If the asset was acquired for less than the specified sum (presently £6,000) a loss will be normally incurred only if it is disposed of for less than the acquisition cost (except perhaps in cases where unusually high enhancement expenditure was incurred). Since the acquisition cost was itself less than the limit, it follows that the provision will always apply in such cases, if the asset is disposed of for less than its acquisition cost.

Where, as in this case, more than one asset is involved, each item falls to be considered separately for the purposes of the restriction.[28]

Motor cars

By virtue of s.263, a motor car (described in the section as a "mechanically propelled road vehicle constructed or adapted for the carriage of passengers, except for a vehicle of a type not commonly used as a private vehicle and unsuitable to be so used") is not a chargeable asset. Thus, no chargeable gain or allowable loss will accrue on its disposal. This may appear at face value to be a generous exemption but since most motor cars are depreciating assets, it is more of a denial of relief in respect of the inevitable losses that will be incurred on the sale of the cars.

Gambling winnings

Section 51(1) provides that winnings from betting, including pool betting, lotteries etc., are not chargeable gains.

Personal injury compensation

Sums obtained by way of compensation or damages for any wrong or injury suffered by an individual in his person or in his profession or vocation are not chargeable gains (s.51(2)).

---

[27] [1991] BTC 408 at 412.
[28] Nicholls V-C at page 412.

Decorations for valour or gallantry

Section 268 provides that a gain accruing on the disposal by any person of a decoration awarded for valour or gallant conduct shall not be chargeable unless the decoration was purchased (for example, by a collector).

Gilt-edged securities

Section 115(1) exempts gains on disposal of gilt-edged securities or qualifying corporate bonds or on disposal of an option or contract to acquire or dispose of any of these.

Works of art

Section 258 exempts gains accruing on a gift of works of art to an organisation falling within s.26(2) of IHTA 1984, if the Treasury gives a direction in relation to the asset under s.26(1) of IHTA. The Treasury may in this sort of case require an undertaking to be given with respect to the proper maintenance and preservation of the asset, and reasonable public access thereto.

Disposals by charities

A gain is not a chargeable gain if it accrues to a charity and is applicable and applied only for charitable purposes (s.256(1)). For this purpose, a charity which gives money to another charity is applying the funds for charitable purposes and is therefore entitled to the exemption. The principle, according to Slade J in *IRC v Helen Slater Charitable Trust Ltd.*,[29] is that:

> Any charitable corporation which, acting intra vires, makes an outright transfer of money applicable for charitable purposes, in such manner as to pass to the transferee full title to the money, must be taken, by the transfer itself, to have "applied" such money for "charitable purposes", within the meaning of [s.256(1)], unless the transferor knows or ought to know that the money will be misapplied by the transferee.

This was upheld by the Court of Appeal.[30]

---

[29]   [1980] 1 All ER 785 at 795-796.
[30]   [1981] STC 471.

Superannuation funds, annuities and annual payments

Section 237 exempts gains accruing on the disposal of a right to, or to any part of:

a. any allowance, annuity or capital sum payable out of any superannuation fund or scheme established solely or mainly for persons employed in a profession, trade, undertaking or employment, and their dependants;

b. an annuity, granted otherwise than under a contract for a deferred annuity, by a company, as part of its business of granting annuities on human life, and

c. annual payments, which are due under a covenant made by any person, and which are not secured on any property.

In *Rank Xerox Ltd v Lane (HMIT)*[31] the House of Lords held that the word "covenant" (in paragraph (c) above) could not be construed in isolation. What fell to be construed was the whole phrase "annual payments which are due under a covenant made by any person".[32] According to Lord Wilberforce,[33] as a matter purely of grammar, the words "due under" and "made by any person" suggest a unilateral promise which is enforceable in spite of the absence of consideration. They are not apt to refer to bilateral agreements in which the annual payments are consideration for some obligation undertaken by the payee. The term should be understood as referring only to unilateral promises of a voluntary character.

Lord Russell said with respect to the same issue:[34]

> In my opinion "due under a covenant" is fairly to be construed as something narrower in scope than "due under an agreement" would have been. I construe the phrase as meaning due by reason of the fact that the promise is under seal, because of the existence of the seal. If the presence of the seal adds nothing to the obligation to make the annual payments, [e.g., if it is already enforceable because of consideration] I do not consider that the payments were "due under a covenant made by a person". This construction is in my view legitimate as avoiding the wholly capricious outcome of exclusion or non-exclusion from chargeable gains depending on the chance of an unnecessary seal.

---

[31] [1979] 3 All ER 657.
[32] Lord Wilberforce at page 660.
[33] Ibid.
[34] At page 664.

The House of Lords also decided in the case that, in Scotland, the phrase should be understood as referring to enforceable gratuitous promises,[35] or to situations "where the gratuitous nature of the undertaking to pay requires it to be evidenced by the writ of the undertaker".[36]

Private Residences

Introduction

Private residence relief is one of the major reliefs available under the CGT legislation. Home ownership has always been seen as something desirable and worthy of encouragement, and the reason is clear. Every one in every society needs a home. And this means that after the daily bread, homes constitute the next major concern of mankind. A society of home-owners is a society that does not rely on the state for its housing needs. This means that scarce resources which are thereby freed, can be diverted elsewhere. Also, property ownership has traditionally been regarded as one of the soundest forms of investment. Such sound investment ensures future stability and security. Furthermore, when a person sells his home, he frequently needs to acquire a new home elsewhere.[37] There are other rationales which were succinctly expressed by Brightman J in *Sansom v Peay*:[38]

> The evil of inflation was evident even in 1965. It must have occurred to the legislature that when a person sells his home to buy another one, he may well make a profit on the sale of one home and lose that profit, in effect, when he buys his new home at the new, inflated price. It would not therefore be surprising if Parliament formed the conclusion that, in such circumstances, it would be right to exempt the profit on the sale of the first home from the incidence of capital gains tax so that there was enough money to buy the new home.

For these and other reasons, relief is given in respect of capital gains made on the sale of a person's home. S.222 describes the types of property which qualify for relief in this manner:

a. dwelling house or part of a dwelling house;

b. which is or has at any time been an individual's only or main residence;

---

[35] Lord Wilberforce at page 661.

[36] See Lord Russell at page 665; Lord Keith at page 666.

[37] Brightman J in *Sansom & Anor v Peay* (HMIT) (1976) 52 TC 1 at 6; [1976] 3 All ER 375 at 397.

[38] Ibid.

c. together with and land enjoyed with the residence as its garden or grounds, up to the permitted area.

By virtue of s.222(2), the permitted area, subject to subsections (3) and (4) is, inclusive of the site of the dwelling house, 0.5 of one hectare. Where the area required for the reasonable enjoyment of the dwelling house as a residence is (having regard its size and character) is larger than 0.5 of one hectare, then that larger size shall be the permitted area (s 222(3)). Note that this is an objective test and the question of how much land is required for the reasonable enjoyment of the dwelling house will not be affected by how the individual taxpayer in fact makes use of the property. This is illustrated by *Longson v Baker*[39] in which the taxpayer and his family kept horses at their farmhouse and the property extended to 7,756 hectares. The High Court rejected the taxpayer's argument that the land was necessary for the reasonable enjoyment of the property as a dwelling. This was not affected by the fact that the taxpayer and his family had made full use of it while living in the property.

The relief that is available here is found in s.223(1), which provides that any gain on the disposal of a dwelling house is exempt if it has been the only or main residence, either:

a. throughout the period of ownership; or

b. throughout the period of ownership except for the last 36 months of ownership.

Dwelling house

Whether a particular building constitutes a dwelling house or not is a question of fact. There are a number of decided cases on this point and most of them turn on their own facts. One such example is *Makins v Elson (HMIT)*[40] where a caravan was held to be a dwelling house. The taxpayer had purchased for £1,800 a building plot of ¾ of an acre in respect of which planning permission for a dwelling house had been granted. The taxpayer had then moved to the site in a mobile caravan. Subsequently essential services – water, electricity, and a telephone, were installed. Although the caravan had wheels, the wheels were actually not on the ground, because the caravan had been jacked up and rested on some sort of supports. The taxpayer then claimed relief in respect of a gain on the sale of the caravan. It was held by Foster J that the caravan was exempt as a

---

[39] [2001] STC 6.
[40] [1977] STC 46; 1 All ER 572.

dwelling house. Factors which he considered important were the facts that services had been installed, and that the wheels were not on the ground.

Contrast however *Moore v Thompson (HMIT)*[41]. The taxpayers had bought an old detached farm house, which had not been inhabited for two years, and which did not have an electricity supply, for use as their family home. The husband later purchased a wheeled caravan which had a sink, table, some chairs, and a settee that could turn into a bed. This caravan was towed into the courtyard of the farm house. It was not connected to any services. The taxpayers stayed in this caravan for various periods, the husband sometimes staying for several weeks, while renovating the farm house. They claimed private residence relief in respect of the caravan. The commissioners decided that, on the facts, neither the farm house nor the caravan in its courtyard was ever a "dwelling house" capable of being regarded as the taxpayers' main residence. They were upheld by Millet J.

Whether ancillary buildings fall to be included as part of the dwelling house or not is also a question of fact. In *Batey (HMIT) v Wakefield*[42] for example, it was held that a separate bungalow, which was adjacent to the taxpayer's house and within the grounds, and which was occupied by a caretaker was exempt as part of the dwelling house. This decisions can be contrasted with *Green v IRC*[43] where the taxpayer's mansion consisted of a central block, and two wings, each of which contained a self-contained flat with its own entrance, but was linked to the central block by connecting passages. One of the wings was occupied by a gardener and his family. The General Commissioners decided that the two wings were not part of the taxpayer's residence, and the Court of Session felt unable to reverse them.[44]

It should be noted that, for the purposes of the main/private residence relief, a dwelling house could comprise more than one building, and that these separate buildings need not be physically connected. This principle is well established but the problem is how it is to be applied. The courts have, in a long line of cases, grappled with this problem. In *Markey (HMIT) v Sanders*[45], the taxpayer had a small country estate consisting of a main house with three bedrooms, and a bungalow, which also had three bedrooms. The bungalow was sited about 130 metres from the main house and was separated from it by a large paddock. The bungalow had been thus sited for privacy, i.e., deliberately sited in order to take it way from the main house. It had its own garden and was protected by a belt of trees deliberately screening it from the main house. The commissioners held that it constituted part of the taxpayer's dwelling house, but they were reversed by Walton J.

According to Walton J[46] two conditions were laid down by the Court of Appeal in *Batey (HMIT) v Wakefield* (above) in order for a separate building

---

[41] [1986] STC 170.

[42] [1981] STC 521.

[43] [1982] STC 458 (Court of Session).

[44] In *Honour (HMIT) v Norris* [1992] BTC 153 at 160, Vinelott J said that *Green v IRC* was a case that "turned on very special facts".

[45] [1987] STC 256.

[46] At page 263.

to qualify as part of the main residence. First, the occupation of the building in question must increase the taxpayer's enjoyment of the main house. This is a necessary but not a sufficient condition. Secondly, the other building must be "very closely adjacent" to the main building. This again is a necessary but not sufficient condition. Walton J himself would prefer to ask the question "looking at the group of buildings in question as a whole, is it fairly possible to regard them as a single dwelling house used as the taxpayer's main residence?" He felt that this was a preferable approach, because the concept of "very closely adjacent" does not of itself indicate that the scale of the building must be taken into consideration, which would appear to be fairly obvious. The expression "very closely adjacent" was, according to him, too imprecise.[47]

In this case the first test was very clearly satisfied but the second was not. According to Walton J[48] although it is true that the test of "very closely adjacent" is an elastic one which is for the commissioners to decide, merely because it is an elastic test does not mean that the commissioners are entitled to apply it absolutely, regardless of the facts. "It is no use the commissioners describing in great detail what is clearly recognisable as an elephant and then concluding that it is a giraffe".[49] Walton J's conclusion was that, either the commissioners had applied no test at all beyond the first condition, or, they had applied the wrong test.

In *Williams (HMIT) v Merrylees*[50], Vinelott J, referring to *Markey v Sanders* said that he found it difficult to spell out of the Batey decision two distinct conditions, each of which must be satisfied, before a separate building can be considered part of a single dwelling house. He felt that both Browne-Wilkinson J at first instance and the Court of Appeal intended to lay down only one test, i.e., "the entity which in fact constitutes the residence of the taxpayer". According to Vinelott J[51] what one is looking for is an entity which can be sensibly described as being a dwelling house though split up into different buildings performing different functions. In deciding whether this test is satisfied on the facts of a particular case, the commissioners must look at all the circumstances, and of course, the propinquity or otherwise of the buildings, having regard to their scale, is a very important factor to be weighed. It however does not seem right to isolate a single factor as one which must be present if the commissioners are to be entitled to conclude that a building physically separate from the taxpayer's main dwelling house, but occupied in such a way that it may be said to increase his enjoyment of the main dwelling house, is part of his residence. The question is one of degree.[52] In this case, a gardener's/caretaker's lodge, situated some 200 metres from the main

---

[47] Ibid.
[48] At page 264.
[49] Ibid.
[50] [1987] STC 445 at 453.
[51] At page 454.
[52] Ibid.

house was held by the commissioners to constitute a single dwelling house with the main house. Vinelott J did not feel able to reverse them even though he doubted whether he would himself have arrived at the same conclusion.

More recently, in *Lewis (HMIT) v Lady Rook*[53] the Court of Appeal in deciding that a cottage, situated some 175 metres from the main house and occupied by the taxpayer's gardener, did not constitute one residence with the main house, emphasised the question of the proximity of the cottage to the main house. After reviewing the case law, Balcombe LJ confessed that he found the current state of the authorities unsatisfactory, and that it was hardly surprising that different sets of commissioners have reached conclusions which are not always easy to understand.[54] In these circumstances it was necessary to go back to the words of the statute. Balcombe LJ said that what first had to be decided was what in the particular case constituted the "dwelling house", an ordinary English word defined in the shorter Oxford English Dictionary as a "house occupied as a place of residence". Following the decision in *Batey v Wakefield*, a dwelling house could consist of more than one building even if the other building itself constituted a separate dwelling house. Nevertheless, he would agree with Vinelott J in *Williams v Merrylees* that what to look for was an entity which could be sensibly described as a dwelling house, though split up into different buildings performing different functions.

How, then, can this entity be identified in any given case? Balcombe LJ said that attention must first be focused on the dwelling-house which is said to constitute the entity. According to him, to seek to identify the taxpayer's residence may lead to confusion, because where, as in the present case, the dwelling-house forms part of a small estate, it is very easy to consider the estate as his residence and from that to conclude that all the buildings on the estate are part of his residence. Balcombe LJ said that in so far as some of the statements made in *Batey v Wakefield* suggest that one must first identify the residence, they must be considered to have been made per incuriam.

According to Balcombe LJ, the proposition that no building can form part of a dwelling-house which includes a main house unless that building is appurtenant to, and within the curtilage of, the main house, was a helpful approach.[55] It involves application of well-recognised legal concepts, and may avoid somewhat surprising findings of fact which were reached in *Markey v Sanders, William v Merrylees*, and the present case. This approach coincides with the close proximity test to which the other cases refer: "very closely adjacent" – per Browne-Wilkinson J in *Batey v Wakefield*, and also avoids the difficulty that a separate lodge or cottage which by any

---

[53] [1992] BTC 102.
[54] At page 108.
[55] Ibid.

reasonable measurement must be outside the one acre "permitted area" of garden or grounds, can nevertheless be part of the entity of the dwelling-house.[56] Thus the correct test in this case was "was the cottage within the curtilage of, and appurtenant to, [the main house], so as to be a part of the entity which, together with [the main house], constituted the dwelling-house occupied by the taxpayer as her residence"?[57] In this case it was impossible to answer the question in the affirmative.

The principles stated by Balcombe LJ in *Lewis v Lady Rook* were applied by Vinelott J in *Honour (HMIT) v Norris*[58] where the question was whether four separate flats, situated in different buildings, in Ovington Square, Kensington, and occupied by the taxpayer and his family, could be regarded as part of a single dwelling-house. The particular flat which was the subject of the dispute was called "Flat 10" and it was situated some 60 to 95 yards by road from the others, but within the same Ovington Square. Answering the question in the negative, Vinelott J said[59] that the proposition that Flat 10, together with the others formed part of a single entity which could sensibly be described as a dwelling-house split into different buildings and performing different but related functions, was an affront to common sense. According to him[60] Flat 10 was acquired because it was a separate dwelling-house conveniently close to the taxpayer's main dwelling-house and with a view to it being used to provide occasional bedroom accommodation for the taxpayer and his wife. It was no more part of a dwelling-house than for example a guest house bought in a neighbouring village by the owner of a country house who found that his house was not always adequate to accommodate his children and guests.

Land used with the house

The exemption in respect of land used as garden or grounds applies where it is used in connection with the dwelling house. Where the dwelling house is sold first and then the garden/grounds is/are sold afterward, it will not qualify for exemption. In *Varty v Lynes*[61] Brightman J held that, in order to be exempt, the garden must be occupied at the time of the disposal. In *Varty* the taxpayer first sold the house and a part of the garden, and then sold the rest of the garden 11 months later, with the benefit of planning permission. It was held that the latter disposal was not exempt.

"Only or main residence"

In order to qualify for main residence relief, a building which is acknowledged to be a dwelling house also has to be the taxpayer's only or

---

[56] At 109.
[57] Ibid.
[58] [1992] BTC 153.
[59] At page 162.
[60] Ibid.
[61] [1976] 3 All ER 447.

main residence. For several years, the courts' approach to this question was to ask whether the building constituted the taxpayer's home.

In *Owen v Elliot (HMIT)*[62] Fox LJ said that the section was concerned with dwelling houses that could reasonably be called "homes". Leggatt LJ said that the concept of occupation as a home was derived not from the use of the term "residence" by itself, but from its use in the phrase "his only or main residence".[63] In *Sansom v Peay (HMIT)*[64] Brightman J said that the scheme of the provision was to exempt from liability to capital gains tax "the proceeds of sale of a person's home". This apparent gloss on the statutory words received close attention in *Goodwin v Curtis (HMIT)*.[65] This case involved the acquisition and sale of three properties by the taxpayer within a nine month period in 1985. The property which is relevant to this discussion was a farmhouse which had its purchase completed on 1 April 1985, but the taxpayer had instructed estate agents to sell it in March 1985 (i.e., before his purchase of the property was completed). At about the time of completion, the taxpayer separated from his wife and took up temporary residence in the farmhouse. On 11 April 1985 the farmhouse was advertised for sale in *Country Life*. In the same month, it was advertised for sale in a number of other publications. A buyer was found almost immediately, and the sale was completed on 3 May 1985. The commissioners decided that, in order to qualify for relief, the taxpayer must provided evidence that his residence at a property showed some degree of permanence, some degree of continuity or some expectation of continuity. Accordingly, since the taxpayer had not intended to occupy the farmhouse as his permanent residence when he moved into it, the farmhouse had not been occupied as his home, and did not qualify for relief as his main residence.

Vinelott J, upholding the commissioners, referred to the Court of Appeal's decision in *Fox v Stirk*[66], in which it was held that students at the Universities of Bristol and Cambridge were "resident" at their halls of residence for the purposes of entry into the electoral register. In that case, Lord Denning MR referred to three principles:[67]

> The first principle is that a man can have two residences. He can have a flat in London and a house in the country. He is resident in both. The second principle is that temporary presence at an address does not make a man resident there. A guest who comes for the weekend is not resident. A shortstay visitor is not resident. The third principle is that temporary absence does not deprive a person of his residence … I think that a person may properly be said to be the 'resident' in a place when his stay there has a considerable degree of permanence.

[62] [1990] BTC 323 at 326; Ch 786; 3 WLR 133; STC 469.
[63] [1990] BTC at page 327; compare Fox LJ at page 326.
[64] Supra.
[65] [1996] BTC 501 and [1998] STC 475.
[66] [1970] 2 QB 463; 3 All ER 7. Applied in *Hipperson v Electoral Registration Officer for the District of Newbury* [1985] 2 All ER 456 (see Sir John Donaldson MR at page 461).
[67] [1970] 2 QB at 475; 3 All ER at 11-12.

Vinelott J also referred to Widgery LJ in *Fox v Stirk*. Before the passage referred to by Vinelott J, Widgery LJ had said that a man cannot be said to reside in a particular place unless in the ordinary sense of the word one can say that for the time being he is making his home in that place[68]. Vinelott J then referred to Widgery LJ's statement that this conception of residence is of "the place where a man is based or *where he continues to live*, the place where he sleeps and shelters and has his home",[69] and that it is imperative to remember in this context that 'residence' implies a degree of permanence:

> In the words of the Oxford English Dictionary, it is concerned with something which will go on for a considerable time ... Some assumption of permanence, some degree of continuity, some expectation of continuity, is a vital factor which turns simple occupation into residence.[70]

In the present case, Vinelott J said[71] that the commissioners were distinguishing permanent residence from mere temporary accommodation and amongst the factors to be weighed by the commissioners are the degree of permanence, continuity, and the expectation of continuity. The facts found by the commissioners were, that the taxpayer had decided to sell the farmhouse and had advertised it widely before completion of the sale to himself, that it was a nine-bedroomed house wholly unsuitable as the residence of a single man who was separated from his wife and in financial difficulties. In the light of these facts, Vinelott J held that the commissioners were entitled to take the view that the farmhouse was used not as a residence but merely as temporary accommodation for a period that the taxpayer hoped would be brief and which in fact was very brief. The taxpayer appealed without success to the Court of Appeal.[72]

Millet LJ supported the arguments of Vinelott J and held that the question was whether the taxpayer had occupied the farmhouse as temporary accommodation or as his settled abode. He held that the commissioners' ruling that the former was the case could easily be supported on the facts:

> Temporary occupation at an address does not make a man resident there. The question whether the occupation is sufficient to make him resident is one of fact and degree for the commissioners to decide.
>
> The substance of the commissioners' finding taken as whole, in my

[68] [1970] 3 All ER at 13.
[69] Ibid. Emphasis added.
[70] [1970] 2 QB at 477; 3 All ER at 13.
[71] [1996] BTC at 518.
[72] [1998] STC 475.

judgment, is that the nature, quality, length and circumstances of the taxpayer's occupation of the farmhouse did not make his occupation qualify as residence. This conclusion was, in my judgment, clearly open to them.[73]

Millet LJ then concluded his judgment by expressing disapproval for the "home" principle:

I do not regard it as helpful to substitute other words as glosses on statutory language by asking whether the farmhouse was his home or whether he lived there since he had nowhere else to live. He manifestly did live there but I do not consider that the commissioners can be faulted for having reached the conclusion that he did not at any stage reside there.[74]

It remains to be seen how the courts will approach this area following this judgment. As has been seen, the "home" principle was quite well established in caselaw and it may be that this relatively brief reference to it will not cause the courts to depart from it.

It is also doubtful to what extent this marks a change of approach. It is notable that, while s.222 makes no reference to homes, neither does it make any reference to the question of whether occupation is permanent or temporary. Both these tests have been abstracted by the courts from the words of the statute referring to "an individual's only or main residence" and so both could be said, to be "glosses on statutory language."

The question is whether it makes any difference which test is applied. As was quoted above, Leggatt LJ in *Owen v Elliot*, stated that the concept of occupation as a home was derived not from the use of the term "residence" by itself, but from its use in the phrase "his only or main residence". If this is the case, then Millett LJ's reluctance to get involved in discussions about homes might stem from the fact that the farmhouse was the only place where the taxpayer lived.

On the other hand, according to the Oxford English Dictionary, a home is "the place where one lives; the fixed residence of a family or household." Since "fixed" can be taken to imply a degree of permanence, it is questionable whether it makes much difference whether the courts ask if the residence was the taxpayer's home or whether the taxpayer was in permanent occupation.

The requirement of permanence could operate to the disadvantage of

---

[73] Ibid.
[74] Ibid.

certain taxpayers. For example, problems may arise in cases where people have to sell their home shortly after buying it, either as a result of an emergency, or as a result of a realisation that the property is somehow not adequate. The same problems might arise in cases where a house is purchased as a temporary measure while the search for the "dream home" continues. In this type of case, if the "dream home" is subsequently found quickly, the taxpayer may be faced with the assertion that the house was not his residence. In these types of case, there might well be no permanence, continuity, or expectation of continuity. Would it then be right to deny main residence relief? If this were the result achieved by decisions such as *Fox* and *Goodwin*, then the gloss introduced by these cases on the statutory provisions would be unsupportable.

However, it may be that escape might be found in the principle that the decision of the matter is a question of fact and degree, and that it would be open to the commissioners to find evidence that a dwelling could be classed as a main residence even in the absence of permanence, continuity or expectation thereof. This gains support from the judgment of Millett LJ, who made it clear that, as well as considering the length of the occupation, the commissioners would also consider the nature, quality and circumstances when deciding whether a taxpayer was resident in a particular property.

Multiple residences

Where an individual has more than one residence, he may determine which is to be treated as his main residence for any period, by notice to the inspector within two years from the beginning of that period, subject to a right to vary that notice by a further notice to the inspector in respect of any period not earlier than two years before the time when the further notice is given (s.222(5)(a).

This provision appears straightforward enough, but the case of *Griffin (HMIT) v Craig-Harvey*[75] shows that that appearance may be deceptive. The taxpayer in the case acquired a farmhouse on 12 August 1985. On 9 July 1986 he completed the sale of another house, and, on the same day completed the purchase of yet another one ("7 Sibella Road"). On 21 January 1988 he gave written notice to the inspector of taxes pursuant to s.101(5) CGTA 1979 (now s.222(5) TCGA 1992) that the farmhouse should be treated as his main residence for capital gains tax purposes. On 26 January 1989 he sold the farmhouse. Since the notice was given more than two years after the acquisition of the farmhouse, the question arose as to when the notice could take effect. The taxpayer contended that the

---

[75] [1994] BTC 3.

notice was effective for a period of up to two years before it was given. The gist of his argument was that the words "from the beginning of that period" in [s.222(5)(a)] relate back to the words "for any period" in the opening part of [s.222(5)], that there is no restriction on the date chosen as the beginning of that period, and that a taxpayer may therefore give notice at any time that a residence is to be treated as his main residence for the period beginning two years before the giving of the notice. Thus, the taxpayer's election would take effect from 21 January 1986 (two years before the notice was given). The Revenue, on the other hand, argued in effect that, a taxpayer who fails to make an election within two years of acquisition of a residence cannot thereafter make any election in respect thereof unless and until he acquires a new residence or makes a change in residence. This meant that the taxpayer's notice could not take effect to make the farmhouse his main residence before the date when he acquired 7 Sibella Road (9 July 1986). It followed that, from 12 August 1985 when the taxpayer acquired the farmhouse, until 9 July 1986 when he acquired 7 Sibella Road, the farmhouse was not his main residence, and that period of ownership did not qualify for relief.

Vinelott J upheld the Revenue's argument. Counsel for the taxpayer put forward a number of examples which illustrated the arbitrary and irrational consequences of the Revenue's argument. The first example was that of a taxpayer who owns two houses, each of which he occupies as a residence. After more than two years, he begins to use a third house as a residence. A new two-year period begins to run at that time so that he can make an election between all three residences during that two-year period. The second example was, if given the same facts as before, the taxpayer ceased, after acquiring a third residence, to use one of them as a residence, a new period will begin at the time of cesser so that, again, he will have a period of two years during which he can elect between the remaining residences. Vinelott J's answer to these illustrations was that they did no more than illustrate the inevitable consequences of [s.222(5)], namely, that it becomes necessary to determine which of two or more residences is an individual's main residence whenever there is a change in the number of properties which he occupies as a residence[76].

The decision that the two year-period begins to run from the acquisition of the property to which the notice relates seems to be right. It does not seem that Parliament would give taxpayers a carte blanche in respect of the time during which they may give notice of their election. Vinelott J said[77] that the reference to "any period" in the opening part of s.222(5) and to "that period" in para. (a) are most naturally read as referring to "the whole or any part of the period of ownership in question". This is

---

[76]   [1994] BTC at page 10.
[77]   At page 9.

obviously correct. If a taxpayer owned two residences in the period between 1 January 1990 and 1 January 1998, any reference to "the period" in s.222(5) would obviously relate to that eight-year period. A notice of election given after 1 January 1992 would be out of time. It cannot possibly be right that the taxpayer may give a notice in respect of this period on 1 January 1997, and then have that notice take effect from 1 January 1995 (the effect of the taxpayer's argument in this case). This decision illustrates the need for prompt action by people who acquire other residences. It may be thought imprudent to commit oneself in this way at the early stages of ownership of new properties – especially when it may not be clear which of them would yield a higher profit figure when they are eventually disposed of, and which should therefore be chosen for main residence relief. However, s.222(5)(a) does provide some amount of relief for those who make their election promptly, by allowing them to vary the earlier notice, by a further notice, with retrospective effect, at any time. This variation notice is also subject to a two-year time limit – but the limit this time attaches to the time when the further notice is given, to make it effective for the preceding two-year period.

While the decision that a fresh two-year period begins each time a change in residence (or acquisition of a new residence) occurs may seem astounding, it could be of benefit to a well advised taxpayer with sufficient means, in that it provides a possible escape route for those who had earlier been tardy. Presumably, all that they would need to do in order to obtain a fresh start would be to acquire another residence.

Married couples

A husband and wife can only have one residence or main residence if living together (s.222(6)). Concessionary relief is available in cases wherein the parties are separated or divorced. ESC D6 applies where a married couple are separated or divorced, and one partner ceases to occupy the matrimonial home, and, subsequently as part of a financial settlement, disposes of the home or an interest in it to the other partner. In these cases, the home may be regarded for the purposes of the main residence relief as continuing to be a residence of the transferring partner from the date his or her occupation ceases, until the day of the transfer (subject to the condition that the home was the other partner's only or main residence throughout this period). According to the text of the concession this means that where a husband leaves the matrimonial home while still owning it, the usual CGT exemption or relief for a taxpayer's only or main residence would be given on the subsequent transfer to the wife, provided that she has continued to live in the house and the husband has not elected that some other house should be treated for capital gains tax purposes as his main residence for this period.

Residence used for trade purposes

Section 224(1) provides that, where part of the dwelling house in respect of which relief is being claimed is used exclusively for the purposes of a trade or business, or of a profession or vocation carried on by the taxpayer, the gain on the house will be apportioned, and the exemption will be applied to the part which is not so used.

Other use of the dwelling house: apportionment

Where the dwelling house has not been the taxpayer's only or main residence throughout his period of ownership (excluding the last 36 months which will invariably attract exemption), only a fraction of the gain is exempt. The fraction is determined according to a formula in (s.223(2)), which can be thus expressed:

$$\frac{A}{B} \times C$$

Where:

A = period of owner-occupation (including last 36 months)
B = total period of ownership
C = gross gain

Letting

Where the property or part of it has been let to tenants, this in effect means that the exemption is lost because the property is not the taxpayer's own residence. There is however a measure of relief. S.223(4) provides that, with respect to houses qualifying for the main residence relief, if the house is or has been either partly or wholly let by the owner as residential accommodation, the gain which would otherwise have been chargeable because of the letting would only be chargeable to the extent that it exceeds the lesser of (a) the part of the gain attributable to the owner-occupation, and (b) £40,000.

In order to apply the relief in s.223(4) it is therefore necessary to apportion the gain into the gain attributable to the letting and the gain attributable to the occupation. Apportionment takes place on the basis of use as well as time.

Examples

Ros has owned a house for 15 years. She sells it in 2002 at a gain of £30,000. For the first five years, she let it out. For the second five years, she occupied half and let the other half out and, for the last five years, she occupied the entire house. It is first necessary to calculate the amount of the gain attributable both to the letting and to the occupation. This works out at half each. The gain attributable to the occupation is therefore £15,000, as is the gain attributable to the letting. As this figure is less than £40,000, this is the relevant figure and, since the gain attributable to the letting does not exceed it, there will be no tax to pay.

Suppose instead that Ros had sold the house at a gain of £90,000. This time, the gain attributable to the occupation and the gain attributable to the letting would each be £45,000. The gain attributable to the letting would exceed £40,000 (this time, the lower of the two figures) by £5,000, so that there would be a £5,000 chargeable gain.

Suppose that Ros had sold the house at a gain of £90,000 but that she had let out a third of the house for the first five years, that she had let out the whole house for the second five years and that she had let out two thirds of it for the last five years. The gain attributable to the letting would be £60,000 (1/3 of £30,000 + £30,000 + 2/3 of £30,000) and the gain attributable to the occupation would be £30,000. This figure is less than £40,000, so is the relevant figure. The gain attributable to the letting exceeds this by £30,000, so this is the chargeable gain.[78]

Note that the section makes no allowance for the actual value of the property at the various times when the use was changed. It would therefore be irrelevant if, in the first example above, the value of the house remained unchanged for the first five years of ownership.

What does "residential accommodation" mean in this respect? Some

---

[78] Note that the gains excluding main residence relief would have been calculated by applying indexation up to 1998. The final figure would also be reduced by taper relief and any remaining gain could be set against the taxpayer's annual exemption.

answers were forthcoming from the Court of Appeal in *Owen v Elliot (HMIT)*.[79] The taxpayer in this case and his wife purchased the Gleneagles Hotel in 1976, and carried on a business of a private hotel and boarding house on the premises. The hotel consisted of two parts, first, a main building, which consisted of ten bedrooms, a kitchen and a lounge, and secondly, an annexe, which consisted of two bedrooms, a lounge, a kitchen and some ancillary facilities. During the period from Easter to September, the hotel received guests who stayed for short terms – usually less than two weeks. During these periods, the taxpayer and his family occupied the annexe. During the period from October to Easter, guests stayed for longer periods, typically three to four months and the taxpayer and his family occupied the whole building together with their guests. The taxpayer sold the whole property on March 24 1982. The inspector agreed that one-third of the gain on the sale of the hotel should be treated as exempt from capital gains tax under s.222 and s.223 TCGA 1992. The taxpayer then claimed further relief in respect of dwelling houses let as residential accommodation under s.223(4) TCGA 1992.

The Crown accepted that as a matter of the ordinary use of the English language "residential accommodation" includes such lettings as were made by the taxpayer, but argued that the provision must be read in its context. It was designed to extend the relief in ss.222 & 223. The concept of a home is central to s.222 and is carried into s.223(4). It is therefore consistent with the relief to extend it to taxpayers who have some surplus accommodation in their homes and which they are proposing to let to a person as his home. Millet J at first instance accepted the Crown's argument but the Court of Appeal disagreed. Fox LJ[80] said that the concept of a home was not conveyed by the use of the word "residence" alone. A person might well have a residence or several residences which were not his home. The language of [s.222] plainly indicated a home, but that of [s.223(4)] was completely different. Fox LJ could see no reason why it should be assumed that because the main residence relief was granted in respect of the home of the taxpayer, the additional relief should only attach to a letting to third parties as their homes. There is no necessary connection between the two. According to him, the provision was designed to encourage householders who had surplus accommodation in their dwelling houses, to make it or some of it available to other persons. The language of the provision is such that the lettings made by the taxpayers in their hotel were within the words "residential accommodation".

Leggatt LJ concurring[81] said that "residential accommodation" does not directly or by association mean premises likely to be occupied as a home.

---

[79]   [1990] BTC 323; Ch. 786; 3 WLR 133.
[80]   At page 326.
[81]   At page 327.

He said that it means living accommodation, by contrast, for example, with office accommodation. According to him:

> No relevant distinction can be drawn between a letting to an undergraduate or nurse or lodger, such as the judge thought would be entitled to relief, and a letting to anyone else. All are lettings of residential accommodation indistinguishable from that which is provided by boarding or guest houses or indeed by hotels, and all are conducted on what the judge called a "commercial basis". They differ from each other, if at all, only in the average length of letting, but it is accepted on behalf of the Crown that the length of the letting is not determinative. This conclusion will not result in relief being extended to a taxpayer the whole or part of whose dwelling-house is exclusively used as an hotel or boarding house. It will apply only where a dwelling-house has at any time been used wholly or partly for that or a like purpose by a person whose only or main residence it is ... [T]here is no limitation imposed by the statute on the scope of residential accommodation entitled to relief ...

Periods of absence

Normally, if an individual is absent from the dwelling house, it will not satisfy the residence requirement. However, some periods during which the taxpayer may not have occupied the dwelling house may still qualify as periods of occupation.

The last 36 months of ownership

Section 223(1) provides that a gain accruing on the disposal of a dwelling house will not be chargeable if it has been the individual's only or main residence throughout the period of ownership, or throughout such period except for the last 36 months. This particular provision covers both periods of absence, and periods during which the house was used for any other purpose, e.g., letting.

Qualifying periods of absence

In addition to the last 36 months of ownership the following periods of absence are treated by s.223(3) as periods of owner-occupation, if both before and after such periods, there was a time when the dwelling-house was actually the individual's only or main residence:

a. a period, or periods of absence not exceeding three years;

b. any period of absence throughout which the individual worked in an overseas employment in which all the duties were performed abroad;

c. any period or periods of absence, not exceeding four years, throughout which the individual was prevented from living in the house because of the situation of his place of work, or because of a reasonable condition imposed by his employer, requiring him to reside elsewhere, being a condition reasonably imposed to secure effective performance of his job.

Concessionary relief is available in ESC D4, to the effect that the requirement of occupation after the period of absence is satisfied where, on a person's return, he is not able to take up residence in his previous home because the terms of his employment require him to work elsewhere.

"Period of absence" is defined in s.223(7) as a period during which the house was not the individual's only or main residence, and throughout which he had no residence eligible for relief under (this) section. This does not include any period before 31 March 1982.

Job-related accommodation

Section 222(8) provides that, if at any time during an individual's period of ownership of a dwelling house, he resides in a job-related accommodation and he intends in due course to occupy the dwelling house as his only or main residence, ss.222–226 shall apply as if the dwelling house were occupied by him as a residence. According to subsection (8A), accommodation will be classed as job related in the following cirumstances:

a. If it is provided either for the employee or for his spouse by reason of their employment in any of the following cases:

   i. here it is necessary for the proper performance of the duties that the employee should reside in the accommodation;

   ii. where the accommodation is provided for the better performance of the duties and the employment is of a kind where it is customary for employers to provide accommodation;

iii. where there is a threat to the employee's security and the accommodation is provided as part of special security arrangements;

b. If either the taxpayer or his spouse is subject to a contract requiring them to carry on a particular trade, profession or vocation and is bound under the terms of the contract:

i. to carry on the trade, profession or vocation on premises provided by another person; and

ii. to live either on those premises or on other premises provided by that other person.

Exceptions to this rule are provided in subsections (8B), (8C) and (9).

Trustees

By s.225, the relief applies also to a gain accruing to trustees on a disposal of settled property which is an asset within s.222(1), where during the trustees' period of ownership, the house has been the only or main residence of a person entitled to occupy it under the terms of the settlement. In *Sansom v Peay*[82] it was held, when beneficiaries under a discretionary trust occupied a house as their main residence in pursuance of an exercise by the trustees of powers to permit those beneficiaries to go into, and remain in, occupation, that the trustees were entitled to main residence relief in respect of accrued gains when they disposed of the dwelling house, under what is now s.225.

Dependent relatives

Section 226(1) extends the relief to a gain accruing to an individual on a disposal of a house which, on 5 April 1988, or at any earlier time in his period of ownership, had been the sole residence of a dependent relative, provided rent-free and without any other consideration. The relief is limited to one dependent relative. The requirement that the provision of the accommodation be rent-free is satisfied where the dependent relative pays all or part of the occupier's rates and the cost of repairs attributable to normal wear and tear (ESC D20). Additionally, the benefit of the relief will not be lost where the dependent relative makes other payments in respect of the property, either to the taxpayer or to a third party, provided that no

---

[82] [1976] STC 494.

[83] Ibid. Because of the time limit of the dependent relative relief, this concession is now obsolescent in the sense that the number of persons who can claim it cannot now increase, and will diminish over time.

net income is receivable by the taxpayer, taking one year with another.[83]

"Dependent relative" is defined in s.226(6) & (7) as:

a. a relative of the individual, or of his/her spouse, who is incapacitated by old age or infirmity from maintaining himself; and

b. the widowed, divorced or separated mother of the individual, or of his/her spouse, or a single woman in consequence of dissolution or annulment of marriage.

Motive

Section 224(3) provides that the relief will not apply to a gain if the acquisition of the house was made wholly or partly for the purpose of realising a gain from the disposal of it.

Roll Over Relief on Transfer of Business to Company

Section 162 provides for roll over relief where an unincorporated business is transferred to a company as a going concern, together with all the assets of the business (other than cash), in consideration wholly or partly of shares in the company. ESC D32 extends the relief to cases where liabilities are taken over by the company on the transfer. In cases qualifying for relief, the gain accruing on the disposal to the company is "rolled over" (deferred) into the shares, resulting in a postponement of CGT until when the shares are eventually disposed of. It works by deducting the gain on the disposal from the cost or value of the shares, thus reducing their base cost. Where the consideration is partly shares, and partly cash, the gain is apportioned, and the part attributable to the cash payment is chargeable immediately.

The formula for determining the part which qualifies for relief is found in s.162(4):

$$\frac{A}{B} \times \text{gain on old assets (the business)}$$

Where:

A = the cost of the new assets (the shares)

B = total consideration for the transfer

The purpose of this provision was explained by Lord President Hope in *Gordon v IRC*[84]:

> It is clear that the section is intended to enable persons who are carrying on a business as individuals or as a partnership to transfer the business to a company without having to pay capital gains tax immediately on the disposal which must then inevitably occur. That company may be one which is controlled by others, or it may be one which the persons have incorporated themselves for the particular purpose of accepting the transfer of the business. It does not seem to me to matter for present purposes which of these alternatives applies...

Two other points emerge from the judgment of Lord President Hope. First, when determining whether or not a business was transferred to a person as a "going concern" the question is whether the transferee's activities could be carried on without interruption, at the date of the transfer.[85] Encompassed within that principle is the second point – timing. According to Lord President Hope[86] the roll over relief does not depend on the date at which the disposal was made, which for example will, in cases of disposals under contract, be the date when the contract was made (s.28(1)). Neither does the relief depend on the state of the business at the date fixed by the contract for the transfer, if the transfer did not in fact take place on that date. What is important is whether the business was a going concern at the date when it was actually handed over from one party to the other.

This leads to another principle. The only thing that must be considered is the state of the business at the date of actual transfer. According to Lord President Hope, there is no requirement that the business shall answer the description of being a going concern at any future date, or that it shall continue to be a going concern for any period after the date of the transfer, nor is the relief said to be affected by what the transferee company may do with the business once it has been received by it. It was Lord President Hope's view that the words "going concern" do not in themselves carry any implication about what may happen in the future or

---

[84] [1991] BTC 130; [1991] STC 174.
[85] [1991] BTC at page 143.
[86] At page 142.

about the length of time which the business must remain in that condition once it has been taken over by the transferee.

Retirement Relief

Introduction

When an individual who has built up a business throughout his or her life wishes to retire from the business, the options available with respect to the business are either to pass the business on (to a member of the family or other beneficiary), or to sell it. If the business had enjoyed anything vaguely resembling financial success, either of these options will normally attract a charge to CGT. Depending on how one looks at it (the political or economic viewpoint) such tax consequences on the results of a life time of toil may either be a desirable thing (redistribution of wealth) or, alternatively, a chilling prospect which will discourage investment, stifle enterprise, encourage planning, and which must therefore be avoided or minimised.

This latter approach has been the philosophy of the CGT system and, until recently, the principal means used to achieve this was the system of retirement relief. This relief is now in the process of being phased out, following the introduction of the new system of taper relief (discussed below). However, retirement relief will still be in force until 5 April 2003 so, for the moment at least, it is still necessary to be familiar with the details of it.

Retirement relief is being phased out by progressively reducing the maximum amount for which relief can be claimed. This is discussed later under "Amount of relief." While the relief is being phased out, the rules for determining whether a taxpayer is entitled to the relief remain the same. These are discussed next.

Section163(1) provides that relief shall be granted to an individual who makes a material disposal of business assets and who either:

a. has attained the age of 50; or

b. retired on grounds of ill health below the age of 50.

Two important concepts are encompassed within this prescription – a disposal of business assets, which is also a material disposal. We shall examine these concepts in turn.

Disposal of business assets

A disposal of business assets is defined by s.163(2) as:

a. a disposal of the whole or part of a business;

b. on cessation of a business, a disposal of assets used for the purposes of that business;

c. a disposal of shares or securities in a company.

Material disposals

What constitutes a material disposal depends much on the type of asset, and the proportion of the asset that is being disposed of.

The whole of part of a business - section163(3)

A disposal of the whole or part of a business is a material disposal if throughout the period of at least one year ending with the date of the disposal:[87]

i. the business is owned by the disponor; or

ii. if the business is owned by a company, the company is a trading company, which is either the disponor's personal company (or a subsidiary thereof), and he is a full-time working officer or employee thereof.[88]

It should be noted that the provisions of s.163(3) relate to a disposal of the whole business or a part of it.[89] They do not relate to a mere disposal of business assets (except on cessation). So for example it is not enough for the taxpayer to establish that he had disposed of an asset, or even an important asset used in his business[90]. Thus Peter Gibson J said in *Atkinson (HMIT) v Dancer:*[91]

---

[87] There is no relief where the conditions are satisfied for only part of the specified period - see *Davenport (HMIT) v Hasslacher* [1977] STC 254.

[88] For definitions see Sch. 6 para 1(2) which defines a "personal company", in relation to an individual, as a company in which not less than 5% of voting rights are exercisable by that individual. A "full time working officer or employee" is an officer or employee who is required to devote substantially the whole of his time to the service of the company in a managerial or technical capacity.

[89] Note that this does not mean that the business must of necessity be sold as a going concern (see Jonathan Parker J in *Pepper (HMIT) v Daffurn* [1993] BTC 277 at 283).

[90] Knox J in *Jarmin (HMIT) v Rawlings* [1995] BTC 3 at 9.

[91] [1988] STC 758 at 764.

[T]he fact that a farmer sells some land alone which he has been
using for a farming business prima facie will not amount to a sale of
his farming business or any part thereof because it is only the sale of
a chargeable business asset and not in itself the sale of the business or
any part of it notwithstanding that it will be virtually inevitable that
the sale of land on which the business has been conducted will
reduce the activity of the farmer and probably his profits.

Although when a business is disposed of there is almost inevitably a
disposal of one or more individual assets which are used in it or which
form part of it, there is an essential difference in that a business is an entity
distinct from the sum of its parts[92]. Whether a particular disposal amounts
to a disposal of the whole or part of a business, or whether it is merely a
disposal of business assets is a question of fact.[93] The distinction between
the two was discussed in *McGregor (HMIT) v Adcock*[94]. A farmer sold some five
acres out of a farm of 35 acres with the benefit of planning permission.
There was nothing to suggest that the scale of his farming business had
been significantly altered by the sale. It was held that he was not entitled
to retirement relief because he had only sold a business asset, and not a part
of the business. Fox J said[95] that the provision requires the taxpayer who is
seeking relief to establish that he has disposed of "the whole or part" of his
business and that in the ordinary use of language, land is not the same thing
as a business. According to him, a business connotes an activity, but land is
merely an asset of a business. Fox J said that, although in order to bring the
section into operation the taxpayer must dispose of the whole or part of a
business, for the purposes of computation, the gains are calculated by
reference to the "chargeable business assets" (i.e., assets used for the
purposes of a trade, profession, etc) comprised in the disposal. According
to Fox J, the provision is therefore merely recognising a distinction which
in fact exists:

In my view there is thus a clear distinction between the business and
the individual assets used in the business. Prima facie, therefore, it
seems to me wrong to assert that the mere sale of farmland is a
disposal of part of the farm business. The true position, I think, is that
the sale is merely a factor which the court has to consider in deciding
whether there has been such a disposal.

In his view, the test was "whether there has been such an interference with
the whole complex of activities and assets as can be said to amount to a

---

[92]   Knox J in *Jarmin (HMIT) v Rawlings* [1995] BTC 3 at 9. A business connotes an activity (ibid, at page 14).
[93]   See Fox J in *McGregor (HMIT) v Adcock* [1977] STC 206 at 209; Peter Gibson J in *Atkinson (HMIT) v Dancer* [1988]
       STC 758 at 765.
[94]   [1977] STC 206.
[95]   At page 209.

disposal of the business or part of the business".[96]

Concerning this test, Peter Gibson J in *Atkinson (HMIT) v Dancer*[97] doubted whether it was particularly helpful or illuminating to rephrase the simple and clear test posed by the wording of the section by a test in terms of interference with the whole complex of activities and assets.[98] However, since both counsel in the case were agreed that this was the appropriate test, he would, in spite of his reservations, follow the test, leaving it to a higher court, if it thinks fit, to lay down some other test. As far as applying the test was concerned Peter Gibson J accepted that the only relevant matters to be considered in relation to the interference are those that are caused by the sale. According to him Fox J was clearly contrasting the position immediately before the sale and the position immediately after the sale. When posing the test of an interference with the whole complex of activities and assets, Fox J was plainly looking to the sale constituting that interference. It was thus implicit in Fox J's remarks that changes in activities and assets caused by something other than the sale are irrelevant.[99] Elaborating on this point Peter Gibson J said:[100]

> But unless the change in [the taxpayer's] activities is attributable to the disposal by way of sale it is simply not material that prior to the sale there had been a connection between the activity that has ceased or been reduced and that which is sold. What the commissioners must do if applying Fox J's test is to look at the position before the sale and the position after the sale and ask the question whether the sale caused any changes in the activities and assets. If the changes caused by the sale lead to the conclusion that the position is wholly different from the position before the sale, the in Fox J's words 'it may well be' ... that an inference will be drawn of the sale of a business or part of a business.

Problems arise where the taxpayer disposes of assets in a number of transactions, and then claims that these transactions constitute a disposal of part of his business. The question in this case is whether the transactions ought to be taken as one single transaction involving a disposal of the business or part of it (therefore qualifying for relief), or as single and independent transactions which are just mere disposals of business assets (therefore not qualifying for relief). The issue arose in *Mannion (HMIT) v Johnston*[101] In this case the taxpayer, after some deterioration in his health, decided to retire partially. He farmed 78 acres of land, and in April 1984, he sold some 17 acres of his farm to a neighbouring farmer. In December

---

[96] [1977] STC at 209.
[97] [1988] STC at 765.
[98] Compare Jonathan Parker J in *Pepper (HMIT) v Daffurn* [1993] BTC 277 at 282.
[99] Ibid.
[100] At page 766.
[101] [1988] BTC 364.

1984, he sold a further 18 acres of the farm to the same purchaser. These transactions were undertaken by the taxpayer in order to sell part of his farm. Counsel for the taxpayer argued that where there were a number of disposals, these could and should be taken together in deciding whether there had been a sale of a business or part of a business. Counsel argued that this was so even if there was no contractual connection between the disposals, or any other link which made the disposals part of the same transaction – otherwise, a taxpayer who chooses to dispose of his business by a number of disposals to obtain a better price would be treated less favourably than a taxpayer who disposes of his business by a single sale. The commissioners accepted the arguments and held that the disposal of 45% of the taxpayer's farm acreage was a disposal of part of the business and thus he was entitled to retirement relief. The Revenue's appeal against this decision was upheld. Peter Gibson J said:[102]

> Where there are two separate disposals not part of the same transaction, I cannot see anything in [s 163] or in the capital gains tax legislation in general which allows or requires such disposals to be treated as one. They are two separate disposals occurring, it may be, in different fiscal years and having separate fiscal consequences accordingly. Unless there be some evidence to enable the two disposals to be treated as one, such as evidence that they were part of the same transaction, they must be treated separately.

Peter Gibson J said[103] that the Commissioners appeared to have treated the two disposals as a single substantial disposal, having referred to the sale (in the singular) of the land and to the disposal of a substantial proportion (also in the singular) of the farmland. He said that this was not correct, and that, each disposal, being a separate transaction, must be treated separately.

This decision is not authority for the proposition that multiple disposals must always be treated separately. The question depends on the facts of each case, and it is quite possible for a number of separate disposals to be taken together as a sale of part of a business. This happened in *Jarmin (HMIT) v Rawlings*.[104] The taxpayer, who was then 61 years old, was a dairy farmer who owned some 64 acres, with a milking parlour and yard, a hay barn, implements shed, cattle sheds and a herd of 34 cattle. He also had the benefit of a milk quota. In October 1988 he sold the milking parlour, yard and storage barn at an auction. Completion took place in January 1989. None of the cattle was sold at the auction (which was solely concerned with the land and buildings) but between the auction and completion 14 cows were sold. At completion, the rest of the cattle were transferred to the

---

[102] At page 373.
[103] At page 375.
[104] [1995] BTC 3.

taxpayer's wife's farm. He retained ownership thereof, but he did not have any financial benefit from their milk. They were eventually sold after a period of time. After completion, the taxpayer ceased dairy farming, but he continued farming on the farm by rearing and finishing store cattle. The commissioners held that the dairy business was a separate and distinguishable part of the taxpayer's business and that, in selling the means of dairy production and the dairy herd, he was disposing of the dairying part of his business. They also found that the sale of the milking parlour and the buildings made it impossible for the taxpayer to continue his business after the sale, and that there was sufficient interference to satisfy the "interference test". Thus the taxpayer was entitled to retirement relief.

Knox J upheld the Commissioners. One issue that arose in this case concerned timing. S. 28(1) TCGA 1992 provides generally that, where an asset is disposed of and acquired under a contract, the time of the disposal and acquisition is the time when the contract is made and not, if different, the time at which the asset is conveyed or transferred. In this respect the Revenue argued that it was only permissible to have regard to what happened at the time of the relevant disposition, which, under s. 27 CGTA 1979 (now s. 28 TCGA 1992) was the date of the auction in October 1988. According to this argument, all that was disposed of at the auction was milking parlour and yard, most of the other disposals having taken place after the auction but before completion. Thus, it was not possible to find that part of a business, as opposed to an asset of a business, was disposed of. The taxpayer on the other hand argued that, the proper subject of inquiry was what was disposed of when the transaction in question took effect and that this could only realistically be assessed by comparing the position immediately before the auction with the position at and immediately after completion. This was all part of the disposal which had to be looked at realistically and included all that happened between contract and completion. He argued that s. 27 CGTA 1979 (s. 28 TCGA 1992) was only a timing provision which enabled a date to be fixed for capital gains tax purposes of a disposal. Knox J preferred the taxpayer's argument, saying:[105]

> It would ... be highly artificial to look only at the date of a contract in order to assess whether there was or was not a sale of part of a business, more especially if the proper subject of enquiry is whether the disposal effected by a contract followed by completion amounted to a disposal of part of a business. To ignore events after the making of the contract would be to ignore the performance of the disposal

---

[105] At page 13.

itself and that in my view cannot be right.

Therefore the sales of cattle between contract and completion could properly be taken into account by the commissioners. However, in respect of the sales subsequent to completion, he felt that the conclusion that there was a disposal of part of a business could not be supported unless there was some connection established at the date of completion, which enabled a subsequent sale of cattle to be treated as part of the same transaction. For these purposes, the fact that the cattle were no longer being used by the taxpayer for his daily farming business would not be a sufficient connection.

On the question of whether the disposals constituted the disposal of a business or part of a business, Knox J said that the right question was whether the sales of cattle were part of the same transaction as the disposal of the farmyard and the milking shed.[106] He said that it was not an easy question[107], and that it could be tested by postulating simultaneous sales by the owner of a business to a wide variety of purchasers not connected between each other, of the totality of the assets of a business:

> An obvious example would be a sale by auction of all the assets used in a business. As regards any individual business asset it would only be possible to say that the disposal was a sale of part of a business if all the other sales of other business assets were taken into consideration. The auction could be regarded as a single transaction at least from the vendor's point of view and it is to be remembered that it is a disposal that is the subject matter of inquiry and not the consequential acquisition by another party.[108]

Knox J said that it is legitimate to have regard to simultaneous disposals entered into of other assets used in the business in assessing whether or not a particular disposal can be categorised as a sale of part of a business. In this case, it was not material that the taxpayer still retained some assets after the disposal because it was not necessary that, for a business or part of a business to be disposed of, all the assets used in the business must be sold. Knox J thus concluded that, on the facts as found by the commissioners, it was open to them to find that the dairy farming was a separate business from the rearing and finishing of store cattle and that the dairy farming business was disposed of by the sale of land at auction coupled with the cessation of milking for profit at completion of that sale.[109] According to him, the critical factor is that a business connotes an activity. The activity

---

[106] Ibid.
[107] At page 14.
[108] Ibid.
[109] Ibid.
[110] At pages 14-15.

in this case was the production and sale of milk, which ceased at completion as far as the taxpayer was concerned. The fact that cows which still belonged to him continued to be milked for other persons' profit, and that he still owned the milk quota (although he did not use it for his own milk production) did not detract from the conclusion that, on completion, the taxpayer's dairying business ceased. Concluding the matter, Knox J said:[110]

> The sale of the milking parlour was a vital ingredient in that cessation so far as to make it indeed possible to say that that sale caused such an interference with the whole complex of activities and assets as to amount to a disposal of part of a business, if that is the correct test. For my part I would prefer to look at it somewhat more broadly and say that the sale by auction and completion of that sale of the milking parlour and yard coupled with the cessation at completion of all milking operations for Mr. Rawlings' benefit amounted to a disposal by him of his dairy farming business.

On the facts of this case, this was obviously the correct decision. However, the point still needs to be emphasised that everything depends on the facts of each case, and that no general rule can be made, as the later decision of *Wase (HMIT) v Bourke*[111] shows. Here, the taxpayer, having decided to give up farming, sold his entire dairy herd in March 1988 at which time he was aged 59 years and four months. At that time the qualifying age for retirement relief was 60 years. After the herd had been sold, the young cattle that remained were fattened up and sold. He leased his milk quota to a third party and then sold it in February 1989, at which time he was 60 years old. The delay in selling the milk quota was due to financial reasons. While the quota remained unsold the taxpayer could have resumed his dairy farming, but did not do so. The only question that arose in this case was whether the disposal of the milk quota was a disposal of the whole or part of a business. It was common ground that the dairy business ceased to be carried on when the taxpayer sold his herd in March 1988. The commissioners found that the taxpayer's decision to give up dairy farming was primarily motivated by the fact that he had developed arthritis in his shoulder, and that each of the transactions were steps taken in implementation or further implementation of that decision. They thus held that the sales were all part of one transaction – the disposal of the taxpayer's dairy farming business. In reaching this conclusion they had asked themselves what it was that amounted to a "major interference with

---

[111] [1996] BTC 3.
[112] At page 12.

the whole complex of activities carried on by the taxpayer". They decided that this was the disposal of the farming business, of which the sale of the milk quota was an integral part. The judge (Anthony Grabiner QC sitting as a deputy judge of the High Court) held that the commissioners had erred by failing to ask themselves the correct question – which was, whether the disposal by the taxpayer of his milk quota amounted to the whole or part of his business.[112] If they had asked themselves the correct question, they would have concluded that the disposal of the milk quota was simply the disposal of an asset which had formerly been used in or which was part of the dairy farming business, and that it was not by itself the disposal of the whole or part of the business. According to Anthony Grabiner QC, the relevant business activity consisted of the production and sale of milk, and that activity ceased upon the disposal of the dairy herd. The subsequent disposal of another asset does not, in the circumstances of this case, amount to a disposal of part of the business. Anthony Grabiner QC said that this case fell on the *Atkinson v Dancer* and *Mannion v Johnston* side of the line, and that the sale of the milk quota does not satisfy the "simultaneous disposals" test identified by Knox J in *Jarmin v Rawlings*. The taxpayer in this case had specific financial reasons for delaying the sale of the milk quota for almost a year after he had sold his herd and given up dairy farming, and these two matters could not be properly described as amounting to a single transaction.

This approach was also applied in *Purves (Inspector of Taxes) v Harrison* in which the taxpayer ran a coach business. He sold his premises to one purchaser in February 1990, but leased them back so that he could continue trading. During the year, he sold some of his vehicles, before selling the business to another purchaser the following December. It was held that the disposal of the premises was a disposal of a business asset and did not qualify for retirement relief.

Cessation: disposal of assets used for business

As seen above, s.163(2)(b) includes in the definition of "disposal of business assets" a disposal of assets which, at the time when a business ceased to be carried on, were in use for the purposes of that business. S.163(4) provides that a disposal of business assets on cessation is a material disposal if:

a. throughout a period of at least one year ending with the cessation, the business was owned by the disponor or his personal company (as in s.163(3) above); and

b. on or before the cessation the had either attained the ago of 50 or retired before attaining that age on grounds of ill health; and

c. the date of cessation falls within the permitted period before the date of the disposal.

"Permitted period" is defined by Sch. 6 para. 1(2) as a period of one year, or such longer period as the Board may allow by notice in writing. If such notice is not given, the period cannot be extended. This was made clear by the High Court in *Hatt v. Newman*.[113]

The Court of Appeal's judgment in *Plumbly v Spencer (HMIT)*[114] concerned the situation where an individual disposed of an asset which had been used by his company. In this case, the individual, H, had granted a lease of land to a company which was a trading company and his family company, and of which he was a full time working director. The letting was for the use of the company's trade, and the company paid rent to H. Within one year of the company ceasing to carry on its trade, H disposed of the land. The question was, whether, upon the true construction of (what is now) s.163(2)(b), use of the land for the purposes of the business carried on by the company was sufficient, or whether it was necessary that the land was used for the purposes of the business carried on by H himself. Lightman J had held that H's personal representatives could not claim retirement relief, but the Court of Appeal reversed this judgment. In allowing the appeal, Robert Walker LJ concluded by stating:

> We do not regard that result as in any way absurd, or even as particularly anomalous. It might be thought more anomalous if Mr Harbour had been denied any business relief, after the company had been farming for 40 years, because of his (or his advisers') omission to take one or other of two otherwise fairly pointless steps (that is the transfer of the farming business to Mr Harbour personally just before its cessation, or the disposal of his shares in the dormant company).[115]

Shares or securities in a company

Section 163(5) provides that a disposal of shares or securities in a company is a material disposal if throughout a period of at least one year ending with the operative date:

---

[113] [2000] STC 113.
[114] [1999] STC 677.
[115] Note the purposive construction of the statute here. The court is not prepared to allow the intention of Parliament to be frustrated by the taxpayer's failure to take otherwise pointless steps.

a. the disponor owns the business, which at the date of the disposal is owned by the company or, if the company is the holding company of a trading group, by any member of the group; or

b. the company is the disponor's personal company, (or a subsidiary) and the disponor is a full time working officer or employee of the company.

Except in situations where either s 163(6) or s 163(7) applies, the operative date is the date of the disposal.[116] S.163(6) provides that, where cessation (of trading) occurs during the permitted period, and on or before cessation the disponor was 50 or retired on ill health grounds before that age, the operative date is the date of such cessation. This date is also deemed to be the date of disposal for the purposes of s 163(5)(a). Where the disponor has ceased to be a full time working officer or employee of the company, the date when the disponor ceased to be a full time working officer or employee is the operative date (S.163(7)).

Other disposals

Section 164(1) extends retirement relief to assets held for the purpose of an office or employment (other than director of a personal company) and s.164(3) extends it to disposals by trustees of settled property, being disposals of shares or securities in a company or of business assets where the conditions attached under subsections (4) and (5) of the section apply to a beneficiary having an interest in possession.

Associated disposals

Where relief falls to be given under s.163 in respect of a material disposal of business assets which is either a disposal by an individual of his interest in partnership assets, or a qualifying (under s.163(5)) disposal of shares or securities of a company, relief is also given in respect of associated disposals made by that individual (s. 164(6)). S. 164(7) provides, for these purposes, that a disposal is associated with a material disposal if it takes place as part of a withdrawal of the individual concerned from participation in the business (carried on by the partnership, or the company, as the case may be). Further conditions are that, immediately before the material disposal (or, if earlier, the cessation of the relevant business) the asset was in use for the purposes of that business, and during any part of the individual's ownership of the asset being disposed of, the asset had been used for the purposes of the business or some other qualifying businesses. Although

---

[116] S.163(5).

s.164(7)(b) refers to the asset being in use for the business immediately before the material disposal or cessation, there is some amount of flexibility in the timing. In *Clarke (HMIT) v Mayo*[117] the Revenue argued that the use of the word "immediately" required that the property must have been in use at the instant immediately before the cessation, such that, when the disposal of property took place four weeks before the cessation of the business, the condition in respect of immediacy was not satisfied. Evans-Lombe J rejected the argument in the following terms:[118]

> The words "immediately before ... the cessation of the business" should not be construed in isolation but in the context of the provisions of [s 163 and 164] as a whole. From those sections it is in my judgment plain that the legislature intended that relief from capital gains tax should be available for associated disposals of assets where those disposals were part of a withdrawal by a taxpayer from participation in a relevant business where he has attained the [prescribed age] or retired earlier on grounds of ill health. The requirement that the asset being disposed of must have been in use in the relevant business immediately before the interest in the business itself was disposed of or that business ceased seems to me to have been provided for so as to ensure that the associated disposal was genuinely part of the withdrawal. It seems to me that where the commissioners are satisfied that such is the case they are justified in so construing the relevant words of subs. (7)(b) so as not to require precisely that at the instant before the material disposal or cessation the asset was in use in the business. The words "immediately before" may be construed as meaning "sufficiently proximate in time to the material disposal or cessation so as to justify the conclusion that the transaction in question formed part of it".

In respect of the principle of "withdrawal from participation", the withdrawal itself must constitute the relevant material disposal of business assets,[119] and "participation" in this context mean holding an interest in the business concerned.[120] Whether the required association exists or not is a question of fact for the Commissioners.[121]

---

[117] [1994] BTC 225.
[118] At page 234.
[119] At page 233.
[120] At page 234.
[121] Ibid.

Amount of relief

The amounts on which retirement relief is available is being gradually reduced so that, between 6 April 1999 and 5 April 2003, the relief is being phased out. The general scheme is to provide relief in relation to a lower monetary limit and an upper monetary limit and it is these limits which are being reduced. Relief is available on gains of up to that upper limit (Sch. 6(13)(1)).

According to Sch. 6 para 13(1), the available relief is the aggregate of:

a. so much of the qualifying gains as do not exceed the appropriate percentage of the lower monetary limit; and

b. half of so much of the gains as exceed the appropriate percentage of the lower monetary limit, but do not exceed that percentage of the upper monetary limit.

In 1996-97 and 1997-98 the lower limit was £250,000 and the upper limit was £1,000,000. The sliding scale of reductions is to be found in s.140(1) FA 1998:

Year	Lower monetary limit (formerly £250,000)	Upper monetary limit (formerly £1 million)
1999–00	£200,000	£800,000
2000–01	£150,000	£600,000
2001–02	£100,000	£400,000
2002–03	£50,000	£200,000

For example, on 2001–02 figures, the appropriate percentage of £100,000 is exempt and half of the appropriate percentage of the next £300,000 is exempt. Any excess over £400,000 is chargeable.[122]

Sch. 6 para. 13(1) also provides that the "appropriate percentage" is one which is determined according to the length of the qualifying period rising arithmetically from 10% for one year to 100% for ten years. For example, on 2001–02 figures, relief is available in respect of:

---

[122] Although taper relief will be available on the excess. See below.

a. £10,000 for each full year, for the first £100,000; and

b. half of £30,000 for each full year, for the remaining £300,000.

Example

A, aged 50, sells his business in May 2001, realising a gain of £1 million pounds. He has owned the business for five years. The appropriate percentage is therefore 50%. Relief is therefore available on £50,000 for the lower monetary limit and £75,000 for the upper monetary limit, giving a total relief of £125,000. The remaining £875,000 is subject to taper relief (see below.)

Had A owned the business for ten years, the total relief would have been £250,000 (£100,000 + £150,000) and the remaining £750,000 would have been subject to taper relief.

Taper Relief

The phasing out of retirement relief and freezing of indexation relief in the 1998 budget were intended to be counterbalanced by the new taper relief. This relief progressively reduced the chargeable gain according to the length of ownership of an asset. The idea was that gains on quick sales should be taxed more heavily than gains on assets that had been held for a longer period.

Example

Bill and Ben each have a valuable painting which they put into an auction. Each painting sells for £50,000. Bill bought his painting fifteen years ago for £10,000; Ben bought his last month for £10,000. The old system would have recognised that Bill's paid more money in real terms for his painting than Ben did, so Bill would have been able to apply indexation relief to increase his acquisition cost, thereby reducing his gain. The aim of this system, however, would have been to put Bill in the same position that he would have been in but for the effects of inflation.[123]

By contrast, under the new system, Bill's gain will be reduced by 40% because he has held the asset for ten years or more. He will therefore pay tax on 60% of his gain, whereas Bill will pay tax on 100%.[124]

---

[123] This example assumes that the new rules have been in force for the full period of ownership. As discussed below, the period of ownership for taper relief is calculated from April 1998.

[124] Applying the rules for taper relief on non-business assets, discussed below.

Another point to note is that, while the legislation refers to the holding period of the asset, it makes no reference to the date of any enhancement expenditure. This means that taxpayers can considerably increase the value of an asset just before disposal and still apply taper relief to the full gain.

Example

Bob bought a painting ten years ago for £10,000. He decides to sell it and spends a further £10,000 on having it restored and cleaned. He then sells it for £50,000. His gain of £30,000 qualifies for full taper relief.

In the absence of increased inflation, taxpayers holding assets for up to ten years are likely to be in a better position as a result of taper relief than they would have been purely on the basis of the indexation allowance. However, taxpayers who hold assets for longer than ten years are likely to be worse off. A taxpayer who holds an asset for twenty years will benefit from maximum taper relief, but this would still have been the case had he only held it for ten. The effect of this is that he is assessed to CGT on purely inflationary gains in the second ten years of ownership. The system therefore encourages taxpayers to dispose of assets after ten years.

Business assets – definition

For the purposes of taper relief, business assets are defined in Schedule A1, paras (4) and (5).

Schedule A1(4) states that, in order for shares to be classed as business assets, the relevant company must be a qualifying company by reference to the disponor. This is the case in relation to individuals[125], trustees of a settlement[126] and an individual's personal representatives.[127] Qualifying companies in relation to all three categories are defined in Schedule A1(6).[128] In each case, the company must be a trading company or the holding company of a trading group and one of a list of other criteria must also be satisfied:

a. the company is unlisted;

b. at least 5% of the voting rights are held by the disponor;

---

[125] Schedule A1(4)(2).
[126] Schedule A1(4)(3).
[127] Schedule A1(4)(4).
[128] Schedule A1(6)(1) relates to individuals, A1(6)(2) to trustees of a settlement and A1(6)(3) to personal representatives.

c. the individual – or, in the case of a settlement, an eligible beneficiary – was an officer or employee of the company, or of a company having a relevant connection with it.

Assets other than shares must be used for one of the following purposes set out in Schedule A1(5) if they are to qualify as business assets:[129]

a. the purposes of a trade carried on by the disponor or, where the disponor is an individual, by a partnership of which he was a member;

b. the purposes of a trade carried on by a company which was a qualifying company by reference to the disponor or, where the disponors are trustees of a settlement, by reference to an eligible beneficiary;

c. the purposes of a trade carried on by a company which was a member of a trading group for which the holding company was a qualifying company by reference to the disponor or, where the disponors are trustees of a settlement, by reference to an eligible beneficiary;

d. the purposes of any office or employment held by an individual – or, where the disponors are trustees of a settlement, by a beneficiary – with a person carrying on a trade.

Business assets – relief available

The relief for business assets is more favourable than for non–business assets, both because the qualifying periods for the relief are shorter and because the relief available is greater.

In order to qualify for relief, the taxpayer must have held the asset for at least one full year and the relief available increases year by year. Originally, the maximum relief was available after ten years of ownership. However, changes introduced in FA 2000 meant that, for assets disposed of after 5 April 2000, maximum relief was available after four years of ownership. A table setting out the percentage of gain chargeable is set out in s. 2A(5) TCGA. For business assets, the position until 5 April 2002 is as set out over:

---

[129] Schedule A1(5)(2) relates to individuals, A1(5)(3) to trustees of a settlement and A1(5)(4) to personal representatives.

Number of whole years in qualifying holding period	Percentage of gain chargeable
1	87.5 (12.5% relief)
2	75 (25% relief)
3	50 (50% relief)
4 or more	25 (75% relief)

In his 2002 budget, the Chancellor of the Exchequer proposed further changes to these limits for disposals made on or after 6 April 2002:

Number of whole years in qualifying holding period	Percentage of gain chargeable
1	50%
2 or more	25% (75% relief)

At the time of writing, these provisions were still subject to enactment by the Finance Act 2002.

The qualifying holding period for business assets is defined in s.2A(8)(a) as the period after 5 April 1998 for which the asset had been held at the time of its disposal. Time before this date does not count towards the qualifying period, probably because the indexation allowance can be claimed on gains up to this date.

Example

Chris sells his factory in May 2002 when it has been used for the purposes of his business for twelve years. Indexation relief is available on the April 1998 value. Taper relief will apply to the gain since this date. This gain will be reduced by 75%, so that only 25% of it will be chargeable.

Taper relief and retirement relief

As discussed above in the context of retirement relief, taper relief can be applied to any gains that are above the retirement relief limits. This will apply until 5 April 2003 when retirement relief is finally phased out. From then on, taper relief will apply to all gains on the sale of a business, assuming that the assets disposed of meet the criteria for the relief set out above.

Some taxpayers will be significantly better off as a result of the move to taper relief from retirement relief. The changes will be particularly beneficial for those who wish to dispose of their businesses when they are under 50 and in good health. Since, unlike retirement relief, taper relief has no upper limit, taxpayers making a gain of significantly more than £1 million pounds will also be better off. Ignoring the period between 1999 and 2003 when retirement relief was being phased out, i.e. comparing full retirement relief to full taper relief, the break-even point is a gain of £500,000.[130] Taxpayers making gains of above this on the disposal of a business will be better off.

However, it also follows that taxpayers who make a gain of below £500,000 on the disposal of a business will be worse off, always assuming that they would have qualified for retirement relief. For example, a taxpayer who makes £250,000 on the disposal of a business would not have had any chargeable gain under retirement relief, but will still have a chargeable gain of £62,500 if he qualifies for full taper relief.

Non-business assets

Taper relief for non-business assets is less generous than for business assets, with no relief being available for the first three years of ownership and full relief of 40% being available only after ten years of ownership. As with business assets, the position is set out in s.2A:

Number of whole years in qualifying period	Percentage of gain chargeable
–	–
–	–
3	95 (5% relief)
4	90 (10% relief)
5	85 (15% relief)
6	80 (20% relief)
7	75 (25% relief)
8	70 (30% relief)
9	65 (35% relief)
10 or more	60 (40% relief)

[130] Full taper relief would mean that only 25% of the gain (£125,000) would be chargeable; full retirement relief would mean that the first £250,000 would not be taxable and half of the remainder up to a maximum of £1 million would be taxable. Half of the remainder in this case would also be £125,000.

When calculating the length of ownership, s.2A(8)(b) provides that, where the asset was acquired before 17th March 1998, the qualifying holding period is the actual length of ownership plus one year.   As described above, indexation allowance is also available for gains up to 5 April 1998.

Taper relief and rollover relief

A taxpayer who chooses to claim rollover relief on the replacement of a business asset under s.152 should be aware that he will lose any taper relief to which he would otherwise have been entitled.   This is because, unlike holdover relief, discussed below, gains are irrelevant for the purposes of rollover relief.   Rollover relief is based on treating the disposal of the old asset as if it had been made for no gain/no loss and then reducing the acquisition cost of the new asset by the amount by which the actual consideration exceeded to no gain/no loss value.   Even though this amount will in most cases be equivalent to the chargeable gain, the language of gains is not used.   Since no gain is identified under rollover relief, there is no gain that can be reduced by applying taper relief.

Taxpayers who qualify for full taper relief on business assets might be advised to consider whether it would be better to claim this relief rather than rollover relief, even though that would mean paying a certain amount of CGT on the disposal of the old assets.

Example

Jean bought a factory in May 1998 for £50,000.   In May 2002, she sells it for £100,000 and buys a new, larger, factory for £200,000.   She has two options:

a.   Claim rollover relief under s.152.   If she does this, she will deemed to have sold the old factory at no gain/no loss.   The amount by which the actual consideration exceeds the no gain/no loss value is £50,000.   This will then be deducted from the acquisition cost of the new factory, giving a revised acquisition cost of £150,000.   She will pay no tax at present, but will face a higher bill when she eventually disposes of the new factory.

b.   Claim taper relief.   Since she has owned the factory for four years, she will qualify for full relief of 75%.   Her chargeable gain will be £12,500.

Which option Jean takes may depend on how long she intends to keep the new factory. If she keeps it for four years or more, any gains on the disposal will again qualify for full taper relief. If she keeps it for less than four years, she will pay more tax on that part of the gain.

Taper relief and holdover relief

Unlike rollover relief, holdover relief operates by deducting the amount of any held over gain both from the chargeable gain and from the transferee's acquisition cost.[131] As a result, taper relief can be applied to reduce the chargeable gain before holdover relief is applied.

Example

Paul gives his consultancy business to his daughter, Lucy, in May 2004 when it is worth £150,000. Paul had established the business in July 1990. The period of ownership is calculated from 5 April 1998, so Paul will qualify for full taper relief and only 25% of the gain will be taxable. If the gain is £100,000, there will be a £25,000 chargeable gain. Paul and Lucy may jointly elect to hold over the gain under s.165. This will mean that Paul is not liable for tax and that Lucy's deemed acquisition cost is £125,000.

Five years later, Lucy gives the business to her son, Peter. It is now worth £325,000. Lucy's gain is therefore £200,000. She qualifies for full taper relief, so that only 25% of the gain will be chargeable. Lucy will be liable to CGT on £50,000.[132]

Note that the parties are significantly better off than they would have been had Paul held onto the business and given it directly to Peter in 2009. Paul's gain would have been £275,000 of which £68,750 would have been chargeable. The combination of holdover relief and taper relief means that maximum taper relief can be claimed on two successive occasions.

---

[131] S.165(4).
[132] Assuming no changes in the law in the meantime.

Further Reading

Riches J, *Changing the Landscape: Revised Taper Relief* [2001] BTR 124.

Pearce-Crump D, *Paddocks Lodge Revisited (or Private Residence Relief Again)* [1993] BTR 12.

Norris W, *Capital Gains Tax: More About Residences* [1993] BTR 24.

Nobes CW, *Capital Gains Tax and Inflation* [1977] BTR 154.

chapter seventeen
Companies and Corporation Tax

Companies resident in the United Kingdom are liable to pay corporation tax on all "profits" wherever arising.[1] "Profits" are defined to include both income and chargeable gains. It is convenient that income and chargeable gains are computed in accordance with income tax principles and capital gains tax principles–thus much of the work has been completed in previous chapters. In this chapter we are going to focus on the problems peculiar to companies. In particular we will consider the issues raised by "groups" of companies; "close" companies; and the problems created by the relationship between the company and its shareholders and any returns (dividends) that shareholders might receive. Before we consider these issues and problems we must first consider why we tax companies.

Why Do We Tax Companies?

This question was considered by the Royal Commission in its Final Report on the Taxation of Profits and Income in 1955.[2] In its own discussion of and reply to that question the Royal Commission appeared to place emphasis on the fact that a company enjoys a personality of its own: it is a legal person distinct and separate from the members, the shareholders, who make up the company.[3] As a legal person perhaps a company like other legal persons should be subject to taxation. However, this reasoning does not explain why a company should be subject to a different regime of taxation nor does it explain why there was a time "lag" between the recognition of the separate legal personality of a company and the introduction of a tax on company profits and gains. The "time lag" is always difficult to explain and account for. The separate legal personality of a company had been recognised for a long period before revenue law caught up with the concept and introduced a separate taxation of companies.[4] In the UK special taxes were introduced and imposed on countries from 1915-1924 and from 1937 onwards. Once again, initiative

---

[1] TA 1988, s.6.
[2] Cmn 9474, para. 45.
[3] For a discussion of the separate legal personality of a company see *Salomon v Salomon & Co Ltd* [1897] AC 22.
[4] It is believed that in Europe, the practice of recognising a separation of the business and its owners was present in the thirteenth century.

for the introduction of these special taxes was the need to finance warfare. In 1965 those special taxes were replaced by a system of corporation tax- it is not applicable to unincorporated associations (partnerships, sole traders) and it recognises the legal status of the company and its separation from the individuals who make up the company. It also provides greater flexibility in allowing the government to operate its fiscal policy knowing that corporation taxes are separate from income taxes. Their independence can be used to promote and encourage investment.

Some believe that the separate taxation of companies is a fair charge for the benefits and privileges that a corporate status confers. One presumes that those benefits or privileges includes the ability to access wider sources of finance, and the privilege of the protection of limited liability. The measure and extent of such privileges is difficult to assess. In many ways those privileges are under threat or, at least, enjoyed at cost. For example, the registration procedure and the annual disclosure requirements impose a cost or charge benefit of incorporation. Similarly, increasing statutory regimes impose liability on individuals instead of or in addition to the company[5]: it is not always possible to "hide" behind the company's existence.

If one still accepts that "incorporation" is a privilege, then a charge for that privilege in terms of a licence and licence fee rather than the inclusion of an uncertain and unquantifiable privilege element in a system of corporation tax is the preferred method of charge. Another major problem of taxing on the basis of benefit or privilege is the difficulty of ascertaining who really pays for that privilege. The incidence of corporation tax or of a benefit charge might fall on the company employees, company owners or the consumers and customers. These might not constitute the intended target.

A very simple perspective of the objective of a company is that it exists to make profits. Cadman (1969) suggested that the centred question was: how does the corporate tax system support or hinder the pursuit of this corporate objective by the operating divisions? Although Cadman used this question to compare the internal and external pressures on a corporation with those on a central government (with some degree of communality), the question should be central in the minds of those studying the concept and detail of corporation tax.

Finally, despite the considerable resources that are expended on compliance, corporation tax in many countries raises only a small proportion of revenue for governments. For example, in the G7 countries, taxes paid by corporations account for less than 8% of tax revenues raised

---

[5]   See ss.213, 214, Insolvency Act 1986.

by governments, except for Japan, where the corporation tax yields about 15% of government revenue. This low yield and high compliance cost have resulted in some experts and politicians questioning the usefulness of corporation tax.

Systems of Corporation Tax

There are three recognised systems of corporation tax: (1) classical, (2) imputation, and (3) integrated. Under the classical system double taxation of the same income often occurs. The company profits are subject to corporation tax and if the company pays dividends out of those taxed profits those dividends are taxed once more in the hands of the recipient shareholder. Thus we find that the same income is taxed twice. First in the hands of the company as corporation tax and then in the hands of the shareholder as income from his investment (the "dividend" on his shareholding). The UK operated a classical system of taxation in 1965-73. The main objection against such a system is the inequitable double-taxation of income. It raises a disadvantage of incorporation if one considers the tax treatment of unincorporated businesses, and it might discriminate against entrepreneurial risk-taking. It also creates a bias against the distribution of dividends: the larger the distribution, the larger is the total tax borne by a company and its shareholders.

The imputation system of taxation mitigates the double-taxation problems of the classical system by imputing to the shareholders some or all of the tax paid by companies. An imputation system was introduced in the UK in 1973 and is present in most EC countries. Imputation systems operate because the income that has been subject to corporation tax and is then distributed as dividends to shareholders will be distributed with a tax credit attached to it. For example, if £1.00 profit had been subject to a corporation tax rate of 35% and then 30 pence dividend had been declared out of the net profit, the money representing the dividend would not be subject to further tax charges in the hands of the shareholder. Instead, the shareholder would receive the dividend (at a grossed-up amount) together with a tax credit to offset against any personal tax liability attending to that income receipt.

The problem that the UK faces is that we have traditionally enjoyed a partial rather than a full imputation system. Under a full imputation system the shareholder would receive a tax credit that equated with both the company's corporation tax liability and the shareholder's individual tax liability. Changes are taking place in the UK with the phasing out and removal of the system of advanced corporation tax. During the phasing out, shareholders are entitled to a limited tax credit (10 per cent of the dividend in 2000). Some companies, such as Germany, do operate full imputation tax systems. Under a partial imputation tax system (UK, France) the taxpayer receives a tax credit equivalent to basic rate liability. For example, if we assumed a basic rate of 25% and a higher rate of 40% a shareholder would receive a dividend plus 25% tax credit. If the shareholder is a basic rate taxpayer no tax liability would ensue, whereas if the shareholder is a higher rate taxpayer, tax liability of 15% (40% rate minus the tax credit) would remain. Thus double taxation at the marginal rate would result.

Finally, before we leave the imputation system of corporation tax we must consider the peculiarities of the system of advance corporation tax (ACT) which operated for many years in the UK until its phasing out and removal was recently announced. In essence ACT was introduced to maintain the government's cash flow under the imputation system of corporation tax. Generally when a distribution was announced a company would pay ACT equivalent to the tax credit granted to the shareholder on that distribution. This ensured that the shareholder's tax credits would always have been paid for. The ACT would then be set-off against the company's corporation tax liability. Two problems occurred with ACT. First, the recipient shareholder may actually be another company. Those companies cannot benefit from the tax credits in the same way as the "non-corporate" shareholder. In this situation the dividends received by the "corporate" shareholder was classed as Franked Investment Income (FII). This FII was used by the recipient company to reduce any ACT due on its own distribution of dividends–thus reducing the amount of tax that it needed to pay in advance.

The second problem caused by the old ACT system relates to "surplus ACT". Surplus ACT was in essence, ACT which a company was unable to set-off against its corporation tax liability–it was sometimes regarded as a dividend tax, Surplus ACT normally occurs in one of two ways. First because a company paid dividends out of reserves, common in a recession, and paid ACT on those dividend payments but found that the ACT payments exceeded the company's mainstream corporation tax liability; or, second, in those companies that earn most of their profits overseas, UK tax liability is usually reduced by the amount of foreign taxes that they pay. Consequently, such companies would also find that the amount of mainstream corporation tax liability that remained, if any, was insufficient to offset any ACT paid. Thus it appeared that foreign profits were taxed twice, abroad and at home. In recognition of this problem the Chancellor announced the issuing of a consultative document based on a proposal that dividends paid out of overseas profits should be separately classified as "foreign income dividends"; companies would be entitled to a refund if the dividend payment gives rise to surplus ACT.[6] Significantly, it was proposed that no tax credit would be available to shareholders who enjoy such dividends. The absence of a tax credit might influence investment decisions.

Finally, the integrated system of company taxation involves an integration of the company's tax liability with the personal income tax liability of the shareholders. Shareholders would pay personal income tax on their share of corporate income or profits irrespective of whether that income is distributed or undistributed. Such a system removes any discrimination between distributed and undistributed income or profit, and it assists in removing any tax deferral control and opportunities of corporations.

An integrated system is similar in operation to the manner in which we deal with the "profits" of a partnership and has recently reared its head in the manner in which we tax European Economic Interest Groupings (EEIGs).[7] In situations where the taxpayer has little (real) control over the declared distributions of a company, an integration system could result in a tax liability in excess of receipts.

Although the removal of ACT came as a surprise to many people, even more surprisingly is the short-term consequences of its removal. In his memoirs 'The Unconventional Minister' the former paymaster general, Geoffrey Robinson, provides a revealing account of the planning of what he calls a "phased hit of £25bn" on corporate cash flow from changes to the system of advanced corporation tax, along with £5bn of annual tax savings from the abolition of tax credits on dividends. The pain of this last measure fell chiefly on companies because of the loss of income to their pension funds.

The rationale for these measures in Labour's first budget was straightforward. The money was needed, says Mr Robinson, "to fund the Welfare to work programme (soon to be called the New Deal); to close the obstinate deficit in the national finances; and for general disinflationary purposes."

Mr Robinson went on to explain that given the political limitation on action in the field of personal taxation, "....the corporate section would have to bear the brunt of the inescapable necessity to raise taxes." John Plender responded in the *Financial Times*[8] with the comment that the outcome must count as one of the greatest raids on corporate cash flow in history. It might also go some way to explaining why government receipts

---

[6] Announced by the Chancellor in his Budget Speech, 16 March 1993.

[7] TA 1988, s.510A.

[8] October 31st 2000.

increased from 3.5% of gross domestic product in 1998–1999 to 3.9% (or move) in 2001–2002.

The Tax Base, Assessment and Rates

Before we discuss European influences on the development and reform of corporation tax, it is important to appreciate the tax base of corporation tax. The tax base and its importance is often overlooked, and was overlooked at European level, when considering the reform of corporation tax. The tax base represents the definition of taxable income. In some countries, particularly France and Germany, the tax base (taxable income) is linked to accounting profit and thus varies with the particular country's rules on the calculation of accounting profit. In the UK, the tax base is not so interrelated with accounting income and profit. The tax base and taxable income is calculated in accordance with statutory requirements and currently consists of a requirement that corporation tax falls on the "income and chargeable gains of a company".[9] Thus the administration of corporation tax is closely linked with that of income tax and capital gains tax.

The tax period for corporation tax is levied by reference to 'financial years', not "years of assessment". Financial years begin on 1 April and end 31 March. They are known by a calendar year of reference being the year of the commencement of the financial year, i.e. 1 April of that year (calendar year 1997 for a year running 1 April 1997 to 31 March 1998). Apportionment of profits will take place where the company's accounting year does not correspond to the "financial year". Generally, assessment is based on a current year basis, and a system of "Pay and File" operates whereby a company "files" a return with the revenue within twelve months following the end of its accounting period and a final assessment is made, albeit that a company initially must comply with a requirement to pay corporation tax within nine months following the end of its accounting period based upon its own assessment: clearly some adjustments may be necessary to accommodate differences in the initial self-assessment and the subsequent "file".

In computing a company's profits, the income and capital gains principles discussed elsewhere in this book generally apply (sections 8 and 9 of the Taxes Act confirm this). For example, a company's income will be allotted to the various Schedules and Cases with the relevant rules for determining assessment and expenses being applied just as they would be for determining the position of an individual. It is then the several classes

---

[9]   TA 1988, s.6(4)

of income of a company together with the total of its chargeable gains that constitutes the total profits of the company.

One broad exception to the application of income tax and capital gains principles to the assessment of corporate profits relates to "loan relationships". Changes were introduced through Chapter II of Part IV of the Finance Act 1996 to loan relationships involving companies as either the borrower or lender. The changes treat all such profits and losses for companies as income, not capital gains nor losses as might previously have been the case. An obvious example of the changes can be illustrated in relation to interest paid on loan capital, debentures. Previously interest paid by a company on its debentures would be treated as a charge on income and thus deductible from profits: the position had now changed. Sections 82 and 83 of the Finance Act 1996 provides that where companies enter into loan relationships (widely defined in section 81) for the purposes of trade, the profits, losses and expenses relating to those relationships will be treated as receipts of the expenses of that trade and thus be part of the Schedule D Case I computation. In the case of profits and losses arising from other (non-trading) loan relationships, any net profit will be taxable under the rules of Case III of Schedule D: Schedule C and Schedule D Case IV are no longer applicable. Any net loss from a non-trading loan relationship can be used in one of four ways: (i) it can be set against profits for corporation tax of the year in which the loss occurred; (ii) it can be used by way of "group relief", (iii) it can be carried back against similar non-trading profits of the preceding three years; (iv) it can be carried forward against non-trading profits of the company for succeeding accounting periods.

Finally, a special note on "distributions". Some payments made by a company are termed as distributions, for example dividends to its shareholders. To the individual taxpayer the receipt of such income is chargeable to income tax under Schedule F.

The meaning of a distribution can be found in section 212 and 218 of the Taxes Act. Broadly it includes dividends and other distributions made in respect of shares, the distribution being made out of the assets of the company and involve a cost falling on the company. It does not cover the situation of the repayment and reduction of capital, nor the situation where the company issues bonus shares, because no cost falls on the company, except where that bonus issue is followed by a repayment of share capital: the latter repayment will then be treated as a distribution up to the extent of the value of the bonus issue. Similarly a rights issue is not included because it is not made out of the assets of a company but involves the company receiving fresh consideration for the issue.

A distinction had been drawn between distributions which are qualifying and distributions which are non-qualifying. Section 14(2) of the Taxes Act declares that a "qualifying distribution" means any distribution other than (a) bonus redeemable shares and bonus securities; and (b) any share capital or security which the company making the distribution has directly or indirectly received from another company in the form of bonus redeemable shares or securities. Thus these non-qualifying distributions confer no immediate benefit to the shareholder although, of course, the benefit can eventually confer a cash benefit, for example through the sale of the bonus shares.

Why make a distinction? The importance lies in the fact that if the distribution is a qualifying distribution, advance corporation tax becomes due from the company and the recipient gets a tax credit. A non-qualifying distribution does not attract advance corporation tax and no tax credit is given.

European Harmonisation and International Influences

It has been suggested that the importance of bringing VAT rates into line is insignificant in comparison to harmonising corporation tax.

> ...The only effect of differences in VAT rates is the encouragement of some cross-border shopping. Differences in corporation taxes affect the location of business and the flow of capital.[10]

Empirical studies and evidence from the Confederation of British Industry appear to support the perceived tax influences on location decisions and actions. Early recognition of the influences of corporation tax and the possible distorting effects were present at European level. Corporation tax systems, tax bases and tax rates differ between EU member countries. Some countries follow the classical system, some the imputation system and some adopt a mixture of the two. Tax bases very because different countries have different rules determining taxable profits; and differences exist in corporation tax rates of the different member states.[11] At various times the European Commission has published reports and proposals on the reform of corporation tax.[12] These proposals have essentially concentrated on tax systems rather than tax bases (although the 1980s did witness consideration of harmonisation of tax bases), and the earlier proposals did favour the classical system but have been replaced with

---

[10]   M Wilson, Taxation, at p 130
[11]   For example, in 1990 corporation tax rates stretched from 35% in the UK, Spain and Portugal, to 50% in Germany and Denmark.
[12]   Early reports include the Report of the Neumark Committee in 1963 (The EEC Reports on Tax Harmonisation) and the van den Tempel Report in 1974.

proposals and a draft Directive focusing on Union-wide adoption of an imputation system of corporation tax.[13] The draft Directive proposed that an imputation system should operate with a single tax rate between 45 and 55%. Imputation credits would be available and compensatory tax like ACT or a pre-compte should be introduced. This draft Directive had received criticism on a variety of grounds.[14] Concerns have been expressed at the failure to consider the treatment of capital gains. This might encourage the wasteful manoeuvring of capital gains tax in order to gain favourable tax treatment in some member states. Similarly, it is suggested that corporation tax must include "turnover and local taxes" if it is to minimise differences in total tax burdens. It has been suggested that total harmonisation is inappropriate. Corporation tax and its influences on location decisions ought to permit regional differences (and favourable treatment) to encourage investment in the "needier" areas and regions of the Union.

Despite this draft Directive and the early recognition of the need to harmonise corporation tax, progress to date has been slow. In fact, some member countries have regarded the Directive as having little influence or constraint on their activities and corporation tax developments[15]- although the situation might be changing.[16]

Two major constraints on the harmonisation of corporation tax are apparent. First, the issue of harmonising tax rates as opposed to tax systems. The determination of corporation tax rates provides an important fiscal tool and opportunity for the governments of each member state. Any request for them to surrender (if they have not already done so) that fiscal and political tool is likely to continue to meet strong opposition - although it has been suggested that a two-stage approach to the harmonisation of "rates" would be appropriate.[17] Second, the need to consider the harmonisation of tax bases had often been repeated. Commenting on the draft Directive, Nobes concluded that:

> Perhaps the most important criticism is that there are some major differences in the calculation of taxable income which it is not proposed to harmonise.[18]

At long last, the Commission has begun to accept concerns in this area and harmonisation of tax bases - as well as rates and tax systems - is now firmly on the agenda. Although it was announced in January 2001 that the

---

[13] Official Journal of the European Communities 5/11/1975 No C253/2

[14] See A Easson, "Tax Harmonisation in the EEC: the Commission's Programme" [1981] BTR 329; C W Nobes, "EEC Imputation Systems of Corporation Tax and the Proposal for a Directive on Harmonisation" (1979) JBL 306.

[15] For example, the Irish Commission on Direct Taxation reported that they did not consider the EC draft Directive to be a significant constraint on their recommendations. First Report of the Commission on Taxation, 1982. Similarly, the UK Green Paper on Corporation Tax (1982, Cmnd 8456) made little reference to EC constraints or recommendations.

[16] The European Commission have reported and recommended the need to revise and continue the harmonisation programme. (Guidelines on Company Taxation—SEC (90) 601).

[17] Easson, supra n 15, at p338-339.

[18] Nobes, supra, at page 309.

European Commission was retreating from its controversial drive to harmonise taxes throughout the Union, it was to refocus on attacking tax rules that contravene the EU's founding treaty. Company taxation was an area identified where the Commission intends to bring forward proposals for pan-European action on cross-border tax obstacles. It has begun studying the problems companies encounter with double taxation and tax barriers, particularly in mergers and acquisitions. In May 2001, the Commission pressed for EU countries to align the way they calculate the tax base on corporate profits to make cross-border comparisons easier, although national leaders will remain free to set company tax rates. Corporation tax rates (standard) vary from 40% in Germany and Greece to 28% in Sweden.

Finally, one should not assume that the harmonisation programme has not resulted in tangible changes Products of harmonisation and change exist; for example, the EC Directives on cross-border mergers and parent/subsidiary companies are beginning to influence practice.[19] What we have yet to experience is the expected, and needed, harmonisation of tax systems and tax bases (and perhaps even tax rates).[20]

Groups and Consortia

It is common for companies to operate their business activities through a group of companies. Groups often involve complex organisational and control structures, especially in the United Kingdom. A group basically involves one company (or individual) acquiring control of another company. The controlling company is known as the holding or parent company and the controlled company is known as a subsidiary company. "Control" is normally achieved through the purchase of shares or through the acquisition of management appointments and rights. Groups of companies exist for a variety of reasons – often very sensible economic decisions in that they might facilitate economies of scale; they might present a steady flow of suppliers or of outlets; they might facilitate the "risk-taking" often associated with new ventures or diversification. Groups of companies might also provide a convenient structure for unwanted business practices and unwanted financial protection of investors, directors and company officers. It has been the task of many areas of English law to try to recognise the reality of groups and to recognise and control potential abuse. Unlike some of our European neighbours we do not enjoy a "Law of Groups".[21] We rely on aspects of competition law, company law and revenue law to provide ad hoc recognition and control of groups. In this

---

[19] See Saunders, *Solicitors Journal*, 1992 at 318.
[20] One interesting suggestion is that if the aim of the harmonisation programme is to prevent "distorted" location decisions, then the solution is not to consider corporation tax rates but to instigate and achieve a change from profits source to residence-based taxation (See Wilson, supra).
[21] Germany, in particular, enjoys a Law of Groups. This has influenced EC debate and proposals in this area.

section we shall attempt to provide an insight into aspects of Revenue law that try to provide some recognition of the group structure and form of business organisation.

Loss relief (sections 402, 403 TA 1988)

The provisions for loss relief are perhaps the most economically significant group relief provisions. These allow one member (the surrender) of a group or consortium to set its losses against the profits of another member (the claimer) of the same group or consortium.

For the purposes of "loss relief", a group consists of a United Kingdom resident parent company plus United Kingdom resident subsidiaries in which the parent company enjoys a 75% interest (essentially "ordinary share capital). A "consortia" consists of 75% interest held by member who each own at least five % in the consortium company.

Restrictions on loss relief demand that the relief must be claimed, with the agreement of all the companies involved, within two years of the end of the surrendering company's relevant accounting period[22]: the claimant company must use the relief in the year of surrender. In the case of a consortia, the claimant is only entitled to that part of the trading loss which is proportionate to the claimant's share in the consortium.

Anti-avoidance controls exist, through sections 409 and 410, to control a temporary group membership or temporary group formation. If a company enjoys temporary membership of a group, loss relief will be time apportioned or adjusted to reflect a just and reasonable allocation of the loss relief. Similarly, if a company is to cease to be a member of a group and "arrangements" are in place to effect his change, that "member" is not entitled to participate in the loss relief provisions. The latter control combats temporary and convenient group formations.

Transfers of assets (section 171, TCGA 1992)

Relief for capital gains tax purposes is available on the transfer of assets between members of the group: the transfer is deemed to result in neither a gain nor a loss. An "exit" disposal will trigger a charge. This occurs when the asset is disposed of outside the group or the company owning the asset leaves the group – provided, in the latter case, that a six year period from the acquisition date had not elapsed. When calculating the gain or an exit disposal, the purchase price must reflect the price paid by the original owner within the group.

For the purposes of the "transfer of assets" provisions, a "group" consists of a 75 per cent group as per the "loss relief" provisions.

---

[22] See *Gallic Leasing Ltd v Coburn* [1991] STC 151.

Close companies

Perhaps in an attempt to prevent the abuse of the corporate form and in an attempt to encourage neutrality of tax in the choice of business organisation and form, provisions have been in existence since 1922 to control close companies.

Close companies are in essence small family companies or similar where the control and the activities of the company are in the hands of a few individuals. The complex statutory definition of close companies essentially provides that a close company is one controlled by five or fewer participators, or by participators who are directors[23].

"Control" is widely defined to include control over the company's affairs (for example, through voting rights) or control through the right or acquisition of the right to receive share capital which confers an entitlement to a majority of the distributable income of the company, or confers the right to the majority of its assets upon winding-up.[24] Rights invested in associates or nominees are deemed to belong to the participator.

"Participator" is defined to include a shareholder and a loan creditor excluding bank's lending in the ordinary course of their business.[25]

"Director"[26] includes a person occupying that post; a shadow director; and a manager who, together with his associates, controls 20% of the company's ordinary share capital.

Certain companies are declared as not being close companies. These include non-resident companies, and companies controlled by the Crown.

Controls on close companies include the following.

Loans to participators and their associates (section 419, TA 1988)

When a close company advances a loan to participator (or their associates) the company is obliged to pay to the Revenue a sum equal to corporation tax (CT) at a special rate of 25% is payable to the company. It is important to appreciate that this sum is not CT, it is merely paid at the special rate. If the participator repays the sum lent, the Revenue will repay the sum that is received. If, however, the loan is released or written-off, the sum paid to the Revenue is forfeited and the borrower is deemed to have received income equal to the grossed-up equivalent of the amount released or written-off. This might result in higher rate tax liability for the borrower.

The purpose of these controls is to prevent a close company being used to confer loans to participators on advantageous terms.[27] Of course

---

[23] S.414, TA 1988.
[24] S.416, TA 1988.
[25] S.417, TA 1988.
[26] Ibid.

"genuine transactions" are not prohibited. These include loans made by a close company in the ordinary course of its business which includes the lending of money; and loans to directors or employees of amounts not exceeding £15,000, provided the borrower works full-time for the close company (or its associates) and does not enjoy a material interest in the company. A material interest is five % of the ordinary share capital.

Expenditure on facilities for participators and their associates (s418, TA 1988)

Whenever a close company incurs expenses in providing living accommodation or other benefits or facilities, for a participator or his associates, that expense is treated as a distribution and must be taxed as such (i.e. the expense it not tax deductible to the company, ACT must be paid; the value of the benefit plus the tax credit is taxable income of the participator).

This provision will not apply if the benefit provided is subject to taxation under other provisions – normally as benefits in kind to directors or higher-paid employees.[28]

Treating the conferment of benefits as a distribution removes the possibility of providing tax advantageous or tax free benefits to participators or their associates.

Statutory apportionment of income

One of the perceived opportunities of close companies was the ability to hoard profits in response to high tax rates. Rather than receiving a distribution, and thus taxable income, a participator might be influenced to declare little or no distribution and retain that profit in the company until income tax rates or personal circumstances favoured dividends or distributions. For example, in 1976/77 a declared distribution might have attracted the top marginal rate of income tax on unearned income of 98% whereas retention of the same profit in the company might attract the main rate of corporation tax of 52%.

In order to influence proper decision-making, the position was that if a close company did not distribute a required proportion of its profits to its shareholders, the Revenue were entitled to apportion the undistributed profits among shareholders and tax them as if the company had distributed a dividend of that amount. This statutory deemed apportionment ought to have influenced proper retention and investment decision-making, although one suspects that it may have tipped the balance in favour of

---

[27] Complimentary controls can be found in the Companies Act 1985, s.330.
[28] TA 1988, ss.153-168

distributable profits.

As income tax rates, capital gains tax rates, and corporation tax rates began to reach almost the same level, it became apparent that the "old" advantages of retention had been reduced or removed and that the regime of statutory apportionment was no longer required. In his 1989 Budget Speech, the Chancellor of the Exchequer confirmed this view and announced the abolition of the statutory apportionment regime. However, the Chancellor did announce the need it introduce controls on a smaller number of close companies known as Close Investment Holding Companies. Close Investment Holding Companies are not trading companies nor are they members of a trading group: they are normally viewed as passive investment companies and as such they are denied access to the small companies' rate of corporation tax.[29] It is hoped that this control will remove the use of small companies for non-trading, passive investment purposes.

Taxation and the Choice of Business Medium

A number of factors influence the choice of business medium. These include issues of retention control; costs of complying with any statutory requirements, particularly annual returns and publicity; statutory restrictions on the number of members; the desirability of limited liability; and financial requirements and access to funds. Tax influences on the choice of business medium might also be apparent. These often involve a comparison of the tax treatment of companies and partnerships. In making such a comparison it is likely that the following will be considered:

1. Tax rates

If the business is carried on as a partnership, the profits are treated as distributed for income tax purposes. Therefore the partners (and proprietors) will pay up to 40% income tax (at current rates) on marginal trade income and on capital gains. If the business is carried on as a company, all profit (including capital gains) will be taxed at the appropriate corporation tax rate (currently 25–35%). (The corporation tax starting rate, the small companies rate or the main rate).

2. Remuneration and distributions

The remuneration that a company pays its employees or the salaries and fees that it pays to its directors are deductible business expenses. It is thus possible to reduce the corporation tax bill, and applicable rate, by the

[29]   See FA 1989, s.105

payments to its directors. In a partnership, increased fees and payments to the partners would simply be reflected in their marginal rate of tax. The deemed distribution of profits would also be reflected in their marginal rate of tax.

3. The treatment of share capital

If the proprietors of a company take their return and profits in the form of shares and dividends then they ought to consider two matters. First, although dividends are treated as though basic rate tax has been paid (grossed–up), tax liability still remains for those subject to higher rate tax liability. This represents "double-taxation" of the company's (and the proprietor's) profits. Second, an eventual sale of the share capital might result in capital gains tax liability.

Careful use of the capital gains tax exemption must be considered. The double-taxation of capital gains is a real danger.

4. Pension arrangements

Pension scheme arrangements have traditionally been more generous to company employees as opposed to the self-employed. Payments by a company to an employee pension scheme are generally tax deductible to the company, and non-taxable benefits to the employee.

5. National Insurance rules

If the proprietor of a business in the form of a company takes out a salary as an employee, Class I National Insurance Contributions are payable (by both the employer and the employee/director). A self-employed person pays National Insurance Contributions in Class 4. The rules allow up to half of the Class 4 contribution to be deductible for tax purposes. The different rates coupled with the rules on deductibility normally favour the self-employed person.

Further Reading

Oliver JDB, *Company Residence - Four Cases* [1996] BTR 505.

Mintz J, *The Corporation Tax* (1995) Fiscal Studies, 23.

Nobes CW, *EEC Imputation Systems of Corporation Tax and the Proposal for a Directive on Harmonisation* [1979] JBL 306.

Watters RM, *To Incorporate of Not to Incorporate - That is the Question* [1977] BTR 34.

Chown J, *The Harmonisation of Corporation Tax in the EEC* [1976] BTR 39.

Knatz T, *Corporation Tax Systems* [1972] BTR 32.

chapter eighteen

Inheritance Tax - Chargeable Persons and Activities

The Background

The tax which is now known as inheritance tax began its life in 1894 as Estate Duty, which was a tax on a deceased's property, whether passing under a will, or on intestacy. The Labour government in 1974 announced its intention to abolish estate duty and to replace it with a tax which would operate in relation not only to transfers on death, but also life time gifts. This was Capital Transfer Tax (CTT), introduced in 1975, and which lasted until 1986. The genealogy of the tax up to the introduction of capital transfer tax was thus traced by Fox LJ in *Inglewood v IRC*:[1]

> From 1894 to 1975 the main instrument of capital taxation was estate duty. It has been described as a voluntary tax. That goes too far but certainly it contained loopholes which enabled its impact to be much reduced. First, it was a tax on death only and while gifts of property or dispositions of life interests were, in effect, taxable on death though made inter vivos, that, in general, only applied to gifts or dispositions made during the statutory period (which was latterly seven years before death).

> Second, discretionary trusts were an effective means of avoiding estate duty. There was normally no charge on the death of one of the discretionary objects leaving more than one other such object surviving him (since no property interest passed or determined by reason of such death); this was so though the deceased had been receiving part or even the whole of the income during his lifetime. The position was altered to some extent by the Finance Act 1969 which imposed a charge for duty on the death of a discretionary object which was geared to the proportion of income which had

---

[1]   [1983] STC 133 at 135.

actually been paid out to him during the statutory period.

The Finance Act 1975 revolutionised the position. It abolished estate duty and created CTT, which was a tax not merely in relation to death but also to other dispositions of capital. Thus a voluntary disposition of property inter vivos to an individual will attract CTT.

Capital transfer tax was replaced with inheritance tax, with respect to transfers on or after 18 March 1986. Inheritance tax is similar to capital transfer tax and estate duty in varying ways, but it is also unlike them in some other ways. Like estate duty, it charges transfers on death, but unlike estate duty, it also imposes an immediate charge on some inter vivos transfers. Like capital transfer tax, it imposes a charge on life time transfers, but unlike capital transfer tax, most life transfers are not immediately chargeable. In effect, inheritance tax is a tax on transfers which occur on death and in the seven year period immediately preceding death. The Capital Transfer Tax Act 1984, rechristened Inheritance Tax Act 1984 (by s.100 FA 1986) is the basic law.[2] Unless otherwise stated all references to statutory provisions are references to provisions contained in the Inheritance Tax Act 1984 (IHTA).

The Charge to Inheritance Tax

Introduction

The charge to inheritance tax is contained in s.1 of the IHTA 1984, which provides that inheritance tax is to be charged on the value transferred by a chargeable transfer. From this statement two clear ideas emerge. First, that there must be a chargeable transfer, and, secondly, that what is to be taxed is the value thereby transferred. What then is a chargeable transfer? S.2(1) defines a chargeable transfer as any transfer of value, which is made by an individual, and which is not an exempt transfer. The second element of this definition of chargeable transfer indicates that inheritance tax is primarily a tax which is imposed on individuals. However there are special provisions in respect of transfers by trustees and close companies, which we shall examine later. The first and third elements of the definition are of more immediate importance. There must be a transfer of value, which is not an exempt transfer. It is clear that these terms relate to specific concepts in the inheritance tax regime, and thus, we need to examine them more closely.

---

[2]   In many ways, Capital Transfer Tax would have been a far more accurate name. A true tax on inheritance would focus on the transferees rather than the transferor.

Transfer of value

The term "transfer of value" is defined in s.3(1) as a disposition made by a person, as a result of which the value of his estate immediately after the disposition is less than it would be but for the disposition. The amount by which the estate is so reduced is the value which is transferred by the disposition. What then is a disposition for these purposes? The term "disposition" is not defined in the Act, but taken in its ordinary sense, it appears to be wide enough to cover any transaction by which a person disposes of an interest in an asset. In addition to the ordinary meaning there is an extended definition in s.3(3) which provides that, where a person's omission to exercise a right leads to a decrease in the value of his estate, and an increase in the value of the estate of another person (for example, a failure to sue on a debt until the limitation period has elapsed), the person whose estate is so reduced will be treated as having made a disposition, unless it is shown that the omission was not deliberate. This disposition will be deemed to have taken place at the time, or the latest time when he could have exercised the right the exercise of which was omitted. This is the only occasion when the estate of someone other than the transferor is relevant for inheritance tax purposes, i.e., by the transferor's omission to exercise a right, the other person's estate was increased. But even so, the value transferred is not the amount by which the other person's estate was increased, but rather, the amount by which the transferor's estate was diminished.

As is evident from the above discussions, the reduction or diminution in the value of the transferor's estate is central to the theme of inheritance tax (see e.g., s.3(1)). This would mean for example that, the sale of an asset at full market price, while being a disposition, will not be a transfer of value, since because of the full price paid, there is no reduction in the transferor's estate. In other words, inheritance tax is basically a tax on gifts, particularly those made within seven years of death. A reduction in a person's estate can occur however, without any element of gift, e.g., a commercial arrangement which is a bad bargain, or the purchase of an immediately depreciating asset such as a new car[3] – these would prima facie be transfers of value and chargeable to inheritance tax. Such situations would however be covered by one of the instances of statutory non-transfers of value. S.10(1) provides that a disposition is not a transfer of value if it was not intended to confer any gratuitous benefit on any person, and either (a) was made in a transaction at arms length between unconnected persons, or (b) it was such as might be expected to be made in a transaction at arms length between unconnected persons (emphasis added).

Section 270 provides that the term "connected persons" for these

---

[3]   See Lord Jauncey in *Macpherson v IRC* [1988] 2 All ER 753 at 757.

purposes has the same meaning as under s.286 of the TCGA 1992. S.286(2) of the TCGA 1992 provides that individuals are connected with their own spouses, their own relatives and their spouses, and with their spouses' relatives and their spouses. The term "relative" is defined by s.286(8) of the TCGA as meaning a person's brother, sister, ancestor, or lineal descendant, but s.270 of the IHTA 1984 also adds the words "uncle, aunt, nephew and niece".[4]

An example of a situation to which s.10(1) of the IHTA 1984 would apply is a sale at an undervalue because of an emergency. There was however another key example in *IRC v Spencer-Nairn*,[5] a case which also tries to explain the purpose and effect of the provision. The taxpayer had sold a farm for £101,305 after he had received advice from his accountant to the effect that he as landlord was obliged to incur expenditure of about £80,000 on replacing farm buildings. Unknown to both the taxpayer and the accountant, at the time of sale, the purchaser had been "connected" with the taxpayer for the purposes of capital gains tax and inheritance tax, which meant that, for capital gains tax purposes he fell to be treated as having disposed of the farm at market value. For the purposes of valuation for capital gains tax purposes, the case was referred to the Lands Tribunal. The Tribunal took the view that the taxpayer had not been obliged to replace the farm buildings and valued the farm at £199,000. The revenue claimed that the sale of the farm was a transfer of value to the extent that the Land Tribunal's valuation exceeded the sale price. The taxpayer on the other hand claimed that since he had no intention to confer a gratuitous benefit by the sale, and since the sale transaction was one which might be expected to be made in a transaction at arm's length between unconnected persons, the sale was not a transfer of value.

The Special Commissioner upheld the taxpayer's argument, holding that the advice that the taxpayer was obliged to replace the farm buildings was reasonable given the unclear state of the law at the time, and that it was unlikely that anyone would have been interested in the farm in a run-down condition. The Commissioner was upheld by the Court of Session. According to Lord President Hope[6] it is clear that transactions which are gratuitous or which were for less than the open market value of the property may nevertheless be taken out of charge if they satisfy the tests laid down by the s.10(1). The fact that the transaction was for less than the open market value cannot be conclusive of the issue, otherwise the subsection would be deprived of its content. The gratuitous element in the transaction becomes no more than a factor, which must be weighed in the balance with all the other facts and circumstances to see whether the onus which is on the taxpayer has been discharged. Lord President Hope

---

[4] With respect to the meaning of "connected persons" in the context of trustees, partnerships and companies, see s.286(3), (4) and (5) of the TCGA 1992, respectively.

[5] [1991] BTC 8003; STC 60.

[6] [1991] BTC at page 8012.

accepted that the question of open market value is crucial to the question whether there has been a diminution in value of the transferor's estate.[7] But the purpose of the subsection is to enable the transferor, if he can, to escape from a rigid application of the open market test, in cases in which there was no intention to confer a gratuitous benefit on anyone, and the other conditions are satisfied. This is necessary if the inevitable bad bargains which occur from time to time are not to be subjected to the tax, and if the great mass of transactions which take place at arm's length between persons not connected with each other are to be exempted from scrutiny. In this case, it was important that the taxpayer and his adviser were both unaware that they were dealing with a connected person, that the accountant's advice was sound, and that the actions of the taxpayer were reasonable in all the circumstances.

Another example of a statutory non-transfer of value is s.11, which relates to dispositions for the maintenance of family. S.11(1) provides that a disposition is not a transfer of value if it is made by one party to a marriage in favour of the other party or in favour of a child of either party, and is (a) for the maintenance of the other party, or (b) for the maintenance, education training of the child, while he is under 18 or, if above that age, while he is undergoing full-time education or training. S.11(2) similarly excludes a payment for the education, maintenance or training of a child who is not in the care of a parent, who is under the age of 18, or who is receiving full-time education or training if over that age, and who has, for substantial periods, been in the care of the person making the disposition. Furthermore s.11(3) covers dispositions for the reasonable care and maintenance of a dependent relative.

For the purposes of s.11, a "child" includes a step-child and an adopted child, and "parent" shall be construed accordingly.[8] "Dependent relative" means, in relation to any person, any relative of his, or of his spouse, who is incapacitated by old age or infirmity from maintaining himself, or the widowed, divorced or separated mother of the person or of his spouse.[9]

Sections 12-17 contain examples of other sorts of dispositions which are not transfers of value.

Exempt transfers

As seen earlier in this chapter, a chargeable transfer is a transfer of value, made by an individual, which is not an exempt transfer. Implicit in this statement is the proposition that some transfers of value are exempt – and there are numerous examples, e.g. s.18, which relates to transfers between spouses, and s.23, which relates to gifts to charities. These exemptions will

---

[7] At page 8014.
[8] S.11(6).
[9] Ibid.

be explored more fully in our discussions on exemptions and reliefs.

Potentially Exempt Transfers (PETs)

Apart from exempt transfers, there are some transfers which are only chargeable if they occur within seven years of death, i.e., they are not immediately chargeable. These are referred to as potentially exempt transfers, even though the term "potentially chargeable transfers" may be more appropriate. Most life time gifts by individuals, and certain favoured trusts, fall within this category of transfer (see s.3A). If the transferor dies within seven years of the transfer, the transfer will be said to have "proved chargeable", and tax will be levied at death rates. References to "chargeable transfer" do not include PETs.

The value transferred

Section 3(1) provides that the value transferred by a disposition is the amount by which the transferor's estate is less than it would be but for the disposition. For these purposes, "estate" is defined by s.5(1) as the aggregate of all the property to which a person is beneficially entitled.

The consequences of the provision that the value transferred is the amount by which the transferor's estate is reduced by the transfer are:

The relevant estate is that of the transferor and not that of the transferee. Thus, the value transferred by the transferor is not necessarily the same as the value received by the transferee.

Example

Elena has a set of three pearls, worth £5,000 each, but £30,000 as a set. She gives one to Yannish. Yannish receives a pearl worth £5,000 but Elena has now 2 pearls, which, because the set is no longer complete, are worth not £25,000, but £10,000. Thus Elena's estate has been diminished by £20,000, and that is the value transferred.

Any consideration received for the transfer will be taken into account in determining how much decrease there has been in the value of the estate.

Grossing up

In calculating the value of a transferor's estate immediately after a transfer, any liability of his to inheritance tax (but not any other tax) on the transfer falls to be included (s.5(4)). This means that the transferor's estate diminishes in value by the value of the transferred property plus the inheritance tax due on the transfer, i.e., the value of the property itself is net of inheritance tax (unless the tax is to be borne by the transferee, in which case it is gross) and must be grossed up to determine the total fall in the transferor's estate.

The formula for grossing up the net transfer is:

$$\frac{100}{100 - R} \quad \times \quad \text{Value of the gift}$$

Where:

R = the rate of tax at which the transferor will be chargeable on the gift.

Example

Mokhtair makes a gift of £15,000 after he had already made gifts taking him above the nil rate of tax. He is to pay the tax on the gift.

Grossed up at "life" rates, the total amount transferred by him will be:

$$\frac{100}{100 - 20} \quad \times \quad £15,000 \quad = \quad £18,750$$

This is the figure on which inheritance tax is charged.

This approach was illustrated in *Re Ratcliffe*.[10]   In this case, the testatrix provided that, after payment of her debts and funeral and testamentary expenses, half her residuary estate should be divided between her two cousins and the remainder should be divided between four charities. Since gifts to charity are exempt from inheritance tax, there were two possible interpretations of the will: an unequal division of the estate before inheritance tax so as to give an equal division afterwards or an equal division before tax so as to give an unequal division afterwards. The High Court held that the latter was the correct position and that the inheritance tax payable on the cousins' share was to be taken as part of their bequest.

---

[10]   *Re Ratcliffe (deceased); Holmes and another v McMullan and others* [1999] STC 262

Valuation

Market value

As a general rule, the value of any property is the price which it might reasonably be expected to fetch on a sale in the open market (s.160). This "market price" will not be reduced on the ground that the whole property is to be placed on the market at one and the same time (even though such reduction would normally occur if an actual sale were to take place in an open market in the real world). A number of principles can be gleaned from the cases. According to Peter Gibson LJ in *Walton v IRC*,[11] the valuation required is on the basis of a hypothetical sale in the open market. The hypothesis must be applied to the property as it actually existed and not to some other property, even if in real life a vendor would have been likely to make some changes or improvements before putting it on the market.[12] The concept of the open market automatically implies a willing seller and a willing buyer, each of whom is a hypothetical abstraction. However, the willing buyer reflects reality in that he embodies whatever was actually the demand for the property at the relevant time.[13] Whilst both the seller and the buyer are assumed to be willing, neither is to the taken to be over-eager. Rather, each will have prepared himself for the sale, the seller by bringing the sale to the attention of all likely purchasers, and honestly giving as much information to them as he is entitled to give; and the buyer by informing himself as much as he can properly do.[14]

According to Peter Gibson LJ the statute does assume a sale, and this assumption has a number of implications. First, however improbable it is that there would ever be a sale of the property in the real world, for example, because of restrictions attached to the property, the sale must be treated as capable of being completed, the purchaser then holding the property subject to the same restrictions.[15] This is because the property must be assumed to have been capable of sale in the open market, even if in fact it was inherently unassignable or held subject to restrictions on sale.[16] In this respect, the question is what a purchaser in the open market would have paid to enjoy whatever rights attached to the property at the relevant date.[17] Secondly, the vendor, if he is offered the best price reasonably obtainable in the market, cannot be assumed to say that he will not sell because the price is too low as inadequately reflecting some feature of the property – nor can the buyer be assumed to say that he will not buy because the price is too high.[18] One does not have to ask whether the hypothetical parties would have been pleased or disappointed with the result, for example, by reference to what the property might have been

---

[11] [1996] BTC 8015 at 8020.
[12] Hoffman LJ in *IRC v Gray* [1994] BTC 8034 at 8036. To this extent only, the express terms of the statute may introduce an element of artificiality into the hypothesis (ibid).
[13] Peter Gibson LJ in *Walton v IRC* [1996] BTC 8015 at 8020.
[14] Ibid.
[15] Ibid.
[16] Hoffman LJ in *IRC v Gray* [1994] BTC 8034 at 8036.
[17] Ibid.
[18] Peter Gibson LJ in *Walton v IRC* [1996] BTC at 8020.

worth at a different time or in different circumstances, because such considerations are irrelevant.[19] Because the market is the open market, the whole world is to be assumed to be free to bid – however, the valuer will inquire into what sort of person will be in the market for the property in question and what price the possible purchaser would be likely to pay.[20] According to Peter Gibson LJ in *Walton v IRC*, the statute requires one to assume a sale, but it should be assumed to take place in the real world.[21] This is more or less the same thing as the statement of Hoffman LJ in *IRC v Gray*[22] that, although the sale is hypothetical, there is nothing hypothetical about the open market in which it is supposed to have taken place. The "practical" nature of this exercise, according to Hoffman LJ, will usually mean that, although in principle no one is excluded from consideration, most of the world will usually play no part in the calculation.[23] Thus:

> The inquiry will often focus upon what a relatively small number of people would be likely to have paid. It may arrive at a figure within a range of prices which the evidence shows that various people would have been likely to pay, reflecting, for example, the fact that one person had a particular reason for paying a higher price than others, but taking into account, if appropriate, the possibility that through accident or whim he might not actually have bought. The valuation is this a retrospective exercise in probabilities, wholly derived from the real world but rarely committed to the proposition that a sale to a particular purchaser would definitely have happened.[24]

Related property

Section 161 provides a special regime for "related property", in order to counter the avoidance opportunities presented by asset–splitting. This special regime relates to situations where assets are worth more as a set than they are worth as separate items (e.g., shares, interests in land, etc.). The avoidance in these situations could be achieved by splitting the sets between two or more tax payers, in a situation wherein transfers between them would be exempt, e.g., between spouses. The related property rules apply to frustrate such schemes.

In this respect, s.161(1) provides that, where the value of an asset would be less than its value when aggregated with any related property, the value of the asset will be the appropriate portion of the value of that aggregate. For the purposes of this rule, property is "related" to the property comprised in a person's estate if it is comprised in the estate of the person's

[19] Hoffman LJ in *IRC v Gray*, at page 8037.
[20] Peter Gibson LJ in *Walton v IRC* [1996] BTC at 8020.
[21] [1996] BTC at 8021.
[22] [1994] BTC 8034 at 8037.
[23] [1994] BTC at 8037.
[24] Ibid.

spouse, or if it was, within the preceding five years, the property of a charity, or property held on charitable trusts, etc. (see s.161(2)).

Example

Jake has a five-piece vintage train set, worth £100,000 as a set, but only £5,000 per piece. Jake gives one piece of the set to his wife Winifred. Winifred receives an asset worth £5,000. Jake's estate falls in value by £80,000, because he has lost the set and now only has four pieces, worth £5,000 each; but this transfer is exempt as an inter-spousal transfer. Winifred later gives the asset to their son Wilf. Wilf receives an asset worth £5,000, and Winifred's estate is reduced by £5,000. However, on the related property rules, the asset is valued as one-fifth of a £100,000 five-piece set (£20,000), and that is what Winifred's estate is reduced by.

Close companies

As we have seen earlier, s.2(1) provides that a chargeable transfer is a transfer of value made by an individual. This means that transfers by companies are not chargeable, opening up planning opportunities, whereby a company could for example make transfers to donees specified by an individual. There are special provisions in the Inheritance Tax Act to combat the use of close companies in this way. Generally, s.94(2) provides that, where a close company makes a transfer of value, the value so transferred shall be apportioned to each participator according to his rights and interests in the company immediately before the transfer. Any amount which happens to be apportioned to a close company in this manner shall be further apportioned among its participators, and so on. The participators are treated as having made net transfers of value, so that the values apportioned to the participators must be grossed up at their respective inheritance tax rates (s.94(1)). For these purposes a participator's estate shall be treated as not including any rights or interests in the company.

Note that for these purposes a *bona fide* commercial transaction by a close company will not fall to be treated as a transfer of value (see s.10(1)). By s.3A(6) the definition of PET does not extend to deemed transfers of value such as this, and thus, the values apportioned to each participator will be chargeable transfers.

"Close company" has the same meaning as it has for corporation tax purposes (s.102(1)). It is defined by s.414(1) of the ICTA 1988 as a company which is under the control of five or fewer participators, or of participators who are directors. For inheritance tax purposes, it also includes non-resident companies (s.102(1) IHTA 1984).

"Participator" also has the same meaning as it has for corporation tax purposes, except that, here, it does not include a loan creditor (s.102(1)). It is defined s.417(1) of the ICTA 1988 as any person having a share or interest in the capital or income of the company.

Calculation of Inheritance Tax

Rates of Tax

There are basically three relevant rates, found in Sch. 1 and s.7 of the Act. The first rate is a nil (or 0%) rate, which applies to chargeable transfers of value not exceeding a specified threshold. This threshold generally increases from year to year. Thus, for the 2001/02 year of assessment, it was £242,000, and for the 2002/03 year of assessment, it was £250,000. Taking account of the variations in the nil rate threshold from year to year, the tax rates are:

a. for chargeable transfers of value up to the threshold, tax is charged at a nil rate;

b. for any excess over the threshold, tax is charged at 40%;

c. "life" rates of 20%, i.e., half of the normal rates – this is provided for in s.7(2) which provides that tax is charged on a chargeable transfer made during the life of the transferor at half of the normal rates.

Where death occurs between three and seven years of the transfer, there is relief in form of a tapering reduction in the tax rate. This relief is given under s.7(4):

1. where the transfer was made between three and four years of death, there is relief of 20% of the normal rates. This means that tax is charged at 80% of the death rates (80% of 40%) instead of the full death rate of 40%;

2. where the transfer was made between four and five years of death, there is relief of 40%;

3. where the transfer was made between five and six years of death, there is relief of 60%;

4. where the transfer was made between six and seven years of death, there is relief of 80%;

5. where death occurs within three years of the date of the gift, tax is levied at the full 40% rate.

Cumulation

Inheritance tax involves a principle of the cumulation of all the chargeable transfers made by an individual. S.7(1) requires the tax chargeable on a transfer by an individual to take account of the chargeable transfers already made by him. This principle of cumulation applies to all chargeable transfers made in the seven year period ending with the relevant one. Transfers made more than seven years previously fall out of the cumulation. The latest transfer is treated as the top slice of the cumulative total and taxed as such.

Example

On 1 January 1992, Seamus made a transfer of 200, 000 (the transferee to pay the tax). If this was his first transfer of value, he would have a cumulative total of 200,000. On 1 January 1996, he made another transfer of 200,000. He would then have a cumulative total of 400,000. Seamus dies on 1 January 2002. The 1992 gift, having been made more than 7 years previously, has fallen out of cumulation.

However, the fact that the 1992 transfer has become exempt does not mean that it is irrelevant for inheritance tax purposes. Since the 1996 PET is within seven years of death, it does not become exempt. Instead, it is taxed on the basis of Seamus's cumulative total at the date of the gift, not on the basis of his cumulative total at the date of death. The 1992 gift was made within seven years of the 1996 gift and so the cumulative total on 1 January 1996 is 200,000. This means that only 42,000 of the 2001/02 nil rate band remains to be set against the 1996 PET and the remaining 158,000 is chargeable but, since the transfer was made within six and seven years of death, there is relief of 80%.

It follows from this example that it is not automatically more tax efficient to dispose of property before death. Suppose Seamus had not made the 1996 gift, but had instead bequeathed 200,000 to the donee. His cumulative total on death would have been nil, so the whole 242,000 nil rate band would have been available for his death estate. Seamus would have been well advised to have waited until the first gift had fallen out of cumulation before making his second one. Had he lived long enough to do this, there would have been no tax to pay on either gift when he eventually died. The first gift would have fallen out of cumulation and the second one would have fallen within the nil rate band.

PETs are not cumulated in this way during the life of the transferor and so do not affect the amount of the nil rate band to set against lifetime transfers while the transferor is still alive.

Liability for Inheritance Tax

Introduction

One curious feature of inheritance tax is that more than one person may be liable for the tax chargeable on any particular transfer of value. In this respect, s.205 stipulates that, except as otherwise provided, where two or more persons are liable for the same tax, each of them shall be liable for the whole of it. This seemingly draconian provision is tempered by limits imposed on the quantum of the liabilities that fall on the various persons who may be subject to tax. The issue of liability to tax depends partly on when the transfer of value took place, i.e., *inter vivos* or on death, and partly on the nature of the transferred property, i.e., was it settled property or not. The applicable rules are contained in ss.199-204 and the discussion that follows addresses first, the question of liability to tax on life time transfers, followed by liability on death.

Liability on life transfers

Generally speaking, liability to tax on life transfers depends upon whether the transfer was made by an individual, by trustees or by close companies.

Individuals

In the case of chargeable lifetime transfers by an individual, s.199(1) provides for the liability of:

a. the transferor;

b. the transferee;

c. any one in whom the transfer vests the property or who has an interest in possession therein;

d. where the property becomes settled property, the beneficiary.

With respect to potentially exempt transfers which later become chargeable and chargeable transfers made within seven years of the transferor's death which then become subject to a supplementary charge on the death, s.199(2) replaces the reference to the transferor in (a) above with a reference to his personal representative.

The liabilities so indicated, of persons who are not the transferor or the transferor's personal representative are supplemental, in the sense only that the persons lower down the list are only liable to the extent that the tax has not been paid by the transferor at the time when it ought to have been paid. Thus for example, the transferor is primarily liable and the transferee only becomes liable if the full tax has not been recovered from the transferor, and so on (see s.204(6)).

Trustees

When chargeable transfers are made by trustees, s.201(1) provides for the liability of:

a. the trustees of the settlement;

b. any person entitled to an interest in possession in the settled property;

c. any person for whose benefit any of the settled property or the income thereof is applied at or after the transfer;

d. in cases of transfers made during the life of the settlor and in which the trustees are not resident in the United Kingdom, the settlor.

For the purposes of these provisions the trustees of a settlement shall be regarded as not being resident in the United Kingdom unless the general administration of the settlement is carried on in the United Kingdom, and the trustees or a majority of them are resident in the United Kingdom (s.201(5)).

As with the case of transfers by individuals (above) the liability of persons who are not trustees attach only to the extent that the tax remains unpaid by the trustees after it ought to have been paid (s. 204(6)).

Close companies

When a close company makes a chargeable transfer of value the persons liable are, primarily, the company making the relevant transfer, and, so far as the tax remains unpaid after it ought to have been paid, the persons to whom any amounts have been apportioned under s.94, and any individual the value of whose estate is increased by the transfer.

Liability on death transfers

Section 200(1) provides for liability to tax in cases in which a chargeable transfer is made on death. Generally, the persons who may be liable to inheritance tax on death are personal representatives, trustees, and beneficiaries/legatees.

Personal representatives

By virtue of s.200(1)(a), so far as the tax is attributable to the value of property which either was not comprised in a settlement immediately before the death, or consists of settled land situated in the United Kingdom which devolves upon or vests in the deceased's personal representatives, the persons liable to tax are the deceased's personal representatives. This provision relates to the tax due on the estate itself. In relation to the extra tax payable on transfers made within seven years of the transferor's death, the transferee alone is liable to pay the extra tax.[25]

The liability of the personal representatives under s.200(1)(a) is subject to further limitations. In cases where the tax is attributable to settled land in the United Kingdom, s.204(1)(b) provides that a personal representative's liability is limited to so much of the property as is at any time available in his hands for the payment of the tax, or might have been so available but for his own neglect or default. In cases where the tax is attributable to the value of any other property, s.204(1)(a) limits the liability of a personal representative to the assets (other than settled land in

---

[25] S.199(2), s.204(6) & (7).

the United Kingdom) which he has received as personal representative or which he might have so received but for his own neglect or default.

For these purposes the liability of a personal representative is a personal liability. It was thus explained by Scott J in *IRC v Stannard*:[26]

> ... the liability in respect of capital transfer tax for which a personal representative becomes liable is not and could never have been a liability of the deceased. It is necessarily an original liability which is in terms imposed on the personal representative. There is nothing in the statutory scheme which in express terms limits the liability of the personal representative to assets of the estate except in so far as such limitation is found in [s.204] of the Act which I have just read. There is, in my judgment, nothing in [s.200(1)] which justifies limiting the liability of a personal representative to liability in a representative capacity only.

Trustees

With respect to settled property in which the deceased had an interest in possession (other than settled land in the United Kingdom) s.200(1)(b) provides for the liability of the trustees of the settlement. The liability of a trustee of any property is limited by s.204(2) to:

a. so much of the property as he has actually received, disposed of, or is liable to account for to the persons beneficially entitled thereto, and

b. so much of any other property as is for the time being available in his hands as trustee for the payment of the tax, or which might have been so available but for his own neglect or default.

Beneficiaries/legatees

The above provisions specify those who are liable to tax in the first instance. There are others who may be liable to tax on death. S.200(1)(c) provides that, so far as tax chargeable on death is attributable to the value of any property, any person in whom the property is vested or who is beneficially entitled to an interest in possession in the property at any time after the death is liable for the tax. S.200(1)(d) further provides that, so far as the tax is attributable to the value of any property which was comprised in a settlement immediately before the death, any person for whose benefit

---

[26]   [1984] STC 245 at 249-250.

the any of the property or the income thereof is applied after the death is liable for the tax. The quantum of the liability is limited by s.204(5) to the amount of the property or income so applied for his benefit.

General limitations of liability

Section 204(6) imposes limitations (some of which have been mentioned above) on the liabilities of persons who are liable otherwise than as transferor, personal representative, or trustee of a settlement. Such persons are only liable if the tax remains unpaid after it ought to have been paid. However, by s.204(7) this limitation does not apply where the tax is more than it would have been if the transferor had died more than seven years after the transfer, i.e., it does not apply in relation to potentially exempt transfers – here, the transferee is equally liable to the tax arising on death.

Duty to render account

We have spoken at length about transfers of value and liability to tax thereon. One may begin to wonder how the revenue will acquire information about the occurrence of a transfer so as to be able to levy tax. The answer is in s.216 which provides that any person who is liable to inheritance tax on a chargeable transfer must render an account of the transfer to the Board. This must generally take place within 12 months of the transfer, and there are penalties, in s.264, for late reporting of transfers, and, in s.245, for failure to deliver an account.

Death and Inheritance Tax

Introduction

Inheritance tax is primarily a tax on the property of a person on his death. The reason for the charges on lifetime transfers is to prevent taxpayers from enjoying the benefit of property until the moment before death, and then making death bed transfers free of inheritance tax. This is the reason for the incentives to make gifts as soon as possible (PETs), and for gifts dropping out of cumulation after seven years, if the transferor is still alive.

The charge on death arises by treating the death as a deemed transfer of value. S.4(1) provides that, on the death of any person, tax shall be charged as if, immediately before his death, he had made a transfer of value equal to the value of his estate immediately before his death. For the purpose of s.4, where it is uncertain which of two or more people died first, they shall be assumed to have died at the same instance (s.4(2)).

Gifts with reservation

The rules relating to gifts with reservation are designed to combat the obvious planning device of making a lifetime gift, and then "borrowing" the asset for the rest of one's life. If the original gift was made to an individual more than seven years before death, this would, without more, have been a successful PET. The rules here provide generally that property which is subject to a reservation is to be treated as continuing to form part of the transferor's estate at his death. The applicable law is in s.102, FA 1986, which applies where an individual disposes of any property by way of gift, and either possession and enjoyment of the property is not bona fide assumed by the donee, at or before the beginning of the relevant period; or, at any time in the relevant period the property is not enjoyed to the entire exclusion or virtually to the entire exclusion of the donor, and of any benefit to him by contract or otherwise.[27]

"The relevant period", during which "significant" benefits to the donor are forbidden, is the period of seven years ending with the date of the donor's death. (s.102(1) FA 1986). By s.102(3) any property which is subject to a reservation is treated as still continuing to be comprised in the donor's estate. This means that the so-called transfer has no effect whatsoever, and that the donor will, in effect, just be "borrowing" his own property. It will still be part of his estate for the purposes of valuation. If the property ceases to be subject to a reservation during the relevant period, that occasion is treated as a PET (s.102(4) FA 1986).

The meaning of "property" in this context was considered in *Ingram v IRC*.[28] Lady Ingram wished to transfer land to her children and grandchildren, while retaining the right to occupy and to receive rents, so she transferred the freehold to her solicitor as nominee. He then transferred to her a twenty-year lease at no rent and then transferred the freehold to her children and grandchildren. The House of Lords held, reversing the Court of Appeal, that the scheme succeeded. According to Lord Hoffmann, the "property" for the purposes of s.102, was not the land itself, but the interest in the land. The Revenue's approach ignored the fact that various interests in the same land were each regarded as separate items of property, and Lady Ingram had not reserved a benefit in the interest that she had transferred. Unsurprisingly, statutory intervention followed, with FA 1999 inserting sections 102A, 102B and 102C into FA 1986. The basic effect of these provisions is that a gift of an interest in land will be a gift

---

[27]   See s. 102(1).

[28]   *Ingram and another (Executors of the Estate of Lady Ingram, decd.) v Inland Revenue Commissioners* [2000] 1 AC 293 [1999] STC 37.

with reservation under s.102 if it entitles or enables the donor or his spouse to enjoy some right in relation to the land otherwise than for full consideration. The reference to "land" rather than "property" in this context gives statutory effect to the Revenue's approach in *Ingram*.

It is important to note here that there are exceptions in s.102(5) to this "gifts with reservation" rule. The exceptions apply mainly to exempt transfers, for example, transfers between spouses, transfers to qualifying political parties, charities, small gifts, and other sundry exempt transfers. Presumably, these exceptions exist because it would make no sense to tax gifts with reservation in situations where gifts made without reservation would be exempt.

It is clear from the definition in s. 102(1) that substantial enjoyment by a donor of the donated property would fall to be considered as a "reservation". But does this indicate that any enjoyment of the property would be so treated? We note here the phrase "enjoyed to the entire exclusion or *virtually* to the entire exclusion of the donor" in the definition.[29] This seems to indicate that a question of degree arises. The principle of virtual exclusion implies the applicability of the de minimis rule. While a significant or substantial benefit would cause a gift to fail, the Inland Revenue's interpretation[30] indicates that a gift will not fail in situations where a benefit to the donor is "insignificant" in relation to the donated property. Obviously, the determination of whether a benefit enjoyed by the donor is "insignificant" or not would be a question of fact and degree. The intention however is clear – that donors are not prevented unreasonably from having limited access to property which they have given away. The Revenue statement itself gives examples, such as stays in the absence of the donee for not more than two weeks each year, and stays with the donee for less than one month each year.

Other consequences of death

There is, in general, no grossing up on death. Chargeable transfers (already taxed at 20%) made within seven years of death become liable to a supplementary charge at death rates (40%), with credit for the tax already paid, and subject to tapering relief for transfers between three and seven years from death. Chargeable transfers made more than seven years from death escape the death supplementary charge. PETs made within seven years of death become chargeable at death rates (40%) subject to tapering relief where available. The PETs are deemed to have been made at the time of the original disposals and fall into cumulation during that period. This will involve a recalculation of tax.

[29] Emphasis added.
[30] RI 55, November 1993.

Variations of dispositions made on death

Section 142(1) provides that, where within the period of two years after a person's death any of the persons who would benefit under the dispositions made on the death make an instrument in writing varying the dispositions or disclaiming the benefit conferred by any of the dispositions, the Act shall apply as if the variation had been effected by the deceased, or (as the case may be) as if the disclaimed benefit had never been conferred. Subsection (2) of the section requires an election by written notice to the Revenue within 6 months of the date of the instrument, either by the persons making the variation, or, in cases where the variation results in additional tax being payable, by the personal representatives of the deceased.

The typical type of situation in which it may be helpful to make such a variation would be in a case where a person leaves property to another by will, in circumstances giving rise to no tax liability (e.g. husband and wife), and the legatee wishes to pass on the property, so that it will not fall to be aggregated with the rest of his own personal estate.[31] This may result in a lower inheritance tax burden. Note that for these purposes when a will has already been varied, a variation which merely varies that earlier variation is not within this section.[32]

Further Reading

Dobris JC: *Marshalling the Arguments in Favour of Abolishing the Capital Transfer Tax* [1984] BTR 363.

McCutcheon B: *Partnerships and Capital Transfer Tax* [1980] BTR 417.

Goodhart W: *Too Good to be True? A Proposal for the Reform of Taxes on Gifts and Inheritances* [1980] BTR 473.

Wheatcroft GSA: *First Thoughts on the Capital Transfer Tax* [1974] BTR 265.

MacDonald G: *From Estate Duty to Inheritance Tax - Towards an Income Tax on Capital?* [1973] BTR 306.

Chamberlain, E. *Ingram and the Finance Bill - a Case of Sour Grapes* [1999] BTR 430.

Chamberlain, E. *Ingram and the Revenue View - an Inconsistency?* [1999] BTR 152

Miller, A. *Finance Act Notes: Lease Carve-Out Schemes - Section 104.* [1999] BTR 367

---

[31]   See e.g., *Lake v Lake* [1989] BTC 8046.

[32]   *Russell v IRC* [1988] 1 WLR 834; BTC 8041 (Knox J); *Seymour v Seymour* [1989] BTC 8043 (Mervyn Davies J at 8045).

chapter nineteen

Inheritance Tax - Exemptions and Reliefs

The inheritance tax legislation features a host of exemptions and reliefs from the full rigour of the tax. This chapter examines a selection of these exemptions and reliefs.

Potentially Exempt Transfers (PETs)

The PET is a device to implement the principle that inheritance tax is largely a tax on death. It is designed to encourage the transmission of property as early as possible, by operating to relieve completely transfers made within a certain period from a person's death. S.3A(1) provides that a PET is a transfer of value, made by an individual on or after 18 March 1986, which apart from the section would be chargeable, and which constitutes either a gift to another individual, or a gift into an accumulation and maintenance trust or a disabled trust. S.3A(4) provides that a PET which is made seven years or more before the transferor's death is an exempt transfer, and that any other PET is a chargeable transfer. Thus, people of substantial means who have dependants/heirs will be able to avoid the charge to inheritance tax by giving away their property while still young.

It is normally presumed (until the contrary is shown) that a PET will prove to be an exempt transfer.[1] If a PET later proves chargeable, tax is payable as if the deceased had made a chargeable transfer at the time of the original disposition. Tax is then calculated by reference to the cumulative total of chargeable transfers made by the transferor in the seven years prior to the transfer.

[1] S.3A(5).

Conditionally Exempt Transfers

A conditionally exempt transfer generally involves a designation by the Treasury under s.31 and is dependent upon a claim for designation being made by the taxpayer. For these purposes, s. 30(1) of the IHTA 1984 exempts a transfer of value if the value transferred thereby is attributable to property which has been designated by the Treasury under s. 31, and in respect of which an "undertaking" has been given. Conditional exemption also includes transfers of value which are exempt under s. 76 FA 1976.[2] One restriction is that, subject to certain exceptions, the exemption applies only to the deemed transfers of value occurring on death, under s. 4 IHTA 1984.[3] The restriction is removed in certain cases, making the transfers of values in those cases conditionally exempt. First, the restriction does not apply in cases where the transferor and the transferor's spouse, have, jointly or severally, been beneficially entitled to the property throughout the period of six years immediately preceding the transfer.[4] Secondly, the restriction does not apply in cases in which the transferor acquired the property on the occasion of the death of another person, if the deemed transfer of value occurring on the death of that person was conditionally exempt.[5]

As earlier indicated, s. 31 requires designation by the Treasury, and, undertakings by the taxpayer. Under s. 31, the Treasury may designate such articles as, pictures, prints, books, manuscripts, works of art, scientific collections, or other non-income-yielding items which appear to the Treasury to be of national, scientific, historic or artistic interest; land, which in the opinion of the Treasury is of outstanding scenic, historic, or scientific interest; buildings which in the opinion of the Treasury require special steps to be taken in respect of their preservation, by reason of their historic or architectural interest, etc. In cases in which a claim for designation is made in respect of a potentially exempt transfer which has proved chargeable, the question whether a designation is appropriate falls to be determined by reference to circumstances existing after the death of the transferor.[6] With respect to undertakings by the taxpayer, the required undertakings vary according to the type of property concerned. With respect to items like books, pictures, and manuscripts, the required undertakings are, first, that, until the death of the owner of the property, or until the disposal of the property, the property will be kept permanently in the UK, (except temporarily, for a purpose and period approved by the Treasury); and, secondly, that the person giving the undertaking will take steps, agreed with the Treasury, to preserve the property and allow the public reasonable access thereto.[7] If the property concerned is land of historic or scenic or scientific interest, an undertaking is required, until the

---

[2] S. 76 applies to other types of property which have been designated by the Treasury, which are also the subject of specific undertakings by the taxpayer.
[3] S.30(3).
[4] S.30 (3)(a).
[5] S.30(3)(b).
[6] S.31(1A).
[7] S.31(2).

death of the owner, or until disposal thereof, to take steps, agreed with the Treasury, to maintain the land and preserve its character. Other properties require an undertaking in respect of the maintenance, repair and preservation thereof.[8]

Where the designation and undertakings have been made, a transfer of value in relation to the property concerned is an exempt transfer.[9] The transfer is exempt even if the property concerned is comprised in a discretionary trust[10] and, in such cases, the exemption extends to the "ten-year anniversary charge" which is levied on trusts in which there is no qualifying interest in possession.[11] The exemption is lost if certain events occur, triggering a tax charge. For example, s. 32(2) provides for a loss of exemption if the Treasury are satisfied that there has been a failure in a material respect to observe an undertaking given in respect of the property concerned, and s. 32A(3) provides for a loss of exemption if there a failure to observe materially an undertaking for the maintenance, repair, preservation, access or keeping of the associated properties of certain buildings. With respect to other types of property, the death of the owner of the property and the disposal of the property are also "chargeable events", unless either the transfer of value thereby effected is also conditionally exempt, or, any undertaking given in respect of the property is replaced by a corresponding undertaking by such persons as the Treasury consider to be appropriate in the circumstances.[12]

The relief given in respect of conditionally exempt transfers is disregarded in determining whether a transfer of value is a PET (s.30(3A)), and a transfer which is a PET cannot be the subject of a claim for conditional exemption under s.30(1) until the transferor has died (s.30(3B)). Furthermore, a PET cannot be conditionally exempt if the property transferred has been disposed of by sale between the date of the transfer and the death of the transferor (s. 30 (3C)). Exemptions given to transfers between spouses under s. 18, and to transfers to charities unders s.23 (see below) have priority over conditional exemption (s. 30(4)), in the sense that conditional exemption would apply only where the transfer of value is not otherwise exempt under those provisions.

Husband and Wife

Section 18(1) exempts transfers between spouses from inheritance tax, without limit, whether the transfer took place during the life time of the transferor, or on the transferor's death. However, by virtue of s.18(2) if the transferor is domiciled in the United Kingdom but the spouse is not so

---

[8]   S.31(4).
[9]   S.30(1).
[10]   S.78.
[11]   S.79.
[12]   S 32(3) & (5).

domiciled, the relief is limited to £55,000.

Annual Exemption

Like the income tax and capital gain tax legislation the Inheritance Tax Act allows transferors an annual tax-free amount. S.19(1) provides that, transfers of value made by a transferor in any one year are exempt to the extent that the values transferred by them (calculated as values on which no tax is chargeable- i.e., as gross sums) do not exceed £3,000. If the value transferred in any year falls short of £3,000, the unutilised portion may be carried forward to the next tax year only (s.19(2)).

Where a particular transfer is a PET, this will be ignored in the original allocation of the annual exemption since it is assumed that the PET will not require the exemption. Rather, the exemption will conferred on other transfers which are immediately chargeable (s.19(3A)). If the PET later proves to be a chargeable transfer, it will be assumed that it was made later than any transfer in the same year which was immediately chargeable, so that it obtains relief only to the extent that the relief has not already been exhausted in that year.

Small Gifts

Transfers of value made in any year by way of outright gifts to any one person are exempt if the values transferred do not exceed £250 (s.20(1)). Thus it is possible to make gifts to the value of £250 to different people in the same year, and to have them each of them exempt. The gifts must not exceed £250 in value, and this sum cannot be severed from a larger sum. Thus if the value transferred by the gift is worth £251, no part of it is exempt. This is quite independent of the £3,000 annual exemption.

Normal Expenditure out of Income

A transfer of value is exempt if it is made as part of the normal expenditure of the transferor, was made out of his income, and, after allowing for all transfers of value forming part of his normal expenditure, leaves the transferor with sufficient income to maintain his usual standard of living (s.21(1)). This exemption was examined in *Bennett v IRC*.[13] The case involved two series of payments, each of which amounted to substantial sums, made to B's children (£9,300 to each child, and £60,000 to each child, in two consecutive years) under a "form of authority" to trustees, of income accruing to B from a trust, which was surplus to her financial requirements. B was 87 years old and in good health when the form of

[13]   [1995] BTC 8003.

authority was made by her solicitor. She died suddenly and unexpectedly shortly after the second series of payments were made. The question was whether these payments were exempt as normal expenditure out of income. Lightman J held that they were so exempt. Lightman J.[14] referred to the Oxford English Dictionary, which defined the word "normal" to mean "constituting, conforming to, not deviating from or differing from, the common type of standard; regular, usual". He then referred to the decision of the Court of Appeal of Northern Ireland in *A-G for Northern Ireland v Heron*[15] on the interpretation of s.59(2) FA 1910 which exempted from estate duty inter vivos gifts made by the deceased which were both part of the normal expenditure of the deceased and were reasonable. In that case, Lowry J (at page 4) said that the adjective in the subsection is used in a qualitative and not a quantitative sense, and that it seemed to refer to type or kind, and not size. Lightman J said[16] that in the context of s.21 of the IHTA 1984, the term "normal expenditure" connotes expenditure which at the time it took place accorded with the settled pattern of expenditure adopted by the transferor. According to him, the existence of the settled pattern may be established in two ways:

> First, an examination of the expenditure by the transferor over a period of time may throw into relief a pattern, e.g., a payment each year of ten percent of all income to charity or members of the individual's family or a payment of a fixed sum or a sum rising with inflation as a pension to a former employee. Second, the individual may be shown to have assumed a commitment, or adopted a firm resolution, regarding his future expenditure and thereafter complied with it. The commitment may be legal (e.g. a deed of covenant), religious (e.g. a vow to give all earnings beyond the sum needed for subsistence to those in need) or moral (e.g. to support aged parents or invalid relatives). The commitment or resolution need have none of these characteristics, but none the less be likewise effective as establishing a pattern, e.g. to pay the annual premiums on a life assurance qualifying policy gifted to a third party or to give a pre-determined part of his income to his children.[17]

Lightman J said that there need be no fixed minimum period during which the expenditure should have been incurred in order for it to be "normal". All that is necessary is that the totality of the evidence shows that the pattern of actual or intended regular payments has been established, and that the relevant expenditure conforms with that pattern.[18]

---

[14] At page 8007.
[15] (1959) 63 TR 3.
[16] [1995] BTC at page 8008.
[17] Ibid.
[18] Ibid.

He said that, if a prior commitment or resolution can be shown, then a single payment implementing it may be sufficient, but that, if no such commitment or resolution can be shown, then a series of payments may be required before the existence of the necessary pattern will emerge. According to Lightman J, although the pattern does not need to be immutable, it must be established that it was intended to remain in place for more than a nominal period. Barring unforeseen circumstances, it must be shown that the pattern was intended to remain in force for a "sufficient period" in order for any payment to be fairly regarded as a regular feature of the transferor's normal expenditure. This means that a death bed resolution to make periodic payments "for life", and a payment made in accordance with such a determination, will not suffice. He also said that the amount of the expenditure need not be fixed. It is sufficient that a formula or standard has been adopted by application of which the payment (which may fluctuate in amount) can be quantified (e.g. ten percent of the earnings, whatever they may be, or, the costs of a sick and elderly dependant's residence at a nursing home). Furthermore, the recipients need not be the same. It is sufficient that their general character, or the qualification for benefit, is established (e.g. members of the family, or needy friends).[19] Lightman J also said that there is no need for the expenditure to be reasonable or to be such that an ordinary person might have incurred in the circumstances (although the existence or non-existence of this characteristic may be relevant in deciding whether the evidence establishes the necessary pattern). Finally, he said that the fact that the objective behind the expenditure is tax planning (e.g. to prevent an accumulation of income in the hands of the transferor liable to inheritance tax on his death) is no impediment. Rather,

> [w]hat is necessary and sufficient is that the evidence should manifest the substantial conformity of each payment with an established pattern of expenditure by the individual concerned – a pattern established by proof of the existence of a prior commitment or resolution or by reference only to a sequence of payments.[20]

Lightman J referred in *Bennett v IRC* to premiums for life insurance policies. It is important to note that, by s.21(2), a life insurance premium or a gift which is applied directly or indirectly to pay such premium will not be regarded as normal expenditure if an annuity has been purchased on the transferor's life at any time, unless it can be shown that the purchase of the insurance and annuity were not associated operations.

---

[19]   Ibid.
[20]   Ibid.

Gifts in Consideration of Marriage

Section 22 exempts gifts made in consideration of marriage, up to certain limits, depending on the relationship between the transferor and the transferee. The limits are £5,000 in the case of gifts by a parent of either party to the marriage, £2,500 in the case of gifts by remoter ancestors (e.g., grandparents) of either party to the marriage, £2,500 in the case of gifts by one party of the marriage to the other, and £1,000 in any other case. A disposition by way of outright gift will not be treated as a gift in consideration of marriage under this section unless it is a gift to a person who is a party to the marriage (s.22(3)).

Gifts to Charities

Section 23(1) provides an exemption for transfers of value to the extent that the values transferred by them are attributed to property which is given to charities. Property is "given to charities" for the purposes of this exemption either if it becomes the property of charities, or if it is held on trust for charitable purposes only (s.23(6)). The latter requirement is taken strictly. According to Lord President Hope in *Guild v IRC*[21] it is not sufficient that one of the purposes of the relevant trust is seen to be charitable, since what the exemption requires is that the property be held in trust for charitable purposes only.[22] This makes it necessary to examine the relevant gift bearing in mind that what one is looking for is whether, viewing the matter in a reasonable sense, its *predominant or sole* purpose is charitable.[23] In *Guild*, the testator had left the residue of his estate to a local authority for use in connection with its sports centre or "for some other similar purpose in connection with sport". The first part of the bequest was held to be a charitable purpose. However with respect to the second part, while the bequest may have been wide enough to enable the property to be applied in the provision of, or to assist in the provision of, facilities which are charitable, there were no words of restriction or limitation to prevent their being used in some way which falls outside the scope of what may be regarded as charitable purposes. Lord President Hope said that any non-charitable element which is merely incidental or ancillary to the bequest can be overlooked.[24] But here there was a provision of such width and generality that the possibility of some benefit which is non-charitable was both real and substantial. Thus, according to a majority of the Court of Session, the Revenue were right to refuse to grant the exemption. While this outcome was reversed on appeal to the House of Lords[25] the principles remain valid. The House of Lords differed from the Court of Session only on the point whether the words "for some other similar purpose ...". in the

---

[21] [1991] BTC 8055; [1991] STC 281 (Court of Session sitting as the Court of Exchequer).
[22] [1991] BTC 8055 at 8060.
[23] Emphasis added.
[24] At page 8064.
[25] [1992] BTC 8046; [1992] 2 All ER 10.

bequest were so wide that they might include non-charitable purposes. On this point Lord Keith accepted the submission that the court should adopt the "benignant" approach which has regularly been favoured in the interpretation of trust deeds capable of being regarded as evincing a charitable intention.[26] Adopting this benignant construction of the bequest, he inferred that the testator's intention was that any other purpose to which the local authority might apply the bequest or any part of it, should also be charitable. This meant that the whole bequest was for charitable purposes only and qualified for exemption. Lord Keith also said that a Scottish court, when faced with the task of construing and applying the words "charity" and "charitable" in a United Kingdom tax statute, must do so in accordance with the technical meaning of those words in English Law.[27]

There are further restrictions in s.23(2). The exemption in respect of gifts to charities will not apply in relation to any property if the testamentary or other disposition by which that property is given either:

a. takes effect on the termination of any interest or period which is subsequent to the transfer itself, or

b. depends on a condition which is not satisfied within the 12 month period subsequent to the transfer, or

c. is defeasible.

For these purposes, any disposition which has not been defeated 12 months after the transfer, and which is not defeasible after that time, will be treated as not being defeasible.

Gifts to Political Parties

Gifts made to a qualifying political party are exempt from inheritance tax (s.24(1)). For this purpose, a "qualifying political party" is one which at the last general election preceding the transfer either had two members elected to the House of Commons or had one member elected to the House of Commons and no fewer than 150,000 votes were given to candidates of that party (s.24(2)).

Gifts for National Purposes

Section 25 exempts gifts made to certain bodies listed in Sch. 3 to the Act. Examples of bodies mentioned specifically include the British Museum,

---

[26] [1992] BTC 8046 at 8052.
[27] [1992] BTC at 8048.

the National Museums, of Scotland and Wales, the Ulster Museum, local authorities and local authority museums and art galleries, universities and university libraries, museums and art galleries, and government departments. However, the Schedule also refers to

> [a]ny other similar national institution which exists wholly or mainly for the purpose of preserving for the public benefit a collection of scientific, historic or artistic interest and which is approved for the purposes of this Schedule by the Treasury.

Agricultural Property

General

Relief for agricultural property is contained within sections 115-124. "Agricultural property" is defined in s.115(2) as meaning agricultural land or pasture, including woodland, and any building used in connection with the intensive rearing of live stock or fish, if that building is occupied with agricultural land or pasture, and that occupation is ancillary to that of the agricultural land or pasture. The term also includes such cottages, farm buildings and farmhouses, together with the land occupied with them, as are of a character appropriate to the property.

According to Blackburne J in *Starke (Executors of Brown deceased) v IRC*,[28] the expression "agricultural land or pasture" is a composite one. Pasture is bare uncultivated land used for the grazing of animals, and, "agricultural land" when used in association with pasture suggests land of a broadly similar nature, i.e., undeveloped land in the sense of land, without buildings or other structures, used for agricultural purposes such as the cultivation of crops. He therefore held that buildings on a piece of land used for agricultural purposes (a six-bedroomed farmhouse, outbuildings used for egg production, a Danish piggery and a covered yard with loft over for housing cattle) did not fall within the definition of agricultural property.

The Court of Appeal affirmed the decision [29] although not necessarily agreeing with the narrowness of the approach. Morritt LJ said[30] that it is common in some parts of the country for pasture to include buildings for the storage of winter feed or to provide shelter for the animals using the pasture. Also, the Interpretation Act 1978 (which in s.5 defines "land" to include a number of structures, unless the contrary intention appears) requires the word "land" to be read as including "buildings or other

[28] [1994] BTC 8029 at 8032.
[29] [1995] BTC 8028.
[30] At page 8032.

structures" unless the contrary intention appears. Thus, neither by itself nor in conjunction with the word "pasture" can the words "agricultural land" be read as bare land. Morritt LJ said that the intention that "buildings or other structures" should not be read into the word "land" must appear, if at all, from other parts of the definition or the Act. Morritt LJ could find no assistance in the part of the definition in s.115(2) which defines incorporates woodland and any building used in connection with the intensive rearing of live stock or fish, saying that that was required so that woodland might be included, and to resolve doubts which might be entertained as to the status of buildings used for intensive farming whether of livestock or fish. However, the part which referred to "cottages, farm buildings and farmhouses ..." was very important since it referred expressly to the buildings and structures which would most obviously be included in the words "agricultural land" if the Interpretation Act applied in full.[31] This seemed to him to be an indication contrary to the inclusion of the relevant words said to be derived from the Interpretation Act. Another indication of a contrary intention could be found in s.115(4), which referred to the breeding, rearing and grazing of horses, and buildings used in connection with those activities. Morritt LJ said that this indicated that Parliament thought it necessary to deal with the buildings used in connection with those activities, which treatment would not be necessary if the words "agricultural land" included "buildings and structures" and the breeding and rearing of horses was taken to be agriculture.[32]

According to Morritt LJ it is necessary to consider the structure of the definition as a whole:

> With the exception of the inclusion of "woodland" all that follows the words "agricultural land or pasture" is concerned with the buildings of one sort or another which are to be included. In such a context it would be surprising to find that buildings were already included in the phrase "agricultural land or pasture". It is as though the draftsman had started with the land and then dealt with what should be treated as going with it.[33]

Morritt LJ concluded that, the indications earlier referred to, and the general structure of the definition, together show a contrary intention sufficient to exclude the words "buildings or other structures" from the definition of the word "land" otherwise required by s.5 of the Interpretation Act.[34] Thus, while the term "agricultural land" is not necessarily limited to bare land, in the context of this relief, there is

---

[31]   [1995] BTC at 8032.
[32]   At 8032-8033.
[33]   At page 8033.
[34]   Ibid.

sufficient indication in the statute that it should be so limited (i.e. the term could include buildings or other structures, but in this instance, it does not).

It is also important to note that pasture in itself does not necessarily qualify for agricultural property relief unless it is used for agricultural purposes. In *Wheatley v IRC*[35] the testator had entered into a grazing agreement whereby he was paid to allow horses to graze on his pasture. However, the horses were not kept in connection with agriculture and so the land did not qualify for agricultural property relief.

The relief in respect of agricultural property is given by reducing the value which is transferred by a transfer of value by various amounts, such that the tax chargeable will be reduced or eliminated. The available relief is specified in s.116(1) which provides that, where any part of the value transferred by a transfer of value is attributable to the agricultural value of agricultural property, that value will be reduced by the appropriate percentage. "Agricultural value" is defined by s.115(3) as the value of property, if it were subject to a perpetual covenant prohibiting its use "otherwise than as agricultural property" (i.e., it has no development value whatsoever). The "appropriate percentage" is 100 % (i.e., there is a 100% reduction in the value transferred) if certain conditions are fulfilled, and, generally, 50% in any other case.[36] The conditions for 100% relief are:

a. immediately before the transfer, the transferor had the right to vacant possession, or the right to obtain it within the next 12 months; or

b. the transferor had been beneficially entitled to his/her interest before 10th March 1981, and certain other conditions (specified in s. 116(3)) are satisfied; or

c. the transferor does not have the interest specified in paragraph (a) above only because the property is let on a tenancy beginning on or after 1st September 1995.

The Inheritance Tax Act specifies a minimum period of ownership or occupation before the agricultural property relief can apply. S.117 denies relief in respect of any agricultural property unless:

---

[35] *Wheatley and another (executors of Wheatley, deceased) v Inland Revenue Commissioners, Special Commissioners* Decision [1998] STC 60.
[36] S. 116(2).

a. it was occupied by the transferor for the purposes of agriculture throughout the period of two years ending with the date of the transfer, or

b. it was owned by the transferor throughout the period of seven years ending with that date and was throughout that period occupied (by him or another) for the purposes of agriculture (i.e., if the land is tenanted, then there is a seven year ownership period required for the transferor).

Section 118 provides for relief where the property has been sold and the proceeds used to buy replacement agricultural property. In this case, the relief will apply if the old and new properties were occupied for periods which together total two out of the previous five years (in the case of s.117(a)) or seven out of the previous ten years (in the case of s.117(b)).

Agricultural property relief on death

Section 124A provides extra conditions to be met where a PET of agricultural property proves chargeable, or where extra tax becomes due on a chargeable transfer on account of death within seven years of the transfer. S.124A(3) provides in such cases that:

a. the original property must have been owned by the transferee throughout the period between the transfer and the transferor's death (the relevant period) and must not have been subject to a binding contract for sale at the time of death; and

b. the original property must still be agricultural property immediately before the transferor's death and occupied by the transferee or another for agricultural purposes, throughout the relevant period; and,

c. where the original property consists of shares in or securities of a company giving the transferor control of the company before the transfer, the value of which reflects the agricultural value of agricultural property owned by the company, that agricultural property must have, throughout the relevant period, been owned by the company and occupied (by the company or another) for the purposes of agriculture.

Section 124B extends this relief to cases where, although the original property has been sold, the whole proceeds of sale have been used to buy replacement agricultural property.

Business Property

Sections 103–114 give relief for transfers of relevant business property. The types of property that constitute "relevant business property" are described in s.105(1), subject to exceptions in s. 105(3), and the amount of the available relief (either 100% or 50%) differs in respect of each type.

100% relief

There are three main types of property which qualify for 100% relief. The first type is property which consists of a business, or an interest in a business (s.104(1)(a) and s.105(1)(a)). For the purposes of this relief s.110(a) and s. 110(b) provide that the value of a business or an interest in a business shall be taken to be its net value, and that the net value of a business is the value of all the assets used in the business (including goodwill), reduced by the aggregate amount of any liabilities incurred for the purposes of the business.

The types of problem that may arise in connection with the assets that fall to be included in such a valuation are highlighted by *Finch v IRC*.[37] The deceased was a life tenant of settled land which he had used for the purposes of his farming and forestry business. It was common ground that the business constituted relevant business property for the purposes of relief, but the question was whether the value of the land used by the deceased for his farming and forestry business fell to be included in the value of the business. Vinelott J held that it did not. According to him:[38]

> ... the phrase "assets used in the business" cannot be construed in isolation. It is part of a provision the stated purpose of which is to prescribe a rule for ascertaining the "net value of a business". That last phrase is one the meaning of which would be perfectly well understood if it stood alone. The net assets of a business are the balance of the assets after deducting the liabilities of the business. In striking a balance only those assets which can be said to be assets of the business would be brought in. [Section 110(b)] should not, I think, be read as giving the phrase "the net value of a business" an

---

[37] [1983] STC 157.
[38] At page 160.

artificial meaning wholly divorced from its ordinary meaning.... In my judgment, therefore, the words "assets used in the business" should be construed as meaning "assets of the business which are used in the business". So construed, [s.110(b)] in effect excludes assets which in an exceptional case might be considered assets of a business and included in a balance sheet or statement of assets and liabilities but which at the relevant time were not used in the business; similarly [s.110(b)] makes it clear that the liabilities to be deducted are only those 'incurred for the purposes of the business'. So construed, settled land occupied by a tenant for life and used by him in his farming business is not an asset of that business.

Other types of business property which qualify for 100% relief are, securities of a company which are unquoted and which either by themselves or together with other such securities and any unquoted shares owned by the transferor give the transferor control of the company immediately before the transfer (s.104(1)(a) and s.105(1)(b)); and, any unquoted shares in a company (s.104(1)(a), s.105(1)(bb)).

For these purposes, the word "quoted", in relation to shares or securities, means "listed on a recognised stock exchange", and "unquoted" means "not so listed" (s. 105(1ZA)). By s.269(1), a person has "control" of a company at any time "if he then has the control powers of voting on all questions affecting the company as a whole which if exercised would yield a majority of the votes capable of being exercised on them". The word "them" in this definition refers to all questions affecting the company as a whole.[39] In *Walding v IRC*[40] the question was whether, in a case where W owns 45% of the shares in a company, and her infant grandson owns 24% of the shares, because of the infant's legal incapacity to exercise his voting rights, his shareholding is irrelevant to the question of control, and W has control of the company. It was argued for the taxpayer that the question is a subjective one, and that it requires the court to have regard to the personal capacity or incapacity of the registered proprietor, who is the person who has conferred on him the votes attached to the shares. The taxpayer contended that the words "capable of being exercised" in s.269(1) must have been inserted for a reason, and that, that reason was to introduce the question of the capacity of the person who has the shares in question registered in his or her name.

Knox J rejected this argument. He said[41] that the inclusion of the words "capable of being exercised" is attributable to the rest of the sentence (i.e., "on them"), and that the reason why the words are found in the section is by way of explanation of the category of votes that is being referred to.

[39]   Knox J in *Walding v IRC* [1996] BTC 8003 at 8005.
[40]   [1996] BTC 8003.
[41]   At page 8005.
[42]   At 8005-8006.

Knox J said that, implicit in the subsection are two categories of votes that may exist – first, votes on questions that do not affect the company as a whole (e.g., a voting right attached to particular classes of shares); and, secondly, voting rights on all questions affecting the company (which are the rights that count for the purposes of s.269).[42]

Knox J pointed to serious practical objections to the taxpayer's contention. If one were to have regard to the personal capacity of the registered shareholders in order to determine whether the taxpayer has control under s.269(1), this could lead to serious complications – people may suffer from incapacity on grounds of age, or mental incapacity:

> If it is right that one has to have regard to the personal capacity of the registered shareholder at the relevant time – the date of death – there must potentially be a substantial number of people who, at the date of death, are mentally incapable but who would not have a receiver appointed, notwithstanding the fact that they had substantial estates … There may be a mentally disabling disease that overtakes the deceased in question not very long before his or her death and there may not be time to get a receiver appointed. If the argument for the taxpayer is right, that would have the effect of disentitling the estate of that person to business property relief.
>
> From the point of view of considering what Parliament is likely to have intended, it also involves the very unfortunate investigation into the mental powers of the deceased at the date of his or her death. That would be both a difficult and, in many cases, invidious task which I suspect would not be welcomed either by the Revenue or taxpayer.[43]

While the taxpayer's argument in this case is understandable, Knox J is clearly right to reject it. The taxpayer's contention would have introduced a totally undesirable and unnecessary subjectivity to the test of control, and would only have served to complicate an otherwise straightforward provision.

The question of control was considered by the Special Commissioners in *Walker's Executors v IRC*.[44] In this case, the deceased had had a 50% interest in a company but, since she was chairman of the board of directors, had also had the casting vote. It was held that she had control of the company.

Note that the fact that property is used as security to raise money for a business does not mean that that property is used in the business and qualifies for relief. This issue was raised in *IRC v Mallender*[45] in which the

---

[43] At 8006-8007.
[44] [2001] STC (SCD) 86.
[45] *Inland Revenue Commissioners v Mallender and others executors of Drury-Lowe, deceased* [2001] STC 514.

deceased was a Lloyd's name who had provided a bank guarantee. Under the terms of the guarantee, the bank had taken charge of an interest in land held by the deceased. The executors argued that this interest in land was an asset used for the purposed of the deceased's business and should therefore qualify for 100% relief. The High Court disagreed. Jacob J accepted that the deceased might not have been able to get the guarantee unless he had had the land, but that did not mean that the land qualified for relief:

> Although commercially it may have been the case that to get the guarantee, the deceased had to charge the land, there is actually no nexus between the underwriting business and the charge. The business is only concerned with the guarantee being in place. How it was obtained, and whether or not a charge or other specific security is provided, is immaterial to the business …
>
> One can perhaps test the point another way. What matters for the business is only the amount of the guarantee. The bank will be unlikely to give a guarantee up to 100% of valuation of the land – normally the maximum loan/value ration is about 70%. So if the executors were right they would be getting relief on a land value greater than that of the guarantee. That is manifestly absurd. The absurdity would be even greater if the loan were at a lower ratio. It is in fact at a much lower ratio in this case, the guarantee being about 10% of the value of the land.[46]

50% relief

Quoted shares or securities which, either by themselves or together with other such shares or securities owned by the transferor, gave the transferor control of the company immediately before the transfer attract a 50% reduction (s.104(1)(b) and s.105(1)(cc)). Land or building or machinery or plant which, immediately before the transfer, was used wholly or mainly for the purposes of a business carried on by a company controlled by the transferor, or by a partnership of which he was a partner, will also attract a 50% reduction (s.104(1)(b) and s.105(1)(d)). So will any land, building, machinery or plant, which, immediately before the transfer, was used wholly or mainly for the purposes of a business carried on by the transferor, and which constituted settled property in which the transferor had an interest in possession (s.104(1)(b) and s.105(1)(e)). There is a restriction in respect of the types of land, building, machinery and plant described above, to the effect that they will not constitute relevant business

---

[46]   Ibid.

property in relation to a transfer of value unless the business or the transferor's interest therein, or the shares/securities of the company carrying on the business, as the case may be, are relevant business property in relation to the transfer (s.105(6)).

Minimum period of ownership

Section 106 provides that property will not be regarded as relevant business property unless it was owned by the transferor throughout the two years immediately preceding the transfer. S.107 applies to extend the relief to property which is acquired to replace other property which was owned for two of the five years immediately preceding the transfer. S.113A provides extra conditions for transfers within seven years of the transferor's death. In this respect, the combined effect of s. 113A(1), s. 113A(3), and s.113A(3A) is that, in cases where any part of the value transferred by a PET would otherwise be reduced by the business property reliefs, such reduction would be subject to the conditions that:

a. the original property was owned by the transferee throughout the period between the transfer and the death of the transferor, and

b. the original property would (apart from the period of ownership required by s. 106) be relevant business property, except to the extent that the original property consists of shares or securities, which were either quoted at the time of the transfer, or which were unquoted throughout the period between the transfer and the death of the transferee.

Reliefs Available only on Death

There are a number of reliefs in the inheritance tax legislation which are available only on the death of the transferor. The discussion that follows examines some of them in outline.

Woodlands

As has been seen above, agricultural property relief may be available in respect of woodlands the occupation of which is ancillary to occupation of other land used for agricultural purposes. However, even if no such relief is available under ss.115-124, there may be some relief under ss.125-130, available only on death. S.125(1) and (2) provide that where any part of a person's estate immediately before his death is attributable to the value of land in the United Kingdom on which trees or underwood are growing but which is not agricultural property, an election can be made to leave the value of the trees and underwood out of account in determining the value transferred on death. The relief is subject to a qualifying period of ownership of five years immediately before death, unless the deceased had received the woodlands as a gift (s.125(1)(b)), and, there may be a charge when the trees and underwood are eventually disposed of (see s.126). This last section is an anti-avoidance device to prevent a taxpayer from spending large amounts of money purchasing woodland which his beneficiaries can then sell after his death.

Death on active service

Section 154 provides that no inheritance tax is payable under s. 4 in relation to the death of a person where the Defence Council or the Secretary of State certify that he died from a wound inflicted, accident occurring or disease contracted at a time when he was engaged on active service against an enemy, or, on other service of a warlike nature, or which in the opinion of the Treasury involved the same risks as service of a warlike nature. This relief is dependent on the condition, that the deceased was a member of any of the armed forces of the Crown, or, not being a member of any of those forces, was subject to the law governing any of those forces by reason of association with or accompanying any body of these forces (s. 154(2)). The exemption extends to the death of such a person from a disease contracted at some previous time, if the death was due to, or was hastened by, the aggravation of the disease during the specified periods of service.

Quick succession relief

Section 141 provides relief where the value of a person's estate has been increased by a chargeable transfer, and that person (the transferee) then dies, or makes a chargeable transfer of the same property, within five years of the original transfer of the property to him. The relief is given as a reduction of a percentage of the tax which is charged on so much of the value of the original transfer as is attributable to the increase in transferee's estate, by the second transfer. The appropriate percentages are specified by s.141(3). If less than one year has elapsed between the date of the first and last transfer the reduction is 100%. If the elapsed period is between one and two years, the reduction is 80%; if between two and three years, the reduction is 60%; if between three and four years the reduction is 40%, and if the elapsed period exceeds four years, the reduction is 20%.

Further Reading
Harris DR: *The Quick and the Dead* [1995] BTR 39.

chapter twenty
Inheritance Tax - Settled Property

The inheritance tax treatment of settled property depends on whether or not there exists someone with an interest in possession in that property. Generally, settlements in which no one has an interest in possession are not favoured by the inheritance tax regime, with the exception of certain favoured trusts like accumulation and maintenance trusts. The tax that is chargeable upon the creation of a settlement is determined generally according to the ordinary rules relating to chargeable transfers of value. The subsequent tax treatment of the property comprised within the settlement may however differ significantly, according to the type of settlement. Most of the discussions that follow relate to the inheritance tax treatment of settled property, after the creation of the settlement.

Settlement

The term "settlement" is defined in s.43(2) as any disposition or dispositions of property whereby the property is for the time being:

a. held in trust for persons in succession (e.g., to Clare for life and then to Emily)) or for any person subject to a contingency (e.g., to Clare when she attains 30); or

b. held by trustees on trust to accumulate the whole or part of any income of the property or with power to make payments out of that income at the discretion of the trustees or some other person, with or without power to accumulate surplus income (e.g., discretionary trusts and accumulation trusts); or

c. charged or burdened (otherwise than for full consideration in money or money's worth) with the payment of any annuity or other periodical payment payable for a life or any other limited or terminable period.

Section 43(3) further provides that a lease for life or lives granted otherwise than for full consideration shall be treated as a settlement (e.g., A grants B a lease of a house for B's life at a nominal rent).

Where there is more than one settlement, in circumstances in which the settlements may be seen as a "composite settlement", they may be regarded as associated operations within the meaning of s.268(1) and they may therefore be taken as effecting a single disposition for the purposes of the Act.[1] In this respect s.268(1) defines "associated operations" as

a. any two or more operations of any kind, being operations which affect the same property, or one of which affects some property and the other or others of which affect property which represents, whether directly or indirectly that property or income arising therefrom; or

b. any two operations of which one is effected with reference to the other, or with a view to enabling the other to be effected or facilitating its being effected, and any further operation having a like relation to any of these.

Generally, where a transfer of value is made by associated operations carried out at different times it shall be treated as having been made at the time of the last of those operations (s.268(3)).

Settlor

"Settlor" is defined in s.44(1) to include any person by whom the settlement was made directly or indirectly, and, in particular, it includes any person who has provided funds directly or indirectly for the purposes of, or in connection with the settlement, or who has made with any other person a reciprocal arrangement for that other person to make the settlement. Where there is more than one settlor in relation to a settlement and the circumstances so require, the settled property shall be treated as comprised in separate settlements (s.44(2)).

Trustee

The term "trustee" should normally be taken according to its ordinary meaning in trust law. However there is an extended definition in s.45, which provides that "trustee", in relation to a settlement for which there would be no trustee apart from this section, means any person in whom

---

[1]   See Chadwick J in *Hatton v IRC* [1992] BTC 8024 at 8043-8045; [1992] STC 140.

the settled property or its management is for the time being vested.

Types of settlement

There are three main types of settlement for inheritance tax purposes. First, there are those settlements in which a person has an interest in possession, e.g., where an annuity is payable to a person for life. Secondly, there are settlements in which there is no subsisting interest in possession, e.g., discretionary trusts. Thirdly, there are some settlements in which there is no subsisting interest in possession, but which are nevertheless treated more favourably than other "no-interest-in-possession settlements", e.g., disabled trusts and accumulation and maintenance trusts. The inheritance tax treatment of each of these types of settlement is quite different, and a change from one type of settlement to another will normally involve an "exit charge".

Interest in Possession

The term "interest in possession" has featured prominently in the discussion on the different types of settlement above. The fact that settlements are classified and taxed by reference to the presence of an interest in possession indicates that the question whether or not a person has an interest in possession in settled property is of the utmost importance. However, the term "interest in possession" is not defined in the Act and an examination of the case law is therefore necessary. The leading case on this point is the decision of the House of Lords in *Pearson v IRC*[2] in which it was held that an interest in possession exists when a person who has an interest in settled property has an immediate entitlement to any income produced by that property as the income arises. In this case three beneficiaries were entitled to all the income arising under a settlement, subject to a power in the trustees to accumulate income. It was held that the overriding power in the trustees to accumulate the income was fatal to the existence of an interest in possesion. There had to be a present right to present enjoyment of the income. Viscount Dilhorne said[3] that one should first seek to determine the ordinary and natural meaning of the words "interest in possession" and then consider whether there is anything in the context in which they are used to lead to the conclusion that the proper interpretation thereof involves a departure from the ordinary and natural meaning. He referred to Preston's Treatise on Estates which states that an estate in possession is one which gives "a present right of present enjoyment". This was contrasted with an estate in remainder, which, it was said, gave "a right of future enjoyment". Viscount

[2]   [1980] STC 318.
[3]   At page 323.

Dilhorne then referred to Fearne's "Contingent Remainders" where it was said that an estate is vested when there is an immediate fixed right of present or future enjoyment; that an estate is vested in possession when there exists a right of present enjoyment; that an estate is vested in interest when there is a present fixed right of future enjoyment; and that an estate is contingent when a right of enjoyment is to accrue on an event which is dubious and uncertain. In the light of these statements, it appeared that words "an interest in possession" would ordinarily mean the possession of a right to the present enjoyment of something. This, was the meaning that it had to bear in the present case.

Lord Keith said[4] that the provisions appeared to contemplate that the entitlement to income which is spoken of, is an entitlement which, for the time being at least, is absolute. If that is true of the part, it must also be true of an interest which extends to the whole of the property. In the present case, the beneficiaries certainly did not have an absolute right to any income of the property as it accrued. At that moment, their interest was qualified by the existence of the trustees' power of accumulation, to the effect that they had no immediate right to anything, but only a right of later payment of such income as the trustees, either by deliberate decision or by inaction for more than a reasonable time, did not cause to be subjected to accumulation. In his opinion, a right of that nature is not a present right of present enjoyment.

The gist of this decision is that an overriding power to accumulate (e.g., to Ben absolutely subject to the trustees' power to accumulate income during the next 21 years) deprives a beneficiary of an interest in possession because he would only be entitled to the net income of the trust fund if the trustees decided not to accumulate. It cannot be said of any trust income, as soon as it arises, that it belongs to the beneficiary, since this would be the case only if the trustees decided not to accumulate. On the other hand, an appointment to Ben for life, and then to Emily, subject to a power in the trustees to revoke Ben's interest, would give Ben an interest in position because although the trustees could revoke the right and thus deprive him of future income, they cannot deprive him of income which has already arisen, even if it had not yet been paid to him. This is the distinction drawn by Viscount Dilhorne[5] between the exercise of a power which prevents a present right of present enjoyment arising, and the exercise of a power to terminate a present right to present enjoyment.

The distinction here has sometimes been likened to a tap - if all that pours out goes to Ben, then he has an interest in possession even if there is a person who can deprive him of future income by turning off the tap. If on the other hand, someone can divert part of what is flowing out of

4   At page 334.
5   At page 325.

the tap to Emily or some other person, then no interest in possession exists.

The question of interest in possession arose again in a different context in *Moore and Osborne v IRC*.[6] A settlor made a settlement directing the trustees to hold the income of the trust funds during the life of the settlor upon protective trusts, and, in their discretion, to pay or apply the same to or for the benefit of the settlor, and any wife whom he may marry, and the child or children or issue of the settlor. The powers were to be exercised by the trustees only with the consent of the settlor during his life time. The settlor died without having married or having had any children. The question was whether he had an interest in possession in the settled property on his death.

Peter Gibson J held that he did not. According to him,[7] in the light of the decision of the House of Lords in *Pearson v IRC*, the expression "interest in possession" connotes a present right of present enjoyment, or "an immediate entitlement, which for the time being is absolute, to income as it accrues." In this case the settlor was, from the date of the settlement until his death the sole beneficiary in existence under the discretionary trust, but until his death there was always the possibility that the class of beneficiaries might increase were he to marry. According to Peter Gibson J:[8]

When income is received by the trustees of a discretionary trust of income, the sole object of a class which is not yet closed cannot in my judgment claim an immediate entitlement to that income. It is always possible that before a reasonable time for the distribution of that income has elapsed another object will come into existence or be ascertained and have a claim to be considered as a potential recipient of the benefit of that income. So long as that possibility exists, the sole object's entitlement is subject to the possibility that the income will be properly diverted by the trustees to the future object once he comes into existence or is ascertained. Indeed in strictness the entitlement of the sole object is only an entitlement that the trustees should consider whether to pay income to him. In respect of income already received it may be possible to say that such an entitlement has arisen, but for present purposes I must consider the position before the death of the settlor not in relation to income previously received by the trustees but in relation to the settlor's rights to income then or thereafter accruing. Such income as it accrued was subject to the possibility that it could properly be

---

[6]   [1984] STC 237.
[7]   At page 241.
[8]   At page 243.

withheld by the trustees from the settlor and diverted to a future beneficiary, unlikely though the possibility of such beneficiary coming into existence or being ascertained undoubtedly was in the present case. On that footing the settlor did not immediately before his death have an interest in possession.

It should also be noted that there is no need for the trust property to produce income in order to give rise to an interest in possession. Such an interest is a right to present enjoyment. In many cases, this will be enjoyment of income, but this is not necessarily the case. For example, in *IRC v Lloyds Private Banking*[9] the right to live in a house was held to be an interest in possession. In this case, the testatrix had left her share in the house to the bank, as her trustees. They were to allow her husband to live in the house for his lifetime and then were to transfer the interest in the property to her daughter absolutely. The Special Commissioner had held that there was no interest in possession, since the husband's own share in the property meant that he could reside there irrespective of his wife's will. The High Court allowed the Revenue's appeal. Lightman J held that the wife's will made a significant difference to the husband's right of occupation. Had the wife left the property to her daughter, the husband's position would have been that of joint occupier with his daughter and the daughter could have sought an order for sale. The effect of the will was to make the husband sole occupier.

Administrative and dispositive powers

The question whether a person has an interest in possession depends on the existence of a power in someone else to deprive him of trust income which has already arisen, and not on the exercise of that power. Furthermore, entitlement to trust income refers to the net income of the trust, not all (i.e. gross) income.[10] The concept of net income is designed to allow for the administrative expenses of the trust. Thus, a distinction is drawn between "administrative powers", i.e., power of trustees to have recourse to income for purposes of administering the trust, (e.g., expenses incurred in the management of the trust), and "dispositive powers" (i.e., powers to dispose of the net income). A life tenant for example has an interest in possession, but his interest only extends to the net income of the property, that is to say, after deduction from the gross income of expenses, etc., properly incurred in the management of the trust by the trustees in the exercise of their powers. In *Pearson v IRC*, Lord Keith[11] summed up the matter thus:

[9] *Inland Revenue Commissioners v Lloyds Private Banking (as trustees of Irene Maude Evans, decd)* [1998] STC 559.
[10] See e.g., Viscount Dilhorne in *Pearson v IRC*[1980] STC at 323.
[11] At pages 333-334.

I consider that a distinction is properly to be drawn between powers directed to the preservation of the trust estate for the benefit of life tenant and remainderman alike, and discretionary powers the exercise of which is intended to have an effect on the actual benefits which the beneficiaries as such became entitled, by virtue of their several interests, to receive. It is not at all appropriate, in my view, to equate a power to execute repairs with a power to distribute income at discretion among a class of beneficiaries, from the point of view of a person who is entitled to receive any income not dealt with under the power. And the considerations applicable in the case of a discretionary power to distribute income apply equally to a discretionary power of accumulation, the exercise of which in effect rolls up income for the benefit of a class of beneficiaries or objects contingently entitled.

A problem arises in this respect, where there is a power to have recourse to income for the payment of what will normally be a capital expense. In *Miller v IRC*[12] a trust deed provided for payment, to the beneficiary, of the free income of the trust property, during her life. The trustees had the power, before determining the free income of the trust for any year, to appropriate revenue to meet depreciation of the capital value of any of the assets, and for any other purpose thought advisable or necessary. When the beneficiary died the revenue assessed tax on the basis that she was, on her death, entitled to an interest in possession in the whole of the funds held by the trustees. The trustees contended that their powers of appropriating revenue deprived the beneficiary of an interest in possession. The question therefore was whether the said powers were dispositive so as to be fatal to the existence of an interest in possession, or merely administrative, so that they would not deprive the beneficiary of an interest in possession. The Court of Session held that the powers were administrative and that the beneficiary had an interest in possession.

Lord Kincraig,[13] referring to *Pearson v IRC*, said that Lord Keith in that case considered that the feature of a dispositive power is that it is a power which, if exercised, has the effect of diverting the income so that it accrues for the benefit of others. The feature of an administrative power on the other hand, is that it is a power the exercise of which is intended to preserve the estate for the benefit of both the income beneficiary and his successors. Administrative powers are those relating to prudent management in the discharge of the trustees' duty to maintain the trust estate. According to Lord Kincraig[14] the question whether powers contained in a trust deed were dispositive or administrative depends upon

[12]   [1987] STC 108.
[13]   At page 111.
[14]   Ibid.

a construction of the declarations relating to those powers in the context of the trust deed as a whole. He concluded that, in this instance, the powers of the trustees were administrative powers, being intended to preserve the capital value of the trust estate by meeting the sum required to maintain those values.[15] He said that "appropriation" in this context means the setting aside for a particular purpose, and the use of the word "meet" limits the appropriation to what is necessary for keeping the value of the estate up to that which it had when the trust fund vested in the trustees. It is not a power to set aside the income for any other purpose as for example, to preserve it for the benefit of future beneficiaries, even though they might benefit incidentally from the exercise of the power. According to Lord Kincraig "[a] power to meet depreciation is not one to increase the capital value of the estate by diverting the income to those in right to the capital".[16]

Settlements with an Interest in Possession

Section 49(1) provides that a person who is beneficially entitled to an interest in possession in settled property shall be treated as being beneficially entitled to the property in which the interest subsists. Where the beneficiary is only entitled to part of the income of the settled property, s.50(1) stipulates that he is to be treated as being entitled only to a proportionate part of the settled property. The effect of s.49(1) and s.50(1) is that a beneficiary who has an interest in possession in settled property is treated as owning the capital of the fund, or the settled property itself. Accordingly, the value of the beneficiary's estate will be increased by the full value of the settled property (or the appropriate proportion thereof).

With respect to close companies, s.101(1) provides that, where a close company is entitled to an interest in possession in settled property, the persons who are participators in relation to the company shall be treated as being the persons entitled to that interest, according to their rights and interests in the company. This will mean for instance that where the close company is not resident in the United Kingdom but the participator is so resident, exemptions based on the non-resident status of the transferee will be lost.[17]

An *inter vivos* creation of a settlement in which an individual has an interest in position is a PET since the settled property which he is thereby treated as owning will be property which increases the value of (and which

---

[15] At page 112.
[16] Ibid.
[17] See for example *IRC v Brandenburg* [1982] STC 555.

is comprised in) his estate (s.3A(2)). This would presumably apply also to those cases in which s.101(1) treats participators in close companies as being entitled to an interest in possession.

Creation of a settlement with an interest in position on death will attract the usual charges that are raised on death.

The Charges to Tax

Death

On the death of any person, tax is charged as if, immediately before his death, he had made a transfer of value equal to the value of his estate immediately before death (s.4(1)). Since the settled property in which a person has an interest in possession is treated as belonging to that person, the value of such property will form part of his estate on death for valuation and tax purposes.

Exit charge

Section 51(1) provides that where a person who is beneficially entitled to an interest in position in settled property disposes of it, the disposal is not treated as a transfer of value, but shall be treated as the coming to an end of his interest and tax shall be charged under s.52. This means that the relevant value is that of the property itself and not the value of the disponor's interest in it.

The charge under s.52(1) is to the effect that, where during the life of the beneficiary, his interest comes to an end, tax is charged as if he had made a transfer of value equal to the value of the property in which his interest subsisted. S.52(2) provides that any consideration received in respect of the termination of such interest will be deducted from the value transferred. Such a transfer would be a PET (see s.3A(6)) if the property becomes part of the estate of another individual.

The charge also applies in cases wherein s.101(1) attributes interests in possession held by a close company to the participators therein. This point is illustrated by *Powell-Cotton v IRC*.[18] The taxpayer had a life interest in some settled property. He sold his life interest to a close company in return for shares in the company. He later transferred some of these shares by way of gift to named individuals as the trustees of a registered charity. It was not disputed that at all material times the company had been a close

---

[18]   [1992] BTC 8086; [1992] STC 625.

company which was entitled to an interest in possession in the parts of the taxpayer's former life interest that it still had. It was also accepted that, immediately before the transfer, the taxpayer fell to be treated as if he had been entitled to a part of that interest in possession, and that the effect of the transfer was that the part of the interest to which he was to be treated as being entitled, had become smaller. The question that arose was whether in these circumstances the taxpayer must be deemed to have disposed of part of his interest under s.51(1) (and was consequently liable to tax under s.52). Answering the question in the affirmative Vinelott J said[19] that the overriding purpose of s.101(1) was to ensure that the participators in a close company which is entitled to an interest in possession are to be treated for all the purposes of inheritance tax as if they were entitled to interests in possession according to their rights and interests in the company. The legislative intention must have been to give rise to a charge whenever there is a change in the proportion of the settled property in which any participator is deemed to be entitled to an interest in possession – whether the change arises on death or on termination of the interest, or on a disposition or deemed disposition inter vivos, and in the latter case, whether as a result of a disposal by the company, or of a change in the participators or in the rights and interests of the participators inter se. According to Vinelott J this result could be arrived at by the ordinary process of construction and does not require recourse to "intendment or equity" or any presumption to tax in order to meet the obvious anomaly that would result if a taxpayer could avoid inheritance tax on a disposal of an interest in possession in settled property by first transferring it to a close company in which he owned all the shares, and then transferring the shares to the intended beneficiary.[20]

Exceptions to the Charges

Excluded property

Section 53(1) provides that tax shall not be chargeable under s.52 if the settled property is excluded property. "Excluded property" is defined in s.48. S.48(1) provides that a reversionary interest is excluded property unless:

a. it has at any time been acquired for money or money's worth; or

b. the settlor or the settlor's spouse is or has been beneficially entitled

---

[19] [1992] BTC 8086 at 8091-8092.

[20] The transfer did not fall within the exemption for gifts to charities in this case because of a restriction in s.56(3) which denies exemption in cases where the property transferred is an interest in possession in settled property and the settlement does not come to an end in relation to that settled property on the making of the transfer.

thereto; or

c. it is interest expectant on termination of a lease treated as a settlement by s.43(3).

Where the settled property is situated outside the United Kingdom s.48(3) provides that such property is excluded property unless the settlor was domiciled in the UK at the time of making the settlement (i.e., if the settlor was non-domiciled at the creation of the settlement, foreign settled property is excluded property).

Beneficiary acquiring another interest

Section 53(2) provides another exception to the charge under s.52 in cases in which the person whose interest in settled property comes to an end becomes on the same occasion entitled to that settled property or to another interest in possession in it.

Reverter to settlor

Tax is not chargeable under s.52 if an interest in possession in settled property ends during the settlor's life and on that occasion the property in which the interest subsisted reverts to the settlor (s.53(3)).

Reverter to settlor's spouse

There is no charge under s.52 if on the occasion on which the interest comes to an end the settlor's spouse (who is domiciled in the United Kingdom) becomes beneficially entitled to the settled property (s.53(4)). This exception also extends to the settlor's widow or widower, who is domiciled in the United Kingdom, and who becomes beneficially entitled to the settled property not later than two years from the death of the settlor.

Exemption from the charge on death

Section 54(1) and s.54(2) provide that, if on the death of the beneficiary during the settlor's life, the settled property reverts to the settlor, or to the settlor's spouse, or widow(er) (if domiciled in the United Kingdom), the value of the settled property shall be left out of account in determining the value of the deceased's estate immediately before his death.

Settlements without an Interest in Possession

The inheritance tax legislation looks upon settlements in which there is no interest in possession with particular disfavour and subjects them to a number of charges. The thinking behind this is that, since interest in possession trusts are linked to the life of the beneficiary, the property within the trust will at some point become subject to the death charge. This is not the case for trusts without an interest in possession and since, unlike individuals, trusts do not die, some other method must be found of making the trust subject to inheritance tax.

The typical example of a settlement without an interest in possession is the discretionary trust – a type of trust which, because of its potential as a planning tool, has always been unpopular with the revenue. Property comprised in these types of settlement will be "relevant property" for the purposes of the inheritance tax charges. S.58(1) defines relevant property as settled property in which no qualifying interest in possession subsists. Certain items are excluded from this definition, e.g., accumulation and maintenance trusts, disabled trusts, and excluded property. The term "qualifying interest in possession" is defined by s.59(1) as an interest to which an individual is beneficially entitled. Although the term is defined in the context of an interest owned by an individual, in certain cases a company can have a qualifying interest in possession. S.59(2) indicates that, in order for a company to have an interest in possession, the business of the company must consist wholly or mainly of acquiring interests in settled property, and the company must have acquired the interest for full consideration in money or money's worth from an individual beneficially entitled to it.

The Charges to Tax

Creation of the settlement

The creation of a settlement in which there is no qualifying interest in possession will be a chargeable transfer, since such a settlement does not fall within those types of transfer of value which are PETs.

The ten-year anniversary charge

This ten-year anniversary charge is perhaps the most troublesome of all the consequences of creating a settlement without a qualifying interest in possession. The term "ten-year anniversary" in relation to a settlement means (subject to some exceptions) the tenth anniversary of the date on which the settlement commenced, and subsequent anniversaries at ten-year intervals (s.61(1)). S.64 provides that, where immediately before a ten-year anniversary, all or part of the property comprised in the settlement is relevant property, tax shall be charged on the value of that relevant property. The ten-year anniversary involves a notional transfer by a person who has the cumulative transfers of the settlor at the date on which the settlement was created. This notional transfer is defined by s.66(4) as the aggregate of:

a. the value of the relevant property comprised within the settlement;

b. the value immediately after coming into the settlement of non relevant property which has since not become relevant property while remaining in the settlement ;

c. value of property comprised in a related settlement immediately after being so comprised.[21]

This is a transfer of value made by a notional person having the cumulative transfers of (a) the chargeable transfers made by the settlor in the seven years before creating the settlement, and (b) any amounts charged under s.65 (the exit charge).

The tax is charged at 30% of the "effective rate" at which tax will be charged on that notional transfer (s.66(1)). This effective rate is found by expressing the tax chargeable as a percentage of the amount on which it is charged.

Example

Justin sets up a discretionary trust in which there is relevant property to the value of £200,000. This transfer takes his cumulative total of chargeable transfers to £50,000 above the nil rate threshold. If the first £150,000 were taxed at the nil rate, and the last £50,000 at 20%, this would result in a tax liability of £10,000.

---

[21] For these purposes two settlements are related only if they are made by the same settlor and commenced on the same day (s.62(1)). Two settlements are not related if all the property comprised in one or both of them was, immediately after commencement, held for charitable purposes only, without limit of time (s.62(2)).

The effective rate would in this case be:

$$\frac{10,000}{200,000} = 0.05 \ \ (\text{or } 5\%)$$

The ten-year anniversary charge will be levied at 30% of this effective rate (i.e., 30% of 5%, which equals 1.5%)

The highest rate at which the ten-year charge can presently be levied is 6% because the highest rate for life time transfers is 20% (30% of 20% = 6%).

Where the whole or part of the property was not relevant property throughout the period of ten years ending immediately before a ten-year anniversary, or was not comprised in the settlement throughout that period, the rate at which tax is charged on that part will be reduced by one-fortieth for each of the successive quarters in that period which expired before the property became or last became relevant property comprised in the settlement (s.66(2)).

The exit charge

Section 65 imposes a charge to tax on the occurrence of certain events in the midst of a ten-year period. S.65(1) provides that tax shall be charged where the property comprised in the settlement, or any part thereof, ceases to be relevant property, whether because it ceases to be comprised in the settlement or otherwise (e.g., where an interest in position is acquired). A charge is also imposed under the subsection in cases in which the trustees make a disposition as a result of which the value of the relevant property comprised in the settlement is diminished. By s.65(2) the tax is charged on the amount by which the value of the relevant property is diminished as a result of the event, or, where the tax is payable out of relevant property in the settlement, on the grossed up sum. The tax is charged at differing rates, depending on whether the occasion is prior to the first ten-year anniversary (s.68) or between ten-year anniversaries (s.69).

There are a number of exceptions to this exit charge. First, there will be no charge where the triggering event occurs in the first quarter of a ten-year period (s.65(4)). Even though this provision could lead to some undesirable results, it is applied strictly.[22] Secondly the charge will not

---

[22] See *Frankland v IRC* [1996] BTC 8034 (Rattee J).

apply in respect of a payment of costs or expenses fairly attributable to relevant property, in respect of a payment which is (or will be) the income of any person for income tax purposes, or in respect of a liability to make such a payment (s.65(5)). Thirdly there will be no charge in cases in which s.10 would apply if the trustees were an individual – i.e., if they can show that they did not intend to confer a gratuitous benefit on anyone (e.g., a bad bargain by trustees).

Accumulation and Maintenance Trusts

As has been stated earlier in this chapter there are some types of settlement in which there is no qualifying interest in possession but which are nevertheless not treated as harshly as, for example, a discretionary trust. Examples are disabled trusts and accumulation and maintenance trusts. The discussion that follows examines the inheritance tax treatment of accumulation and maintenance trusts only.

Section 71(1) specifies the conditions that have to be satisfied before a settlement can qualify as an accumulation and maintenance trust. First, no interest in possession subsists in the settlement, and the income from it is to be accumulated so far as it is not applied for the maintenance, education or benefit of a beneficiary (s.71(1)(b)). Secondly, one or more persons (i.e., the beneficiaries) will, on or before attaining a specified age, not exceeding 25, become beneficially entitled to the settled property or an interest in possession in it (s.71(1)(a)).[23] Thirdly, either not more than 25 years have elapsed since the commencement of the settlement, or all present or past beneficiaries are (or were) grandchildren of a common grandparent, or children, or widow(er)s of such grandchildren beneficiaries who died before they would have become entitled to an interest in position (s.71(2)).

As seen above, s.71(1)(a) speaks about persons being entitled to an interest in possession at a "specified age" not exceeding 25. In most cases the age will be that imposed by s.31 of the Trustee Act 1925 – 18 years. Thus that condition will be satisfied where s.31 of the Trustee Act applies. The second condition (in s.71(1)(b) – that the income is to be accumulated to the extent that it is not applied for the maintenance, education or benefit of a beneficiary) will also be satisfied where s.31 of the Trustee Act applies. Indeed, s.71 is really directed towards relieving cases where infant beneficiaries would have had an interest in position in settled property but for the interposition of s.31 of the Trustee Act. S.31 of the Trustee Act 1925 provides that, where an infant has an interest which is not

---

[23] Concessionary relief is available in ESC F8, to the effect that this particular requirement is regarded as being satisfied even if no age is specified in the trust instrument, provided that it is clear that a beneficiary will in fact become entitled to the settled property, or to an interest in possession in it, by the age of 25.

reversionary, the trustees shall (even if the infant would otherwise have a vested interest) accumulate the income during the infancy of the beneficiary in so far as they do not use it for his maintenance, education or benefit. On reaching the age of 18, the beneficiary obtains an interest in position (a vested right).

Example

Emily sets up a trust which provides that income from certain property should be held on trust for such of Maria's children as attain the age of 30.

1. Maria's children are aged 10, 12, and 15.

This is a case in which s.31 Trustee Act 1925 will apply, because the beneficiaries are minors. The age of 30 which is specified in the trust instrument will be overridden, and the children will be entitled to an interest in possession when they attain 18 (under s.31 Trustee Act 1925). Thus the provisions of s.71(1)(a) IHTA 1984 are satisfied.

2. Maria's children are aged 20, 22, and 24.

Section 31 Trustee Act 1925 will not apply because the children are all over the age of 18. Since the age specified in the trust instrument is above 25, the provisions of s.71(1)(a) IHTA 1984 are not satisfied.

Apart from the effect of s.31 of the Trustee Act 1925 discussed above, the requirement that the beneficiary "will" become entitled to the property or an interest is possession in it is taken strictly. This strict approach was evident in *Inglewood v IRC*,[24] in which property was held on trust for such of the settlor's children then living, or born during the life of the settlement, as should attain the age of 21. The trustees also had powers of maintenance and accumulation, and powers to revoke (and reappoint in their discretion) any of the trusts appointed. The question was whether in these circumstances one or more persons will, on or before attaining a specified age not exceeding 25, become entitled to, or to an interest in possession in the settled property. The Revenue argued that, having regard to the power of revocation, it could not be postulated of any beneficiary that he or she "will" become entitled to an interest in possession in the

[24] [1983] STC 133.
[25] At page 139.

settled fund on or before an age not exceeding[25]. The trustees on the other hand claimed that the word "will" must be construed to mean "will if no event happens to disentitle him or her."

The Revenue's argument was upheld. Fox LJ said that the word "will" in [s.71(1)(a)] does import a degree of certainty which is not satisfied if the trust can be revoked and the fund reappointed to some other person at an age exceeding 25. A trust for A if he attains 25 is within the provision. So also is a trust for A if he attains 25 and with a power of advancement. According to Fox LJ[26] if property is given to A for life but subject to a power of revocation, A is entitled to the income from the inception of the trust until it is revoked. That is an interest in possession. What the court is concerned with here is however something quite different. It is whether it can be said that somebody "will" become entitled to an interest if it is capable of revocation. With respect to this question, Fox LJ concluded:[27]

> [section 71(1)(a)] leaves on us the strong prima facie impression that its provisions are not satisfied by a trust subject to a power of revocation and reapppointment under which the beneficiary's interest can be destroyed and reappointed to another person at the absolute discretion of the trustees. The word "will" involves a degree of certainty which is inconsistent with such a power.

He suggested however[28] that a power which is limited to permitting appointments to persons on attaining an age not exceeding 25 would be within the provision.

The Tax Treatment of Accumulation and Maintenance Trusts

Creation of the settlement

Section 3A(1)(c) provides that a gift into an accumulation and maintenance trust (and a disabled trust) is a PET if made on or after 18 March 1986. Thus, there will be no charge on the creation of such a settlement, or on occasions in which further gifts are made into it. Furthermore, s.58(1)(b) provides that property comprised in such a settlement is not "relevant property" for the purposes of the ten-year anniversary charge which is imposed on settlements in which there is no qualifying interest in possession. This means that accumulation and maintenance trusts will not be subject to the ten-year anniversary charges.

---

[26] At page 141.
[27] Ibid.
[28] At page 140.

Exit charge

As said earlier in this chapter, a change from one type of settlement to another will trigger an exit charge. With respect to accumulation and maintenance trusts s.71(3) imposes a charge in situations in which the settled property ceases to be held on accumulation and maintenance trusts as defined, and in situations in which the property does not cease to be held on such trusts, but the trustees make a disposition diminishing the value of the settled property. There are exceptions to the charge, in cases in which a beneficiary becomes entitled to settled property or an interest in position in it on or before the specified age (e.g., where the trustees make an advancement of capital to or for the benefit of an infant beneficiary or when a beneficiary obtains an interest in possession, for example on attaining 18 under s.31 of the Trustee Act) and there will be no charge on the death of a beneficiary before attaining the specified age (s.71(4)).

Further Reading

Jopling J: *Interests in Possession* [1982] BTR 105.

Goodhart W: *Capital Transfer Tax on Discretionary Trusts - A New Approach* [1980] BTR 393.

chapter twenty one
Value Added Tax

Historical Background

The development of VAT

Value-added tax (VAT) was first introduced by France in 1954 and was then introduced by Finland ten years later. However, it is fair to say that it was the decision by the European Community to adopt VAT which led to the tax's wider acceptance. As a result of this decision it took little more than thirty years for the tax to become the accepted world system of sales taxation. The decision to adopt VAT was taken by the original six Member States and those Member States that joined the Community afterwards had to agree to introduce VAT as a condition of entry. The United Kingdom joined the Community on 1 January 1973 and applied a system of VAT from the beginning of April that year. VAT therefore has a strong identity at EC level as well as at national level.

When the European Community was founded in 1957, the most popular form of sales taxation was the so-called cascade tax. This was used by Belgium, the Netherlands, Luxembourg, Germany and Italy. It was also used by France at a local level. Like VAT, the cascade tax was imposed at each stage in the production chain but, unlike VAT, it did not allow traders to reclaim the tax they had paid to their suppliers.

For example, suppose that a manufacturer spent £1,000 on materials. If the rate of cascade tax was 10%, he would pay his supplier £1,100. If he used the materials to produce goods worth £2,000, he would then have to charge his customer (possibly a wholesaler) £2,200. Similarly, if the wholesaler were to sell the goods on for £3,000, he would have to add £300 tax. The end result would be that the authorities had received a total of £600, only £300 of which would be listed as tax on the final invoice. The other £300 would be hidden in the price of the goods.

There were two major disadvantages with this type of tax system. The first was that it was not neutral, since it encouraged the vertical integration of businesses. In the example above, the manufacturer and the wholesaler could have saved £200 on that transaction alone had they merged.

The second disadvantage was that it was impossible to make accurate border tax adjustments since it was difficult to determine what proportion of the final selling price was tax. This posed a serious threat to a common market based on the free movement of goods, persons, services and capital. Because of this, Article 99 of the Treaty of Rome (now Article 93 EC) allowed the Commission to draw up proposals for the harmonisation of indirect taxation. In 1960, the Commission appointed two committees of experts under this Article. The first body was a set of three working groups appointed to address the problems and issues involved in the harmonisation of the various systems of taxation within the Community. Of these groups, Group I was given the mandate of considering the harmonisation of turnover taxation. Since this group divided itself into three subgroups, A, B and C, its report is normally known as the ABC Report. The second body was the Fiscal and Financial Committee which was chaired by Professor Fritz Neumark and which was to produce the Neumark Report.[1]

Both reports supported a form of VAT which did not extend to the retail stage, arguing that retailers would not be able to deal with the administration involved. However, the Commission did not accept this limitation and it produced proposals in 1965 which were to result in the First and Second VAT Directives.[2] These were followed in 1977 by the Sixth VAT Directive.[3] This, with subsequent amendments, is still the central piece of Community VAT legislation. Before going any further, though, it is necessary to discuss the basic structure and advantages of the type of tax that the Community had decided to adopt.

Structure and advantages of VAT

The key difference between VAT and the cascade taxes discussed above is that VAT is designed to allow a trader who makes taxable supplies to claim a refund of tax that he has paid to his supplier or to offset this tax against the tax that he in turn collects from his customers before passing the difference on to the tax authorities.

To return to the example given above, a manufacturer spends £1,000 on materials. If the rate of VAT is 10%, he will pay his supplier £1,100. He then sells his products on to a wholesaler for £2,000, or £2,200 including VAT. This time, though, he can deduct the £100 that he has paid to his supplier from the £200 he has collected from his customer and pass the remaining £100 on to the tax authorities. In the same way, the

---

[1] "The EEC Reports on Tax Harmonization, the Report of the Fiscal and Financial Committee and the Reports of Sub-Groups A, B and C, An Unofficial Translation prepared by Dr H. Thurston," International Bureau for Fiscal Documentation 1963

[2] Directive 67/227/EEC and Directive 67/228/EEC.

[3] Directive 77/388/EEC.

retailer who buys these goods for £3,300 inclusive of VAT can deduct the £200 that he has paid to the wholesaler from the £300 that he collects from his customer before passing the remaining £100 on to the authorities.

This system addresses the two main disadvantages of the cascade tax described above. Firstly, the same amount of tax is payable regardless of how many stages of production the goods have gone through. Had the original supplier of raw materials decided to process them himself and to sell the products directly to the final consumer, the amount of tax payable would have been the same. Secondly, at any stage in the production chain, it is possible to identify what proportion of the price consists of tax. Because of this, it is then possible to refund that tax to the last trader in the supply chain if the goods are exported.

Community Aspects of VAT

In order to understand VAT, it is necessary to place it in its Community context. Even though the systems of VAT operated in the Member States differ from each other in important aspects, they are based on the same basic principles. The authorities in all the Member States are bound by the framework of Community VAT legislation and the national courts are obliged to apply the jurisprudence of the European Court of Justice.

The role of VAT in the Community budget

VAT is also a source of Community revenue as well as national revenue, although this happens in rather an indirect way. A proportion of the VAT collected by Member States forms an important part of the Community's budget. Prior to 1970, the Community was financed by direct contributions from the Member States, but it had always been intended that it should have a certain degree of financial independence from them.[4] The development of the present system of own resources has taken place since then.[5] At present, there are basically four main categories of resources:

i.   sugar levies and agricultural levies;

ii.   revenue from customs duties on trade with third countries;

iii. a fixed percentage of VAT;

iv.   the "fourth resource" consisting of top-up payments based on Member States' GNP.

---

[4]   Article 201 (now Article 269) of the Treaty of Rome provided that the budget should eventually be financed wholly from own resources.

[5]   For a full explanation of the Community's budget and the development of the system of own resources, see Brigid Laffan, "The Finances of the European Union", MacMillan 1997.

The fixed VAT percentage was originally set at one per cent in 1970. This was increased to 1.4% in 1984. In the so-called Delors I round of budgetary negotiations, from 1988 to 1992, the percentage remained the same, but it was agreed that no Member State's VAT contribution should exceed 55% of its GNP. In the Delors II round, which began in 1993, the fixed percentage was reduced back to one %.

Although VAT plays a key role in the Community budget the Community itself has no mechanism for collecting the tax, so that it is not paid directly to the Community. Instead, the Member States pay to the Community an amount based on the amount of VAT that they collect. This amount is not equivalent to one per cent of the actual VAT collected since it is not based on the VAT rates applied by the Member States.[6] If the VAT resource had been based on the actual VAT collected, a Member State would have been able to reduce its contribution to the Community budget by lowering its VAT rates to the minimum permitted level.[7]

Because of this system, the different VAT rates applied in the various Member States do not result in a lack of equity between their nationals. For example, if there had been a Community mechanism for collecting VAT based on the tax actually paid, it would have been the case that a German consumer contributed to the Community budget when buying basic foodstuffs, whereas a UK consumer did not.[8] Nevertheless, this has not prevented the European Commission from arguing that the zero-rating of products sold to final consumers disrupts the Community tax base.[9]

The relationship between Community law and national law

The main principle to note here is that Community law takes precedence over national law. This principle of supremacy was laid down by the European Court of Justice (ECJ) in *Flaminio Costa v ENEL*.[10] The ECJ has also made it clear that, if there is a conflict between Community law and a piece of national legislation, the national court must disapply the national legislation and apply Community law.[11] Courts in the United Kingdom have accepted this principle, although they have interpreted it in a slightly different way from the ECJ.[12] Their acceptance of this principle is clear from Lord Bridge's speech in *Factortame Ltd v Secretary of State for Transport (No. 2)*:[13]

---

[6] See Council Regulation 1553/89 for full details of how the VAT resource is calculated.
[7] Article 12(3)(a) of the Sixth Directive permits Member States to apply reduced rates of not less than 5%. This is discussed later in the context of VAT rates and exemptions.
[8] Basic foodstuffs are zero-rated in the UK.
[9] European Community, "Further Harmonisation of VAT," *Intertax*, April 1983, p.139.
[10] Case 6/64, [1964] ECR 585, [1964] CMLR 425.
[11] Case 106/77, *Amministrazione delle Finanze dello State v Simmenthal SpA* [1978] ECR 629, [1978] 3 CMLR 263.
[12] For example, in *Costa*, the ECJ referred to a permanent limitation of sovereign rights. By contrast in *Macarthys v Smith* [1979] 3 All ER 325, Lord Denning stated that, if Parliament were to make it clear that it intended to legislate in contravention of Community law, it would be the duty of the courts to follow the will of Parliament.
[13] [1991] 1 AC 603.

Under the terms of the 1972 Act [the European Communities Act 1972] it has always been clear that it was the duty of a United Kingdom court, when delivering final judgment, to override any rule of national law found to be in conflict with a directly enforceable rule of Community law. Similarly, when decisions of the Court of Justice have exposed areas of United Kingdom statute law which failed to implement Council directives, Parliament has always loyally accepted the obligation to make appropriate and prompt amendments.

The different types of Community legislation

There are five different types of Community legislation: directives, regulations, decision, recommendations and opinions. The vast majority of VAT legislation has been enacted by directive. There is also a relatively small number of regulations. Decisions have also been used, primarily to permit Member States to derogate from directives. Recommendations and opinions have no binding force and are not discussed in this section.

The difference between the various types of legislation is set out in Article 249 of the EC Treaty:

A regulation shall have general application. It shall be binding in its entirety and directly applicable in all Member States.

A directive shall be binding, as to the result to be achieved, upon each Member State to which it is addressed, but shall leave to the national authorities the choice of form and methods.

A decision shall be binding in its entirety upon those to whom it is addressed.

Recommendations and opinions shall have no binding force.[14]

For the purposes of VAT, the most significant type of legislation is the directive. In order to have full effect in national law, a directive must be implemented.[15] Member States have a certain amount of flexibility as to how they do this, provided that they achieve the results set out in the directive.

Regulations and decisions, on the other hand, are binding in their entirety. A Regulation becomes part of the national law in all Member States from the time that it comes into force. There is no need for

---

[14] This was formerly Article 189, before the EC Treaty was renumbered by the Treaty of Amsterdam.
[15] Enforcement of Community legislation is discussed below.

Member States to implement a regulation; indeed, the ECJ has made it clear that it is a breach of Community law for a Member State to purport to do so.[16] Decisions have been used to permit Member States to derogate from the terms of a directive under certain circumstances.

Because directives allow Member States so much more flexibility, it is not surprising that the Community has used directives to set out the main substance of the common system of VAT. It is doubtful whether the Member States would have agreed to the use of regulations in this context, as this would have meant total harmonisation of national VAT systems, including tax rates and registration thresholds. Regulations have been used more for procedural matters, for example to put systems in place for collecting statistics and to require administrative co-operation between the authorities in the Member States.

Enforcement of Community legislation

The enforcement of regulations is relatively straightforward; as Article 249 states, these are directly applicable. They can therefore be enforced in national courts both by individuals and by Member States.

The enforcement of directives is more problematic. Although they are not stated in Article 249 to be directly applicable, the ECJ has nevertheless held that they can have direct effect. In other words, even though they do not become part of the national law in the same way as a regulation, individuals can still enforce them in national courts, provided that their provisions are "unconditional and sufficiently precise."[17]

Under normal circumstances, there will be no need to rely upon the direct effect of a directive. Article 249 envisages that the Member States will implement directives by passing national legislation. If the Member State has implemented the directive correctly, then proceedings will be based upon the implementing legislation. The aim of the ECJ in developing the principle of direct effect of directives was to prevent Member States from being successful before their national courts by relying upon the fact that they had breached their obligations under Community law by failing to implement a directive or by implementing it incorrectly.[18]

It is clear from the ECJ's judgments in this area that an individual can rely as against a Member State upon an unimplemented or incorrectly implemented directive.[19] It is also clear that a Member State cannot rely

---

[16] Case 34/73, *Variola v Amministrazione delle Finanze*, [1973] ECR 981. However, the ECJ has accepted that Member States could use national legislation to provide sanctions for breach of a regulation provided that this did not obscure the fact that the regulation was Community law and therefore took precedence over any conflicting national law - Case 50/76, *Amsterdam Bulb BV v Produktschap voor Siergewassen* [1977] ECR 137, [1977] 2 CMLR 218.

[17] See Case 41/74, *Van Duyn v Home Office*, [1974] ECR 1337, [1975] 1 CMLR 1, and Case 148/78, *Pubblico Ministerio v Tullio Ratti*, [1979] ECR 1629, [1980] 1 CMLR 96.

[18] It follows from this that an individual cannot rely upon the direct effect of a directive until the date for its implementation has passed, as the Member State is not in breach of EC law until then.

[19] The ECJ has also made it clear that an individual cannot rely upon such a directive as against another individual: Case 152/84, *Marshall v Southampton and South West Hampshire Area Health Authority*, [1986] ECR 723, [1986] 1 CMLR 688. Since revenue law is concerned with the relationship between individuals and the state, this issue is not addressed here.

upon such a directive against an individual. For example, in 1985, the Commission brought two cases against the United Kingdom arguing that it was in breach of its obligations under the relevant VAT directives. *Commission v UK*[20] concerned the zero-rating of spectacles and contact lenses and *Commission v UK*[21] concerned the zero-rating of items not supplied to final consumers. In both cases, the Commission was successful and the United Kingdom had to amend the relevant legislation. However, the United Kingdom had to wait until the amended legislation came into force before it could collect the extra VAT from the parties affected by the changes.

If a Member State wishes to rely upon the provisions of a directive against an individual, it must make sure that it has implemented the directive correctly so that it can then rely upon the provisions of the implementing legislation. The reason for this is the same as the reason why an individual can enforce a directive against a Member State: the Member State cannot be allowed to succeed by relying on its own breach of Community law.

Note, though, that this principle does not apply if the Member State is attempting to enforce a directive against a public body. This issue was addressed in *Arts Council of Great Britain v Commissioners of Customs and Excise*.[22] The Commissioners were seeking to enforce a provision of the Sixth Directive against the Arts Council. The Arts Council argued that the provision had not been implemented into national law and that the Commissioners were therefore not able to rely upon it. The VAT Tribunal held that the provision had been implemented but stated that, even had this not been the case, the Commissioners would still have been able to rely upon it. This was because the Arts Council was a public body. It was therefore not an individual but an arm of the state and directives could be enforced against it, whether implemented or not. It follows from this that arms of the state can enforce unimplemented directives against each other.

The status of national legislation

National VAT legislation is implementing legislation. Because of this, it is not the highest source of law and can therefore be set aside by the courts if it is found to be inconsistent with the directives. This is clear from Lord Bridge's speech in *Factortame*, quoted above.

The preliminary reference procedure

If faced with an inconsistency between Community law and national law, national courts must set aside national legislation. They are unlikely to do

---

[20]   Case 353/85, [1988] ECR 817, [1988] STC 251.
[21]   Case 416/85, [1988] ECR 3127, [1988] STC 456.
[22]   [1994] VATTR 313.

this, however, without first making a reference to the ECJ under Article 234 of the EC Treaty. This provides that the ECJ shall have the jurisdiction to give preliminary rulings on points of law when requested to do so by a court or tribunal in a Member State. Two separate types of courts are referred to in the Article. Paragraph 2 provides that any court or tribunal may make a reference to the ECJ if it considers that a decision on a point of EC law is necessary for it to give judgment. Paragraph 3 provides that a court or tribunal must make a reference if there is no judicial remedy against its decisions under national law.

Where such a reference is made, the national court will send a question of law to the ECJ. The ECJ will send its reply back to the national court which will then decide the case on that basis. It must be stressed that this is not an appellate process. It is the national court that refers the case and individuals cannot appeal to the ECJ.

The difference between paragraphs 2 and 3 of Article 234

It is clear that the House of Lords falls within the third paragraph of Article 234. However, the ECJ has interpreted this paragraph as having a wider scope than that. In *Costa v ENEL*, an Italian magistrates' court made a reference to the ECJ. The court was clearly not the highest court within the Italian legal system, but it was the highest court in which that particular case could be heard because there was such a small sum involved. The ECJ treated the court as one that fell within the third rather than the second paragraph of Article 234.

On this approach, it is arguable that any court brings itself within the scope of the third paragraph if it refuses leave to appeal. On the other hand, the possibility of seeking leave to appeal from the appeal court if the lower court refuses it could be classed as a "judicial remedy" against the ruling of the lower court, meaning that the latter still falls within the second paragraph.

When must a reference be made to the ECJ?

Courts falling within the second paragraph of Article 234 have a discretion as to whether to refer. The ECJ gave guidance as to when courts falling within the third paragraph should refer in *Srl CILFIT and Lanificio di Gavardo SpA v Ministry of Health*.[23] It set out three situations in which a court was not required to make a reference, in spite of the fact that there was no judicial remedy against its decision and that a question of Community law was involved. These situations are known as the *CILFIT* exceptions.

---

[23]   Case 283/81, [1982] ECR 3415, [1983] CMLR 472.

Cases where the question cannot affect the outcome of the case

The national court is only obliged to refer where the question of Community law is necessary to decide the case. Hence, a question of Community law may arise, but the court will not be obliged to refer it to the ECJ unless it will affect the outcome. For example, the authorities may put forward two reasons why a trader is liable to VAT. One of these reasons may be based on an uncertain point of Community law, but the other one may be completely clear. If the second reason means that that trader is liable to VAT in any event, there will be no reason to make a reference in respect of the first.

This point is really clarifying the distinction between the second and third paragraphs of Article 234. Unlike the second paragraph, the third paragraph does not contain the words, "if it considers that a decision on the question is necessary to enable it to give judgment." In *CILFIT*, the ECJ is making it clear that this is equally applicable to the third paragraph.

Cases where the ECJ has already decided that point of law

Here, the ECJ referred to its earlier judgment in *Da Costa en Schaake*[24] and stated that, if it had already given a judgment on that particular point of law, the national court could refer to that judgment instead of making a reference.

The acte clair *exception*

This was the new exception that the ECJ added in *CILFIT*. It stated that, even if neither of the first two exceptions applied, a national court that fell within the third paragraph of Article 234 could still decline to make a reference and could decide the question of Community law itself if the correct application of Community law was so obvious that there was no scope for any reasonable doubt as to how the question should be resolved. This is known as the *acte clair* doctrine.

It may seem here that the ECJ has given the national courts a significant amount of control over the development of Community law. However, the ECJ made it clear that, before deciding that the question was *acte clair*, the national court should be convinced that the matter was equally obvious to the courts of the other Member States as well as to the ECJ itself.

---

[24] Cases 28-30/62, *Da Costa en Schaake NV, Jacob Meijer NV and Hoechst-Holland NV v Nederlandse Belastingadministratie*, [1963] ECR 31, [1963] CMLR 224.

Sources of Law

The main sources of VAT law in the United Kingdom are summarised below:

EC legislation

As discussed above, the main legislation setting out the framework of the common system of VAT has been enacted by directive. The main directives are:

The First Directive – Directive 67/227.

The Sixth Directive – Directive 77/388.

The Eighth Directive – Directive 79/1072.

The Thirteenth Directive – Directive 86/560.

The First Directive set out some of the main principles of VAT and provided that the Commission should put forward a proposal for the Second Directive[25]. The Second Directive was the main piece of Community VAT legislation until 1977 when it was replaced by the Sixth Directive. The Eighth and Thirteenth Directives respectively provide for refunds of VAT to traders established in other Member States and traders established outside the Community.

UK legislation

The main piece of legislation implementing the VAT directives in the UK is the Value Added Tax 1994 (VATA 1994). This came into force on 1 September 1994 and acts as a consolidating act for previous VAT legislation, including VATA 1983.

VATA 1994 also acts as the parent act for a significant amount of secondary legislation. Section 97 provides that such legislation shall take the form of statutory instruments. Among other things, statutory instruments can change the rate of VAT, end zero-rating and exemption in respect of certain supplies and disallow the deduction of input tax in certain cases.

Customs and Excise notices and extra-statutory concessions

Customs and Excise issue a large number of notices giving their interpretation of certain aspects of VAT law. The vast majority of these

---

[25] Directive 67/228.

notices do not have the force of law, but traders are well advised to follow them if they are not prepared to challenge the Commissioners' rulings before the VAT Tribunal.

The main exception to this is Notice 727, which concerns retail schemes and is passed under Regulation 67 of the Value Added Tax Regulations 1995. Notice 48 sets out the Commissioners' extra-statutory concessions.

Case law

Appeals from the Commissioners' decisions are made to the VAT Tribunal. Appeals against VAT Tribunal decisions can then be made to the High Court, then the Court of Appeal and finally to the House of Lords. As discussed above, a reference to the ECJ can be made at any point during this process.

Both the VAT Tribunal and the courts make use of ECJ judgments. In the following chapters, relevant ECJ judgments will be considered before UK judgments, but no attempt has been made to segregate EC issues into separate chapters. Since the whole of the UK VAT system has been put in place to implement EC directives, it would be artificial to attempt to draw a clear line between EC law and UK law in this area.

The Charge to VAT

This section gives a very brief outline of the charge to VAT. The issues identified here will be considered in detail in later chapters.

Article 2(1) of the Sixth VAT Directive provides that VAT shall be charged on the supply of goods or services effected for a consideration within the territory of the country by a taxable person acting as such.

This charge breaks down into four main elements:

a.   A supply of goods or services.
b.   Consideration.
c.   Territorial scope.
d.   Taxable person.[26]

Article 17 of the Sixth Directive provides that a taxable person shall be entitled to deduct the VAT that he has paid to his suppliers in relation to taxable transactions from the VAT that he has collected from his customers.

---

[26]   The domestic legislation implementing this provision is to be found in Sections 1 and 5 and Schedule 4 of the Value Added Tax Act 1994. This adopts a slightly different approach in that it includes the requirement for consideration in the definition of supply. Under the Sixth Directive, a supply may not be subject to VAT unless there is consideration; under the 1994 Act there cannot be a supply in the first place unless there is also consideration. The end result is the same whichever approach is followed.

Taken together, these two articles give effect to the principle set out in Article 2 of the First VAT Directive:

> The principle of the common system of value added tax involves the application to goods and services of a general tax on consumption exactly proportional to the price of the goods and services, whatever the number of transactions which take place in the production and distribution process before the stage at which the tax is charged.[27]

These issues are discussed in the following five chapters. Chapter 22 discusses supplies of goods and services and the territorial scope and Chapter 23 discusses consideration. Chapter 24 deals with VAT rates and exemptions and Chapter 25 with the right to deduct input tax. Chapter 26 considers some of the more theoretical issues relating to VAT.

Further Reading

Dame Valerie Strachan: *Twenty-five Years of VAT* [1998] BTR 547.

Oliver S, Q.C., *Twenty-five years of the VAT Tribunals: A View from the President* [1998] BTR 552.

Voge AWB, *Twenty-five years of the VAT Tribunals: The Views of a Lay Member* [1998] BTR 558.

Hamilton P, *Twenty-five years of the VAT Tribunals: An Advocate's View* [1998] BTR 560.

Conlon M, *A Tide in the Affairs of Men* [1998] BTR 563.

Cordara R, Q.C., and Cargill–Thompson P, *Judicial Review in the Context of VAT: Effective Supervison of the Commissioners?* [1998] BTR 573.

"The EEC Reports on Tax Harmonization, the Report of the Fiscal and Financial Committee and the Reports of Sub-Groups A, B and C, An Unofficial Translation prepared by Dr H. Thurston," International Bureau for Fiscal Documentation 1963.

Directive 67/227/EEC and Directive 67/228/EEC.

Directive 77/388/EEC.

---

[27] Article 2 of Directive 67/227/EEC.

chapter twenty two

Value Added Tax - Supplies of Goods and Services

Section 4(1) of VATA 1994 provides that VAT shall be charged on any supply of goods or services made in the United Kingdom, where it is a taxable supply made by a taxable person in the course of or furtherance of any business carried on by him. Section 4(2) provides that a taxable supply is a supply of goods or services made in the United Kingdom other than an exempt supply.

It is therefore necessary to know the meaning of a supply of goods or services and to know how to determine whether such supplies are made in the United Kingdom. These two issues are considered in this chapter.

Supplies of Goods and Services

The Sixth Directive refers to two separate types of supply: supplies of goods and supplies of services. This is reflected in s.5(3) of VATA 1994.[1]

Supplies of goods

A supply of goods is defined by Article 5 of the Sixth Directive as "the transfer of the right to dispose of tangible property as owner." The main text of VATA 1994 makes no attempt to give a general definition of a supply of goods. Section 5(2)(a) merely states that "supply" includes all forms of supply, but not anything done otherwise than for a consideration. Schedule 4 of the 1994 Act provides that the following are to be treated as supplies of goods:

1. Any transfer of the whole of the property in goods.

2. The transfer of the possession of goods under an agreement for sale or under agreements that provide that title will pass in the future.

---

[1] Section 5(c) also refers to supplies of neither goods nor services. This allows the Treasury to remove certain supplies from the scope of VAT. It has done this, for example, in relation to the transfer of a business as a going concern and for supplies within groups of companies.

3. The supply of power, heat, refrigeration or ventilation.

4. The grant, assignment or surrender or a major interest in land.

5. The transfer of goods forming part of the assets of a business, whether or not for consideration.

These provisions are all consistent with EC law, as follows:

1. Article 5(1) of the Sixth Directive provides that the supply of goods shall mean the transfer of the right to dispose of tangible property as owner.

2. In *Staatsecretaris van Financien v Shipping and Forwarding Enterprise SAFE BV*,[2] the ECJ considered the question of whether the transfer of the possession of goods could be classed as a supply even if the ownership was not to be transferred until a later date. It held that such a transfer could be classed as a supply of goods, provided that the person making the transfer had the right to transfer ownership as well as possession.

3. This is consistent with Article 5(2) of the Sixth Directive which provides that "electric current, gas, heat, refrigeration and the like shall be considered tangible property."

4. This is consistent with Article 5(3) of the Sixth Directive, which allows Member States to treat immovable property as tangible property.

5. This is consistent with Article 5(6) of the Sixth Directive, which deals with business assets which are either disposed of free of charge or used by the trader for his own use. The disposal of such business assets is to be treated as a supply for consideration, although there is an exception for samples and gifts of small value. Article 11(6) provides that the taxable amount for such supplies is the purchase price of the goods or, in the absence of this, the cost price.[3] The ECJ applied these provisions in *Kuwait Petroleum (GB) Ltd v Customs and Excise Commissioners*.[4] The case involved a promotion by a petrol company. Every time customers bought fuel, they were given vouchers which they could collect and exchange for items in a catalogue. It was held that the catalogue items were gifts but that they were taxable supplies because of Article 5(6). The VAT Tribunal followed this approach in *Gallaher v Customs and Excise Commissioners*,[5] which involved a similar promotion by a tobacco company.

---

[2] Case 320/88, [1990] ECR I-285
[3] See Chapter 23
[4] Case C-48/97, [1999] ECR I-2323, [1997] STC 488.
[5] LON/96/1928, (14827, 16395).

Supplies of services

A supply of services is defined by Article 6 of the Sixth Directive as "any transaction which does not constitute a supply of goods within the meaning of Article 5." This definition of a supply of services may at first seem unhelpful, but its effect is to make sure that a transaction cannot fall outside the scope of VAT merely because it does not fall within the definition either of a supply of goods or of a supply of services.

VATA 1994 takes a similar approach; s.5(2)(b) provides that anything which is not a supply of goods but is done for a consideration (including, if so done, the granting, assignment or surrender of any right) is a supply of services.

Schedule 4 of the Act provides that the following shall be treated as supplies of services:

1. The transfer of any undivided share of the property.

2. The transfer of the possession of goods.[6]

It can be seen from this that the transfer of the possession of goods can be either a supply of goods or a supply of services, depending on the circumstances. Mere transfer of possession will be a supply of services, whereas transfer of possession as part of the transfer of the goods themselves will be a supply of goods.

The Distinction Between Supplies of Goods and Supplies of Services

In a large number of cases, the distinction between the two types of supply is immaterial, provided that they are made within one Member State and that the same rate of VAT applies. For example, Article 5(2) of the Sixth Directive specifically states that electric current is to be classed as tangible property. Anyone who has ever had an electric shock may disagree with this conclusion, but its effect is that the supply of electricity is to be treated as a supply of goods rather than a supply of services. Within a purely domestic context, it would have made very little difference had the authors of the Sixth Directive decided that the supply of electricity was to be classed as a supply of services.

However, in cases with an intra-Community aspect, the difference between the two types of supply is crucial. This is because one of the key

---

[6]   As opposed to the transfer of the whole property in goods, which is a supply of goods. See above.

differences between supplies of goods and supplies of services is the place of supply rules that apply to each. These are the rules that determine which Member State collects the revenue from a particular transaction. They are discussed later in this chapter.

The importance of distinguishing between the two types of supply was illustrated in *Faaborg-Gelting Linien A/S v Finanzamt Fiensburg*.[7] This case concerned the VAT paid on restaurant meals served on ferries travelling between the ports of Faaborg and Denmark and Gelting in Germany. The place of supply of any services provided on the ferries would have been the supplier's place of establishment, in this case Denmark; the place of supply of any goods would have been the place where the goods were when the supply took place.[8] The ferry company argued that the restaurant meals were supplies of services and so did not include the restaurant transactions in the tax returns that they submitted to the German tax authorities. On the other hand, the German authorities argued that the meals were supplies of goods and laid claim to the VAT that had been paid on meals bought when the ferries were in German waters.

The European Court of Justice (ECJ) held that restaurant meals were supplies of services and that the place of supply was therefore the operator's place of establishment. However, they did suggest that supplies of take-away food might be classed as supplies of goods:

> Consequently, restaurant transactions are characterized by a cluster of features and acts, of which the provision of food is only one component and in which services largely predominate. They must therefore be regarded as supplies of services within the meaning of Article 6(1) of the Sixth Directive. The situation is different, however, where the transaction relates to "take-away" food and is not coupled with services designed to enhance consumption on the spot in an appropriate setting.[9]

While the case illustrates the importance of distinguishing between the two types of supply in certain cases, it also illustrates how nice that distinction can be. The VAT paid by a passenger who pays for a restaurant meal in German waters will go to the Danish authorities whereas as the VAT paid by a passenger who buys sandwiches in German waters and takes them out on deck to eat them will go to the German authorities.[10]

---

[7] Case C-231-94, [1996] ECR I-2395
[8] Articles 8 and 9 of the Sixth Directive. These are discussed below.
[9] Paragraph 14 of the judgment
[10] A similar difficulty exists for supplies of computer software, which can be treated as either supplies of goods or supplies of services, depending on whether it is "off the shelf" or written to a customer's specific requirements. Software downloaded from the internet is treated as a supply of services, as is the supply of a licence to use software: Customs and Excise Notice 702/4, "Importing Computer Software." See Etienne Wong and David Saleh, "When VAT Met the Internet," Computers and the Law, December 1997/January 1998, pp. 31-34. As Wong and Saleh point out, the main component of the sale of software is the licence to use it and the distinction between customised and off the shelf software is difficult to maintain once it is admitted that the supply of a software licence is a supply of services.

Composite and mixed supplies

As stated above, for VAT to be chargeable, there must be a supply of goods or services. Each identifiable supply is therefore subject to VAT and a great deal of VAT litigation centres around whether any given transaction consists of one composite supply or a number of separate supplies. The normal reason for attempting to split supplies in this way is to take advantage of the more favourable tax treatment of one type of supply. Many of these cases turn on whether there is a single supply of services or separate supplies of goods and services, but the distinction between goods and services in these cases is not the central issue in the same way that it was in *Faaborg-Gelting*. That case concerned which Member State should receive the tax that had been paid; the cases discussed below concern whether a transaction can be split into separate elements so that some elements can escape VAT or take advantage of a lower rate.

The approach taken by the European Court of Justice

The two leading cases from the ECJ on the issue are *Commission v United Kingdom*[11] and *Card Protection Plan Ltd. v Commissioners of Customs and Excise*.[12]

Commission v United Kingdom concerned the question of whether medicines and other goods were part of the services of providing medical care. The ECJ's approach was as follows:

> ... apart from minor provisions of goods which are strictly necessary at the time when the care is provided, the supply of medicines and other goods, such as corrective spectacles prescribed by a doctor or by other authorised person, is physically and economically dissociable from the provision of the service.[13]

However, the Court took a slightly different approach in *Card Protection Plan*. This concerned a company that offered various services to holders of credit cards. In return for an annual fee, CPP would notify the credit card companies involved if the cards were lost and would provide insurance against the unauthorised use of the cards. Various other services were offered such as notifying the card companies of any changes of address. Until 1990, Customs and Excise classed the service provided by CPP as exempt.[14] However, in 1990 the Commissioners altered their assessment and argued that the plan was a package of services which was subject to VAT at the standard rate.

There were various possible approaches to these facts. One, as argued

---

[11]   Case 353/85, [1988] ECR 817, [1988] STC 251.
[12]   Case C-349/96, [1999] ECR I-973.
[13]   Paragraph 33 of the judgment.
[14]   Article 13B(a) of the Sixth Directive and Group 2 of Schedule 6 of the Value Added Tax Act 1983 provide that insurance services are exempt.

by CPP, was that the supply was a single exempt supply of insurance services. Another, as argued by the Commissioners, as that it was a single taxable supply of a card registration service. Each of these approaches is based on arguing that the taxation of the whole supply should be determined by that of its principal element. An alternative approach, as taken by the High Court was that the total amount paid should be apportioned and that the amount relating to the card registration service should be taxable and the amount relating to the insurance services should be exempt. This decision was reversed by the Court of Appeal which supported the Commissioners' view, stating that the insurance elements were merely incidental to the supply of a card registration service. Leave was granted to appeal to the House of Lords which in turn made a reference to the ECJ. The ECJ's approach was as follows:

> There is a single supply in particular in cases where one or more elements are to be regarded as constituting the principal service, whilst one or more elements are to be regarded, by contrast, as ancillary services which share the tax treatment of the principal service. A service must be regarded as ancillary to a principal service if it does not constitute for customers and aim in itself, but a means of better enjoying the principal service supplied.
>
> In those circumstances, the fact that a single price is charged is not decisive. Admittedly, if the service provided to customers consists of several elements for a single price, the single price may suggest that there is a single service. However, not withstanding the single price, if circumstances such as those described in paragraphs 7 to 10 above [setting out the terms of the contract between CPP and its customers] indicated that the customers intended to purchase two distinct services, namely an insurance supply and a card registration service, then it would be necessary to identify the part of the single price which related to the insurance supply, which would remain exempt in any event.[15]

When this reference was referred back to the House of Lords,[16] the House unanimously allowed CPP's appeal, holding that the relevant supply was a principal exempt insurance supply and that the other supplies were ancillary to this.

---

[15] Paragraphs 30 and 31 of the judgment.
[16] [2001] STC 174.

The approach taken by courts in the United Kingdom

One of the earliest and most often quoted cases UK in this area is that of *Mander Laundries v The Commissioners of Customs and Excise*[17]. This involved a firm which owned coin-operated launderettes. Customs and Excise argued that the firm was supplying a taxable service and that VAT was payable on the total amount of money that the customers put into the machines. Mander Laundries appealed against this decision, arguing that a proportion of the money paid was in return for zero-rated supplies of goods, namely water, oil and gas used for heating, electricity and salt used for softening the water. It argued that the twenty pence paid by each customer for the use of a washing machine should be apportioned as between the amount paid for zero-rated goods and the amount payable for standard-rated services and that only the latter should be subject to VAT.

The Birmingham VAT Tribunal dismissed the appeal. It drew the distinction between a taxable person who supplied zero-rated goods and one who used such goods in order to provide a service:

> There is, for example, the dentist who uses power in his electric drill but he could hardly be said to be selling the electricity. He is using the electricity to provide the service which the patient obtains. Therefore what is supplied in this case is a service by way of a licence to use the machine and the water, gas and electricity are really supplied to the launderette; the customer gets the use of these merely through the agency of Mander Laundries who supply the overall washing or drying services.

A similar approach was taken by the Court of Appeal in *British Airways plc. v Customs and Excise Commissioners*.[18] Here, the Commissioners attempted to argue that British Airways should apportion the price of air fares into the amount paid for zero-rated passenger transport and that paid for standard-rated in-flight catering. This argument had been successful before the London Value Added Tax Tribunal, where Lord Grantchester had given weight to the argument that catering could not be seen as a necessary ingredient of supplies of transport.[19] British Airways appealed against the ruling to the High Court and were successful.[20] Otton J held that the tribunal had made an error of law in asking whether in-flight catering was a necessary ingredient of supplies of air travel and that the correct test was whether or not the supply of catering was incidental to the supply of air travel. This approach was upheld unanimously by the Court of Appeal. According to Stuart-Smith LJ:

[17]   [1973] VATTR 136.
[18]   [1990] STC 643.
[19]   [1987] VATTR 120.
[20]   [1989] STC 182.

The test, as both Lord Grantchester QC and Otton J recognised, is 'in substance and reality is the in-flight catering and integral part of the transport?'. Yet ... It seems to be that Lord Grantchester effectively answers the question by saying that it is not a necessary part of the transportation. While something that is necessary for the supply will almost certainly be an integral part of it, the converse does not follow. ... It may not be necessary for passengers to wash their hands on a short-haul flight yet it would be astonishing if the supply of soap was to be regarded as a separate supply of goods.

Some of the more recent significant UK cases have concentrated on the question of whether delivery or postal charges can be treated as separate supplies. Two cases are of particular interest here. *Customs and Excise Commissioners v British Telecommunications plc*[21] reached the House of Lords in July 1999. The case of *Customs and Excise Commissioners v Plantiflor Ltd* has so far been considered by the VAT Tribunal,[22] by the High Court[23] and by the Court of Appeal.[24] The Commissioners have successfully petitioned the House of Lords for leave to appeal.

British Telecom concerned delivery charges on the supply of new motor vehicles bought by BT direct from the manufacturers. BT tried to argue that the supply of the delivery services was a separate supply and was not integral to the supply of the vehicles. This was important because VAT paid on the supply of motor vehicles cannot be offset by way of input tax.[25] Therefore, BT had to argue that the delivery was a separate supply in order to offset the VAT paid on the delivery costs. The VAT tribunal held that BT could deduct the delivery costs.[26] The High Court reversed this decision holding that it could not.[27] This decision in turn was reversed by the Court of Appeal[28] which was then reversed by the House of Lords.

Plantiflor concerned a Dutch company that sold plants and other garden products through catalogues. The catalogues gave customers the option to collect their goods in person from the company's garden centre in the Netherlands or from its premises in Spalding, but the vast majority of customers chose to have their goods sent to them via Parcelforce.

In 1993, Plantiflor had decided to bring its conditions of business in the UK into line with those used in Germany and the Netherlands by other companies in the group. It renegotiated its delivery contracts to state that it was acting as its customers' agent in arranging delivery with Parcelforce

[21] [1999] 3 All ER 961, [1999], [1999] STC 758.
[22] [1997] V & DR 375.
[23] [1999] STC 51.
[24] [2000] STC 137.
[25] The Value Added Tax (Input Tax) Order 1992 (S.I. No. 32222 of 1992).
[26] LON/96/14072.
[27] [1997] STC 475.
[28] [1998] STC 544.

on their behalf. Plantiflor argued that there were then two separate supplies: a supply of garden products to the customer by Plantiflor and a supply of delivery services to the customer by Parcelforce.

Plantiflor argued that the result of this change was that no VAT was payable on the costs of postage.[29] Customs and Excise initially accepted Plantiflor's arguments. However, the Commissioners changed their minds two years later in 1996 and informed Plantiflor that they no longer accepted the arrangement. They assessed Plantiflor to VAT on the delivery charges. The VAT Tribunal accepted Plantiflor's argument that there were two separate supplies. This ruling was reversed by the High Court only to be reversed again by the Court of Appeal. In the context of mixed supplies, the important point to note is that it was decided as a matter of fact that there were two separate supplies: one of goods and one of delivery services.[30]

Questions of law and questions of fact

In this area, it is important to bear in mind the distinction between questions of law and questions of fact. The law is reasonably clear: if a supply consists of more than one element, any elements which are ancillary or incidental to the main supply will be treated as part of the one integral supply.

The courts can reverse the rulings of the VAT tribunals on questions of law, but not on questions of fact. For example, as discussed above, the ruling in *British Airways* was reversed because the High Court held that the tribunal had applied the wrong test to determine whether or not there was a composite supply. On the other hand, in *Customs and Excise Commissioners v Peninsular and Oriental Steam Navigation Co Ltd*,[31] the High Court refused to reverse a VAT tribunal decision that a cruise was a single zero-rated supply of passenger transport. Since the tribunal had correctly applied the law in reaching this decision, it was not subject to appeal.

The law in this area now seems to be reasonably settled, but the issue is still the subject of much VAT litigation. It seems that the difficulty does not lie so much in formulating an appropriate test as in deciding whether or not that test is satisfied. The following cases illustrate some of the difficulties.

In *Hermolis & Co Ltd v Commissioners of Customs and Excise*,[32] sealed kosher meal packs supplied to airlines and hospitals for consumption by orthodox

---

[29] The conveyance of postal packets by the Post Office are exempt from VAT under the Value Added Tax Act 1994. This provision implements Article 13A of the Sixth VAT Directive which states that certain activities in the\ public interest shall be exempt from VAT. It includes in this category "the supply by the public postal services of services other than passenger transport and telecommunications services and the supply of goods incidental thereto."

[30] The question of whether there was another separate supply by Plantiflor of arranging the delivery services is considered in Chapter [VAT3] in the context of disbursements. See also "Postage, packing and all VAT: some issues involved in *Customs and Excise Commissioners v Plantiflor Ltd*." [2001] BTR No. 2 at p.100, where the sections concerning Plantiflor were first published.

[31] [1996] STC 698.

[32] [1989] VATTR 199.

Jews were held to be mixed supplies. An apportionment therefore had to be made between the standard-rated cutlery and mints and the zero-rated foodstuffs contained in the pack.

In *Pilgrims Language Courses Ltd v Customs and Excise Commissioners*,[33] the Court of Appeal held that meals, accommodation and transport to and from the airport for students on residential language courses were ancillary supplies and that the main supply was a single supply of exempt educational services.

In *Virgin Atlantic Airways Limited v Customs and Excise Commissioners* and *Canadian Airlines International Ltd v Customs and Excise Commissioners*[34] both airlines successfully appealed against the VAT tribunal's decision that a limousine service for first class passengers was a separate standard-rated supply rather than an integral part of a zero-rated supply of passenger transport. As in *British Airways*, the VAT tribunal had placed reliance on whether a supply was a necessary part of the main supply. In reversing the tribunal's decision, Turner J referred to the judgment of Lord Widgery CJ in *Customs and Excise Commissioners v Scott*:

> I think that it would be a great pity if we allowed this subject to become over-legalistic and over-addressed with legal authorities when, to my mind, once one has got the question posed, the answer should be supplied by a little common sense and concern for what is done in real life and not what is ... too artificial to be recognised in any context.[35]

The dividing line between questions of law and of fact in this area is always going to be a fine one and the battle between traders and Customs and Excise is ongoing. Cases such as *Plantiflor* indicate that traders are deliberately renegotiating their contracts to categorise supplies in the most VAT-efficient manner. Lord Widgery's hopes looks set to be disappointed.

The Place of Supply of Goods and Services

The place of any supply determines the Member State that receives the revenue in respect of it. This position is reflected in the UK legislation in s.4(1) VATA 1994 which provides that VAT shall be charged on any supply of goods or services made in the United Kingdom.

There are separate rules determining the place of supply of goods and the place of supply of services. Since services tend to be intangible, it is not possible to base the place of supply rules on their physical movement

---

[33] [1999] STC 874.
[34] [1995] STC 341.
[35] [1978] STC 191 at paragraph 195e.

around the Community.

The place of supply of goods

The place of supply rules for goods are set out in Article 8(1) of the Sixth Directive. This sets out three basic rules governing the place of supply:

a. Where goods are despatched or transported, the place of supply is the place where the goods are when the transport begins. However, where goods are installed or assembled, the place of supply is the place where installation or assembly takes place.

b. Where goods are not despatched or transported, the place of supply is the place where the goods are when the supply takes place.

c. Where goods are supplied on board ships, aircraft or trains during the course of passenger transport, the place of supply shall be the point of departure of the passenger transport.

The UK legislation implementing these provisions is to be found in s. 7 of the 1994 Act.

The place of supply of services and the reverse charge

The place of supply rules for services are set out in Article 9 of the Sixth Directive. Since it is not possible to base these on the location of the services themselves, the general rule, set out in Article 9(1) provides that the place of supply is the place where the supplier has established his business or has a fixed establishment from which the service is supplied. In the absence of such a place of business, the place of supply is the place where he has his permanent address or where he usually resides.

However, Article 9(2) goes on to provide certain exceptions to this general rule:

a. The place of supply of services connected with immovable property and construction shall be the place where the property is situated. This includes services provided by estate agents, architects and construction firms.

b. The place of supply of transport services shall be the place where the transport takes place, having regard to the distances covered.

c. The place of certain other services shall be the place where they are physically carried out. These services include: cultural, artistic, sporting, scientific, educational and entertainment services, ancillary transport services such as loading, valuation of and work on movable tangible property.

d. [36]

e. This paragraph sets out a number of services which are to be treated as supplied where performed, provided that they are performed for customers established outside the Community or for customers established within the Community, but in a different Member State from the supplier. [37] Such services include the transfer and assignment of copyrights and patents, advertising services, services of lawyers, accountants, consultants and engineers, banking and financial services, the hiring of movable, tangible property with the exception of means of transport, and telecommunications services.

Article 9(3) permits Member States to depart from the rules set out in Article 9(2) in order to avoid double taxation, non-taxation or the distortion of competition.

The UK legislation implementing these provisions is to be found in s. 7, 8 and 9 of the 1994 Act. Section 7(10) provides that a supply of services shall be treated as made in the UK if the supplier belongs in the UK and treated as made in another country if the supplier belongs in that country. Section 7(11) empowers the Treasury to vary this rule by statutory instrument. The implementing legislation for Article 9(2)(e) is the Value Added Tax (Place of Supply of Services) Order 1992. [38] Section 9 sets out the rules for determining where the supplier or recipient of services belongs. Section 8 is considered next.

The reverse charge

The question whether Article 9(1) or 9(2) applies will determine which Member State collects the revenue. If the supply falls within Article 9(1), the supplier's Member State collects the revenue whereas, if it falls within Article 9(2)(e), the customer's Member State will collect it. The collection mechanism for this second type of supply is known as the reverse charge and is found in s.8 of the 1994 Act.

Section 8 refers to services specified in Schedule 5 to the Act, which contains a list of services supplied where received. The services listed in

---

[36] Article 9(2)(d) is no longer in force.

[37] Where the supplier and the customer are established within the same Member State, there is no need to apply Article 9(2)(e), as the general rule in Article 9(1) provides that the supply is made where the supplier has his establishment. There is therefore no need to refer to the customer's place of establishment where this is the same as the supplier's.

[38] SI 1992/3121. This revoked the earlier Value Added Tax (Place of Supply) Order 1984 and came into force on 1st January 1993.

Schedule 5 correspond very closely to those listed in Article 9(2)(e) of the Sixth Directive. Section 8 provides that, where the supplier of such services does not belong in the UK and the recipient does belong in the UK, the recipient of the services is to be treated as if he himself had made a taxable supply of the services. He must therefore account for output in respect of the VAT he has charged himself but, assuming that he makes taxable supplies, he can then offset the input tax in the usual way. The effect of this provision is that traders who make exempt supplies cannot avoid paying tax on services merely by acquiring them from overseas traders.

The following examples may help to illustrate these provisions.

A owns a haulage business based in the UK. One of his lorries is involved in a crash while he is in France and he has it repaired at a French garage. This is a service on movable, tangible property under Article 9(2)(c), and so the place of supply is France, because that is where the service is physically carried out. A pays VAT to the garage, which the latter passes on to the French authorities. A may be able to reclaim this amount directly from the French authorities under the Eighth Directive.

B is a manufacturer based in the UK, who wishes to market his products in France. He pays a French advertising agency to handle the advertising in France. Advertising falls under Article 9(2)(e) as a service supplied where the customer is established, i.e. in the UK. The place of supply is therefore the UK and the service is outside the scope of French VAT. Under Article 8 of the 1994 Act, the UK trader must charge himself VAT on the value of the advertising services.

C is a bank based in the UK. It obtains telecommunications services from a company based Jersey. Such services fall under Article 9(2)(e) It must apply the reverse charge to these services. Because banks make exempt supplies of financial services, they are unable to deduct a large proportion of their input tax. As a result of the reverse charge, it will be in the same position as if it had bought services from a company based in the UK. This retains the neutrality of the tax.

Telecommunications services were only recently added to Article 9(2)(e) by Directive 99/59/EC. Before this, they used to fall within Article 9(1) since they were not mentioned in Article 9(2). Because of this, it was possible for exempt traders, such as banks, to avoid paying VAT on them. They did this by rerouting the services through offshore companies. Under this system, the company would set up a subsidiary in, say, Jersey. The subsidiary was set up to supply telecommunications services to the main company and would do this by buying the services in from another company such as BT. The subsidiary would then enter into an arm's length contract with the main company.[39]

The place of supply of the services supplied to the subsidiary was the UK. Because the subsidiary was based outside the Community, it was able to claim a refund of the VAT paid under the Thirteenth Directive. The supply of telecom services to the main company also fell under Article 9(1), so the place of supply was Jersey where the subsidiary was established. Because of this, the main company was not subject to a reverse charge as it would have been had the services been deemed to be supplied where they were received. The result of routing telecom services through a subsidiary established outside the Community was that the main company received VAT free telecom services. Moving the supply of telecommunications services into Article 9(2)(e) means that this device is no longer possible.

Further Reading

Doran N, *The Time of Supply Rules: How Far Do They Go?* [1998] BTR 602.

Roxan I, *Locating the Fixed Establishment in VAT*, [1998] BTR 608.

---

[39] This device was known as the "Jersey route." See John Carnie, "Assessing and Understanding the Far Reaching Implications of the Change of VAT Rules for Telecommunications and Internet Services," Conference Paper given at the ICM Conference "Minimising European VAT Liability" at the Cafe Royal, London on 12th -13th May 1997.

chapter twenty three

Value Added Tax - Consideration and the Taxable Amount

Once the relevant supply has been identified – or, according to UK legislation, if a relevant supply is to be identified[1] – the requirement for consideration must be satisfied. Closely linked to the concept of consideration is that of the taxable amount. This can be seen from Article 11A(1)(a) of the Sixth Directive which provides that the taxable amount shall be:

> In respect of supplies of goods and services ... everything which constitutes the consideration which has been or is to be obtained by the supplier from the purchaser, the customer or a third party for such supplies including subsidies directly linked to the price of such supplies.

Despite the close relationship between these two concepts, though, a distinction needs to be drawn between them. If there is no consideration, then there is no need to define the taxable amount because there is no taxable supply. If there is a taxable supply, it is then necessary to determine the taxable amount. In other words, cases that just involve consideration turn on whether any VAT is payable; cases that involve consideration and the taxable amount turn on how much VAT is payable.

What is Meant by Consideration?

One of the leading cases on the meaning of consideration is *Staatssecretaris van Financien v Cooperatieve Aardappelenbewaarplaats*.[2] This case was referred to the ECJ by the Dutch courts and concerned an agricultural co-operative association. The association decided that it would not make any charges to its members for storing potatoes during 1975 and 1976. Because it made no charge, the association did not account for VAT on its supply of

---

[1] Compare Article 2(1) of the Sixth Directive to Sections 1 and 5 of Schedule 4 VATA 1994.
[2] Case 154/80, [1981] ECR 445.

storage services for those two years. In spite of this, the authorities issued an assessment to VAT. They argued that the members' shares in the association had reduced in value because no storage charges had been collected and that the consideration for the supply of the storage services was the reduction in the value of the shares. The association appealed against this assessment and a reference was made to the ECJ.

The ECJ held that no VAT was payable because there was no consideration. It made three main points in relation to this:

1. The meaning of consideration is to be determined by Community law and not by national law.[3]

2. There must be a direct link between the supply and the consideration received.[4]

3. The consideration must be capable of being expressed in money. The taxable amount is the consideration actually received and not a value assessed according to objective criteria.[5]

Hence, in this case, there was no direct link between the reduction in the value of the shares and the benefits received by the members. The fact that the association had not made a charge for the storage services was decisive and the authorities were not permitted to charge VAT on their assessment of the value of the services.

The requirement for a direct link

The Court next considered the requirement for a direct link in *Apple and Pear Development Council v Commissioners of Customs and Excise*.[6] The Apple and Pear Development Council was a body which was funded by a levy on all commercial apple and pear growers in England and Wales. It was set up at the request of the growers to advertise, promote and improve the quality of the fruit that they grew. The Council also operated an additional promotion scheme which registered growers could choose to join upon payment of an additional fee.

The parties were agreed that the activities funded by the optional additional fee were subject to VAT. However, the Commissioners argued that the activities funded by the levy did not fall within the scope of VAT. It was in the Council's interests to argue that all its activities were subject to VAT, as this would mean that it could offset all its input tax. The Commissioners, on the other hand, were arguing that the input tax should

---

[3] Paragraph 9 of the judgment.
[4] Paragraph 12 of the judgment.
[5] Paragraph 13 of the judgment.
[6] Case 102/86, [1987] ECR 3379.

be apportioned. Because the levy was imposed by a Statutory Instrument,[7] they accepted that it was outside the scope of VAT, so there was no question of collecting output tax on the levy.

The London VAT Tribunal held in favour of the Council,[8] but the High Court allowed the Commissioners' appeal.[9] The Court of Appeal dismissed the Council's appeal[10] and the Council appealed to the House of Lords.[11] The House of Lords made a reference to the ECJ.

The ECJ held that, although the Council made supplies of services, the supplies funded by the levies were not made for consideration and hence were not taxable.[12] It gave the following reasons for this.

1. The benefits provided by the Council accrued to the industry as a whole rather than to the individual growers. Benefits received by individuals were received indirectly from benefits accruing to the industry.

2. There was no relationship between the amount that an individual grower paid and the level of benefit that he received.

3. The charges were imposed by law and were payable regardless of whether any benefit was received.

As Farmer and Lyal have pointed out,[13] neither the second nor the third condition can be a sufficient test on its own, as this could have the effect of excluding flat-rate charges and supplies by public bodies from the scope of the tax. They suggest that the decisive factor is the combination of the second and third conditions since these indicate that the amount paid is a tax rather than a payment for services. They cite Sir Gordon Slynn's opinion in support of this:

> It is possible for persons to pay the same amount for different degrees of benefit and for that payment to be consideration. Such a position seems more likely to indicate that the money paid is more in the nature of an across-the-board tax than a true payment for services.[14]

The question of whether a payment is a tax is of some help when deciding whether it constitutes consideration, but it does not give a complete answer, as is demonstrated by the fact that VAT is charged on prices inclusive of excise duty. It is a section later in the same paragraph of Sir

---

[7]   The Apple and Pear Development Council Order 1966 (SI 1966/1579).
[8]   [1983] VATTR 142.
[9]   [1984] STC 296.
[10]   [1985] STC 383, [1987] CMLR 634.
[11]   [1986] STC 192, [1987] 2 CMLR 635.
[12]   Note that, in the language of the United Kingdom legislation, this amounts to a decision that there were no supplies, since a supply is defined as being made for consideration.
[13]   *EC Tax Law*, OUP 1994 at p.125
[14]   Paragraph 18 of the opinion.

Gordon Slynn's opinion which gives a more helpful test:

> Although I do not consider that it is necessary to be able to attribute particular parts of a consideration to particular services, since a direct overall charge for an overall service could be sufficient, I am not satisfied that the necessary reciprocity or direct link has been established between the payment and the services in this case.

The next leading case on the question of a direct link was *Tolsma v Inspecteur der Omzetbelasting Leeuwarden*.[15] Mr Tolsma used to play a barrel organ on the streets in the Netherlands. He used to hold out a collecting tin to ask for contributions from passers-by and sometimes knocked on the doors of houses and shops to ask for donations. Because of this, the Dutch authorities argued that he was supplying services in return for consideration and they assessed him to VAT on the money that he collected. Mr Tolsma appealed against this assessment and the Dutch court made a reference to the ECJ.

The authorities argued that there was a direct link between the music and the payments since the latter were made in return for the former. Mr Tolsma argued that the payments did not constitute consideration because they were made voluntarily.

The Court followed the opinion of Advocate General Lenz in holding that there was no consideration:

> It follows that a supply of services is effected "for consideration" within the meaning of Article 2(1) of the Sixth Directive, and hence is taxable, only if there is a legal relationship between the provider of the service and the recipient pursuant to which there is reciprocal performance, the remuneration received by the provider of the service constituting the value actually given in return for the service supplied to the recipient.

> Firstly, there is no agreement between the parties, since the passers-by voluntarily make a donation, whose amount they determine as they wish. Secondly, there is no necessary link between the musical service and the payments to which it gives rise. The passers-by do not request the music to be played for them; moreover, they pay sums which depend not on the musical service but on subjective motives which may bring feelings of sympathy into play. Indeed some persons place money, sometimes a considerable sum, in the musician's

---

[15] Case C-16/93, [1994] ECR I-743.

collecting tin without lingering, whereas others listen to the music for some time without making any donation at all.[16]

This test ties in with the first test put forward by the Court in *Apple and Pear Development Council*. The music was played to passers-by as a group and not to individuals. An individual could receive the services offered without making any payment and without being under any obligation to do so. This differs from the situation where people pay to go to a concert, where only those who buy tickets are entitled to seats.

Following Tolsma, the direct link test means that there must be an obligation to pay that results from a legal relationship between the parties. As *Apple and Pear Development Council* shows, though, this is not in itself sufficient. As Sir Gordon Slynn pointed out, there must be a reciprocal relationship between the parties. Perhaps this requires a supplier of services to be able to prevent any individual who does not pay from benefiting from them. In other words, he should be able to restrict his supplies to paying customers.

This test would fit in with the decisions in *Tolsma* and *Apple and Pear Development Council*. Mr Tolsma was not in a position to prevent anyone from listening to the music; if people were less than generous, his only option would have been to move to a different street. In the same way, all apple and pear growers benefited from the activities of the Apple and Pear Development Council. The Council was not in a position to ensure that those who did not pay did not benefit even though, unlike Mr Tolsma, it was in a position to demand payment. The levies that funded the Council only applied to growers who had at least five acres of orchards, but there was no way that the Council could prevent the owners of smaller orchards from benefiting from its activities.

Voluntary payments

A further question that arises in relation to the taxable amount is whether tips and other voluntary payments are included. This question involves determining the scope of the judgment in *Tolsma*, discussed above. *Tolsma* makes it clear that, in cases in which the only payment to change hands is a voluntary payment, there is no consideration because there is no legal relationship. It does not automatically follow from this, though, that voluntary payments that are made in addition to consideration are not part of the taxable amount since there is a legal relationship between the parties in those cases.

---

[16] Paragraphs 14 and 17 of the judgment.

The ECJ has not yet been given an opportunity to decide whether *Tolsma* means that voluntary payments cannot be included in the taxable amount, or whether it just means that they cannot in themselves give rise to a legal relationship.

The question is crucial in relation to tips. If *Tolsma* means that voluntary payments cannot be included in the taxable amount, then tips are not subject to VAT. On the other hand, if it only means that they cannot give rise to a legal relationship, then they can be subject to VAT, in cases where a legal relationship already exists between the parties. The ECJ has not had the opportunity to develop this issue further.

One of the first cases that the VAT Tribunal considered on this issue was *Commissioners of Customs and Excise v Kenealy*[17] in which it decided that a taxi driver was accountable to VAT on his tips as they formed part of the consideration that he received from his customers. However, later cases, both before and after the *Tolsma* judgment, have taken a different approach and have held that tips are not subject to VAT as long as they are freely given and there is an element of choice.[18]

For example, in *NPD Co Ltd v Commissioners of Customs and Excise*[19] the VAT Tribunal held that a voluntary service charge on a restaurant bill did not constitute consideration and so was not part of the taxable amount. Service charges were handed over to one of the waiters at the end of each day to be shared amongst the staff. Contrast this case with *Potters Lodge Restaurant v Commissioners of Customs and Excise.*[20] Here, the service charges were also passed on to the staff, but the difference was that they were stated to be part of the bill, so that the customers could not choose not to pay them. The Tribunal held that such charges were classed as consideration.

Note that the courts will decide on the facts whether or not a payment is voluntary. A trader cannot avoid being accountable to VAT on a payment by labelling it as voluntary if it is in fact compulsory. In *Glasgow Miles Better Mid-Summer 5th Anniversary Ball v Commissioners of Customs and Excise*[21] tickets for a charity ball were sold for £50 each. At the bottom of each ticket, it was printed that the price "for VAT purposes" was £20, since the other £30 was a minimum voluntary donation to the local hospice. The tribunal held that the £30 could not be classed as a voluntary donation since it was not an option only to pay £20 for a ticket. Presumably, if a purchaser had chosen to make a "donation" of more than £30, the extra amount would have been classed as a voluntary payment and so would not have been subject to VAT.

The issue was considered again in Friends of the *Ironbridge Gorge Museum v Commissioners of Customs and Excise.*[22] The Friends of Ironbridge was an

---

[17] LON/77/208 (466).
[18] Contrast this to the income tax treatment of tips. Presumably the rationale for this distinction is that tips still form part of a trader's income even if they are not received by way of consideration for the supplies that he makes.
[19] [1988] VATTR 40.
[20] LON/79/286, unreported.
[21] EDN/89/85, unreported.
[22] [1991] VATTR 97.

organisation established to support the Ironbridge Gorge Museum and to allow members to become involved in its work. Half of each member's subscription was donated to the museum and the other half was used to fund the group's running expenses. Members received free admission to the museum sites, a ten per cent reduction on purchases in the museum shop, a quarterly newsletter and a programme of talks, visits and social events. The benefits were at the discretion of the Museum and were not given by the Friends organisation itself. The VAT Tribunal distinguished *Glasgow Miles Better* and held that the subscriptions were not subject to VAT. The subscriptions could be regarded as donations since they far exceeded the average benefits which the members received. For example, family membership cost £23.50 per year and it was calculated that the average value of benefits received was £2.97. The case also differed from *Glasgow Miles Better* in that the body that received the subscriptions and the body that allowed the members the benefits were not the same.

Note that the whole question of voluntary payments would have to be reviewed if a suitable case were to reach the ECJ. As discussed earlier, it does not automatically follow from the judgment in *Tolsma* that voluntary payments are not to be included in the taxable amount; it only follows that they may not in themselves give rise to a legal relationship. Voluntary payments are really a specific example of the general rule which requires that there should be a direct link between the supply and the payment if the payment is to be classed as consideration.

As described above, as well as establishing a direct link, the Court in *Aardappelenbewaarplaats* required that consideration should be capable of being expressed in money. It should not be inferred from this, though, that VAT cannot be charged unless money changes hands. Although the consideration must be capable of being expressed in money, this does not mean that it must consist of money. The question of non-monetary consideration is considered next.

Non-Monetary Consideration[23]

Non-monetary consideration could fall into two basic categories: payment in goods and payment in services. The approach taken by the courts to both types of non-monetary consideration is essentially the same and is discussed below.

---

[23] The text relating to non-monetary consideration and vouchers was first published as "Non-monetary consideration in the context of VAT: the status of the judgment in *Empire Stores v Commissioners of Customs and Excise* in the light of later judgments" EC Tax Review 2001. Vol 10, pages 234-241.

The approach taken by the ECJ

The ECJ has made it clear that services as well as goods can be classed as consideration. Two of the leading cases on this point are *Naturally Yours Cosmetics Ltd v Commissioners of Customs and Excise*[24] and *Empire Stores Ltd v Commissioners of Customs and Excise*.[25]

Naturally Yours Cosmetics was sent to the ECJ on a preliminary reference from the London VAT Tribunal. Naturally Yours Cosmetics (NYC) was a cosmetics wholesaler. It supplied goods to retailers who were known as beauty consultants. The beauty consultants would approach friends and acquaintances, known as hostesses, and ask them to organise parties at their homes so that the guests could buy NYC products. The consultants would buy the products from NYC at wholesale prices, sell them at retail prices and would be entitled to keep the profit. In return for organising the party, the consultant would give each hostess a free pot of face cream. The normal wholesale price of this cream was £10.14, but NYC sold it to the consultants for £1.50. If, having bought the pot of cream for £1.50, the consultant was unable to find a hostess to organise a party, she either had to return the cream or pay the full price.

HM Customs and Excise assessed NYC to VAT on the normal wholesale price of £10.14 on all the pots of cream that it sold. NYC appealed against this assessment, arguing that the consideration for the cream sold to be given to the hostesses was only the £1.50 that the consultants had to pay. The Court had to decide whether the service provided by the consultant in arranging for the hostess to organise the party was part of the consideration for the pot of cream. If it decided that this service was part of the consideration, it then had to decide how it should be valued.

The Court decided that the service did form part of the consideration and that its value was the difference between the price paid and the ordinary wholesale price. It referred to its judgment in Aardappelenbewaarplaats and said that it was clear that the consideration had to be capable of being expressed in monetary terms. The value was a subjective value since the basis of assessment was the consideration actually received and not a value estimated according to objective criteria.[26] It stated that, in this case, the wholesale price of the cream had been reduced by a specific amount in return for the supply of a service by the consultant. Since the lower price was only available if the consultant provided this service, it could be inferred that there was a direct link between the provision of the service and the lower price. The value of the service was therefore the difference between the price paid and the normal price. The

[24] Case 230/87, [1988] ECR 6365
[25] Case C-33/93, [1994] ECR I-2329
[26] Paragraph 16 of the judgment.

taxable amount was therefore the normal wholesale price since this was the sum of the value of the service and the price actually paid.

The Court explained what it meant by "subjective" in *Argos Distributors Ltd. v Customs and Excise Commissioners*:[27]

> It is acknowledged in the observations submitted in this case that, in this context, the word "subjective" is not used here in its normal sense in English, but rather to describe the value placed by the parties on key elements in a transaction; a meaning which is equally capable of being characterised as "objective". The effect of these cases is to distinguish and exclude, for the purpose of assessing the consideration for a sale, any supposed independent valuation, different from that adopted by the parties. [28]

The Court returned to the question of whether services could count as consideration in *Empire Stores v Commissioners of Customs and Excise*. This concerned the VAT payable on gifts made by a catalogue company to its customers. The company offered a selection of gifts to new customers. Similar gifts were also offered to existing customers who introduced a new customer. In both cases, the gifts were despatched after the new customer had placed an order and made the first payment on it. The items that were offered as free gifts were not available for purchase through the catalogue.

Empire Stores received a VAT assessment for the gifts based on 150 % of the cost price. This was the Commissioners' estimate of the price at which the goods would have been sold in the catalogue. Empire Stores appealed against the assessment, arguing that the taxable amount was the cost price of the goods. The Manchester VAT Tribunal made a reference to the ECJ.

Surprisingly, neither Advocate General Van Gerven nor the ECJ held that there was any significant difference between the two types of offer, in spite of the fact that the Portuguese government argued that such a distinction should be drawn. They held that, in both cases, there was a supply of goods by Empire Stores. The consideration for these supplies was the services provided by the customers, either by introducing themselves or by introducing friends. The taxable amount was the price that Empire Stores had paid for the goods involved in the promotion. Advocate General Van Gerven considered that it was significant that Empire Stores was in the habit of selling its list of established customers to third parties. The customers' details provided in return for the promotional items therefore had a value over and above the money that the customers

---

[27] Case C-288/94, [1996] ECR I-5311, [1996] STC 1359.
[28] Paragraph 21 of the judgment.

paid for their purchases from the catalogue.

This decision has been criticised by Paul Farmer and Richard Lyal. They argue that the Court should have drawn a distinction between the two schemes:

> The "introduce a friend" scheme unquestionably involved an exchange of supplies between the existing customer and the supplier. The former received the non-catalogue goods from the supplier in exchange for the service of introducing another person as a customer. The "self-introduction" scheme, on the other hand, did not involve any act of agency on the part of the potential customer. It must be clear that, in the absence of other factors, the mere fact of agreeing to be a customer cannot constitute additional consideration over and above the price paid for any supplies.[29]

Farmer and Lyal go on to argue that the goods sent to the new customers were gifts whereas the goods sent to the existing customers were supplies for consideration, the consideration being the service provided by the existing customer in introducing a new customer. As a result, they argue that, while the taxable amount in respect of the first supply was the cost to the supplier, the taxable amount for the second supply should have been the estimated retail value.

There is much to be said for this approach. After all, if a customer in a restaurant found that he could not pay his bill and were lucky enough to find that the manager would let him do the washing-up instead, the value of the services that he provided would clearly be the amount that he should have paid for the meal and not the amount that it had cost the restaurant to provide it.

However, the approach also causes difficulties in cases where there is no retail price specified. In such cases, estimating the retail value seems to come very close to using "a value assessed according to objective criteria" since the items involved were not offered for sale in the catalogue. On the other hand, suppose that the items had been included in the catalogue. It would then have been possible, as it was in Naturally Yours Cosmetics, to give a precise retail value.

The Court was aware of this problem in *Empire Stores*, as is clear from the following extract:

---

[29] *EC Tax Law*, Oxford University Press 1994 at pp. 123-125.

Moreover, since the services provided to Empire Stores are remunerated by the supply of goods, the value of the services can unquestionably be expressed in monetary terms.

As for the determination of the that value ... the Court held in *Naturally Yours Cosmetics* (cited above) at paragraph 16, that the consideration taken as the taxable amount in respect of a supply of goods is a subjective value, since the taxable amount is the consideration actually received and not a value estimated according to objective criteria.

Where that value is not a sum of money agreed between the parties, it must, in order to be subjective, be the value which the recipient of the services constituting the consideration for the supply of goods attributes to the services which he is seeking to obtain and must correspond to the amount which he is prepared to spend for that purpose. Where, as here, the supply of goods is involved, that value can only be the price which the supplier has paid for the article which he is supplying without extra charge in consideration of the services in question.[30]

At the start of paragraph 19 above, the Court makes it clear that its use of cost price as the taxable amount only applies where the parties have not already agreed a cash price. In cases where a cash price has been agreed, as in the example of washing up in a restaurant, the consideration can be taken to have the same value as the cash price. This approach draws an effective distinction between *Naturally Yours Cosmetics* and *Empire Stores*, since the goods involved in the former had an agreed retail price.

The approach taken by courts in the United Kingdom

Both cases were referred to in the UK in the case of *Customs and Excise Commissioners v Westmorland Motorway Services Ltd.*[31] This case concerned various benefits given to coach drivers by motorway service areas. Any coach driver who brought at least twenty passengers onto a service area and remained for at least half an hour was entitled to a free packet of cigarettes (or cash in lieu) and a free meal.

The Commissioners assessed Westmorland to VAT on the retail price of the meal and the cigarettes. Westmorland appealed to the VAT Tribunal arguing that they should only be assessed on the cost price. They were successful and the Commissioners appealed to the High Court.

Note at this point that it was common ground between the parties that

---

[30] Paragraphs 17-19 of the judgment.
[31] [1997] STC 400.

Westmorland made a supply to the coach drivers for which they gave consideration. The appeal concerned the taxable amount.

The Commissioners conceded that the taxable amount for the supply of cigarettes was the amount of cash payable in lieu rather than the full retail price. Lightman J referred to *Naturally Yours Cosmetics* and *Empire Stores*. He held that the taxable amount was the retail cost of the meal and the cash payable in lieu for the cigarettes. He pointed out that, if a coach driver were to receive his free meal and cigarettes and then were to discover that there were only nineteen passengers on the coach, he would be obliged to pay the retail price for these items. The situation was therefore analogous to *Naturally Yours Cosmetics*. The case differed from *Empire Stores* in that the items were offered for retail sale so that their retail value could be determined. The judgment was upheld unanimously by the Court of Appeal.[32]

An alternative approach to non-monetary consideration

The approach taken by the ECJ offers a consistent way of distinguishing between the type of scenario involved in *Naturally Yours Cosmetics* and that involved in *Empire Stores*. The High Court applied this in *Westmorland*. However, another look at the issues involved in *Westmorland* shows that there is another possible approach.

In *Westmorland*, the Commissioners accepted that the taxable amount for the supplies of cigarettes was the amount of cash in lieu that was offered to the drivers. Counsel for Westmorland referred to this sum, but only to argue that the taxable amount of any cigarettes supplied should be reduced. Neither party appears to have based their arguments on the situation where a driver chose to accept the cash instead of the cigarettes.

In such a situation, the approach of the ECJ and of the High Court would mean accepting that there was a taxable supply of cash for which the driver provided services by way of consideration. This seems to be a very dubious argument and any party who wanted to rely on it would first have to establish that a cash payment was either a supply of goods or a supply of services.

A far more coherent approach seems to be to argue that, far from being the supply, the cash payment to the driver was the consideration for the services that he supplied in bringing his passengers to the service station. This possibility was not mentioned in *Westmorland* as neither party seemed to have looked beyond the assumption that any taxable supplies were made by the service area.

---

[32] [1998] STC 431.

If this approach is correct, Lightman J's analogy with *Naturally Yours Cosmetics* in *Westmorland* may not be as sound as it first appeared. Naturally Yours Cosmetics concerned a taxable supply of goods for which the purchaser could either pay cash or a combination of cash and services. The lower price was only available if the services were provided. On the other hand, *Westmorland* could be said to involve a supply of services for which the supplier could choose to accept payment in cash or in kind. If it were to turn out that there were only nineteen passengers on the coach, the driver would have to refund the money to the service area, not because he had not provided the consideration but because he had not provided services for which he had received consideration.

It is also arguable that this approach provides an alternative rationale for the judgment in *Empire Stores*. It is clear from paragraph 19, quoted above, that the ECJ sees two different ways of valuing non-monetary consideration: in cases where the consideration is in lieu of an agreed cash price, the taxable amount is the cash price whereas, in cases where no cash price has been agreed, the taxable amount is the amount that the supplier is prepared to pay to receive the consideration.

Let us return to the example of washing up in a restaurant. Suppose that, at the end of an evening, five people are washing up in a restaurant kitchen and all five of them have been provided with a meal. Four of them have been sent by an agency that provides casual staff whereas the fifth went into the restaurant as a paying customer, was unable to settle his bill and offered to wash up instead. The Court's approach in *Empire Stores* can be used to distinguish between the staff and the customer, since a cash price had been agreed for the customer's meal but not for the staff meals. In this case, though, it makes far more sense to ask who is providing the services; the customer is doing the washing up as the consideration for the meal that he has eaten, whereas the staff have received a meal and a pay cheque as consideration for doing the washing up.

In *Empire Stores*, the ECJ refers to how much money the supplier is prepared to pay for the services which constitute the consideration. It assumes that the services are the consideration and does not consider the possibility that they might be the supply. If the services were the supply, this would be consistent with the more usual situation where it is the purchaser who asks himself whether he is prepared to pay the price asked by the supplier.

It is arguable that the question of who is the supplier would be a far more satisfactory way of distinguishing between *Naturally Yours Cosmetics* and *Empire Stores* than the question of whether a cash price has been agreed. The ECJ's approach means that traders who use promotional items that are not offered for general sale are treated differently from those who use items from their trading stock. It also assumes that the fact that an item is offered for sale means that the retail price is the value agreed between the two parties. Another difficulty with this approach concerns offers of cash in lieu, as in *Westmorland*. If it is accepted that a cash payment cannot be a taxable supply,[33] then a further distinction must be drawn depending on whether the customer chooses to take the item on offer or the cash in lieu.

The rationale behind the principle that consideration can be non-monetary as well as monetary is surely correct. If consideration were limited to cash payments, the opportunities for avoidance would be endless and there would be a lack of neutrality between parties who were paid in cash and those who were paid in kind. However, when looking at cases involving non-monetary consideration, it is important to realise that the question of who is the supplier and who is the customer may not be as straightforward as it is in cases involving cash. If, as in *Empire Stores*, goods are handed over in return for services, then this could either be a supply of goods or a supply of services. Rather than first asking whether the parties have agreed on a price, it might helpful to start by asking who is making the supply.

Vouchers and Credit Card Payments

The issues involved with vouchers and credit card payments are closely linked to the question of non-monetary consideration. In some cases, vouchers have been held to constitute non-monetary consideration whereas in others they have been held to be a mere mechanism for reducing the taxable amount. The basic distinction to be drawn here is between vouchers such as book tokens, for which money has been paid, and money-off coupons.

The issue of credit card payments does not involve non-monetary consideration but the issues involved in determining the taxable amount for credit card transactions have much in common to those in some of the voucher cases.

Coupons and cash-back offers

Article 11(A)(3)(b) of the Sixth Directive provides that the taxable amount shall not include "price discounts and rebates allowed to the customer and accounted for at the time of the supply."

---

[33] The Court of Appeal accepted this point in *Westmorland*, although the High Court did not. According to Hutchinson LJ, it had been common ground between the parties that no VAT was payable in respect of the cash in lieu, but Lightman J was under the impression that it was common ground that the cash in lieu constituted a taxable supply.

Article 11(C)(1) provides:

> In the case of cancellation, refusal or total or partial non-payment, or
> where the price is reduced after the supply takes place, the taxable
> amount shall be reduced accordingly under conditions which shall be
> determined by the Member States. However, in the case of total or
> partial non-payment, Member States may derogate from this rule.

In *Boots v Commissioners of Customs and Excise*[34] Boots accepted various money-off coupons from customers. Some of these coupons were distributed as leaflets or appeared in magazines and newspapers. Others were printed on the back of products sold in the store, so that the customer had to make a purchase in order to obtain the coupon. The case revolved around the question of whether the coupons counted as consideration or whether they were just a mechanism for offering a discount.

The case only concerned offers that Boots funded itself. It was common ground between the parties that, where Boots had to send coupons to a third party, such as the manufacturer, to reclaim their face value, the coupons constituted consideration since they were of some value to Boots.

HM Customs and Excise accepted that the coupons printed on leaflets and in magazines did not count as consideration because of Article 11(A)(3)(b) of the Sixth Directive. However, they argued that coupons obtained by purchasing other products were consideration because the customer had had to spend money in order to get such coupons. They issued a VAT assessment on this basis and Boots appealed to the London VAT Tribunal. When the Tribunal dismissed this appeal, Boots appealed to the High Court, which made a reference to the ECJ.

The ECJ held that there was no difference between the two types of coupon and that both were ways of giving discounts under Article 11(A)(3)(b). In reaching this decision, it followed the opinion of Advocate General Van Gerven. The Advocate General agreed that a coupon would constitute consideration if the person who issued it had himself received consideration in return:

> Having regard to the decisions of the Court ... it must, however, be assumed
> that a coupon no longer incorporates the right to a price reduction if and
> to the extent to which the issuer, in return for the obligation he enters into
> in issuing the coupon, obtains consideration value in monetary terms – and
> thus not only the expectation of increased turnover.[35]

[34] Case C-126/88, [1990] ECR I-1235.
[35] Paragraph 13 of the opinion.

However, he argued that, as Boots had received no consideration – or at least no separate consideration – in return, the coupons could not constitute consideration in this case.[36]

This approach is clearly sensible. Coupons attached to products tend only to be available for a limited period of time. It is very often the case that the price of the product involved is the same before during and after the promotion. If all the consideration is paid in return for the product itself, it is difficult to see how any of it could be said to be paid for the coupon attached to it.

Suppose that a certain item retails for £2.50 and carries a coupon for fifty pence off the next purchase. On the first purchase, the customer hands over £2.50 but, on subsequent purchases for the duration of the offer, hands over £2 and a fifty pence coupon. If the coupon is classed as consideration, it is necessary to value it. Any valuation other than the face value would run contrary to the decision in *Aardappelenbewaarplaats* as a valuation according to objective criteria. If the coupon is to count as consideration, it must have been received for consideration. If this is the case then the original selling price of £2.50 should be divided into £2 for the item and fifty pence for the coupon. If fifty pence is consideration for the coupon, then that is not subject to VAT. In other words, the Commissioners cannot have it both ways. If they argue that the coupon constitutes consideration then they must also accept that the taxable amount for the original supply is reduced by the face value of the coupon; if they argue that there is no such reduction on the taxable amount for the first purchase, then they must accept, as did the ECJ in *Boots*, that there is a reduction on the taxable amount for the second purchase. Whichever way the question is resolved, the retailer receives £4.50 instead of £5 for two purchases of the same item. There must therefore be a decrease of fifty pence in the taxable amount for one of the items.

Bearing in mind Advocate General Van Gerven's approach in *Boots*, though, it is surprising that he did not take a similar approach in *Empire Stores*. He argued that the customer in *Boots* paid no separate consideration for the coupon. Although the customer handed money over when he acquired the coupon, that money was the consideration for the goods and the customer would still have had to pay this had there been no coupon attached. Similarly in *Empire Stores*: the customer provided the catalogue company with his name, address and personal details, but it is difficult to see how anyone can become a customer of a catalogue company without supplying such details. The customer would still have had to give the details even had the company not been sending out the promotional items.

---

[36] Paragraph 12 of the opinion.

The next leading case in this area was *Elida Gibbs v Customs and Excise Commissioners.*[37] This again concerned tokens on packaging. Elida Gibbs operated two types of promotion: money-off coupons and cash-back coupons. The money-off coupons were distributed to members of the public who handed them to retailers when buying the products in question. The retailers then reclaimed the face value of the coupons from Elida Gibbs. The cash-back coupons were part of the packaging of some of Elida Gibbs' products. The customer would cut out the coupon and send it to Elida Gibbs, which would refund the face value of the coupon directly to the consumer.

Elida Gibbs argued that the effect of both types of offer was to reduce the taxable amount in respect of the products involved. It therefore wrote to Customs and Excise requesting a repayment of output tax equal to the total repayments that it had made to retailers and final consumers during the course of the promotion. Customs and Excise refused this request and Elida Gibbs appealed to the London VAT Tribunal. The Tribunal referred the case to the ECJ.

Unusually, the ECJ did not follow the opinion of the Advocate General. Advocate General Fennelly had held that neither promotion had the effect of reducing the taxable amount, whereas the ECJ held that both promotions had this effect. Although they agreed about little else in this case, the Advocate General and the Court did agree that both schemes should be treated in the same way and that it was immaterial whether it was the retailer or the final consumer who sent the coupon back to the manufacturer for a refund of its face value.

Advocate General Fennelly considered the cash-back scheme first. He thought that it was significant that Elida Gibbs was not a party to the contract between the retailer and the final consumer:

> The retailer is a stranger to the transaction between the manufacturer and the retail customer comprised in the cash-back schemes. To attempt, like the company, to maintain that the acceptance by the retail customer of the 'offer' printed on the coupon, affecting the retail sale, can alter the agreed price in the earlier transaction involving the supply of goods by the manufacturer to the retailer, would distort commercial realities and introduce an unacceptable and unjustifiable degree of uncertainty into the Community VAT system.[38]

In relation to the money-off coupons, he referred to the *Boots* case and

---

[37] [1997] QB 449, [1996] STC 1387, Case C-317/94. [1996] ECR I-5339
[38] Paragraph 21 of the opinion.

pointed out that Boots had conceded that coupons issued by third parties constituted consideration. Elida Gibbs' argument, he said, involved accepting that Boots had been incorrect to concede this point:

> The company, in the model transaction presented to the court, treats the retail price as being reduced by the amount of the coupon and omits from the retailer's taxable amount the refund obtained from the company. It is only by making this important, and, in my view, incorrect, assumption, that the company succeeds in leaving the retailer's position unaffected by the reduction in the taxable amount which it claims for itself. Without that reduction, the redemption of the coupons would automatically increase the margin between the retailer's outputs and inputs and, accordingly, the retailer's VAT. In view of the analogy drawn with *Boots*, it is worth pointing out that this was clearly not the approach adopted by the company in accounting for the proceeds of a similar scheme. Boots included in its gross takings for VAT purposes and thus conceded liability for VAT on any payments received from manufacturers in the reimbursement of coupons. This approach was accepted by all parties to that case and did not have to be addressed by the court. ... The company's argument implies that Boots was wrong to concede that liability. I think that Boots acted on a correct interpretation of Art 11(A)(1)(a).[39]

As stated above, the Court rejected both these arguments. Unlike the Advocate General, it concentrated on the whole supply chain between the manufacturer and the final consumer instead of the single transaction between the retailer and the final consumer. It emphasised the nature of VAT as a tax on final consumers and the traders' roles as collectors of that tax:

> The basic principle of the VAT system is that it is intended to tax only the final consumer. Consequently the taxable amount serving as a basis for the VAT to be collected by the tax authorities cannot exceed the consideration actually paid by the final consumer which is the basis for calculating the VAT liability ultimately borne by him.
>
> In circumstances such as those in the main proceedings, the manufacturer, who has refunded the value of the money-off coupon to the retailer or the value of the cash-back coupon to the final

---

[39] Paragraph 34 of the opinion.

consumer, receives, on completion of the transaction, a sum corresponding to the sale price paid by the wholesalers or retailers for his goods, less the value of those coupons. It would not therefore be in conformity with the directive for the taxable amount used to calculate the VAT chargeable to the manufacturer as a taxable person, to exceed the sum finally received by him. Were that the case, the principle of neutrality of VAT vis-à-vis taxable persons, of whom the manufacturer is one, would not be complied with.[40]

In spite of the Advocate General's opinion that Article 11(C)(1) did not apply because the refund was not made by a party to the taxable transaction, the ECJ decided to the contrary:

It is true that that provision [Article 11(C)(1)] refers to the normal case of contractual relations entered into directly between two contracting parties, which are modified subsequently. The fact remains, however, that the provision is an expression of the principle, emphasised above, that the position of taxable persons must be neutral. It follows therefore from that provision that, in order to ensure the observance of the principle of neutrality, account should be taken, when calculating the final taxable amount for VAT, of situations where a taxable person who, having no contractual relationship with the final consumer but being the first link in a chain of transactions which ends with the final consumer, grants the final consumer a reduction through retailers or by direct repayment of the value of the coupons. Otherwise, the tax authorities would receive by way of VAT a sum greater than that actually paid by the final consumer, at the expense of the taxable person.[41]

In reaching this conclusion, the ECJ did not make any reference to Advocate General Fennelly's argument based on *Boots*, but it is worth pointing out that this argument does not necessarily follow. The fact that the value of a coupon issued by the manufacturer can be deducted from the manufacturer's taxable amount does not mean that the same value can also be deducted from the taxable amount of the retailer who accepts such a coupon. To hold otherwise would mean that the authorities were obliged to refund the VAT component of the same coupon twice in respect of a single price reduction for the final consumer While the authorities must not receive a greater sum by way of VAT than that paid by the final consumer, it surely also follows from the ECJ's judgment in *Elida Gibbs* that

---

[40]   Paragraphs 19 and 28 of the judgment.
[41]   Paragraph 31 of the judgment.

neither must they receive a lesser sum.

It is appears from *Boots* and *Elida Gibbs* that, if a coupon is issued free of charge, it has the effect of reducing the taxable amount and does not count as consideration. It is a discount which at some point will be honoured by the original issuer. This is the case regardless of whether the trader who supplies the final consumer is the same trader who issues the coupon.

This was the approach that was taken by the VAT and Duties Tribunal in *Conoco Ltd. v Customs and Excise Commissioners*.[42] In this case, the company distributed vouchers entitling traders and final consumers to money off fuel. Customs and Excise had originally argued that the value of the vouchers could not be deducted from the taxable amount. A reference to the ECJ had originally been made in this case, but the Tribunal allowed Conoco's appeal following the ruling in *Elida Gibbs*.

Note, though, that it only makes sense to refer to a discount when a supply is made for consideration. *Kuwait Petroleum (GB) Ltd. v Commissioners of Customs and Excise*[43] involved a promotion scheme in which customers were given vouchers when they purchased petrol. They could collect such vouchers and exchange them for gifts. The ECJ held that there was no consideration in this case and hence no discount. It held that the supplies were taxable under Article 5(6) of the Sixth Directive as supplies for no consideration.

Vouchers issued for consideration

It is clear from the above line of case law that coupons that are not issued for consideration cannot themselves constitute consideration. A different approach applies, however, when the trader who issues the vouchers receives payment for them. The classic example of this type of voucher is a book token.

Such vouchers involve two distinct transactions: the sale of the voucher and the redemption of the voucher. It would not be consistent to hold that both transactions were taxable supplies, as this would mean that the authorities would receive twice the VAT that they would have received on a cash purchase of the same item. For this reason, Schedule 6, paragraph 5 of the Value Added Tax Act 1994 provides:

> Where a right to receive goods or services for an amount stated on any token, stamp or voucher is granted for a consideration, the consideration shall be disregarded for the purposes of this Act except to the extent (if any) that it exceeds that amount.

---

[42] [1997] VATDR 47 (14679).
[43] Case C-48/97, [1999] ECR I-2323, [1999] STC 488.

In cases where vouchers are sold for their redemption value, the position is fairly straightforward: the original sale of the voucher is not a taxable supply. When the voucher is redeemed, the position is the same as it would have been had the customer paid cash.

The position is slightly more complicated in cases where the vouchers are sold for less than their face value. The leading case on this point is *Argos Distributors Ltd. v Customs and Excise Commissioners.*[44]

Argos produced vouchers which it sold to other businesses. These businesses provided the vouchers as incentives to their employees or agents, who could redeem the vouchers at face value against items in the Argos catalogue. Argos was assessed to VAT on the retail price of goods which were bought with such vouchers. It appealed against the assessment to the London VAT Tribunal, arguing that the taxable amount was the amount that the businesses concerned had paid for the vouchers and not the face value of the voucher which was available to the customer to spend on catalogue items.

Both parties based some of their arguments on the principle that consideration should be valued subjectively rather than objectively. Argos argued that a subjective valuation was based on the money that it had actually received, whereas the Commissioners argued that the consideration actually received was the face value of the voucher, since the customer was unaware that the voucher had been sold for less than this.

The Tribunal clearly thought that Customs and Excise had the stronger case. It stated that it would accord with commercial reality to take the value of the voucher as its face value. A customer who was asked how much he had paid for an item would refer to this amount, as would the manager of an Argos store if asked to itemise his takings. Having highlighted the main questions to be decided and indicated his view, the tribunal chairman made a reference to the ECJ.

Advocate General Fennelly also argued that the consideration should be the face value of the voucher:

> Accordingly, it is clear in my opinion that, in the circumstances described, the consideration represented by the voucher is its face value. This is the value which is attributed to it by the parties to the transaction. If a customer wishes to purchase a product, he will have to produce consideration either by way of voucher or some other means of payment to the amount of the catalogue price. The goods will not be handed over unless that consideration is forthcoming. Thus, if a voucher is used, the consideration which it represents in that transaction is its full face value.[45]

---

[44]   Case C-288/94, [1996] ECR I-5311, [1996] STC 1359.
[45]   Paragraph 25 of the opinion.

Advocate General Fennelly does not refer directly to *Empire Stores* in this passage, but his reasoning is clearly based on the test laid out in that case that, in cases where an amount has been agreed between the parties, that amount is taken to be the value of any non-monetary consideration.

As in *Elida Gibbs*, the ECJ did not follow Advocate General Fennelly's opinion. It held that the taxable amount was the amount received by Argos in return for the vouchers and not the face value of the vouchers:

> In order to ascertain the actual money equivalent accruing to Argos when it takes a voucher in payment, regard must be had only to the transaction which is relevant in that regard, namely the initial transaction comprising the sale of the voucher at a discount or otherwise. In view of the nature of that transaction, the actual money equivalent which the voucher represents for Argos, when the latter accepts it in payment, is the sum of money which it received upon the sale of the voucher, namely its face value less any discount allowed.

> The fact that a buyer of Argos goods does not know the real money equivalent of the voucher used by him is irrelevant: the important issue in this case is to determine the actual money equivalent received by Argos when it accepts the vouchers in payment for its goods, since only that actual equivalent can constitute the taxable amount.[46]

Elida Gibbs was not cited in this case. Strictly speaking, it is not relevant since the coupons involved were not classed as consideration at all. In *Argos*, it was common ground that the vouchers were consideration but the parties disagreed over the taxable amount. However, some of the wider issues involved in *Argos* have much in common with those in *Elida Gibbs* and it is interesting to compare the two cases from this point of view. In particular, both cases concerned the question of whether the Court should focus on the single supply from the retailer to the final consumer or whether it should look at the whole supply chain. In both cases, Advocate General Fennelly focused on the single supply whereas the ECJ focused on the whole chain. Both cases also turn to a certain extent on whether the transaction should be seen from the point of view of the final consumer or from the point of view of the trader. Both parties in *Argos* could have argued that the principles used by the Court in *Elida Gibbs* favoured their case. *Argos* could have argued that the Court in *Elida Gibbs* showed a willingness to look at the supply chain as a whole and to admit

---

[46] Paragraphs 20 and 21 of the judgment.

that earlier transactions in the chain could affect the taxable amount of the supply to the final consumer. Customs and Excise, on the other hand, could have argued that *Elida Gibbs* emphasised that it was the final consumer who was being taxed, so that the taxable amount should be determined by looking at how much the final consumer actually paid.

The Court's approach in *Argos* is inconsistent with its earlier approach in *Empire Stores*. According to the test in *Empire Stores*, the value of the non-monetary consideration (the voucher) should have been the price agreed between the parties, so the value of the voucher should have been its face value. This inconsistency will no doubt have to be resolved in future cases. Two possible ways of doing this spring to mind.

One possibility is that the Court could change its mind as to whether the vouchers themselves constituted the consideration. It could argue that the consideration for the supply of goods to the final consumer was the money paid to Argos in return for issuing the vouchers. Argos could then be seen as a monetary consideration case. It would involve third party consideration, which falls within the scope of Article 11(A)(1)(a). The voucher could then be seen as evidence of third party consideration rather than consideration in itself. As Advocate General Fennelly points out, Argos did not attempt to argue this. Taking this approach would involve accepting that the consideration was paid for an as yet unknown supply to an as yet unknown customer.[47] The approach is a possibility, though, and the consideration would be the amount that Argos had actually received.

The alternative is to return to an argument put forward earlier, namely that the Court's approach in *Empire Stores* was incorrect and that the distinction between that case and *Naturally Yours Cosmetics* should be based on the question of who was making the supply to whom rather than that of whether the promotion goods were included in the catalogue. It is arguable that the Court's approach in *Elida Gibbs* and then in *Argos* means that the *Empire Stores* approach of concentrating on an agreed cash price is no longer tenable. This is because both cases involved an acceptance by the Court that the taxable amount did not depend solely on the contract between the retailer and the final consumer since events earlier in the supply chain could have a bearing on the taxable amount. This being the case, any agreed cash price between the parties could be altered by earlier events in the chain. In both cases, Advocate General Fennelly's approach was consistent with Empire Stores but this was not followed by the ECJ.

---

[47]   Paragraph 17 of the opinion.

Credit card payments

Similar issues to those involved in *Argos* had also been involved in *Chaussures Bally SA Belgian State*.[48] Both Customs and Excise and Advocate General Fennelly had relied on this judgment in *Argos*.

Bally was a shoe supplier and, like many retailers, accepted payment by credit card. Once a customer had paid using a card, the credit card company forwarded the price to the retailer, but would retain a commission of 5%. Bally argued that, because of this commission, the taxable amount was only 95% of the retail price because this was the amount that it had actually received. The Court held that the taxable amount was the full retail price.

> The harmonization sought by Article 11(A)(1)(a) of the Sixth Directive could not be achieved if the taxable amount varied according to whether the calculation was for the VAT to be borne by the final consumer or for determining the sum to be paid to the revenue authorities by the taxable person. It follows that when the supplier has calculated on the full price the VAT to be paid by the purchaser so as to charge it on behalf of the revenue authorities, it is the same taxable amount which must be taken into account to determine the corresponding amount of VAT which the supplier as a taxable person is to pay to the revenue authorities.
>
> It should be added that the method of payment used in the relations between the purchaser and the supplier cannot alter the taxable amount.[49]

The issues here have much in common with those in *Argos*. In both cases, the trader's agreement with a third party means that he receives less than the cash price when the customer, who has a connection with the same third party, pays by a method other than cash.

However, there are key differences between the two cases. In *Argos*, the taxable amount was held to be the amount that the companies paid for the vouchers. That was the amount that Argos actually received. Bally was also trying to argue that it only received 95% of the retail price, but this position was rather different; as the Court pointed out, the 5% difference was the consideration for a separate supply:

> It should be pointed out in that respect that the fact that the purchaser did not pay the price agreed direct to the supplier but

---

[48] Case C-18/92, [1993] ECR I-2871.
[49] Paragraphs 14 and 17 of the judgment.

through the intermediary of the organization issuing the card, which retained a percentage calculated on the price, cannot change the taxable amount. That deduction made by the card–issuing organization represents the consideration for a service rendered by it to the supplier. That service represents an independent transaction in respect of which the purchaser is a third party.[50]

Bally only received less than the retail price from the credit card company because the amount sent was settling two separate debts: the amount that the company owed to Bally and the amount that Bally owed to the company. The second debt could not be allowed to alter the taxable amount in respect of the supply that Bally made to the final consumer.

Unlike Bally, Argos was offering a discount in that it was prepared to accept less for its goods under certain circumstances. Unlike coupons, vouchers supplied for consideration cannot themselves be classed as discounts; the discount lies in the difference between the face value of the voucher and the amount for which it is sold. To put it another way, Argos' VAT position would have been exactly the same if, instead of supplying vouchers to businesses at a discount, it had issued cards to the employees of those businesses entitling them to a discount on all products in the catalogue. The same cannot be said of Bally. The VAT system allows a trader to offset his input tax against his output tax, but it does not normally allow him to deduct the cost of making a supply from the taxable amount.[51]

However, this principle does not necessarily apply when a trader makes his profits purely by exchanging cash. The main examples of this are gambling transactions and currency exchange. These are considered next.

Pure Cash Transactions

The leading case on this point is *Glawe Spiel und Unterhaltungsgerate Aufstellungsgesellschaft mbH & Co KG v Finanzamt Hamburg-Barmbek-Uhlenhorst.*[52] The case concerned a trader who operated slot machines in bars and restaurants. The machines were so set that they paid out in winnings 60% of the money paid in by way of stakes. There was no meter on the machines, so there was no record kept of how much money had been paid in. The German tax authorities assessed the trader to VAT on the total stakes paid into the machines. The trader appealed, arguing that the taxable amount was the 40% of the stakes that he collected from the machines. The German court made a reference to the ECJ.

---

[50] Paragraph 16 of the judgment.
[51] Exceptions to this rule are the special margin schemes in place. For example, tour operators and those dealing in second-hand goods are permitted to calculate VAT on the margin rather than on the total price. Special schemes are also in place for retailers, as detailed in Customs Notice 727.
[52] Case C-38/93, [1994] ECR I-1679.

Advocate General Jacobs and the Court were agreed that the taxable amount was the net amount that the trader collected from the machine and not the total stakes paid in. Having set out the facts of the case and the issues involved, the Advocate General first turned to the provisions of the Sixth Directive dealing with gambling. Article 13(B)(f) of the Directive provides that "betting, lotteries and other forms of gambling" shall be exempt from VAT, "subject to conditions and limitations laid down by each Member State." However, Article 33 of the Directive permits Member States to impose other taxes on gambling. Advocate General Jacobs pointed out that the Commission and some Member States had interpreted this as meaning that Member States could subject certain gambling transactions to VAT if they so wished and his view was that this was consistent with Community law.[53] Having said this, he went on to state that VAT was ill suited to deal with gambling transactions and that the aim of the Court should be to seek an interpretation which was consistent with the aims and principles of the VAT system.[54]

The Advocate General rejected the German government's argument that the taxable amount was the total amount of money paid into the machine. He gave the example of two individuals who engaged in a private bet. Each placed an amount on the table and the winner would collect the sum of the two amounts. He argued that it would be ridiculous to state that each was making a supply of services to the other by providing the chance of winning. He then went on to consider how this scenario differed from commercial gambling and concluded that the commercial organisation was providing a service by drawing together a group of individuals who wished to gamble and managing the process. The value of this service was therefore the amount that the organisation could keep once it had paid out the winnings.[55] This meant that the taxable amount was the money that the operator collected when he emptied the machine:

> From the foregoing analysis it follows that, in so far as it is appropriate to charge VAT on gaming machine transactions, the taxable amount should be limited to the operator's actual takings, i.e. his net receipts after payment of winnings to the players. The correctness of this view is confirmed by looking at the transaction from the players' viewpoint. What players as a group pay for the operator's services is the amount retained by the machine and collected by the operator. For the rest, the machine acts as a means of collecting players' bets and paying them out to winners.[56]

---

[53] Paragraph 10 of the opinion.
[54] Paragraph 16 of the opinion.
[55] Paragraphs 20 and 21 of the opinion.
[56] Paragraph 24 of the opinion.

This case may at first seem to contradict the requirement that the taxable amount should be the amount actually received. However, if the supply is defined as the management of the gambling process, only the amount retained by the trader was actually received for that supply. The rest went into the pot of money which was distributed amongst the players. This is consistent with the argument put forward by the United Kingdom, which argued that each stake put into the machine had to be broken down into two separate elements: the 40% that was retained by the machine and the 60% that was paid out in winnings.

The VAT treatment of gambling transactions was considered again in *Fischer v Finanzamt Donaueshingen*.[57] Under German law, roulette games could only be operated by owners of licensed casinos. Such games were exempt from VAT. The trader in *Fischer* did not own a licensed casino; he had an official permit to operate a game similar to roulette, but he departed from the terms of this permit. As a result, the game that he operated was classed as an illegal roulette game. The German authorities sought to charge VAT on the stakes in the game. The German court asked the ECJ two questions: whether the roulette game was subject to VAT because it was illegal and, if so, how the VAT should be calculated.

In the event, the ECJ only considered the first question since it decided that the game should be exempt. However, Advocate General Jacobs considered both questions and he argued that, if the transaction was subject to VAT, the ruling in *Glawe* should be extended to roulette.

The Advocate General had to decide between three possible methods of determining the taxable amount. The German government argued that the taxable amount was the value of the chips placed on the table, the Commission argued that it was the value of the total chips purchased and the UK government argued that the ruling in *Glawe* should be extended to roulette.

This case, even more so than *Glawe*, illustrates the difficulties that arise when VAT is applied to gambling transactions. As Advocate General Jacobs pointed out, the German government's approach cannot work, since it fails to distinguish between chips that a player has bought and chips that he has won.[58] Suppose that, at the end of an evening, a player stakes and loses one hundred chips. He started the evening with two chips which he bought and he won the other ninety-eight in the course of the evening. Following the German government's approach, tax would be payable on the value of one hundred chips, even though the player had only bought two.

The Commission's approach is slightly less problematic. As Advocate General Jacobs points out, the casino will be aware of how many chips have been sold. However, there is a further problem with this approach which he does not address. Supposing that two players each buy two pounds worth of chips and each one wins a further hundred pounds. The first player cashes in his chips and the second does not. Later in the evening, the first player repurchases his chips and both players stake and lose the full amount. It is difficult to see why a distinction should be drawn between these two players and it does not seem sensible to say that the services provided by the casino to the first player are worth more than fifty times more than those provided to the second.

This leaves the *Glawe* approach. However, unlike *Glawe* itself, there was no obligation in *Fischer* to pay about a certain percentage of each stake as winnings. However, as Advocate General Jacobs pointed out, the proportion could be calculated exactly by reference to the way that the odds were set.

The Court applied applied the same approach to currency exchange transactions in *Commissioners of Customs and Excise v First National Bank of Chicago*.[59] In this case, the amount that the bank could take for itself was limited to the spread between the bid and the offer prices.

The precise scope of the *Glawe* principle has yet to be established. It seems likely that it will be confined to pure cash transactions. This view is supported by Lord Slynn in *Nell Gwynn House Maintenance Fund Trustees v Customs and Excise Commissioners*:

> Cases involving simply the exchange of money on which a profit is made are really in a category of their own.[60]

One case which may clarify the scope of the principle is *Town and Country Factors Ltd. v Commissioners of Customs and Excise*. This case concerned a "spot the ball" competition for which various prizes were offered, including a QE2 cruise, a Concorde flight and a jackpot of £200,000. The rules of the competition stated that the transactions were "binding in honour only." The case concerned the period between June 1994 and November 1995. Customs and Excise argued that the company was liable to VAT on the total entry fees, whereas the company argued that it was only liable on the entry fees less the value of the prizes. The company appealed against the assessment to the VAT Tribunal.[61]

Two main issues of law were involved. The first was whether the ECJ's judgment in *Tolsma* could be applied to argue that the "binding in honour only" clause meant that there was no legal relationship between the parties

---

[59]   C-172/96 ECR 1998 I-4387
[60]   [1999] 1 All ER 385, [1999] 1 WLR 174, 32 HLR 13, [1999] STC 79. This case is discussed below in the context of disbursements.
[61]   27th August 1996 and 4th April 1997, unreported.

and hence no consideration. The second was whether the judgment in *Glawe* applied. As the parties had not raised the *Tolsma* issue, the Tribunal listed the appeal for a further hearing on this matter.

The Tribunal decided to make a reference to the ECJ on the *Tolsma* issue but not on the *Glawe* issue. It stated that *Glawe* did not apply. This was because the "spot the ball" competition differed from the gaming machines in the following ways. Firstly, the operators were not obliged to pay out a set amount of the takings as winnings; secondly, the trader was able to take for himself the total stakes paid. He could pay the prizes out of it as a matter of convenience but he was not in the same position as the gaming machine operator who could not touch the sixty per cent of the takings that had to be paid out as winnings. On this point, the Tribunal argued that it was bound by the Court of Appeal judgment in *Nell Gwynn House Maintenance Fund v CEC*.[62] In this case, Sir Christopher Slade stated:

> Though the court did not explicitly repeat the Advocate General Jacobs's reference to "turnover", the clear ratio of its decision, in so far as it rejected the German government's contentions, was that the proportion of the stake money payable out as winnings could not be regarded as "consideration . . . obtained by the supplier" because the supplier could not deal with that proportion as his own or receive any benefit whatsoever from it; the supplier could not "actually take it for himself".[63]

At the second hearing to consider the *Tolsma* point, the company asked the Tribunal to reconsider this issue, but it refused. Both parties then appealed to the High Court, the Commissioners arguing that a reference should not have been made on the *Tolsma* point and the company arguing that a reference should have been made on the *Glawe* point. By the time the case reached the High Court, Advocate General Jacobs had given his opinion in *Fischer*, although the ECJ had not then given its judgment.[64]

In the High Court, Carnwath J. referred to the opinion in *Fischer* and said that it showed that the ECJ had not conclusively settled the boundaries of the *Glawe* principle.[65] He stated that a reference should be made on both points.

Advocate General Stix-Hackl gave her opinion in September 2001. She argued that the clause that the agreement was binding in honour only should not have the effect of bringing it within the scope of the *Tolsma* judgment and that the taxable amount was the value of the stakes and not the value of the stakes less the cost of the prizes. At the time of writing,

---

[62] [1996] STC 310.
[63] At page 324h.
[64] Advocate General Jacobs' opinion was given on 20th March 1997, just over a fortnight before the second Tribunal hearing, but had not been published at the time of the second hearing.
[65] 23rd January 1998, unreported.

the ECJ had not given its judgment.

Disbursements

A disbursement is a sum of money that passes through a trader's hands without becoming part of his turnover.   He therefore does not have to account for VAT on this amount.

Article 11A(3)(c) of the Sixth Directive provides:

> The taxable amount shall not include ... (c) the amounts received by a taxable person from his purchaser or customer as repayment for expenses paid out in the name and for the account of the latter and which are entered in his books in a suspense account.

Disbursement cases based on agency

One of the leading cases on disbursements is *Rowe & Mawe v Customs and Excise Commissioners.*[66] The case involved travelling expenses for solicitors. The expenses were listed on the client's bill as disbursements. The firm argued that it was acting as agent for its client in buying the tickets and that the cost of the tickets did not form part of its turnover.

Both the VAT Tribunal and the High Court dismissed the appeal. The held that the fact that an item of expenditure had to be treated as a disbursement under the Solicitors' Accounts Rules did not mean that they were not part of the solicitor's turnover for VAT purposes. According to Bridge J:

> I also agree and I only add a word in order to emphasis the importance of the distinction between two different classes of disbursement which a solicitor may expend on his client's behalf which lead to different consequences in respect of the incidence of value added tax. On the one hand a solicitor (like any other agent) may purchase goods or services for his client, as for instance when paying stamp duty, court fees or buying, say, a travel ticket to enable the client to travel. The goods or services purchased are supplied to the client, not to the solicitor, who merely acts as an agent to make the payment. Naturally no value added tax is payable (if the goods or services in question are themselves exempt or zero-rated) because such payments form no part of the consideration for the solicitor's own services to his client. But on the other hand quite different

---

[66] [1974] VATTR 271, [1975] 2 All ER 444, [1975] STC 340.

considerations apply where the goods or services purchased are supplied to the solicitor, as here in the form of travel tickets, to enable him effectively to perform the service supplied to his client, in this case to travel to the place where the solicitor's service is required to be performed. In such case, in whatever form the solicitor recovers such expenditure from his client, whether as a separately itemised expense or part of an inclusive overall fee, value added tax is payable because the payment is part of the consideration which the client pays for the service supplied by the solicitor.

The distinction, then, is based upon whether the trader is paying out the money on his customer's behalf or whether he is paying it on his own account to enable him to make the supplies to his customer. In the former case, the payment is a disbursement, and does not form part of the trader's turnover whereas, in the latter case, the payment attracts no special treatment.

A similar approach was taken nearly twenty years later in *Shuttleworth & Co. v Commissioners of Customs and Excise*.[67] This case also involved solicitors' expenses. This time, the payment that the solicitor sought to treat as a disbursement was the fee paid to a bank for the telegraphic transfer of funds on behalf of a client during the conveyancing process. The London VAT Tribunal held that this sum was not a disbursement. It drew a distinction between expenses such as search fees and stamp duty, which were disbursements, and expenses that the solicitor had to incur in order to provide the service to his client, which were not. In the former case, the solicitor was acting as agent for his client in making payments on his behalf. He could then recover these payments from his client without their being classed as part of his turnover.

This issue was considered further in *Nell Gwynn House Maintenance Fund Trustees v Customs and Excise Commissioners*.[68] The case concerned a block of 435 luxury flats and studio apartments. Each tenant was liable for 1/435 of the total annual maintenance bill and the landlord paid this amount for each unlet property. The money was paid into a fund for which the trustees were three partners from a firm of solicitors. The trustees could retain £17,000 per year in return for their services and held the rest of the money on trust to provide services for the flats. It was their responsibility to employ porters and cleaning staff and such staff were employed by the trustees and not by the tenants. The Commissioners issued an assessment to VAT in respect of all moneys paid into the fund, arguing that this was consideration for the services that the trustees provided. The trustees argued that the consideration for their services was limited to the £17,000.

---

[67]   [1994] VATTR 355, LON/94/986A.
[68]   [1999] 1 All ER 385, [1999] STC 79.

The main arguments concerned the question of agency and the ECJ's judgment in *Glawe*. The trustees argued that they were acting as agents for the tenants and that the moneys spent were spent on their behalf. They also argued, following *Glawe*, that the consideration for their services was limited to the amount that they could take for themselves. The VAT Tribunal and the High Court held for the Commissioners, the Court of Appeal reversed the judgment of the High Court and the House of Lords reversed the judgment of the Court of Appeal. However, all judgments were in agreement upon the agency point and held that the expenses incurred by the trustees were made in the course of making supplies to the tenants, since the staff provided their services to the trustees and not to the tenants directly. The trustees employed the staff, so could not argue that they were acting as someone else's agent in paying wages to their own staff. They therefore provided staff to the tenants and not just the services of managing the trust fund. Sir Christopher Slade in the Court of Appeal stated that Article 11(A)(3)(c) was not restricted to a relationship of agency but held that the facts of *Nell Gwynn* did not fall within the scope of that provision.

Although the Court of Appeal also held that the trustees could not win on the basis of the agency argument, it held that the ECJ's judgment in *Glawe* was applicable and that the amount of consideration was limited to the amount that the trader could take for himself. In the present case, that amount was £17,000.

The House of Lords reversed this decision. As quoted above, Lord Slynn held that the principle in *Glawe* was limited to cases involving the exchange on money on which profit was made. However, Lord Slynn did agree with Sir Christopher Slade in holding that there did not have to be a relationship of agency for a payment to be classed as a disbursement.

It is clear from these cases that, where a trader acts as his client's agent in making payments on his behalf, these payments will be treated as disbursements, but it is also clear that a relationship of agency is not necessary for this to be the case. The next section considers two recent cases that were not based on the principle of agency.

Disbursement cases not based on agency

Customs and Excise Commissioners v Emap MacLaren Ltd[69] involved a publishing company which offered a prize for scientific research. It invited firms to sponsor the award. In return, the sponsors received benefits in the form of publicity at conferences and in scientific journals published by Emap.

[69] [1997] STC 490.

Emap did not take any expenses from the sponsorship that it received and it put all the money into the prize fund. The Commissioners argued that all the money paid by the firms was consideration for the publicity offered by Emap and was therefore chargeable to VAT. Emap appealed against this assessment to the VAT Tribunal, which upheld its appeal. The Commissioners then appealed to the High Court.

The High Court dismissed the appeal. Given the Court of Appeal's judgment in *Nell Gwynn*[70] McCullough J. said that he saw no reason not to apply the principle in *Glawe*. VAT was not payable on the sponsorship money because Emap was not able to deal with it as its own. Given that this was the case, he also argued that that meant that there was no direct link, as was required following *Aardappelenbewaarplaats*.

Following the House of Lords' judgment in *Nell Gwynn*, the status of the *Emap* judgment appears doubtful, given that McCullough J. placed so much reliance on the Court of Appeal's approach to the *Glawe* principle, which the House of Lords reversed. McCullough J. also made it clear that his argument based on the direct link test was only applicable if his application of the *Glawe* principle was correct, so the case cannot be distinguished on that basis. No reliance was placed upon the principle of agency and it would not seem to be arguable that *Emap* was acting as agent for the sponsoring firms. The prize awarded was the Laboratory News Award for Science and Laboratory News was published by *Emap*, not by its sponsors. It is also doubtful whether the facts of Emap fall within the scope of the *Glawe* principle as defined by Lord Slynn in *Nell Gwynn*, as it did not involve the exchange of money on which a profit was made.

One argument that could have been put forward in Emap's favour was the argument used in *Friends of the Ironbridge Gorge Museum v Commissioners of Customs and Excise*.[71] The sponsorship money could then have been classed as a donation, depending on the relationship between the amount paid and the benefits received. Emap suggested appropriate levels of donation for sponsors based on their turnover, but it made no effort to check whether the donation actually received was at the level suggested. The only difficulty with this approach is that, unlike in *Ironbridge*, the party receiving the payments and the party giving the benefits in Emap were one and the same, but it is arguable that Emap could have succeeded on the donation point alone.

One of the most recent cases involving disbursements was *Customs and Excise Commissioners v Plantiflor* which involved plants supplied by mail order. As discussed earlier in the context of mixed supplies, the Court of Appeal accepted that there were two separate supplies in this case: a supply of plants by Plantiflor to the final consumer and a supply of delivery services

---

[70]   Note that *Nell Gwynn* had not reached the House of Lords at this point.
[71]   [1991] VATTR 97.

by Parcelforce to the final consumer.[72] The question of disbursements arose because the final consumer had no direct dealings with Parcelforce, but forwarded the consideration for both supplies to Plantiflor. Plantiflor kept the moneys for the postal charges in a separate account and argued that they did not form part of its turnover. It argued that the delivery charges paid by the customers were consideration for supplies made by Parcelforce, not by Plantiflor, so Plantiflor was not liable for VAT in respect of them. The moneys passed through Plantiflor's books, but they did not form part of its turnover since they were not consideration for any supplies that Plantiflor had made.

The VAT Tribunal allowed Plantiflor's appeal[73], but this was reversed by the High Court.[74] Laws J. held that Article 11(A)(3)(c) could not apply since there was no relationship of agency between Plantiflor and its customers:

> Where on the facts all along the specific fund is not intended to be treated as in any sense the taxpayer's property but as the property of the party to whom it is to be paid, that will generally be a conclusive indication that it does not form part of the taxpayer's consideration. In the English jurisdiction, trust and agency form the clearest instances of this concept's application. ...
>
> Once agency is ruled out, there is in truth nothing left in the evidence here to lift the case out of the ordinary situation where the taxpayer incurs debts in the course of his business which, of course, he has to pay.[75]

This judgment predates the House of Lords' judgment in *Nell Gwynn* and was also reversed by the Court of Appeal. However, it is still not completely clear whether the passage quoted above remains good law. Both the Court of Appeal and the House of Lords in *Nell Gwynn* accepted that a relationship of agency was not necessary for a payment to be classed as a disbursement. However, *Nell Gwynn* involved a trust, so it is arguable that there has either to be a trust or a relationship of agency. The Court of Appeal held that this was not necessary and ruled in favour of Plantiflor, but the Commissioners have now petitioned the House of Lords for leave to appeal.

It is possible that the House of Lords will reverse the Court of Appeal's judgment as it did in *Nell Gwynn*. The main difference here, though, is that the Court of Appeal did not rely on *Glawe* to rule in favour of Plantiflor; it relied to the text of Article 11(A)(3)(c) and said that there did not have

---

[72] [2000] STC 137.
[73] [1997] V&DR 375.
[74] [1999] STC 51
[75] At pages 64 - 65a.

to be a relationship of agency for this provision to apply. The Court of Appeal held this in both *Nell Gwynn* and *Plantiflor* and, as stated above, Lord Slynn accepted this point in the House of Lords. The House of Lords' ruling in *Plantiflor* will settle the matter.

Like cases concerning mixed supplies, cases dealing with disbursements tend to arise because of the different tax treatments used for different types of supply. If postal services had been standard-rated rather than exempt, the issue would not have made any material difference in *Plantiflor* and the case would not have come to court. Since the amount that Plantiflor collected for delivery services was the same amount that it paid to Parcelforce, the input tax and output tax would have been identical and so would have cancelled each other out. The effect of this would have been the same as if the delivery charges had been treated as disbursements.

Another link with the mixed supply cases is that, if a trader is arguing that a sum of money is a disbursement, he must be able to separate out the supply to which that money relates. If it had been held in *Plantiflor* that there was a single supply of delivered plants by Plantiflor to the final consumer, it would have followed from this that the supply of delivery services was made by Parcelforce to Plantiflor. There would then have been no question of arguing that the delivery charges were disbursements.

Cases involving disbursements can sometimes be difficult to distinguish from cases in which a trader who purchases goods or services from his suppliers incorporates those supplies into the taxable supplies that he makes to his customers. This is illustrated by Laws J's consideration of *Plantiflor* in the High Court. Laws J held that the customer paid the delivery costs in return for Plantiflor's supply of arranging the delivery service. The Commissioners' arguments and Laws J's judgment placed a great deal of reliance on an earlier judgment of Laws J in *Customs and Excise Commissioners v Reed Personnel Services Ltd.*[76]

This case involved an agency which supplied nursing staff to hospitals. The Commissioners refused to allow it to deduct input tax in respect of this business, arguing that it was making an exempt supply of nursing services. The agency successfully appealed to the VAT Tribunal arguing that it was supplying nursing staff rather than nursing services. The Commissioners then appealed to the High Court and Laws J dismissed the appeal.

In *Plantiflor*, Laws J made the following reference to his judgment in *Reed*:

Mr Paines' [counsel for the Commissioners] principal purpose in

[76] [1995] STC 588.

referring to this decision was to demonstrate that there is no anomaly, in the law of VAT, in a situation where A makes a supply to B which consists in arranging for the services of C to be supplied to B. There are then two separate supplies, and it matters not that the supply of services by C to B is an exempt supply under the legislation. In *Reed*, the provision of the nurses to the hospitals (B) was a taxable supply by Reed (A) and the provision by the nurses (C) of their own services was an exempt supply. Upon Mr Paines' argument, the same is true here: Plantiflor (A) makes a taxable supply to the customer (B) consisting of arranging for delivery by Parcelforce (C), which then supplies actual delivery, which is exempt.[77]

Laws J. appeared convinced that the issues in *Reed* were analogous to those in *Plantiflor*, but it is nevertheless possible to highlight certain key differences between the two cases. In particular, *Reed* turned on the nature of the supply whereas *Plantiflor* turned on the identity of the supplier. In *Plantiflor*, the supply was identical whether it was held to be made by Plantiflor or by Parcelforce. On the other hand, there were differences between the services provided by the nurses and the services provided by Reed. This is shown by the ruling that, whereas the nurses provided nursing services, Reed provided nursing staff. It is possible to point to extra benefits that the hospitals derived from booking their casual staff through Reed. For example, Reed as an agency provided a reliability that individual casual workers could not provide. It also provided the convenience of making one 'phone call to arrange for extra staff instead of having to telephone individual nurses to see if they were available. Consequently, it is arguable that the service of providing nursing staff provided by Reed was a composite supply consisting of a combination of nursing services and staff management. Therefore Reed, like any other supplier of composite supplies, put various components together and added value in the process. This is reflected by the fact that the money paid by Reed to the nurses was not as much as that paid by the hospitals to Reed.

If *Reed* is viewed as a case concerning composite supplies, it is uncontroversial. However, since *Plantiflor* involved separate supplies of goods and services, it does not automatically follow that the principle in *Reed* can be applied to the facts of *Plantiflor*. In the context of delivery services, *Reed* would certainly apply in the case of delivered goods, where the supplier undertakes to deliver the goods to his customer and remains responsible for them until they have been delivered.[78] It is also consistent with the later House of Lords judgment in *British Telecom*.[79] The fact that

---

[77] At page 58g.

[78] See Customs and Excise VAT Notice 700/24/94 "Postage and Delivery Charges." The previous five paragraphs were first published in Postage, packing and all VAT: some issues involved in *Customs and Excise Commissioners v Plantiflor Ltd.* [2001] BTR 100.

[79] [1993] 3 All ER 961, [1999] STC 758.

an analogy could so easily be drawn between the issues in *Plantiflor* and those in *Reed*, though, shows how difficult it can be to distinguish between a disbursement and a payment on a trader's own account.

Further Reading
The Rt. Hon. Sir John Laws, *Law and Fact* [1999] BTR 159.

chapter twenty four

Value Added Tax - Tax Rates and Exemptions

Supplies for VAT purposes can be divided into two categories: taxable supplies and exempt supplies. In the United Kingdom there are three different rates applicable to standard-rated supplies: the standard rate of 17.5%, the reduced rate of 5% and the zero rate. Section 4(2) of VATA 1994 defines a taxable supply as any supply of goods or services made in the United Kingdom which is not an exempt supply.

Section 2(1) of VATA 1994 provides that the standard rate of VAT is 17.5% and s.2(1A) provides that a reduced rate of 5% shall apply to supplies falling within Schedule A[1]. S.30 provides that items falling within Schedule 8 shall be zero-rated and s.31 provides that items falling within Schedule 9 shall be exempt.

Reduced Rate Supplies

Until recently, the UK only used two rates of VAT: the standard rate and the zero rate. The existence of the reduced rate is due to EC law. Article 12(3)(a) of the Sixth Directive permits Member States to apply reduced rates of not less than 5 per cent. Member States that use zero-rating may continue to do so but, once they have departed from the zero-rate, they cannot return to it.

Reduced rate supplies are set out in Schedule 7A to the 1994 Act.[1] Supplies listed here are ones for which the rate of VAT applicable has at some point been reduced. The relevant supplies are as follows:

i.   supplies of domestic fuel or power;

ii. installation of energy-saving materials;

iii. grant-funded installation of heating equipment;

---

[1] The 2002 budget proposed widening the scope of the reduced rate for grant-funded installation of heating equipment and for residential conversions. These measures are due to come into force on 1 June 2002. See Customs Notices CE 40/02 and CE 41/02.

iv.   women's sanitary products;

v.   children's car seats;

vi.   residential conversions;

vii.   renovation and alteration of dwellings which have been empty for at least three years.

Domestic fuel used to be zero-rated in the UK, but the UK was not able to return to the zero rate once it had departed from it. The main residential conversions covered by the Schedule are those where the end result of the conversion is that more households can occupy the building.

Zero-Rated Supplies

Zero-rated supplies are technically charged to VAT at 0%. Because such supplies are taxable supplies, this means that the supplier is entitled to deduct input tax in respect of those supplies. This should be contrasted with exempt supplies since there is no deduction of input tax in respect of these.

Supplies which are zero-rated are set out in Section 30 and Schedule 8 of VATA 1994. The main groups under Schedule 8 are as follows:

Group 1 - food

Group 2 - sewerage services and water

Group 3 - books

Group 4 - talking books for the blind and handicapped[2]

Group 5- construction

Group 6 - protected buildings

Group 7 - international services

Group 8 - transport

Group 9 - caravans and houseboats[3]

Group 10 - gold

Group 11 - bank notes

Group 12 - drugs and medicines

Group 13 - imports and exports

Group 14 – tax free shops[4]

Group 15 - charities

Group 16 - children's clothing and footwear.

---

[2]   The zero-rating only applies where the supply is made to the RNIB, the National Listening Library or to a similar charity.

[3]   Note that this Group only covers caravans above the maximum towing weight and houseboats without their own means of propulsion.

[4]   This Group was repealed by the Value Added Tax (Abolition of Zero-Rating for Tax Free Shops) Order, SI 1999/1642 which took effect on 1st July 1999.

Some of these groups have given rise to a considerable amount of case law, whereas others, such as sewerage services and talking books, have hardly given rise to any. Food, books, clothing and transport are considered in more detail below, because they best illustrate the very nice distinctions that have to be drawn when deciding whether certain supplies fall within the scope of the zero rate. A basic outline of the main rules relating to construction is also given. Supplies with an international aspect are discussed, but for a different reason, as will be explained.

Food

Group 1 includes four general items which are classed as food:

1. food of a kind used for human consumption;

2. animal feeding stuffs;[5]

3. seeds or other means of propagation of plants comprised in item 1 or 2;

4. live animals of a kind generally used as, or yielding or producing, food for human consumption.

The Act provides that anything included in these general items is zero-rated unless:

a. it is a supply in the course of catering; or

b. it falls within the list of exceptions to the general items and does not fall within the list of items overriding those exceptions.

The structure of Group 1 is that it gives a broad list of items, a more specific list of exceptions and an even more specific list of exceptions to the exceptions. This structure may appear complex, but it has its advantages. For example, the first item on the list of exceptions is ice cream, ice lollies, frozen yoghurt and similar products. Therefore, even though these fall within the general item of food of a kind used for human consumption, they are still standard rated because of the exception. The first item of the items overriding the exceptions is yoghurt unsuitable for immediate human consumption when frozen. This would cover yoghurt that was frozen for other reasons than to turn it into an ice cream substitute, so this would still be zero-rated.

---

[5] See for example *Fluff Ltd (trading as Mag-it) v Customs and Excise Commissioners* [2001] STC 674, in which it was held that maggots supplied to fishermen did not qualify for zero-rating under this item since their aim was to catch rather than to feed fish. The fact that they were of nutritional value to the fish was irrelevant. It was accepted that maggots supplied as food to fish farms would qualify for zero-rating, but Fluff Ltd did not supply any maggots for this purpose.

Supplies in the course of catering

As described above, supplies in the course of catering are standard-rated rather than zero-rated. Note 3 to Group 1 provides that a supply in the course of catering shall include:

a.   any supply of food for consumption on the premises;

b.   any supply of hot food for consumption off the premises.

Presumably one of the aims of this provision was to prevent meals in restaurants enjoying the same tax treatment as basic foodstuffs. When VAT was first introduced in the United Kingdom, it was presented as a tax on luxury items; the zero rate was used so that final consumers were not taxed on the purchase of essentials.

The end result of this provision, though, is that a customer who buys a hot pie in a baker's may be charged VAT whereas a customer who buys a cold pie will not be. This depends to a certain extent upon the reason why the food is hot. If it is hot because it has just been cooked, then it may still be zero-rated. In *John Pimblett & Sons Ltd v Customs and Excise Commissioners*,[6] the appellant sold freshly-baked pies. It argued that it carried out its baking on the premises so that the smell would encourage customers to go into the shop. Both the High Court and the Court of Appeal accepted this argument. This case can be contrasted with *Pret A Manger (Europe) Ltd v Customs and Excise Commissioners*[7] in which the VAT Tribunal held that the sale of hot croissants was a supply in the course of catering. The appellant argued that the croissants were kept warm to keep them fresh rather than to enable them to be eaten hot. The Tribunal held that this distinction was artificial.

One final point to note on the subject of hot food is that tribunals will be reluctant to class it as a supply in the course of catering if it is not suitable for immediate consumption. In *The Lewis Group Ltd v Customs and Excise Commissioners*,[8] the Commissioners tried to argue that roast chickens were supplies in the course of catering. The appellant did keep the chickens hot, but argued that this was for hygiene reasons. The Manchester VAT Tribunal accepted this argument, pointing out that customers would not be expected to eat whole roast chickens in the same way that they would eat hot pies.

The notes to Group 1 are not exclusive and it is perfectly possible for a supply to be made in the course of catering if the food is neither hot nor consumed on the premises. An example of such a supply would be one

[6]   [1988] STC 358.
[7]   LON/C/1423 (16246)
[8]   MAN/89/389 (4931)

made by a mobile catering firm which laid on a cold buffet at a customer's home or at a hired venue such as a church hall.

This point was accepted in *Customs and Excise Commissioners v Safeway Stores plc*[9] in which both parties and Keene J accepted that a supply of catering could cover the supply of cold food for consumption off the premises. The case involved the supply of "party trays" from a supermarket delicatessen counter. These trays were made up to serve either 12 or 20 people and customers ordered them in advance. A selection of food from the counter was placed on foil trays and customers could either place the food straight onto the table or transfer it onto their own crockery.

Customs and Excise argued that the supply of the trays was a supply in the course of catering. Safeway was successful in its appeal to the VAT Tribunal[10] and the Commissioners appealed to the High Court. Keene J dismissed the appeal.

> The problem which arises in this case is one of where the dividing line is to be drawn. The fact is that these days a lot of food is ready to eat when sold. ... Most of these things can be obtained at delicatessen counters of supermarkets or delicatessens of free-standing shops. Many ordinary families, no doubt, find that purchasing such items individually in a supermarket or superstore is a very convenient way of reducing meal preparation to the minimum and with a large family one can see that purchasing a tray of the kind which Safeway here provide would be an easy way of minimising the number of calls one has to make within the shop at various departments or counters. The same may obtain, to varying degrees, even when the purchasing is being done for a dinner party or similar occasion.
>
> The tribunal, as a tribunal of fact and law, has to draw that line between supplies of food on the one hand, and supplies which occur in the course of catering. I accept that the test which has to be applied is that of the normal meaning which would be attached to that phrase 'in the course of catering' in the ordinary usage of the English language. As was said by the tribunal in the case of *Armstrong v Customs and Excise Comrs* [1984] VATTR 53 at 62: "Taking the word in its ordinary and popular meaning, we think an ordinary person can recognise catering when he sees it." [11]

As with many areas relating to zero-rating, the distinction between supplies

---

[9] [1997] STC 163.
[10] VAT Decision 14067 of 9th April 1996.
[11] At p.168g.

of food and supplies in the course of catering can be a difficult one to draw. It is clear from *Safeway Stores* that supplying food ready to eat does not in itself count as catering. The notes to Group 1 expressly state that supplies on the premises and supplies of hot food are to be treated a supplies in the course of catering, but the courts have not been prepared to extend the scope of this by analogy. For example, they could have compared the party trays in *Safeway Stores* to hot take-away meals, but did not. Hot food is classed as catering because of the text of the Act, but it is doubtful whether an "ordinary person" who recognises catering when he sees it, would class the sale of a hot pie in baker's as a supply in the course of catering.

The difference between food and confectionery

Another difficult distinction to draw in this context is that between supplies of food and supplies of confectionery. Item 2 of the excepted items states that confectionery does not include, "cakes or biscuits other than biscuits wholly or partly covered in chocolate or some product similar in taste and appearance."

The distinction between a cake and a biscuit was considered in *United Biscuits (UK) Ltd v The Commissioners of Customs and Excise.*[12] United Biscuits had appealed against the Commissioners' assessment that Jaffa Cakes were standard-rated chocolate biscuits rather than zero-rated cakes. The London VAT Tribunal allowed the appeal, and held that Jaffa cakes were cakes rather than biscuits. The Chairman accepted that, in some ways, Jaffa cakes were more like biscuits in terms of size and location on the supermarket shelves. He also described their packaging as "uncakelike" but he held that they were, on balance, cakes. This was because the base was made from a mixture almost identical to sponge mixture and because, like cakes, they became brittle when they went stale, as opposed to biscuits which tended to go soft.

Cases such as this make interesting reading, although they sometimes seem to border on the surreal. In *Customs & Excise Commissioners v Ferrero UK Ltd*, [13] Lord Woolf warned the VAT Tribunals against trying to create legal principles out of what were essentially questions of fact.

> I commend the tribunal for the care which it took over this matter, but I am bound to say that, no doubt because of the submissions which were made to it by the parties, the treatment of the issue which was before it, was far more elaborate than was necessary. I do urge tribunals, when considering issues of this sort, not to be misled

[12]   LON/91/160.
[13]   [1997] STC 881, CA.

by authorities which are no more than authorities of fact into elevating issues of fact into questions of principle when it is not appropriate to do so on an inquiry such as this. The tribunal had to answer one question and one question only: was each of these products properly described as biscuits or not? If it had confined itself to that issue which is, and has to be, one of fact and degree, then the problems which subsequently arose would have been avoided.

Defining the boundaries of zero-rated supplies is always going to involve drawing very fine distinctions. In the context of foodstuffs, the courts have made it clear that such distinctions are essentially ones of fact rather than of law.

Books and publications

Group 3 provides that books, newspapers, periodicals, printed music and maps are zero-rated. As with food, the question of whether a supply falls into one of these categories is one of fact and the line can sometimes be a difficult one to draw.

For example, in *Richard Salmon Ltd v Commissioners of Customs and Excise*[14], the VAT Tribunal held that an art diary containing photographs of an artist's work and a series of blank pages headed with the months of the year should be classed as a book and therefore zero-rated. The book contained no printed dates or days of the week and did not relate to a specific year. On the other hand, in *Customs and Excise Commissioners v Colour Offset Ltd*,[15] the High Court held that diaries and address books were not to be classed as books for VAT purposes. May J held that the word "book" should be taken as having its ordinary English meaning:

> As Mr Richards submitted ... people generally think of books as things to be read rather than as blank pages bound together. A filled-in diary of historical or literary interest may be a book because it is retained to be read or looked at. But a blank diary is not a book in the ordinary sense of the word. Likewise a blank address book is not in the ordinary sense a book and it does not become one simply because its name includes the word "book". A cheque book is plainly not a book nor, in my view, is it a booklet in the ordinary sense of that word. The fact that in some contexts you would say of a blank diary that it is a book within one possible meaning of that word does not mean that it is a book within the ordinary meaning of the word.

[14] LON/92/2893A.
[15] [1995] STC 85.

The VAT Tribunal took a similar approach to defining "periodical" in *EMAP Consumer Magazines Ltd v Commissioners of Customs and Excise*[16] and *European Publishing Consultants Ltd v Commissioners of Customs and Excise*.[17] In both cases, it held that the word should be given its ordinary English meaning. Both cases concerned poster magazines aimed at the teenage market.

Clothing and footwear

Group 16 of Schedule 8 provides that the following items are to be zero-rated:

1. articles designed as clothing or footwear for young children and not suitable for older persons;

2. the supply of protective boots and helmets for industrial use, other than for use by employees;

3. motorcycle crash helmets.

The third item is self-explanatory. The effect of the second is that people who are buying industrial protective clothing for their own use should be able to take advantage of the zero-rate, but that such clothing should be standard-rated when supplied to employers for use by their employees.

The item that has given rise to most litigation is the first. In order to qualify for the zero-rate, it is not sufficient for the clothing to be designed for young children; it must also be unsuitable for older persons. The aim of this is to prevent smaller than average adults being able to buy their clothes at zero-rate.

In *Charles Owen & Co (Bow) Ltd v Commissioners of Customs and Excise*,[18] the Manchester VAT Tribunal held that a range of riding hats manufactured by the appellant could be zero-rated. The riding hats bore the logo "Kids' Own" and even counsel for the Commissioners accepted that a teenager "would not be seen dead in one." The Tribunal accepted that the hats were large enough to fit many older persons, because of the fact that young children's heads are disproportionately large. The Chairman said that some adults might be prepared to wear the hats because they were considerably cheaper, but suggested that any adult who did so would be exposed to "ridicule and contempt." He stated that "suitable for older persons" did not merely mean "capable of being worn by older persons." In deciding whether a garment was suitable, it was necessary to consider its fashion and style as well as its size.

---

[16]   LON/94/1710.
[17]   LON/94/698A.
[18]   [1993] VATTR 514.

Transport

Group 8 zero-rates a number of supplies in relation to transport. Among other things, it includes the supply of passenger transport and the supply of ships and aircraft above a certain weight and which are not designed or adapted for recreation or pleasure.

In *Customs and Excise Commissioners v Peninsular and Oriental Steam Navigation Company (No 2)*,[19] the High Court held that a holiday cruise was a single supply of passenger transport. The Commissioners had argued that the supply should be apportioned. The court held that the fact that the purpose of the cruise was pleasure did not prevent it from being a supply of passenger transport. However, the courts will require that the aim of the transport is to move passengers from one place to another. In *Customs and Excise Commissioners v Blackpool Pleasure Beach Co*,[20] the appellants failed to convince the High Court that a big dipper should be classed as passenger transport.

Construction

Group 5 of Schedule 8 zero-rates certain types of construction, the most significant of which is the building of new homes.

In particular, the group covers:

1. the grant of a major interest in a building by a person constructing a building designed as a dwelling or intended for use solely for a relevant residential or charitable purpose;[21]

2. the grant of a major interest in a building by a person converting that building from a non-residential building into a dwelling or a building intended for use solely for a relevant residential purpose;[22]

3. the supply in the course of construction of a building designed as a dwelling or intended for use solely for a relevant residential or charitable purpose;[23]

4. the supply in the course of construction of civil engineering work necessary for the development of a permanent park for residential caravans;[24]

5. the supply to a relevant housing association of a building which has been converted from a non-residential building to a dwelling, a number of dwellings or a building designed for a relevant residential purpose.[25]

---

[19] [1996] STC 698, QB.
[20] [1974] STC 138, [1974] 1 WLR 540, [1974] 1 All ER 1011.
[21] Group 5, Item 1(a).
[22] Group 5, Item 1(b).
[23] Group 5, Item 2(a).
[24] Group 5, Item 2(b).
[25] Group 5, Item 3.

Note that it is only the construction or first sale which is zero-rated; the subsequent sale of such buildings is exempt.[26] Construction services which are not covered by Group 5 are standard-rated or, if they fall within the scope of Schedule 7A, charged at the reduced rate.

Note 4 provides that a relevant residential purpose covers a number of uses, such as hospices, residential homes for children, the elderly, the disabled, the mentally ill and people who are dependent on alcohol or drugs. It also covers residential accommodation for students or school pupils or members of the armed forces. Homes for religious orders are covered as is any institution which is the sole or main residence of at least 90% of its residents. However, hospitals, prisons, hotels and inns are specifically excluded.

Note 6 provides that a relevant charitable purpose covers the use of a building by a charity otherwise than for business purposes. It also covers the use by a charity of a building as a village hall or similar building which is intended to provide social or recreational facilities for a local community.

Group 5 also zero-rates the supplies of any services related to the construction, apart from any services provided by architects, surveyors and people acting as consultants or in a supervisory capacity. Such supplies are standard-rated. However, if the final supply is zero-rated, the constructor will be able offset the VAT paid on such supplies.

It is important to note that Group 5 does not cover alterations or improvements to buildings; these are either standard-rated or charged at the reduced rate. The most VAT-efficient way of building is therefore to have as much work done as possible at the initial stage. For example, the building of an extension at a later date will be standard-rated,[27] whereas the same work would have been zero-rated had it been done as part of the initial construction process.

Customs and Excise have produced guidance on the distinction between building materials and furniture.[28] For example, cupboards, other than kitchen cupboards, are classed as furniture. As in many cases involving zero-rating, the extremes are easy to identify: a free-standing wardrobe is clearly a piece of furniture, whereas the cupboard under the stairs is clearly part of the house. Examples between these two extremes are more difficult to classify and Customs' guidance on the point at which a walk-in wardrobe ceases to be part of the building and becomes classed as a piece of furniture makes interesting reading.

---

[26] See below.
[27] Unless the extension will change the number of dwellings in the building, in which case it may qualify for the reduced rate. See above.
[28] See Notice 708, "Buildings and Construction."

Imports, exports and international services

The zero-rating of imports, exports and international services is a different type of zero rating from the other examples discussed in this section. The other examples are based on the principle that consumers should not have to pay VAT on certain items; export zero-rating is a question of assigning the revenue collected to the correct tax authority.

For example, suppose that a trader in France sells coffee and brandy to a trader in the United Kingdom. Both of these supplies will be zero-rated. As a result, the French trader will be able to reclaim from the French authorities the amount of VAT that he paid on the items when he bought them.[29] When the items are sold on to final consumers in the UK, the coffee will be zero-rated and the brandy standard-rated, but this is a completely separate issue from the zero-rating of the intra-Community supply[30] from the French trader to the UK trader. This latter type of zero-rating ensures that it is the UK government rather than the French government which receives the revenue charged on the sale of goods to final consumer in the UK.

This system of zero-rating both imports and intra-Community acquisitions is provided for by s.30 VATA 1994 and is supplemented by Group 13 of Schedule 8. Group 7 makes similar provisions for international services. As a result of these provisions, it is the Member State of supply that receives the revenue in respect of that supply.

Exempt Supplies

The crucial difference between exemption and zero-rating is that here traders are not permitted to deduct input tax in respect of exempt supplies. Zero-rated supplies are taxable, albeit at 0%, and so input tax can be deducted as for any other taxable supply.[31] Exempt supplies, on the other hand, are not taxable supplies, so input tax cannot be deducted. This means that a certain amount of VAT is hidden in the price of exempt supplies. The result of this distinction is that the authorities receive no revenue from zero-rated supplies – which are supposed to be taxable – yet do receive revenue as a result of exempt supplies – which are supposed to be outside the scope of VAT.

Exempt supplies are dealt with by s.31 and Schedule 9 of VATA 1994. S.31 refers to Schedule 9 and permits the Treasury to vary its content by statutory instrument. The main groups under Schedule 9 are as follows:

---

[29] France does not zero-rate foodstuffs, so VAT would have been paid on the coffee.
[30] Since the completion of the single market at the end of 1992, the words "import" and "export" only refer to trade with traders outside the Community. The terms "intra-Community supply" and "intra-Community acquisition" are used for trade between Member States. This is reflected by S.30(3) VATA 1994 which refers to goods "acquired in the United Kingdom from another member State or imported from a place outside the member States."
[31] The right to deduct input tax is discussed in the next chapter.

Group 1 - land
Group 2 - insurance
Group 3 - postal services
Group 4 - betting, gaming and lotteries
Group 5 - finance
Group 6 - education
Group 7 - health and welfare
Group 8 - burial and cremation
Group 9 - subscriptions to trade unions and professional bodies
Group 10 - sport
Group 11 - works of art
Group 12 - charitable fund-raising
Group 13 - cultural services
Group 14 - supplies where input tax cannot be recovered.

These groups reflect Article 13 of the Sixth Directive which gives two separate groups of exemptions: exemptions in the public interest (Article 13A) and "other exemptions" (Article 13B). This distinction is not found in the UK legislation, but it is worth bearing in mind that, of the list given above, groups 1 – 5 relate to "other exemptions" and groups 6 – 13 to exemptions in the public interest.   Group 14 is a special case, and is discussed in the next chapter.

Land

Since VAT is seen as a tax on consumption[32] it is arguably inappropriate to apply it to land, a commodity which cannot be consumed.

Group 1 exempts the grant of any interest in or right over land or any licence to occupy land. It then goes on to give a list of exceptions to this general rule.   The main exceptions are as follows:

1. The sale of an uncompleted building which does not qualify for zero-rating.

2. The sale of a building under three years old which does not qualify for zero-rating.

---

[32]   This point is discussed in detail in the next chapter.

3. Uncompleted civil engineering works.

4. Civil engineering works under three years old.

5. The rights to take game or fish unless person acquiring such rights acquires the fee simple of the land at the same time.

6. Holiday accommodation, rooms in hotels and pitches for caravans or tents.

7. The right to fell timber.

8. Facilities for parking cars, mooring boats or housing aircraft.

9. Seats at concerts and sporting fixtures and entry to sports facilities.

The rules on new buildings mean that the sale of any commercial property is standard-rated if it takes place within three years of construction. If the sale takes place later than this, then it is exempt.

Paragraphs 2 and 3 of Schedule 10 provide for an election to waive the exemption when land is sold or leased. This is sometimes referred to as the option to tax and its aim is to allow the developer to recover his input tax.

Insurance

Group 2 provides that insurance and reinsurance services are exempt if supplied by an authorised person.

As is clear from the text of the Sixth Directive, insurance is not exempt for reasons of public interest. It would be very difficult to make insurance transactions subject to VAT because of the difficulties involved in valuing the supplies. Very similar issues are involved in gambling transactions, as was discussed in the previous chapter.

Both transactions involve the trader collecting money from customers and paying it out again. Different customers receive different amounts, with some breaking even, some paying in more than they get out and others getting out more than they pay in. In both cases, the question is whether the value of the services provided is the total amount that the customers pay or the net amount that the trader can keep. For this reason, VAT is not particularly suitable for either type of transaction.

Postal services

Group 3 covers "the conveyance of postal packets by the Post Office." This exemption only covers Royal Mail and Parcelforce and does not extend to any privately owned carrier. As was discussed in the previous chapter, the *Plantiflor* litigation centred around this exemption.

Betting, gaming and lotteries

Group 4 exempts the following items:

1. the provision of any facilities for the placing of bets or the playing of any games of chance;

2. The granting of a right to take part in a lottery.

The notes to this group exclude, among other things, admission to premises and the provision of a gaming machine from the scope of Item 1.

As was discussed in the context of the *Glawe-Spiel* judgment, the taxable amount for gaming machine transactions is the difference between the amount paid in and the amount paid out; it is not the total amount paid into the machine.

Finance

This is the last item that is exempt for reasons other than the public interest and the rationale behind this exemption is similar to that for insurance and gambling transactions.

Group 5 and its accompanying notes give detailed lists of transactions that do and do not fall within the scope of the exemption. In particular, the granting of credit and the management of bank and building society accounts are exempt and credit reference services and the supply of coins and notes for investment purposes are taxable.

It is very difficult to see how the lending of money could be valued for VAT purposes. Borrowers pay interest to banks, but lenders also receive interest from them. One possible approach is based on the approach in *Glawe*[33] and holds that the value of the services provided by a bank is the difference between the interest it receives from borrowers and the interest that it pays to lenders. This was the approach taken in a recent report undertaken at the request of the European Commission.[34] However, this approach would cause difficulties if the VAT were to be passed on to

---

[33] See the discussion of pure cash transactions in Chapter 23.

[34] "Value Added Tax: A Study of Methods of Taxing Financial and Insurance Services, A study carried out for the European Commission by Ernst and Young." This report was published by Ernst and Young in 1996.

account holders at the bank since its logic is that, the more interest a lender receives on his account, the lower the value of the investment services that he has received from the bank. The greatest amount of VAT would therefore be paid by the holder of a current account which paid no interest. At the moment, there is no sign of any legislative proposals from the Commission in this area and it seems likely that financial services will remain exempt for a considerable time.

Exemptions in the public interest

The other items in the list above are exempt because the Community has taken the view that consumers should not be subject to tax when they buy them. Because traders cannot deduct input tax in respect of exempt supplies, the VAT that the traders themselves have had to pay will be passed on to the consumer in the form of a higher price. The right to deduct input tax is considered in the next chapter.

Between them, exemption and zero-rating account for a high proportion of VAT litigation. Cases based on mixed supplies and disbursements only arise because of the different tax rates applicable to different supplies. However, taxing all supplies at the same rate would mean taxing consumers on the most essential purchases. These issues are considered further in the final VAT chapter.

chapter twenty five

Value Added Tax - The Right to Deduct Input Tax

As discussed previously, one of the key features of VAT is traders' ability to offset input tax against output tax. The provisions governing this are set out in Article 17 of the Sixth VAT Directive and sections 24-26 of the 1994 Act and related secondary legislation. In order to deduct input tax, the following conditions must be met:

1. The trader must be a taxable person.

2. The supply must be a business supply.

3. The supply must be made to the trader.

The Finance Bill 2002 also proposes the insertion of a new provision, s.26A, which will disallow the deduction of input tax in cases where the consideration for the supply has not been paid. Even if these conditions are met, input tax may not be deducted in respect of exempt supplies or supplies for which deduction is blocked. Further special rules are applicable to traders who make a combination of taxable and exempt supplies. Each of these areas is considered below.

Taxable Persons and Business Supplies

Section 3 of the 1994 Act merely defines a taxable person as one who is required to be registered under the Act. The more detailed provisions relating to registration are contained in Schedules 1, 2, 3 and 3A, which contain far more detailed provisions than are contained in the Sixth Directive.[1] From the UK point of view, then, a taxable person is a registered trader. Traders are obliged to register for VAT once their turnover reaches a certain level. They are then not permitted to deregister until their turnover reaches a lower level. For example, 2002-2003, the

[1] The detailed rules for registration are not discussed here.

registration threshold was £55,000 and the deregistration threshold was £53,000; in 2001-02 the thresholds had been £54,000 and £52,000 respectively. Traders whose turnover is below the registration threshold may register if they so wish, but are treated as final consumers if they do not. Such traders may choose to register to enable them to deduct input tax and, possibly, because they think that a VAT registration number gives their business more credibility.

The EC approach is different: Article 4(1) of the Sixth Directive defines a taxable person as "any person who independently carries out in any place any economic activity specified in paragraph 2, whatever the purpose or results of that activity."

Article 4(2) defines such economic activities as, "all activities of producers, traders and persons supplying services, including mining and agricultural activities and activities of the professions." It goes on to provide that "the exploitation of tangible property for the purpose of obtaining income therefrom on a continuing basis shall also be considered an economic activity."

This does not mean that there is an inconsistency between EC and UK law in this area; it merely means that the particular expression "taxable person" is not being used in the same context in the 1994 Act as it is in the Sixth Directive. The section of the Act that corresponds to the EC definition of "taxable person" is s.4(1) of the Act, which provides that:

> VAT shall be charged on any supply of goods or services made in the United Kingdom, where it is a taxable supply made by a person in the course or furtherance of any business carried on by him.

"Business" is defined in s.94 as including "any trade, profession or vocation."

ECJ cases on the meaning of "economic activity"

In *Staatssecretaris van Financien v Hong-Kong Trade Development Council*[2] the Hong Kong Trade Development Council offered services, such as advice, to promote trade between Hong Kong and traders in other countries. The body was partly financed by levies and party by government grants and it made no charge for its services. Since it wanted to claim a refund of the input tax that it paid on its overheads, it argued that it should be treated as a taxable person. The ECJ held that it could not since it did not charge for its services. In *Apple and Pear Development Council v Commissioners of Customs*

---

[2] Case 89/81, 1982 ECR 1763
[3] Case 102/86, [1987] ECR 3379.

and Excise[3] the ECJ held that the Council was not a taxable person because the supplies that it made were not made for consideration. The cases show that there is a close link between making supplies for consideration and carrying out an economic activity.

In *Polysar Investments Netherlands BV v Inspecteur der Invoerrechten en Accijnzen te Arnhem*[4] the ECJ held that a holding company whose sole purpose was to acquire interests in other companies without becoming involved in their management was not a taxable person and therefore had no right to deduct input tax. The mere holding of financial interests did not constitute economic activity. While the holding of interests is undoubtedly "economic" the ECJ's point here appears to be that it is not sufficiently "active" to qualify as an economic activity.

UK cases on the meaning of "business"

Although the definition of "business" in s.94 of the 1994 Act appears to have much in common with income tax legislation, there are important differences. Firstly, there is no such concept for VAT purposes as an "adventure in the nature of business." This is illustrated by *Three H Aircraft Hire v Customs and Excise Commissioners.*[5] In this case, a partnership acquired an aircraft for its own use. Since the partners did not use the aircraft full time, they hired it out to an aircraft hire company, on the condition that it would still be available for their use at certain times. Later, the partners sold the aircraft and bought a larger one, which they also hired out to the same company on similar terms. The partnership tried to obtain VAT registration so that it could deduct the input tax paid on the aircraft. Customs and Excise refused to allow them to do this. Both the VAT Tribunal and the High Court dismissed the partnership's appeal. They held that, for a business to exist, there had to be some degree of continuity and that the purchase and subsequent sale of a single asset was not sufficient.

In *Customs and Excise Commissioners v Lord Fisher*[6] a landowner organised shoots on his estate and asked for financial contributions from the guests. The guests were mainly his friends and relations and he also contributed at least half the cost of the shoot himself. He did not make a profit and his aim in asking for a contribution was to enable the shoots to go ahead. Customs and Excise argued that he was providing services in return for a consideration and assessed him to VAT. Lord Fisher successfully appealed. The High Court held that he was not carrying on a business; the main purpose of the shoots was pleasure and social enjoyment and the fact that the participants shared the costs did not alter this.

In other cases, the Commissioners will argue against an organisation

[4]   Case C-60/90, [1991] ECR I-3111.
[5]   [1982] STC 653.
[6]   [1981] 2 All ER 147, [1981] STC 238

being classed as a business. For example, in *Compassion in World Farming v Commissioners of Customs and Excise*[7] the organisation sought registration to allow it to reclaim input tax. Its appeal was unsuccessful.

Customs and Excise Commissioners v British Field Sports Society[8] is an interesting example of the Commissioners wanting to have it both ways. They held that the Society's activities were not business activities and that its ability to recover input tax should be restricted accordingly. At the same time, they held that the Society was accountable for output tax on the all subscriptions received, allowing for an apportionment where these related to zero-rated and exempt supplies.[9] The VAT Tribunal allowed the Society's appeal and the High Court dismissed the Commissioners' appeal. In both cases, it was held that the Society provided an advantage to its members by campaigning for their interests. The court took notice of the fact that the Society's activities were done in return for its members' subscriptions; this was to be distinguished from cases where members paid subscriptions to organisations for charitable or altruistic purposes.

The Supply Must be to the Trader

The fact that a trader has paid for a supply does not necessarily mean that the supply is made to the trader, although the recent House of Lords' judgment in *Customs and Excise Commissioners v Redrow Group plc*[10] has marked a significant change in the courts' approach to this area of law. The issue is probably best illustrated by *Redrow* itself, together with two cases involving British Airways, one before the *Redrow* judgment and one after.

British Airways plc v Customs and Excise Commissioners[11] involved vouchers for free drinks and meals that British Airways issued to its passengers if flights were delayed. Passengers could exchange these vouchers at various participating restaurants and food outlets within the airport. They had the option of paying extra if they ordered food in excess of the value of the vouchers issued, but no change was given if the food ordered was of a lower value.

British Airways argued that it, rather than its passengers, was the recipient of the supplies and that VAT paid on the food was therefore deductible input tax; Customs and Excise argued that the supplies were made directly to the passengers and that British Airways could not deduct input tax. The VAT Tribunal dismissed British Airways' appeal against the assessment, pointing out that the airline did not acquire ownership of any food supplied to its passengers. An appeal to the High Court was also dismissed.

Redrow was a construction company which agreed to pay the estate

---

[7] [1997] V & DR 281
[8] [1998] 2 All ER 1003, [1998] STC 315, [1998].
[9] The provision of books and insurance services respectively.
[10] [1996] STC 365
[11] [1995] V & DR 258; [1996] STC 774.

agents' fees involved in selling its customers' existing homes. It claimed that the VAT on these fees was deductible input tax. Customs and Excise disagreed, arguing that the estate agents provided their services to Redrow's customers rather than to Redrow itself. Redrow was successful before the VAT Tribunal[12] and the Commissioners' appeal to the High Court was dismissed.[13] However, their subsequent appeal to the Court of Appeal was upheld.[14] Redrow appealed to the House of Lords.

The House of Lords allowed Redrow's appeal. According to Lord Millett:

> The commissioners begin by describing the services in question as the ordinary services of an estate agent instructed to market and sell his client's house. They then ask: to whom were those services supplied? Inevitably they answer: to the householder. They concede that Redrow derived a benefit from the services supplied by the agent and was accordingly prepared to pay for them; but they insist that this is irrelevant. The question is: to whom did the agent supply his services, not who derived a benefit from them.
>
> But this approach begs the question to be decided. The way in which the commissioners describe the services dictates the answer. But it is equally possible to begin with the services which Redrow instructed the agents to perform. This would lead to a different definition of the services in question. They would not be the ordinary service an agent instructed to market and sell his client's house, but the services of an agent instructed to market and sell a third party's house. The fact is that the nature of the services and the identity of the person to whom they are supplied cannot be determined independently of each other, for each defines the other.

Lord Millett held that the starting point should be Redrow's claim to deduct tax. Firstly, Redrow had to identify supplies of goods or services for which it had paid. Once it had established this, it had to show that it received in return something that was to be used for the purposes of its business. Lord Millett held that, while this would normally consist of goods or services supplied to the trader, it could also consist of the right to have goods or services delivered to a third party and that this right was in itself a supply of services. In reaching this conclusion, he also bore in mind that Redrow chose the estate agents and instructed them and that the householders were not able to override Redrow's instructions. The householders therefore did not have the same sort of control that they

---

12   [1995] VATTR 115.
13   [1996] STC 365.
14   [1997] STC 1053.

would have had had they instructed their own estate agents.

Relating Lord Millett's approach to the facts of *British Airways*, a sandwich seller handing a sandwich to a customer in return for a voucher could either be seen as making a supply of goods (the sandwich) to the customer or a supply of services to the airline by feeding its passengers during the delay. The approach taken by the VAT Tribunal of asking whether the airline ever acquired ownership of its passengers' meals is therefore begging the question. Not surprisingly, British Airways brought another case challenging this view. The VAT Tribunal referred to Lord Millett's approach and held that the right to have its delayed passengers fed at its expense was a supply of services to the airline.[15]

It seems likely that *Redrow* will spark a number of similar appeals and that the scope of the ruling will therefore be clarified by further judgments.

Supplies for which Deduction is Blocked

Even if all the above criteria are satisfied and the supply is a business supply made to a trader who is a taxable person, deduction of input tax may still be blocked by statute or statutory instrument. The main types of supply for which input tax is blocked are as follows.

1. Accommodation for a director of a company. S. 24(3) of the 1994 Act provides that the cost of such accommodation shall not be treated as expenditure for the purpose of the company's business.[16]

2. Works of art, antiques, collectors' items and second-hand goods. These are blocked by Article 2 of the Value Added Tax (Input Tax) Order 1992.[17]

3. Supplies for the purpose of business entertainment. (Article 5 of the Order.) There is an exception covering the entertainment of employees and company directors and managers, provided that such entertainment is not incidental to the entertainment of others, for example, customers.

4. Goods other than building materials which are incorporated in zero rated building work under Schedule 8 of the 1994 Act. (Article 6 of the Order.)

5. Motor cars. (Article 7 of the Order.) Input tax recovery on cars is blocked unless they are used exclusively for business use. This is interpreted strictly, so any car that is made available for private use

---

[15] *British Airways plc v Commissioners of Customs and Excise* [2000] V & DR 74, No. 16446.
[16] Technically, this should have been considered under the heading of business supplies, but it is more convenient to consider it as an example of a supply for which there is no deduction of input tax.
[17] SI 1992/3222.

by any person will not qualify. Conditions are less strict for taxis and driving school cars, where the requirement is that the car is used primarily for business use. There are exceptions for car-hire firms and for car dealerships where the cars are classed as trading stock.

It has been held that the rules on business entertainment in Article 5 of the Order allow for apportionment. In *Thorn EMI plc v Customs and Excise Commissioners*[18] Thorn used to exhibit electronic equipment at airshows. It had chalets built for this purpose which were largely used for entertaining customers, although they were partly used for business purposes. The Court of Appeal held that there should be an apportionment since to hold otherwise would be contrary to the right to deduct provided for by Article 17(3) of the Sixth VAT Directive.

The compatibility of Article 7 of the Order with Community Law was considered in *Royscott Leasing and Allied Domecq v Commissioners of Customs and Excise.*[19] The appellants argued that Article 7 was contrary to Article 17(3) of the Sixth Directive. The Court of Appeal referred the question to the ECJ, which held that Article 7 did not contravene the Directive. This is because Article 17(6) of the Directive provides that Member States may retain all exclusions of input tax under their national laws until harmonised legislation comes into force. It also provides that VAT shall not be deductible on expenditure which is not strictly business expenditure.

Royscott Leasing therefore makes it clear that the whole of the Input Tax Order is compatible with Community Law because of Article 17(6) of the Sixth Directive.

Exempt supplies

As discussed in the previous chapter, there is no deduction of input tax in respect of exempt supplies. In its simplest sense, this means that a trader who only deals in exempt supplies, for example a money-lending agency, cannot reclaim that VAT that it has paid on its overheads. However, the position can be more complicated for traders who make both taxable and exempt supplies. Such traders are required to apportion their general overheads, but it does not follow from this that all input tax is apportioned; input tax that relates only to exempt supplies is not deductible at all and input tax that relates only to taxable supplies is fully deductible.

When deciding whether expenditure relates to taxable or exempt supplies, the courts take a strict view, as was confirmed by the ECJ in *BLP Group Plc v Commissioners of Customs and Excise.*[20] BLP needed to raise money to pay debts which related to its taxable transactions and did this by selling

---

[18]   [1995] STC 674.
[19]   Case C-305/97, [1999] ECR I-6671.
[20]   Case C-4/94, [1995] ECR I-983.

shares in a subsidiary. In the process of selling the shares, it had to pay for advice from a merchant bank, a firm of solicitors and a firm of accountants and it sought to offset the VAT paid on these fees as input tax.

Customs and Excise argued that the VAT was not deductible, since it related to an exempt supply of shares. BLP agreed that the sale of the shares was an exempt supply, but it argued that the money was raised for the purposes of its taxable transactions. It relied on Article 17(2) of the Sixth Directive which provides that a taxable person can deduct input tax in so far as the goods and services are used for the purposes of his taxable transactions.

The VAT Tribunal held in favour of the Commissioners,[21] as did the High Court,[22] the latter also refusing to make a reference to the ECJ. BLP appealed to the Court of Appeal against the High Court's refusal to refer and this appeal was upheld. The Court of Appeal referred the case back to the High Court which made a reference to the ECJ.

Like the VAT Tribunal and the High Court, the ECJ held that the VAT was not deductible. The ability to deduct input tax depended on the nature of the supply and not the trader's purpose in making that supply. The ECJ referred to Article 17 of the Sixth VAT Directive:

> Paragraph 2 of Article 17 of the Sixth Directive must be interpreted in the light of paragraph 5 of that Article. Paragraph 5 lays down the rules applicable to the right to deduct VAT where the VAT relates to goods or services used by the taxable person "both for transactions covered by paragraphs 2 and 3, in respect of which value added tax is deductible, and for transactions in respect of which value added tax is not deductible." The use in that provision of the words "for transactions" shows that to give the right to deduct under paragraph 2, the goods or services in question must have a direct and immediate link with the taxable transactions, and that the ultimate aim pursued by the taxable person is irrelevant in this respect.[23]

Note that the "direct and immediate link" test is only applicable where a trader makes both exempt and taxable supplies; traders who make only taxable supplies can offset all their input tax and traders who only make exempt supplies can offset none. It is important only to apply the test in the correct context. In *Redrow*, the Court of Appeal used it to rule against the construction company. It argued that the direct and immediate link existed between the estate agent and the householder and not between the

---

[21] [1992] VATTR 448.
[22] [1994] STC 41.
[23] Paragraphs 18 and 19 of the judgment.

estate agent and Redrow and that the supply was therefore made to the householder. Lord Millett in the House of Lords held that this was a misreading of the test in BLP; the test was not to be used to determine the recipient of the supply but to determine whether the supply was attributable to the trader's taxable supplies. The confusion probably arose because both these issues relate to a trader's ability to deduct input tax.

A similar issue reached the ECJ in *Commissioners of Customs and Excise v Midland Bank plc.*[24] Midland Bank was the representative member of a VAT group. Another member of the group was sued for breach of contract in respect of services provided to a customer in the United States[25] and incurred considerable legal costs. Midland claimed that, since the company was allowed to deduct all the input tax in relation to the services provided, it should also be allowed to deduct all the input tax on legal costs incurred as a result. It argued that this satisfied the *BLP* test of a direct and immediate link. Customs and Excise disagreed; they argued that the legal costs related to the company's business as a whole and not just to that specific transaction. As a result, the input tax should be apportioned. The High Court made a preliminary reference to the ECJ.

The ECJ held that there was not a direct and immediate link between the legal costs and the services provided to the American company. Although the legal costs were incurred as consequence of providing these services, they did not form part of the cost components of the services, so the input tax was not deductible in full. By contrast, the legal costs were part of the trader's general costs so that there was a direct and immediate link between the legal costs and the trader's business as a whole. Because of this, the input tax had to be apportioned. The fact that the legal costs were incurred as a consequence of providing the services was not sufficient to establish a direct and immediate link

The ECJ's approach in *BLP* was followed by the High Court in *Mirror Group Newspapers Ltd v Customs and Excise Commissioners*[26] The Mirror Group made an issue of shares in 1992 and incurred over £1.5 costs in connection with this. It used the proceeds of the issue to expand its business and argued that it should therefore be allowed to deduct the VAT on these costs as input tax. The High Court applied *BLP* and held that the costs were incurred in relation to an exempt supply and so were not deductible.

The capital goods scheme

In the vast majority of cases, the VAT system draws no distinction between income and capital expenditure. It may therefore be quite normal for a trader in the first year of business to reclaim tax from Customs and Excise,

---

[24] Case C-98/98, [2000] ECR I-4177
[25] Even though the financial services in question would have been exempt, Article 17(3)(c) of the Sixth Directive provides that input tax is deductible if such services are provided to a trader established outside the Community.
[26] [2000] STC 156

since the VAT that he has paid on his plant and equipment will exceed that which he has collected on his sales.

Traders who make both taxable and exempt supplies will have to apportion the input tax on capital items in the same way that they would for their overheads, always assuming that the item is used for both taxable and exempt supplies.

This is unproblematic if the ratio of taxable to exempt supplies remains the same, but there would be considerable scope for avoidance here if rules were not put in place to deal with changes in this ratio.

For example, A sets up in business making only taxable supplies. He spends £75,000 on a computer system for his business. He offsets the VAT paid on this against his output tax and claims a refund from Customs and Excise. The following year, A expands his business so that one third of his supplies are exempt. Had this been the case when he started, he would only have been able to offset two thirds of the input tax on the computers.

The capital goods scheme operates by requiring a continual adjustment over a period of years should the ratio between taxable and exempt supplies change. The scheme is set out in Part XV of the Value Added Tax Regulations 1995[27] and applies to the following capital items:

i. a computer or an item of computer equipment worth £50,000 or more;

ii. land, buildings or civil engineering works worth £250,000 or more.

Adjustments are made over a period of five years, or ten years for certain interests in land. At the end of each year any change in the ratio between exempt and taxable supplies results either in an increased VAT liability for that year or, if the amount of exempt supplies has decreased in relation to the initial assessment, in a refund to the trader from Customs and Excise.

Applying this to A, the VAT paid on the computer will be divided into five equal parts, since the adjustment period for computer equipment is five years. In A's second year, Customs and Excise will require a payment equal to one third of one of the amount relating to the second year, so A will have to repay one fifteenth of the total VAT on the computer. If, in the third year, he only makes exempt supplies, he will have to repay another fifth of the VAT. On the other hand, if he only makes taxable supplies in the third year, no repayment will be necessary.[28]

Further Reading

Warburton J, *Value Added Tax: Business and the Predominant Concern Test* [1995] BTR 534.

---

[27] SI 1995/2518.
[28] Full details of the methods of calculation are set out in Article 115 of the VAT Regulations.

chapter twenty six
Value Added Tax - VAT as a Tax on Consumption

This chapter concludes the discussion of VAT by considering two more theoretical issues. The first is the extent to which the principle that VAT is a tax on consumption has influenced the ECJ and, in turn, courts in the UK. The second is the question of the extent to which VAT can be said to be a tax on final consumers.

The Consumption Tax Principle[1]

It is clear from the text of the First VAT Directive that VAT was intended to operate as a tax on consumption.

> The principle of the common system of value added tax involves the application to goods and services of a general tax on consumption exactly proportional to the price of the goods and services, whatever the number of transactions which take place in the production and distribution process before the stage at which the tax is charged.[2]

However, this principle was largely neglected until February 1996, when the European Court of Justice (ECJ) gave its judgment in *Jurgen Mohr v Finanzamt Bad Segeberg*[3]. This was followed in December 1997 with the ECJ's judgment in *Landboden-Agrardienste GmbH & Co KG v Finanzamt Calau*[4]. In both cases, the ECJ based its decision on the nature of VAT as a tax on consumption.

---

[1]   The sections of this chapter relating to the consumption tax principle were first published as "VAT as a Tax on Consumption: Some Thoughts on the Recent Judgment in *Parker Hale Ltd v Customs and Excise Commissioners*" [2000] BTR 545-553.

[2]   Article 2 of Directive 67/227/EEC.

[3]   (Case C-215/94) [1996] STC 328, [1996] ECR I-959, ECJ.

[4]   (Case C-384/95) [1998] STC 171, [1997] ECR I-7387, ECJ.

The approach of the European Court of Justice on VAT as a tax on consumption

The Gaston Schul *case - an example of the Court's earlier approach*

Until relatively recently, the European Court of Justice did not base any of its decisions upon the fact that VAT was a tax on consumption, although it did expressly recognise VAT as a tax on consumption in the *Gaston Schul* case[5]. The Court's approach in its earlier case law was based upon the text of the Sixth Directive[6] and also of the EC Treaty itself.

The *Gaston Schul* case concerned the import of a second-hand boat into the Netherlands from France on behalf of a private individual. The Dutch authorities charged VAT on the import at 18% of the sale price and this was challenged by Gaston Schul, the company that had imported the boat. In reaching its decision, the Court relied on Articles 25 (then 12) and 90 (then 95) of the EC Treaty as well as the text of the Sixth Directive. It concluded that the charge was not a customs duty or a charge having equivalent effect to a customs duty contrary to Article 25 since VAT was part of a Member State's internal system of taxation. As a result, the relevant article of the Treaty was Article 90. The Court then concluded that there was a breach of Article 90 to the extent that VAT already paid on the boat when it was originally sold in the exporting country had not been taken into account by the authorities in the importing country. In other words, the Dutch authorities should have calculated what percentage of the sale price of the boat represented the VAT paid by the original purchaser. They should then have deducted this amount from the amount they proposed to charge.

What is striking about the Court's decision in this case is that it makes no attempt to use arguments based on VAT's identity as a tax on consumption. For example, the original purchaser of the boat would have paid VAT on the full sale price as a tax on consumption. The fact that he was able to sell the boat demonstrates that he had not, so to speak, fully consumed it. If the boat had sunk, there would have been nothing left to sell and the first and only owner would have borne the full tax burden. On the other hand, given that the boat was sold, a certain percentage of the sale price would represent the original VAT so, by the time of import, the second buyer had already paid the consumption tax that was hidden in the second-hand price of the boat.

The Court did consider that some of the original tax was included in the second-hand price, but it did not relate this fact to the consumption tax argument. Instead, it based its decision on the principle of non-discrimination contained in Article 90:

---

[5] Case 15/81. In paragraph 10 of the judgment, the Court refers to Article 2 of Directive 67/227/EEC (The First VAT Directive).

[6] Articles 12 and 95 are renumbered as 25 and 90 respectively by the Treaty of Amsterdam.

Article 95 [now 90] of the Treaty ... prohibits not only the direct but also the indirect imposition of internal taxation on products from other Member States in excess of that on similar domestic products. That prohibition would not be complied with if imported products could be subject to the value-added tax applicable to similar domestic products without account being taken of the proportion of value-added tax with which those products are still burdened at the time of their importation.[7]

The approach taken by the ECJ in *Gaston Schul* is therefore based on the principle that there should not be discrimination against products from other Member States rather than on the principle that an individual consumer should not be taxed twice in respect of the same consumption.

This approach is consistent with the Court's earlier decisions on double taxation[8]. For example, in *Statens Kontrol med aedle Metaller v Larsen*[9], the Court stated:

The EEC Treaty does not contain any rules intended to prohibit the effects of double taxation with regard to products placed on the market in various Member States of the community. The abolition of such effects, which is desirable in the interest of the freedom of movement of goods, can however only result from the harmonization of national systems under Article 99 [now 93] or possibly Article 100 [now 94] of the Treaty.[10]

However, it is arguable that this judgment is not consistent with the Court's more recent case law.

The decision in Jürgen Mohr – *the ECJ's new approach to the consumption tax principle*

The Court's approach changed noticeably in the *Jürgen Mohr* case. This case concerned a German dairy farmer who was given a compensation payment by the government under Council Regulation 1336/86 for discontinuing milk production[11]. The German authorities argued that this payment was subject to VAT as the discontinuation of milk production was a supply of services within the meaning of Article 6(1) of the Sixth Directive[12]. This Article defines a supply of services as, "any transaction that does not constitute a supply of goods within Article 5." It expressly includes, "obligations to refrain from an act or to tolerate a situation."

---

[7] Paragraph 35 of the judgment.
[8] For a discussion of the approach taken to double taxation both by the ECJ and by the US Supreme Court, see Michel De Wolf, "The Power of Taxation in the EU and in the US," EC Tax Review1995/3 at p. 124.
[9] Case 142/77, [1978] ECR 1543.
[10] Paragraph 3 of the judgment.
[11] For a discussion of the Court's approach in this case, see Alfons L. C. Simons, "EC Court of Justice recognizes the legal character of VAT," EC Tax Review 1996, vol. 2 at p. 88.
[12] Directive 77/388/EEC.

The Court's judgment was a marked departure from its previous approach:

> It should be recalled that, according to Article 2(1) of the First Council Directive ... on the harmonization of legislation of Member States concerning turnover taxes, ... VAT is a general tax on consumption. In a case such as the present one, there is no consumption as envisaged in the Community VAT system. As the Advocate General notes, ... the Community does not acquire goods or services for its own use but acts in the common interest of promoting the proper functioning of the Community milk market. In those circumstances, the undertaking given by a farmer that he will discontinue milk production does not entail either for the Community or for the competent national authorities any benefit which would enable them to be considered consumers of a service. The undertaking in question does not therefore constitute a supply of services within the meaning of Article 6(1) of the Directive.[13]

As has been discussed earlier, the Court's previous decisions on this type of issue had concentrated on the question of a direct link between the service provided and the consideration paid. This was the approach taken in *Staatsecretaris van Financien v Cooperatieve Aardappelenbewaarplaats*[14] in which the Court held that the basis of assessment for VAT purposes was the money actually received and not a value assessed according to objective criteria. This case was relied upon by the German and Italian governments in *Jürgen Mohr* to argue that the compensation payment should be subject to VAT.[15]

The decision in **Landboden-Agrardienste** - *a confirmation of the ECJ's new approach*

The issues involved in this case were very similar to those involved in Jurgen Mohr. The compensation in question was paid by the German government to a farmer who agreed to reduce his potato production by 20%. The ECJ followed its decision in *Jürgen Mohr* and held that it made no difference that the compensation in question was paid by a Member State and not by the Community. It repeated its conclusion that the undertaking given by the farmer did not fall within the scope of the Sixth Directive because it did not constitute consumption.[16]

---

[13] Paragraphs 19-22 of the judgment.
[14] Case 154/80 [1981] ECR 445.
[15] See paragraphs 16 and 17 of the judgment.
[16] Paragraph 23 of the judgment.

The approach taken to the consumption tax issue in the United Kingdom

The main United Kingdom case to date which concerned the consumption tax issue is *Parker Hale v Customs and Excise Commissioners*.[17] Parker Hale was a manufacturer and retailer of guns. Following the Firearms (Amendment) Act 1997, it became an offence to possess, manufacture, sell or purchase many of the handguns in Parker Hale's stock. Parker Hale claimed payment under the Large-Calibre Handgun Compensation Scheme. This scheme had been set up by the government to allow payments to be made to individuals and dealers who surrendered handguns to the police. Claimants under the scheme had to sign a declaration stating that they relinquished any entitlement to the ownership or use of the handguns.

Parker Hale received an assessment to VAT from the Commissioners of Customs and Excise in respect of the payment received under the scheme. The Commissioners argued that the surrender of the guns constituted a supply of goods within the meaning of s.1 of the Value Added Tax Act 1994 and Article 5 of the Sixth VAT Directive.

Parker Hale appealed against the assessment to the London Value Added Tax Tribunal. When this appeal was dismissed, it appealed to the Queen's Bench Division of the High Court.

In the High Court, counsel for Parker Hale, Mr Robert Venables QC, relied on the judgments in *Jürgen Mohr* and *Landboden-Agrardienste*. He argued that the government's acquisition of the guns for the purposes of destruction could not be classed as consumption within the meaning of the Sixth Directive. The government could not be classed as a consumer because it was not acquiring the guns for its own use but was merely acting in the common interest and making sure that they were taken out of circulation. He argued that the compensation payment for the guns was analogous to the compensation payments for reducing production in *Jürgen Mohr* and *Landboden-Agrardienste*. He also pointed out that no distinction was made in *Jürgen Mohr* between the supply of goods and the supply of services.

Moses J. rejected these arguments. In doing so, he relied heavily on the opinion of Advocate General Jacobs in *Landboden-Agrardienste*, in particular paragraphs 22 and 23:

> In that regard it is necessary to distinguish between supplies of goods and supplies of services. As the German government illustrates ... a supply of goods by a taxable person always entails consumption regardless of the use, if any, to which the goods are put. Consumption in the context of VAT

---

[17] [2000] STC 388.

does not mean actual use but merely the acquisition of the right to dispose of the goods as owner. Where goods pass down the commercial chain they must be subject to VAT - it would be unworkable if tax authorities had to inquire whether there was actual enjoyment of the goods.

Thus, if a public authority acquires land with a view to the construction of a motorway but in the event does nothing with it, there is still a supply of goods. Moreover, the fact that the purchase is made in the public interest of a sound transport policy does not remove it from the scope of VAT.

Moses J applied this to the facts of *Parker Hale* as follows.

> I conclude, in reliance upon the Advocate General's statement of principle - which seems to me to have been endorsed by the Court of Justice - that the fact that the government acquired the guns for destruction is irrelevant. The significant feature of the transaction was that the appellant transferred title to the guns to the government. Thus, the supply of guns gave rise to consumption by the government. Consumption does not depend on questions of whether there was any further use for the guns, or if they were destroyed, but upon the acquisition of title to the goods. The acquisition in the instant case was no different from the purchase of a portrait of a well-known politician for purposes of destruction by his wife.[18]

It is clear from these extracts that both Moses J and Advocate General Jacobs see the consumption principle as applying to the supply of goods and the supply of services in completely different ways. The question of whether this distinction is satisfactory is considered next.

Should the consumption tax principle distinguish between supplies of goods and supplies of services?

Paragraph 22 of Advocate General Jacobs' opinion in *Landboden-Agrardienste* (quoted above) can be contrasted with paragraph 27 of his opinion in *Jürgen Mohr*.

> The scope of the tax is nevertheless limited by its character as a tax on consumption. A trader must supply goods or services for

---

[18] Page 397f.

consumption by identifiable customers in return for price paid by the customer or by a third party.

The different use of the consumption principle in the context of supplies of goods and supplies of services can be seen from these two passages. For supplies of services, it is treated as an extra requirement which goes beyond the text of Article 6 of the Sixth Directive. In other words, a supply can appear to satisfy the text of Article 6 and yet still not be within the scope of the Sixth Directive because no consumption can be identified. This was the case both in *Jürgen Mohr* and *Landboden-Agrardienste*. By contrast, for supplies of goods, it is assumed that a supply that satisfies the definition given in Article 5 of the Sixth Directive automatically involves consumption.

It should be pointed out, however, that the ECJ has never made a ruling on this point. The two cases in which it has applied the consumption tax principle have both been concerned with the possible supply of services. The passages relied on by Moses J in support of the distinction between goods and services in the context of consumption are taken from Advocate General Jacobs' opinion. This, while persuasive, is not binding.

Furthermore, it is arguable that the examples given by the Advocate General can be distinguished from the facts of *Parker Hale*, so it is at least possible that he would have reacted differently to this case. In paragraphs 22 and 23 of his opinion in *Landboden-Agrardienste* (quoted above), two main points stand out.

Firstly, the VAT system would be unworkable if the authorities had to enquire whether goods were actually used before they could tax them. Secondly, the fact that a public body is acting in the public interest does not mean that it cannot at the same time be a recipient of a supply of goods for the purposes of the Sixth Directive.

These arguments are both perfectly sound, but it is quite possible to accept them and yet still hold that the appeal in *Parker Hale* should have been allowed. To do this, it is necessary to argue that the consumption principle should be applied in exactly the same way to supplies of goods under Article 5 of the Sixth Directive as it is to supplies of services under Article 6. In each case, it should be possible for the supply to fall within the text of the Article and still be outside the scope of the Directive because there is no identifiable consumption.

Adopting this approach would still mean that the examples given by Advocate General Jacobs would be classed as supplies of goods. A public body acquiring land to build a motorway is analogous to a private body acquiring land to build a housing estate. In each case, there is consumption.

At this point, it is necessary to draw a distinction between the role of the state and the role of private parties. Suppose that the farmers in *Jürgen Mohr* and *Landboden-Agrardienste* had agreed with neighbouring farmers to reduce their production in return for a lump sum. This would clearly have been a supply of services within Article 6 and the neighbouring farmers would have been the consumers of those services. In the same way, suppose that a pressure group concerned about the number of handguns in circulation offered to buy guns in order to destroy them. This would clearly be a supply of goods within Article 5 and would be analogous to Moses J's example of the purchase of Churchill's portrait. Both purchases are made by consumers and VAT is a tax on consumption.

On the other hand, it is arguable that the government in *Parker Hale* is acting in a different capacity and that this is not an example of consumption at the end of the production chain; on the contrary, the government is removing the guns from the production chain to prevent them from being sold to final consumers. Advocate General Jacobs stated that goods had to be subject to VAT when they were passed down the commercial chain[19], but it is arguable the guns in *Parker Hale* were not being passed down that chain but removed from it. Applying the consumption tax argument to supplies of goods as well as to supplies of services does not mean that the tax authorities would have to find out whether goods had actually been used before they could tax them and it does not mean that government purchases in the public interest cannot be classed as consumption. What it does mean is that there should be a recognition that government purchases of goods and services do not necessarily fall within the scope of a tax on consumer spending.

Given that the underlying aim of VAT is that of a tax on consumer spending, it is arguable that the compensation for the handguns should not have been subject to VAT because the role of the government in acquiring them was not comparable to that of a final consumer. By contrast, there would have been a supply of goods had the Ministry of Defence bought the guns for issue to the forces.

To suggest that the consumption argument is not limited to the supply of services is to suggest that the courts should be prepared to look beyond the detailed provisions of Community and national VAT legislation to the underlying goal of the tax. In *Parker Hale*, this would have involved discussion of whether the government's compensation scheme was analogous to consumer spending and whether the Home Office had considered VAT in calculating the payments to be made.[20]

---

[19] Paragraph 22 of the opinion in Landboden-Agrardienste, quoted above.
[20] It is interesting to note that no mention of VAT is made in the Large-Calibre Handgun Compensation Scheme. Perhaps it would be advantageous if in future such schemes were to make it expressly clear whether or not VAT was included in the payment.

There is one further problem with retaining the distinction between goods and services in the context of consumption. Advocate General Jacobs' argument in paragraph 24 of his opinion in *Landboden-Agrardienste* is based on the lack of an identifiable consumer:

> The transaction in the present case does not fit in with that definition [the definition of consumption in Article 2 of the First Directive]. There is no consumption. The farmer does not supply goods to a consumer, he does not supply services to an identifiable consumer and he does not provide any benefit capable of forming a cost component of the activity of another person in the commercial chain.

Specific examples of the supply of services are given in Article 6 of the Sixth Directive. One, as already discussed, is the obligation to refrain from an act or to tolerate a situation. Another is the assignment of intangible property, whether or not it is the subject of a document establishing title.

It is very difficult to see how Advocate General Jacobs' argument could apply to this second example. If the person to whom tangible property is transferred is automatically a consumer under Article 5, then surely the person to whom intangible property is transferred is automatically a consumer under Article 6. Bearing this in mind, the distinction between goods and services for the purpose of the consumption argument no longer looks very strong. It was this distinction which formed the main basis of the judgment in *Parker Hale*.

Future development of the consumption tax principle

The ECJ has recently shown a willingness to consider the consumption tax principle in the cases discussed above. However, it is not yet clear how far it will be prepared to take this line of reasoning. It is disappointing that the *Parker Hale* case was not sent to the Court on a preliminary reference under Article 234 of the EC Treaty, as the case offered an ideal opportunity for the Court to clarify the scope of the consumption tax principle.

This is a principle that needs clarification on a Community-wide basis, as the present situation is unsatisfactory. The judgments in *Jürgen Mohr* and *Landboden-Agrardienste* make it clear that a transaction that falls within the text of Article 6 of the Sixth Directive can still fail to fall within the scope of that Directive because no consumption is involved. However, the opinion of Advocate General Jacobs in *Landboden-Agrardienste* suggests that this new approach does not extend to supplies of goods under Article 5 of the Sixth Directive since supplies of goods are automatically deemed to involve consumption. It may be that the ECJ would have taken this approach had a reference been made in *Parker Hale*. Alternatively, the Court could have held that the facts of *Parker Hale* were significantly different from the examples that Advocate General Jacobs gave of purchases by governments that were classed as taxable supplies. In short, a decision needed to be taken as to whether money paid by the government to acquire the guns was comparable to the payments made by the governments in *Jürgen Mohr* and *Landboden-Agrardienste* or whether it was comparable to the money paid in Advocate General Jacobs' example of a government buying land to build a motorway. The failure to make a reference in *Parker Hale* meant that the ECJ did not have the opportunity to make a definitive statement as to whether a transaction that fell within the definition of a supply of goods under Article 5 of the Sixth VAT Directive automatically involved consumption as set out in Article 2 of the First VAT Directive.

VAT as a Tax on Final Consumers

VAT as an indirect tax

As confirmed by Article 93 of the Treaty of Rome, VAT is an indirect tax. Such taxes were defined by John Stuart Mill as:

> ... those which are demanded from one person in the expectation that he shall indemnify himself at the expense of another: such as the excise or customs. The producer or importer of a commodity is called upon to pay a tax on it, not with the intention to levy a peculiar contribution upon him, but to tax through him the consumers of the commodity, from whom it is supposed that he will recover the amount by means of an advance in price.[21]

It can be seen from this that there is a split between the formal and effective burdens for VAT. Although traders are formally classed as taxpayers, the purpose behind the tax is that they should act as tax collectors. This view of VAT has been expressed by Peter Wilmott:

> VAT is nominally a tax on value added. However, governments regard its real purpose as to tax final consumption and the tax

---

[21] Principles of Political Economy, Book V, Influence of Government.

collected in instalments at each stage in the distribution process where value is added "rolls forward" to the final purchaser (who cannot deduct it) and is equal in its sum to the product of the value of the final sale and the tax rate to which it is liable. Hence the taxation of value added becomes a mere mechanism for collecting the tax rather than the underlying goal of the tax.[22]

This split between the formal and effective burdens of the tax can sometimes give rise to inconsistency within the tax structure as to whether the trader is treated as a taxpayer or a tax collector. Although the legislation refers to traders as taxpayers, there are some points in the legislation that recognise that they are in substance tax collectors.

For example, s.36 of the 1994 Act provides a certain amount of recovery for VAT that traders have paid on bad debts.[23] Provided that the trader has written off the amount in his books as a bad debt and it is more than six months since he made the supply, he is able to recover VAT that he has already paid in respect of that supply. This recognises in the longer term that traders are tax collectors; in the short term, it does little to help their cash flow. In the 2002 budget, it was announced that simplification measures for bad relief would be introduced after FA 2002 had received Royal Assent.

Another example is s.80(3), which allows the Commissioners not to refund overpaid VAT to traders where the cost of the extra VAT has been borne by someone other than the trader. This provision was applied in *Marks and Spencer plc v Customs and Excise Commissioners*.[24] This case concerned VAT which was mistakenly paid on chocolate teacakes. Supplies of these had been standard-rated since 1973 and the Commissioners acknowledge in 1994 that the supplies should have been zero-rated. In 1995, Marks and Spencer claimed a refund of all VAT paid on supplies of chocolate teacakes. The Commissioners allowed 10% of the claim, but claimed that to repay the remaining 90% would amount to unjust enrichment contrary to s.80(3) since Marks and Spencer had passed most of the VAT on to its customers and so had not itself borne the extra cost. The Commissioners' decision was upheld by the VAT Tribunal, the High Court and the Court of Appeal.

The defence of unjust enrichment has been strongly criticised by Graham Virgo.[25]

Why should it matter that the effect of overpaying the VAT is that the taxpayer is unjustly enriched? Surely this is better than that the

---

[22]   Peter Wilmott, "A Common VAT System for the European Union" EC Tax Review 1997, vol 2 at p.7.

[23]   Note that, since it is the supply that triggers the charge to VAT and not the receipt of payment, traders are liable to pay VAT on supplies for which they have not themselves received payment.

[24]   [2000] STC 16.

[25]   "Restitution of Overpaid VAT" [1998] BTR 582-591.

Commissioners should retain the money to which they are clearly not entitled. Since the justification for the taxpayer's restitionary claim is that the Commissioners had not been authorised to receive the overpaid VAT in the first place, the taxpayer's claim to restitution should outweigh the Commissioners' claim to retain the tax.[26]

The defence is certainly an acknowledgement that traders are tax collectors rather than taxpayers in that the burden of the tax is intended to fall on the final consumer. It would clearly be impracticable for either the Commissioners or the trader to refund any overpaid VAT to the consumers themselves, but this does not seem to be a particularly strong reason for refusing to refund the money to the trader.

Another feature of VAT that is consistent with seeing the trader as a tax collector rather than a taxpayer is the existence of the zero-rate. The system of exemption, however is aruably less consistent in this respect. This is discussed next.

Zero-rating and exemption

Even though the structure of VAT focuses for the most part on the trader rather than to the final consumer, zero-rating, the reduced rate and some of the categories of exemption exist to reflect the final consumer's interests. If VAT were really nothing more than a tax on traders, there would be no point in having different rates of tax. It is difficult to see why a trader who makes a profit out of selling basic foodstuffs should pay less tax than a trader who makes a profit out of selling alcohol, but it is quite sensible that a government should charge final consumers a lower rate of tax when they buy bread than it does when they buy whisky.

On the other hand, the need for different tax rates has to be balanced against the need for a neutral tax. How many of the cases considered in the previous five chapters would have arisen had there only been one rate of tax and no exemptions? Exemptions and different rates make the VAT more complicated and less neutral. Zero-rating in particular can give rise to some puzzling distinctions, as is shown by the fact that smoked salmon and caviar are basic foodstuffs whereas crisps and chocolate biscuits are not.

Of the two approaches, though, zero-rating is arguably more consistent with a tax on consumption than is exemption. The difficulty with exemption is that it prevents the trader from recovering input tax. Traders will then pass on the irrecoverable input tax to final consumers in the form of higher prices. When people are told that certain supplies are exempt

---

[26] Ibid. at p.590.

from VAT they assume, quite reasonably, that this means that no VAT is payable on those supplies. There was a public outcry in the UK recently when VAT was imposed on supplies of domestic fuel. Perhaps there would be a similar outcry if it were realised that VAT was in fact charged on services to do with funerals and cremation but that it was passed on to the customer in the form of undertakers' increased overheads.[27]

The Commission has expressed its dissatisfaction with the exemption system. It gave the following reasons for this in a Commission Services Technical Note published in 1996:[28]

i.   Distortion due to the cascade effect because suppliers of these types of services are unable to recover VAT on their purchases which is, in turn, reflected in charges for their services to customers;

ii.   distortions due to the existence of a number of options either to exempt or to tax;

iii.   the need for taxable persons who are involved in both taxable and exempt transactions to carry out often complicated apportionment calculations to determine their entitlement to deduction of VAT;

iv.   the problem for tax authorities of assessing the merits or quantum of claims for repayment of VAT under the 8th Directive from businesses which may be exempt or partially exempt in their own Member States.

These reasons are convincing. However, the Commission does not state how supplies that are currently exempt would be treated under a new system. The only two options are for them to be zero-rated or for them to be taxed and the Commission has made its opposition to zero-rating very clear. Its argument is that zero-rating threatens the efficiency of VAT and must therefore be abolished:

The Commission Services insist that, apart from the existence of a reduced rate, the VAT system and the fixing of rates should not directly pursue social objectives. Member States have other social-policy instruments at their disposal which generally have much more direct effects and are therefore much more efficient than VAT. Moreover, the incorporation of social objectives considerably complicates the application of the tax and runs the risk of producing distortions of competition. Consequently, the Commission Services do not intend, at present, to propose the retention of a zero rate,

---

[27]   Schedule 9 of the Value Added Tax Act 1994 provides that the disposal of the remains of the dead and the making of arrangements for or in connection with such disposal are exempt (Group 8, items 1 and 2). See further, "Burial, cremation and the commemoration of the dead," Customs and Excise notice 701/32.

[28]   "A Common System of VAT- A Programme for the Single Market, Description of the General Principles," Commission Services Technical Note XXI/1156/96 at p. 15.

[29]   Ibid. at p.49.

which is often justified by means of social consideration.[29]

Thus, the Commission's statement that it wants to see the abolition of exemption amounts to a statement that it wants all types of supplies of goods and services to be subject to VAT. Put this way, the argument appears rather more controversial.

When the Commission refers to "other social policy instruments," it presumably means national benefits systems and its arguments in this context have been strongly supported by Vidar Christiansen:

> It is very hard to see what can be achieved by reduced rates that cannot be achieved more efficiently by the use of better targeted instruments such as child allowances and other benefits. The economic arguments have been pointed out repeatedly. A reduced rate will introduce distortions. It will benefit the rich more than the poor, assuming only that goods are non-inferior. It will induce lobbying or rent seeking by those who have not (yet) been favoured by a reduced rate.[30]

A similar view has been expressed by Peter Sorensen:

> Such a reduced rate is normally defended on the ground that it helps to redistribute real income towards the lower income groups. However, it is widely recognized that indirect taxation is a very imprecise and inefficient means of income redistribution, and that it would be much more efficient to implement such redistribution by direct government grants to the poor.[31]

The essence of this argument is that, since only a minority cannot afford to pay VAT on essentials, there is no need to give such a concession to everyone when it would be more efficient simply to pay extra benefits to the minority. There is much to be said for this argument. On the other hand, it is questionable whether a reduced VAT rate can be dismissed as an "imprecise and inefficient means of income redistribution."[32] As Adrian Ogley has pointed out, all taxation involves income redistribution:

> ... because the principal beneficiaries of government expenditure are unlikely to be the principal contributors to tax revenue. Adam Smith

---

[30] "VIVAT, an Alternative VAT for the EU" Economic Policy, October 1996 at p. 415.

[31] "Tax Harmonization in the European Community: Problems and Prospects," Bank of Finland Research Department, 20/2/1990 at p. 23.

[32] It should be pointed out here that Peter Sorensen also argues that the Common Agricultural Policy produces artificially high food prices and that, if the CAP were to be dismantled, the case for a uniform VAT rate would be stronger. However, this argument ignores the point that reduced VAT rates are not confined to basic foodstuffs.

suggested that this redistribution should be on the basis of ability to pay and it is not easy to improve on this suggestion."[33]

Income redistribution is therefore not an optional extra but an intrinsic part of any tax system. The question is not whether the VAT system should be used to redistribute income but whether the way in which it in fact does so is an equitable one. Looking at it this way, the thinking behind reduced VAT rates is not that they help to "redistribute real income towards the lower income groups" but that they help to mitigate the effects of the tax in redistributing income away from such income groups.

The indirect nature of VAT means that the balance between the interests of the final consumer, the interests of traders and the interests of the government is always going to be a difficult one to strike. In addition, the Community aspects of VAT and the requirements of the single market mean that such a balance cannot be struck in a purely national context. VAT is in some ways a national tax and in others a Community tax; in some ways a tax on consumers and in other ways a tax on traders. It is arguable that the tax owes many of its complexities to the need to balance these various interests.

---

[33] Adrian Ogley, "Principles of Value Added Tax: A European Perspective," Interfisc Publishing 1998 at p. 191.

chapter twenty seven
Tax Planning

Whenever one activity is taxed more highly than others there is a
ceteris paribus argument that people will switch to the lightly taxed
(or untaxed) activity.[1]

Tax planning normally involves a deliberate arrangement of the taxpayer's
financial affairs such as to take advantage of the fiscal opportunities
presented by relieving provisions and/or loopholes in tax legislation.
During times of high rates of tax, the tax avoidance and planning industries
thrived through their ability to present the taxpayer (for an appropriate
fee) with "off the peg" tax planning schemes.[2] Early judicial responses to
these planning endeavours were informed and coloured by peculiar rules
developed by the courts specifically in relation to the interpretation of
taxing statutes. By virtue of the Bill of Rights 1688, taxes can only be
levied by Parliamentary legislation.[3] The imposition of income taxes in the
beginning (to finance the Napoleonic wars)[4] was seen as a mischief,
contrary to natural justice[5], and an infringement of privacy and other civil
liberties,[6] which had to be kept within its due bounds. Indeed, there were
some rather extreme responses from some very senior judges. It was Lord
Esher MR who said in *Grainger & Son v Gough*[7]:

It is no use to tell us that an Income Tax Act is assessing somebody
contrary to natural justice; it is a very solemn thing to say, no doubt,
but the truth is that all taxes in a certain sense are contrary to natural
justice; they are very hard on a great many people, but those who

---

[1] *CV Brown v PM Jackson*, "Public Sector Economics". Page 425 (4th Edition Blackweel, 1990).
[2] See *IRC v Plummer* [1979] STC 793. See also *Vestey v IRC* [1980] STC 10 (reviewed by A Sumption [1980] BTR 4) for
    an insight into the success of these schemes.
[3] The Bill of Rights provides that "the levying of money for or to the use of the Crown by pretence of prerogative without
    grant of Parliament for longer time or in other manner than the same is or shall be granted is illegal".
[4] See generally S Dowell, "A History of Taxation and Taxes in England", Vol II, page 225 (3rd edn, Frank Cass & Co Ltd,
    1965); S James and C Nobes, "The Economics of Taxation", page 125 (4th edn, Prentice Hall, 1992).
[5] See Lord Esher MR in *Grainger & Son v Gough* (1894) 3 TC 311 at 318.
[6] See S James and C Nobes, op. cit.
[7] 3 TC at 318.

impose taxes care nothing whatever on earth about the justice of the thing with regard to people, or about the injury that it does to people or hurting the feelings of people, they care nothing about that; the imposers of taxes are unpleasant tyrannical monsters – they do not care about the feelings of people, all they want to get at is the amount of the tax ...

Hence the emergence of the principles, that the subject is not to be taxed "unless the words of statute unambiguously impose the tax on him";[8] that where a statutory provision is ambiguous, the taxpayer must be given the benefit of any doubt,[9] and that the onus is on the Revenue to show that a taxing statute imposes a charge on the taxpayer. As Lord Cairns explained in *Partington v AG*[10]:

> If the person sought to be taxed comes within the letter of the law, he must be taxed, however great the hardship may appear to the judicial mind to be. On the other hand, if the crown, seeking to recover the tax, cannot bring the subject within the letter of the law, the subject is free, however apparently within the spirit of the law the case might otherwise appear to be. In other words, if there be admissible, in any statute, what is called an equitable construction, certainly such a construction is not admissible in a taxing statute, where you can simply adhere to the words of the statute.

This statement of Lord Cairns is echoed more dramatically by Rowlatt J in *Cape Brandy Syndicate v IRC*[11] when Rowlatt J was explaining the principles of construction of taxing statutes.

> [I]n taxation you have to look simply at what is clearly said. There is no room for any intendment; there is no equity about a tax: there is no presumption as to a tax; you read nothing in; you imply nothing, but you look fairly at what is said and at what is said clearly and that is the tax.

To this literalist approach to interpreting tax statutes, and the concomitant judicial responses to tax planning, has been attributed the initial successes of the tax avoidance industry – a success which has been described as being

---

[8] Per Lord Simonds in *Russell v Scott* [1948] AC 422 at 423; compare Lord Normand in Ayrshire Employers Mutual Ins. Assoc. v IRC, 27 TC 331 at 344. In CIR v Angus & Co (1889) 23 QB 579 Lord Esher MR went as far as saying: "the Crown ... must make out its right to the duty and if there be a means of evading the duty, so much the better for those who can evade it." See also Sankey J in *S W Hawker v J Compton* (1922) 8 TC 306 at 313: "If certain documents are drawn up, and the result of those documents is that persons are not liable to a particular duty, so much the better for them."
[9] Lord Thankerton in *IRC v Ross and Coulter* [1948] 1 All ER 616.
[10] [1869] LR 4 HL 100 at 122.
[11] [1921] 1 KB 64; 12 TC 358 at 366;

"to the detriment of the general body of taxpayers".[12] Some in the House of Lords inevitably have come to the conclusion that this literalist approach to the construction of taxing statutes is no longer tenable. In *IRC v McGuckian* Lord Steyn[13] referred to the advances in the law of interpretation of statutes wherein there was a shift away from literalist to purposive methods of construction. However, "tax law remained remarkably resistant to the new non-formalist methods of interpretation", and was "by and large left behind as some island of literal interpretation". He then proceeded along the lines that the literalist approach has been discarded even in this area of law. Referring to the landmark decision of the House of Lords in *IRC v Ramsay*[14] Lord Steyn said that in that case:

> Lord Wilberforce restated the principle of statutory construction that a subject is only to be taxed upon clear words ... To the question "what are clear words"? he gave the answer that the court is not confined to a literal interpretation. He added "There may, indeed should, be considered the context and scheme of the relevant Act as a whole, and its purpose may, indeed should, be regarded". This sentence was critical. It marked the rejection by the House of pure literalism in the interpretation of tax statutes.[15]

Whether or not one agrees with the conclusions of Lord Steyn in respect of the role now played by literalism in statutory construction, the nail in the coffin of literalism in tax legislation presented by him in *IRC v McGuckian* is significant. It represents the latest shot in the seemingly relentless onslaught of the House of Lords on artificial tax planning schemes. This onslaught is part of a "new approach" to tax avoidance schemes. The "old" approach was an approach that is alleged to have unduly favoured the taxpayer. That approach lay in the recognition by the House of Lords in *IRC v Duke of Westminster* that, every man is entitled if he can to order his affairs so as that the tax attaching under the appropriate Acts is less than it would otherwise be,[16] and had its high watermark in *IRC v Plummer*.[17] This seemingly blanket permission of all activities that can reduce one's taxes was however subject to the constraints of legality. This constraint had earlier been alluded to by Lord Clyde in *Ayrshire Pullman Motor Service v IRC*[18] when he said:

---

[12] Per Lord Steyn in *IRC v McGuckian* [1997] 3 All ER 817 at 824. According to Lord Steyn, the result was that the court appeared to be relegated to the role of a spectator concentrating on the individual moves in a highly skilled game, wherein the court was mesmerised by the moves in the game and paid no regard to the end result, or the strategy of the participants.

[13] [1997] 3 All ER at page 824.

[14] [1981] 1 All ER 865.

[15] [1997] 3 All ER at page 824.

[16] (1936) 19 TC at page 520 (per Lord Tomlin).

[17] [1979] STC 793.

[18] (1929) 14 TC 754 at 763-764.

No man in this country is under the smallest obligation, moral or other, so as to arrange his legal relations to his business or to his property so as to enable the Revenue to put the largest possible shovel into his shares. The Inland Revenue is not slow - and quite rightly - to take every advantage which is open to it under the taxing statutes for the purpose of depleting the taxpayers pocket. And the taxpayer is, in the like manner entitled to prevent, so far as he honestly can, the depletion of his means by the Revenue.[19]

The phrase "so far as he honestly can" in this statement is crucial, for lack of honesty in one's dealings with the Revenue is a sure recipe for trouble. Thus, there was and still is a need to distinguish between tax avoidance and tax evasion[20] - the former being perfectly lawful, while the latter is not.[21] Indeed, for the taxpayer and his/her professional advisers, tax planning schemes can be a potentially dangerous venture and need to be approached with great caution. The recent (unsuccesful) attempt by the Revenue to charge an accountant with conspiracy to defraud the Revenue in the matter of a tax-saving scheme shows.[22] The new offence of fraudulent evasion of income tax introduced by FA 2000, s.144 adds to the pressure on tax advisers and makes the need to understand clearly the distinction between tax avoidance and evasion more pressing.[23]

The distinction between tax avoidance and tax evasion was considered by the Royal Commission on the Taxation of Profits and Income in 1955. In its Final Report, the Commission stated that tax evasion:

denotes all those activities which are responsible for a person not paying the tax that the existing law charges upon his income. Ex hypothesi, he is in the wrong, though his wrongdoing may range from the making of a deliberately fraudulent return to a mere failure to make his return or to pay his tax at the proper time.[24]

In *Commissioner of Inland Revenue v Challenge Corporation Ltd*[25] Lord Templeman said that tax evasion occurs when the Commissioner is not informed of all the facts relevant to an assessment to tax. We may also add to this those cases in which the Commissioner or Inspector is actually deceived or deliberately misled as to the relevant facts.[26] Thus any action which amounts to tax evasion is as such an illegal act and does not fall within the

---

[19] Emphasis added.

[20] There is growing recognition of a concept of "tax mitigation". This is an imported concept which we shall discuss later.

[21] For a general discussion on the various descriptions of tax planning, see *A J Sawyer* [1996] BTR 483.

[22] See *R (on the application of Inland Revenue Commissioners) v Kingston Crown Court* [2001] EWHC Admin 581; [2001] BTC 322.

[23] FA 2000, s.144(1) provides that " a person commits an offence if he is knowingly concerned in the fraudulent evasion of income tax by him or any other person".

[24] Cmnd 9474, para 1016.

[25] [1987] 1 AC 155 at 167.

[26] See for example Stanley Burnton J in *R (on the application of Inland Revenue Commissioners) v Kingston Crown Court* [2001] EWHC Admin 581, para [2].

permitted "ordering of affairs" referred to by Lord Tomlin in the *Westminster* case.

On the other hand, tax avoidance is generally permitted, although the effectiveness of a tax avoidance plan will often be a contentious issue between the Revenue and the taxpayer. As to the meaning of tax avoidance, Lord Hoffmann said in *Westmoreland Investments Ltd v MacNiven*[27] that, unless statutory provisions use words like "avoidance" or "mitigation", it is not helpful to talk about them. However, we are not short of definitions – both judicial and otherwise.

Lord Nolan in *IRC v Willoughby*[28] described the concept of tax avoidance as "elusive" although he accepted as "helpful" some definitions offered in that case by counsel[29] and he then proceeded to define tax avoidance as a course of action designed to conflict with or defeat the evident intention of Parliament. Lord Hope of Craighead adopted this definition when he said in *Westmoreland Investments Ltd v MacNiven*[30] that "a course of action that was designed to defeat the intention of Parliament would fall to be treated as tax avoidance".

This definition indicates that tax avoidance involves attempts to take advantage of tax legislation in a way that Parliament did not envisage or intend. This would normally be achieved by exploitation of loopholes in the legislation, or by attempts to construct schemes which fall within the letter of the legislation but perhaps not its spirit. According to the Royal Commission on the Taxation of Profits and Income, tax avoidance consists of some act by which a person so arranges his affairs that he is liable to pay less tax than he would have paid but for the arrangement. Thus the situation which he brings about is one in which he is legally in the right.[31] The word "arrangement" is a crucial concept in this context. In Commissioner of *Inland Revenue v Challenge Corporation Ltd*[32] Lord Templeman said that income tax is avoided and a tax advantage derived from an arrangement when the taxpayer reduces his liability to tax without involving him in the loss or expenditure entitling him to that reduction. According to him, the taxpayer who is engaged in tax avoidance does not reduce his income or suffer a loss or incur expenditure but nevertheless, obtains a reduction in his liability to tax as if he had. Thus most tax avoidance involves a pretence, because the reality of the situation is normally that "in an arrangement of tax avoidance the financial position of the taxpayer is unaffected (save for the costs of devising and implementing the arrangement)".[33] Lord Goff of Chieveley waxed lyrical in *Ensign Tankers (Leasing) Ltd v Stokes*,[34] saying:

---

[27] [2001] 1 All ER 865 at 884.
[28] [1997] 4 All ER 65 at 73.
[29] Counsel for the Revenue had proffered a definition of tax avoidance as being when a taxpayer reduces his liability to tax without incurring the economic consequences that Parliament intended to be suffered by any taxpayer qualifying for such reduction in his tax liability
[30] [2001] 1 All ER 865 at 889.
[31] Cmnd 9474, para 1016.
[32] [1987] 1 AC at page 168.
[33] at page 169.
[34] [1992] BTC 110 at 128.

Unacceptable tax avoidance typically involves the creation of complex artificial structures by which, as though by the wave of a magic wand, the taxpayer conjures out of the air a loss, or a gain, or expenditure, or whatever it may be, which otherwise would never have existed. These structures are designed to achieve an adventitious tax benefit for the taxpayer, and are in truth no more than raids on the public funds at the expense of the general body of taxpayers, and as such are unacceptable.

Tax planning is often equated with tax avoidance because tax evasion cannot even come into the equation. However, as we have just seen from the speeches of two Law Lords, tax avoidance is hardly regarded as a virtue. While tax avoiders and their advisers would naturally view tax avoidance as, at worst, morally and ethically neutral[35] (they may even see it as being a commendable exercise[36]), some elements of tax avoidance can conjure images of inequity and unacceptability. Tax planning and avoidance schemes often introduce artificial "losses" or "gains" that would not have existed in straightforward transactions, and often lack genuine business and commercial intent other than the intent to avoid one's "fair share of the tax burden". Often, only the rich can afford the type of specialist advice needed to secure a successful scheme, and so, tax planning can be seen as an instrument of the rich, employed brazenly in their bid to cast their tax burden which they clearly can bear, onto the shoulders of others who often find the increased tax burden unbearable. Such considerations would then lead naturally to a perception that such behaviour is "unacceptable" and ought not to be permitted. It is this type of "unacceptable tax avoidance" that has been the focus of judicial debate and consideration in recent years. At times judicial attempts to grapple with the situation and/or to articulate the unacceptability of the taxpayer's activities has resulted in some apparent confusion over the concepts of "evasion" and "avoidance".[37] More recently, the House of Lords have admonished that:

The fact that steps taken for the avoidance of tax are acceptable or unacceptable is the conclusion at which one arrives by applying the statutory language to the facts of the case. It is not a test for deciding whether it applies or not.[38]

This serves as a warning against instinctive or emotional conclusions of unacceptability divorced from the language of the charging or exempting

---

[35] For a general discussion on the ethical issues raised by tax planning see P F Vineberg [1969] BTR 31.

[36] Contrast the view expressed about tax avoiders by Viscount Simon LC in *Latilla v IRC* [1943] AC 377 at 381: "There is, of course, no doubt that they are within their legal rights, but that is no reason why their efforts, or those of the professional gentleman who assist them in the matter, should be regarded as a commendable exercise of ingenuity or as a discharge of the duties of good citizenship."

[37] Most strikingly this was seen in *Furniss v Dawson* [1984] AC 474, when Lord Scarman appeared to refer to unacceptable 'tax avoidance' schemes as 'tax evasion' (at 513). This drew a comment from Lord Goff that "... unacceptable tax avoidance schemes which Lord Scarman described as 'tax evasion' - a label which is perhaps better kept for those transactions which are traditionally so described ...".

[38] Per Lord Hoffmann in *Westmoreland Investments Ltd v MacNiven* [2001] 1 All ER 865 at 884.

statutory provisions which are relevant to the taxpayer's transactions.

The UK does not currently have a general statutory anti-avoidance rule, and the response to the threats of tax avoidance has been left to the courts. Before we examine the judicial approaches to tax planning, there are a number of matters that we should note. First, accurate information about the level and practice of evasion and avoidance is difficult to obtain.[39] The Inland Revenue have indicated that it is "not implausible" that incomes not declared for tax purposes could amount to 7.5 % of gross domestic product. Some academic commentators say that levels of tax evasion might be high and that professionals are keen to advise on tax avoidance schemes – albeit that there was some resistance to the consideration of complex artificial tax avoidance schemes.[40] Secondly, just as accurate information on the extent of avoidance and evasion is difficult to obtain, accurate information on the causes of evasion and avoidance is just as difficult to obtain. High tax rates[41], imprecise and incomprehensible legislation, weak investigatory and legal penalties[42] might all contribute to the encouragement of tax avoidance and evasion. Some of these points are encapsulated by Kay in a statement which also highlights causes of tax avoidance[43].

> The incidence of evasion is a function of the mechanisms by which tax is assessed and collected, and the extent to which they can be controlled and monitored; the incidence of avoidance is a function of the tax base and depends on the extent to which legislation is successful in expressing the underlying economic concepts. Avoidance depends on the base: evasion on assessment procedures. There is an area which lies in between the two, and this is mainly where the tax treatment of some transaction depends on the reason for undertaking the transaction. This is bound to prove difficult to police and offers scope for distorting and misrepresenting activities which gradually shade from tax avoidance into tax evasion.

Social attitudes are also important. In some countries tax evasion is perceived as a national sport or even a moral duty. In the United Kingdom, apart from criminal liability, the social penalties of evasion are probably high (as they also appear to be in relation to complex artificial tax avoidance schemes) – although we may sympathise with the unintended evasion of the example of an elderly neighbour making and selling her home-made jam to a few close friends without any appreciation of the tax liability that should have attached to her "profits". Thirdly, one might

---

[39] See generally, M O'Higgins [1981] BTR 286 and 367; P Dean et. al. [1980] BTR 28.
[40] See M W Spicer [1975] BTR 152; Sandford, "Hidden Costs of Taxation", Institute for Fiscal Studies (1973).
[41] Brown and Jackson ("Public Sector Economics", page 424) note that the "incentives" for illegal evasion are likely to rise as marginal tax rates rise.
[42] See *Brown and Jackson*, op. cit., page 429.
[43] J A Kay, "The Economics of Tax Avoidance" [1979] BTR 354.

question why we should be concerned with the practice of tax evasion and avoidance. The answer extends beyond the social unacceptability and inequity of evasion and avoidance.[44] Included in the answer must be a consideration of the economic costs of the activity. These costs include the resource costs of the time and effort devoted to the development of evasion and avoidance schemes; the "loss" to any wealth redistribution and planning schemes; and the costs of policing and responding to evasion and avoidance developments. These costs might be seen as providing sufficient reason to pursue and regulate evasion and artificial avoidance schemes and their creators.

Judicial Responses - the Old and the New

We begin our journey through the changing and developing judicial responses to tax planning by examining what is often regarded as the "traditional approach" – one which was put forward by the House of Lords in *IRC v Duke of Westminster*.[45] The traditional or *"Westminster"* approach demands that the authorities impose a tax on the individual in accordance with the legal effects of his arrangements, and rejects the notion that one must ignore the form of a transaction to look for "the substance" of the matter. This approach demands recognition of the legal and tax result of the taxpayer's arrangements.[46] These arrangements and their legal effects are not to be undone or ignored – except in very rare circumstances, and certainly not for the sole purpose of imposing a greater tax burden on the taxpayer. In *IRC v Duke of Westminster* itself the Duke entered into a covenant to pay his gardener a yearly sum by weekly payments (£1.90 per week) for a period of seven years or during their joint lives. The covenant was expressed to be without prejudice to the gardener's normal weekly wage (£3.00), although there was an understanding that the gardener would only take the balance of £1.10 per week as his wage. The purpose of the scheme was to enable the Duke to deduct the covenanted sum in computing his total income for surtax purposes. The Revenue claimed that the covenanted sum represented the gardener's wages and could not therefore be deducted for surtax purposes. The House of Lords disagreed and held (Lord Atkin dissenting) that the covenanted sums were annual payments under Schedule D Case III and thus were deductible for surtax purposes.

The Revenue had argued that, in accordance with the doctrine that the court may ignore the legal position and have regard to "the substance of the matter", here the substance of the matter was that the gardener was serving the Duke for something equal to his former salary or wages and

---

[44] Kay points out that the opportunities for avoidance are not evenly distributed between individuals or across activities (J A Kay, "The Economics of Tax Avoidance" [1979] BTR 354 at 355-356).

[45] (1936) 19 TC 490.

[46] See Lord Atkin at page 511: "... it has to be recognised that the subject, whether poor and humble or wealthy and noble, has the legal right so to dispose of his capital and income as to attract upon himself the least amount of tax. The only function of a Court of Law is to determine the legal result of his dispositions so far as they affect tax ...".

[47] at page 520.

that, therefore, while he was so serving, the annuity must be treated as salary or wages. Lord Tomlin said[47] that this argument was based on misunderstanding of language used in some earlier cases. He said that the doctrine seemed to involve substituting "the uncertain and crooked cord of discretion" for "the golden and straight mete wand of the law".[48] Lord Tomlin emphasised the taxpayer's freedom to enjoy the benefits of the tax consequences of his affairs. The Courts must recognise and tax the legal status and effects of the taxpayer's arrangements. In a famous passage, he declared[49]:

> Every man is entitled if he can to order his affairs so that the tax attaching under the appropriate acts is less than it otherwise would be. If he succeeds in ordering them so as to secure this result, then however unappreciative the Commissioners of Inland Revenue or his fellow taxpayers may be of his ingenuity, he cannot be compelled to pay an increased tax. This so-called doctrine of "the substance" seems to to be nothing more than an attempt to make a man pay notwithstanding that he has ordered his affairs that the amount sought from him is not legally claimable.

Lord Wright said[50] that he did not understand the Revenue's arguments on the expression "payments for continuing service *ejusdem generis* with wages or salaries". He said that the payments must be one thing or the other – either annual payments or wages – and that there was no room for anything intermediate or in the nature of *cy pres*. According to him, once it is admitted that the deed is a genuine document, there is no room for the phrase "in substance" – "or, more correctly, the true nature of the legal obligation and nothing else is "the substance".[51] In this case, the legal effect and substance of the transaction were both that the Duke had entered into a legally binding and enforceable deed of covenant, the private understanding with the gardener notwithstanding. In this respect, Lord Macmillan[52] referred to the risk to which the Duke left himself exposed, "namely, that his servants may quit his employment and take their services elsewhere and yet continue to exact the covenanted weekly payments from him." This obviously would have been sufficient to indicate that payments under the covenants were not wages, because they were still payable as such even if the gardener left the Duke's employment.[53]

---

[48] ibid.
[49] ibid.
[50] at page 529.
[51] ibid.
[52] at page 527.

Thus the *Westminster* doctrine invites the taxpayer to arrange his or her affairs so as to enjoy maximum tax benefits and invites the courts to recognise the status of those arrangements and apply tax benefits and tax rules accordingly. One may take the view that this is a recognition of form over substance. Although this might be a convenient way of explaining the *Westminster* case, it is not entirely accurate. The Courts have always been willing to look beyond the presented "form" to ascertain the true status of the taxpayer's arrangements. This formally appears when the courts declare the form or label to be a "sham". Less formally it appears when the courts find that the substance dictates the form. In the determinant of legal status and in the attaching of the appropriate tax consequence, the process demands recognition of both substance and form. For example, in the *Westminster* case Lord Tomlin referred[54] to the statement of Warrington LJ in In re *Hinckes, Dashwood v Hinckes*[55] that the court does look at the substance, but that in order to ascertain the substance, the court must look at the legal effect of the bargain which the parties have entered into. Lord Tomlin thus concluded[56]:

[H]ere the substance is that which results from the legal rights and obligations of the parties ascertained upon ordinary legal principles, and, ... the conclusion must be that each annuitant is entitled to an annuity which, as between himself and the payer is liable to deduction of income tax by the payer and which the payer is entitled to treat as a deduction from his total income for surtax purposes.

Many principles have been derived from the approach exemplified by the *Westminster* case. First, it is said that one import is that a transaction which on its true construction, is of a kind that would escape tax, is not taxable on the ground that the same outcome could have been produced by entering into a transaction in another form which would have attracted tax. What this simply means is that a person ought to be taxed by reference to the transactions into which he has actually entered, and not by reference to transactions into which he might have entered to achieve the same object or result. Thus, if the object is to make a donation to my favourite charity, I have a number of possible methods of achieving this object. One method, which is not tax efficient, is to send the funds to the charity, without any ceremony. Another method is to complete the necessary formalities and give the money as a lump sum through the "gift aid"

---

[53] In *Ensign Tankers (Leasing) Ltd v Stokes*, [1992] BTC 110 at 118-119, Lord Templeman pointed out that, on the basis that the gardener was enjoying his annuity to the full, but worked voluntarily for the Duke for half wages, the embarrassments would not all be on the Duke's side. The gardener would incur liability to income tax for wages to which he was entitled but voluntarily omitted to draw. He thus preferred Lord Atkin's dissenting analysis that the gardener worked full time for full wages, and volunteered that he would not take his annuity until he had retired - "gardeners do not work for Dukes on half-wages". With respect, this analysis is as problematic as Lord Templeman thinks that the first analysis is. For one, it does not seem to accord with the actual facts of the case, and it appears to be nothing more than an attempt to reconstruct the taxpayer's transactions.

[54] at page 521.

[55] [1921] 1 Ch 475 at 489.

[56] 19 TC at page 521.

scheme. This is tax efficient and attracts tax relief. If I choose the tax efficient method, I cannot be treated "as if" I had chosen the first (and tax inefficient) method. In the context of income tax, Lord Greene MR famously explained this principle in *IRC v Wesleyan and General Assurance Society*[57].

> In dealing with income tax questions it frequently happens that there are two methods at least of achieving a particular financial result. If one of those methods is adopted, tax will be payable. If the other method is adopted, tax will not be payable. It is sufficient to refer to the common case where property is sold for a lump sum payable by instalments. If a piece of property is sold for £1,000 and the purchase price is to be paid in ten instalments of £100 each, no tax is payable. If, on the other hand, the property is sold in consideration of an annuity of £100 a year for ten years, tax is payable. The net result, form the financial point of view, is precisely the same in each case, but one method of achieving it attracts tax and the other method does not.

To relate this to *Westminster*, if the Duke wished to make regular payments to his gardener, and chose to do so by a deed of covenant rather than by a pay rise or a regular wage payment, he cannot be treated as if he did the latter. The difficulty here lies in the private "understanding" between the Duke and his gardener and whether this should be seen as part of the formal transactions, or as extraneous to it. It seems that the court preferred the latter approach, although the former also seems tenable.

Another principle that emerges from the "old" or "traditional" approach is that it is not the function of the court to stretch statutory provisions so as to "catch" a person who is involved in a tax avoidance scheme. It was Lord Simon of Glaisdale who said in *Ransom v Higgs*[58]:

> It may seem hard that a cunningly advised taxpayer should be able to avoid what appears to be his equitable share of the general fiscal burden and cast it on the shoulders of his fellow citizens. But for the courts to try and stretch the law to meet hard cases (whether the hardship appears to bear on the individual taxpayer or on the general body of taxpayers as represented by the Inland Revenue) is not merely to make bad law but to run the risk of subverting the rule of law itself. Disagreeable as it may seem that some taxpayers should escape what might appear to be their fair share of the general burden

[57] [1946] 2 All ER 749 at 751.
[58] (1974) 50 TC 1 at 94.

of national expenditure, it would be far more disagreeable to substitute the rule of caprice for that of law.

It is also clear that, unless statute otherwise provides, the fact that the taxpayer had fiscal motives for entering into the transactions do not invalidate the transactions.[59] These principles are eminently sensible and probably unassailable. Yet their application led to a thriving tax avoidance industry involving schemes of the kind which were probably never envisaged by their Lordships in *Westminster*. In particular, they seemed to encourage transactions that were so artificial that they could never have been ordinary or normal commercial transactions. But is the traditional approach really so porous so as to allow taxpayers to get away with almost anything, and, in particular, "abusive" transactions? It seems not. The traditional approach does not envisage a blinkered or blind approach to the taxpayer's activities. Although a genuine transaction may not be ignored and has to be treated as such, the court will not necessarily accept the parties' formal description of their own transactions as conclusive. Thus, "sham" transactions or documents will be disregarded. Lord Tomlin recognised this in the *Westminster* case, when he said that there may be cases where documents are not *bona fide* or intended to be acted upon, but are only used as a cloak to conceal a different transaction.[60] However, he said that no such case was made or even suggested in the case. While Lord Tomlin did not use the word "sham" to describe the types of transaction or document that he was referring to, the term has been attributed thereto in subsequent cases. The concept is still very much alive today, and the principle, even under the new approach, is that sham transactions will be disregarded. Such transactions are "void".[61]

Diplock LJ addressed the issue of sham documents in *Snook v London and West Riding Investments Ltd*[62] referring to them as those which are executed by the parties to the "sham" which are

> intended by them to give to third parties or to the court the appearance of creating between the parties legal rights or obligations different from the actual legal rights and obligations (if any) which the parties intended to create... All parties thereto must have a common intention that the acts or documents are not to create the legal rights and obligations which they give the appearance of creating. No unexpressed intentions of a "shammer" affect the rights of a party whom he has deceived.

Lord Wilberforce in *Ramsay v IRC*[63] preferred to define "sham" as referring

---

[59]   See for example Lord Wilberforce in *Ramsay v IRC* [1982] AC 300, at 323; (1981) 54 TC 101 at 184; Viscount Dilhorne in *Lupton v FA & AB Ltd* [1972] AC 635 at 655; Lord Morris in *Finsbury Securities Ltd v IRC* [1966] 1 WLR 1402 at 1417;
[60]   19 TC at page 521.
[61]   Per Arden LJ in *Hitch & Ors v Stone* [2001] BTC 78 at 96.
[62]   [1967] 2 All ER 518 at 520.
[63]   54 TC at page 184.

to documents or transactions, which, while professing to be one thing, are in fact something different, while "genuine" transactions or documents are described as those which are, in law, what they profess to be. However it is important to note that the concept of "sham" appears to enjoy a rather limited scope in that it may have become too technical in its requirements. In essence it demands evidence of an intention (common to the parties) to conceal or deceive – a fact that may make it more appropriate to be linked to tax evasion than tax avoidance. In *IRC v McGuckian*[64] Lord Steyn made it clear that tax avoidance does not necessarily mean that a transaction is a sham, and in *Hitch & Ors v Stone*[65] Arden LJ said that the fact that an act or document is uncommercial or even artificial does not mean that it is a sham. According to him a distinction should be drawn between situations where parties make an agreement that is unfavourable to one of them, or one that is artificial, and situations in which they intend some other arrangement to bind them. In the former case the agreement is intended to take effect according to its tenor, while in the latter case, the agreement is not to bind their relationship.[66]

The result is that an inquiry into whether an act or document is a sham "requires careful analysis of the facts."[67] In such an analysis, the court is not restricted to examining the parties' documents, and may examine "external evidence" – which will include the parties' explanations and circumstantial evidence such as evidence of the subsequent conduct of the parties.[68] With respect to the question of the requisite intention, the test of intention is subjective[69] and it seems that there are two parts to it.

> The parties must have intended to create different rights and obligations from those appearing from (say) the relevant document, and in addition they must have intended to give a false impression of those rights and obligations to third parties.[70]

Although the intention to deceive must be common and Diplock LJ said in *Snook* that it must be common to "all parties", it seems that the courts will not require that "in every situation every party to the act or document should be a party to the sham".[71] Arden LJ in *Hitch & Ors v Stone* rejected the "all or nothing" principle put forward by counsel for the taxpayer that, save in very exceptional circumstances, the intention must be common to all the parties. According to Arden LJ[72] the effect of this submission will be

---

[64] [1997] 3 All ER 817 at 826.
[65] [2001] BTC 78 at 92.
[66] Ibid.
[67] Per Arden LJ in *Hitch & Ors v Stone* [2001] BTC at 92.
[68] Ibid. However Arden LJ noted that the fact that parties subsequently depart from an agreement does not necessarily mean that they never intended the agreement to be effective and binding, and that the proper conclusion to draw in such a case may be that the parties agreed to vary their agreement and that they have become bound by the agreement as varied.
[69] Ibid.
[70] Ibid.
[71] Per Arden LJ in *Hitch & Ors v Stone* [2001] BTC at 96.
[72] At page 96.

that the court is precluded from finding that a document is a sham because it includes an additional provision which is intended to be effective, and this might undermine the doctrine of sham. Inherent in Arden LJ's rejection of the "all or nothing" principle is the proposition that, in proper cases, a document can be held to be partly a sham and partly effective. This type of case will be the exception rather than the rule, and will only occur "where the document reflects a transaction divisible into separate parts.[73]

The New Approach

The limitations of the traditional *Westminster* approach soon became obvious – particularly, in the context of "off the peg", artificial tax avoidance schemes. The purchasers of these "off the peg" schemes (or even tailor-made schemes) would seek to enjoy the tax consequences of each transaction in a multi-transaction scheme, examined in isolation from the whole. They would insist, relying on the *Westminster* case, that the courts should recognise the status and effects of each isolated transaction, and that such recognition should result in the application of appropriate, and often isolated, tax principles and concessions. This was in reality an invitation to ignore the fiscal reality of the overall effects of the whole scheme, but rather to concentrate on each isolated step in the scheme – steps that may well become negated or nullified by subsequent steps. It was clear that the tax system would need to respond to the artificiality of this situation – but that it must respond in a manner which would not undermine the taxpayer's freedom (strongly supported in the *Westminster* case) to organise his or her affairs so as to enjoy the maximum possible tax benefits. Parliament feared to tread here (or at least has been tardy in doing so) and so the courts have rushed in. Their intervention was, and still is controversial, as it led to the development of what clearly was (until the House of Lords recent attempts at denial in *Westmoreland Investments Ltd v MacNiven*) a general anti-avoidance rule for the UK (albeit one in judicial form), with all the problems that this brings (e.g., the lack of a consultation process, and the restrictions that the adversarial litigation procedures impose on factors that can be taken into account).

Ramsay v IRC (above) is usually considered to be the starting point for the development of a "new approach" to tax avoidance schemes. It seems however that the earliest incidences of what is now the new approach can be traced back to Lord Mansfield in the 18th century in a case where he seemed to look to the substance of a transaction that had been devised to circumvent a statutory charge, to the effect that the scheme was unsuccessful.[74] This approach seems to have been lost during the heyday of the *Westminster* approach. After *Westminster*, evidence of a changing judicial

---

[73]   Ibid.
[74]   See I Ferrier [1981] BTR 303.

attitude can be found in the case of *Floor v Davis*[75]. This case involved the disposal of shares from X to Y. In order to avoid capital gains tax, X set up a subsidiary company, and transferred shares to that company in consideration of the issue of shares. The subsidiary would then transfer those shares to Y. Subsequently, the subsidiary was dissolved and all its assets transferred to X. Thus, X had, indirectly, achieved the disposal of shares to Y through this subsidiary. On the issue of whether the "disposal" ought to be treated as one from X to Y, thus removing the capital gains tax advantages, or simply whether each step should be examined in isolation from the whole, the court opted for the latter. The decision was perceived as being in keeping and consistent with the decision in *IRC v Duke of Westminster*. The dissenting judgment of Eveleigh LJ provided an insight into changing attitudes. Eveleigh LJ suggested[76] that the courts were not required to consider each step in isolation. The real question was whether in reality they were faced with a disposal of shares from X to Y. If so, they should treat it as a transfer from X to Y and not a transfer by the subsidiary to Y – at least for tax purposes. This of course is problematic. The drafters of the capital gains tax legislation were well aware of the possibilities offered by company law and should (if that is what they desired) have provided for associated transactions. For the courts to attempt to do what the legislature failed to do is arguably objectionable.

The approach of Eveleigh LJ was later confirmed as principle in *Ramsay v IRC*. This case involved a complex series of transactions designed to create an "allowable loss" for Capital Gains Tax purposes. The true state of affairs was that, at the end of the series of transactions, the taxpayer's financial position was in reality just the same as it was at the beginning. Although the scheme produced a paper "loss", the taxpayer had not, at the end of all the transactions, suffered any real or actual loss in the sense of an appreciable and quantifiable depreciation in their assets or in the value thereof. The House of Lords decided that such artificial schemes should be looked at as a whole for the purpose of determining their tax consequences. The courts should not look to each isolated transaction but to the fiscal reality of the series of related transactions, comparing the taxpayer's position at the beginning and at the end of the scheme. Lord Wilberforce, responding to the argument that the court could not go behind a genuine document or transaction to look for some supposed underlying substance, said:[77]

> This is a cardinal principle but it must not be overstated or overextended. While obliging the court to accept documents or

[75] (1979) 52 TC 609.
[76] at pages 633-634.
[77] 54 TC at page 185.

transactions, found to be genuine, as such, it does not compel the court to look at a document or a transaction in blinkers, isolated from any context to which it properly belongs. If it can be seen that a document or transaction was intended to have effect as part of a nexus or series of transactions, or as an ingredient of a wider transaction intended as a whole, there is nothing in the doctrine to prevent it being so regarded: to do so is not to prefer form to substance, or substance to form. It is the task of the court to ascertain the legal nature of any transaction to which it is sought to attach a tax or a tax consequence and if that emerges from a series or combination of transactions, intended to operate as such, it is that series or combination which may be regarded.

This is the new approach to tax avoidance schemes. It is an approach in which one must look for the real loss or the real gain.[78] In *Ramsay v IRC*, although the scheme produced a "loss", it was not a real loss (since the taxpayer had incurred no loss in the real world), and therefore was not allowable. The principle was followed and applied in *IRC v Burmah Oil Co Ltd*[79] Here, a series of transactions were designed to create an "allowable loss" for Capital Gains Tax purposes. Lord Fraser of Tullybelton, referring to *Ramsay*, said[80] that the question was whether the scheme, when completely carried out, did or did not result in a loss such as the legislation in question is dealing with, that is, a "real loss". In the case, although the transactions involved in the scheme were real, the loss which was the end result of them was not real, and so the scheme failed.

It is interesting to note that in *Burmah Oil* Lord Diplock was careful to stress the differences between the tax avoidance scheme found as acceptable in the *Westminster* case, and the tax avoidance schemes declared unacceptable in *Ramsay* and *Burmah Oil*. The former consisted of simple arrangements between two consenting (real) persons, whereas the later involved inter-connected transactions between artificial persons (limited companies) without minds of their own but directed by a single master-mind.[81] One appeared to be an acceptable arrangement of one's affairs whereas the other appeared to be an unacceptable artificial tax avoidance scheme. Lord Diplock made it clear[82] that the new approach had not overruled the *Westminster* case. However, he also made it clear that the new approach does involve recognising that the famous dictum of Lord Tomlin in the *Westminster* case tells us little or nothing as to the methods of ordering one's affairs that will be recognised by the courts as effective to lessen the tax that would attach to them if business transactions were conducted in a straight forward way.[83] Thus while the true state of the law

---

[78]   See Parker LJ in *Craven v White* [1987] 3 WLR 660 at 704.
[79]   (1981) 54 TC 200.
[80]   at page 220.
[81]   54 TC at page 214.
[82]   ibid.
[83]   ibid.

is still that a man is entitled if he can to arrange his affairs so as to pay less tax than he otherwise have done, it seems that a further truth is that, in many cases, a man cannot do so, no matter how hard he tries.[84] This is because he may be treated under *Ramsay* as having made a different arrangement from that which he believed himself to have made. Lord Diplock clearly stated that *Ramsay* marked a "significant" change in the approach adopted by the House of Lords with respect to preordained series of transactions.[85]

The real problem is that of trying to ascertain when and in what circumstances the courts would adopt this new approach. *Furniss v Dawson*[86] provided some insight into judicial thinking in this area. The case involved a scheme to defer liability to Capital Gains Tax. The Dawsons wished to sell some shares to Wood Bastow. An outright sale would give rise to immediate tax liability under Capital Gains Tax rules. The scheme to defer tax involved the taxpayers transferring the shares (through a share exchange) to a newly incorporated Manx company, Greenjacket Investments Ltd ("Greenjacket"). Greenjacket then sold its acquisition of the taxpayer's shares to Wood Bastow. The eventual sale price equated with the originally planned sale price of £152,000. The Revenue claimed that the reality of the scheme was a chargeable disposal from the taxpayer to Wood Bastow for £152,000. Applying the new approach, the House of Lords agreed with the Revenue's assessment. The transaction was a disposal of the taxpayer's shares to Wood Bastow, and had immediate (as opposed to deferred) tax implications.

Furniss v Dawson has been referred to as the "high water mark" of the new approach. It certainly took the tax avoidance industry by surprise, since the new approach had hitherto only been applied to "circular" or self-cancelling transactions. *Furniss v Dawson* involved what has been termed a "linear" transaction, yet the House of Lords applied the new approach to that transaction. Two distinct approaches were apparent in the House of Lord's analysis of the new approach. The first approach is to be found in the speech of Lord Brightman, although Lord Brightman was careful to stress that he was adopting and following a formulation proposed by Lord Diplock in *Burmah Oil*. According to Lord Brightman[87]:

First, there must be a pre-ordained series of transactions; or, if one likes, one single composite transaction. This composite transaction may or may not include the achievement of a legitimate commercial (i.e. business) end ... Secondly, there must be steps inserted which have no commercial (business) purpose apart from the avoidance of a

---

[84] See McNeill J in *R v Inspector of Taxes, ex p Fulford-Dobson* [1987] 3 WLR at 289-290.
[85] 54 TC at page 214.
[86] [1984] STC 153; 55 TC 324. For comment, see C N Beattie [1984] BTR 109.
[87] 55 TC at page 401.
[88] 55 TC at page 392.

liability to tax - not "no business effect". If those two ingredients exist, the inserted steps are to be disregarded for fiscal purposes. The court must then look at the end result. Precisely how the end result will be taxed will depend on the terms of the taxing statute sought to be applied.

The second approach is to be found in the speech of Lord Bridge. Lord Bridge took strength from the experiences of United States Federal Courts, and suggested that, in cases of composite transactions, it was perfectly legitimate for the court to draw a distinction between the substance and the form of the composite arrangement, without in any way suggesting that any of the single transactions which make up the whole are other than genuine.[88] Under either approach, the scheme in *Furniss v Dawson* would fail.

This decision is open to the same criticism levelled at Eveleigh LJ's approach in *Floor v Davis*. It is one thing to say (as in *Ramsay*) that a step which is later cancelled by another step should be treated as just that (i.e., cancelled, and therefore of no effect), but the notion of disregarding a transaction that has not been cancelled or negated by another, is nonsensical, and ignores fiscal realities. It also raises the question how to determine what is the intermediate step inserted for no commercial purpose. For instance, in *Furniss v Dawson*, is the intermediate step the creation of Greenjacket, or the exchange of shares with Greenjacket? Supposing that, instead of a share exchange with Greenjacket, there was a share exchange with an already existing and established corporation in the Bahamas, or even in the UK, which then proceeds to sell to Wood Bastow: what then would be the result?

After *Furniss v Dawson*, there was some concern over the way in which the new approach would develop - would it confine its area of application to the rather mechanistic and legalistic requirements of Lords Brightman and Diplock, or would it follow the US approach of enjoying a wide application in searching for the substance and fiscal reality of the composite arrangement? The latter (which has been described as analogous to the search for the Holy Grail) would provide a wider scope for judicial discretion but would suffer from uncertainty and imprecision of application. In *Furniss v Dawson*, Lord Bridge resisted[89] any attempt to provide an exposition of all the criteria by which form and substance are to be distinguished. According to him, once a basic doctrine of form and substance is accepted, the drawing of precise boundaries will need to be worked out on a case by case basis. Perhaps if criteria were propounded, the "substance over form" approach would face the danger of becoming as

---

[88]   55 TC at page 392.
[89]   ibid.

mechanistic and restrictive as Lord Brightman's approach.

In any event, it is difficult to see how this "substance over form" could have been adopted without overruling the *Westminster* case, which was definite in its rejection of the "substance of the matter". It would seem that the two-point approach of Lord Brightman is preferable. This is the approach that was adopted by the House of Lords in a decision which developed further the principles of the new approach – the decision in three conjoined appeals – *Craven v White*; *IRC v Bowater Property Developments Ltd*; and *Baylis v Gregory*.[90] Both *Craven v White* and *Baylis v Gregory* involved the *Furniss v Dawson* type of share transfer schemes. In Baylis v Gregory it was originally intended that a sale to X would take place by the taxpayer transferring shares to a Manx company, followed by the Manx company then transferring those shares to X (as in *Furniss v Dawson*). However, following the transfer of the shares by the taxpayer to the Manx, X withdrew from the scheme. Eventually (some twenty months later) another buyer (Z) was found, and the sale to Z took place. The House of Lords unanimously held that the new approach did not apply – the sale was not one by the taxpayer to Z, but rather one by the Manx to Z. In *Craven v White*, the taxpayer company was considering either (i) a merger with X or (ii) a sale of its shares to Z. In preparation for the proposed merger with X, the taxpayer transferred (in a share exchange as in *Furniss v Dawson*) its shares to a Manx company. Before the merger was completed, negotiations with Z were resumed, the outcome of which was the sale of the relevant shares by the Manx company to Z. Once again, the House of Lords held (Lords Templeman and Goff dissenting) that the new approach did not apply – the sale was by the Manx company to Z, not one by the taxpayer to Z. In *IRC v Bowater Property Developments Ltd*, a scheme was devised to provide the maximum tax benefits in a sale of land. Bowater Property Developments Ltd, divided land into five parts and transferred each part to a separate company within its group. Each company then sold their part of the land to Z Ltd. The tax benefits of this arrangement enabled the five companies to enjoy individual statutory allowances under the Development Land Tax regime. If Bowater had directly sold the land to Z Ltd, Bowater only would have enjoyed statutory allowances. The House of Lords unanimously held that the new approach did not apply, and that the transfers of land were transfer by the five individual companies; not a transfer from Bowater to Z Ltd.

The importance of these three joined appeals (hereafter referred to as *Craven v White*) is reflected in how they interpreted *Furniss v Dawson* and applied the new approach. As indicated earlier, the House of Lords favoured the Brightman and Diplock approach to the question of when

---

[90] [1988] 3 All ER 495; STC 476. For comment, see R K Ashton [1988] BTR 482; G Mansfield [1989] BTR 5.

the new approach will apply. Lord Oliver, in a speech which seemed quite critical of *Furniss v Dawson*[91], was careful to emphasise that *Furniss v Dawson* simply brought forth the principles of statutory construction established in *Ramsay*. *Furniss v Dawson* was not an authority for any wider proposition such as a general proposition that any transaction which is effected for the purpose of avoiding tax on a contemplated subsequent transaction and is therefore "planned" is, for that reason, necessarily to be treated as one with that subsequent transaction and as having no independent effect even where that is realistically and logically impossible.[92]

According to Lord Oliver, the question which fell to be determined in *Furniss v Dawson* was (as it in the present case) "whether an intermediate transfer was, at the time when it was effected, so closely interconnected with the ultimate disposition that it was properly to be described as not, in itself, a real transaction at all but merely an element in some different and larger whole without independent effect."[93] He said that this was a question of fact – but one which had to be approached within the bounds of what is logically defensible. As far as *Ramsay* itself was concerned, Lord Oliver asserted that it was no authority for any proposition wider than that "where it can be shown that successive transactions are so indissolubly linked together, both in fact and in intention, as to be properly and realistically viewed as a composite whole, the court is both bound and entitled so to regard them."[94] This theme of the tight binding of the transactions flowed through the whole of Lord Oliver's speech. For example, he later again explained the principles to be derived from *Ramsay* as being that one has to look at the transactions as a whole, and ask whether "realistically they constitute a single and indivisible whole and whether it is intellectually possible so to treat them".[95] We shall examine this theme again when we look at the concept of "preordained". It suffices to say here that this theme eventually led Lord Oliver to reformulate the prerequisites for the application of the new approach. Lord Brightman's two-stage test in *Furniss v Dawson* was to the effect that, first, there must be a pre-ordained series of transactions, making one composite transaction, which may or may not include the achievement of a legitimate commercial or business effect or end, and, secondly, that there must be steps inserted into those transactions which have no commercial or business purpose apart from the avoidance of liability to tax. This test was redefined by Lord Oliver as a four-fold test[96]:

1. that the series of transactions was, at the time when an intermediate transaction was entered into it, pre-ordained in order to produce a given result;

[91]   See for example, Lord Oliver's query ([1988] 3 All ER at page 517) as to whether, apart from the tripartite contract on which reliance was placed in *Furniss v Dawson*, the reconstitution of the parties activities in that case was "rationally and logically possible within the accepted principles of construction provided by *Ramsay* or, indeed, any other principle".
[92]   [1988] 3 All ER at page 523.
[93]   ibid.
[94]   ibid.
[95]   at page 525.
[96]   at page 527.

2. that the intermediate transaction had no other purpose than tax mitigation;

3. that there was at that time no practical likelihood that the pre-planned events would not take place in the order ordained, so that the intermediate transaction was not even contemplated practically as having an independent life; and

4. that the pre-ordained events did in fact take place.

According to Lord Oliver, the court can, in these circumstances, be justified in linking the beginning with the end so as to make a single composite whole to which the fiscal results of the single composite whole are to be applied.

The majority's decision in *Craven v White* was described by Lord Templeman (dissenting) as distorting the effect of *Furniss v Dawson*, with the potential to "revive a surprised tax avoidance industry and cost the general body of taxpayers hundreds of millions of pounds by enabling artificial tax avoidance schemes to alter the incidence of taxation".[97] However, while it may indeed have had the result of distorting the effect of *Furniss v Dawson*,[98] it is arguably more principle-based than *Furniss v Dawson* itself, and, in seeking to formulate clear guidelines, it can be said to have placed the law on a clearer footing. While artificiality is an essential element for applying the new approach[99], the majority were right to reject the notion that the mere presence of an "artificial tax avoidance scheme" permits the court to intervene, and Lord Oliver's four-fold test seems to be a sensible and clear approach to the question – so long as the court is still asking itself whether it is logically, intellectually and realistically defensible to treat all the transactions as a single whole. This test employs a number of important terms, which we shall now examine.

"Pre-ordained"

Craven v White and previous cases talked of a "pre-ordained" series of transactions. It is clear that the "pre-ordained" here relates to the whole series of transactions (or the whole scheme) and not to a subset of it.[100] But what does "pre-ordained" mean? Much of Lord Oliver's speech in *Craven v White*, in pursuing the theme of tight binding of transactions, was in reality concerned with this issue. According to Lord Oliver[101], "pre-ordained" means more than simply "planned or thought out in advance." Rather, it involves a degree of certainty and control over the end result at the time when the intermediate steps are taken. This however does not require absolute certainty (in the sense that every single term of the

---

[97] at page 509.
[98] For example, Lord Keith went to the extent of saying that *Furniss v Dawson* must be restricted to its own facts (at page 501).
[99] See for example Lord Hutton in *Westmoreland Investments Ltd v MacNiven* [2001] 1 All ER at page 892.
[100] See *Fitzwilliam v IRC* [1993] BTC 8003. See especially Lord Browne-Wilkinson at page 8036.
[101] at page 528.

transaction which ultimately takes place must then be finally settled and agreed).[102] It means at least that the principal terms should be agreed to the point at which it can be said that there is no practical likelihood that the transaction which actually takes place will not take place.[103] Lord Oliver was of the view that it was insufficient that the ultimate transaction which finally takes place, although not envisaged at the intermediate stage as a concrete reality, is simply a transaction of the kind that was then envisaged. On the contrary, it must, on the facts,

> be possible to analyse the sequence as one single identifiable transaction and if, at the completion of the intermediate disposition, it is not even known to whom or upon what terms any ultimate disposition will be made, I simply do not see how such an analysis is intellectually possible.[104]

Lord Oliver was careful to emphasise that the court had no business reconstructing the parties' transactions in the quest to ascertain whether a transaction was preordained. That decision had to be made solely on the basis of the facts and events, all of which must clearly establish a "cut and dried" deal – and nothing less would suffice. This approach is linked to *Ramsay* itself. Explaining the link, Lord Oliver said[105]:

> A transaction does not change its nature because of an event, then uncertain, which subsequently occurs and *Ramsay* is concerned not with reforming transactions but with ascertaining their reality. There is a real and not merely a metaphysical distinction between something that is done as a preparatory step towards a possible but uncertain contemplated future action and something which is done as an integral and interdependent part of a transaction already agreed and, effectively, predestined to take place. In the latter case, to link the end to the beginning involves no more than recognising the reality of what is effectively a single operation *ab initio*. In the former it involves quite a different process, viz. that of imputing to the parties, *ex post facto*, an obligation (either contractual or quasi contractual) which did not exist at the material time but which is to be attributed from the occurrence or juxtaposition of events which subsequently took place. That cannot be extracted from *Furniss v Dawson* as it stands nor can it be justified by any rational extension of the *Ramsay* approach. It involves the invocation of a different principle altogether, that is to say, the reconstruction of events into something that they were not, either in fact or in intention, not

---

[102] ibid.
[103] ibid.
[104] ibid.
[105] at page 527.

because they in fact constituted a single composite whole but because, and only because, one or more of them was motivated by a desire to avoid or minimise tax. That may be a very beneficial objective but it has to be recognised that the rational basis of *Ramsay* and *Furniss v Dawson* then becomes irrelevant and is replaced by a principle of nullifying a tax advantage derived from any "associated operation."

Applying these principles in the case itself, in *Craven v White*, the final step was not practically certain or likely at the time of the intermediate step, because the taxpayer had at that time genuinely believed that a sale to Z would not take place. The taxpayer believed that a merger with X was the more probable outcome. Similarly, in *Baylis v Gregory*, the breakdown of negotiations and the subsequent sale to a different purchaser some 22 months later indicated the absence of "certainty". Likewise, in *IRC v Bowater Property Developments Ltd*, no "certainty" or pre-ordained event was present. At the time of entering into the fragmentation of the land, the ultimate purchaser was not a party to the fragmentation arrangements.

While Lord Oliver concentrated on the practical likelihood of all the pre-planned transactions taking place as planned, Lord Keith took a different approach to the question of "pre-ordained". He said[106] that, in ascertaining the true legal effect of a series of transactions, it is relevant to take into account that all the steps in it were contractually agreed in advance, or that they had been determined in advance by a guiding will (normally the taxpayer) which was in a position, for all practical purposes, to secure that all of them were carried through to completion. This is obviously a different test from the "practical likelihood" test. The latter is focused on probability, while Lord Keith's test is focused on contract, or, the ability of the taxpayer to secure the completion of the scheme. Both tests when applied to the same set of facts, may well produce different results in some cases. The "no practical likelihood test" is a "double negative" test which requires a high degree of probability, does not require certainty,[107] but possibly requires a "near certainty".[108] However, it might be more uncertain in application than Lord Keith's test, because while with the benefit of hindsight, one might feel confident to answer the question whether there was no practical likelihood that the scheme would not be carried through, it would be difficult to answer this question at the time that is material – when the intermediate steps were being taken. Invariably, it might involve "second-guessing" – something far removed from the proper judicial function. Lord Keith's test is however also not without its difficulties. How does one assess the ability of the taxpayer to secure

---

[106] at page 500.
[107] Per Knox J in *Pigott v Staines Investments Ltd* [1995] BTC 90 at 113.
[108] Knox J, ibid, at page 108.

completion? This might be easy enough in the context of corporations which are under the control of one or more of the parties to the transaction. But what about natural persons, or corporations which are not under the control of any of the parties?

Perhaps the best approach, if we are stuck with a judicial anti-avoidance rule, is to merge both tests, so that a series of transactions would be preordained if;

a. there is a contractual obligation to carry them through; or
b. there is a master-mind or guiding will who or which can secure their completion; or
c. they are pre-planned, and there is no practical likelihood that they will not be carried through as planned.

Thus it may be that there is no need to adopt an "either, or" approach to the tests. This approach to the question may have been later adopted by Lord Keith himself. In deciding in *Fitzwilliam v IRC*[109] that the scheme in that case was pre-ordained, Lord Keith seemed to apply Lord's Oliver's approach in *Craven v White*, saying that the transactions "all formed part of a pre-planned tax avoidance scheme and that there was no reasonable possibility that they would not all be carried out."

Both the Keith and Oliver tests were criticised (naturally) by Lord Templeman in his dissenting speech in *Craven v White*. First, he said[110]:

> Two transactions can form part of a scheme even though it is wholly uncertain when the first transaction is carried out whether the taxpayer who is responsible for the scheme will succeed in procuring the second transaction to be carried out at all.

And then he later added[111]:

> If the shadowy, undefined and indefinable expressions "practically certain", "practical likelihood", and "practical contemplation" possess any meanings, those expressions and those meanings are not to be derived from *Dawson*.

On that basis, Lord Templeman was able to conclude that the intentions in *Craven v White* were eventually fulfilled as part of the planned arrangements.

---

[109] [1993] BTC 8003 at 8015.
[110] at page 506.
[111] at page 508.

With respect, an approach which allows the court to intervene on the basis that there is a planned tax avoidance scheme (as defined) seems to be more objectionable in principle than the approach which seems restricts the court's intervention to cases which can realistically and intellectually be described as pre-ordained – especially one that also gives a clear definition of "pre-ordained".

"Commercial purpose"

We have examined the concept of "pre-ordained" as one of the prerequisites of the new approach. Pre-ordainment is however not necessarily fatal to a scheme's success. One other essential characteristic of a composite transaction for the purposes of the new approach centres around the question of the purposes of the individual transactions in a composite scheme. Lord Keith said in *Fitzwilliam v IRC*[112] that the fact of pre-ordainment is not sufficient in itself, to negative the application of an exemption from a tax liability which the series of transactions is intended to create, unless the series is capable of being construed in a manner inconsistent with the application of the exemption. For example, pre-ordainment cannot be used as an excuse to re-characterise a "perfectly normal and straightforward commercial transaction into a thoroughly abnormal and unusual transaction whose only merit ... is that it attracts a tax advantage".[113] Lord Brightman in *Furniss v Dawson* and Lord Oliver in *Craven v White* both pointed to a second criterion – that there are steps inserted into the pre-ordained series of transactions, for no commercial purpose, other than the avoidance of liability to tax. Such a step was treated as a "fiscal nullity" (a concept which is not without difficulty – see below) in *Furniss v Dawson*. The position was explained by Vinelott J in *Shepherd v Lyntress Ltd*[114];

> It is a necessary but not sufficient condition for the application of the *Dawson* principle that there should be a finding that the intermediate step which it is sought to disregard as having no fiscal consequence was inserted for no purpose except that of saving tax. The intermediate step is disregarded because if a composite transaction is treated as a single transaction it is evident that it falls outside the purpose of the exemption or the relief of the allowance which the taxpayer seeks to avail himself of.

---

[112] [1993] BTC at page 8015.
[113] Knox J in *Pigott v Staines Investments Ltd* [1995] BTC 90 at 118. See also *Girvan v Orange Personal Communications Services Ltd* [1998] BTC 181 (Neuberger J).
[114] [1989] STC 617; BTC 346 at 396.

According to Lord Keith in *Fitzwilliam v IRC*[115] the reference to the insertion of steps which have no commercial purpose apart from the avoidance of liability to tax indicates that this is a feature that demonstrates the artificiality of the whole scheme. This of course raises the question whether the presence of any commercial purpose demonstrates the non-artificiality of the scheme. The answer to this might be affirmative. Browne-Wilkinson VC said in *Overseas Containers (Finance) Ltd v Stoker*[116] that if essentially the transaction is of a commercial nature and there is a genuine commercial purpose, the presence of a collateral purpose to obtain a tax advantage does not "denature" what is essentially a commercial transaction. On the other hand, if the sole purpose of a transaction is to obtain a fiscal advantage, it is logically impossible to postulate the existence of any commercial purpose.[117] He went on to say[118] that a finding that the dominant purpose (as opposed to the sole purpose) was a fiscal advantage does not by itself inevitably lead to a finding in law that the taxpayer's transactions were not normal trading transactions. This seems to indicate that as soon as any commercial purpose is found, it is impossible to describe the transactions as amounting to an "artificial" tax avoidance scheme.

The problem, when the second prerequisite is found to exist lies in the correct analysis of what happens to the steps that were inserted for no commercial purposes. As indicated earlier, in *Furniss v Dawson*, such a step was treated as a "fiscal nullity" (meaning perhaps that it is treated as generating neither a gain nor a loss). In practical terms, it seems that the inserted step was simply disregarded in *Furniss v Dawson*, and then the tax consequences of the whole scheme were determined without reference to that step. This meant that the "end result" in that case (a sale by the Dawsons of their shares to Wood Bastow) was an edited version of what really happened – arguably amounting not to a construction of the parties activities, but to a reconstruction thereof. It is not difficult to see why Lord Oliver was so critical in *Craven v White* of *Furniss v Dawson*, and why Lord Keith suggested that it should be restricted to its own facts. In *Ensign Tankers (Leasing) Ltd v Stokes*[119] Lord Templeman said:

> The task of the courts is to construe documents and analyse facts and to ensure the taxpayer does not pay too little tax or too much tax but the amount of tax which is consistent with the true effect in law of the taxpayer's activities. Neither the taxpayer nor the Revenue should be deprived of the fiscal consequences of the taxpayer's activities properly analysed.

---

[115] [1993] BTC at page 8011.
[116] (1989) BTC 153 at 159.
[117] Emphasis added.
[118] at page 161.
[119] [1992] BTC at page 120.

In the light of such statements, how can the disregarding of the intermediate steps in *Furniss v Dawson* be explained or justified?

It seems that the courts are not always sure as to how to approach the matter. In *Fitzwilliam v IRC* Lord Keith[120] preferred to explain the *Furniss v Dawson* decision by saying that, in that case, the intellectual basis upon which the House was able to disregard the fiscal consequences of the interposition of Greenjacket was that all the parties involved had formally agreed upon what was to happen, but they were not formally bound to bring it about. Thus the *Ramsay* principle "made it possible to hold that the final result for fiscal purposes was the same as it would have been if the parties had been so formally bound". He subsequently suggested that it was not legitimate "to alter the character of a particular transaction in a series or to pick bits out of it and reject other bits".[121] In *Ensign Tankers (Leasing) Ltd v Stokes*[122] Millet J (as he then was) said that the principles of *Ramsay* and *Furniss v Dawson* do not entitle the court to "disregard" the component elements of a composite transaction by treating them as if they never happened. According to him, the real question is whether some step in a pre-ordained series of transactions is so closely connected with the rest that it is to be treated not as having an independent effect but as merely an element in a different and larger whole. His rationalisation of what happened in *Furniss v Dawson* is that the transfer to Greenjacket was not disregarded, but was rather treated for what it was - a step in the disposal to the ultimate purchaser. Then the question was whether that step fell within the words of a statutory exemption.[123]

These explanations of *Furniss v Dawson* seem to be trying hard to establish that that case did not really involve the disregarding of anything. On that basis, the decision can be supported, and does not contravene any established principle. It would also be able to escape the criticisms rightly directed at any judicial attempt to attribute to the parties something which they had not done. On the other hand, other judicial comment seems to accept that the reality of the situation is that transactions are being disregarded. We have already referred to Vinelott J's statement in *Shepherd v Lyntress Ltd*. That was not a lone voice. In *Fitzwilliam v IRC* Lord Browne-Wilkinson said[124] that the commissioners or the court must identify the real transaction carried out by the taxpayers and apply the words of the taxing provisions to the real transaction - and if this real transaction is carried through by a series of artificial steps, then they must disregard for fiscal purposes the steps artificially inserted. According to him the provisions of the taxing statute are to be construed as applying to the actual transaction that the parties were effecting in the real world, "not to

---

[120] [1993] BTC at page 8012.
[121] at page 8015.
[122] [1989] BTC 410 at 478.
[123] ibid.
[124] [1993] BTC at page 8035.

the artificial forms in which the parties chose to clothe it in the surrealist world of tax advisers".[125] Lord Browne–Wilkinson took the same line again in *IRC v McGuckian*,[126] saying that the approach pioneered in the *Ramsay* case and later decisions is an approach to construction, to the effect that[127]:

> in construing tax legislation, the statutory provisions are to be applied to the substance of the transaction, disregarding artificial steps in the composite transaction or series of transactions inserted only for the purpose of seeking to obtain a tax advantage.

There is no doubt that the latter analysis is the correct interpretation of the principles of and decision in *Furniss v Dawson*. The case did involve the disregarding of the interposed transactions involving Greenjacket, and this is precisely what Lord Brightman himself quite clearly said that he was doing, and what he thought that the court should do when the new approach applies. In so doing, *Furniss v Dawson* extended *Ramsay* perhaps quite unnecessarily, and also created a number of problems, which the courts have since been grappling with. The attempts of other judges and Law Lords thereafter to rationalise the decision in other ways shows the amount of disquiet that it has raised. It could perhaps rightly be described as an extreme and unwarranted form of judicial intervention.[128] The principle of disregarding certain activities, or treating them as fiscal nullities, is not only suspect, but it is also bound to be nonsensical in some cases (we will say more about this later). In *Furniss v Dawson*, the Dawsons were left at the end with shares in Greenjacket, but with no cash. Greenjacket was left with money for the sale of its property, but no capital gains tax liability. The Dawsons had a capital gains tax liability in respect of a disposal made by Greenjacket, of property belonging to Greenjacket. If the facts had been exactly the same, save that Greenjacket had been a United Kingdom as opposed to a Manx company, it is doubtful whether the decision would have been the same. However, if the true principle is that the court is seeking to ascertain the true nature of the taxpayer's activities, then it must be that that "true nature" itself cannot vary depending on whether the intermediate transactions involved United Kingdom or foreign persons. The result is, it is submitted, that the only ways in which *Furniss v Dawson* can be defended are, either to say as Lord Keith in *Craven v White* that it depended on its own facts (another way of saying that it was wrongly decided) or to explain it on the same basis as Lord Keith in *Fitzwilliam* or Millet J in *Ensign*.

Although the concept of "disregarding" transactions has often featured in speeches in the House of Lords, it can hardly be said that the House is

---

[125] ibid.
[126] [1997] 3 All ER 817.
[127] at page 823; compare Lord Steyn at page 827.
[128] This description was not accepted by Lord Steyn in *IRC v McGuckian* ([1997] 3 All ER 817 at 823–824).

unanimous in its approach to that issue, or that such a concept has been wholeheartedly endorsed by the whole House. As long as some of their Lordships continue to toe the "disregarding" line, while some are apparently averse to that form of analysis or approach, it might be argued that the debate is still open. This, coupled with the justified criticisms of judicial attempts to so reconstruct the transactions which the parties have entered into, would seem to raise questions about the defensibility of the "disregarding" approach. The House of Lords has of course been on a damage limitation exercise since *Furniss v Dawson* was decided, and, in one of their recent decisions they have tried to defend the "disregarding" approach. A most interesting analysis of what happened in *Furniss v Dawson* can be found in the ingenious application by Lord Hoffmann of the House of Lords' new "commercial concept" doctrine in *Westmoreland Investments Ltd v MacNiven*.[129] Lord Hoffmann explained[130] that Greenjacket was merely an artificially introduced intermediate party that was never intended to hold the shares for more than an instant, and that, commercially, therefore, the transaction was a transfer by the Dawsons to Wood Bastow in exchange for payment to Greenjacket. Thus, in answering what was the relevant question in that case ("to whom was the disposal made?"), the fact that the shares were routed through Greenjacket was irrelevant. Referring to Lord Brightman's famous statement on the limits of the new approach, Lord Hoffmann said[131]:

My Lords, this statement is a careful and accurate summary of the effect which the *Ramsay* construction of a statutory concept has upon the way the courts will decide whether a transaction falls within that concept or not. If the statutory language is construed as referring to a commercial concept, then it follows that steps which have no commercial purpose but which have been artificially inserted for tax purposes into a composite transaction will not affect the answer to the statutory question. When Lord Brightman said that the inserted steps are to be "disregarded for fiscal purposes", I think that he meant that they should be disregarded for the purpose of applying the relevant fiscal concept. In *Furniss'* case, this was the concept of a disposal by one person to another. For that purpose, and for that purpose only, the disposal to Greenjacket was disregarded. But that does not mean that it was treated, even for tax purposes, as if it had never happened. The payment by Wood Bastow was undoubtedly to Greenjacket and so far as this might be relevant for tax or any other purposes, it could not be disregarded.

---

[129] [2001] 1 All ER 865.
[130] At page 879.
[131] At page 880.

Thus, "disregarded for fiscal purposes" now means "disregarded for the purpose of applying the relevant fiscal concept". The question is whether this new form of words actually adds anything to the analysis or operates as a convincing defence of the disregarding approach. With all respect to Lord Hoffmann, it is submitted that it does not, for it raises as many questions as it endeavours to answer. For example, if, as Lord Hoffmann says, the relevant fiscal concept is the concept of disposal from one person to another, and that that is a commercial as opposed to juristic concept[132], how does that concept (and question) logically permit the disregarding of a disposal from one person to another? It is of no assistance to say that, under some conditions, "the commercial nature of the transaction as a whole would transcend the juristic individuality of its parts".[133] For one, this begs the question of what constitutes the relevant "commercial nature". It also begs the question of what constitutes the relevant transaction the "commercial nature" of which is at issue (something which *Ramsay* and *Furniss v Dawson* indicate is the edited version of the original).

That being so, it may be that the proper approach to steps inserted for no commercial purpose (if anything is to be done to them at all) is not to "disregard" them or treat them as "fiscal nullities", but to treat them as indistinguishable parts of the whole transaction, with no independent existence or effect of their own. And this will only be possible where it is possible in respect of such intermediate steps to say that "realistically they constituted a single and indivisible whole in which one or more of them was simply an element without independent effect", and where it is "intellectually possible so to treat them".[134]

The New Approach: Fixing the Limits

The next question that arises relates to the proper scope of the new approach. It obviously applies to income tax and capital gains tax. Is this the correct scope? Interestingly, there has been an attempt in the Court of Appeal to apply the principles of the new approach to a dispute under the Agricultural Holdings Act 1948 which had no tax connotations whatsoever. In *Gisborne v Burton*[135] Dillon LJ referred to the principles established in *Ramsay* and *Furniss v Dawson* and said:

> It seems to be that a similar principle must be applicable wherever there is a preordained series of transactions which is intended to avoid some mandatory statutory provision, even if not of a fiscal nature. You must look at the effect of the scheme as a whole, instead of concentrating on each preordained step individually, and you do not,

---

[132] [2001] 1 All ER at 879-880.
[133] At page 880.
[134] Per Lord Keith in *Fitzwilliam v IRC* [1993] BTC at page 8014; compare his Lordship at page 8016.
[135] [1988] 3 All ER 760 at 765; distinguished in *Hilton v Plustitle Ltd* [1988] 3 All ER 1051 (CA).

as it were, blow the whistle at half-time.

Russell LJ, concurring with Dillon LJ, said[136] that he had not derived "a lot of assistance" from the tax avoidance cases. However, he "gratefully" acknowledged their theme – "that where there are a number of transactions creating a composite whole the court should be astute not to consider the individual transactions in isolation but should look at the overall result of what is achieved."

It is rather astonishing that a principle which was developed in response to a specific problem – off-the-shelf artificial tax avoidance schemes – can be extended in this way.[137] If this were to be followed, it would amount to a dangerous and unwarranted excalation of judicial activism. Apart from the fact that it is not legitimate to take principles developed in response to one thing and then bolt those principles onto other unrelated areas, the *Ramsay/Dawson* principle bears no analogy with non-tax cases unless certain parts of it are to be taken out of context. It is well enough to refer to a pre-ordained series of transactions which should then be considered as a whole. This however is only half of the cake. The analysis abandons the second limb of the new approach – that there should be steps inserted for no commercial purpose other than to avoid tax, in which case the inserted steps are treated as fiscal nullities. This is where the analogy breaks down. The second limb of the new approach only makes sense in the context of tax cases and therefore it is not clear how the *Ramsay/Dawson* principle can correctly be applied to non-tax cases. It is difficult to fault the approach of Ralph Gibson LJ (dissenting) in *Gisborne v Burton* whereby he was unconvinced that the principles of the tax avoidance cases are applicable to "the construction and enforcement of a transaction in private law between private citizens".[138]

In any event, the House of Lords seems not to be too keen to extend the new approach beyond income tax and capital gains tax. In *Fitzwilliam v IRC*[139] Lord Browne-Wilkinson referred to the provisions in the capital transfer (now inheritance) tax legislation which render taxable dispositions effected by associated operations. He said that the provisions amounted to a statutory enactment, "in much wider terms", of the *Ramsay* principle, and that, accordingly, it could be argued "that there is no room for the court to adopt the *Ramsay* approach in construing an Act which expressly provides for the circumstances and occasions on which transfers carried through by 'associated operations' are to be taxed". He however felt that it was not necessary to express any concluded view on the point at this time.[140] The point raised by Lord Browne-Wilkinson is pertinent. It raises the question whether if statute already covers the field, rules of common

---

[136] [1988] 3 All ER 760 at 774.
[137] For example, in *Fitzwilliam v IRC* [1993] BTC 8003 at 8037, Lord Browne-Wilkinson said that the *Ramsay* principle is essentially based on the construction of statutory taxing provisions.
[138] at page 772.
[139] [1993] BTC at page 8037.
[140] ibid.

law on the same subject can still be applicable. This question has arisen in other areas of law, for example, in respect of the interaction between the royal prerogative and statute. In that context, the principle is that, where Parliament legislates in an area previously covered by prerogative powers, the prerogative powers will for the time being be superceded by the statute.[141] Perhaps this is the analogy being drawn here by Lord Browne-Wilkinson. With respect to statutory anti-avoidance rules, the same approach was adopted in Australia, where the High Court of Australia rejected the *Ramsay* principle on the basis that the statutory rule already covers the field.[142]

One might approach this question in the same way, and say that once Parliament has legislated in an area formerly covered by judicial doctrines, those judicial doctrines will be taken to have been superceded by statute and will become inapplicable *in toto*. Another approach would be that the judicial doctrines would give way to statute, but can lurk in the background as a residual force to be brought into effect if the statutory provision is later found to have gaps. A third approach would be that both the statutory scheme and the judicial doctrines would exist and apply side-by-side.[143] The last two approaches would be problematic in that two different sets of rules may then potentially or actually govern the same situation. The first approach would seem preferable, not least because it is an approach which already been adopted, by the House of Lords in respect of a similar question (prerogatives versus statute), and by Commonwealth courts in respect of the same question (*Ramsay* versus statutory anti-avoidance rules). It would also be preferable because only one set of rules (the statutory scheme) would cover the situation, leading to certainty. Furthermore, this would be in line with two fundamental principles (a) the supremacy of Parliament, and (b) taxation and taxation policy are matters for Parliament, not the courts.

Tax Mitigation

In some jurisdictions the concept of "tax mitigation" has been developed. The development in those jurisdictions is often explicit, entitling taxpayers to the tax benefits of their transactions only if those transactions are genuine, in the sense that the taxpayer has actually suffered the loss which entitles him or her to the tax benefits. In those circumstances the taxpayer would deserve, or would have earned the tax benefits. In an appeal from one such jurisdiction (New Zealand) the Privy Council had the opportunity to consider this term. In *Commissioner of Inland Revenue v*

---

[141] See *A-G v De Keyser's Royal Hotel* [1920] AC 508; generally, AW Bradley and KD Ewing, "Constitutional and Administrative Law", 12th edn., pages 281-282 (Addison Wesley Longman, 1997).

[142] See *John v FCT* (1989) 166 CLR 417, esp. at pages 434-435. For comment, see P Harris [1998] BTR 124; compare the Canadian Supreme Court in *Stubart Investments Ltd v The Queen* [1948] CTC 294 (see Estey J at page 305).

[143] Lord Cooke in *IRC v McGuckian* ([1997] 3 All ER at page 830) said that the *Ramsay* approach does not depend on the type of general anti-avoidance provisions found in Australasia, but is "antecedent to or collateral with them". For a critical view of this statement, see H Appleton [1999] BTR 86 at pages 90-91.

Challenge Corporation Ltd[144] Lord Templeman said that tax mitigation occurs when a tax payer:

> reduces his income or incurs expenditure in circumstances which reduce his assessable income or entitle him to reduction in his tax liability ... the taxpayers advantage is not derived from an "arrangement" but from the reduction of income which he accepts or the expenditure which he incurs.

Increasingly, this concept has crept into United Kingdom tax law. In *Ensign Tankers (Leasing) Ltd v Stokes*, Lord Templeman, who often appears to have a crusade against tax avoidance, seemed to be better disposed to tax mitigation. He took the view that there was "nothing magical about tax mitigation whereby a taxpayer suffers a loss or incurs expenditure in fact as well as in appearance".[145] He gave the example of "bed and breakfast" transactions of selling and repurchasing shares, and said that a taxpayer who carries out such a transaction establishes a loss for capital gains tax "because he has actually suffered that loss at the date of the transaction".[146] The idea is that tax mitigation is good and acceptable (and perhaps always so), because there is nothing artificial about it. This means, according to Lord Goff in *Ensign*[147], that "there is a fundamental difference between tax mitigation and unacceptable tax avoidance", because tax avoidance involves a great degree of artificiality, and is no more than a raid on public funds at the expense of the general body of taxpayers.[148] On the other hand, tax mitigation involves a loss to the pocket of the individual taxpayer, who then is entitled to claim relief for that loss.

It is interesting that no distinction is made (if one exists) between "acceptable tax avoidance" and tax mitigation. The key to tax mitigation obviously lies in its genuine, non–artificial nature, and it would seem that Lord Templeman and Lord Goff equate it with a permitted planning or ordering of one's affairs. This ordering of one's affairs may at first appear to be similar to that referred to in Lord Tomlin's *dictum* in the *Westminster* case. However, the "ordering of affairs" that Lord Tomlin was referring to was a description of acceptable tax avoidance. Logically this invites a conclusion that acceptable tax avoidance and tax mitigation are the same and are to be distinguished from tax evasion, and unacceptable (artificial) tax avoidance. This "logic" might, for the moment, be disturbed by suggesting that "acceptable" tax avoidance and tax mitigation are distinct and separate concepts because of the latter's insistence that the taxpayer "suffers" in fact as well as in appearance. However, if one points to the decision at the very

---

[144] [1987] 1 AC 155 at 167. For comment see D Nicoll [1987] BTR 134.
[145] [1992] BTC at page 124.
[146] ibid.
[147] at page 128.
[148] Lord Goff, ibid.

heart of acceptable tax avoidance (the *Westminster* case), one can see that the taxpayer did "suffer" in fact and in appearance. The covenant was for seven years, irrespective of the length of employment of the gardener. Thus, the gardener was entitled to receive the covenanted sum for the covenanted period, even if his employment had terminated within that period. The Duke had, in fact, "suffered" this obligation to pay the covenanted amount. He might be regarded, therefore, as having earned his tax benefit. This is perhaps what led Lord Templeman to say in *Ensign Tankers (Leasing) Ltd v Stokes*[149] that subsequent events have shown that although Lord Tomlin's dictum in the *Westminster* case "is accurate so far as tax mitigation is concerned it does not apply to tax avoidance."

McGuckian

IRC v McGuckian[150] is one of the more recent landmark decisions of the House of Lords on tax avoidance. In this case the taxpayers (Mr and Mrs McGuckian) were resident and domiciled in the United Kingdom, and owned all the shares in an Irish company, B Ltd. The Irish company had reserves of profits, amounting to Ir£400,055, which were available for distribution as dividends. Payment of such dividends directly to the taxpayers would have attracted an immediate charge to income tax. They thus took the advice of a tax consultant and embarked on a scheme to avoid tax on the dividends. The first step was to settle all the shares of B Ltd on trust for Mrs McGuckian as the sole income beneficiary. The trustee of the settlement was a Guernsey company, S Ltd. A direct payment of dividends by B Ltd to S Ltd (as trustee and the legal owner of the shares) would have still attracted tax, because the income would have been that of Mrs McGuckian, as a beneficiary who had a vested interest in the trust income. Thus, in furtherance of the scheme, S Ltd assigned its right to receive the dividends from B Ltd to M Ltd, a United Kingdom company associated with the tax consultant, in consideration of a payment of Ir£396,054. B Ltd then declared a dividend of Ir£400,055, and paid it to M Ltd as assignee of the right to receive it. M Ltd, in accordance with the assignment deal, paid Ir£396,054 to S Ltd, which then kept it. The difference between the two amounts was 1%, and represented fees and commission. The point of the whole scheme was to establish that the payment of Ir£396,054 to S Ltd was a capital sum – the price for the assignment of the right to receive dividends – and so was not chargeable to income tax. Two weeks before the expiry of the six-year period for raising the necessary assessments, the Revenue raised an assessment under s.478 TA 1970 – an anti-avoidance provision covering situations whereby a transfer of assets by a person ordinarily resident in the United Kingdom

[149] [1992] BTC at page 124.
[150] [1997] 3 All ER 817.

results in income being payable to a person resident or domiciled outside the United Kingdom. The Revenue argued that the assignment by S Ltd of its rights to receive the dividends was a step inserted solely for the purpose of gaining a tax advantage, and that it fell to be disregarded under the *Ramsay* principle. According to that argument, the result was that the payment Ir£396,054 that S Ltd received was a dividend from B Ltd and it was therefore income. Being income and not capital, received by a person not resident or domiciled in the United Kingdom (S Ltd), it fell to be assessed as the income of the taxpayers under s.478 TA 1970. Both the Special Commissioner and the Court of Appeal in Northern Ireland decided in favour of the taxpayers, but the House of Lords decided in favour of the Revenue.

A number of approaches are discernible from the speeches. Lord Browne-Wilkinson was content to simply apply the *Ramsay/Dawson* principles, which he felt were clearly applicable. According to him[151] the artificial step inserted was the assignment by S Ltd to M Ltd, and that step fell "to be disregarded in construing the relevant taxing provisions". His understanding of the *Ramsay* principle was to the effect that statutory provisions had to be applied to "the substance" of the transaction.[152] Lord Clyde simply applied the provisions of s.478 of TA 1970 (s.739 TA 1988) to the "substance of the whole transaction".[153] Here, the effect of the whole transaction was to carry 99% of the dividend to S Ltd, but by a circuitous route. Thus the assessment was correct.

The speeches of Lord Steyn and Lord Cooke were more far-reaching. Lord Steyn took on the whole question of the proper approach to the construction of tax statutes. The proper approach was to reject "pure literalism".[154] According to him, the *Ramsay* principle was not invented on a juristic basis independent of statute, but was rather developed as a matter of statutory construction.[155] Even in this context, it was not based on "a linguistic analysis of the meaning of particular words in a statute", but on a "broad purposive interpretation, giving effect to the intention of Parliament".[156] Therefore, the *Ramsay* principle was based on an "orthodox form of statutory interpretation". Lord Steyn said that in asserting the power to examine "the substance" of a composite transaction, the House was simply rejecting formalism and choosing "a more realistic analysis".[157] As to the current state of the law, there were two points to be made. First, Lord Tomlin's observations in the *Westminster* case still point to "a material consideration" - the liberty of the citizen to arrange his financial affairs as he thinks fit.[158] However, "they have ceased to be canonical as to the consequence of a tax avoidance scheme".[159] Thus, Lord Tomlin's

---

[151] at page 822.
[152] at page 823.
[153] at pages 831-832.
[154] at page 824.
[155] at page 825.
[156] ibid.
[157] ibid.
[158] Compare Neuberger J in *Girvan v Orange Personal Communications Services Ltd* [1998] BTC 181 at 201.
[159] ibid.

observations might be a good starting point, but they do not tell us much about what would be acceptable. Not only that, all the later decisions on the matter do not tell us the whole story either – thus the issue is still, as it were, "up for grabs". This is evident in the statement of Lord Steyn that, in the light of "the reasoning underlying the new approach it is wrong to regard the decisions of the House of Lords since the *Ramsay* case as necessarily marking the limit of the law on tax avoidance schemes".[160]

With regard to the present case itself, Lord Steyn said[161] that, while the declaration of the dividend by B Ltd was an ordinary commercial decision, the other steps (the assignment to M Ltd, the payment to M Ltd, and the payment by M Ltd to S Ltd) were not taken for any business or commercial reason, and tax avoidance was the sole reason for those steps. He said that a formalistic view of the individual tax avoidance steps and a literal interpretation of the statute in the spirit of the *Westminster* case could possibly lead to the conclusion that the money that reached S Ltd was capital. However, the court was no longer compelled to look at transactions in blinkers, and literalism had given way to purposive interpretation.[162] In the present case, he felt that the objective of the composite transaction was that S Ltd should receive the dividend. It was a classic case for the *Ramsay* principle, and the steps involving M Ltd should be disregarded for fiscal purposes.[163] Accordingly, the "end result" was the receipt by S Ltd of 99% of the dividend as income.

For Lord Cooke of Thorndon the matter was quite straightforward. He said[164] that one only had to recount the facts to see that what was received by S Ltd was essentially income. According to him the dividend was intended to be for the benefit of S Ltd, the "circular route" whereby the payment was made was merely "machinery" for giving effect to that intention, the assignment was created as a bridge or vehicle for attaining that end, and the money was unmistakably traceable through a single link.[165] Lord Cooke, like Lord Steyn, felt that the principle of looking at a planned series of steps as one whole transaction was perfectly natural and orthodox – and it was "decidedly more natural and less extreme than the decision which in 1935 a majority of their Lordships felt forced to reach in the *Duke of Westminster's case*".[166] Thus he could understand why the House was unwilling to carry the *Westminster* decision any further in *Ramsay*. The *Ramsay* principle was interpreted by him to be an application to taxing statutes of the general approach to statutory interpretation whereby, in determining the natural meaning of particular expressions in their context, weight is to be given to the purpose and spirit of the legislation.[167]

Lord Cooke took the view that the present case fell within the "limitations" specified by Lord Brightman in *Furniss v Dawson*, but added

---

[160] ibid.
[161] at page 826.
[162] at page 827.
[163] ibid.
[164] at page 828.
[165] ibid.
[166] at page 829.
[167] at pages 829-830 (emphasis added).

that, if the ultimate question is always the true bearing of a particular provision on a particular set of facts, then those limitations cannot be universals, and one must always go back to "the discernible intent of the taxing Act".[168] Thus, as far as the judicial responses to tax avoidance were concerned, "the journey's end may not yet have been found".[169]

Looking at these speeches, the following emerge. The court is entitled to look to the "substance" of a composite transaction[170] and to disregard any artificial steps inserted for no commercial purpose other than tax avoidance.[171] The court is entitled to adopt a "purposive" interpretation – meaning that they are entitled to examine the purpose and intention of the relevant legislation.[172] And, the answer to the question "where will it all end?" is very much open[173] – leaving the courts plenty of room to take their anti-avoidance doctrines as far as they wish. This is regrettable, as it is arguable that they have already taken it much too far, and, since all tax legislation exists in order to collect as much tax as possible, one can only speculate as to what their Lordships will consider to be the purpose and intention of the tax statutes.

The issue of disregarding certain transactions emerges here again with all its problems. As applied in this case, it raises as many questions as it answers. For example, their Lordships all concentrated on the assignment by S Ltd to M Ltd of its rights to receive dividends as being the artificial step inserted for no commercial purpose which should therefore be disregarded. This is rather odd. In a straightforward transaction without any fiscal considerations, B Ltd would simply have paid the dividends that it was waiting to declare directly to Mr and Mrs McGuckian. The whole point of every single step that transpired as an alternative to this straightforward payment was to convert any dividend into capital. The first step in this process was to settle the shares of B Ltd in a Guernsey trust of which S Ltd was trustee. There was no commercial purpose for that first step, or indeed, any of the other steps that followed. The step of creating the Guernsey settlement was no less artificial than the step of assigning the right to receive the dividends. On this analysis, the whole scheme from the beginning to the end should have been disregarded, leaving us with an "end result" which is a straightforward payment of a dividend by B Ltd to Mr and Mrs McGuckian. Now, this is of course not what happened in the real world – but neither is the "end result" reached by the House of Lords. What the House of Lords did was a selective disregarding of transactions – but the analysis being put forward now has the virtue of actually looking at the whole scheme (from the first to the last step), as opposed to only a part or subset of the whole scheme (from the assignment of the right to

---

[168] at page 830.
[169] ibid.
[170] Lord Browne-Wilkinson at page 823; Lord Steyn at page 825; Lord Clyde at page 832.
[171] Lord Browne-Wilkinson at pages 822 and 823; Lord Steyn at page 827.
[172] Lord Steyn at page 825; Lord Cooke at page 830.
[173] Lord Steyn at page 825; Lord Cooke at page 830.

the dividends to the last step). The fallacy of fixating on a subset only of the whole scheme had been pointed out by Lord Browne-Wilkinson himself in *Fitzwilliam v IRC*.[174] That case involved a five-step scheme. Clearly, steps two to five were "pre-ordained", but only after step one had been taken. Thus the Revenue sought to claim tax under what Lord Browne-Wilkinson described as a "mini-*Ramsay*", i.e., that steps two to five (leaving out step one) formed a pre-ordained series of transactions. According to Lord Browne-Wilkinson[175], the Revenue by seeking to set up a "mini-*Ramsay*" were attempting to attach fiscal consequences to all or some of the steps two to five, but his view that it was:

> not legitimate to attach fiscal consequences to artificial transactions designed to carry out the real transaction in question just because an attempt to demonstrate that steps 1 to 5 constituted one transaction failed for some extraneous reason i.e. that they were not pre-ordained prior to step 1.[176]

Yet, what the House of Lords, including Lord Browne-Wilkinson himself have done and have allowed the Revenue to do in *IRC v McGuckian* is to create a "mini-*Ramsay*", also by leaving the first step out of consideration when examining the whole scheme. Thus the Revenue were able to attach fiscal consequences to one of the artificial transactions (the transfer of the shares in B Ltd into the Guernsey settlement with S Ltd as trustee) while treating as a fiscal nullity one of the artificial transactions (the assignment, by S Ltd, of the right to receive dividends, to M Ltd), while also miraculously omitting to treat, for the purposes of the application of the *Ramsay* principle, the transfer of the shares to S Ltd as part of the whole scheme. This rather odd result has of course just set a precedent for the Revenue brazenly to apply "mini-*Ramsays*" whenever it suits them.

The question might be asked what the difference would be if the analysis had been adopted that, if anything was to be disregarded in this case, it had to be every step, starting from the transfer of the shares into the settlement, and ending with the receipt by S Ltd of payment from M Ltd. The simple answer is that the assessment under s.478 TA 1970 would then not have been valid. That section depends on there having been a transfer of assets, the result of which is that income becomes payable to a non-resident or non-domiciled person. If all the artificial steps in the case were disregarded for tax purposes, then no transfer of assets (shares to the Guernsey trustee, S Ltd) would be deemed to have taken place, and no income would be deemed to have become payable to an overseas person. This would leave the Revenue with an assessment which could not be

---

[174] [1993] BTC 8003 at 8036.
[175] ibid.
[176] ibid.

upheld, and (in the absence of fraud or negligence on the taxpayer's part[177]) with no further recourse. Any new assessment would have been out of time, seeing that the original assessment under s.478 TA 1970 had been raised just in the nick of time. It is unlikely that this analysis would have escaped their Lordships, and so one can only speculate as to why they opted for a "mini-*Ramsay*" and the selective disregarding of part of a subset of a partitioned scheme.

Westmoreland

As the discussion on *McGuckian* has shown, the House of Lords in their relentless quest for clarity in their anti-avoidance doctrines have continued to hand down controversial decisions. As has already been submitted, this onslaught by their Lordships seems to be very much a damage limitation exercise. *Westmoreland Investments Ltd v MacNiven*[178] recently provided them with more opportunities for damage limitation. In this case, the Lords held that the payment by a debtor of interest on a loan by means of another loan obtained from the creditor for that purpose constituted a "payment of interest" under s.338 ICTA 1988. The debtor (the taxpayer, Westmoreland) was a company owned by the creditor (ESPS - an approved superannuation scheme exempt from income tax). The total debt was over £70m, which included £40m arrears of interest. Westmoreland was valueless, but it had a substantial accrued interest liability which could not be converted to tax losses, if the interest was paid. This would make Westmoreland, an otherwise valueless company, attractive to some buyers. Westmoreland did not have the resources to pay the interest and could not raise a loan from a third party. ESPS agreed to lend money to Westmoreland for the purposes of paying the interest owed on the original debt. The accrued interest was duly paid, with Westmoreland deducting tax from the interest payments for which it accounted to the Revenue. The trustees of ESPS, as a tax-exempt superannuation scheme, reclaimed this tax from the Revenue. The Special Commissioners found that the transactions were genuine and none of the steps was a sham. Carnwath J reversed the Commissioners and found for the Crown. The Court of Appeal unanimously reversed Carnwath J's decision, and the House of Lords unanimously upheld this. The issue that arose in the case was whether the payment of a debt with a loan obtained from the same creditor was "a payment" under the legislation, or whether this was the type of transaction to which the *Ramsay* principle applied. The House of Lords held that *Ramsay* did not apply.

According to Lord Nicholls of Birkenhead[179], payment of interest in

---

[177] See s.36 TMA 1970; *Re McGuckian* [1999] BTC 152.
[178] [2001] 1 All ER 865.

s.338 has *prima facie* its normal legal meaning, and connotes simply satisfaction of the obligation to pay.[179] Here, Westmoreland's obligation to pay the accrued interest to the trustees of ESPS was discharged by satisfaction. He said that, if the Revenue were to succeed, "payment" in s.338 must bear some other meaning – and he was unable to see what that other meaning could be. According to Lord Nicholls[181], the source from which a debtor obtains the money that he used to pay his debt is, under normal circumstances, immaterial for the purposes of s.338. He concluded thus[182]:

> Leaving aside sham transactions, a debt may be discharged and replaced with another even when the only persons involved are the debtor and creditor. Once that is accepted, as I think it must be, I do not see it can matter that there was no business purpose other than gaining a tax advantage. A genuine discharge of a genuine debt cannot cease to qualify as a payment for the purpose of s.338 by reason only that it was made solely to secure a tax advantage. There is nothing in the language or context of s.338 to suggest that the purpose for which a payment of interest is made is material.

Lord Hutton noted that artificiality was a sine qua non of the application of *Ramsay*,[183] and that the payments of interest by Westmoreland were not artificial or unreal or conjured out of the air because the obligation to pay the interest was a genuine one which existed in the real world.[184] By undertaking to pay the interest, Westmoreland had "incurred the economic burden" which Parliament intended should give rise to the allowances in s.338, and it was entitled to take steps to obtain the advantage that Parliament afforded it in respect of that burden. This point was also important to Lord Hope, who said that an attempt to defeat the intention of Parliament would be treated as tax avoidance and dealt with accordingly, but that one must first discover what the statute means.[185] In this case the relevant statutory word ("payment") is to be given its ordinary meaning, whether a payment has been made is a question of fact, and the Commissioners were satisfied that payments had been made. Therefore the interest was a charge on income because it was a payment of the description in s.338.

So the Revenue lost *Westmoreland* on the facts but their Lordships had much to say about the scope of the *Ramsay* principle. In a statement that seems like an invitation to a change in terminology, Lord Nicholls said that the phrase "the *Ramsay* principle" is potentially misleading because the House of Lords did not enunciate any new principle in the *Ramsay* case.

---

[179] At page 870.
[180] Compare Lord Hope of Craighead at page 889: "The words 'paid' and 'payment' are to be construed according to their ordinary meaning. The question whether a payment has been made is a question of fact."
[181] At page 871.
[182] Ibid.
[183] At page 892.

Rather, what the House did was "to highlight that, confronted with new and sophisticated tax avoidance devices, the courts' duty is to determine the legal nature of the transactions in question and then relate them to the fiscal legislation"[186] (i.e., to the language of the statute). Thus, if a scheme has the apparently magical result of creating a loss without the taxpayer suffering any financial detriment, then the question arises whether this artificial loss is "a loss within the meaning of the relevant statutory provision".[187] Referring to Lord Steyn in *McGuckian*, Lord Nicholls said that this was an exemplification of the established purposive approach to the interpretation of statutes.[188] Lord Nicholls preferred the phrase "the *Ramsay* approach to ascertaining the legal nature of transactions and to interpreting tax statutes" to "the *Ramsay* principle". According to him, observations about the "approach" in subsequent cases should be read "in the context of the particular statutory provisions and sets of facts under consideration"[189], and, in particular, those observations "cannot be understood as laying down factual prerequisites which must exist" before the court may apply the *Ramsay* approach, as this would be to misunderstand the nature of the decision in *Ramsay*, potentially leading to error.[190] Referring to Lord Brightman's famous formulation in Furniss v Dawson, Lord Nicholls readily accepted that "the factual situation described by Lord Brightman is one where, typically, the *Ramsay* approach will be a valuable aid". He said however that the *Ramsay* approach is "no more than a useful aid" and that this is not an area for absolutes[191] since the paramount question is always one of interpretation of the particular statutory provision and its application to the facts of the case. Lord Nicholls thus concluded his analysis[192]:

[A]s I have sought to explain, the *Ramsay* case did not introduce a new legal principle. It would be wrong, therefore, to set bounds to the circumstances in which the *Ramsay* approach may be appropriate and helpful. The need to consider a document or transaction in its proper context, and the need to adopt a purposive approach when construing taxation legislation, are principles of general application. Where this leads depends upon the particular set of facts and the particular statute.

Lord Hoffmann delivered the leading speech, and had many things to say about many of the leading House of Lords judgments on tax avoidance. With respect to *Ramsay* itself, it was his opinion that the innovation in that

---

[184] At page 893.
[185] At page 889.
[186] [2001] 1 All ER at page 868.
[187] Ibid. Emphasis is original.
[188] At page 869.
[189] Ibid.
[190] Ibid.
[191] Ibid.
[192] Ibid.

case was to give the statutory concepts of "disposal" and "loss" a commercial meaning.[193] Unlike Lord Nicholls who said that *Ramsay* did not enunciate "any new legal principle", Lord Hoffmann saw a "new principle of construction" – viz., a recognition that the statutory language was intended to refer to commercial concepts, so that in the case of a concept such as a "disposal", the court was required to take a view of the facts which transcended the juristic individuality of the various parts of a pre-planned series of transactions.[194] According to him, while there was nothing new about terms in tax and other legislation being construed as referring to business or commercial concepts, what was "new and fresh" about *Ramsay* was "the realisation that such an approach need not be confined to well-recognised accounting concepts such as profit and loss but could be the appropriate construction of other taxation concepts as well".[195] And what Lord Wilberforce was doing in *Ramsay* was no more than

> to treat the statutory words "loss" and "disposal" as referring to commercial concepts to which a juristic analysis of the transaction, treating each step as autonomous and independent, might not be determinative.[196]

Lord Hoffmann said that the perceived difficulty of reconciling *Ramsay* with Lord Tomlin's statement in the *Westminster* case that the courts cannot ignore the legal position and give effect to the substance of the matter, lay in an ambiguity in Lord Tomlin's statement – which ambiguity Lord Hoffmann proceeded to clarify thus[197].

> If "the legal position" is that the tax is imposed by reference to a legally defined concept, such as stamp duty payable on a document which constitutes a conveyance on sale, the court cannot tax a transaction which uses no such document on the ground that it achieves the same economic effect. On the other hand, if the legal position is that tax is imposed by reference to a commercial concept, then to have regard to the business "substance" of the matter is not to ignore the legal position but to give effect to it.

With regard to references in the cases to the "real" nature of transactions, and to what happens in the "real world", Lord Hoffmann warned about the need for care about the sense in which these expressions are being used, because of the possibility of being bogged down with "unnecessary

[193] At page 875.
[194] Ibid.
[195] At pages 875-876.
[196] At page 876.
[197] At page 877.

philosophical difficulties about the nature of reality". This was particularly important in the context of questions such as how a transaction can be said not to be a "sham", while being "disregarded" for the purpose of what happened "in the real world".[198] He emphasised that the important point is that "something may be real for one purpose but not for another". Thus, when it is said that the *Ramsay* transactions were not shams, one is "accepting the juristic categorisation of the transactions as individual and discrete and saying that each of them involved no pretence". But when it is said that they did not constitute a "real disposal" giving rise to a "real loss", then one is "rejecting the juristic categorisation as not being necessarily determinative for the purposes of the statutory concepts of disposal and loss as properly interpreted – the relevant contrast being the commercial meaning of those concepts.[199] So, when it is said that the tax legislation was intended to operate in the real world, what is being referred to is "the commercial context which should influence the construction of the concepts used by Parliament".

IRC v Burmah Oil Co Ltd was, according to Lord Hoffmann, an "entirely straightforward" application of *Ramsay*'s construction of the concept of a disposal giving rise to a loss under the CGT legislation – i.e., that the concept refers to "a loss in commercial terms and not a series of preplanned transactions which had no business purpose".[200] Thus for the House in that case to ignore the intermediate stages of the transaction and look at the end result was something that followed logically from "the decision to construe "disposal" and "loss" in a commercial sense which transcends the individuality of the "book entries".[201]

On the difference between *Ramsay* and *Furniss v Dawson* being that between a circular and a linear scheme, Lord Hoffmann recognised the convenience of those metaphors, but thought that it was "more illuminating to concentrate on the question which the legislation required the House to answer".[202] In *Ramsay*, the question was whether there was a disposal giving rise to a loss, but in *Furniss v Dawson*, the question what whether the disposal in the case had been made to one person rather than another. Although the questions were different, the House decided that the commercial characterisation of the relevant concept could also be applied to the identity question raised in *Furniss v Dawson*. In deciding that question, the fact that the shares disposed of in *Furniss v Dawson* were routed through Greenjacket was irrelevant,[203] because, if the statutory language is construed as referring to a commercial concept, it follows that steps that have no commercial purpose but which have been artificially inserted for tax purposes into a composite transaction will not affect the answer to the statutory question.[204] Lord Hoffmann emphasised that, like Lord Diplock's

[198] Ibid.
[199] At page 878.
[200] Ibid.
[201] At page 879.
[202] Ibid.
[203] Ibid.

formulation in *Burmah Oil*, Lord Brightman's formulation in *Furniss v Dawson* is not a principle of construction. His analysis of the Brightman formulation and its impact was thus[205]

> It is a statement of the consequences of giving a commercial construction to a fiscal concept. Before one can apply Lord Brightman's words, it is first necessary to construe the statutory language and decide that it refers to a concept which Parliament intended to be given a commercial meaning capable of transcending the juristic individuality of its component parts. But there are many terms in tax legislation which cannot be construed in this way. They refer to purely legal concepts which have no broader commercial meaning. In such cases, the *Ramsay* principle can have no application. It is necessary to make this point because, in the first flush of victory after the *Ramsay* case, the *Burmah Oil* case and *Furniss'* case, there was a tendency on the part of the Revenue to treat Lord Brightman's words as if they were a broad spectrum antibiotic which killed off all tax avoidance schemes, whatever the tax and whatever the relevant statutory provisions.

On *IRC v McGuckian*, Lord Hoffmann said[206] that the Crown gave itself unnecessary difficulties by not noticing that the question in that case (whether S Ltd. had received income or capital) was different from the question in *Furniss v Dawson* and that therefore it "did not necessarily respond to precisely the same analysis". Thus, while in *Furniss v Dawson* it was reasonable to speak of the middle stage of a chain of disposals being disregarded, it made much less sense in *McGuckian*. According to Lord Hoffmann, the question in *McGuckian* was not whether the assignment of the right (to receive dividends) should be disregarded, but "whether, from a commercial point of view, it amounted to an exchange of income for capital". Lord Hoffmann accepted that such exchanges usually have a commercial reality. He gave the example of the purchase or sale of an annuity, which is an exchange of capital for an income stream, involving a transfer of risk.[207] He felt however that the *McGuckian* transactions were simply an attempt to re-label a sum of money[208] and the fact that the assignment had no commercial purpose did not mean that it was to be disregarded, but rather, the correct analysis was that it failed "to perform the alchemy of transforming the receipt of a dividend from the company into a receipt of a capital sum from someone else." Thus, for the purposes of the relevant fiscal concept (the character of the receipt as income derived from the company), the assignment made no difference.[209]

---

[204] At page 880.
[205] Ibid.
[206] At page 881.
[207] Ibid.
[208] At page 882.
[209] Ibid.

Referring to the suspicion of Lord Cooke of Thorndon in *McGuckian* that advisers of those bent on tax avoidance do not always pay sufficient heed to the theme of the speeches in *Furniss v Dawson* to the effect that the journey's end may not yet have been found, Lord Hoffmann added that it was not only tax avoiders who may not pay sufficient heed to "the necessity of concentrating on the application of the particular taxing provision to the particular facts", and that the Revenue sometimes also fails to do so. According to him, "the journey's end may be different because the journey itself is not the same." [210]

Lord Hoffmann thus described the scope of *Ramsay*:[211]

The limitations of the *Ramsay* principle therefore arise out of the paramount necessity of giving effect to the statutory language. One cannot elide the first and fundamental step in the process of construction, namely to identify the concept to which the statute refers. I readily accept that many expressions used in tax legislation (and not only in tax legislation) can be construed as referring to commercial concepts and that the courts are today readier to give to them such a construction than they were before the *Ramsay* case. But that is not always the case. Taxing statutes often refer to purely legal concepts. They use expressions of which a commercial man, asked what they meant, would say "You had better ask a lawyer." ... If a transaction falls within the legal description, it makes no difference that it has no business purpose. Having a business purpose is not part of the relevant concept. If the "disregarded" steps in *Furniss'* case had involved the use of documents of a legal description which attracted stamp duty, duty would have been payable.

Even if a statutory expression refers to a business or economic concept, one cannot disregard a transaction which comes within the statutory language, construed in the correct commercial sense, simply on the ground that it was entered into solely for tax reasons. Business concepts have their boundaries no less than legal ones.

Comment on Westmoreland

The *Westmoreland* decision is another major landmark in the development of the House of Lords' anti-avoidance doctrine. It is remarkable for Lord Hoffmann's ingenious attempts to rationalise the previous leading cases on the topic by bringing their underlying principles within the broad

---

[210] Ibid.
[211] At pages 882-883.

umbrella of a "commercial construction" of fiscal concepts in tax legislation. In insisting that *Ramsay* is valuable only as and "is no more than a useful aid"[212], and that it only applies where Parliament intended that statutory words be given a commercial as (opposed to legal or juristic construction)[213], it serves as a further limitation to the scope and applicability of *Ramsay* and the new approach. *Westmoreland* confirms the *McGuckian* purposive approach to construing tax legislation and the view that "the end is not yet in sight". However, the likely impact of this decision on judicial anti-avoidance doctrines is far from clear.

First, it is not clear what the relegation of the new approach to "no more than a useful aid" means in a practical context. Secondly, and more importantly, the force of the Brightman formulation in *Furniss v Dawson* (as extended by Lord Oliver in *Craven v White*) is no longer clear. We are now told that it is not a rule of construction – but rather is a statement of consequences. We must not treat it "as laying down factual prerequisites which must exist" before the court may apply the *Ramsay* approach.[214] But we can still refer to it and "apply" it.[215] Thus, it would seem that the formulation is still quite valid - but it is not conclusive, and it has again been added to. One addition relates to the meaning of the legislation – here, it is necessary that the relevant fiscal concept must be intended to have "a commercial meaning". This issue must be decided before we can apply the formulation to the transactions in a case. While any limitation on *Ramsay* (especially one that moves the focus back to the meaning of the relevant legislation rather than whether the taxpayer's activities had a commercial or business purpose) is to be welcomed, the new emphasis on whether the legislative words are intended to have a legal (or juristic) or commercial meaning is likely to be troublesome. For one thing, how does one decide whether a particular word or concept is intended by Parliament to have a commercial meaning and not a legal meaning? This type of analysis would open the proverbial "can of worms", and is likely to lead to much argument and debate. We can already see evidence of such debate in the recent decision of the Court of Appeal in *DTE Financial Services Ltd v HMIT*[216] with the Revenue arguing that "the concept of 'payment' in the context of the PAYE system is par excellence a practical, commercial concept as opposed to a juristic concept of the kind referred to by Lord Hoffmann", while counsel for the taxpayer (naturally) argued that it is not a commercial concept but a "legalistic concept". This type of analysis is hardly the kind of thing that comes up in Parliamentary debates or in Ministers' statements to Parliament, and its introduction seems to be nothing more than an open invitation to judges to apply instinctive or subjective criteria and responses. In *DTE Financial Services Ltd v HMIT*,

---

[212] Per Lord Nicholls at page 869.
[213] Per Lord Hoffmann at page 880.
[214] Per Lord Nicholls at page 869. It is not clear what effect this has on Patten J's decision in *Citibank Investments Ltd v Griffin* ([2000] BTC 323) that "the test laid down by Lord Brightman is exhaustive" (at 339) and that "unless the *Furniss v Dawson* conditions are satisfied there can be no composite transaction to which the *Ramsay* principle can apply" (at 342).
[215] Per Lord Hoffmann at page 880.
[216] [2001] EWCA CIV 455; [2001] BTC 159.
[217] Para. [42].

Jonathan Parker LJ[217] upheld the Revenue's argument that "payment" in the context of PAYE is a practical, commercial concept, and added:

> In some statutory contexts the concept of payment may (as Lord Hoffmann pointed out in *MacNiven*) include the discharge of the employer's obligation to the employee, but for the purposes of the PAYE system payment in my judgment ordinarily means actual payment: i.e. a transfer of cash or its equivalent.

The impact of *Westmoreland Investments Ltd v MacNiven* on the *DTE* case was to convert a quite straightforward *Ramsay* situation (an attempt to convert a bonus to be paid to an employee into a non-PAYE payment by passing the intended bonus through an off-shore trust) into one involving arguments on whether "payment" in s.203 TA 1988 was used in a "commercial" or "legalistic" sense. Without this argument, the courts could simply have applied the Brightman/Oliver formulations to "disregard" the intermediate steps of passing the intended bonus through the off-shore settlement and treat payments from the settlement to the employee as payments from the employer. This, on a formal *Furniss v Dawson* analysis, would have been the "end result". With the input of *Westmoreland Investments Ltd v MacNiven*, the Revenue could very well have lost what may have been a cast iron case. They may still lose it, for it is not so obvious that "payment" (in PAYE terms) refers to or was intended by Parliament to refer to a commercial concept. For example Lord Hope of Craighead said in *Westmoreland Investments Ltd v MacNiven*[218] that "[t]he words 'paid' and 'payment' are to be construed according to their ordinary meaning. The question whether a payment has been made is a question of fact." Lord Nicholls said that "payment" in s.338 TA 1988 could not have any meaning other than its "normal legal meaning".[219] By this they (as well as Lord Hoffmann) were treating it as a legalistic or juristic concept – the unanimous view of the House of Lords. Of course, "payment" in s.338 could be intended to have a "normal legal" meaning, while in s.203 it could be intended to have a "commercial" meaning. But if so, why? Jonathan Parker LJ's statement that payment means "actual payment" could arguably be said to indicate that it has, as in *Westmoreland Investments Ltd v MacNiven*, its "ordinary" or "normal legal" meaning, rather than a commercial meaning. If so, then the *Ramsay* approach cannot, according to *Westmoreland Investments Ltd v MacNiven*, apply – and the Revenue will lose a case that they would have won. Some may well say "good!" – and it may be good for the Revenue to lose every now and then – but such a response

---

[218] [2001] 1 All ER at page 889.
[219] at pages 870-871.

misses the point (which is the lack of clarity that results from *Westmoreland Investments Ltd v MacNiven*). *DTE* is just one example of the types of problems that *Westmoreland Investments Ltd v MacNiven* is likely to cause, and it is not only the Revenue that may be at the receiving end.

Even if easy agreement is reached that a commercial construction was intended by Parliament, the question still arises what that commercial meaning is. This again leaves much room for debate. It is not clear either how a court would arrive at this meaning. It would be disingenious to ask whether judges are commercial people who should understand the correct commercial meaning to give to a fiscal concept which Parliament intended should have a commercial construction. But the spectre of courts and Commissioners hearing evidence from "commercial" experts looms.

A second addition to the Brightman formulation by *Westmoreland Investments Ltd v MacNiven* is the necessity to focus on "the question".[220] The nature of "the question" may well dictate whether and to what extent the Brightman formulation is appropriate (and perhaps whether variations are required). This of course also opens wide the issues, and will provide plenty of scope for argument and debate as to what the relevant "question" is. It also opens the doors to inconsistent decisions. What, for example, was "the question" in *DTE*? Was it whether a payment had been made, or was it the identity of the payer, or was it the nature of the sums received in the end by the employee? Arguably, each pathway could lead to a different result.

Indeed, the main contribution of *Westmoreland Investments Ltd v MacNiven* (apart from a further narrowing of *Ramsay*) would seem to be the hastening of the journey to a case-by-case analysis. This type of approach is much favoured by the Lords in other areas (such as the tort of negligence), and it seems that they have now decided that this is also the preferred option for the judicial anti-avoidance doctrines. This decision has not done much to clarify the law but has rather served to obfuscate matters and a case-by-case approach is unpredictable. The tax planning industry might be forgiven a smile or two, but it would be optimistic to think that the chances of tax avoidance schemes being successful have been increased.

A General Statutory Anti-Avoidance Rule?[221]

The United Kingdom's judicial anti-avoidance doctrines are the direct result of the absence of a statutory general anti-avoidance rule (GAAR) in the United Kingdom. This type of rule exists in New Zealand, and was referred to briefly by Lord Cooke in *IRC v McGuckian*.[222] It also exists in Australia,[223] Canada,[224] and Holland.[225] Judicial anti-avoidance doctrines of

---

[220] Lord Hoffmann at pages 879 and 881.
[221] See generally, Ward et. al. "The Business Purpose Test and Abuse of Rights" [1985] BTR 68.
[222] [1997] 3 All ER at page 830.
[223] See generally, P Harris [1998] BTR 124.
[224] See generally, I Roxam [1998] BTR 140; B J Arnold [1995] BTR 541.
[225] See generally, E van Der Stok [1998] BTR 150.

the type now being applied in the United Kingdom are arguably objectionable[226] for four reasons; (a) the courts are now claiming to be seeking to apply the intention or purposes of legislation – however, Parliamentary legislation has not shown any tendency towards a general anti-avoidance rule – which is arguably what the *Ramsay* principle, even with the limitations in *Westmoreland Investments Ltd v MacNiven* amounts to[227]; (b) the question of the proper response of a jurisdiction to the threats and problems posed to the State by tax avoidance is a matter of taxation policy, for the Treasury and the tax authorities, and, ultimately, Parliament[228] – not a matter for the judiciary, which is not subject to any political control, and which is not accountable to the taxpayers or the electorate for its policy choices; (c) issues of tax policy are not the types of issues that should be developed on an ad hoc or case-by-case basis, subject to conflicting formulations by different judges, and the element of chance as to which issues arise in the courts and the intervals between such issues arising, as judicially developed policy is bound to be (d) the judiciary has no mandate to develop this type of policy and the forensic process whereby it is developed does not allow for the fullest range of consultation to be carried out, or for the fullest range of relevant information to be admitted.[229]

Obviously, tax avoidance is a matter of concern to the Revenue, but while the judicial anti-avoidance doctrines have continued to favour them, they have not always had the incentive to press for a general anti-avoidance legislation. Perhaps now, after *Westmoreland Investments Ltd v MacNiven*, they may have a greater incentive to press for one. To its credit, the current Labour Government indicated a desire to introduce wide legislative provisions in this area following a period of consultation.[230] Such legislation would arguably be preferable to the kind of judicial activism that has been seen on the issue in recent times. The Tax Law Review Committee in its report on Tax Avoidance favoured such a rule.[231] However, others are not convinced, taking the view that a general anti-avoidance rule is likely to introduce uncertainty into the law.[232] There are many arguments on both sides. Most of them have been well aired elsewhere, for example, by Arnold[233] and Masters (above), and we shall not rehash them here. The position that one takes on this issue would be much coloured among other things by one's perception of the proper role of judges in the formulation (as opposed to the implementation) of tax policy. As indicated earlier, it is arguable that the judges have gone too far

---

[226] Contrast P Gillett, "The consultative document on a general anti-avoidance rule for direct taxes - a view from business" [1999] BTR 1 at 5: "What constitutes acceptable and unacceptable tax planning is in my view a matter for the courts to determine, in accordance with the social and political mores of the time. It is far too complex and judgmental an area for it to be established with any degree of certainty by statute"; compare I Roxam [1998] BTR 140 at 148.

[227] For a debate about the constitutionality of the *Ramsay* principle, see R T Bartlett [1985] BTR 338.

[228] For some interesting implications of this, see D Wilde[(1995) BTR 137.

[229] For an analysis of the types of issues involved in the development and implementation of tax policy, thereby arguably making it an inappropriate task for the courts, see S James and C Nobes, "The Economics of Taxation", pages 115-120.

[230] For comment, see "Tax ploy warning", Accountancy Age (1997) 4 July, p5.

[231] For comment see H McKay [1998] BTR 86.

[232] See for example C Masters [1994] BTR 647.

[233] B J Arnold: "The Canadian General Anti-Avoidance Rule" [1995] BTR 541.

already and that the time has come for Parliament to step in. The issue is not whether the UK should have a GAAR at all, but whether, if the UK is to have one, the rule should be statutory or judicial. We have already argued that (in spite of recent judicial denials) the "new approach" may well amount to a judicial GAAR. If so, then the question whether there should be a GAAR at all has already been answered by the emergence of a *de facto* judicial rule. The question then becomes "should the UK keep the judicial GAAR or enact a statutory GAAR"? This is a question of principle, and arguments about the merits and weaknesses of particular permutations of a statutory GAAR are not relevant. The Labour government, in accordance with its earlier promise published a consultative document on a general anti-avoidance direct taxes. Initial reactions were not very positive[234] and the government has since become very quiet about this topic. Thus it may well be that the judicial GAAR will reign for some time to come, as the political will to tackle the implementation of a statutory GAAR seems to be presently lacking.

Although the United Kingdom does not currently have any general statutory anti-avoidance provision, the legislature has at times recognised potential planning and avoidance "loopholes" in statutory provisions and has sought to take anti-avoidance measures in relation to those, actual or potential, loopholes.[235]

These anti-avoidance measures are limited in their application and they are broadly of two types. The first type apply irrespective of the intentions or motives of the taxpayer, while the second type only apply when it is shown that there exists a tax avoidance motive behind the transaction. Included in the first type of provision are these contained in the Taxes Act 1988, Part XV (ss.660A–694). These apply to "settlements" and are discussed in the chapter on Trusts and Settlements. Examples of the second type of provision can be found in Part XVII of the Taxes Act, 1988. These include the provisions in ss.703–709 which are designed to counteract tax avoidance schemes in relation to certain transactions in securities. Ss.703–709 recognise the tax benefits and potential in relation to activities relating to the distributable assets of a company, but declare that those benefits cannot be enjoyed unless the person concerned can show that the transaction was carried out for either bona fide commercial reasons or in the ordinary course of making or managing investments and obtaining a tax advantage was not one of the main objects of the transactions.[236] Another example of the second type is s.739 TA 1988 (s.478 TA 1970) the effect of which we have already seen in *IRC v McGuckian*.[237]

---

[234] See for example, P Gillett [1999] BTR 1; E Troup [1999] BTR 5.
[235] A recent example of this process can be found in the March Budget, 1993, when the Chancellor announced that he intended to "... close a number of loopholes which have been exploited to avoid tax." Those loopholes related to the Business Expansion scheme and to some Corporation Tax matters.
[236] s.703(1).
[237] See also R K Ashton [1990] BTR 251.

Further Reading

Sandford C, *Hidden Costs of Taxation*.

James S and Nobes C, *The Economics of Taxation*.

Brown CV and Jackson PM, *Public Sector Economics*.

Dowell S, *A History of Taxation and Taxes in England*, Vol II.

Tiley J, *First Thoughts on Westmoreland* [2001] BTR 153.

Gillett P, *The consultative document on a general anti-avoidance rule for direct taxes - a view from business* [1999] BTR 1.

Stopforth D, *Creating Anti-Avoidance Legislation – A Look Behind the Scenes* [1999] BTR 106.

Arnold B J, *The Canadian General Anti-Avoidance Rule* [1995] BTR 541.

Masters C, *Is there a need for a General Anti-Avoidance Legislation in the United Kingdom?* [1994] BTR 647.

Popkin WD, *Judicial Anti-Avoidance Doctrines in England: A United States Perspective* [1991] BTR 283.

Mansfield G, *The "New Approach" to Tax Avoidance. First Circular, Then Linear, Now Narrower* [1989] BTR 5.

Tiley J, *Judicial Anti-Avoidance Doctrines* [1987] BTR; 1988 BTR 63, 108.

Kay J A, *The Economics of Tax Avoidance* [1979] BTR 354.

C V Brown and P M Jackson, "Public Sector Economics", page 425 (4th edn, Blackwell, 1990).

Index

Printed in the United Kingdom
by Lightning Source UK Ltd.
103626UKS00001B/1-3

9 781903 499054